SICILY

CONTENTS

- **Sicily** 5
  - Sicily's Top Destinations 11
  - Planning Your Trip 17
  - Travel Smart 26
- **Palermo** 29
- **Day Trips from Palermo** ... 107
  - Sanctuary of
    Santa Rosalia 107
  - Mondello 110
  - Monreale Cathedral 111
  - Segesta 129
- **Cefalù** 133
- **Trapani &
  the West Coast** 152
  - Trapani 154
  - Erice 174
  - Favignana &
    the Egadi Islands 182
  - Mozia Island & Salt Flats 186
  - Selinunte 197
- **Agrigento & the Valley
  of the Temples** 203
- **Villa Romana del Casale** . 233
- **Ragusa & the Southeast** ... 251
  - Ragusa 252
  - Southeast
    Countryside Drive 273
  - Noto 283

- **Siracusa** 290
- **Catania** 334
- **Mount Etna** 360
  - Mount Etna Volcano Visit .. 364
  - Mount Etna Wine Country . 375
- **Taormina** 388
- **Sicilian History** 420
- **Practicalities** 435
  - Travel Tips 435
  - Resources from
    Rick Steves 436
  - Money 440
  - Staying Connected 445
  - Sightseeing 448
  - Sleeping 451
  - Eating 460
  - Transportation 481
  - Conversions 496
  - Packing Checklist 498
  - Italian Survival Phrases 499
- **Index** 501
- **Map Index** 514

Welcome to Rick Steves' Europe

Travel is intensified living—maximum thrills per minute and one of the last great sources of legal adventure. Travel is freedom. It's recess, and we need it.

I discovered a passion for European travel as a teen and have been sharing it ever since—through my bus tours, public television and radio shows, and guidebooks.

Over the years, I've taught millions of travelers how to best enjoy Europe's blockbuster sights—and experience "Back Door" discoveries that most tourists miss.

This book offers a balanced mix of Sicily's lively cities and cozy towns, from bustling Catania to sleepy Cefalù. It's selective: Rather than listing dozens of archaeological sites, I recommend only the best ones. My self-guided museum tours and city walks provide insight into the island's history and today's living, breathing culture.

I advocate traveling simply and smartly. Take advantage of my money- and time-saving tips on sightseeing, transportation, and more. Try local, characteristic alternatives to expensive hotels and restaurants. In many ways, spending more money only builds a thicker wall between you and what you traveled so far to see.

We visit Sicily to experience it—to become temporary locals. Thoughtful travel engages us with the world, as we learn to appreciate other cultures and new ways to measure quality of life.

Judging by readers' positive feedback, I believe this book will help you enjoy a fun, affordable, and rewarding vacation—whether it's your first trip or your tenth.

Bon viaggiu! Happy travels!

Rick Steves

SICILY

Sicily is a fertile, uncommon mix of geology and culture. Eruptions from its volcano, a glowing sun, generations of hard work, and wave after wave of civilizations storming through over the centuries—they all come together here, giving visitors a full-bodied travel experience that engages all the senses.

If Italy is one of the most dramatic, flamboyant places in Europe, Sicily is its distilled and intensified sibling—pure passion set in wild beauty. To those who have traveled in other parts of Italy, Sicily may feel similar—but it's not the same. The beauty is more rugged, the food is more flavorful, and the highs and lows of human history are more extreme. Coming to this island requires not only patience and a sense of adventure, but a willingness to be open to its seductions.

Sicily floats just off the toe of Italy's boot, like a soccer ball about to be kicked. At about 9,900 square miles, the island can be driven end to end in three hours—a journey that traverses a variety of landscapes, climates, and cultures. This is the only place I can think of where you can marvel at a well-preserved Greek temple, wander through Carthaginian ruins, listen to the Arab-influenced sales pitches of market vendors, dine on African couscous, and admire the glittering mosaics of a Norman cathedral...all in a single day.

Western Sicily is home to Palermo, the busy capital. Ringed by mountains and citrus groves, the once-elegant city has a 19th-century center spiced with fragments of Arab and Norman buildings from a thousand years ago. Nearby is the

Rick Steves Sicily

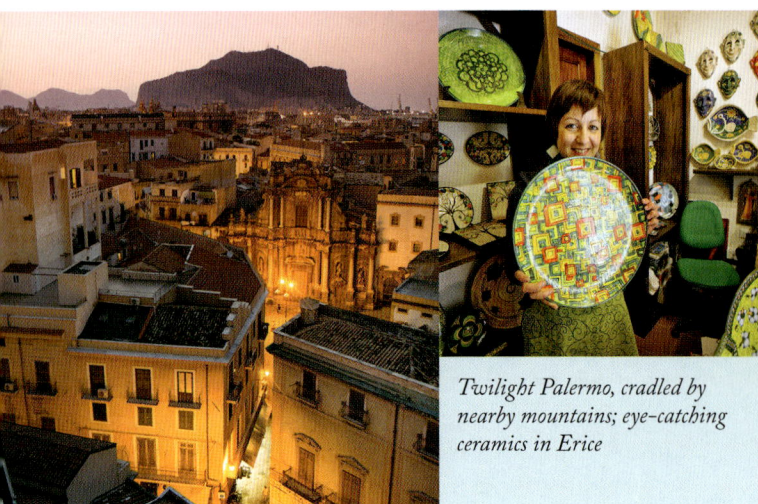

Twilight Palermo, cradled by nearby mountains; eye-catching ceramics in Erice

magnificent Norman cathedral at Monreale. Outside Palermo, this region is quiet and untamed—and often wet and windy— with rolling hills punctuated by jagged mountains and aquamarine waters lapping at windmill-sprinkled salt flats. On the southwest coast is Agrigento, home to an amazing ensemble of cliff-hanging Greek temples.

Things get drier as you move inland, with rolling fields of wheat. In the island's arid midsection, dusty medieval hill towns crown peaks scattered along dry riverbeds. Burrowed here, in the middle of nowhere, is the ancient, mosaic-rich Villa Romana del Casale.

Sicily's sunny eastern side is dominated by Europe's most active volcano, Mount Etna. From her smoking peak, the mountain slopes gently down to the southeast coast. Surrounding Etna are thriving cities (earthy Catania, historic Siracusa, and resorty Taormina), ancient wonders, and a tropical natural beauty. This side of the island bustles with shopping centers, factories, urban sprawl, and traffic. To the south, deep valleys and rolling green hills lead to a sunny coast strewn with ancient artifacts and wide sandy beaches.

Sicily's location at the center of the Mediterranean made it a strategic base for successive waves of long-ago settlers and invaders—each leaving a mark on the culture and landscape. And that too has had an effect on Sicily's regional differences.

A Sweet Trip Through Sicily

Typical Italian desserts, such as tiramisu and biscotti, are lightly sweetened and made with little butter. But Sicilian sweets pull out all the stops—they're packed with calories and sugary goodness.

The difference in desserts stems from 200-plus years of Arab rule. When the Arabs arrived in 827, they brought date palms, oranges, lemons, almonds, ginger, and most important, sugar. New farming techniques, such as irrigation, made it possible to cultivate these delicacies—which thrived. Today's Sicilian desserts owe their sweetness to this Arabic heritage.

Most pastries are made with some combination of sugar, almonds, citrus, and ricotta. Every town has a *pasticceria* crafting the local version of each sweet, and many desserts have funny names and backstories (like the *minnuzze*, or breasts, of St. Agatha—a round spongy cake topped with a cherry). Sicilian sweets are eaten any time of day, not just after a meal. A typical breakfast is a sweet one, with cakes, cookies, and pies, all washed down with a cappuccino.

Pasta di mandorla is an almond cookie. Made with almond flour, sugar, and egg whites, this basic recipe comes in many variations, usually named for the shape: little pyramids (*tette delle monache,* "nuns' breasts"), wavy wafers (*foglie da té,* "tea leaves"), or clumps of dough dropped roughly in the pan (*brutti e buoni,* "ugly but good").

Cassata is a classic, colorful, sugar-bomb cake. The simplest *cassata* is a crust filled with lightly sweetened ricotta. More elaborate versions ▶▶▶

Authentic Sicilian pastries include cassata *cake, the cherry-topped "breasts of St. Agatha," and almond cookies stuffed with pistachios.*

Rick Steves Sicily

▶▶▶ might have a base of liquor-infused cake topped with sweet ricotta cheese and chocolate chips, then crowned with a layer of neon green marzipan and a sugar glaze.

Gelato is found all over Sicily, with local varieties such as *pecorino* (sheep's milk), *fichi d'india* (prickly pears), and *cassata,* a gelato version of the cake.

Sicilians also enjoy a light, refreshing frozen treat called **granita.** Similar to a slushie, it's served only during the warmer months (April-Oct). Traditional flavors are *mandorla* (almond), *limone* (lemon), and *gelsi* (mulberry), but you'll find many others. Sicilians enjoy a *granita* for breakfast, topped with whipped cream. For a truly local treat, order your *granita* with a warm brioche bun to use as a scoop.

Cannoli are the most famous Sicilian sweet. A crispy fried pastry tube is filled with sweetened ricotta, then dusted with powdered sugar. The ends can be dipped in nuts, chocolate chips, or candied fruit, depending on the local style. The mark of a high-quality *cannolo* is one that's filled right when you order it—otherwise, the shell gets soggy and loses its crunch.

Choosing a Sicilian sweet from a pastry case can be a challenge, as they are all beautiful and enticing. If you can't decide, ask for *un vassoio misto,* a mixed tray of shop selections. ∎

In Sicily, gelato comes in a cone, a cup, or spread on brioche. slushy granita *is ideal any time of day. Choose a* cannolo, *but only if it's filled at the last moment.*

Carthaginians from North Africa used the west side of the island as a trading base. Meanwhile, the Greeks settled the east side. Ancient ruins lie just beneath the surface all along this coast—remnants of Greek colonies that grew to surpass their homeland in splendor. Today, a cultural divide remains. The west has traditionally been poorer and more rural, and the east more affluent and cosmopolitan.

The people of Sicily are warm and welcoming. Although English can be spotty outside of big cities, that's never a barrier to conversation, as most Sicilians speak more with their hands than with words.

Sicilians live outdoors, flooding piazzas and al fresco cafés. Early evening is the time for the ritual *passeggiata* promenade up and down the main drag. Sit in the town square and soak in the atmosphere, eavesdropping on spirited conversations. Most people are talking about the same thing: food.

While food may be an art form in Italy, it's more like a religion in Sicily. Even if you know Italian food well, Sicilian cuisine will surprise you with its complexity—a legacy of its multicultural background. Sicily grows everything from citrus to nuts to tomatoes and feeds the rest of Italy with its harvests. Produce is fresh, cheap, and plentiful—and sold at markets that more closely resemble an Arab souk than a European marketplace.

Family has been the thread that holds this cultural tapestry together. Several generations often live in close proximity.

Segesta's photogenic Greek temple; Catania's Baroque buildings, built from volcanic basalt

Taormina, in Mount Etna's shadow; locals celebrating one of Sicily's many religious processions

Most Sicilians can say they reside within a few miles of where their great-grandparents lived. Sundays are set aside for family, with a big lunch or a drive in the country.

Sicily, like Italy, is almost entirely Roman Catholic. Attendance at Mass has sharply declined in the past 20 years, but that hasn't dampened a spirited participation in religious festivals. Every city has a patron saint who is celebrated effusively with processions, fireworks, and of course, eating.

Sicily lags behind mainland Italy in terms of modernization but is quickly catching up. Some travelers are put off by the chaotic traffic, broken infrastructure, garbage, and graffiti. Public transit is spotty, opening hours change without notice, and Wi-Fi works when it wants to. Things won't go the way you expect, and "island time" is firmly in effect.

Rather than seeing these as problems, use them as an invitation to enjoy *il dolce far niente* ("the sweetness of doing nothing"), and surrender to the island's charms. Slow your pace, linger over a glass of local wine, and breathe the sea air. Embrace the chaos, and open yourself up to the wonders of a place that lives by its own rules.

Sicily's Top Destinations

Mamma mia! There's so much to see in Sicily and so little time. This overview categorizes Sicily's top destinations into must-see places (to help first-time travelers plan their trip) and worth-it places (for those with extra time or special interests). I've also suggested a minimum number of days to allow per destination.

MUST-SEE DESTINATIONS

Sicily's top cities show off the historical and cultural diversity of the island. For the best quick visit, focusing on these two destinations will give you a sampler platter of ancient Greek, Arab, Norman, and late Baroque Sicily, set against a modern backdrop.

▲▲▲Palermo (2 days)
Sicily's sprawling capital is gritty on its face, but its colorful markets and bustling shopping streets signal a fun-loving city in regeneration. Top activities include eating your way through the thriving Ballarò or Capo street markets, touring the massive Teatro Massimo, marveling at glittering mosaics at the Palatine Chapel or Church of La Martorana, visiting the eerie Capuchin Crypt, and simply exploring the city's maze of back streets.

▲▲▲Siracusa (1-2 days)
Once the greatest ancient Greek city on Sicily, today's Siracusa centers around the lovely historic island of Ortigia, boasting shabby-chic lanes, a grand Baroque piazza, and a lazy seafront promenade, plus a charming puppet museum/theater and a unique cathedral built on the skeleton of an ancient temple. Even the drab, urban, mainland part of town is worth a visit for its ancient sites, archaeological museum, spooky catacombs, and modern church.

Sicily's Top Destinations

Byzantine mosaics of Monreale (opposite); Palermo back street; Palermo's Ballarò street market; Siracusa's Puppet Museum; Siracusa's Baroque main square

Rick Steves Sicily

Monreale Cathedral; beach fun in Cefalù; sunset in Trapani; mosaic floor at Villa Romana del Casale; Monreale's cloister (opposite)

Sicily's Top Destinations

WORTH-IT DESTINATIONS

You can weave any of these destinations—rated ▲ or ▲▲—into your itinerary. It's easiest to add destinations based on proximity (if you're going to Palermo, Cefalù is next door), but some out-of-the-way places can merit the journey, depending on your time and interests.

▲▲Day Trips from Palermo (half-day)
Several worthwhile sights are within an hour of Palermo, including the hilltop ▲▲▲ Monreale Cathedral with its striking interior, wallpapered with golden Byzantine mosaics. The Sanctuary of Santa Rosalia, the beach town of Mondello, and the ancient city of Segesta are also close by.

▲▲Cefalù (1 day)
An hour from Palermo, this fishing village turned beach-bum paradise has a charming old town center with a Norman cathedral, fine seafood options, and an inviting, sandy beach.

▲▲Trapani & the West Coast (2 days)
The laid-back port town of Trapani, famous for its nearby salt flats, makes an easy home base for day trips to the hilltop village of Erice, fishing island of Favignana, Carthaginian ruins at Mozia, and ancient ruins of Selinunte.

▲▲Agrigento & the Valley of the Temples (1 day)
This town, on the southern coast, is home to Sicily's premier ancient attraction: the Greek ruins at the Valley of the Temples, with a fine archaeological museum nearby.

▲▲Villa Romana del Casale (half-day)
Deep in the middle of the island, this remote palace ruin has the largest collection of Roman mosaics ever found in situ—with 38,000 exquisite square feet of scenes of Roman life.

Rick Steves Sicily

▲▲Ragusa & the Southeast (1-2 days)
The southeastern corner of Sicily is packed with rolling hills and picturesque towns—the finest being Ragusa, with higgledy-piggledy stone homes blanketing two adjacent hilltops. From here, Modica (famous for chocolate), the valley village of Scicli, the scenic southern coastline, and the showcase Baroque city of Noto are within reach.

▲Catania (half-day)
Sicily's second city and the de facto capital of the east, workaday Catania is most useful as a transportation hub. Still, its rejuvenated Baroque city center is worth a visit for its splashy fish market, hidden Roman theater, and rare-in-Italy WWII museum.

▲▲Mount Etna (1 day)
The most active volcano in Europe is also the top tourist sight in Sicily. Activities include hikes in a lunar landscape, a visit to the steaming summit, and tours and tastings at up-and-coming wineries on its north slope.

▲Taormina (1 day)
Perched cliffside overlooking the sea, this cushy resort town with a Grand Tour vibe offers picture-perfect views of Mount Etna, a dramatic Greek-Roman theater, easy access to the island's east side, and the chance to rub shoulders with high-end tourists.

Catania fish market; Ragusa spills over two adjoining hills.

Planning Your Trip

Planning Your Trip

To plan your trip, you'll need to design your itinerary—choosing where and when to go, how you'll travel, and how many days to spend at each destination. For general advice on sightseeing, accommodations, restaurants, and more, see the Practicalities chapter.

DESIGNING AN ITINERARY

As you read this book and learn your options...

Choose your top destinations.
My recommended itineraries (see the sidebar on the next page) give you an idea of how much you can reasonably see in one or two weeks, but you can adapt the plans to fit your own interests and speed.

City lovers could spend three or four days in Palermo, taking in the 19th-century atmosphere, exploring the churches and many interesting museums, and day-tripping to nearby sights. Wine connoisseurs could spend several days in the countryside (especially along the slopes of Mount Etna) sampling regional vintages. And beach bums could easily lose a week idling on the sandy beaches at Cefalù.

Decide when to go.
Sicily is one of the few European destinations that is open year-round. April, May, June, and October are ideal, with fewer crowds, lots of festivals, and mild weather. The days leading up to Easter are full of celebrations, and worth planning around. July and August are hot and can be crowded—

Rick Steves Sicily

Sicily's Best Two-Week Trip by Car

To get the most from your time in Sicily, it's best to have a car. This two-week itinerary covers the island's top sights.

Day	Plan	Sleep
1	Fly into Palermo, begin sightseeing there	Palermo
2	Sightsee Palermo; side-trip to Monreale	Palermo
3	Pick up car, visit Segesta en route to Trapani	Trapani
4	Day-trip to Mozia and the salt flats, and up to Erice	Trapani
5	Morning drive to Agrigento to tour the Valley of the Temples	Agrigento
6	Morning drive to Villa Romana del Casale, sightsee there, then afternoon drive to Ragusa	Ragusa
7	Follow my southeast Sicily countryside drive (with stops in Scicli and Modica)	Ragusa
8	Morning drive to Noto, then to Siracusa; start sightseeing there	Siracusa
9	Sightsee Siracusa	Siracusa
10	Drive north, choosing between Catania (fish market and WWII museum) or Mount Etna (volcanic sights and wineries); end your day in Taormina	Taormina
11	Vacation from your vacation in Taormina (or day-trip to Etna wineries)*	Taormina
12	Morning drive to Cefalù, afternoon on the beach	Cefalù
13	Return to Palermo, drop off car, fly out of Palermo	

With More Time: Add days in Palermo and/or Trapani, and include both Catania and Mount Etna.

With Less Time: To see Sicily in one week, from Palermo (2 nights) head to Agrigento (1 night) and the Valley of the Temples. From there, visit Villa Romana del Casale on the way to Siracusa (2 nights). Then drive north, sightseeing at Catania or Mount Etna on the way to Taormina (2 nights). The next day, drive to Catania and fly out.

Getting to the Boot: Daily ferries take passengers, buses, and trains across the Strait of Messina to mainland Italy (see page 483).

Planning Your Trip

Sicily's Best One-Week Trip by Bus and Train

If you're relying on public transportation, it's wise to group overnights in big cities and day-trip from there.

Day	Plan	Sleep
1	Fly into Palermo, begin sightseeing there	Palermo
2	Sightsee Palermo; side-trip to Monreale	Palermo
3	Day-trip to beachy Cefalù (1 hour by train) or the Valley of the Temples in Agrigento (2 hours by train)	Palermo
4	Morning in Palermo, afternoon bus to Siracusa (3.5 hours)	Siracusa
5	Sightsee Siracusa	Siracusa
6	Morning in Siracusa, afternoon train to Taormina (2 hours)	Taormina
7	Join an excursion tour to Mount Etna or take it easy in Taormina	Taormina
8	Bus to Catania Airport (1.5 hours) and fly out from there	

With More Time: You can stretch out this itinerary by doing any of the following: overnight in Cefalù (train); add Trapani (bus); spend a night or two in Catania (train/bus); or relax in Ragusa for a night or two (train), with a side trip (by bus) to Noto.

The vertical Baroque city of Modica, best known for its chocolate; the salt flats near Mozia, with its medieval windmills

especially at beaches and resorts as Italians and other Europeans descend on the island (especially in August). September is a busy month and rates at hotels can soar (as at other busy times, especially in popular places like Taormina). But even at its liveliest, the island is less crowded than the big, mainland Italian cities.

In the off-season (roughly November through March), Sicily can be chilly (low temperatures in the 40s and snow at high altitudes), but you'll have the island to yourself. Bring plenty of layers, and be prepared for cooler inside temperatures, as Sicilians don't heat their houses the way Americans do. Expect shorter hours, more lunchtime breaks at sights, and fewer activities. In the dead of winter, stick to bigger cities, as remote areas shut down.

Connect the dots.

Link your destinations into a logical route. Determine which cities you'll fly into and out of. Catania in the east and Palermo in the west have the biggest airports. Begin your search for transatlantic flights online at Google Flights or Kayak.

Decide if you'll travel by car or public transportation, or a combination. A car is particularly helpful for exploring west and southeast Sicily (where public transportation can be sparse) but is useless in big cities (park it). Trains connect

Planning Your Trip

Trip Costs Per Person

Run a reality check on your dream trip. You'll have major transportation costs in addition to daily expenses.

Flight: A round-trip flight from the US to Palermo costs about $1,000-2,000, depending on where you fly from and when.

Public Transportation: For a two-week trip, allow $75 for buses and trains.

Car Rental: Allow $350-500 per week (booked well in advance), not including tolls, gas, parking, and insurance (theft insurance is mandatory in Italy).

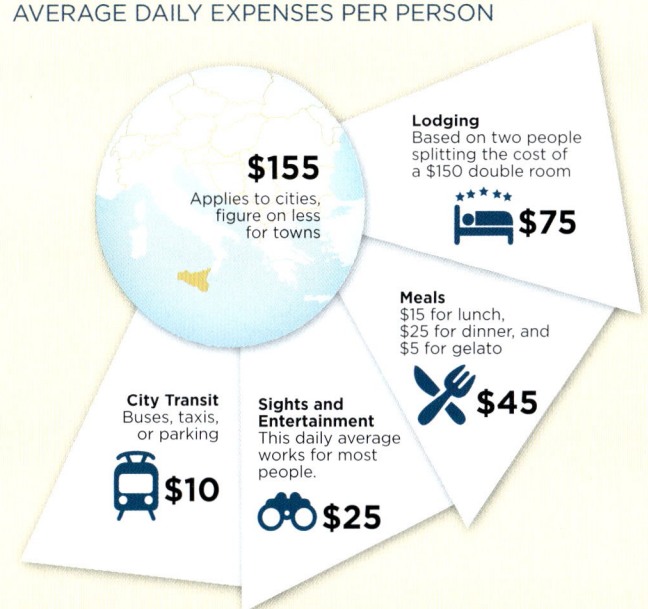

AVERAGE DAILY EXPENSES PER PERSON

$155 Applies to cities, figure on less for towns

Lodging Based on two people splitting the cost of a $150 double room — $75

Meals $15 for lunch, $25 for dinner, and $5 for gelato — $45

Sights and Entertainment This daily average works for most people. — $25

City Transit Buses, taxis, or parking — $10

Budget Tips

To cut your daily expenses, use public transit in cities rather than taxis, enjoy picnics rather than restaurants, and look for alternatives to fancy hotels. Seek out free sights and experiences (people-watching counts). Save splurges for experiences you'll always remember (hiring a private guide, taking a food tour, scaling that volcano). Reserve your rooms directly with the hotel. Some hotels, restaurants, and tour companies offer discounts to my readers. Look for the RS% symbol in the listings in this book.

Greek-Roman theater in Taormina; a wine bar featuring typical Sicilian drinks; welcoming hotel staff in Palermo; a vineyard near Catania

some cities, but not all. Long-distance buses fill in the gaps, but few run on Sundays and holidays.

For approximate travel times between destinations, study the driving map in the Practicalities chapter or check Google Maps. Bus and train travel times are given in this book (in the "Connections" sections per chapter). Confirm bus schedules locally and see trenitalia.com for train times. To go beyond Sicily, check budget intra-European flights at skycanner.com.

Work out a day-by-day itinerary.

Figure out how many destinations fit comfortably in your time frame. Don't overdo it—few travelers wish they'd hurried more.

Allow enough days per stop (see estimates in "Sicily's Top Destinations," earlier). Minimize one-night stands. It can be worth taking an afternoon drive or bus ride to settle into a town for two consecutive nights—and gain a full uninterrupted day for sightseeing. Allot sufficient time for transportation; whether you travel by train, bus, or car,  it'll take a half-day to get between most destinations.

Staying in a home base (like Taormina or Trapani) and making day trips can be more time-efficient than changing locations and hotels.

Take sight closures into account. Avoid visiting a town on the one day a week its must-see sights are closed. Check if any holidays or festivals fall during your trip—these attract crowds and can close sights (for the latest, visit Italy's tourist website, italia.it).

Give yourself some slack. Every trip, and every traveler, needs downtime for doing laundry, picnic shopping, people-watching, and so on. Pace yourself. Assume you will return.

Rick Steves Sicily

BEFORE YOU GO

You'll have a smoother trip if you tackle a few things ahead of time. For more details on these topics, see the Practicalities chapter and ricksteves.com, which has helpful travel-tip articles and videos.

Make sure your travel documents are in order. If your passport expires within six months of your return date, you need to renew it (allow eight weeks for a new passport or renewal). Get passport and country-specific info at travel.state.gov. Be aware of entry requirements; you may need to register with the European Travel Info and Authorization System (ETIAS, travel-europe.europa.eu/etias_en), and if traveling in the United Kingdom, you'll need an Electronic Travel Authorization (ETA, gov.uk/visa-immigration).

Arrange your transportation. Book your international flights. Figure out your local transportation options: If renting a car, reserve it before you go. (If relying on trains and buses, buy tickets in Sicily.) If traveling beyond Sicily, book any cheap European flights you'll need.

Drivers need to bring an International Driving Permit (sold at AAA offices in the US, aaa.com) along with a license.

Book rooms and key experiences well in advance, especially if your trip falls during peak season or any major holidays or festivals. Availability for rooms tightens (and rates skyrocket) on the coast in the busy summer months. Popu-

Planning Your Trip

lar local guides and experiences like food tours can also get booked up.

Consider travel insurance. Compare the cost of insurance to the cost of your potential loss. Understand what protections your credit card might offer and whether your existing insurance (health, homeowners, or renters) covers you and your possessions overseas.

Manage your money. "Tap-to-pay" or "contactless" credit cards are the simplest way to pay for many things in Europe (you can also set up your smartphone or smartwatch for contactless payments). You may need your credit card's PIN for some purchases—request it if you don't have one. Don't bring euros from home; it's cheaper to withdraw cash from a bank ATM in Europe.

Use your smartphone smartly. Check what type of international service your carrier offers, or plan to rely on Wi-Fi. Download any apps you'll want on the road, such as maps, translators, and Rick Steves Audio Europe (see sidebar).

Pack light. You'll walk with your luggage more than you think. I travel for weeks with a single carry-on bag and a day pack. Use the packing checklist on page 498 as a guide.

Rick's Free Audio Tours and Video Clips

Rick Steves Audio Europe, a free app, makes it easy to download audio content to enhance your trip. Use the app to listen to audio tours of Europe's top sights, plus my public radio show interviews with travel experts from around the globe. Scan the QR code to find it in your app store or visit ricksteves.com/audioeurope.

Rick Steves Classroom Europe, a powerful tool for teachers, is also useful for travelers. This video library contains about 600 short clips excerpted from my public television series. Enjoy these videos as you sort through options for your trip and to better understand what you'll see in Europe. Check it out at classroom.ricksteves.com.

Travel Smart

Sicily can fray nerves with its carefree approach to time and rules. If you have a positive attitude, equip yourself with good information (this book), and expect to travel smart, you will.

Read—and reread—this book. To have an "A" trip, be an "A" student. Note opening hours of sights, closed days, and any crowd-beating tips (in Sicily, make sure to confirm hours locally). Check the latest at ricksteves.com/update.

Be your own tour guide. As you travel, book ahead for events and tours, reconfirm hotels, and check transit connections. Upon arrival in a new town, lay the groundwork for a smooth departure; confirm the road, bus, or train you'll take when you leave.

Outsmart thieves. Pickpockets abound in crowded places—especially where tourists congregate. Treat commotions as smokescreens for theft. Take commonsense precautions with your valuables, especially phones, credit cards, and cash (store them securely). Don't set important items down on counters or café tabletops, where they can be stolen or easily forgotten (and don't hang day packs on the backs of chairs).

Minimize potential loss. Keep expensive gear to a minimum. Bring copies or take photos of important documents to aid in replacement if they're lost or stolen. Back up devices to the cloud as you travel.

Beat the summer heat. If it's hot, start your day early, take a midday siesta, and resume your sightseeing later. Use sunscreen and hydrate. Churches offer a cool haven (though dress modestly—no shorts or bare shoulders). Take frequent *granita* breaks. Join the *passeggiata*, when locals stroll in the cool of the evening.

Guard your time and energy. Taking a taxi can be a good value if it saves you a long wait for a cheap bus or an exhausting walk across town. To avoid long lines, follow my crowd-beating tips, such as sightseeing early or late. For example, visiting Villa Romana del Casale early will let you enjoy the mosaics with fewer crowds on its narrow catwalks.

Be flexible. Even if you have a well-planned itinerary, expect changes, strikes, closures, sore feet, bad weather, and so on. Your Plan B could turn out to be even better.

Attempt the language. Many Sicilians speak English—especially young people and those in the tourist trade. And apps such as Google Translate work for on-the-go translation help. But if you memorize and use some Italian, even just a few

Taormina's main street entices strollers at night. Don't be afraid to negotiate at a market—it's a Sicilian sport.

pleasantries, you'll get more smiles and make more friends. The survival phrases near the end of this book are a good starting point.

Connect with the culture. Interacting with locals carbonates your experience. Enjoy the friendliness of the Sicilian people. Ask questions; most locals are happy to point you in their idea of the right direction. Set up your own quest for the best *arancine* (fried rice balls). When an opportunity pops up, make it a habit to say yes.

Sicily…here you come!

PALERMO

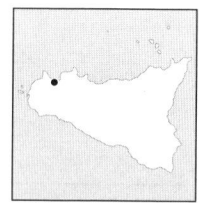

Misunderstood, underrated Palermo may be Sicily's most delightful surprise. For years, its touristic reputation was tarnished: gritty, run-down, polluted, traffic-clogged, crime-ridden, and synonymous with Mafia violence. But those days are long gone. The city has revitalized itself with new museums, gentrified neighborhoods, pedestrianized streets, and upscale shops and hotels. The attitude towards the Mafia has also changed, and its influence has significantly diminished. Today, travelers are surprised by how much Palermo (pop. 680,000) entertains them with striking architecture, a cosmopolitan vibe, and a fun-loving energy—while maintaining the wonderful edge that makes travel in Sicily such a treat.

Spend a day (or two) exploring Palermo's wide, lively, endearingly potholed streets. Dodge motor scooters on "pedestrianized" lanes as you visit interesting museums (art, archaeology, aristocratic palazzos, marionettes, and more). Tour some of Italy's most exuberantly decorated churches, and rub shoulders with the *palermitani* (as the locals are known) at one of the city's famous landmarks (the Quattro Canti intersection, or the nearby Fountain of Shame). Commune with the dearly departed at the thought-provoking Capuchin crypt, and ogle stunning golden mosaics.

Palermo is also home to Italy's most vivid street markets. Make a point to wander amidst a cacophony of musical sales pitches and let yourself be tempted by some of Italy's best street food. If spleen sandwiches and boiled octopus are just too much, stick to saffron-scented *arancine* rice balls and other deep-fried goodies. And be sure to look up—otherwise you'll miss the city's spectacular set-

30 Rick Steves Sicily

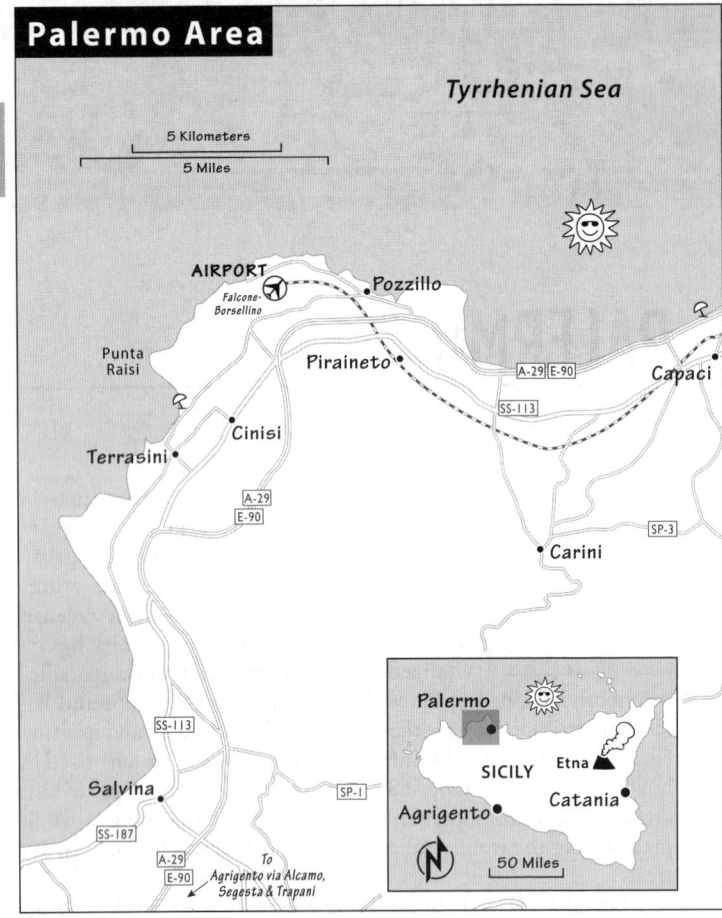

Palermo Area

ting, facing the sea and filling the mouth of a lush valley tucked between dramatic mountains.

If you've been to Naples, you'll recognize Palermo's brand of "organized chaos." Traffic is a mess (pedestrians: keep your head on a swivel). And even the city's prettiest public spaces are rough around the edges. But Palermo's decaying elegance is one of the reasons I like it so much. Don't be afraid to fully experience Palermo. Let its grime get under your fingernails. While a few timid travelers may run screaming, most dive in, fall in love with this warts-and-all city, and leave wanting more.

PLANNING YOUR TIME
On a quick visit, Palermo deserves at least one very full day. Start with my Palermo City Walk to get a handle on this unruly city, then branch out to explore Palermo's fascinating nooks and cran-

Palermo 31

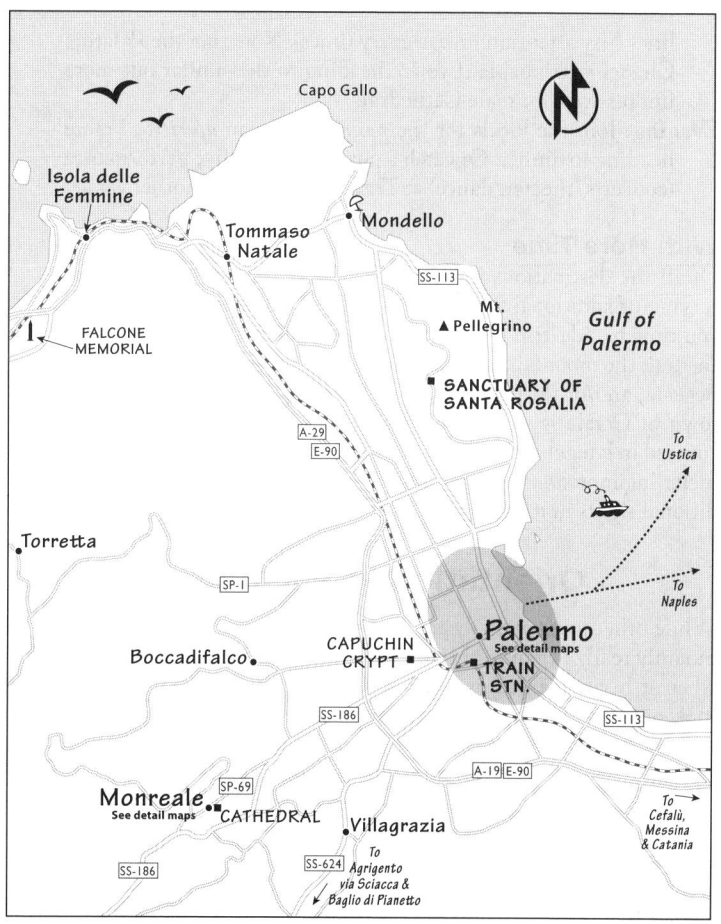

nies. While crowds are generally not a concern, the exception is the Palatine Chapel, where lines can be long with cruise-ship groups. You'll save time by visiting as soon as it opens or at the end of the day.

Palermo in One Day

On Sundays, when the Norman Palace and the Palatine Chapel close early, rearrange this plan to arrive at the palace when it opens.

Morning: Tour the Teatro Massimo, then follow my self-guided walking tour of the city's historic core. Finish in time for a street-food lunch at Ballarò Market (where grazing also counts as sightseeing).

Afternoon: After lunch, tour the elegant Palazzo Conte Federico, then head to the Palermo Cathedral and the Palatine Chapel in the Norman Palace, arriving late in the day to avoid long lines (pay attention to last-entry times). Note that the Palatine Chapel is skippable if you're heading to the similar but more impressive Monreale Cathedral.

Evening: Join the locals for the *passeggiata* or an *aperitivo* before heading to dinner. Or catch a puppet show or live performance (concerts, theater, dance) at Teatro Massimo or another venue.

With More Time

Of all the destinations in this book, Palermo is the one most deserving of additional time. A second (or third or fourth) day gives you time to side-trip to see the stunning interior of Monreale Cathedral, the mountaintop Sanctuary of Santa Rosalia, the temple at Segesta, and/or the beachy burg of Mondello. The laid-back resort town of Cefalù is another good day-trip option. All of these are covered in later chapters. And there's plenty more to do in Palermo, including more market browsing, a street-food tour, and seeing additional sights in town.

Orientation to Palermo

While other parts of Sicily are known for their ancient sites, Palermo only really began to thrive under Arab rule (9th-11th century), when it became an impressive metropolis. The Norman invaders took note and claimed Palermo as their capital. And since then, with each successive wave of rulers, Palermo has remained Sicily's leading city—layered with fascinating artifacts of each era.

The city center is ringed by sprawling suburbs—especially to the north—hastily erected and cheaply built in the postwar years. Fortunately, the tourists' Palermo is its fairly compact city center; you can walk briskly from one end to the other in 30 minutes. This zone is bounded by the Norman Palace to the west, Teatro Politeama to the north, the main Stazione Centrale train station to the south, and the harbor to the east.

Downtown Palermo is built on a predictable grid street plan, but within its ancient Arab quadrants, the side streets can spin around in confusing curlicues. It can be doubly confusing to get oriented because tourist maps tend to show the city the way locals think of it: with the harbor—which is actually to the east—at the bottom. (This book's maps, however, show north on top).

The intersection called **Quattro Canti**—"Four Corners," for its quartet of sculpted facades—is considered the center of the city. (Just around the corner are other major landmarks—the Fountain of Shame and the three stunning churches on Piazza Bellini.) Quattro Canti is the point from which the city core is divided into four medieval quadrants—called *mandamenti*—which locals and savvy visitors use as a shorthand for navigating the city: The northeast quadrant is Castellammare (better known as the **Vucciria**), the southeast is the district known as **La Kalsa,** the northwest is **Capo,** and the southwest is Albergheria (also known as **Ballarò**).

Quattro Canti is also where two big streets meet: The north-south **Via Maqueda** is the pedestrian-only shopping and strolling hotspot, passing in front of Teatro Massimo. And the east-west **Via Vittorio Emanuele** leads west to the cathedral and Norman Palace, and east past a thriving restaurant zone to the harbor. A few blocks east of Via Maqueda is **Via Roma,** the main traffic artery through the center. It runs from the main train station in the south to Piazza Struzo (near Teatro Politeama) in the north, parallel to Via Maqueda.

While most Palermo sightseeing is easily done on foot, outlying sights such as the Capuchin Crypt, the Sanctuary of Santa Rosalia, the beach resort of Mondello, and the Monreale Cathedral are too far to walk. The crypt and Monreale are on the same bus line, making them easy to connect. To reach the others in one day it's more efficient to hire a taxi for a few hours (or a private driver—see "Getting Around Palermo," later). The Capuchin Crypt is covered in this chapter; for the rest see the Day Trips from Palermo chapter.

TOURIST INFORMATION

Palermo's main TI sits just below the Church of San Cataldo on Via Maqueda. It has bus schedules and current sightseeing information (daily 8:00-19:00, near Quattro Canti at Via Maqueda 191, +39 091 740 8020, turismo.comune.palermo.it). You can also find a TI desk at Teatro Massimo (Mon-Fri 9:30-14:30, Sat-Sun until 15:30) and a TI kiosk at Piazza Marina (in Palazzo Galleti; generally Mon-Fri 9:30-13:30, closed Sat-Sun).

ARRIVAL IN PALERMO

By Train: Palermo's main train station—Stazione Centrale—is at the southern edge of the central core, facing straight up Via Roma. Inside the station are basic eateries and predictable services; pay WCs are near track 1, and a luggage-storage office is near track 3. The main building has a ticket desk, and ticket machines are out by the tracks. A tobacco shop sells local city-bus tickets. To exit, with your back to the tracks, walk straight out the front door of the station onto Piazza Giulio Cesare, where you'll find city buses and taxis. Via Roma and the center of town is straight ahead; it's about a 15-minute walk to Quattro Canti. A taxi to most of my recommended hotels should cost around €10—but only catch a taxi where you see an official, orange *TAXI* sign (or use Uber). You can also take bus #101 or #102 straight up the Via Roma artery (buses

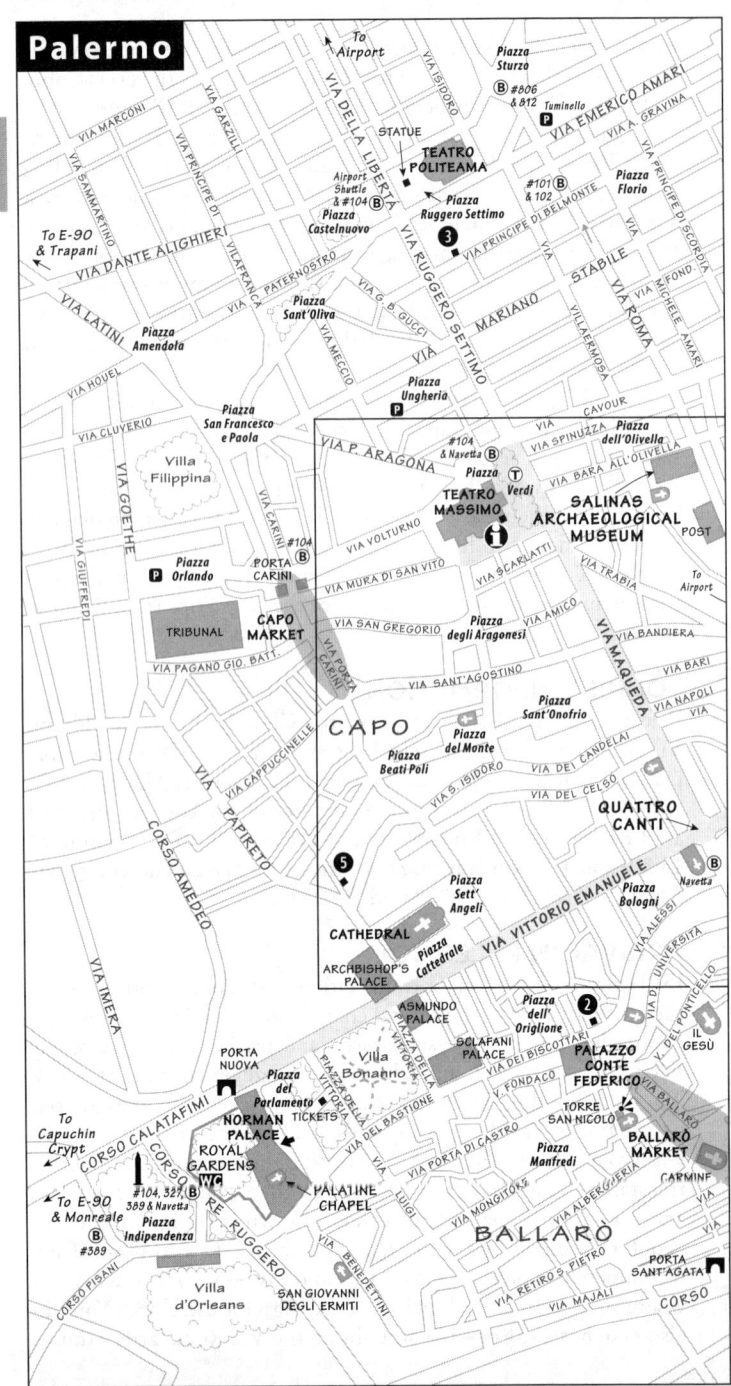

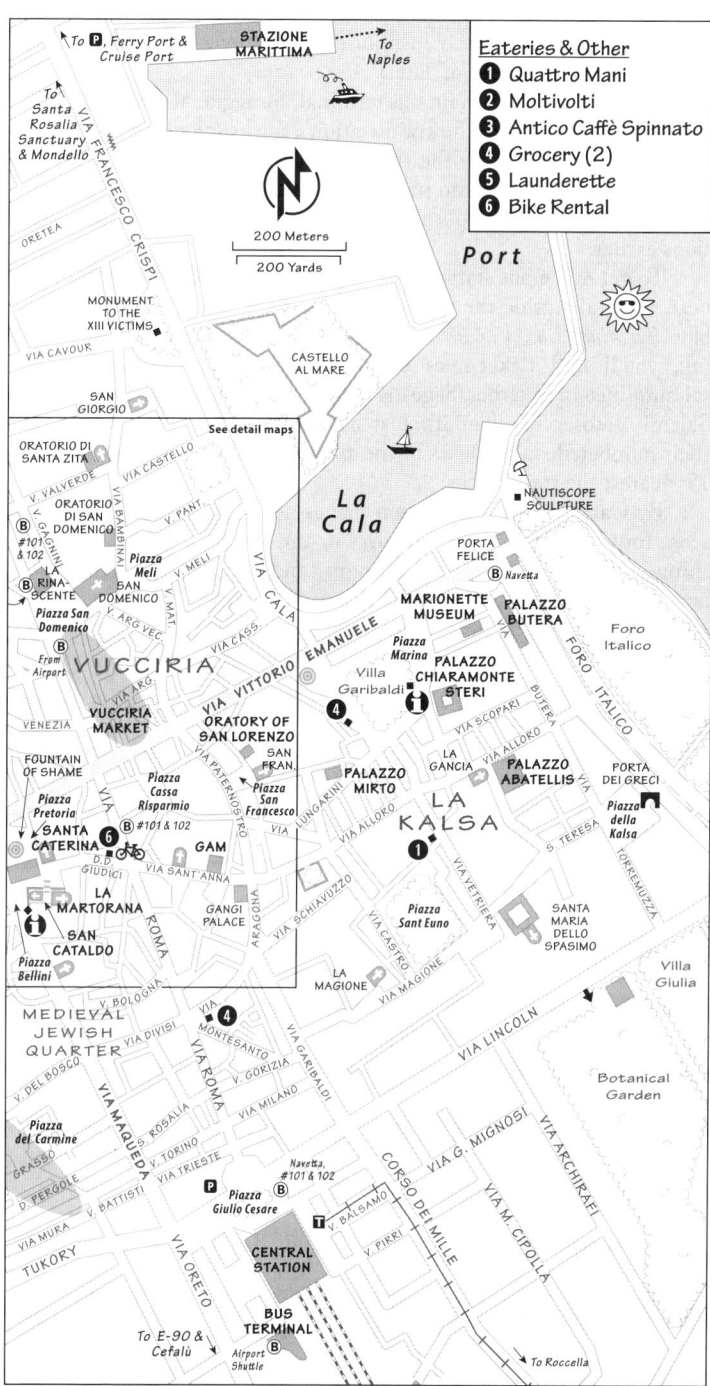

leave from the stop directly in front of the station; for details, see "Getting Around Palermo," later).

By Bus: Palermo's main bus terminal, for regional and airport buses, clings alongside the train station's tracks (along track 10). Leaving your bus, follow the tracks (past the little terminal with ticket offices) into the main part of the train station; walk straight through the station and out the front door, then follow the directions earlier.

To get *to* the bus station, first go inside the train station, then bear right, alongside the outer platform of track 10 (look for the blue *Terminal Bus, Via Fazello* sign). At the bus-terminal building, you'll find ticket-sales offices for most operators (SAIS, saisautolinee.it; Interbus/Segesta/Etna Trasporti, interbus.it; and Salemi, autoservizisalemi.it). Just beyond that, buses line up in their numbered stalls. Buses to the airport usually leave from stall 15, nearest the train tracks.

By Car: Driving in Palermo makes no sense for the sightseer. Traffic moves in anything but a straight line; lights, signs, and laws are flagrantly ignored; buzzing motor scooters swarm everywhere; and double- or triple-parking while blocking traffic is common. I'd skip the stress and pick up your rental car at the airport when you leave town. If you do decide to drive in Palermo, be aware that the town center is a **Zona Traffico Limitato** (ZTL) that requires a special pass to enter. For details and parking advice, see "Palermo Connections," at the end of this chapter).

By Plane or Boat: See "Palermo Connections" at the end of this chapter.

HELPFUL HINTS

Safety Tips: While Palermo is generally safe, your wallet may not be—particularly near the train station, at Ballarò Market, and near the cruise port. As in any other big Italian city, use common sense, wear a money belt, and be very careful with your day bag. Secure your phone and don't wear flashy jewelry. Crowded street markets with lots of distractions are common territory for thieves.

Bike Rental: Centrally located **Social Bike,** near Quattro Canti, rents regular and e-bikes (Mon-Fri 9:00-18:00, Sat-Sun until 17:00, Discesa dei Giudici 13, +39 328 284 3734, palermonbike.com). They also offer bike tours (see "Tours in Palermo," later).

Laundry: There are a few small, self-service launderettes scattered around the center. A reliable one is **The Blue Bubbles,** near the cathedral (daily 7:00-21:30, Via Matteo Bonello 17, +39 329 256 4791).

Parking "Help": If you have a car and must park it on the street, local men may offer to "assist" you in finding street parking. It's smart to give them a euro or two, as they make it their business to "keep an eye on your car." Sadly, if you don't pay the local man sitting on a chair nearby, there's a chance your car will be robbed or damaged while you're sightseeing. It's also possible they'll just pocket the money and disappear.

Best Views: Many Palermo sights (including the cathedral and the Church of Santa Caterina) offer a "rooftop visit" for a few euros extra. While any of these can give a nice overview of the city, doing all is redundant—pick one (the cathedral is probably best). For a free view (mostly over the Piazza San Domenico), ride up to the top-floor cafeteria at the Rinascente department store (Via Roma 289).

GETTING AROUND PALERMO

For most visitors, the best way to see Palermo is on foot. The streets of Via Maqueda and Via Vittorio Emanuele are nominally pedestrianized (but keep an eye out for bikes, scooters, and occasional cars) and enjoyable to stroll. Taxis and buses connect outlying sights.

I'd avoid the tuk-tuks and horse-drawn carriages that loiter in the tourist zones waiting to fleece unsuspecting visitors. Their scam is to quote a price upfront, but later claim that price is per person.

By Bus

Palermo's local bus company is AMAT. Single tickets are valid for 1.5 hours, including transfers; you can buy one at a newsstand or tobacco shop for €1.40 and sometimes on board for €1.80. Ask for *biglietto autobus* (beel-YEH-toh OW-toh-boos). A 24-hour ticket costs €3.50. All tickets must be validated in the blue machines on the bus (amat.pa.it).

Bus stops are indicated by large signs with either *AMAT* or *fermata* written across the top. The sign lists all stops on each route, with an arrow indicating the direction. A red dot indicates your current stop. The frequency of bus departures is listed to the side but rarely reflects reality. When your bus approaches, be sure to wave to the driver so they know to stop for you.

Bus hubs in the center include the train station (Stazione Centrale), Piazza Indipendenza (behind the Norman Palace—from here buses fan out to the Capuchin Crypt and Monreale), and Piazza Ruggero Settimo (in front of Teatro Politeama).

Palermo at a Glance

▲▲▲**Palatine Chapel** and **Norman Palace** Glittering mosaic-clad chapel inside Europe's oldest royal residence. **Hours:** Mon-Sat 8:30-16:30, Sun until 12:30 (chapel closed Sun 9:30-11:30). See page 69.

▲▲**Church of Santa Caterina** Sicilian Baroque architecture at its most extravagant. **Hours:** Daily 10:00-18:00. See page 56.

▲▲**Church of La Martorana** Oldest Byzantine-Norman mosaics in Sicily. **Hours:** Mon-Sat 9:30-13:00, closed Sun. See page 58.

▲▲**Teatro Massimo** Landmark Art Nouveau opera house—the largest in Italy. **Hours:** Daily 9:30-19:00. See page 42.

▲▲**Capuchin Crypt** Fascinating, albeit morbid, collection of embalmed bodies. **Hours:** Daily 9:00-12:30 & 15:00-17:30. See page 80.

▲▲**Il Ballarò Market** Palermo's oldest and most authentic street market. **Hours:** Generally open Mon-Sat 6:00-14:00, closes earlier Sun. See page 79.

▲**Church of San Cataldo** Time-warp church with interesting mix of Arab and Norman architecture. **Hours:** Daily 10:00-14:00 & 14:30-18:00. See page 59.

Most useful for travelers are buses #101 and #102, which stop all along Via Roma between Stazione Centrale and Teatro Politeama (including at Discesa dei Giudici just south of Via Vittorio Emanuele, and at the post office). Bus #104 links the Norman Palace, Capo Market, Teatro Massimo, and Teatro Politeama.

AMAT buses also conveniently serve several nearby day-trip destinations. From Piazza Stuzo, behind Teatro Politeama, bus #812 links to the Sanctuary of Santa Rosalia and bus #806 heads to the beach town of Mondello. Bus #389 to Monreale leaves from Piazza Indipendenza. You can also reach Monreale or Mondello on the hop-on, hop-off bus (see later).

Free Shuttle Bus: An electric minibus (painted white, orange, and blue and labeled *Navetta*) runs around the historic center of Palermo; though it's designed for locals, visitors are welcome to hop on (no tickets needed, runs every 30 Sicilian minutes, less frequent Sun and holidays). It does a handy, one-way, clockwise loop past major landmarks in the city center, stopping at the following

▲**Salinas Regional Archaeological Museum** Top-notch collection of ancient Greek, Roman, and Carthaginian artifacts with a wing dedicated to Selinunte. **Hours:** Tue-Sat 9:00-19:00, Sun until 13:30, closed Mon. See page 60.

▲**Oratory of San Lorenzo** Playful Baroque space and site of notorious theft of Caravaggio masterpiece. **Hours:** Daily 10:00-18:00. See page 50.

▲**Palermo Cathedral** City's favorite church with a wild mix of architectural styles. **Hours:** Mon-Sat 7:00-19:00, Sun from 8:00. See page 65.

▲**Palazzo Chiaramonte Steri** Palace that also served as a prison for victims of the Spanish Inquisition. **Hours:** Daily 10:00-20:00. See page 74.

▲**Regional Art Gallery at Palazzo Abatellis** Palermo's top art museum, with Antonello da Messina masterpiece. **Hours:** Tue-Sat 9:00-19:00, Sun until 13:30, closed Mon. See page 75.

▲**Palazzo Conte Federico** Tour of elegant palace with an aristocrat as your guide. **Hours:** Generally Thu-Tue, tours on the hour 11:00-14:00, closed Wed. See page 78.

▲**Il Capo Market** Classic street market in city center. **Hours:** Generally open Mon-Sat 6:00-14:00, closed Sun. See page 79.

---

places in this order: the train station (in front), Piazza Indipendenza and the Norman Palace, Teatro Massimo (north side, near the taxi stand), and the harbor area near Porta Felice, where it takes a break. Finally, it runs back through the center of town to Quattro Canti.

Because it's a one-way loop, it's much handier for getting, for example, from the station to the Norman Palace than vice versa. These shuttles can be crammed, so they work best if you're patient and not in a hurry. As with all public buses in Palermo, watch for pickpockets. You may even find it enjoyable to simply hop on and joy ride through the kaleidoscopic wonder of Sicily's biggest and liveliest city.

By Taxi

Palermo is a fine taxi town—especially when it's hot. You can find taxis at orange-signed *TAXI* stands, usually near major attractions such as Teatro Massimo or the Norman Palace. If you can't find a taxi stand, ask someone at a bar or tobacco shop to call one for you. A typical ride—say, from Teatro Massimo or the train station to the Norman Palace—should run about €15. Make sure the meter is running; if you're going somewhere more distant, agree to a fixed price and have the driver write down the amount before you get in the cab. Taxis can be hired hourly (about €40/hour, €150/half-day), and most drivers can suggest a nice sightseeing itinerary for a fixed price. Avoid hawkers at tourist destinations offering rides—stick to official taxis (+39 091 6878, 6878.it). Uber also operates in Palermo.

By Private Driver
Salvatore "Sal" Coppola and his team of English-speaking drivers can take you to outlying sights, such as Monreale and the beaches of Mondello (€350/about 8 hours for up to 3 people); or farther afield, on side trips to Cefalù, or to Segesta and Erice near Trapani (€420/8 hours). Sal also offers help tracking down your Sicilian roots in the countryside near Palermo and runs multiday tours around Sicily (ask for prices for larger groups or custom trips, +39 339 466 1233, insightsicily.com, salcop@libero.it).

Tours in Palermo

Bus Tours
Several hop-on, hop-off outfits offer tours in the city. **City Sightseeing**'s buses run generic tours with recorded narration in two loops—one that hits most of the highlights with an optional extension to nearby Monreale Cathedral or the beach town of Mondello, and another that stops at lesser sights. This can be a low-stress, if expensive, way to reach these day-trip destinations (€30/48 hours including either Monreale or Mondello—but not both, April-Oct runs every 30 minutes 9:30-17:00, fewer departures off-season, Monreale bus departs from Piazza del Parlamento in front of the Norman Palace, +39 346 004 6435, city-sightseeing.it). Those arriving in Palermo on a cruise can use the Politeama stop, a short walk from the port.

Cheapskates can see many of the sights by riding the free **shuttle bus** *(navetta)* that loops around the city center (see "By Bus," earlier).

Bike Tours
Social Bike offers morning tours around the city in places that buses can't go. Their three-hour Palermo Old Town tour glides by the major sights and includes street-food stops (€40); they also have longer rides into the outskirts (Discesa dei Giudici 13, +39 328 284 3734, palermonbike.com, Anthony). They also offer bike rentals (see "Helpful Hints," earlier).

Walking Tours
Domenico Aronica, a professional photographer and guide, leads easygoing walking tours around the back streets of Palermo with entertaining commentary sprinkled with dad jokes. His tour varies each day and usually includes a stop for street food (€45, most days at 9:30, 3 hours, maximum 15 people, reservations required; private small-group tours available, +39 347 133 6788, palermowalkingtour.com, domenico@domenicoaronica.com).

Local Guides
Jacqueline Alio is a tour guide and author, raised in the US, who has returned to her homeland to share her passion for Sicily. Her tours make the complex history of Palermo accessible, and her depth of knowledge works well for novices and historians alike. She can also arrange custom day trips with a driver to nearby sights (€140/2 hours, €210/half-day, palermoguide.net).

Andrea Masi is an archaeologist who grew up in England and calls both places home. His strength is the archaeology of Sicily, such as at Mozia and Segesta, but he also guides in Palermo (€180/half-day, €300/day, +39 339 440 9377, masitourguidesicily.com).

Food Tours
Streaty Tours offers several entertaining walks that combine nibbles and history. Select from the original street food walk, Sicilian wine, or cooking a meal in a *palermitano's* home. This is a great way to spend time exploring Palermo with an energetic local (€69-129, maximum 12 people, streaty.com, booking@streaty.com).

Culinary Backstreets offers a five-hour tour that includes market visits and tastings of street food, wine, and various other Sicilian delights ($150-175, culinarybackstreets.com).

Market Tour and Cooking Class
Duchess Nicoletta, who rents apartments in her palace (see page 93), is also a well-known culinary artist offering a cooking and cultural experience. She'll lead you on a tour of a local market, then return to her palace, where you prepare lunch together (contact for price and schedule, includes palace tour, +39 366 414 3887, palazzolanzatomasi.it, info@cookingwiththeduchess.com).

Palermo City Walk

Your first impression of Palermo might be grit and traffic. But with this city, more than most, you have to get under its skin to see what makes it special. This walk will help you do that.

We'll loop from Teatro Massimo through the historic core of the city, exploring back streets and checking out churches. It's best to do this walk in the morning; if you finish by lunchtime, you can

42 Rick Steves Sicily

1. Teatro Massimo
2. Via Bara all'Olivella
3. Salinas Regional Archaeological Museum
4. Via Roma
5. La Vucciria Market
6. Via Alessandro Paternostro
7. Piazza San Francesco
8. Oratory of San Lorenzo
9. Piazza Aragona
10. Piazza Bellini
11. Piazza Pretoria
12. Quattro Canti

head to the Ballarò or Capo markets for street food (Capo Market closed Sun). While the walk could be done without stops in an hour, there are several sightseeing opportunities en route; the most worthwhile stops (Teatro Massimo at the beginning, three churches on Piazza Bellini at the end) add another two to three hours.

1 Teatro Massimo

Close to the heart of Palermo and its people, Italy's largest opera

Palermo City Walk

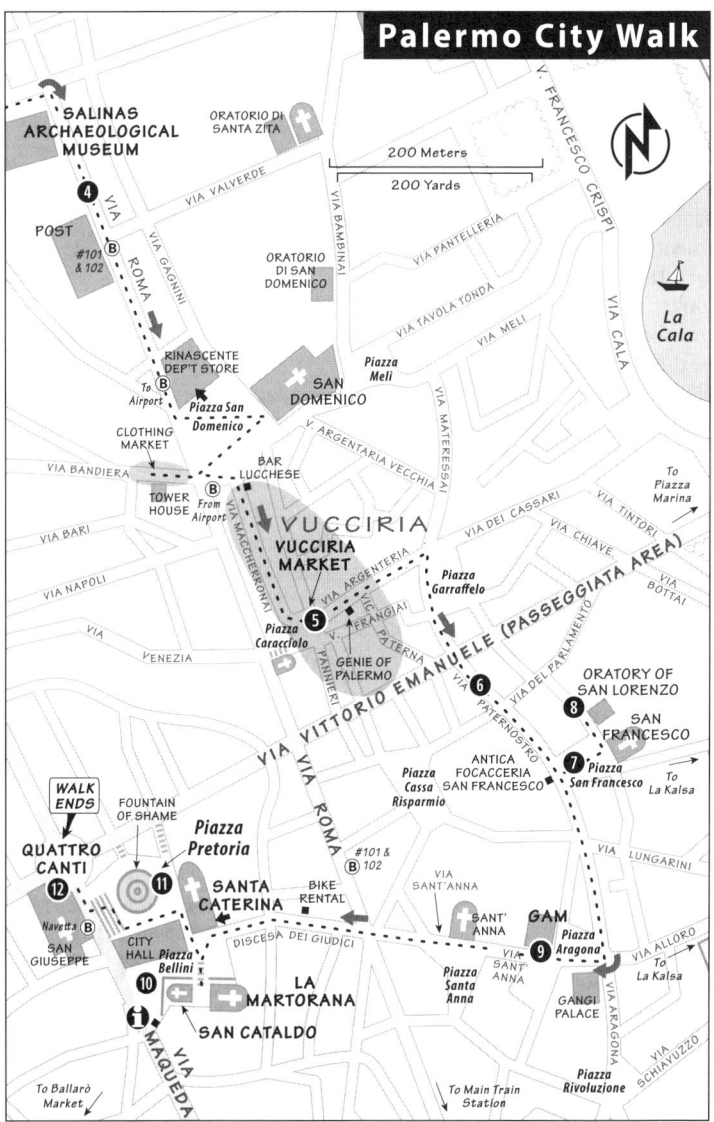

house (and Europe's third largest, rated ▲▲) fills Piazza Verdi in a dramatic, Neoclassical fashion. Started in 1875, soon after the Risorgimento united Italy and civic pride was at a peak, the massive theater took 22 years to build and became a symbol of the up-and-coming city as a magnet for arts and culture. The Massimo (Maximus) Theater was inaugurated on May 16, 1897, with a performance of *Falstaff*, the last opera written by then-80-year-old Giuseppe Verdi, to whom this square was dedicated.

True to its name, Teatro Massimo has a footprint of nearly two acres, half of which houses the massive backstage. While it may not appear so at ground level, this is also one of the tallest buildings in Palermo, accommodating a towering fly-space used to house scenery (hidden behind the pediment and dome).

If the grand front staircase looks familiar, you might remember it from the final scene of the *Godfather* trilogy. The two elegant kiosks on either side of the piazza facing the opera house were the original ticket booths. The theater's classy Giardini del Teatro café, to the right of the staircase, is open until late daily.

While the exterior is stern Neoclassicism, the interior is a frillier and more playful Art Nouveau (called Liberty Style in Italy), viewable only on a worthwhile 30-minute guided tour or if you attend a performance (tour and performance details on page 59).

• *With the grand staircase at your back, walk straight across the street and jog slightly right to head up the lane called....*

❷ Via Bara all'Olivella

Enjoy a stroll along this little street, which is filled with small artisan shops and touristy restaurants. Along the way, check out a few vignettes of local culture.

While Palermo's sometimes dirty and broken streets may turn off some visitors, remember to look up—where you'll see an entirely different city. Balconies (adorned with flowers or laundry) are common here. Older residents sit and chat with friends in adjacent buildings, or talk to passersby on the street. Some balconies come wrapped in curtains, offering privacy and protection from the sun. Conventional wisdom is that there are no secrets in Sicily, as there are always eyes on the street.

On the right, stop in at #60, and say *ciao* to **Signore Puccio** if he's open. He runs a workshop where he makes small, inlaid-wood art pieces and paints a variety of traditional handicrafts, such as colorful papier-mâché boxes and nativity scenes.

Down a bit on the left at #95 is the **Teatro dei Pupi** of the Cuticchio family. Sicilian puppetry is an art form that uses puppets on rods, unlike marionettes, which are controlled by strings. The plays staged by the puppeteers reenact fictional episodes from the epic story of the life of Charlemagne and his chivalrous yet merciless knights (€10, shows usually Sat-Sun at 18:30, schedule posted on theater door, +39 091 323 400, figlidartecuticchio.com).

Just beyond, on the corner to the right at #42, peek inside to watch a wood craftsman at work on the lathe, fabricating candlesticks and reproduction parts for antique furniture.

Continue down Via Bara all'Olivella until you reach Piazza Bara all'Olivella. The building on the right is the ❸ **Salinas Regional Archaeological Museum,** with one of Sicily's best archaeological collections (described later, under "Sights in Palermo").

• *Continue straight along the side of the museum. At the corner, turn right onto…*

❹ Via Roma

Opened in 1865 to celebrate the newly unified kingdom of Italy, this street throbs with cars, buses, and shoppers. This is the last artery still open to traffic through downtown Palermo, as the city has pedestrianized the other two major streets, Via Maqueda and Via Vittorio Emanuele. Traffic congestion has increased dramatically in Sicily as more and more people buy cars. To minimize traffic, the city created a limited-traffic zone (ZTL)—charging a fee to drive in the city center—and added a free electric shuttle bus that circulates around the historic core.

The huge building on the right, dominating the street, is the main **post office,** built in the 1930s. This austere, imposing fascist style of architecture was favored by Italy's fascist dictator, Benito Mussolini. Using materials and architectural language reminiscent of ancient Rome, Mussolini's architecture-as-propaganda sends one message: You are small. Individualism is eclipsed by the all-powerful state.

Cross the street, take in the scope of the post office, and then continue up the street; you'll find a sleek, blocky department store on the left: **Rinascente.** This is the Italian version of Nordstrom. Admire their high-fashion window displays, and step inside if you're in the mood for a bit of air-conditioning. If you're hungry, their top-floor €€ terrace café offers great views as well as salads, sandwiches, pizza, and a mozzarella bar (daily, enter on Piazza San Domenico and find the elevators to your right).

Rinascente abuts Piazza San Domenico, which is dominated by the huge Baroque **Church of San Domenico**—the city's second largest. (For more on Sicily's Baroque history, see the sidebar on page 66.) If the church is open, step inside (free, Mon 17:00-19:00, Tue-Sun 9:00-13:00 & 17:00-19:00).

This very long church is bigger than it looks from the outside. The aisles are lined with tombs of famous Sicilians. To the right as you enter, you'll find the elaborate **float** of the Virgin of the Holy Rosary, which is carried on people's backs through town each year. This is a tradition you'll see all over Sicily, where religious processions are a fixture of life. Mary, supported by a cloud of angels, carries Jesus as San Domenico (St. Dominic) kneels at her side.

Farther down the right aisle, in a plainly adorned chapel, look for the **tomb** of Giovanni Falcone, marked *Magistrato—Eroe della Lotta alla Mafia* ("Magistrate—hero of the fight against the Mafia"). A Sicilian judge and prosecutor, Falcone led efforts to crack down on the Mafia, first in Palermo and later in Rome. After winning a series of convictions against Mafia leaders, Falcone, his wife, and several police officers were killed by a Mafia bomb in 1992. Falcone's death, intended to assert Mafia power, instead helped to turn public opinion against this social scourge. (For more on the Mafia in Sicily, see the sidebar on page 50.)

Back out on Piazza San Domenico, with your back to the church, pass through the square and (carefully) cross Via Roma to Via Bandiera, then continue about 50 yards up the street. On the left at #14, you can see a Spanish Gothic **tower house**, the Palazzo Alliata di Pietratagliata, built in 1573. Even though Palermo has a long history, most buildings you see today are Baroque, dating from the 1600s and 1700s, when the city was renovated by prosperous noble families. Prior to that (back when leading families needed to provide their own security), most of the city was made up of stone fortress-like tower houses similar to this one.

• *Head back across the street into the square and turn right to find the lane with the sign overhead reading* La Vucciria. *Before leaving Piazza San Domenico, consider a snack break at the recommended* **Bar Lucchese** *(on your left), well known for quality* granite, gelato, *and* spremuta— *fresh orange juice. Consider it a palate cleanser for our next stop.*

When you're ready, head down Via Maccheronai (the "Street of the Pasta Makers") and wind your way through the stalls of...

Palermo's History

Like much of Sicily, Palermo has a complicated history of domination. But unlike much of the island, it doesn't have Greek roots. The city was founded in the eighth century BC by Phoenician traders, near the natural harbor between two rivers.

Although the town was never conquered by the Greeks, it adopted a Greek name, Panormus (meaning "all port"), because it was a critical trading center for the mostly Greek island. Palermo's prized location—with its excellent port and the fertility of the thriving valley behind it—attracted a parade of successive invaders.

Palermo was a small settlement until the Arabs arrived (in AD 827) and put it on the map by making it the capital of the island. Under Arab rule, Palermo flourished and became one of Europe's leading cities. With a population of 100,000, it was the second-largest city in Europe (only Córdoba was bigger). During those times, Palermo had an estimated 300 mosques. Eventually the city covered up its rivers to allow expansion. (For more on the important Arab period in Palermo, see the "Arab Palermo" sidebar, later in this chapter.)

Then came the Normans, who arrived in the late 11th century after conquering England and southern Italy. The first Norman king of Sicily, Roger II (r. 1130-1154), found a multicultural island ruled by Arabs. Rather than impose his own culture and Roman Catholic religion, he allowed the ethnic groups to stay—each continuing in their traditional businesses: the Arabs as master engineers and craftsmen, the Byzantine Greeks as teachers, and the Jews in finance and trade. This tolerant attitude, allowing each community to play to its strengths, led to a period of economic prosperity that ushered in a golden age for Sicily.

Norman rule was followed by a series of other overlords: the German Hohenstaufen dynasty (1194-1250), French Angevins (1250-1282), Spanish Aragons and Bourbons (1282-1860), and, finally, a unified Italy (the Risorgimento of the 1860s). And, as throughout Sicily, each period of rule left its mark on Palermo. But Palermo's colonial heritage has been a blessing in disguise. Today's city is a wonderful patchwork of architecture, works of art, traditions, dialects, and delightful food cultures.

❺ La Vucciria Market

Browse the shops and stalls of Palermo's oldest marketplace (dead on Sunday). While this small market falls conveniently along the route of this walk, it pales in comparison to Palermo's biggies (Ballarò and Capo—see page 78), which are much busier and more sprawling. The Vucciria Market (likely named for the French *boucherie*—butcher) is less about the vendors and all about experiences.

Exploring, you can find butchers, household goods, produce, fish, and deli meats and cheeses. At #30 (after the first set of stalls, on the right), a knife store sharpens knives the old-fashioned way, with the *arrotino* whetting stone.

Several blocks down, on the left at #9, saunter into **Taverna Azzurra** and sidle up to the bar for a quick glass of wine with the local characters. This gritty dive bar cultivates a clientele that's an oddly harmonious mix of blue-collar locals and gregarious tourists.

At the end of the market street, **Piazza Caracciolo** bustles with food stands, open-air grills, and plastic tables. This ragtag space is a handy one-stop shop for Palermo's famous street food—from boiled octopus *(polpo bollito)* and spleen sandwiches *(pane con milza),* to less adventurous dishes such as grilled meats, deep-fried rice balls *(arancine)*, and chickpea fritters *(panelle)*. For more on your options here, see page 99.

Before leaving, take a moment to notice what isn't there: Traditional market stalls would have once filled this square. Competition from modern supermarkets has hit traditional markets hard. Now you'll find more cocktail bars and pop-up restaurants than fruits and vegetables. If you come back here in the evening, you'll find the Vucciria entering its next evolution—as a nightlife hotspot.

From the small fountain in the middle of the square, turn left and head down unmarked Via Argenteria Nuova ("New Street of the Silver Shop"). After a short block, step into the tiny piazza on the right to see the statue of the **"Genie of Palermo"** (in a niche in the wall on your right). This is a common symbol of the city, with a snake biting its chest and sucking its blood—a commentary on foreign domination. If you keep an eye out, you'll find other genies around Palermo.

Back on Via Argenteria Nuova, you are now walking above the subterranean Kemonia River, which once defined one side of Palermo.

Turn right to enter the next piazza, named for the water that flows under your feet—**Piazza Garraffello,** from the Arab *gharraf,* meaning "water in abundance." Survey the damaged buildings here, especially the one on the left. This area—located close to the strategic port—was heavily bombed by Allies during World War II, and even after all these years, many buildings still await reconstruction. The money received from the Marshall Plan was not used to restore the historic center, as it should have been, but instead funded cheap, sketchy apartment blocks on Palermo's outskirts.

• *With the "Genie of Palermo" behind you, take the first right-hand exit down...*

❻ Via Alessandro Paternostro

Cross Via Vittorio Emanuele and enjoy strolling along one of Palermo's most characteristic streets. With its sturdy paving stones, bulky balconies, and delightful shops, Via Alessandro Paternostro is one of Palermo's most appealing residential streets to wander. And it's a great place for browsing craft shops—the best of which are marked with the logo of the local artisan association, ALAB (see "Shopping in Palermo," later).

• *Carry on until you reach...*

❼ Piazza San Francesco

You've now crossed from the Vucciria into the edge of the Kalsa district. This neighborhood—even closer to the port—was also hit hard during WWII bombings, and the wealthier residents moved out, leaving this a poor and dangerous area. But recently, this district has been at the heart of the city's regeneration, and now the Kalsa is full of trendy boutiques and restaurants.

This beautiful square is one of the district's finest, where you'll find the famous, recommended **Antica Focacceria San Francesco** (a good place for a snack) and, opposite, a church also named for St. Francis. In a town with a Baroque facade on every corner, the Romanesque simplicity of the **Church of San Francesco d'Assisi** is a delightful surprise. Franciscans arrived in Palermo in 1224, two years before St. Francis' death, and built this church in 1255. Later remodeled in Baroque style, it was damaged by WWII bombs—triggering a restoration process that brought the church back to its original design. If it's open, step inside. It's typical of Franciscan churches: large but less decorated, in keeping with the order's philosophy of poverty and simplicity. Notice the elegant arch of the Mastrantonio Chapel (third on the left)—one of only a few Renaissance sculptures in the city.

The Mafia

Many travelers' first introduction to Sicily is *The Godfather*, the 1972 drama about the fictional Corleone family and the Sicilian crime syndicate known as the Mafia. While the Mafia still exists, it no longer holds sway over the island, and the violence that erupted in the 1970s and '80s is long past.

The origins of the Mafia—which referred to itself as Cosa Nostra ("Our Thing")—are murky but probably date back to the transition out of feudalism after the unification of Italy in the 1860s. The nobility were no longer in control, but the fledgling Italian state did not have the resources to impose the rule of law in far-flung Sicily. After generations of colonial rule, Sicilians found that they couldn't rely on the government to protect them.

Instead, they looked to people they knew for help. In rural areas, clans formed to provide protection from theft of valuable livestock and fruit. But before long, these "security guards" became a racket in cahoots with the thieves. The clans looted and dominated the people they "protected" and ensured silence with threats. Without anyone to challenge them, the Mafia clans grew stronger and moved into politics, consolidating power by requiring the people under their "protection" to vote for Mafia-controlled candidates.

That system came to a halt under Mussolini, Italy's fascist dictator (r. 1922-1943). Mussolini brutally crushed the Sicilian Mafia in the 1920s, imposing national government control—and driving some crime bosses to America. But after the Allied invasion in 1943 and the fall of the fascist government, chaos reigned in Sicily. The Allies looked for local help to control the island—and opened the door to the return of the Mafia clans. Corrupt politicians channeled Marshall Plan reconstruction funds to Mafia-run companies, which explains the cheaply built postwar housing sur-

• *Back outside, facing the church, follow the small brown signs to the* Oratorio di San Lorenzo *(to the left).*

ⓘ Oratory of San Lorenzo

Tucked away about 50 yards down the street, the Oratory of San Lorenzo (Oratorio di San Lorenzo), worth ▲, might warrant a quick visit. An *oratorio* was a Christian service organization—a kind of medieval Rotary Club—designed to provide social work not provided by governments. Each had its own oratory—a meet-

rounding Palermo (much of the money simply disappeared).

The Mafia had a successful M.O.: They'd show up at a business owner's shop and request a tribute, called a *pizzo*. Sometimes they'd say that someone in the community needed help, and they were simply passing the hat. Any refusal to pay would result in physical intimidation, injury, arson, or even murder. And nothing was discussed—the Mafia ruthlessly enforced a code of silence, called the *omertà*. Their dominance continued into the 1980s, reaching a violent frenzy as drug trafficking and turf wars mixed with politics. Those who openly opposed the Mafia were threatened or killed.

The tide turned in the early 1990s, beginning with the convictions of several high-profile Mafia leaders. In 1992, the two leading anti-Mafia judges, Giovanni Falcone and Paolo Borsellino, were murdered. A year later, a popular anti-Mafia priest, Giuseppe "Pino" Puglisi, was assassinated at point-blank range. But rather than strengthen the Mafia, the brazen murders fueled a growing resistance. Small acts, like shopkeepers refusing to pay the *pizzo*, emboldened the public. The *omertà* broke down and people started to report what they knew. One by one, crime families were taken down, some with claws deep in the Italian government. Today, the Mafia still exists, but is less active on the neighborhood level. However, organized crime remains big business: Criminal gangs operate on a worldwide scale, dealing in drugs, weapons, fraud, cybercrime, and human trafficking.

The typical visitor to Sicily will never directly encounter the Mafia but will see monuments recalling events leading to its fall from power. The tombs of Father Puglisi and Giovanni Falcone are inside Palermo Cathedral and the Church of San Domenico, respectively. The council room in City Hall (which you can ask to see) is lined with plaques dedicated to victims of the Mafia. On the road to the airport are pillars marking the sites of the Falcone assassination. The facade of the Nautical Institute has an evocative mural honoring Falcone and Borsellino (facing the marina on Via Cala). And on Piazza Marina is a memorial plaque for Joe Petrosino, an American policeman assassinated on that spot in 1909 while gathering information against the Sicilian Mafia in the US.

---

ing/worship hall/headquarters—and informally competed to have the most beautiful buildings, and the Baroque Oratory of San Lorenzo is no exception. But it is most (in)famous as the site of a theft of a priceless Caravaggio masterpiece. (For details on visiting the interior, see "Sights in Palermo," later.)

• *Head back to Piazza San Francesco and stand facing the popular* focacceria. *Turn left to continue down boutique-filled Via Alessandro Paternostro. After a few blocks, turn right at...*

⑨ Piazza Aragona

This wide medieval street has even more fun-to-browse little shops and sidewalk cafés and is jammed with people in the evenings. At the far end of the square, the big stone palace houses the **Galleria d'Arte Moderna (GAM),** featuring mostly Sicilian artists from the 19th and 20th centuries (for details, see "Sights in Palermo," later).

Head straight up Via Alloro, with GAM on your right. You'll soon reach the facade of the ultra-Baroque **Church of Sant'Anna,** which faces a lovely square with lively cocktail bars (another fun place to hang out after dark). At the next corner, before the busy street, look on your right for the **street sign** for *Via Lattarini* (from the Arab *attariin,* or grocery vendor)—one of the few surviving that's still written in three languages: Italian, Hebrew, and Arabic.
• *Cross busy Via Roma and continue straight uphill, past a row of inviting bars. You'll pop out at a church-ringed square.*

⑩ Piazza Bellini: Palermo's Trio of Churches

This tiny square is surrounded by three of the city's most famous churches. On your right as you enter the square, up the stairs, is **Santa Caterina**—with a boisterous Baroque interior that's a feast for the eyes. Across the square, up on a little plateau, are two other churches: On the left is **La Martorana,** with gorgeous gilded mosaics. And on the right is little **San Cataldo,** with its Arab architecture. Take time to tour these three, then head for  the next stop (for details on visiting each church, see the listings under "Sights in Palermo," later).
• *Before leaving the square, consider pausing for a fresh* cannolo *at the* **bakery** *tucked away in Santa Caterina's cloister. When you're ready to move on, face the Church of Santa Caterina and take the little alley on its left side to...*

⑪ Piazza Pretoria

At the center of this piazza is the Fontana Pretoria, better known as the **Fountain of Shame.** While fountains like this one may seem "typically Italian," they are actually quite rare in Sicily. The Renaissance never really took hold here, and this is

Arab Palermo

Palermo's ancient roots go back to the Phoenicians, but it wasn't a major city until the arrival in AD 827 of the Arabs—the first inhabitants who really spurred the city's development. Sicily's Arabs were from the Fatimid dynasty, whose caliphate stretched along the North African coast and beyond. They ruled Sicily for more than 200 years, reinventing what was a Byzantine colony, making the most of its strategic location and fertile soil. The Arabs brought new crops like citrus, nuts, sugar, dates, and cotton, and were marvels at water engineering, turning dry areas into farmland. Considered the most modern of its time, Arab culture was admired for its commitment to education and advances in mathematics, medicine, and astronomy.

Palermo also benefited from the Arabs' urban-planning skills. The city was enlarged as the two rivers surrounding it, the Papireto and Kemonia, were channeled underground. With the newly formed land, the Kalsa district was laid out with wide streets and gardens, some of which still exist. Palermo became one of the largest and most modern cities in Europe; at the turn of the millennium, it was considered the jewel of the Mediterranean.

In the 11th century, the Normans came from northern France to conquer and re-Christianize Sicily. They succeeded—but were so impressed that they chose to keep the Arab community and incorporate their skills into the new kingdom. Arab mathematics, cartography, and architecture merged with the Norman culture, bringing on a golden age. The 1200s were the heyday of "Arab-Norman" art and architecture, a unique hybrid of two distinct cultures sharing one island.

Arabian influence can still be found today throughout the city. The architecture of Palermo Cathedral, San Cataldo Church, the Norman Palace, and other buildings of the Norman era incorporate Arab decoration and engineering. And their influence can be found in the sweet shops and in the singsong of the merchants in the Ballarò and Capo markets, which began as Arab souks.

---

one of the few Renaissance works in the city. The fountain, made of Carrara marble, was originally crafted in 1555 for the Tuscan villa of a Spanish viceroy. It was sold to the city of Palermo by the viceroy's son, who had become Palermo's governor. His workers broke the fountain down to about 640 pieces and rebuilt it in front of the City Hall. (Locals note the irony that one of their most famous landmarks is the least *palermitano* thing about their city.)

This fountain's gathering of statues includes gods, goddesses, and grotesques on several levels. The nickname "Fountain of Shame" comes from the nude figures—considered quite racy in conservative Sicily. To make things worse, the fountain was assembled right under the windows of the Dominican convent of Santa Caterina (notice the adjacent dome). Local folklore claims that the nuns tried dressing the figures, but to no avail. Eventually, they slipped out of their convent—chisel and hammer in hand—and chipped away some of the offending parts. The iron fence was added in the 19th century to prevent further "remodeling."

The **City Hall** (Palazzo Pretorio) flies four flags: the blue EU flag; the red, white, and green Italian flag; the Sicilian flag with the Trinacria symbol (see the sidebar, later); and the red-and-yellow flag of Palermo. Below the flags stands the imperial eagle—the symbol of Palermo since the reign of Frederick II. And up at the top of the building is a statue of St. Rosalia, the city's patron saint (for more on Rosalia, see the sidebar on page 110). The bell to the left of the flags used to announce city assemblies. Don't be surprised to find *polizia* in riot gear loitering, as people usually gather here for protests. If you ask politely, you can often peek at the city-council chambers, with their walls covered in plaques dedicated to victims of Mafia assassinations.

• *With City Hall on your left, go down the steps to Via Maqueda and turn right. At the intersection, look around at the four fancy facades.*

⓬ Quattro Canti ("Four Corners")

The Quattro Canti, or "Four Corners," is the heart of the city of Palermo. This intersection of Via Maqueda and Via Vittorio Emanuele divides the city into its four major historical neighborhoods. Officially named Piazza Vigliena, the intersection's four concave corner facades create a great example of the Sicilian delight in Baroque architecture. It was built under Spanish rule to lure nobles to move from country villas into urban townhouses, in an effort to revitalize the city.

Starting from the bottom, Quattro Canti's three levels of statues represent the four seasons, each one personified as a woman (from a young maiden for Spring, to an elderly woman for Winter), Spanish kings (Charles V and Philip II, III, and IV—a reminder of the colonial overlords this island has endured), and four patron saints of Palermo (Cristina, Ninfa, Oliva, and Agatha). Wondering why St. Rosalia, the adored local saint, didn't make it to the Final

The Trinacria

The Trinacria, or Triskeles, is the ancient symbol of the island. Although there are variations, it typically shows a face in the center with three disjointed legs bent around it. Often it is portrayed with wings on the sides as ears and shafts of wheat sprouting from the center. Two pairs of tangled snakes, above the head and below the chin, create a hissing headdress.

The face is often referred to as Medusa, one of the three Gorgons, who, along with her two sisters, had the power of turning enemies into stone with a single glance. Because of this, the symbol could be a reference to the stone-creating mama herself, Mount Etna. The first existing example of the symbol was found on a bowl dating from the seventh century BC (now in the archaeological museum at Agrigento's Valley of the Temples), but the symbol itself is very likely much older. It is possible that early colonists, intent on keeping the fertile island for themselves, used this scary symbol to ward off superstitious Greek settlers.

The wheat shafts represent the fertility of the island, as Greek myths claimed that wheat grew wild here. The three legs are likely a representation of the three corners of the island, which links to the name "Trinacria," meaning three promontories.

The symbol has become the centerpiece of the Sicilian flag, which features the Trinacria on a red-and-yellow background split diagonally: red symbolizing Corleone and yellow representing Palermo—the first two territories to rebel against the French in 1282.

Four? Quattro Canti was finished before she became the city's patron saint. (To make up for it, they added a statue of Rosalia—higher than any of these—on top of the City Hall building, in the square we just left.)

After "reading" the Quattro Canti vertically, scan it horizontally, noticing the complete circle created by the **four seasons:** Spring (holding flowers; she's on your left, as you enter the square), Summer (holding fruit), Fall (holding pinecones), and Winter (with a flame). Baroque architects often hide a trick in their buildings—some sort of optical illusion. In this case, the contrast of sunlight and shadows *(chiaroscuri)* on the facades at this intersection changes progressively as the sun moves across the sky. As you pass through this intersection at different times of the day, notice how the light shifts: starting in the early morning with Spring, then moving clockwise as the day goes on, until illuminating Winter just before sunset. That's why Quattro Canti is also called the "Theater of the Sun."

Notice the elegant **lampposts** that ring the square. On the base of each lamppost, you'll find a face with three legs surrounding it. This is the symbol of Sicily, the Trinacria, which has represented the island for more than 3,000 years. On our walk today we've seen the fragments of many civilizations that have arrived and departed, but the Trinacria remains, watching over her island from flags, pottery, and decorative elements like these.

• *Our walk is over. From here, you have several excellent options. You could continue straight up the lovely, mostly traffic-free Via Maqueda; in about 10 minutes, you'll reach the* **Teatro Massimo***—where we began our walk. The* **Capo Market***, a great stop for lunch, is a few minutes' walk behind the theater.*

Or you could turn 90 degrees to the left and head up Via Vittorio Emanuele. In about 10 minutes, you'll reach the **Palermo Cathedral***; then, about 10 minutes past that is the* **Norman Palace***, with its mosaic-encrusted Palatine Chapel. Or to reach the* **Ballarò Market***, go back the way you came on Via Maqueda (passing the Fountain of Shame on your left). After two blocks, follow signs on the right to* Mercato Ballarò *and* Palazzo Conte Federico *on Via del Ponticello.*

All of these sights are described in the next section. You're in the center of Palermo life. Enjoy!

Sights in Palermo

CHURCHES ON PIAZZA BELLINI

This trio of glorious churches—facing each other across Piazza Bellini—are just a few steps from the Quattro Canti intersection and the Fountain of Shame.

Discount Deal: These three churches are part of a group called Il Circuito del Sacro. If you have a ticket for any one of these, show it to get a euro off at the others.

▲▲Church of Santa Caterina

Baroque—a hyperdecorative architectural style from the 1600s and 1700s—is at its most colorful and exuberant extreme in Sicily, as demonstrated in this church. Santa Caterina's simple exterior hides an explosive Sicilian Baroque interior, a riot of *marmi mischi e tramischi* (mixed and remixed) marble-inlay decoration.

Cost and Hours: €3 church entry, daily 10:00-18:00, last entry 45 minutes before closing; €10 rooftop visit, daily 9:30-13:30 & 15:00-17:00.

Visiting the Church: Here's a quick tour: The base of the first column on the right shows a three-dimensional depiction of the story of Jonah, where the ship and the whale's mouth appear ready to jump right out of the wall. Scenes on other column bases are nearly as dynamic—look for Abraham about to slay his son, Isaac.

This marble-inlay technique was popular in Florence during the Renaissance, later making its way down to Sicily. It's a type of mosaic, but rather than using small tiles, larger slabs are pieced together like a puzzle—taking advantage of the marble's color and pattern to heighten the design.

Walking farther down the nave—toward the over-the-top altar area—consider the history of this church, dedicated to Saint Catherine of Alexandria. This was the church of a prestigious convent, active until the early 2000s. In noble families of the past, the first-born daughter was given a dowry and strategically married off. Subsequent daughters, who lacked funds to marry into aristocracy, were instead "married to Christ" and sent to convents. Posh families sent their spare daughters here to Santa Caterina, giving a handsome donation for acceptance in this exclusive convent. The funds were used to take good care of the sisters...and to enrich the decor of their church.

Look up and find the golden screens. The families of the nuns could come for Mass on special days, and while they were not allowed to meet face to face, the sisters could observe from the hidden upper galleries.

This convent was famous for making sweets. On the right, near the altar, is a door where traditionally you could place your order and money on a lazy Susan and sweets popped out, allowing nuns to avoid contact with the public. Today a line forms in the cloister at *I Segreti del Chiostro* where you can buy the same sweets made using the original recipes. Their cannoli are freshly assembled as you watch (customize your order with pistachio, chocolate, candied orange, or cherries). Even if you're not ready for a snack, you can pop into the cloister to look around.

▲▲Church of La Martorana

This jewel-box church (officially called Santa Maria dell'Ammiraglio) is a typically Sicilian architectural fusion, combining Baroque with the oldest Byzantine-Norman mosaics on the island.

Cost and Hours: €2, Mon-Sat 9:30-13:00, closed Sun, +39 345 828 8231.

Visiting the Church: The core of the church dates from the 12th century. But that's not what you see when you first enter. Over the centuries, what started as a squat Byzantine church was eventually enlarged, with a Baroque extension at the front and back. (Since the standard-issue frilly Baroque altar dominates your view as you enter, it's easy to look right past the church's Norman highlights.)

In the first side chapel on the left is a **mosaic** of a man kneeling before Mary. This is George of Antioch, who commissioned the church in the 12th century. In a similar altar opposite George, you'll find his boss, King Roger II. Unlike George, the king stands proudly before Christ. This mixture of religious and political themes reinforces Roger's divine rule, as he receives a crown from Christ who hovers only ever-so-slightly above him.

Now walk slowly up the **nave.** Look up at the ceiling decor, and you can't miss where you step from the Baroque extension into the gilded mosaic-clad original core of the church. Looking down, you'll notice the floor changes at the same point.

On the underside of the arch just before the cupola (in the gilded mosaic) are scenes from Mary's life: on the left, a sweet Nativity scene, and on the right, the Dormition of the Virgin. Based on the belief that Mary didn't "die," but rather went into a deep, peaceful sleep before being assumed to heaven, this subject is rare in Italian Catholic churches—but common in Greek Orthodox ones. Although always devoted to the Greek Orthodox rite, in 1937 the church was officially handed over by the archdiocese of Palermo to the Albanian Orthodox community, who still celebrate their liturgy here today. Notice that the seats of the pews can be flipped up—in Eastern Orthodox worship services, the congregation stands rather than sits.

Stand under the **main dome** and appreciate the other glittering mosaics. You'll see Jesus seated on a throne, as he's typically depicted in Eastern Orthodox churches: Christ Pantocrator ("All Powerful").

Sights in Palermo

Exploring the rest of the church, think of this: Sicilians associate La Martorana with marzipan. In the past, nuns from the adjacent Benedictine convent (founded in the 12th century by Eloisa Martorana) raised funds making and selling fruit-shaped marzipan. That convent is long gone, but the traditional candies called "Frutta Martorana" live on in every sweet shop in town.

▲Church of San Cataldo

While built around the same time as La Martorana, the architectural contrast between the two churches is striking. Sicily was transitioning from Arab to Norman rule in the 12th century, and this church blends both styles of architecture. The solid Norman walls are lightened with the three round, red, Arab-inspired domes on top. This church remained unspoiled by its neighbor's  Baroque influence. In the 18th century, it was converted into a post office. During the fascist period, a restoration stripped it of its interior decoration, leaving it plain. Even so, it will make you feel like you've gone back in time 900 years.

Cost and Hours: €2.50, daily 10:00-14:00 & 14:30-18:00, Piazza Bellini 3.

OTHER SIGHTS IN THE CITY CENTER

These are listed roughly in the order you'll reach them on my self-guided Palermo City Walk, earlier.

▲▲Teatro Massimo

Palermo has two landmark theaters, Teatro Massimo and Teatro Politeama. Teatro Massimo—closer to the center and with the more impressive interior—can be seen on a concise, interesting 30-minute tour. (The theater's history and exterior are described earlier, at the beginning of my Palermo City Walk.)

Cost and Hours: €12, tours run daily 9:30-18:20—enter through the  door to the left of the grand staircase and ask about the next tour, classy Giardini del Teatro café, +39 091 605 3267, teatromassimo.it.

Visiting the Theater: On the tour, your guide will lead you through the Liberty Style (Italian Art Nouveau) interior—beginning with the original detailed wooden model of the theater, which the architect used to win the commission. Then, stepping into the impressively huge auditorium, understand the forgotten elegance and importance of Palermo in the past. The auditorium boasts near-perfect acoustics thanks to the horseshoe shape of the seats and mahogany wood used for the construction of the boxes, which naturally amplifies the sound. Very modern for its day, the theater even has an early form of climate control: the 11 fresco panels in the ceiling, arranged like the petals of a daisy, can be raised to let out hot air. From the auditorium, you'll head up to the royal box (with the best seats—and acoustics—in the house), then visit the Pompeiian Room, a domed lounge modeled after the frescoes from that ancient Roman city.

Performances: The theater hosts performances year-round, and tickets can be affordable (sometimes available day of show, box office open Tue-Sun 9:30-15:30, closed Mon, same contact info as above).

▲Salinas Regional Archaeological Museum (Museo Archeologico Regionale Antonino Salinas)

Palermo's easily appreciated archaeological museum shows off the rich mix of ancient civilizations that shaped Sicily. You'll see Egyptian hieroglyphs, Phoenician sarcophagi, and Greek vases. But the museum's highlight is the fascinating trove of sculpture from Selinunte, the ancient Greek city on Sicily's southwest coast (see page 197). Whether you visit Selinunte or not, these impressive fragments from its ruined temples are

striking reminders of the enormous influence that ancient Greece had on Sicily.

Cost and Hours: €8; Tue-Sat 9:00-19:00, Sun until 13:30, closed Mon; worthwhile €5 audioguide; Piazza Olivella 24, +39 091 611 6805, coopculture.it (search "Salinas").

Visiting the Museum: Entering the museum, pass through a serene little courtyard (say hi to the turtles) and into a second courtyard. Get oriented. The Selinunte sculptures are straight ahead, through the Selinus Hall. But first, we'll see artifacts from the civilizations that preceded Selinunte.

• *Explore the rooms circling the courtyard, starting with the room immediately to your right.*

The **Palermo Stone**—a slab of black basalt covered in Egyptian hieroglyphics—is as old as the pyramids (c. 2450 BC). The text (read right to left) is one of the oldest histories in existence, a boon to scholars. It lists every Egyptian pharaoh from 3100-2300 BC, including Khufu, who built the Great Pyramid of Giza. It's also a calendar, with years named after important festivals and births. So why is an Egyptian *stele* (monument stone) in Sicily? Though Egyptian culture was the foundation of all Mediterranean culture, the Egyptians didn't settle Sicily. A Sicilian family donated this *stele* to the museum in the late 1800s.

• *Now let's see artifacts of the next great Mediterranean civilization—the Phoenicians—who first docked their ships in Sicily around 1000 BC. Exiting the Palermo Stone room, turn left and start circling the exhibits clockwise.*

Find the **Torso of the Stagnone**—a Phoenician sculpture from the sixth century BC. Appropriately for the sea-trading Phoenicians, this stone fragment was discovered on the sea floor near Marsala. And appropriately for the Egyptian-influenced Phoenicians, the statue is wearing an Egyptian-style kilt (a *shenti*) and has the stiff pose of Egyptian art. But because the statue is made of a local limestone, it was likely made here in Phoenician Sicily.

• *Continue into the next small room, with more Phoenician treasures.*

The **Sarcophagi of Cannita** (fifth-century BC)—two large stone caskets in the shape of women—were discovered near the Phoenician port town of Palermo. The Phoenician burial practice (preserving a body for the afterlife) borrows from Egyptian traditions, but the women's elaborately carved dresses show the influence of the next great civilization to touch down in Sicily: the Greeks.

• *Now we turn to Sicily's Greek legacy. Continue along the courtyard rooms, where you'll pass by red-and-black Greek vases (kraters) and ancient jewelry. Stop in the room with four vases.*

The **Centuripe vases** put a Sicilian spin on the typical Greek vase. Unlike the kraters, these have molded decorations and tempera painting. As the painted scenes depict, these vases were typically used for weddings and funerals. The first vase shows a tribute to the bride. The second (a low bowl with handles, which once had a lid) held wedding gifts. The third vase features a colorful parade of bridesmaids. Finally, on the fourth vase, notice the Gorgon head, possibly used for funeral rituals.

• *Now for the museum's high point: a wing dedicated to remains of the ancient Greek city of Selinunte—one of the greatest of the Greek settlements on Sicily (c. 628-250 BC). Start at the end of the courtyard, in the main room.*

Take in the **model of the Selinunte site.** Perched on the northwest tip of the island, Selinunte was one of many colonies the energetic Greeks founded as they expanded around the Mediterranean. At its zenith, Selinunte was a thriving city of some 30,000, with an impressive skyline of towering temples on its high points. Though those temples are now mostly ruined, the best sculptures have been brought here to this museum. On the model, locate the temples featured on this tour: Temples X and Y, Temple C, and Temple E. (Scholars use letters because the temples are so ruined no one knows what god they were dedicated to.)

• *Now let's see some of the treasures that graced Selinunte. Start with one of the oldest—the large stone to the left of the model.*

This *stele* (560 BC) dates from the era when the Greeks first founded the city. It's dedicated to the great Greek hero Hercules: the last line reads "I am sacred to Heracles." The deep cuts in the stone occurred as it was being unearthed.

• *Facing the model of Selinunte, turn right, into the room housing small relief panels called metopes. These bas reliefs portray Greek myths with a distinctive thick-bodied Sicilian style.*

The **metopes from Temples X and Y** are some of the oldest. Chained together, these panels formed a decorative frieze running around the upper part of the temples. They told stories, like the panels of a graphic novel. On the far left, a winged female sphinx crouches, ready to pounce. Next to her is Europa riding atop a bull. This myth was especially meaningful to the Selinuntians. Europa was a Phoenician princess abducted by  the Greek god Zeus (in the form of a bull)—symbolically merging Phoenician and Greek culture and laying the foundation for "Europe." Three metopes down, check out the impressive four-horse chariot driven by the queen of the gods, Hera, and wise Athena.

• *For more metopes, turn left and enter the large room.*

The wall to your left is lined with **metopes from Temple C**, the largest and most important of Selinunte's temples. These particular panels graced the temple's main entrance, facing a sacred sacrificial area, and depict well-known myths of the day. There's Apollo on his four-horse chariot *(quadriga)* carrying the sun across the sky. Next, the great hero Perseus coolly decapitates the hideous monster

Medusa. The blood spilled by Medusa results in the next panel: the birth of the winged horse Pegasus. And finally, a fed-up Hercules punishes the rascally Cercope twins by dangling them from poles. Before moving on from Temple C, note that it once had one more very impressive piece of sculpture…which we'll see in a bit.

• *For now, turn your attention to sculptures from another Selinunte temple here in the same room.*

Along the far wall are **metopes from Temple E**—the best preserved of Selinunte's temples, which still has its full complement of stout Doric columns. Above those columns ran this row of metopes with their dramatic scenes. Find Hercules grabbing an Amazon warrior by the hair to carry her off. There's Zeus casually leaning back and toasting his wife Hera. Then the hunter Acteon, after angering Artemis, is attacked by his own dogs. And finally, the myth that' so important to Sicily: Athena pushes down the giant Enceladus, burying him under Mt. Etna… where he occasionally erupts in anger to this day.

• *Flesh out your vision of ancient Selinunte in the next long hallway. You'll pass by various architectural decorations, ancient gutters, etc.*

In the third room, find the **Corinthian wine jug**. It shows Artemis, goddess of the hunt, holding a vividly rendered swan and ram. This and the accompanying alabaster ointment vase and iron dagger were buried with their owner, a wealthy Selinuntian.

• *Continue through the long hallway, past pottery, jewelry, Roman coins, terracotta busts, and amphorae (containers used to transport wine and olive oil). Make your way into the covered central courtyard, filled with impressive pieces.*

Dominating the courtyard wall is a **Gorgon mask**—the largest found anywhere in the ancient Greek world. This was the centerpiece of (the aforementioned) Temple C's pediment. Masks like this were both decorative and thought to protect the temple from evil spirits. Arranged purposefully atop a life-size schematic drawing, you get a feel for the large scale of the temple—and of Greek culture at its peak. Greek-based Selinunte thrived for four centuries (c. 628-250 BC), before falling to the Carthaginians and finally being destroyed when the Romans took over Sicily.

To complete your visit, check out the various **lion head** waterspouts—once brightly painted—which also warded off evil spirits. These were from Selinunte's neighboring city of Himera—one final

▲Oratory of San Lorenzo (Oratorio di San Lorenzo)

An oratory was like a proud chapter house of a service club, funded by a local guild and associated with a neighborhood church. Stepping inside this oratory you'll be immersed in a luxurious and exquisite Baroque world. While Baroque architecture was common enough throughout Italy in the 17th and 18th centuries, Sicilian Baroque—like Sicily itself—goes a step further, adding drama and intensity. And, thanks to the spirit of competition between the brotherhoods of various *oratorio*s, this chapel isn't shy of artistic exuberance.

Cost and Hours: €3, daily 10:00–18:00, Via Immacolatella 5, +39 091 611 8168, amicimuseisiciliani.it.

Visiting the Oratory: Enter the garden patio, buy a ticket, then cross over to the oratory.

The patron saint of this brotherhood was **San Lorenzo** (St. Lawrence), who was martyred. As you enter, look high on the right to see him being grilled to death. Throughout the space, look for other symbolic grills (for example, in the center of the floor). Notice also the mischievous cupids engaged in joyful—if occasionally painful—examples of their juvenile love of life. The decor is stucco (lightweight plasterwork over a frame, made to look like carved stone).  The family that decorated this space, the Serpottas, is famous in Sicily for developing a technique called *allustratura*, a process that makes plaster so shiny it looks like fine marble.

The **Nativity altarpiece** is a reproduction. The original, by Caravaggio, hung here for over 350 years. It was stolen on October 17, 1969, and has never been recovered. Someone slipped in with a knife, cut it out of its frame, rolled it up, and vanished. The brazen theft of this venerated religious artwork was symbolic for Palermo, as it signaled the depth of depravity in a city under Mafia control. More than 4,000 pieces of art were stolen from churches in the 1960s, and many of them were never found.

Today, the whereabouts of the priceless Caravaggio—unsalable on the legitimate art market—is shrouded in mystery. This reproduction, *Nativity 2.0,* was installed here in 2015 and inaugurated by the president of Italy—whose brother was assassinated by the Mafia. But the case isn't closed, and this theft remains in the top 10 on the FBI's list of unsolved art crimes.

GAM (Galleria d'Arte Moderna)
In Italy, "modern" is a relative term. This art collection—featuring mostly Sicilian artists from the 19th through early 20th century—may not sport any names familiar to Americans. But it's beautifully presented in a fine Spanish Gothic palazzo, and fans of Romanticism, Neoclassicism, and Impressionism enjoy seeing how those movements found expression in Sicily—including landscapes that give a flavor of the island in the past.

Cost and Hours: €10; daily 9:30-18:30, last entry one hour before closing; slow but decent audioguide-€4, Via Sant'Anna 21, +39 335 545 3277, gampalermo.it.

Visiting the Museum: The permanent exhibit begins on the ground floor. You'll see lots of fleshy nudes, epic and large-scale historical scenes, Neoclassical sculpture, and misty landscapes evocative of everyday life in the burgeoning kingdom. In the adjoining cloister, head up the stairs to continue through the permanent collection: realism (genre scenes), expressive portraits, and more landscapes from around Sicily. Then climb up one more flight of stairs for a look at Sicilian Modernism. The treasure of the collection is on the landing at the entrance to the first room—Franz Von Stuck's *Il Peccato (The Sin)*. From there, explore a world of Pointillism, Cubism, Expressionism, and works by the "Group of Four" (Gruppo di Quattro).

WEST END OF DOWNTOWN
To reach these sights, head west from the main Quattro Canti intersection along the mostly traffic-free Via Vittorio Emanuele.

▲Palermo Cathedral (Cattedrale Metropolitana della Santa Vergine Maria Assunta)
Palermo's cathedral is a crazy quilt of architectural styles and patterns. Much like the city itself, it was added to and changed with each new ruling power. While the city has no lack of interesting churches, the cathedral is most dear to the locals, as it houses the bones of their celebrated patron, St. Rosalia. Because it's free to enter, the cathedral is often jammed with cruise-ship crowds.

Cost and Hours: Cathedral—free, Mon-Sat 7:00-19:00, Sun from 8:00; rooftop—€7, includes entrance to royal tombs, daily

Sicily's Unique Baroque

While Baroque art is everywhere in Europe, "Sicilian Baroque" is distinct. In the 1700s, the convivial Sicilians took the already ornamental Baroque style to even higher levels of beauty and knock-your-socks-off drama. From soaring towers to sumptuous chapels to playful palaces and cozy piazzas, Sicilian Baroque dazzles.

Traditional Baroque was first forged in Rome in the 1600s. This over-the-top art featured curves and curlicues, cherubs on billowy clouds, chandeliered ballrooms, and corkscrew columns. As the chosen style of Europe's nobles and powerful Catholic Church, it was meant to impress.

Sicily was an early adopter of Baroque. Palermo's **Quattro Canti** ("Four Corners")—four elegant townhouses angled theatrically—features the kinds of curved facades, sensuous statues, and inviting fountains that would look right at home in Baroque Rome (see page 54).

Sicilian Baroque really began on one very specific day. On January 11, 1693, a 7.4 magnitude earthquake rocked Sicily, leveling entire towns...and leaving a blank canvas for rebuilding. Whole cities—Noto, Catania, Ragusa, Modica, Scicli—had to be rebuilt from scratch. Many started fresh with a logical grid plan, punctuated with delightful piazzas enclosed by elegant buildings, creating a kind of communal "living room." The rebuild was financed by a close-knit circle of rich and devil-may-care nobles. They built glitzy new *palazzi* to host lavish parties for their friends, and remade churches in grand style to show off their generosity and sophistication.

By the mid-1700s, homegrown Sicilian architects were taking Baroque to new heights with their own distinctive style. Perhaps

9:30-18:00, closed in bad weather and afternoons off-season; Via Vittorio Emanuele, +39 091 334 373, cattedrale.palermo.it. You can pay to see the rest of the "monumental area" (which includes the crypt and treasury), but I'd skip it.

Background: When the Norman kings took over Sicily in the

Sights in Palermo

the most instantly recognizable feature of Sicilian Baroque is the church with a tall central bell tower (such as Ragusa's **Cathedral of San Giorgio** and **Church of San Giuseppe,** and Modica's **Cathedral of San Giorgio**). Many churches also gained wide, grand staircases (also seen at both San Giorgio cathedrals mentioned above).

Sicilian church facades are rarely flat. They bulge out (convex) or curve in (concave). Columns stick out prominently from the surface, creating clear horizontal-vertical lines. In the bright Sicilian sun, such irregular facades cast dramatic light-and-dark shadows. Inside, churches can be mind-bogglingly ornate. Sicilian decorators loved marble inlay, intricately carved. Walls come alive, crawling with intertwined vines, embracing cherubs, animals or shells—often executed in the local gray-white volcanic stone (Palermo's **Santa Caterina** and **La Martorana** churches are good examples).

Baroque theatricality was baked into Sicilian life. On holy days, the robed faithful would parade through town (and still do) bearing colorful floats with emotion-packed statues of Mary and the saints (see page 159). Everyday buildings remain adorned with distinctive Sicilian balconies, ornamented with curvy iron railings and playful faces of people, animals, or fantastic beasts (see Noto's **Palazzo Nicolaci**

and Ragusa's **Palazzo La Rocca**). Such whimsical touches are a testament to Sicilian Baroque in full flower.

But as the 1700s waned, so did Sicilian Baroque. A trendy new style was coming out of France: Neoclassicism. And those free-spending aristocrats, having neglected their feudal estates, were running out of money. For the next two centuries, there was virtually no new construction. Sicily's Baroque structures were frozen in the glacier of economic decline. As a result, visitors today can enjoy the enduring legacy of those high-living Sicilians, who gave us such beauty as they blithely went Baroque.

1100s, they had a mission from the pope to consolidate the power of the western Roman church. Palermo was a melting pot—with Muslims, Jews, and Eastern Orthodox Christians—so building this new, bigger cathedral on the site of an older one was a political statement. Beginning in 1168, a powerful cardinal oversaw its construction, following an ambitious plan that was meant to intimidate the new young king, William II. But William had the last laugh when he diverted funds to building Monreale, an even more grandiose cathedral in the nearby hills. While Monreale was finished within a matter of decades (and is more impressive to visit today—see the next chapter), Palermo's underfunded cathedral project limped along for centuries, changing in style depending on the period. (For more on these two cathedrals, see the sidebar on page 115.)

Visiting the Cathedral: From the **exterior,** your eyes are drawn to wild graphic patterns—such as the crenellated fringe at the top of the walls and the geometric tracery over the side door. These features are typical of the Byzantine-Norman style that was born in 12th-century Sicily, when the geometrical, fortified-church architecture of the Normans blended with the decorative Arabic style that preceded them.

The **portico** of the church—over the side door—dates from Spanish rule in the 1400s, in Gothic-Catalan style. Look for a carving on the farthest column to the left, which has inscribed verses from the Quran in Arabic—likely recycled from a mosque—and the entire structure is capped by a (much later) Sicilian Baroque dome.

Now step **inside.** The drab Neoclassical interior (renovated this way in 1801), full of somber Baroque side chapels, is a jarring contrast to the wild exterior. Head to the nave, turn right, stroll toward the altar, and try to imagine this space before its remodel. It would have had soaring Gothic arches, wallpapered with shining gold mosaics.

Near the altar, locate the brass line inlaid in the floor, illustrated with signs of the zodiac. This **meridian line** acts as a solar calendar. A small hole in the dome above lets in sunlight that pinpoints the zodiac, and therefore the month.

To the right of the main altar, a massive silver altar houses the bones of Palermo's patron saint, **St. Rosalia.** During the plague of 1624, the saint appeared to a hunter and revealed her resting place on nearby Monte Pellegrino. Once her bones were brought back to Palermo, the plague ended. Rosalia has delivered miracles to locals ever since. (For more on Rosalia, see the sidebar on page 110.) Palermo's other four patron saints—who don't command nearly the devotion of Rosalia—are squeezed into one crowded chapel, on the right aisle, about halfway down.

Opposite the church entrance and a bit toward the front is a modern marble altar celebrating another miracle worker, **Father Giuseppe Puglisi.** This priest served in Palermo's poor neighborhoods in the 1980s and focused his ministry on vulnerable kids, encouraging them to stay away from the Mafia. His anti-Mafia stance led to his assassination on his birthday in 1993. The guilt-ridden assassins eventually turned themselves in, becoming Mafia informants.

Puglisi's death ignited local fury and helped to bring about the end of Mafia domination in the city. Notice how Father Puglisi is depicted: always smiling and happy, and with oversized hands (representing his hard work to serve his community). Considered a martyr and believed to be the last person killed by the local Mafia, Father Puglisi was beatified by Pope Francis in 2013.

Before you exit, at the back of the church near the entrance door, a screened-off section houses mildly interesting **royal tombs,** most with elaborate canopies (requires admission—skip it).

▲▲▲Palatine Chapel (Cappella Palatina) and Norman Palace (Palazzo Normanni)

This sprawling palace (sometimes called the Palazzo Reale, "Royal Palace") has been home to the various rulers of Sicily since the ninth century. On weekends, a visit includes the somewhat-interesting royal apartments, where Sicily's regional assembly meets. But the main reason to visit is the sumptuous Palatine Chapel, a unique cross-cultural work of architecture from the 1100s.

While the cathedral at Monreale is much bigger and displays more impressive mosaics, if you won't make it out there or prefer to see mosaics close up, you won't be disappointed by the elegance of the Norman-Byzantine mosaics here. Because the chapel is included in every cruise-ship excursion for Palermo, expect crowds (and consider skipping it if you're going to Monreale).

Cost: €14.50, audioguide-€5.

Hours: Mon-Sat 8:30-17:30, Sun until 13:30; chapel closed Sun 9:30-11:30, apartments open Fri-Mon only; last entry one hour before closing.

Information: +39 091 705 5611, federicosecondo.org.

Getting There: The Norman Palace sits at the west end of Via Vittorio Emanuele, past the cathedral, about a 15-minute **walk** from the main Quattro Canti intersection. Walking up Via Vittorio Emanuele, you'll head toward the Porta Nuova—a gigantic decorative gateway that sticks out from the side of the palace, spanning the street. Before the gate, you'll pass a park, Villa Bonanno, on your left (peek in to see an enclosed Roman mosaic—one of the rare few traces of Rome that remains in Palermo). At the top of the park, you'll find the ticket kiosk. The entrance to the palace is opposite the kiosk, up a few steps, in Piazza del Parlamento—it's the big grand doorway. (To trace this route, see the "Palermo" map near the beginning of the chapter).

If you don't want to walk, the palace is served by **bus** #104 and the free **shuttle bus** *(navetta)* that circulates around central Palermo. A **taxi** from the station to the palace is around €10-15.

Crowd-Beating Tips: The Palatine Chapel is tiny, and only a few dozen people can enter at a time. Big cruise-excursion and noisy student groups often create long waits for much of the day (peaking in the late morning). Try visiting right when it opens or in the late afternoon.

Services: WCs are located at the entrance after security and on the far side of the palace from where you enter. You'll find a tranquil café in the Royal Gardens.

Background: This palace, the oldest royal residence in Europe, was the seat of the Arab emirs, who began it in the ninth century—building it upon original Carthaginian foundations from the fifth century BC. Palermo was not the largest city on the island when the Arabs arrived, but over their two centuries of rule, they built Palermo into a capital, with sprawling palaces and gardens. Upon arriving in the late 11th century, the Normans were impressed with the city they found, and decided to adapt what was already there—making the Arab palace their own royal seat and adding onto it. Other rulers who succeeded the Normans also made it their capital. In the 1500s, the Spanish Bourbon and Habsburg governors who ruled the island moved in and added opulent royal apartments, which today house the Sicilian Regional Assembly—the modern version of a traditional parliament that dates all the way back to Norman times. (Sicily and Iceland have little in common, but both claim to have the "world's oldest parliament." I'll leave that fight to the historians.) While Sicily is fully part of Italy, it's allowed to operate a "parliament" with a greater degree of self-rule than most other regions.

Visiting the Palace: Before heading inside, look up and scan the building's eclectic **exterior.** You'll see a patchwork of archi-

Sights in Palermo

tectural styles suggesting traces of each culture that shaped this building.

After buying your ticket, pass through security and the bookshop, following signs to *Cappella Palatina*. Enter the main courtyard of the palace, Cortile Maqueda, and walk straight ahead, then climb the grand staircase on the opposite side. On the first landing, you'll see the Palatine Chapel entry queue on the left. The royal apartments are up another flight of stairs. (If

the apartments are open and the chapel line is long, try touring the royal chambers first while waiting for the chapel line to die down.)

Palatine Chapel: While waiting in line, get ready for the glittering glass mosaics you're about to see by learning about the king who commissioned them: Roger II (r. 1130-1154), who ruled over a complicated island. Yet somehow, he was able to honor each culture (see the "Palermo's History" sidebar, near the beginning of this chapter). In 1132, he commissioned a chapel to be built inside the royal residence, using architects and craftsmen from the different communities. That's why you'll find a mix of Norman, Byzantine, and Arab artistic traditions, architecture, and craftsmanship.

Upon entering the chapel, let your eyes adjust to the low light. The artistic style is eastern, coming from Constantinople (today's Istanbul), but the craft is rooted in ancient Roman mosaic tradition. The mosaic artists were Byzantine Greeks, and many of the motifs and imagery in this Catholic chapel are Eastern Orthodox. For example, over the altar, rather than Christ on the cross, you'll find Christ Pantocrator—the typical representation of the Eastern Orthodox Christ.

The **architecture** of the chapel is a unique mishmash. The rectangular, basilica-style plan, with heavy walls and small windows, links to Norman traditions, while the arches supporting the nave are in an Arab-style high horseshoe shape. The lower walls have abstract, geometric designs and stylized palm trees—Muslim artists were forbidden from representing the human form, so they excelled at colorful patterns. Look up to find decorative Arabic writing hidden in eight-pointed stars. The wooden ceiling, covered in *muqarna*s—stalactite-like decorations seen in traditional Islamic architecture—is the most unusual feature in the chapel. Usually a church with *muqarna*s has been converted from a mosque, but this is the only original church in Europe to have a ceiling with this type of ornament from Muslim cultures.

The chapel's **mosaics** are set up to be read like a book. In the dome above the altar, Christ Pantocrator ("All Powerful") appears as a multiracial mascot: Jesus' nose and lips are straight like a Byzantine Greek, his eyebrows and mustache are brown as an Arab's, and his hair is blond and his eyes are light hazel in color, like the Normans. He was not just an icon, but the symbol of the melting-pot Norman kingdom in Sicily.

Flanking Jesus are domes featuring Peter (left, white beard) and Paul (right, balding). The stories of each of these saints' lives fill the walls of both side aisles. Higher up and farther down the central nave are stories of the Old Testament, beginning with the Creation in the top-right corner (to find the beginning of the story, look for the lands of the earth being cut up like a pie). Facing the high altar, in the back of the church, is another  Christ Pantocrator (strategically placed directly above where the king would sit on his throne, reminding congregants of his divine right to rule), again flanked by Peter and Paul. Amazingly, 95 percent of the mosaics in the chapel are original.

A recent restoration found more evidence that Roger II was a tolerant and inclusive king. Hidden in the decoration was an inscription in Arabic reading "Roger is the chosen one of Allah," next to lines of the Quran. This is a truly remarkable statement about a Catholic French Norman knight who was sent by the pope to reclaim the island from the Arabs; it shows the respect he must have earned from the Sicilian people.

Royal Apartments: The Sicilian Regional Assembly is in session Tuesdays, Wednesdays, and Thursdays. On other days, it's possible to head up one more flight of stairs to see the rooms where they meet.

At the top of the stairs, walk down the long hall but look for open doors on the left, through which you can see the "Stanza da Ercole" or Hercules room. This is where the Sicilian assembly meets and makes decisions for the island. If the scenes on the wall are any indication, getting Sicilians to agree to anything must be the 13th Labor of Hercules.

Sights in Palermo

Continuing on, you'll come to the Hall of Viceroys, with large portraits of governors from the centuries of Spanish domination. The rooms that follow are each decorated in a different style, matching the tastes of the last Bourbons who lived here. You'll pass through a blue "Pompeii-style" room, painted to mimic the frescoes discovered when Pompeii was first uncovered in the 1700s.  The adjacent room is in Chinese style. Maria Carolina, a Habsburg archduchess who became queen of Naples and Sicily (and was a sister of Marie Antoinette), designed this room to show off her collection of Chinese porcelain.

At the end of the series of rooms is the **Tower of the Winds,** which resembles architectural styles from North Africa. It's the only one of the original towers open to the public. While there used to be four towers, just two remain—and the other one houses the office of the president of Sicily. Check out the elegant mosaic decoration in **King Roger's Hall,** similar to that  of the Palatine Chapel but showing off exotic plants and animals and abstract, glittering patterns. The final rooms are less spectacular but display large-scale paintings of Sicilian scenery from the 19th century. Stop for a moment and admire these pastoral scenes. Fix them in your mind so you can think back on them later in your trip, when you're enjoying similar views—in person—around Sicily.

Before you leave the palace complex, it's worth taking a quick stroll through the breezy **Royal Gardens** (exit on the ground floor, to the left as you come down the monumental staircase). They're built on top of an old defensive bastion. Those who really want to go deep into Palermo's history should follow the signs for the *Halls of the Duca di Montalto.* Stairs lead down (through a massive hall often hosting a contemporary-art show) into a small exhibit on the city's ancient roots—interesting for the archaeologically inclined, since the exhibit weaves through the oldest foundations of the palace.

The Fading Sicilian Aristocracy

Prior to the mid-19th century, Sicily was ruled under a feudal system. Wealthy noble families had large land holdings in the countryside and hired peasants to work the land; income from the estates supported the lifestyles of the noble and famous. Palermo is full of palaces built by those families, but today many are dilapidated and deserted. So, what happened?

In the mid-1800s, the fever of nationalism fell over Europe, and a call to unite the Italian peninsula was answered by the Risorgimento—the unification of Italy. A civil war swept from Sicily to Piedmont, and the foreign powers controlling Italy were deposed. The country was at last united under a common flag, with a new king.

As the old regimes ended, so did the social order. Lands from noble families were "redistributed" to the workers, and the upper classes began a long decline. The famous book *The Leopard (Il Gattopardo),* by the Sicilian author Giuseppe Tomasi di Lampedusa (and recent Netflix series of the same name) documents this shift. With its nostalgia for a lost time, it's a Sicilian *Gone with the Wind*. World War II and Mussolini exacerbated the situation, as the monarchy was abolished and Palermo's city center was damaged by Allied bombs. Many of the noble families ran out of money and luck, and abandoned their palaces for good.

These days, a few noble descendants remain, hanging on to their palaces as best they can. Many look for ways to support their heritage, sometimes by welcoming tourists into their homes. (As a local "princess" in Palermo says, you can't eat a title.) One of my favorite places to sneak a glimpse of the aristocratic life is at the Palazzo Conte Federico in the Ballarò neighborhood.

IN LA KALSA, NEAR THE HARBOR

These sights cluster in the eastern end of central Palermo, just before the harbor, in the neighborhood called La Kalsa. Most are close to the delightful park called Villa Garibaldi—a fenced, shady retreat with inviting benches under gigantic trees, centered in Piazza Marina.

▲Inquisition Cells at Palazzo Chiaramonte Steri

Palazzo Chiaramonte was the former home of the powerful Chiaramonte family during the Middle Ages (this is a famous name in Sicily—you'll find it all over the island). In 1392, the head of the family, Andrea Chiaramonte, refused to surrender to the Spanish Aragonese and was beheaded in the piazza in front of his home, ending the family line. The Spanish mounted his head on the palace wall and moved in, basing their administration here.

During the Spanish Inquisition of the 1600s, the stables were converted into jail cells for those awaiting trial (the Inquisition hit Sicily hard, expelling many of its ethnic minorities and ending the period of religious tolerance). On the included guided tour, you'll see those cells (covered in drawings by prisoners) and learn about the history of the Inquisition.

Cost and Hours: €8 one-hour guided tour; daily 10:00-20:00, multilingual tours depart generally hourly at the top of the hour—check at the ticket office for the next departure, last tour departs one hour before closing; Piazza Marina 61, +39 091 2389 3780, coopculture.it (search "Steri").

Visiting the Palazzo: On the tour, you'll see about a half-dozen original cells, plus one that has been restored. The cells are elaborately decorated with detailed drawings, writing, and some carvings by bored prisoners waiting for an uncertain fate. As art supplies weren't readily available, prisoners used bodily fluids and dirt to paint the walls. Many of the drawings are religious, praying for a favorite saint to intercede on their behalf. Some drawings are more imaginary, but all tell a little about who the prisoners were. Keep an eye out for writing in Shakespearean English: Palermo was a trade capital, and foreigners were occasionally rounded up for an "interview."

▲Regional Art Gallery at Palazzo Abatellis

Built at the end of the 15th century for the magistrate of Palermo, Francesco Abatellis, and badly damaged during World War II, this fine Spanish-Gothic palazzo has housed Palermo's major art museum since 1954. While the building itself is basic, its treasures are considerable. If you're a fan particularly of Gothic and Renaissance art, this museum is worth a stop—though its Baroque gallery is respectable too.

Cost and Hours: €10; Tue-Sat 9:00-19:00, Sun until 13:30, closed Mon; Via Alloro 4, +39 091 623 0011.

Visiting the Museum: After getting your ticket, head across the courtyard to the entrance. The first large room displays one of the museum's highlights: ***Triumph of Death*** *(Trionfo della Morte)*, a mysterious fresco by an unknown artist portraying imminent death. It represents the Bubonic Plague as a skeletal knight on a white horse striking down clergy and nobles with laser-like precision. It's not complete, because it was detached from the walls of Palermo's former hospital, the Palazzo Sclafani. While a grim image for a hospital, it was fitting, as medieval hospitals were usually places you didn't walk out of. If it looks familiar, you might be seeing hints of Picasso's famous anti-war painting, *Guernica*. Scholars say Picasso was aware of *Trionfo* before completing his masterpiece—intended or not, there are recognizable similarities between the two paintings.

Continuing through the small door to the right, the next few galleries highlight two of Sicily's most notable Renaissance sculptors. First, look for the gracious bust of **Eleanor of Aragon,** a masterpiece by Francesco Laurana. The next room features several of Antonello Gagini's statues including the ***Madonna del Neve*** proudly breastfeeding *Bambino* Jesus. Note that the sculptures in this room show traces of their original Renaissance paint job.

Exiting back into the small courtyard and taking the stairs to the left, you'll arrive in the painting galleries. Wind your way through medieval altarpieces to find the most famous work in the collection, framed in white: ***Annunciation of the Virgin*** by Antonello da Messina. Unlike most depictions of the Annunciation, here there's no angel—just Mary at her desk with her book. Mary's gesture is an artistic shorthand that this is an Annunciation scene. We can imagine the angel standing somewhere outside of the painting. The darkness in the background, contrasted with Mary's light skin and the thoughtful expression on her face, draw us in and make us wonder what she's thinking. Da Messina is the most famous Renaissance artist from Sicily and one of the first to paint in oil. His oil technique was considered cutting edge for his time, but perhaps the bigger advance was the psychological tension this image created. (For more about Antonello da Messina, see the sidebar on page 145.)

Palazzo Butera

The Valsecchi family's private collection of 16th- to 20th-century art, furniture, and other decorative objects is displayed throughout three floors of a thoughtfully restored historic palace overlooking Palermo's waterfront. Unless you're an art historian, chances are you won't know any of the pieces, but that doesn't make it any less interesting to wander through. In fact, the entire museum is purposefully free of any identifying labels—instead, visitors are meant to enjoy whatever speaks to them.

On the ground floor, you'll find contemporary art displayed in the former stables and carriage house, along with an ancient jacaranda root growing beneath 18th-century tiles. Upstairs, the first floor offers a few frescoed salons and a lush garden terrace promenade, while the 20 rooms on the second floor are packed with a hodgepodge of more frescoed ceilings and parqueted floors, delicate porcelain and glassworks, household silver, Industrial Revolution-era furniture, and four centuries of paintings. There's also a chance to visit the attics, to see the backbones of the building's vaulted ceilings, and climb the turret for a panoramic view.

Cost and Hours: €10; Tue-Sun 10:00-20:00, closed Mon, last entry one hour before closing; Via Butera 8, +39 091 752 1754, palazzobutera.it/en/ (study their helpful website before your visit; they also offer loaner museum books to help you know what you're viewing).

International Museum of Marionettes (Museo Antonio Pasqualino)

The Sicilian puppet tradition is alive and well. This compact, nicely presented museum displays puppets and marionettes from cultures around the world, with TV screens showing them in action. It's mostly in Italian, but the puppets are easy to appreciate, the care for the craft is evident, and it's all a bit more compelling than you might expect—fans of quirky attractions will  like it. As you browse, remember the trick to telling a marionette from other puppets is marionettes use strings (which are never attached to the head). The ones controlled by rods are considered puppets, not marionettes. The culmination of the tour is a huge hall where dozens and dozens of vintage puppets hang on racks, ready for their next performance. Their theater presents *spettacoli* (puppet shows) in an airy space surrounded by the collection. For more on the Sicilian art of puppetry, see page 327.

Cost and Hours: Museum—€5, Tue-Sat 10:00-18:00, Sun-Mon until 14:00; puppet show—€10 (includes museum entry), typically Mon at 11:00 and Tue-Sat at 17:00, check schedule online; Piazzetta Pasqualino 5, +39 091 328 060, museodellemarionette.it.

Palermo Botanical Garden (Orto Botanico)

This botanical garden is one of the oldest in the Mediterranean, and is an active research garden for the University of Palermo. Considering Palermo's mild climate, it grows one of the most diverse collections in Europe, with more than 12,000 species from all over the world, including citrus, water lilies, bamboos, and an ancient fig tree. Though it's a little shabby and unkempt, a walk through this peaceful garden will delight the avid horticulturalist and soothe everyone else with the scent of orange blossoms.

Cost and Hours: €7, daily 9:00-20:00, closes earlier off-season, Via Lincoln 2, +39 091 238 91236, ortobotanico.unipa.it.

IN BALLARÒ
▲Palazzo Conte Federico

This elegant and extremely lived-in mansion, built upon the Carthaginian city wall, offers a rare opportunity to get a personal glimpse into Sicilian aristocratic life. Count Federico's family has lived here for centuries, but now that the perks of nobility no longer pay the bills, the family has opened its doors to the paying public. The current count (Alessandro) is a vintage-racecar enthusiast happy to show off some of his favorite toys; most tours are led by one of his sons (Nicolò or Andreas). The countess, Alwine, is from Salzburg and fills her home with both joy and a respect for the family's illustrious history.

Cost and Hours: €15; tours generally run Thu-Tue on the hour 11:00-14:00, closed Wed; 45-minute tour in English and Italian, reservations not necessary—just show up before the top of the hour; near the Ballarò Market at Piazza Conte Federico 2—from Quattro Canti, take Via Maqueda toward Piazza Bellini and watch for signs on the right; +39 091 651 1881, contefederico.com.

MARKETS

Sicily has some of the best street markets in Europe, and Palermo has two of the most famous. The island—the garden patch of Italy—offers a wealth of produce, from ripe tomatoes to purple eggplants to comically long zucchinis to fragrant citrus. But markets aren't just for greengrocers—you'll also see fishmongers, butchers, spices, herbs, and everyday items like clothing and housewares. As you stroll the narrow lanes of a Palermo market—your senses assaulted by sights, smells, and sounds—you'll enjoy an almost Arabian vibe, echoing the rise of Palermo 1,200 years ago. Vendors here still maintain the tradition of calling out to passersby in a singsong way, like an auctioneer. Street-food carts are scattered among the stalls, selling *panelle* (chickpea fritters), *sfincione* (fluffy pizza with anchovies), and lots of other eats (see the street-food sidebar under "Eating in Palermo," later).

Hours: Palermo's markets are generally open Mon-Sat 6:00-

Sights in Palermo

14:00 (with some stalls—especially imperishable items—staying open later), and all but the Ballarò Market are closed Sun.

Market Tips: Join in the fun by buying some olives, cheese, or fruit. Food is sold by the kilo (2.2 pounds), and a tenth of a kilo is called an *etto*. If you're buying cheese, cold cuts, or a snack sold by weight, *un etto* (about a quarter-pound) or *due etti* (roughly a half-pound) is a standard amount for a picnic. *Attenzione!* Don't touch the food on display. Vendors here consider themselves artists in their trade, so ask for what you want and tell them how and when you plan to eat it; they'll select a fruit or vegetable at the correct degree of ripeness.

▲▲Il Ballarò Market

Of all the street markets in Palermo, Ballarò is the oldest, most authentic, and liveliest, stretching from Piazza Ballarò (a few blocks east of Palermo Cathedral) to the train station. A thousand years ago, when Palermo was still bounded by its now-underground rivers, this market was here with its singing merchants. The market's neighborhood is diverse and unpolished,

with immigrant families squatting in dilapidated buildings a few steps off the main shopping street...real-life Palermo. It's best to wear sturdy shoes on the broken pavement. While a visit here is not dangerous, pay close attention to your belongings.

▲Il Capo Market

More central and almost as colorful as Ballarò, the Capo Market (from the Latin *caput*, "head"), winds its way behind Teatro Massimo, with the main entrance at Porta Carini. This one preserves the traditional character of a daily market, featuring food on its main street and mostly household goods on side streets. Similar merchants—fabric sellers, cleaning suppliers, clothing shops—tend to cluster together.

La Vucciria Market
Described on my Palermo City Walk, earlier, the waning Vucciria Market used to be the city's beating heart. Now you'll find a smattering of butchers, fruit-and-veggie vendors, antiques, and fun street life. Although it's no longer a traditional Palermo street market, it still has one of the city's best street-food scenes, with stalls hawking freshly fired eats. And the Vucciria neighborhood—especially Piazza Caracciolo—is a youthful, bohemian, and often boisterous hangout after dark.

AWAY FROM THE CENTER
▲▲Capuchin Crypt (Catacombe dei Cappuccini)
Perhaps Palermo's quirkiest sight is the crypt of its Capuchin monastery. The Capuchins, monks known for their brown robes (and the namesake of cappuccino), are a branch of the Franciscan order. Capuchins have a passion for reminding people of their mortality, called *memento mori* (a Latin phrase that translates to "remember that you will die"). Generally, when their brothers passed away, the Capuchins put their bones on display to send

the macabre message: "What you are, we once were; and what we are, you will be." In other words, live a noble life, and put yourself right with God while you still have time...because your time will come, and soon.

The monks of Palermo have taken this tradition a step further: Rather than just saving bones, they preserved the bodies. Later, the monks realized they could charge wealthy parishioners for the privilege of being mummified, which became a fashionable way to leave this life. By 1887, the practice had become forbidden except in special cases, and about 4,000 bodies had been collected in their crypt. Today, the public is welcome to wander the halls of this collection of fully clothed and remarkably preserved bodies.

Cost and Hours: €5, cash only; daily 9:00-12:30 & 15:00-17:30; scan QR code on-site for audioguide; out of respect for these bodies without souls, photography is not allowed—but plenty of postcards are on sale; Piazza dei Cappuccini 1, +39 091 652 7389, palermocatacombs.com.

Sights in Palermo

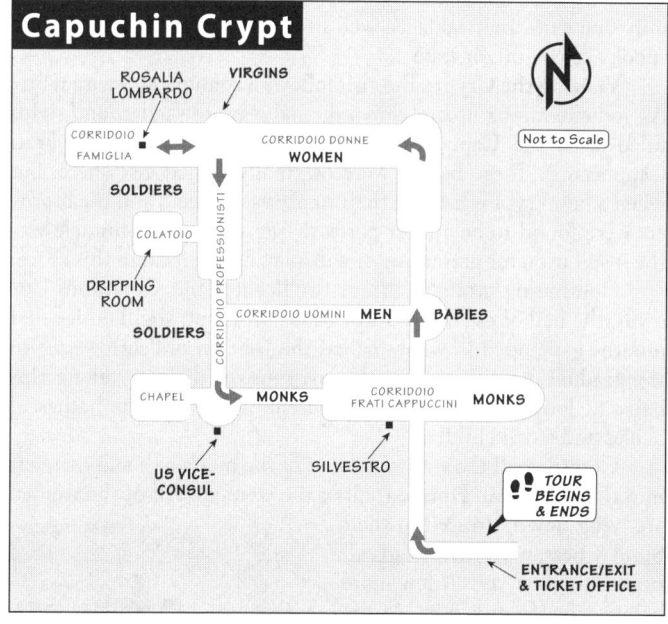

Getting There: It's on the western edge of Palermo, about 1.5 miles from Quattro Canti. To **walk,** follow Via Vittorio Emanuele past the cathedral and through the Porta Nuova gate at the Norman Palace; at the far end of Piazza Indipendenza, veer right on Via Cappuccini. After several blocks, turn right on Via Pindemonte, which dead-ends at the crypt. You can also take **bus** #327 or #389 from the stop behind the Norman Palace on Piazza Indipendenza—but in the time it takes to wait for the bus, you could just walk. Smart travelers can stop at the catacombs after visiting Monreale using bus #389 (stop: Calatafimi-Pindemonte), where you can walk the rest of the way following my instructions from Via Pindemonte, above. A **taxi** from central Palermo to the crypt costs about €15. **Drivers** can park in front (officially free, though you'll likely have to give a few coins to the "attendant").

Warning: This morbid site isn't for everyone—it's a below-ground crypt jam-packed with corpses in various states of decay, some with facial hair and others with disturbing expressions, and

only one exit. That said, it's well lit and not nearly as musty and spooky as you might expect.

Visiting the Crypt: The visit follows a counterclockwise route. As you enter, look up and down the hallways to the left and right, filled with the Capuchin brothers themselves (Corridoio Frati Cappuccini). These bodies were originally buried elsewhere, but when a new crypt was built, their tomb was opened, and the brothers were found to be almost perfectly preserved. This miracle was the inspiration for preserving and displaying the dead in this space.

Continuing straight ahead, you'll enter the **Corridoio Uomini** (the hall of the men). Throughout the crypt, you'll notice that mouths gape open in what's called the "scream of death"—due to the gradual deterioration of the jaw muscles. Partway along this hallway, look for a small alcove on the right with the bodies of babies and small children.

Continue all the way to the end of the men's hall and turn left into the **Corridoio Donne** (hall of the women). All of the women are lying down, dressed in their Sunday best, with their heads all turned to greet you. A few more babies are also mixed in. At the next junction, you'll find another alcove on the right, dedicated to virgins (Cappella Vergini).

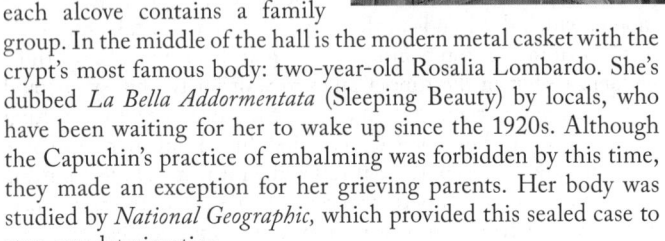

In the dead-end hallway ahead **(Corridoio Famiglia)**, each alcove contains a family group. In the middle of the hall is the modern metal casket with the crypt's most famous body: two-year-old Rosalia Lombardo. She's dubbed *La Bella Addormentata* (Sleeping Beauty) by locals, who have been waiting for her to wake up since the 1920s. Although the Capuchin's practice of embalming was forbidden by this time, they made an exception for her grieving parents. Her body was studied by *National Geographic,* which provided this sealed case to stop any deterioration.

Returning to the main path, you'll pass the bodies of men of different professions **(Corridoio Professionisti).** Watch on the right for the small doorway marked *Colatoio*—the dripping room, where monks drained the body and cleaned the skin with vinegar and herbs. When the body was properly dried out (and stench-free), families brought clothing and did their dead

loved ones' hair, and the body was put on display. The exact process used to preserve the bodies is unknown, but a recent CAT scan of the most well-preserved body, the last to be embalmed, revealed that the internal organs are as equally well preserved as the facial skin and hair.

Continue down the hall; you'll pass a hall on your left lined with bodies of priests **(Preti).** Keep going straight, and at the end of the hall, to the left of the chapel up four steps, you can just make out a long casket with a glass cover, which houses the only American, Giovanni Paterniti, the vice-consul for the United States, who died here in Palermo in 1911.

Now head along the final hall, back to where you entered. The oldest body, Brother Silvestro from 1599, is at the very end, above and to your right, bidding you: Go in peace...for now.

Shopping in Palermo

Palermo has a variety of shopping experiences—from gritty street markets, to inviting artisanal shops, to the typical big-city department store.

Artisanal Crafts: The **Kalsa district**—near the port—has the city's most appealing assortment of one-off craft boutiques (for location, see the "Palermo" map, earlier). Around 50 artisan shops in the city center have formed the Associazione Liberi Artigiani-Artisti Balarm (alabpalermo.it); their shops are marked with an orange *ALAB* logo— watch for it as you window  shop in the old center. If you like what you see, look for a free map locating all of ALAB's shops across Sicily.

Via Alessandro Paternostro is lined with creative boutiques selling leather bags, clothes, accessories, ceramics, and books. If you follow this from Via Vittorio Emanuele south, you'll enjoy one of Palermo's most atmospheric walking streets (also covered on my Palermo City Walk). Eventually you'll spill out onto the skinny **Piazza Aragona,** with several fine shops, including **LaboRiuso** (creative, youthful jewelry and accessories). Turning left at Piazza Aragona, along **Via Alloro,** you'll find a few more interesting shops.

Food: Sicilian sweets, particularly cookies and marzipan fruit, have a long shelf life. Cafés and sweet shops all over the city sell boxes of colorful sweets, including stalls at the Ballarò Market.

> ## Sicilian Souvenirs
>
> Palermo is a great place to find Sicilian handicrafts and gifty edibles to take home.
>
> **Pottery** shops sell typical, colorful wares—hand-painted with bright colors and intricate designs. Popular pottery items are decorative ceramic pinecones (representing divinity, health, renewal, and prosperity) and the "Head of the Moor" flower vases (described on page 400). Sicily's pottery capital is Caltagirone, in the middle of the island; you'll see work from that town sold everywhere.
>
> The island's symbol, the three-legged **Trinacria,** is featured on pottery, flags, T-shirts, and magnets. The island's triangular shape is another popular subject for handicrafts, from wallets to trivets. You'll see traditional Sicilian **puppets** for sale, in varying sizes and priced according to their detail and workmanship.
>
> A wide variety of **jewelry** is also available, from modern styles to pieces shaped like Sicilian symbols: the shape of the island, the Trinacria, traditional horse carts, and puppets. Men may want to pick up a **"coppola"**—a woven cap with a brim, traditionally worn by men.
>
> Sicilian **wines** are excellent and generally affordable; Nero d'Avola is the most typical, but there are many unique local varieties in each part of the island. For more on Sicilian wines, see page 480. Also consider Sicily's high-quality **olive oil,** produced in the south, near Castelvetrano.
>
> Canned **tuna** was invented in the western part of the island, and real Sicilian tuna packed in olive oil is a culinary treat. While it's not possible to take home cannoli, which are perishable, other sweets have excellent shelf life. **Almond cookies** stay fresh for months and make a great gift; they have different names in every city—look for *mandorla* in the name.

Near Teatro Politeama, **I Peccatucci di Mamma Andrea** sells a seasonal variety of sweets, jams, and cakes that are beautifully packaged (Via Principe Scordia 67).

Department Stores and Big Chains: Rinascente is the pick for a major department-store fix in the very center, selling clothes and upscale housewares. Their top-floor food hall has a terrace with views over Palermo (daily 10:00-20:00, food hall until 23:00). Beyond that, the most popular shopping area is between Teatro Massimo and Teatro Politeama, along **Via Ruggero Settimo,** which hosts big-name retailers like H&M, Benetton, and OVS. **Antica Sartoria** sells clothing and jewelry with traditional southern Italian motifs (Via Maqueda 336). The Italian bookstore chain **Feltrinelli** also has a branch near Teatro Massimo that sells some English books and accessories for booklovers (Via Cavour 133). Higher-end shops are in the new part of town, just past Teatro Politeama on **Via della Libertà**.

Street Markets: The **Capo, Ballarò, and Vucciria** street markets mostly sell food, but they also have sections of souvenirs, cheap clothing, and household goods. **Via Bandiera,** near Piazza San Domenico, has a small clothing market (Mon-Sat 7:00-14:00, Cappo and Vucciria closed Sun while Ballarò has shorter hours).

Antiques: A weekly antiquarian market pops up in **Piazza Marina** in the Kalsa, selling furniture, jewelry, books, and all sorts of flea-market treasures (Sun 10:00-14:00).

Nightlife in Palermo

Palermo has become a hotbed for events and nightlife in recent years. Music, food, and art festivals happen frequently from May through October. Two websites (in Italian) keep updated schedules of upcoming events: palermotoday.it and balarm.it.

LOW-IMPACT NIGHTLIFE

Passeggiata: The evening *passeggiata* gets underway about 17:30 and lasts well into dinnertime. The best places to stroll and people-watch are **Via Maqueda** (the traffic-free zone stretching north from Quattro Canti to Teatro Massimo) or **Via Vittorio Emanuele** (the restaurant-lined street between Quattro Canti and the harbor). Following the route of my Palermo City Walk in the evening lets you mix and mingle with the locals for a memorable experience.

Aperitivo: As in other parts of Italy, Palermo has a thriving *aperitivo* (Italian happy hour) scene. In the early evening hours, buying a drink at any bar will net you some free nibbles. Some bars even offer a small, complimentary buffet—ask before you order. Some bars offer *apericena* (a term combining *aperitivo* and the word for "dinner"). Several of the places described under "Lively Nightlife Areas," later, offer *aperitivo* nibbles if you arrive at the right time.

Theater: Teatro Massimo is the home of opera in Palermo, but also hosts concerts, dance, and special events such as literature readings. There are performances every month except July-August, and events almost every day in May and June. Summer performances take place outside of the theater, typically at Teatro di Verdura on the outskirts of the city, but tickets can be booked through Teatro Massimo. For evening performances, Sicilians tend to dress up. Same-day tickets are often available (+39 091 605 3267, teatromassimo.it). The city's second grand theater, a few blocks north—**Teatro Politeama**—is another fine venue and home to the Sicilian Symphony Orchestra, which performs from October through May (orchestrasinfonicasiciliana.it).

Summer Classical Music: From July through early September, **Palermo Classica** hosts music events across the city in memorable venues, such as Palazzo Chiaramonte Steri (+39 091 332 208, palermoclassica.it).

LIVELY NIGHTLIFE AREAS
To sample Palermo after hours, wander through the city's core and connect a few lively squares that are magnets for young and old.

Nightlife in Palermo 87

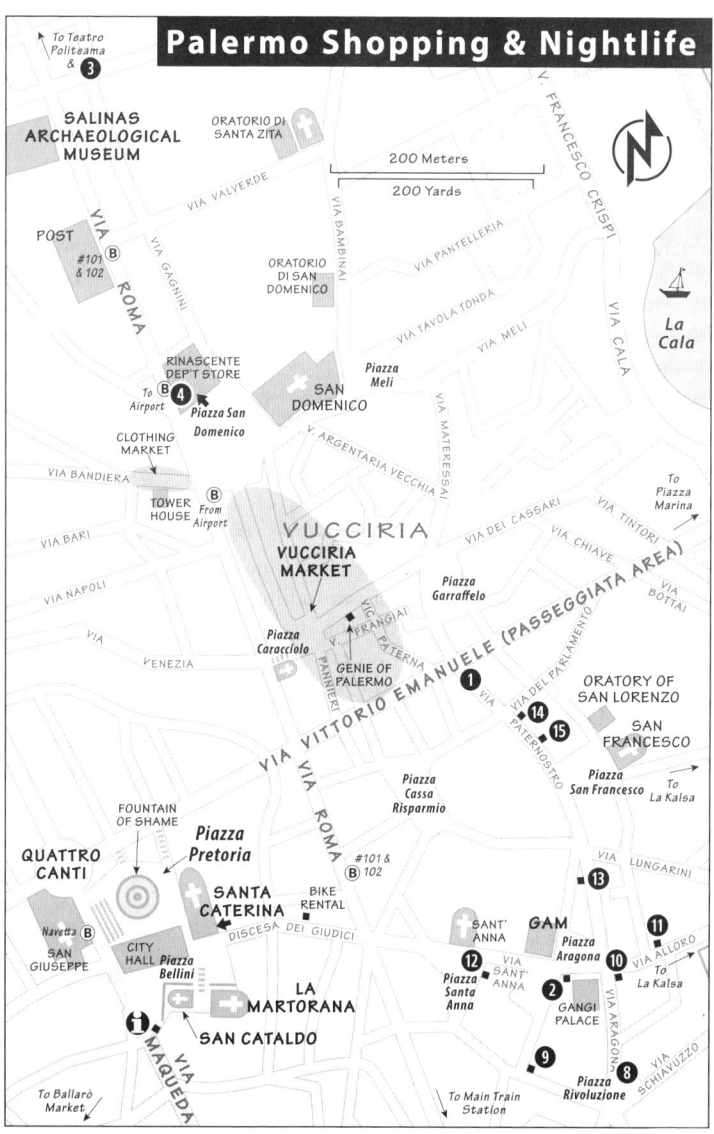

Most of these places are in La Kalsa, south of Via Vittorio Emanuele and east of Via Maqueda. For locations, see the "Palermo Shopping and Nightlife" map.

Piazza Rivoluzione and Nearby: This colorful square, tucked a short walk from Via Roma and north of the train station, is a delightful place to hang out. Early in the evening, it hums with a happy *aperitivo* scene, where locals and visitors nurse €6 cocktails and munch a free little spread of light food under balconies of drying laundry while watching the gurgling "Genie of Palermo" fountain. Later, it becomes a boisterous nightlife zone. Anchoring the scene at #5, **Qvivi** has a rock-n-roll vibe, pleasing to backpackers and backpackers-at-heart. At #35, **Zammù** is a pre-fab cocktail bar. Around the corner, at Via Cantavespri 15, you'll find **Extra Hop**, with an extensive beer menu.

Piazza Aragona and Nearby: A block away from Piazza Rivoluzione, this square is a livelier scene—full of people spilling out of the bars and into the streets. The main watering hole here, **New Art 108,** has abundant outdoor tables and a long list of drinks. A block down Via Alloro, **Farmacia Alcolica** is an eclectic medley of oddities with fun drinks and good nibbles. Two short blocks west of Piazza Aragona, Piazza Santa Anna is

enlivened by a couple of popular bars, including the thriving **Monkey Pub,** with an energetic local crowd spilling out into the square.

Via Alessandro Paternostro: The street heading north from Piazza Aragona is lined with a variety of bars and cafés that are lively after hours. Hidden down the little alley Vicolo dei Corrieri, **Botanico** (at #38), with kindergarten chairs, feels totally hipster and local—until *you* show up. **Dal Barone** (at #87) is a popular wine bar that takes over much of the street. **Colletti** (#77) is more old-school cabaret, while **Goccio** (#79) has a hip cocktail vibe. This up-and-coming area is changing fast—stroll here to see what's new.

Vucciria Market and Nearby: This area has bars with music and a fun, youthful scene after dark. A bohemian crowd spills from the bars into the cobbled lanes on nice nights. The tangle of streets from Vucciria to Piazza Marina is hopping with a constantly changing scene of new and trendy bars and cafés. The recommended **Franco ù Vastiddaru** street-food shop on Via Vittorio Emanuele is an epicenter for late-night eats and drinks

(for location, see the "Palermo Restaurants" map, later).

A bit farther away is **Piazzetta della Canna,** deep in some back streets a five-minute walk west of Via Maqueda. This younger-skewing scene fills a little square under big trees with shared tables of happy drinkers, ringed by mostly interchangeable bars.

This scene doesn't really get rolling until later and often comes with live music.

Near Teatro Massimo: In this neighborhood, locals hit **Bottiglieria Massimo** before or after dinner for a drink and conversation (daily 10:00-very late, Via Salvatore Spinuzza 59). This area, called the "Champagneria," is filled with lively drinking spots open late, some with live music.

And to reach a very local-feeling, traffic-free street with some appealing spots for the *aperitivo* happy hour, walk a few short blocks north of the Teatro Massimo to **Via Principe di Belmonte.** In this workaday, urban-feeling area are several fine bars and cafés with generous outdoor seating, including the recommended **Antico Caffè Spinnato.** This is a nice place to sip a drink and people-watch before dinner.

Sleeping in Palermo

Palermo is a busy, noisy, crazy city full of fun and excitement... which are not characteristics you want in a hotel room. Considering how affordable Palermo is in comparison to other big Italian cities, it's smart to splurge a little here and pick a hotel with some extra comforts (unless noted, all of my recommended places have air-con and elevators).  That said, some of Palermo's smaller, boutique B&Bs are a great value, offering hotelesque quality at *pensione* prices. For some travelers, short-term, Airbnb-type rentals can be a good alternative; search for places in my recommended hotel neighborhoods. Parking here is either tricky or not available—which is why I recommend picking up your car on departure (if you must drive in Palermo, ask your hotel for parking advice, and be sure to get a ZTL pass—described later, under "Palermo Connections").

For more details on reservations, short-term rentals, and more, see the "Sleeping" section in the Practicalities chapter.

CENTRAL PALERMO

This is the thick of the action. My listings along Via Roma contend with traffic noise, while those along Via Vittorio Emanuele or Via Maqueda are victim to street noise. Thankfully, most hotels have double-paned windows to counter the impact; still, if you're sensitive, request a room at the back. The shuttle bus from the airport

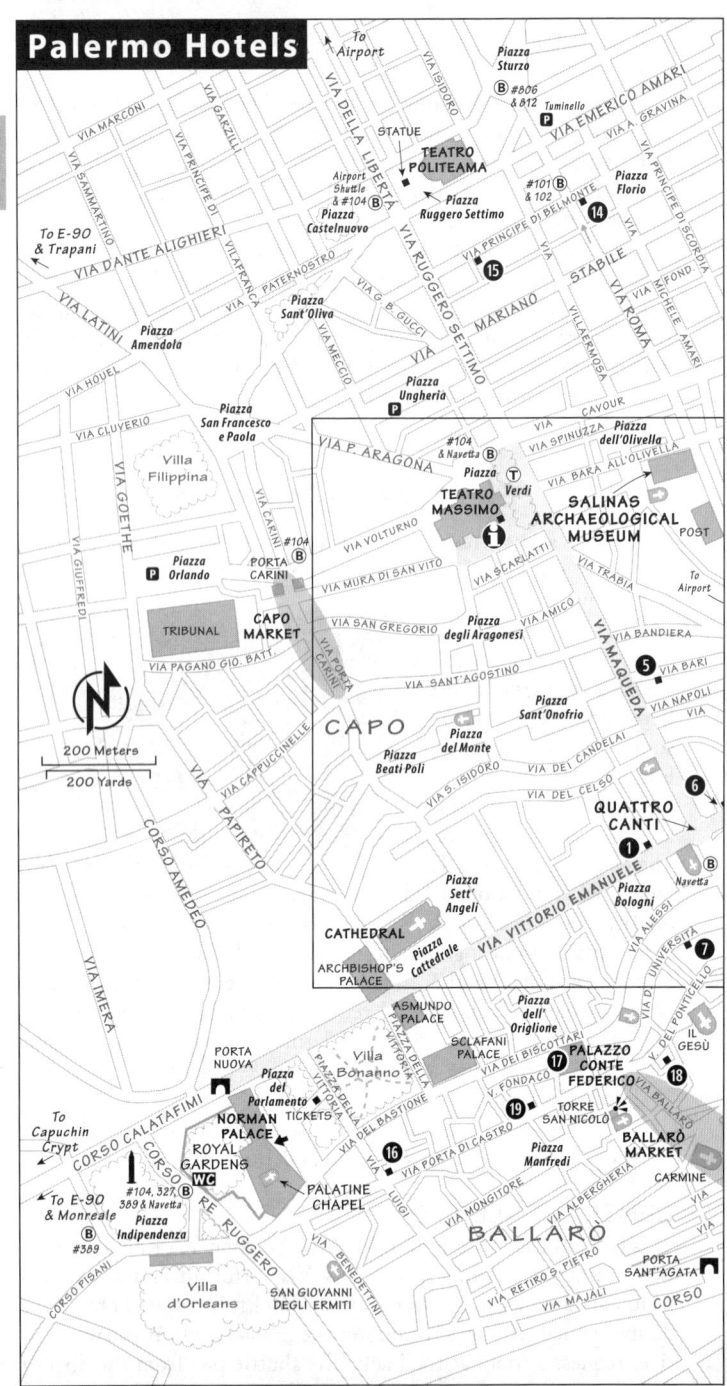

Sleeping in Palermo

stops along Via Roma near the Vucciria Market, which may be closer to your hotel than riding all the way to the train station.

€€€€ Eurostars Centrale Palace is indeed central, just steps from Quattro Canti and within easy walking distance of the main sights. Housed in a large former noble palace, with a stuffy vibe to match, you can pretend you're an aristocrat. The 104 well-appointed rooms are quiet, and a few have small terraces (abundant breakfast, rooftop restaurant, Via Vittorio Emanuele 327, +39 091 366 6666, eurostarscentralepalace.com, info@eurostarscentralepalace.com).

€€€ BB22 is tucked away on a quiet lane behind San Domenico, like a hidden city retreat. The seven rooms have a trendy panache in neutral tones, and come with a warm welcome (but no elevator, Via Pantelleria 22, +39 091 326 214, bb22.it, info@bb22.it, Emanuela). **BB22 Palace,** run by BB22, is in a palazzo just off Via Roma. While not as cozy as BB22, the rooms are upscale and quiet, with white walls and simple but tasteful furnishings. For families, they offer a larger apartment (Via Bandiera 11, family rooms, small terrace, same contact info as BB22).

€€€ Hotel Ambasciatori, right along Via Roma, has 26 rooms—some with stately furniture and wood floors, others a bit worse for wear. The top-floor breakfast terrace has views of the Palermo skyline and is extremely popular for dinner (Via Roma 111, +39 091 616 6881, ambasciatorihotelpalermo.com, booking@ambasciatorihotelpalermo.com, Aida).

€€ Delle Vittorie is a boutique bed-and-breakfast shoehorned into a palazzo just off Via Maqueda. Its nine rooms are clean and modern, with thoughtful touches. The breakfast room looks out onto a curious empty courtyard, built by the fascist government to display its victories...that never happened (family rooms, Via Bari 52, +39 091 335 453, bbdellevittorie.it, info@bbdellevittorie.it, Giuseppe).

€€ Despite its name, **B&B Hotel Quattro Canti** is a 140-room hotel, not a hole-in-the-wall B&B. Though it has no historic charm, if you're seeking businesslike, efficient, super-central, quiet, and reasonably priced accommodations, look no further (rooftop terrace, Via Vittorio Emanuele 291, +39 091 332 082, hotelbb.com, palermo@hotelbb.com).

€€ La Terrazza sul Centro, warmly run by Barbara and Emiliano, has 15 clean, modern rooms in a great location a short walk from Quattro Canti, where you can join in the action or take in the scene from the peaceful view terrace (no elevator, Via dell'Università 20, +39 333 456 7678, laterrazzasulcentro.it, info@laterrazzasulcentro.it).

€ AdHoc Rooms is run by kind and helpful Luca, with five bright, modern, comfortable rooms in a real Palermo apartment. Every room has a theme—music, library, superheroes—and all share a delightful terrace. This place offers an ideal combination of good value, hospitality, and unbeatable location just a stone's throw from Piazza Bellini and the Fountain of Shame (no elevator, Discesa dei Giudici 15, mobile +39 393 929 0900, adhocrooms.it, info@adhocrooms.it).

€ **Mantegna Rooms** is cozy and a good value. The five light and breezy rooms are modest but well designed. Each is named after a different Sicilian author and equipped with a small balcony. This place is a little step up in style from my two budget listings below and energetic Luca makes sure you feel at home (no breakfast, Via Roma 174, +39 091 784 7897, mantegnarooms.it, info@mategnarooms.it).

€ **Hotel Concordia** is a simple, clean, budget place with welcoming warmth on the fourth floor a short walk from the train station. Friendly Dario mans the desk at his family's hotel, renting 12 colorful, comfortable, no-frills rooms with high ceilings (family rooms, Via Roma 72, +39 091 616 9062, hotelconcordiapalermo.it, info@hotelconcordiapalermo.it).

€ **Bed and Breakfast D'Angelo,** located on the second floor of a dowdy apartment, offers quality cheap sleeps. The four old-timey rooms are spotlessly well maintained, hearkening a bygone era. Two have en suite bathrooms and the other two each have a private WC in the hall (Via Roma 83, +39 091 784 7302, beb.it/bedandbreakfastpalermodangelo, info@bedbreakfastdangelo.com, Angelo).

LA KALSA

This area is a bit quieter than central Palermo, with a touch more historic atmosphere thanks to plenty of crumbling palaces. Both recommendations are at the end of Via Vittorio Emanuele, close to the *navetta* shuttle bus terminus and Familia supermarket.

€€€ **Hotel Porta Felice,** near the harbor, has a business-like feel. Its 33 rooms are decorated with leather accents and dark wood, making it the conventional choice in this neighborhood (Via Butera 45, +39 091 617 5678, hotelportafelice.it, info@hotelportafelice.it).

€€€ **Butera 28 Apartments** are scattered around an actual palace, which is still lived in by a duchess (her late husband was the adopted son of the famous author of *The Leopard*). Duchess Nicoletta rents out 12 rambling apartments filled with antique furniture, colorful tiles, and the ambience of bygone Sicily. She also offers cooking classes—see page 41 (no breakfast, Via Butera 28, +39 366 414 3887, palazzolanzatomasi.it, info@butera28.com).

NORTH OF THE CENTER

This area, near Teatro Politeama, has easier access to parking and more modern conveniences than the other neighborhoods. It's also more lived-in by locals, and has several inviting sidewalk cafés. The shuttle bus from the airport stops at Piazza Ruggero Settimo in front of the theater, a few short blocks from the next two listings.

€€€€ **Palazzo Planeta** rents nine apartments and four suites in a classy palazzo near a lively district. The elegantly furnished apartments have cozy living areas, kitchens, and washing machines; the suites have a common kitchen and laundry available. The property is run by a winery, so you'll find complimentary wine and olive oil stocked in the kitchen (Via Principe Belmonte 68, +39 0925 195 5460, planetaestate.it, palazzoplaneta@planeta.it).

€ **Operà B&B** is well located on an inviting pedestrian street. Its six rooms are a good value and chatty Marco is your welcoming host (Via Principe Belmonte 102, +39 091 982 5946, bedandbreakfastopera.com, info@bedandbreakfastopera.com).

BALLARÒ

The neighborhood surrounding Palermo's most lively market can be chaotic and noisy during the day and intimidating at night. But those who don't mind a more authentic experience will find it convenient to most sights. When you first arrive, stick to the main streets: From Via Maqueda (heading south from Quattro Canti, or north from the train station), angle into the Ballarò area on the tourist-friendly Via del Ponticello, passing the big Il Gesù church. Better yet, splurge for a taxi to take you right to your hotel's front door. (Forging a different path—or simply following a mapping app—could take you through some rougher parts of the Ballarò.)

€€€€ **Porta di Castro**—at the western edge of the Ballarò, near the Norman Palace—is perfect for artsy, eclectic types who like their cities gritty and their boutique hotels full of character. Alessandro is a collector, and his 19 rooms in a converted church showcase his pieces. Every room has interesting furniture, and many feature one of his 40 vintage Vespas (family rooms, pool, spa, Via Porta di Castro 223, +39 328 263 9433, bebportadicastro.it, bebportadicastro@gmail.com).

€€€€ **Palazzo Conte Federico,** listed earlier under "Sights in Palermo," rents seven tastefully furnished, eco-friendly apartments (Piazza Conte Frederico 2, call or WhatsApp +39 388 997 5267, matteo@contefederico.com, contefederico.com/newsite/en/booking).

€€€ **Palazzo Brunaccini,** set in a hidden courtyard in the Ballarò chaos, is surprisingly peaceful and elegant. The 21 stylish rooms are spacious and spotless, with all the comforts, including high-end mattresses. As the neighborhood can seem a little shabby, enter from Vicolo S. Michele Arcangelo to avoid loiterers (Piazzetta Brunaccini 9, +39 091 586 904, palazzobrunaccini.it, info@palazzobrunaccini.it, Adrianna).

€€€ **Il Giardino di Ballarò** is another gem, tucked into a historic building surrounding a small garden and sun terrace. While the streets outside can be scruffy, the creatively decorated common spaces feel like a friend's home, and the seven rooms are a nice combination of artsy and modern (some street noise, Via Porta di Castro 75, +39 091 212 215, ilgiardinodiballaro.it, info@ilgiardinodiballaro.it).

Eating in Palermo

The mix of cultures that contributed to the makeup of today's Palermo also created a vibrant food scene. Fish is the mainstay, but also look for local veggies, North African ingredients like couscous, and anything made with ricotta. Dishes *alla Palermitana* usually mean they are topped with breadcrumbs (yesterday's scraps of bread were an affordable substitute for those who couldn't afford grated cheese).

Most of my restaurant listings are open daily for lunch and dinner; I've noted exceptions. For more advice on eating in Sicily, including ordering, tipping, and Sicilian cuisine and beverages, see the "Eating" section in the Practicalities chapter.

The restaurants listed here are popular with both locals and visitors; it's smart to book ahead, especially in high season, and as you approach the weekend.

PALERMO'S STREET-FOOD SCENE

One of the most memorable ways to eat in Palermo is also one of the cheapest: street food. Fearless eaters will head to the Capo or Ballarò markets and simply try a nibble from each cart, with choices ranging from sesame bread to veal penis. Several spots have open-air grills where you can order your raw meat at the counter and watch it cook. Notice the oversized plume of smoke that pours out of some of the hissing grills. Vendors wipe down their grills with fat to generate extra smoke—not for the flavor, but as a sort of advertisement. To make things easier, join a street-food tour, such as the one offered by Streaty (see "Tours in Palermo," near the beginning of this chapter).

Lunch at Ballarò or Capo Markets: These two sprawling markets are each spread out along a large area: With almost as many street-food stands as traditional stalls, either can be an easy

96 Rick Steves Sicily

1. To Ballarò Market
2. To Capo Market
3. Vucciria Market
4. Gagini
5. Bocum Fuoco
6. Buatta Cucina Popolana
7. Casa del Brodo
8. Franco ù Vastiddaru
9. Ferramenta
10. Bar Lucchese
11. Ferro di Cavallo
12. Casa Stagnitta
13. Passami ù Coppu
14. Occhiovivo & Osteria dei Vespri
15. Antica Focacceria San Francesco
16. A'nìca
17. Trattoria del Massimo
18. La Taverna di John
19. Assud Pizzeria
20. Trattoria Al Vecchio Club Rosanero
21. Bisso Bistrot

place to fill up. I'd walk through the market to survey your choices, then circle back to the places that appeal, assembling a moveable feast. Most food stands at the Ballarò and Capo markets are only open at lunchtime and the Capo Market is closed Sunday.

Ballarò: On the train station end of the Ballarò Market, **Da Giovanni** fries your selection on the spot, and **Gioé** (near Via Ballarò and Vicolo del Carmelo) is a good place to try *pane con milza*

Eating in Palermo 97

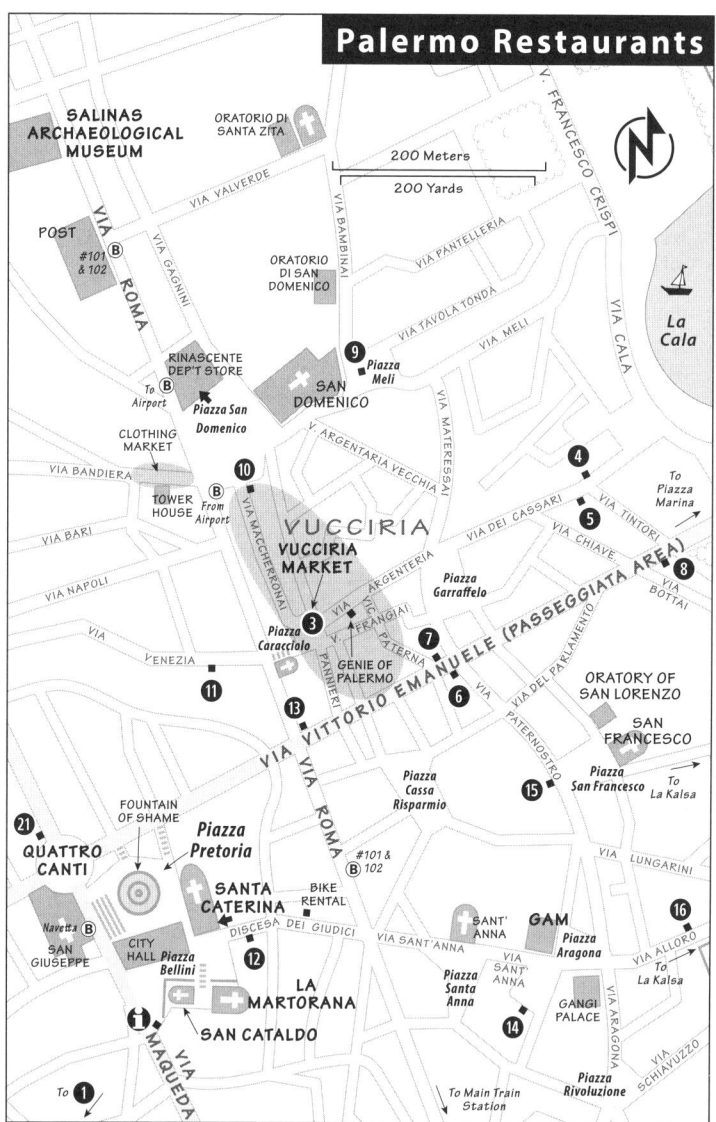

Palermo Restaurants

(spleen sandwich). Just up the street in the Piazza del Carmine, **Mu Manciu** tempts hungry shoppers with grilled octopus.

Capo: At the Capo Market, look for seasonal treats like mulberries (in season late spring through early summer) and refreshing blood orange *spremute fresca* (fresh-squeezed juice). Another typical Palermo dish you'll see here are heaping trays of *anniletti al forno* (a baked pasta casserole resembling SpaghettiOs). About midway through, on the corner of Via San Gregorio (just after the twin

Sicilian Street Food

Palermo, with its strong street-food culture, is considered a capital for finger foods in Europe. The quintessential street-food experience is to hop-scotch between vendors at one of the city's street markets. Prices are affordable (any of the items below shouldn't cost more than €1-2). Don't be intimidated—just point to what you want and dig in.

Arancina (plural *arancine*): A breaded, deep-fried rice ball filled with meat sauce or other ingredients. Traditionally, Palermo's *arancine* are flavored with vivid yellow saffron and contain no tomatoes. (Catania calls this dish *arancino* and adds tomato to the filling.)

Cazzilli and *crocché:* Potato croquettes, usually filled with mashed potato, parsley, and mint. *Cazzilli* are a smaller version of *crocché*.

Frittola: Leftover cow parts, like cartilage and bone, fried up and assembled into a chewy meat fluff. It's the ultimate for the adventurous eater and is usually found only at market carts (and sells out quickly).

Mangia e bevi: Thin strips of pork around green onion

Panelle: Deep-fried chickpea fritters. *Panelle* and *cazzilli* are often served together.

Pane con milza (or *pani c'a meusa*): Deep-fried spleen, lung, and other veal organ meat, served on a roll. It can be dressed with cheese *(maritatu),* or without *(schiettu).*

Polpo bollito: Octopus (large or small) that's been boiled in salty water, then chopped up and spritzed with lemon

Rascatura: A mix of leftover *panelle* and *cazzilli* with some onion and lemon, refried into little pieces of greasy goodness

Sfincione: Fluffy pizza topped with tomato (and sometimes anchovy and cheese) and sold on carts by the greasy slice. It doesn't look appetizing in the cart's display case, but the vendor will grill it on a hidden oven.

Stigghiole: Lamb intestines wrapped around green onions. They may not sound appetizing, but they smell and taste great and are easy to find—just look for the grills spewing smoke. For something a bit tamer, look for *mangia e bevi* (described above). Often, other meats are also available to throw on the grill.

churches straddling the street), **Dainotti's** is a solid option for Sicilian street food staples like *arancine* (fried rice balls) and *panelle* (deep-fried chickpea fritters on bread).

Lunch at Vucciria Market: To sample a smorgasbord of classic Palermo street food in a graffiti-slathered square, make your way to Piazza Caracciolo in the heart of the Vucciria Market. Most of this market's traditional meat, fish, and produce vendors have moved elsewhere. But taking their place is an array of ramshackle food stands and cocktail bars. (It's particularly lively after hours, when this area transforms into one of Palermo's trendiest nightlife spots.) Take a spin around to consider your options: a classic cart selling *pane con milza* (spleen sandwiches), an octopus man serving up *polpo bollito,* a fry stand selling *panelle* and *cazzilli* (chickpea fritters and potato croquettes), and a sizzling grill with *stigghiola, mangia e bevi,* and other meaty choices (see sidebar on page 98). Once you've got your food, pull up a chair at a rickety plastic table near the fountain in the middle of the square. Palermo street food doesn't get more adventurous, or accessible, than this.

Off the Street: In the neighborhood eating sections next, I've included several eateries that serve essentially the same food you'll find at the grungy markets, but in a more sane and sanitized setting—less fun but perhaps a little more convenient. Good choices include the Antica Focacceria San Francesco, Franco ù Vastiddaru, and Passami ù Coppu.

ON AND NEAR VIA VITTORIO EMANUELE

To quickly survey several good dining options, walk down Via Vittorio Emanuele—lined with cheap street food, high-end gourmet restaurants, trendy hotspots, and everything in between. The first three listings are part of the same restaurant family, serving high-quality food in completely different ways.

€€€€ **Gagini,** set in a former sculpture workshop, has a candlelit interior and attentive staff. The carefully prepared pre-set menus are beautifully presented, even if the portions are small. Sit inside, under the massive stone vaults, or out on the back-streets sidewalk (reservations smart, closed Mon, Tue dinner only, a block off Via Vittorio Emanuele at Via dei Cassari 35, +39 091 589 918, gaginirestaurant.com).

€€€ **Bocum Fuoco,** across the street, is a charming place, with creative drinks, wine, small plates, and wine-crate stools. It's a great place for a pre- or post-dinner drink, or a full meal (Tue-Sun for dinner, closed Mon, Via dei Cassari 6, +39 091 332 009, bocum.it).

€€€ **Buatta Cucina Popolana,** a destination for foodies, offers high-end versions of Sicilian classics. Chef Fabio subscribes to the slow-food approach, emphasizing territory, seasonality, and sustainability. You can order a la carte, or go all-in for an appealing fixed-price menu (reservations smart, daily, Via Vittorio Emanuele 176, +39 091 322 378, buattapalermo.it).

€€ Casa del Brodo, a Palermo institution, is an old-school place for a reliably good meal. While it's just steps from the noisy Vucciria Market scene, it feels sedate and sophisticated, with photos of celebrity diners hanging on the walls. You're there for the *brodo*, a clear broth with tortellini that's warmed bellies for generations (closed Sun, Via Vittorio Emanuele 175, +39 091 321 655, casadelbrodo.it).

€ Franco ù Vastiddaru bustles day and night, slinging out typical Palermo street-food dishes such as *panelle e cazzilli* and *pane con milza*. Choose the deep-fried snack of your dreams for takeaway from the window, or pull up a plastic chair in the piazza out front (long hours daily, Via Vittorio Emanuele 102, +39 091 325 987).

ON AND NEAR VIA ROMA

Via Roma—Palermo's busy north-south thoroughfare—is generally less atmospheric with simpler and more functional eateries. The exception is my first listing, on a lively square tucked behind the San Domenico church on Piazza Meli.

€€ Ferramenta serves generous charcuterie boards and offers a nice mix of hearty pastas and seafood *secondis* (main course) on a rustic, sprawling outdoor terrace just begging you to stop for an afternoon drink and stay for a meal (Wed-Sun lunch and dinner, Mon-Tue dinner only, Piazza Giovanni Meli 8; +39 392 294 3548).

€ Bar Lucchese, on Piazza San Domenico, is a classic old café with a fine selection of gelato and *granite*, Italian ices often made with fresh fruit (long hours daily, Piazza San Domenico 11).

€ Ferro di Cavallo ("The Horseshoe") is an old-time eatery, serving simple dishes at basic prices since 1944 (Mon-Tue lunch only, Wed-Sat lunch and dinner, closed Sun, opposite Piazza Caracciolo at Via Venezia 20, +39 091 331 835, ferrodicavallopalermo.it).

€ Casa Stagnitta is a longstanding, respected coffee roaster with a fancy coffee bar attached. You can try different varieties of coffee from the menu, then pop in the shop to watch the roasting in action. Better than the coffee, though, is their pistachio *granita* and the lovely outdoor seating. This is particularly handy for a break near the Fountain of Shame and Piazza Bellini churches (long hours daily, Discesa dei Giudici 50, +39 091 547 317, casastagnitta.it).

€ Passami ù Coppu sells little cones of fried bits from their lengthy menu at the busy intersection of Via Roma and Via Vittorio Emanuele. Pay at the register and pick up your paper cones from the "Sweet" or "Savory" window (long hours Tue-Sun, closed Mon, Via Roma 195, +39 091 584 498, passamiucoppustreetfood.it).

Groceries: A huge and handy **Lidl** supermarket sits on Via Roma, between the train station and city center (daily, Via Roma 59—for location see the map on page 35).

LA KALSA

While this neighborhood sprawls all the way to the port, the restaurants I recommend cluster on the western edge of La Kalsa, close to Piazza Aragona and about a 10-minute walk from Quattro Canti.

€€ **Occhiovivo,** on charming Piazza Croce dei Vespri, is small, cool, and attracts a stylish crowd. It does Sicilian tapas—such as fried polenta with creamed cod, or baby squid with Noto almonds—plus a few veggie options (occhiovivobistrot.it). Its sister restaurant across the square, €€€€ **Osteria dei Vespri,** is a nice choice for a splurge meal (both closed Sun, Nov-March dinner only, Piazza Croce dei Vespri 7, +39 091 617 1631, osteriadeivespri.it).

€€€€ **Quattro Mani** focuses on quality, with thoughtful twists on classic dishes, and is my pick for a fancy, yet affordable, dinner. Choose between the spacious interior under high vaults or the expansive outdoor terrace. Chef Chiara's flavorful, seasonal menu highlights the best of Sicilian seafood (reserve ahead, dinner served Tue-Sat, lunch and dinner Sun, closed Mon; Via Francesco Riso 3—for location see the "Palermo" map on page 35; +39 091 616 5046, quattromaniristorante.it).

€ **Antica Focacceria San Francesco** has a vintage photo-op storefront with a long history (since 1834). It's such a venerable Palermo institution that it has spun off a chain of imitators—the original has become touristy and lost a bit of its cachet, but it still offers decent food on an atmospheric square. The main part of the shop has counter service for street food—including *pane con*

milza (spleen sandwiches), fried goodies (*arancine, panelle,* and *cazzilli*), *sfincione* (Sicilian pizza), and more. They also have table service at higher prices (daily, Via Alessandro Paternostro 58, +39 091 320 264, anticafocacceria.it).

€€ **A'nìca** is a trendy, modern pizzeria a block off Piazza Aragona. The breezy interior is clean, white, and modern, but I prefer the seating out on the terrace. While the creative pizzas are a favorite, they also have pricier pastas and *secondi*, plus salads (daily, Via Alloro 135, +39 091 982 6011, anicapalermo.it).

Groceries: Famila is a large supermarket hidden in the Kalsa, just in front of Palazzo Mirto (daily, Salita Partanna 1—for location see the "Palermo" map on page 35; +39 091 611 0322).

BALLARÒ

Most people come to Ballarò to eat at the market, but if you want a little altruism with your meal, € **Moltivolti** is a restaurant and community center with a mission to bring the diverse groups of the area together. Their menu features Sicilian and African dishes, served in a colorful communal atmosphere (long hours daily, Via Giuseppe Mario Puglia 21—for location see the "Palermo" map on page 34; +39 091 271 0285, moltivolti.org).

NEAR TEATRO MASSIMO

€€ **Trattoria del Massimo,** directly behind Teatro Massimo, is a barn-sized dining room popular with locals and families that will make your mouth water the minute you open the door. It's known especially for its pastas, but reasonably priced fish and meat dishes round out the menu (daily, Piazza Giuseppe Verdi 25, +39 091 326 155).

€ **La Taverna di John** is an unpretentious, rollicking pizzeria packed with families enjoying friendly service, good-value pizzas and salads, and each other's company (Thu-Tue, closed Wed, Via Sperlinga 57, +39 091 334 678, latavernadijohn.it).

€ **Antico Caffè Spinnato,** set on a wide, pleasant shopping street under shady trees, a few minutes' walk past the Teatro Massimo, is a classic spot for coffee, cocktails, light lunch, or tempting sweets (they also have fine *arancine*). Belly up to the bar for a quick snack or linger at their outdoor tables (long hours daily, Via Principe di Belmonte 107—for location see the "Palermo" map on page 34, +39 091 329 220).

NEAR VIA MAQUEDA

Via Maqueda, stretching north from Quattro Canti to Teatro Massimo, is lined mostly with chains or tourist traps—handy for a quick bite, but hardly ideal for a good meal. However, a couple of more enticing places lie just west of Via Maqueda, in a characteristic (and somewhat run-down) maze of streets.

€ **Assud Pizzeria** slings Trapanese-style pizzas in a laid-back taverna with just the right amount of action and enthusiasm thrown in. Their signature is a slightly thicker, chewier dough (compared to normal wood-fired Italian pizzas), along with their specialty pies—the *rinata* or *rinelle*—with anchovies and garlic (daily, Via del Celso 5, +39 091 736 3230).

€ **Trattoria Al Vecchio Club Rosanero,** a seriously local restaurant, is dedicated to the only thing the people here love more than St. Rosalia—their soccer club. Diners discuss and watch sports while slurping up the special of the day. The menu offers basic comfort food at prices that will make you do a double take (Mon-Wed lunch only, Thu-Sat lunch and dinner, closed Sun, Vicolo Caldomai 18, +39 349 409 6880).

€ **Bisso Bistrot,** filling a former bookstore (still marked *Libreria Dante*) around the corner from one of the Quattro Canti fountains, is a trendy spot for traditional Sicilian dishes in a homey, Old World interior with communal seating (long hours daily, Via Maqueda 172a, +39 328 131 4595).

Palermo Connections

BY PLANE
Falcone-Borsellino Airport

Palermo's small and easy-to-manage Falcone-Borsellino (aka Punta Raisi) Airport is located on the coast, 20 miles northwest of Palermo and surrounded by a dramatic landscape (airport code: PMO, aeroportodipalermo.it). Note that if you are arriving on an international connection (for example, you flew in from the US with a change in Rome), your bags may appear on a separate carousel, often belts 1-2 (look for the international baggage claim). In the arrivals hall, signs point to taxis, buses, and the train station. Car rentals are on the ground floor, straight ahead. There's an ATM and pharmacy near the entrance to the train station.

Connecting the Airport to the City Center: You can link the airport and Palermo by train, bus, taxi, or shared taxi.

Trains connect the airport and Palermo's main train station, Stazione Centrale, in just under an hour (€6.80 one-way; 2/hour, typically departing from platform 2 at :26 and :45, runs 4:00-22:40, some **express trains** make the journey in 30 minutes—confirm schedule at trenitalia.com). At the airport, the train station is to the left after you exit arrivals: Take the stairs or escalator down and buy a ticket from the machines at the end of the underground passage, nearest the tracks. Most sights and hotels are walkable from the train station—or take a taxi or bus the rest of the way (see "Arrival in Palermo" at the beginning of this chapter.) Trains *to* the airport from Stazione Centrale typically depart from platform 8 or 10 at :12 and :42 (2/hour, runs 5:20-22:45).

Airport shuttle buses (Prestia e Comandè) can drop you along the main axis of the city: near Teatro Politeama (on Piazza Ruggero Settimo at the north end of the center), on Piazza San Domenico on Via Roma (near the Vucciria Market, handy for many of my listings), or at Stazione Centrale (main train station, the last stop, at the south end of the center). Exiting the airport, buses are to the far right, beyond the end of the terminal. You'll load your luggage under the bus before boarding, but keep smaller bags and valuables with you (€6, buy ticket online in advance or at desk in airport lobby; 2/hour, runs from the airport 5:00-01:00, to the airport 03:30-21:30, takes about 50 minutes depending on traffic; +39 091 586 351, prestiaecomande.it).

Taxis are twice as fast and eight times the cost. Take only official taxis, waiting at the taxi stand. The fare to central Palermo should be about €40-55, depending on the day, time, or mood of the driver. Negotiate, ask several drivers the price, be firm, and set a *prezzo fisso* (fixed price) rather than the metered price. Have the driver write down the price before you depart. To be sure there will be no other charges added later, ask, *"È tutto?"* (Is that everything?).

Shared minivan taxis are a compromise between a bus and a taxi, running the same route as the bus with minivans for up to eight people. They line up to the right of the airport exit, just before the bus parking (follow signs). Drivers wait to gather a group (minimum of five) and drop at the same downtown points as the public bus: at Teatro Politeama and at the main train station. Your driver may be willing to drop you halfway along Via Roma—ask when you board. Compared to the bus, these leave more frequently and are slightly faster (€8). These taxis wait at the airport, but you can try to reserve the journey *to* the airport at 6878.it.

Connecting the Airport to Cefalù: On weekends, some direct trains run straight from the airport to the beachy town of Cefalù (2/day Sat, 4/day Sun, 1.5 hours, Cefalù Line). Otherwise take the train from the airport to Palermo's Stazione Centrale and connect to Cefalù from there (1-2 hour, allow 2 hours total). Two taxi companies offer direct transfers from the airport to Cefalù (see page 151).

BY BUS

Long-distance buses arrive and depart from the main bus terminal alongside the train station's track 10 (for details, see "Arrival in Palermo—By Bus" at the beginning of this chapter). Purchase bus tickets online or in the bus-terminal building. Large luggage is stored beneath the bus; for efficient loading, they may ask for your destination.

It's smart to ask your hotelier or the TI for help confirming schedules. Fewer buses depart on Saturdays, and very few on Sundays.

From Palermo by Bus to: Catania (hourly, 2.5 hours, SAIS Autolinee), **Trapani** (hourly, 2 hours, Segesta Autolinee; from Trapani you can catch a Cuffaro bus to **Segesta**), **Siracusa** (4/day direct, 3.5 hours, Etna Trasporti; more with a change in Catania), **Piazza Armerina** (near Villa Romana del Casale, 5/day Mon-Fri, less on Sat, not workable on Sun, 2 hours, SAIS), **Ragusa** (4/day, 4 hours, AST). You'll need to change in Catania to reach **Taormina** (hourly, 4 hours, SAIS to Catania, then Etna Trasporti to Taormina). You can catch a bus to **Agrigento** (7/day Mon-Fri, fewer on weekends, 2 hours, Cuffaro) but the train may be better.

For mainland Italy, SAIS and Salemi run daily overnight buses to several destinations, including **Rome** (12 hours) and **Milan** (20-24 hours).

Bus info: AST (aziendasicilianatrasporti.it), Cuffaro (cuffaro.info), Interbus/Segesta/Etna Trasporti (interbus.it), SAIS (saisautolinee.it), Salemi (autoservizisalemi.it), Segesta Autolinee (segesta.it).

BY TRAIN

Train connections leave from Stazione Centrale, at the southern end of the city center (for details on arriving by train and station services, see "Arrival in Palermo—By Train" at the beginning of this chapter). Sicily's train network is sparse; buses are often more efficient and frequent. Many cities, particularly in the west, have infrequent or no train service at all.

Trains to the mainland cross at the Strait of Messina, to the east. Train cars are loaded on a ferry for the 20-minute crossing, allowing passengers to walk around the ferry during the crossing. Once on the other side, the cars are reconnected to the rails and continue north.

From Palermo by Train to: Cefalù (1-2/hour, 1 hour), **Agrigento** (hourly, 2 hours; from Agrigento town a taxi or hourly bus gets you directly to the archaeological site), **Catania** (7/day, 4.5-6 hours, 1-2 changes), **Taormina** (7/day, 4.5 hours, change in Messina), **Rome** (3 direct/day, 11-13 hours), **Naples** (2 direct/day, 9-11 hours).

BY FERRY

Two companies run overnight ferries between Palermo and Naples, leaving from Stazione Marittima and taking about 10 hours: **GNV** (+39 010 209 4591, gnv.it) and **Tirrenia** (tirrenia.it).

Ships dock near the city center at Palermo's Stazione Marittima, a reasonable walk (20-30 minutes) or quick taxi ride from the sightseeing core. Taxis that meet arriving ships are more likely to overcharge; it's better to walk farther into town to find a more honest cabbie. The trip to the city center should cost no more than €15.

BY CAR

Car-rental agencies are located near the port and at the main train station. However, driving in Palermo is stressful, and parking is limited and expensive. For many, a better plan is to enjoy Palermo car-free, then return to the airport to pick up a car for further Sicilian adventures. That way, your first Sicilian driving experience will be on a highway with light traffic, rather than in the thick of an urban jungle.

ZTL Pass and Parking Tips: If you do need to drive into the historic core of Palermo, you'll have to purchase and register a **ZTL** *(Zona Traffico Limitato)* **pass** online (€5/day). If staying multiple days, you'll need to register a new ZTL pass each day (ztl. comune.palermo.it, hotels can sometimes help).

Parking spots inside the ZTL are scarce. The easiest parking option is in a secured underground parking lot under the courthouse, near the entrance to the Capo Market (Vittorio Emanuele Orlando 49). Other underground garages are a bit farther out: several options near Teatro Politeama, such as Parking Tuminello on the corner of Via Roma and Via Amari; and at Piazzale Ungheria. An easy surface parking lot is at the port, at the end of Via Amari.

Route Tips for Drivers

Leaving Palermo, your goal is to make your way through the snarled traffic to the ring road. For most destinations, you'll aim for the E-90 highway that runs north to south along the western edge of the city center.

Going north on E-90 takes you to the **airport** (about 30 minutes from downtown), near which the road becomes the A-29 expressway to **Segesta** (1 hour from Palermo), then **Trapani** (1.5 hours from Palermo).

Heading south/east on E-90 takes you toward **Catania** (2.75 hours from Palermo), along autostrada A-19—which serves as the island's spine. To reach **Siracusa** (3.75 hours), head to Catania, then south to Siracusa.

To reach **Cefalù** (1 hour east of Palermo), begin by heading south/east on E-90. Don't turn off when the road forks onto the A-19 toward Catania; instead, stay on E-90, following the coast. This is also a good plan if you're heading to **Messina** (3.5 hours) or even **Taormina** (4.25 hours)—it's more scenic to follow the coastal E-90 tollway past Cefalù, then turn south on E-45 at Messina.

Finally, to reach **Agrigento** (2 hours from Palermo), you won't get on the E-90 highway—instead, you'll head south on SS-121 toward Sciacca (on the south coast), then head east.

DAY TRIPS FROM PALERMO

Sanctuary of Santa Rosalia • Mondello • Monreale Cathedral • Segesta

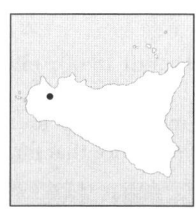

Several worthwhile destinations are within day-trip distance of Palermo, all in Sicily's northwest corner. Just a few miles north of Palermo, around Monte Pellegrino—a hill the German writer Goethe called "the most beautiful promontory in the world"—lie the beach town of Mondello and the Sanctuary of Santa Rosalia. And to the south and west are the intriguing 12th-century cathedral at Monreale and the ancient city of Segesta. I've listed these sights according to their proximity to Palermo, but even the farthest is within just an hour's drive.

One other day-trip possibility—the charming beach town of Cefalù—is described in the next chapter.

North of Palermo

Two sights within a few miles north of the city can be combined as a day trip—one a mountaintop church, the other a pleasant beach getaway.

SANCTUARY OF SANTA ROSALIA

On top of Monte Pellegrino sits the Sanctuary of Santa Rosalia, dedicated to the patron saint of Palermo. If you don't mind making the trek out here, the ride up the mountainside comes with impressive views. Worth ▲, the sanctuary—burrowed into a rock face with dripping walls and reverent locals—is an unusual, low-key sight. A visit here with the right mindset will help you appreciate

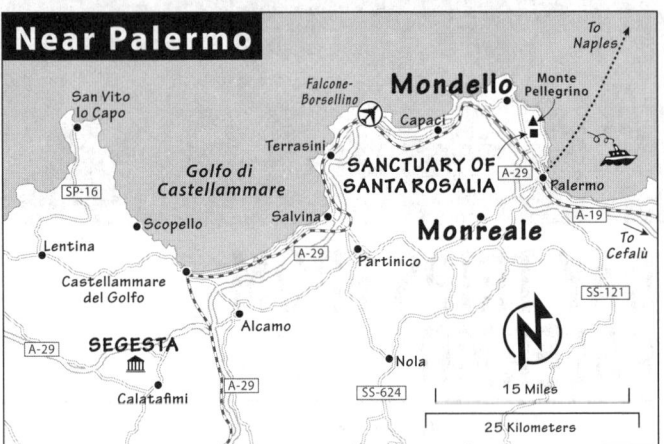

why locals say that, in their pantheon of saints, there is St. Rosalia...then everyone else.

Hours: Free, daily 8:00-19:00, Nov-March until 18:00, +39 091 540 326, santuariosantarosalia.it.

Getting There: The chapel perches on a mountaintop four miles north of Palermo's city center (but the drive is twice that far, thanks to many switchbacks). The journey to the top of Monte Pellegrino is scenic, with sprawling views over busy Palermo, the mountains, and the sea. AMAT **bus #812** departs from the stop in the middle of Piazza Sturzo, a block behind Teatro Politeama (departs every 1.5 hours Mon-Sat, roughly hourly on Sun, trip takes about 30 minutes depending on traffic, amat.pa.it). **Drivers** go north along the port, then head out of town on Via Montepellegrino, which becomes Via Isaac Rabin. Reaching the base of the hill, bear right and follow Via Pietro Bonanno as it switchbacks steeply all the way to the top (figure at least 30 minutes' drive, depending on traffic). As you twist up, consider that many devout *palermitani* make this trek on foot from the city center each year in mid-July.

Visiting the Sanctuary: This church and convent were built on the place where Rosalia's bones were discovered. But the facade is just...a facade. Once inside, the roof cuts away to the open sky and the church blends into a dramatic cave, complete with dripping rock formations.

In this entryway—before passing through the gate of the church itself—you'll see a staggering variety of **votive** items, offered as thanks to Rosalia by those who pray to her for help. On the left wall hang hundreds of little silver plaques, some shaped like body parts—left by people who have recovered from illness or Vespa accidents. On the right is a pile of more modern ex-voto items, such as wedding dresses and baby clothing, surrounding the gigantic anchor of a ship that survived a rough journey in the seas near Palermo.

Now step into the **church interior.** The altar on the left houses an ivory sculpture of the saint (in the glass enclosure below)—though her actual bones are in Palermo Cathedral. The metal channels attached to the cave ceiling seem artistic, even surreal, but they're entirely practical—they're an elaborate system for channeling dripping water, which is believed to have miraculous properties. You can follow the water from the ceiling, across the top of the altar, and down into the holy-water fonts.

This sanctuary is a powerful place for the faithful. People come to drink the water or rub it on troubled body parts. According to the sanctuary's custodian, even skeptical doctors have been healed here. It's poignant to simply step back and observe the steady stream of visitors who come to pay their respects and to thank St. Rosalia for her help.

Connecting to Mondello: Drivers wanting to combine the Sanctuary of Santa Rosalia with the alluring beach town of Mondello may find a shortcut road open: Carry on down the mountain road past the sanctuary, and you may be able to twist directly down to Mondello (with stunning views as you approach). However, this road is often closed (especially off-season) due to rockslides, in which case you'll need to backtrack and loop around the bottom of the mountain. The seaside road is pleasant and avoids congested city streets.

> ## Santa Rosalia
>
> St. Rosalia (Santa Rosalia)—whose name comes from the words for "rose" and "lily" (signifying beauty and purity)—was a Norman noblewoman and possibly the niece of Sicily's King William II. According to tradition, 15-year-old Rosalia refused her arranged marriage to a nobleman and decided to dedicate herself to Christ. She lived out her life as a hermit on Monte Pellegrino, where she died in 1166. During the plague of 1624, Rosalia appeared to a local hunter and told him where to find her remains. He discovered the bones in a cave (now the sanctuary) on July 14 and brought them down into the city...and the plague ended. Rosalia is the most venerated saint in Palermo. She's also the patron saint of epidemics—and of volcanoes and fires (fitting for this volcanic island).
>
> Thanks to Rosalia, July 14 and 15 are the most festive days of the year in Palermo. The mayor kicks things off by placing flowers at the Quattro Canti intersection (while the public either cheers or—more often—jeers, depending on the mayor's current popularity). Then the crowd marches down to the harborfront, where they watch fireworks and eat snails, the traditional food of the feast of St. Rosalia. (Snails, which live in solitude in a little "house" they carry on their backs, are a common symbol for hermits.) After the celebration, everyone walks home—empty snail shells crunching underfoot. The festivities also include a long, laborious pilgrimage—by foot—from the city center to the Sanctuary of Santa Rosalia, high atop Monte Pellegrino.

MONDELLO

A favorite summer resort on the other side of Monte Pellegrino, Mondello, worth ▲, is a popular hangout for families, teens, and tourists who are tired of city congestion. Crystal-clear blue waters and a crescent of soft, sandy beach beckon sun worshippers. The town offers turn-of-the-century boardwalk atmosphere, a cancan line of Liberty Style (Italian Art Nouveau) villas, and beautiful views along the coast—and occasionally all  the way to Mount Etna. This area was originally a swamp, which was drained to create a beach community (with the help of Belgian engineers—notice the Belgian and Italian flags on the main pier). In the 1910s, this was *the* place for aristocrats to build their seaside villas. Overcrowded in summer and dead in the winter, Mondello is perfect on a warm spring or fall day.

Getting There: From Palermo, you can reach Mondello by bus or car. AMAT **bus #806** runs to Mondello from Piazza Struzo, a block behind Teatro Politeama (runs May-Aug only, 3/hour, takes about 40 minutes, amat.pa.it). City Sightseeing's **hop-on hop-off bus** from Palermo combines narrated sightseeing with transport (see page 40 for details). For **drivers,** Mondello is about 20 minutes from downtown Palermo—if there's no traffic.

Eating: For a seafood treat, try the *polpo bollito* (freshly chopped boiled octopus) at one of the restaurants near the seafront, such as €€ **L'Angolo di Mondello** (closed Mon, Via Mondello 15, +39 329 701 0382). For a splashy meal, the old-time bathing pavilion houses €€€€ **Alle Terrazze,** a pricey restaurant with killer views (closed Tue, +39 091 626 2903).

Southwest of Palermo

One of Sicily's most important sights is just six miles southwest of Palermo: the stunning Norman cathedral of Monreale. The surrounding town offers a few enjoyable places to grab a bite, but there's nothing of importance to see other than the amazing cathedral.

Monreale Cathedral

Built between 1174 and 1189, this Romanesque building is an amalgam of Byzantine, Norman, and Arab elements—reflecting the intermingling of cultures and religions in this period. While the exterior, with its elaborate stonework, and the cloister, with its decorated capitals, are both notable, the stars of the show are the intricate golden mosaics completely covering the church interior.

Illustrating Old and New Testament stories, they form the largest cycle of Byzantine mosaics in Italy.

The cathedral, worth ▲▲▲, sits on a hillside that once held an Arab manor house. The Norman kings used it as a private hunting reserve and built a palazzo called Mons Regalis ("Royal Mountain")—the origin of "Monreale." William II, Sicily's last Norman king, chose this site for a magnificent cathedral, a Benedictine monastery, and a palace for his newly minted archbishop.

Most cathedrals under construction in the 1100s, such as Paris' Notre-Dame, took more than 100 years to finish, but Monreale was built in only 15 years, spurred by Norman wealth and political urgency (see the "Dueling Cathedrals" sidebar). The result is an unusually cohesive architectural style for a structure of its size.

Over time, a village grew around the cathedral; modern Monreale has a population of over 30,000. Although the original Norman palace and part of the monastery are long gone, the cathedral and cloister are well preserved.

GETTING THERE

By Public Bus: From Palermo, AMAT **bus #389** departs from Piazza Indipendenza, behind the Norman Palace (hourly, 30 minutes, amat.pa.it). The bus drops you in Monreale at a roundabout below the cathedral complex at the bottom of Via d'Acquisto (return buses leave from the same spot). From there, you'll hike about 10 minutes uphill on Via d'Acquisto to reach the church. Note that bus #389 also stops at the Capuchin Crypt just outside Palermo (see page 80), making it possible to see both in one day. This bus is often packed—a pickpocket's dream. *Attenzione!*

By Hop-On, Hop-Off Bus: The **City Sightseeing** tour bus from Palermo combines narrated sightseeing with transport (see page 40 for details).

By Taxi: A one-way ride from downtown Palermo to the cathedral door takes about 30 minutes (roughly €40, negotiate and confirm price in advance—traffic jams are common and can be costly). When you're ready to return to Palermo, you'll find taxis waiting at Piazza Vittorio Emanuele, near the cathedral entrance.

By Car: It's a 30-minute drive to Monreale from Palermo. Head west from central Palermo on Corso Calatafimi (SS-186). About a mile after crossing over the E-90 ring road, bear left at the intersection with SP-69, continuing on SS-186 (ignore the sign that indicates you should go right for *Monreale*). After about 1.5 miles, turn right onto Via Ferrata. Follow it slightly left and uphill, then hook right onto Via Ignazio Florio. At the end of Via Ignazio Florio, pull into the big pay parking lot. From this lot, you can climb 92 steps up to the town, or take a taxi shuttle (€15/up to 5

Monreale Cathedral

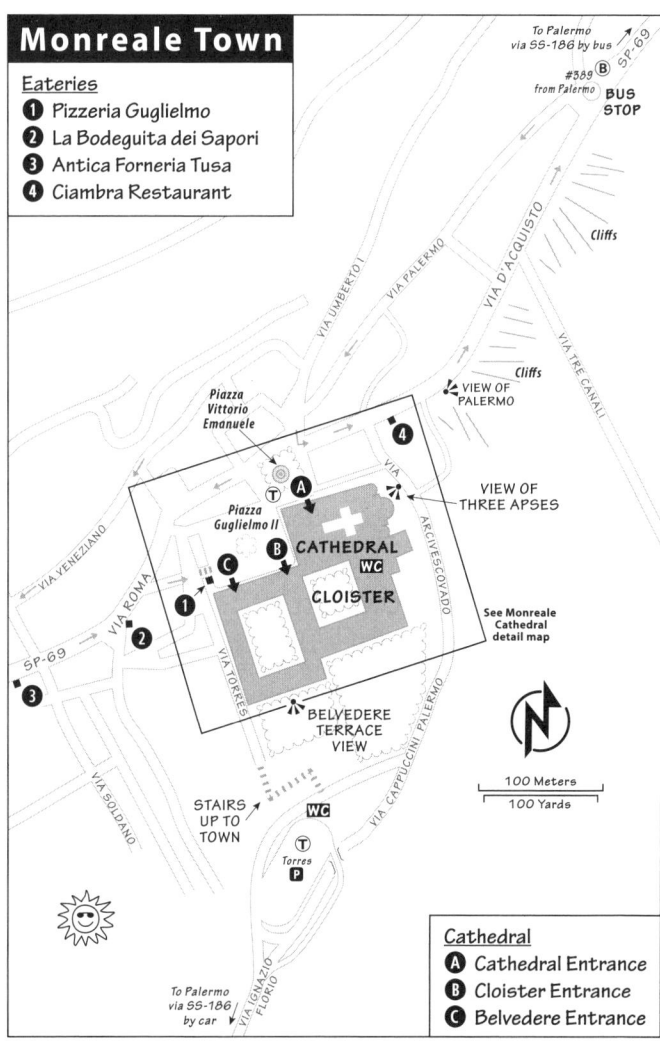

people) to Monreale's main square, Piazza Vittorio Emanuele, near the cathedral entrance.

PLANNING YOUR TIME

Monreale, just 30 minutes from downtown Palermo, is an easy side trip if you go at the right time. Morning traffic can be bad; visiting around lunchtime is often a better bet (I'd aim to arrive at 11:30 or so). If you arrive close to the midday closure (see hours later), visit the cloister first, grab some lunch, and see the cathedral when it

> ## Eateries in Monreale
>
> The following spots make for a nice lunch or snack break. For locations, see the "Monreale Town" map.
>
> **€ Pizzeria Guglielmo:** Enjoy fine pizza and outdoor seating on the square facing the church (daily, Piazza Guglielmo II 2).
>
> **€ La Bodeguita dei Sapori:** This bistro, just uphill from the cathedral, prepares *focaccie* and salads good for a light meal (closed Sun, Via Roma 85).
>
> **€ Antica Forneria Tusa:** Pizza and other Sicilian baked goods provide a quick carryout bite (daily, just up from La Bodeguita dei Sapori—it's on the left at Via Pietro Novelli 25).
>
> **€€ Ciambra:** Downhill from the cathedral, with grand views over Palermo, this classy dining room is nice for an upscale meal (closed Tue, Via d'Acquisto 18).

reopens. Avoid Sundays, when the cathedral is closed most of the morning and the cloister is closed in the afternoon.

ORIENTATION TO MONREALE

Cost: Cathedral—free (you'll still have to wait in line; tell the ticket checker you're coming just for the mosaics); cloister—€8.

Overachievers can buy a €13 ticket that lets you enter the cloister, climb up to the **roof terraces** (closed in bad weather), tour the ho-hum **Diocesan Museum** (entrance in south transept), or check out some royal tombs and an ornate chapel in the **north transept.**

Hours: The cathedral is open Mon-Sat 9:00-12:45 & 14:00-17:00, Sun 8:00-9:15 & 14:30-17:00; in winter (Nov-March) all closing times are 15 minutes earlier. The cloister is open Mon-Sat 9:00-18:30, Sun until 13:00. The roof terraces, Diocesan Museum, and north transept have similar hours to the cathedral.

Information: +39 327 351 0886, monrealeduomo.it.

Dress Code: Knees and shoulders must be covered; disposable cover-ups are provided at the door.

Visitor Information: The gift shop to the left of the cathedral entry sells a detailed map of the mosaics.

Tours: Pick up the fine and thorough **audioguide** at the ticket counter (€5, 45 minutes, must leave ID, return audioguide 30 minutes before closing).

Length of This Tour: Allow 1.5 hours.

Services: At the cathedral, a good pay WC is within the Diocesan Museum. In town you'll find WCs in cafés near the church, on Piazza Guglielmo II, and on Piazza Vittorio Emanuele; there's also a pay WC at the stairway near the parking lot.

Dueling Cathedrals: The Rivalry of Monreale and Palermo

The story of Monreale's construction begins with a legend. While out hunting, young King William II stopped for a siesta under a tree. The Virgin Mary appeared to him in a dream and revealed the location of a treasure hidden by his father. There was one condition: The fortune must be spent entirely on the construction of a basilica dedicated to her.

A more secular explanation is that William built Monreale Cathedral for political reasons. He sought to curb the growing power of his former tutor, the Englishman known as Walter of the Mill. Walter, who had the support of the pope, had worked the system to become archbishop of Palermo—according to some, "less by election than by violent intrusion."

To counterbalance Walter, William needed his own archbishop—and in a hurry. He built this impressive church and its abbey, handing them over to Benedictine monks. Doing so automatically elevated the Benedictine abbot to archbishop status. Constructed in just 15 years (some of the mosaics took longer), the grandiose church became Sicily's second archbishopric, despite being just six miles from the cathedral in downtown Palermo. William had his archbishop and his cathedral.

Monreale Cathedral was consecrated in 1189, and its diocese was endowed with large parcels of land throughout the province of Palermo. It quickly overshadowed Walter's diocese as the most influential in the kingdom, effectively blocking Walter's aspirations. But later that year, William II died suddenly at age 36—without an heir. William left Sicily with a grand cathedral, but his lack of a clear successor also spelled the end of the island's Norman golden age.

Tips: Bring small binoculars to help make out mosaic details, and use the "Monreale Mosaics" map in this chapter to identify specific scenes.

Starring: A cathedral with 68,000 square feet of glittering golden mosaics and a peaceful cloister with carved column capitals.

◑ SELF-GUIDED TOUR

Begin on Piazza Guglielmo II, in front of the main church doors, facing the two towers. Monreale Cathedral was built on this hilltop by the young Norman king of Sicily, William II. For such an elaborate building, construction was completed very quickly: William was in a hurry to finish and show up the cathedral over in Palermo (see the "Dueling Cathedrals" sidebar, earlier).

EXTERIOR
• *Position yourself on Piazza Guglielmo II to take in the...*

❶ View of the Main Facade
If you didn't know this was a church, from this side you might mistake it for a fortress. The Normans were exceptional military architects, and their style of church is called *ecclesia munita* ("church-fortress")—it's both a place of worship and a last line of defense. Two mighty square **towers** frame the facade. The one on the left was never completed and sports slit windows at the bottom and crenellations at the top.

The Neoclassical **portico** between the towers was added in 1770 to protect the main bronze doors—and to help the church look a little less like a fort. The **doors,** completed in 1186, were made by Bonanno Pisano, architect of the Leaning Tower of Pisa. Luckily, Pisano was a better sculptor than architect. Blending Byzantine and classical elements, his doors feature 46 panels: lions and griffins at the bottom, Old Testament scenes on the lower bands, New Testament scenes on the upper bands, and the Virgin Mary and Christ at the top. Remember these scenes; we'll compare them to another set of doors in a few minutes.

• *Now head left and curve around the back side of the cathedral, passing by the entrance and under the arch of the side chapel, to look up at the cathedral's back side.*

❷ Three Apses
Examine the richly ornamented apses you see here. Decorated with a series of interlacing pointed arches of different heights, the three apses (unlike the more restrained main facade) beautifully show off Monreale's fusion of Arab and Norman styles. One can imagine that the complex geometric forms, interlacing patterns, and intricate inlays are the creations of Arab craftsmen,

in particular. Remember the black lava-stone inlay—we'll see more of it later on our tour.

• *It's time to go inside. Retrace your steps to the cathedral entrance opposite Piazza Vittorio Emanuele.*

❸ Cathedral Entrance

Just inside the iron fence at the entry, look left and right. You're in the middle of a *sacra conversazione* ("holy conversation") between two modern bronze statues, made in 1997 by Italian sculptor Arnaldo Pomodoro. The "holy conversation" was a typical way to imagine interactions between God and the saints in medieval and Renaissance art. In this case, William II (on your right) is humbly offering the church of Monreale to Mary (on your left)...and you are invited to witness the donation.

❹ North Doors

The bronze doors before you are only a decade older (1179) than the Bonanno doors we saw a few minutes ago, but they are more firmly in traditional Byzantine style. The 28 panels represent the lives of saints and the evangelists, with each panel showing a single static figure. Compare these doors with the pair we saw earlier: The art of the east, represented here, remains rooted in well-established tradition, while the art of the west, on the other doors, is anticipating the slow march toward the realism and humanism of the Renaissance.

• *Enter the church and walk straight ahead, to the center of the nave, and face the altar. Spin around to take it all in.*

INTERIOR

This imposing basilica, at 335 feet long by 130 feet wide, is slathered with over 68,000 square feet of golden **mosaics**—a third more than at St. Mark's Basilica in Venice. While this is a fine example of the interplay between architecture and visual art, it's also the perfect illustration of something uniquely Sicilian: the fusion among classical, Byzantine, Arab, and Norman craftsmanship.

It's estimated that the walls of the cathedral hold about two

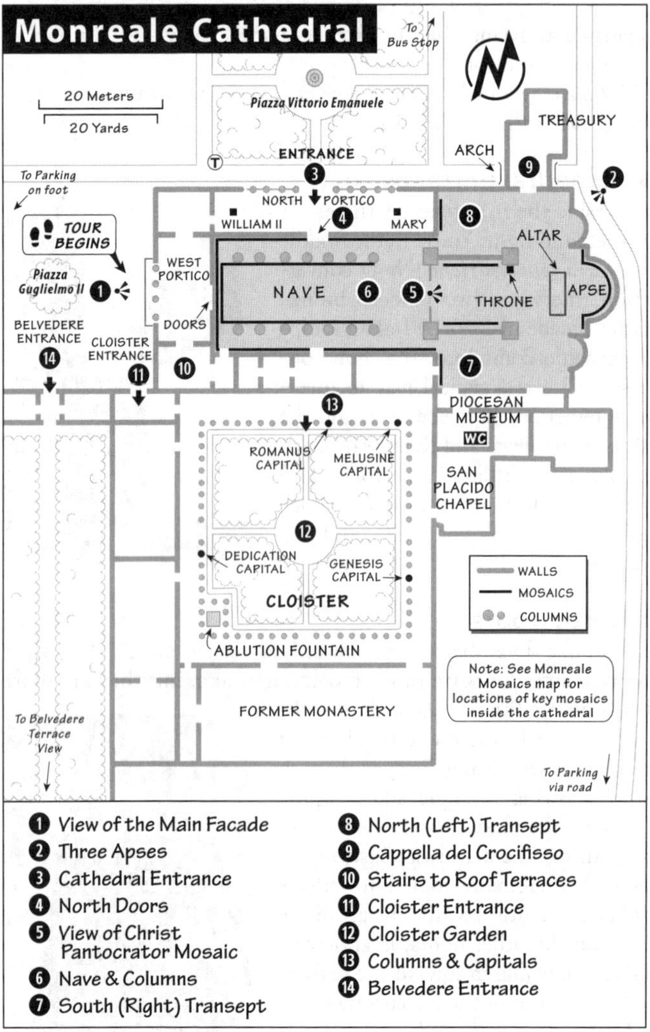

Monreale Cathedral

- ① View of the Main Facade
- ② Three Apses
- ③ Cathedral Entrance
- ④ North Doors
- ⑤ View of Christ Pantocrator Mosaic
- ⑥ Nave & Columns
- ⑦ South (Right) Transept
- ⑧ North (Left) Transept
- ⑨ Cappella del Crocifisso
- ⑩ Stairs to Roof Terraces
- ⑪ Cloister Entrance
- ⑫ Cloister Garden
- ⑬ Columns & Capitals
- ⑭ Belvedere Entrance

Map labels: Piazza Vittorio Emanuele, Entrance, Arch, Treasury, North Portico, William II, Mary, Altar, Apse, Throne, Nave, West Portico, Doors, Piazza Guglielmo II, Belvedere Entrance, Cloister Entrance, Tour Begins, To Parking on foot, To Bus Stop, Diocesan Museum, WC, San Placido Chapel, Romanus Capital, Melusine Capital, Dedication Capital, Genesis Capital, Cloister, Ablution Fountain, Former Monastery, To Belvedere Terrace View, To Parking via road, Walls, Mosaics, Columns.

Note: See Monreale Mosaics map for locations of key mosaics inside the cathedral.

---

tons of gold. The Byzantines perfected the technique of sandwiching pieces of paper-thin gold leaf between glass. The uneven surface of the tiles captures and reflects light, helping to illuminate small-windowed, lantern-lit churches. Just as important, the golden glow of the mosaics symbolizes the divine light of heaven (for more on mosaics, see the sidebar on page 243).

The **roof** above you, with gilded and painted trusses, is a faithful reproduction of the original, which burned after a lightning strike in 1811.

The **floor** is original and was added to over time. The oldest

portions are found in the sanctuary, while the remainder took 300 years to complete. Floors like this—using marble scavenged from ancient buildings—were common in this time period. Marble often cracked as it was removed, leaving small pieces like the ones used in this patchwork floor.
• *Face the altar. Focus on the top mosaic above the altar in the central apse.*

❺ View of Christ Pantocrator Mosaic

Christ Pantocrator ("All Powerful") is shown with his right hand raised in the classical gesture of a Byzantine blessing. Each finger represents a letter: The straight finger is the letter I, the crossed fingers make an X, and the two curved fingers are for two Cs—that's IC XC, the first and last Greek letters for the name Jesus Christ. The mosaic's dimensions are impressive—the right

hand alone is over six feet long. Christ is benevolent and welcoming, with flowing hair and beard. With outstretched arms, he seems to embrace you and everyone else in the cathedral at once. In his left hand he nimbly holds the Gospel, open to John 8:12, which reads (in both medieval Latin and Greek), "I am the light of the world. Whoever follows me shall not walk in darkness."

Seated beneath Christ is the **Virgin Enthroned with Child,** flanked by Greek letters spelling *panakrontas* ("All Immaculate"). Surrounded by heavenly gold skies, Mary is draped in heavy, colorful clothes like a Byzantine empress. To either side are the archangels Gabriel and Michael and the apostles.

Below Mary, a row of saints flanks the window. The second saint on the right, in green vestments, is the earliest representation anywhere of **St. Thomas Becket.** Martyred on December 29, 1170, in Canterbury, England, Becket was sainted just one year before the construction of this cathedral began. Becket was a friend of William II's mother, Margaret of Navarre, and supported her while she ran the kingdom during William's childhood. (Ironically, seven years after

Becket's murder, William II married Joan of England, daughter of Henry II—the man who ordered Becket's assassination.)
• *Turn around to look at the columns.*

❻ Nave and Columns

Notice the ancient Roman columns dividing the central nave from the two side aisles. These monolithic columns and their fine Corinthian capitals are unusually well preserved and certainly recycled—probably taken from an ancient Roman temple. (Look for faces surrounded by cornucopias in the centers of some of the capitals; these are portraits of Rome's pagan goddesses.) The columns were shipped here from Rome—a gift from Pope Lucius III, who was happy to support and affirm Norman (Western and Christian) control of Sicily.

This was a challenging time for popes: The Great Schism (a century before this cathedral was built) had split Christendom between the Orthodox east and the Catholic west, and the Church faced ongoing threats from Islam (including the Arabs who controlled Sicily before the Normans arrived). Then some smug archbishop in Palermo had the nerve to build a cathedral as a statement of his own power. Monreale Cathedral was King William II's answer to Palermo.

• *Look high above the arches at the mosaics between the windows.*

Genesis Mosaics

The story of Genesis runs like a comic strip around the top of the nave. Start in the upper-right corner, closest to the altar, and work your way clockwise from there, reading each scene in order—just as illiterate medieval peasants would have done. (The mosaics mentioned here are keyed to the "Monreale Mosaics" map on page 121.)

• *To the left of the first window is...*

❶ **Creation of Heaven and Earth:** Notice the stylized face whose flowing hair and beard fuse into the rippling waters.

• *The next mosaic in the series is between the first two windows; the series continues along the south wall from there.*

❷ **Let There Be Light:** God, seated comfortably on a giant bouncy ball, creates a fireball of light, from which the angels emerge.

❸ **Separation of Waters:** In the circle over his head, God separates the waters. One will be the sea, and the other will be the sky.

❹ **Creation of the Earth:** God commands the earth to rise from the sea. Some unusual trees grow.

Monreale Cathedral

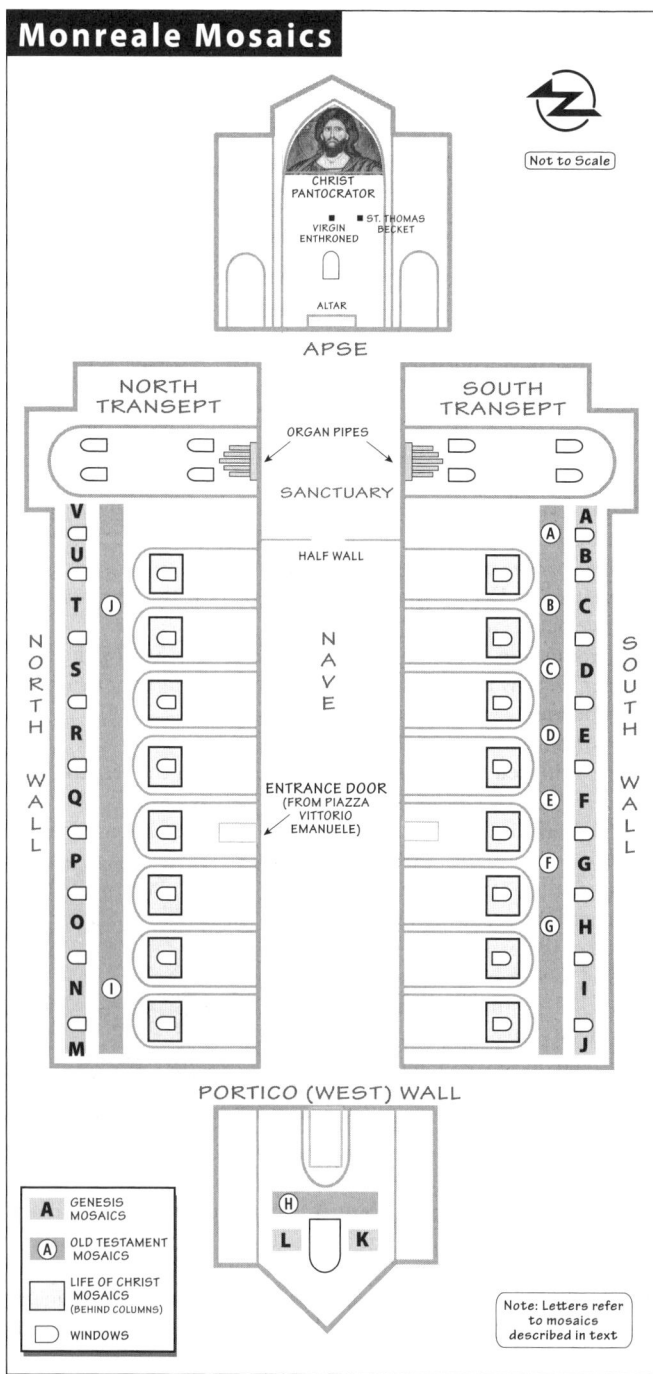

❺ **Creation of the Stars:** God grabs a star, finds a clear shot, and goes in for the dunk.

❻ **Creation of the Fish and Birds:** The sea at God's feet teems with fish, and the mountain displays a variety of birds, including a flying white dove (symbol of the Holy Spirit), a peacock, a common crane, and a spotted owl.

❼ **Creation of Animals and Man:** Using a very long straw, God breathes life into Adam, who gestures back at his father and seems to say, "Thanks, Dad, now can I have 20 bucks and the keys to the car?"

❽ **And on the Seventh Day:** God rested. He clearly needs it—he looks like a dazed tourist at the end of a hot day of looking at mosaics.

❾ **Garden of Eden:** God places Adam in the Garden of Eden.

❿ **Adam Alone in Eden:** Adam is lonely.

• *Continue to the west portico, looking way up to the top (on either side of the window).*

⓫ **Creation of Eve:** While Adam lazily plays with the grass, God lifts Eve out of his rib.

⓬ **Introduction of Adam and Eve:** God escorts Eve by the hand to meet her new beau. Adam points at God, asking if he's sure this is a good idea.

• *Turn to face the north wall to continue the story.*

⓭ **Eve Tempted by the Serpent:** Eve chats with the serpent, who insists that everyone else is doing it.

⓮ **Original Sin:** Eve takes a bite of the apple of knowledge and hands one to Adam. The malicious reptile, after inviting in innocent Eve, seems to stick his tongue out at her.

⓯ **God Confronts Adam and Eve:** God gestures toward the pair, who have now covered their nakedness with large fig leaves, and asks who's to blame. Adam points to Eve, Eve points

to the snake, and the snake looks back at God, closing the circle of blame—proving that some things are eternal.

⓰ **Expulsion from the Garden:** A fiery seraphim and the archangel Michael force the pair out of paradise and into some fluffy fur coats.

⓱ **Adam and Eve Suffer:** Adam works the land while Eve laments her fate. Cradling a spindle with her right hand—procrastinating in her new work-to-live lifestyle—she realizes that maybe ignorance was bliss.

❶ to ❷ Cain and Abel: The narrative shifts as the next four panels tell the story of Cain killing Abel, then Cain being killed by their other brother, Lamech. Notice how profusely Abel's blood gushes from his mortally wounded forehead.

❸ God Commands Noah to Build an Ark: God plans to flood the earth, but he's got a plan for Noah.

• *Turn back to where you started, looking at the south wall. In the lower band beneath the Creation, find more scenes, this time from the Old Testament.*

Old Testament Mosaics

Ⓐ **Building of Noah's Ark:** Notice Noah's tools for this building project. You'll more or less see how ships were built at the time of this church's construction. The saw shown is a type used in Sicily until the 20th century.

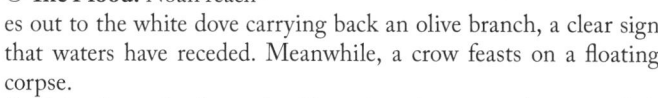

Ⓑ **Loading the Animals:** While the people wait patiently inside, Noah loads the uncooperative animals.

Ⓒ **The Flood:** Noah reaches out to the white dove carrying back an olive branch, a clear sign that waters have receded. Meanwhile, a crow feasts on a floating corpse.

Ⓓ **Unloading the Animals:** Now that the waters have receded, Noah carefully unloads the still skeptical animals while the people again wait patiently.

Ⓔ **The Rainbow:** God seals his covenant with a rainbow.

Ⓕ **The Drunken Noah:** Noah overdoes it in the vineyard.

• *Continue circling the nave. If you're familiar with the Old Testament, you should be able to identify the construction of the…*

Ⓖ **Tower of Babel,** the Ⓗ **Destruction of Sodom** (look for Lot's wife shown as a pillar of salt), the Ⓘ **Sacrifice of Abraham,** and Ⓙ **Jacob's Ladder.**

• *Now, beneath the arches in the side aisles, find the…*

Life of Jesus Christ Mosaics

This series progresses down and around the nave, starting under the Noah's Ark panel (south wall), with the **Healing of the Possessed Woman.** See if you can pick out other miracles, such as the **Healing of the Leper** (the fellow covered with open wounds) and the **Multiplication of the Loaves and Fishes,** when Christ fed 5,000 followers with just five loaves of bread and two fish (last scene, south side). Christ's story continues along the opposite wall: Look for **Christ Expelling the Money Changers from the Temple** (midway on the north side) and **Mary Magdalene Washing Jesus' Feet** (last scene before the transept).

• *Now, refer back to the map on page 121. Walk toward the altar, to the right side of the nave, and up a few steps into the...*

❼ South Transept

Notice the large red porphyry and colored marble disks in the floor here. These are ancient columns that have been recycled—sliced like salami.

The large stone coffins are **royal tombs.** The red porphyry tomb belongs to William I. Long and cylindrical, it was carved from an ancient Roman column. The white marble tomb is for William II, who built this church. These tombs were originally covered with red porphyry canopies *(baldacchini),* like the royal tombs in Palermo's cathedral.

• *Walk beyond the tombs and climb a few steps, then turn left and look across the altar.*

The **throne** directly across from where you stand is where the king sat for Mass. Notice that it's higher than the archbishop's throne on the opposite side. Above the king's throne, a mosaic shows the king, dressed in the precious gem-covered robes of a Byzantine emperor, being crowned directly by God. After his power struggle with the archbishop of Palermo, William II needed to reinforce who was boss. This cathedral and this throne sent a clear message.

• *You've seen the most interesting parts of the cathedral interior. To see a bit more, you can pay to enter the **Diocesan Museum** (enter through the south transept, WC). Or, circle around to the other side of the altar and pay to enter the (skippable)...*

❽ North Transept

Along the outer (left) wall of the north transept are the **tombs** of Margaret of Navarre, mother of William II, and of his two brothers.

There's also a sarcophagus containing the heart of King Louis IX of France. Also known as St. Louis, he died—probably of dysentery—in 1270 while on crusade in Tunisia. His body was temporarily interred here but, except for his heart, eventually made it back to France.

Also here is the ❾ **Cappella del Crocifisso,** a frothy Baroque chapel from the 1700s that contrasts sharply with the rest of the church's interior.

• *Before leaving the church, consider paying to climb the narrow stairs to the* ❿ *roof terraces for an enjoyable view of the cloister and the surrounding countryside (stairway entrance is in the west portico).*

When you're ready to continue to the cloister, exit the cathedral and return to Piazza Guglielmo II, where we started this walk. One more paid option is through the doorway straight ahead: the ⓫ *cloister.*

BENEDICTINE CLOISTER

This cloister was the main outdoor space for the Benedictine monks, who would have rarely ventured out of the monastery. Imagine the monks pacing the square path, deep in prayer. In the past, the cloister would have been a lush garden, probably used to grow produce for the brothers. Today, it's one of the greatest in-situ sculpture galleries of the Middle Ages, exemplifying the Norman-Arab style of Sicily.

• *You'll enter the cloister on its north side. Walk straight ahead, stepping into the garden through the gap in the colonnade and finding the center to get oriented.*

⓬ Cloister Garden

The monks divided the garden into quadrants, each with a different tree planted in its center: date palm, fig, olive, and pomegranate. These are the four species described as symbolizing paradise both in the Bible and the Quran. The arcade is a perfect square of 154 feet, with 26 arches per side. The 228 twin columns are made of Carrara marble from Tuscany. Arab influences can be seen in the shafts of the columns, which are decorated with carved arabesque motifs or golden mosaics inlaid in geometrical patterns.

• *Now let's look at the...*

⓭ Columns and Capitals

The Romanesque capitals atop each column are the highlight of the cloister. Each is an individual artwork depicting intricate mythological or religious scenes populated with a profusion of animals, people, birds, plants, and fantastical creatures. Made by several teams of craftsmen, the capitals vary in complexity and style—no two are alike.

On the walls opposite the colonnade, patterns are inlaid with black stone. The monks who came to establish this monastery were transferred from near Mount Vesuvius on the mainland. As they left their homeland, knowing they would probably not return, the monks are said to have brought chunks of lava with them—to have a bit of home built into the new monastery.

• *We'll circle the cloister clockwise (starting at the north side, where you entered). While it's fun to discover your own favorite details, I'll point out a few capitals worthy of your attention. The best way to track them down is to count columns (starting with the one next to the gap through which you first entered the garden).*

North Side: The fifth column after the gap has a capital with a Roman phrase carved into its top: *EGO ROMANVS FILIVS CONSTANTINVS MARMVRARIVS* ("This is Romanus, son of Constantinus the marble carver"). In the 12th century, artists were humble craftsmen, and it is uncommon to find a signed work. This is the only signed capital in the cloister.

Skip one column and stop in front of the seventh, where you'll find the story of Samson *(SANSON)* carved on all four sides.

Skip two more columns, stopping in front of the tenth one, to find a cruel, vivid scene of the **Massacre of the Innocents.**

Skip one column and stop in front of the twelfth, where you may recognize an international logo: Melusine, also known as the **Starbucks Mermaid.**

Melusine the mermaid fell in love with and married a human. Hiding her true nature from him, she snuck away once a week to return to fish form in the sea. One day, curiosity got the best of him and he discovered her secret. A furious Melusine declared that because he hadn't trusted her, she had to leave him. This may seem a strange topic in a monastery, but the message was clear to the brothers: You need faith and trust to be close to God. On the four corners of the same capital are symbols of the Four Evangelists: eagle (John), angel (Matthew), winged lion (Mark), and ox (Luke).

East Side: Soon you'll reach the first corner of the cloister. The corner columns, in groups of four, are decorated with floral motifs. On this corner the capitals depict stories from the **Life of the Virgin Mary.** Find these scenes: the journey of the Three Kings, the presentation of the gifts, the Annunciation, and the Nativity.

Now continue down the east side of the cloister. After the gap halfway down, find the sixth column, with scenes from Genesis, featuring **Adam, Eve, Cain,** and **Abel.**

South Side: Head to the south side of the cloister. Three columns before the garden entry on this side, find a column carved with scenes of **winemaking.** Now carry on to the fountain in the corner. Just before it, the last column shows armored **Norman knights** with long shields, sword-fighting against Arabs brandishing sabers.

In the corner is an **ablution fountain**—strategically located for monks to wash up before entering the dining hall next door. The fountain is in the shape of a palm-tree trunk. If the water is flowing, the pressurized streams at the top take on the shape of palm fronds. The stylized palm-tree motif is repeated all over the cathedral walls, as a symbol of life, rebirth, martyrdom, and purification. In the Middle Ages, religion was considered a lush oasis of spirituality in the arid desert of mortal sins.

Pause at the corner, where the capitals show scenes from the **life of infant Christ** and the **mission of the apostles.**

West Side: From the fountain enclosure, count to the fifth column—the one with the capital that's brighter than the rest. This is the **dedication capital:** King William II holds a model of the church, offering it to Mary.

Before exiting, take a moment to savor the spirit of the cloister. The word "cloister" comes from the word "enclosed"—a protected paradise for reaching a higher state of spirituality. Feel the tranquility the monks must have experienced as they meditated in this unique space.

• *Return to Piazza Guglielmo II, where you entered the cloister, and take a last look at the cathedral.*

Consider everything you've just seen: Norman towers, a Latin basilica floor plan, Arab arches and abstract geometric patterns, Byzantine mosaics, and columns and capitals both sacred and profane. You are admiring the apex of Norman "syncretism"—the Sicilian Normans' unique knack for creating a balanced fusion of styles, cultures, and traditions. Understanding this ability to gracefully merge conflicting ideas and cultural symbols is key to appreciating not just Monreale, but Sicily in general.

• *From the southwest corner of Piazza Guglielmo II, an archway leads through a series of courtyards to the* ⓮ *belvedere for a view over the landscape below (may be closed for construction when you visit).*

Between Palermo and Trapani

Just off the freeway halfway between Palermo and Trapani, an ancient theater perches atop a hill with a temple in the valley below. This is the ancient city of Segesta...or what's left of it (worth ▲▲). The theater with its lovely views and the unfinished temple are good places to contemplate the rise and fall of civilizations.

Segesta

Segesta (seh-JESS-tah) was a city of the mysterious Elymians, people from Asia Minor who settled here, at Erice, and around the tip of western Sicily. The Greeks thought they were colonists from Troy. We don't know much about them, as their language has never been deciphered, but we do know that they intermingled with Greeks and adopted their culture. Segesta played an important role in the Peloponnesian War, and their diplomatic flirtation with Athens contributed to the eventual decline of the great Greek city-state. More on that later...

GETTING THERE

From **Palermo,** Segesta is about a one-hour **drive.** Coming from there on the A-29 expressway, take the right fork for Trapani and the Birgi airport. A few miles later, be ready for the Segesta exit—it's immediately after a long tunnel, on the right. Exiting here (from either direction), follow the brown signs for *Segesta*.

From **Trapani,** Segesta is 30 minutes by car. It's also possible to reach the archaeological site from Trapani via **public transit,** though the timing isn't very convenient. Your best bet is to catch the 10:20 bus, returning to Trapani at 13:10 (40-minute ride, buses depart from the Piazza Montalto station in Trapani, confirm schedule at tarantolacuffaro.it).

ORIENTATION TO SEGESTA

Cost and Hours: €16; daily 9:00-19:30, Oct and March until 18:30, Nov-Feb until 17:00; last entry 1.5 hours before closing, +39 0924 952 356, parchiarcheologici.regione.sicilia.it/segesta.

Sun Warning: Bring sun protection, as the Segesta site has very little shade.

Services: Near the main parking lot are the ticket office, some

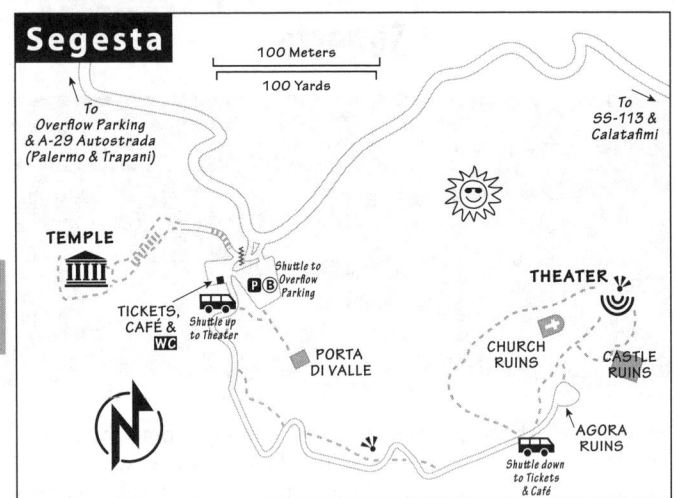

gift shops, a basic café, and WCs. An overflow parking lot is linked to the main lot by a shuttle.

Shuttle Bus to Theater: Within the site, a shuttle bus runs from the entrance most of the way up the hill to the theater (€2.50, about 4/hour or with demand, 5 minutes, pay when you buy your entry ticket). You can ride the bus back down, too, but it's a very scenic walk...and much easier downhill.

VISITING THE SITE

The visit to the site is in two parts: the temple and the theater (keep your entry ticket handy, as you'll need to show it at both areas). The temple is a short but steep 10-minute walk (trail begins directly across from the café). The theater is a long, steep, 30-minute uphill hike (about three-quarters of a mile, with 500 feet of elevation gain; road leads up to the left as you face the café). If you don't want to walk, take the shuttle bus.

It makes sense to start with the temple, then head up to the theater for the grand finale. But if the theater bus is leaving soon, you might as well hop on.

Temple

This temple is a beautifully preserved example of Doric Greek architecture, spanning 6 columns by 14 columns. At 69 feet by 183 feet, it is a petite temple for the Greek world of the time. It was built about 420 BC,

roughly 25 years after the Parthenon in Athens, and possibly with the help of a Greek architect.

But the temple was never finished. Typically, temple columns are made of round, stacked stones connected with pins, and would be fluted after construction to make each column look like one smooth piece. But these columns were never fluted. Look for the cube-shaped "tabs" sticking out on the base of the columns, used to move the heavy blocks and normally chiseled off when a temple was completed. And the temple is missing other important features as well: It has no cella (the central room used for worship), no roof, and no altar in front. (For more on the layout of a Greek temple, see the sidebar on page 200.)

Historians are unclear as to why the temple was left unfinished, although a plausible story has emerged: Around 450 BC, Segesta sought an alliance with Athens against their common enemies. The Segestans were not particularly powerful, so to impress the Athenians, they built this Greek-style temple. It can almost be seen as a stage set rather than a temple—made to impress visiting dignitaries. Once the Athenians signed the pact, the Segestans never bothered to finish the temple. But Segesta's plan failed—Athenian troops never arrived, and the enormous Greek fleet went instead to Syracuse (and was destroyed—eventually leading to the decline of Athens...but that's a story for another guidebook).

Theater

Segesta's small theater has been restored. But its seats, in a concentric semicircle, have many of the original stones. Where you see the view, there would have been a backdrop—the *scena*. Imagine the plays produced here—both tragedies and comedies. Greek plays were not all blood and pathos...they even had fart jokes, which suggests that some comedy is timeless.

The genius of this theater is the acoustics. Hams enjoy taking the stage and trying it out: Walk to the floor of the theater, find the center of the stage and take a big step forward. Say something. Sing something. Move around a little until you find the right spot. When you've found the focal point, you'll know it—you'll hear your own voice in your head as if you were wearing headphones. The Greeks used geometry and architecture to create ideal acoustics, so that every seat could hear perfectly and the actors didn't need to strain their voices. If you're in the focal point, people in the cheap seats can even hear you whisper.

In the hilltop area around the theater, you'll find other ruins from the ancient city, marked by informative plaques in English. For example, the large area where the shuttle bus turns around was the agora. These ruins are extremely scant, as the city was built over by the Arabs and Normans before being abandoned 700 years ago.

From the theater, you could ride the shuttle bus back down to the entrance. But consider hiking down the hill (stick to the road, as the gravel paths are slippery). You'll be rewarded with ever-changing views of the temple, framed by flowers and trees. In this setting, you can almost imagine you're in ancient Sicily.

CEFALÙ

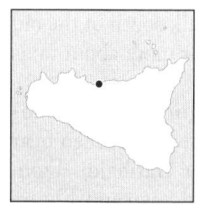

An hour east of Palermo sits the salty fishing village of Cefalù (cheh-fah-LOO). Tucked under the towering rock called La Rocca, Cefalù entices with narrow lanes, medieval charm, and an imposing Norman cathedral. These days, Cefalù is a popular beach destination, but it still has the feel of an old Sicilian fishing hub. Cefalù's creaky character, stretches of wide sandy beach, and parade of shops and restaurants make this a popular, laid-back tourist resort. If you're going to settle in for a beach break anywhere in Sicily, I'd do it here for a night—or two.

PLANNING YOUR TIME

With few major sights, Cefalù makes an easy day trip from Palermo (about an hour by train or car). Or, for an easygoing start to a Sicilian trip, consider heading here directly from the Palermo airport by car or taxi (about 2 hours) or by train (1.5 hours direct on weekends only, otherwise 2 hours with change at Palermo's Stazione Centrale).

With one day in Cefalù, start early with a hike to the summit of La Rocca for expansive views. Then descend into town, where you can follow my self-guided walk, visiting Cefalù Cathedral along the way, and tour the local museum (Museo Mandralisca). Or simply enjoy a bit of beach time. If you're spending the night, finish your day with a *passeggiata* and a candlelit seafood dinner on the harbor.

Orientation to Cefalù

Cefalù (pop. 14,000) is wedged between its Gibraltar-like mountain and a long stretch of sandy beach. At the north end of town, the historic center is a grid of narrow, pedestrian-only streets. The town's spine is Corso Ruggero, which runs past Cefalù's main landmark—its Norman-style cathedral—and the central Piazza del Duomo. The old town stretches south to Piazza Garibaldi, where the modern city begins. The train station marks the southern city limits.

Tourist Information: Two TI offices sit side-by-side on Corso Ruggero, one managed by the region and the other by the city. The regional TI is open most mornings and afternoons and offers local maps. The city TI has sporadic hours (Corso Ruggero 77 and 79, +39 0921 421 458 and +39 0921 421 050).

Arrival in Cefalù: Trains from Palermo and Messina arrive at the Cefalù train station, about a 15-minute walk south of the old town center and beach (about €15-20 by taxi; for more about taxis see "Helpful Hints," below).

To walk into town, exit the station, turn right onto Via Antonio Gramsci, jog onto Via Aldo Moro, cross Via Roma, then bear right onto Via Matteotti to continue to Piazza Garibaldi. From here, the beach is downhill to the left, and the old town and TIs are straight ahead, down the pedestrianized Corso Ruggero.

Drivers arrive in Cefalù in the new town on SS-113, near the train station. The no-traffic zone begins at Piazza Garibaldi, but you have several parking options. For cheap long-term parking, there's a garage next to the train station. Pay parking is also available along the waterfront promenade, Lungomare Giardina, either on the street (€1/hour within blue lines) or at the huge gravel parking lot just south of the waterfront Hotel Riva del Sole—near the start of my self-guided city walk.

Helpful Hints: Taxis line up at the train station and along the beach near Piazza Cristoforo Colombo. To call a taxi, try Taxi Service Cefalù (WhatsApp +39 0921 440 740). On Saturday mornings off-season, a **market** selling household goods pops up along the waterfront near Hotel Riva del Sole.

Cefalù Town Walk

Get to know this old Sicilian fishing village by following this 45-minute self-guided walk from the beach, out to the pier, and through some of Cefalù's most characteristic alleyways and piazzas. You'll end at the cathedral on grand Piazza del Duomo.

• *Start your walk on the beach promenade opposite the recommended Al*

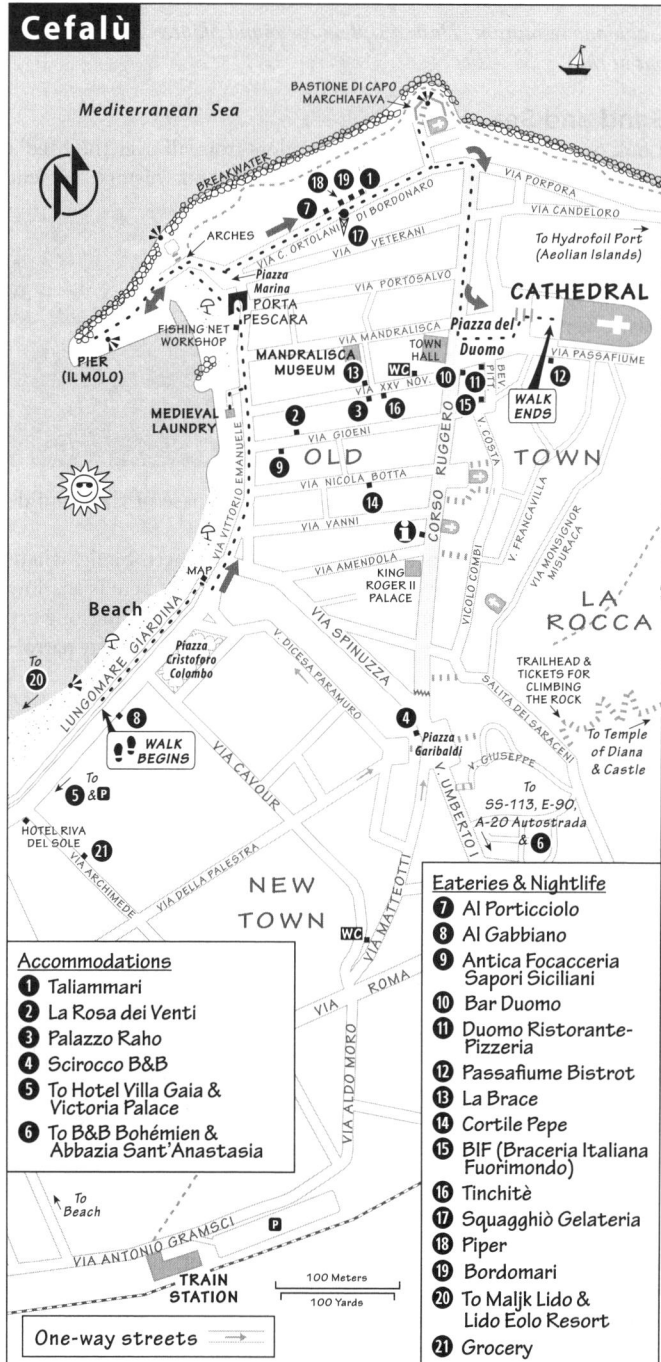

Gabbiano restaurant. Have a seat on the round planter bench and gaze out at the...

Sand and Sea

Look out at the sea and ponder the sailors from all over the Mediterranean who landed on this beach throughout history: ancient Greeks, shipwrecked Normans... and pirates looking for an easy target.

Look to the right for a classic view of Cefalù. The sun-drenched buildings that face the sandy harbor—the oldest part of town—were built into a curved defensive wall protecting the knot of streets inland. You can still see surviving stretches of the wall at the base of these buildings.

This sandy beach is one of the best in northern Sicily, where most beaches are either pebbly or rocky. The water here is shallow and warm. If you're here in the summer, listen for the singsong cry of *"Coc-co! Coc-co bello!"*—the sales pitch of coconut vendors patrolling the beach.

• *Walk along the promenade toward the historic center. On your right, you'll pass the parklike Piazza Cristoforo Colombo. Continue to the end of the promenade, where you'll find a big city map fastened to the battered wall. Use it to get oriented to the...*

Historic Center

The old city is a stack of tight, neatly gridded lanes, likely a legacy of 12th-century Norman King Roger II, who relied on Byzantine and Arab builders. The nine almost parallel streets are aligned east-west to maximize sun exposure while taking advantage of prevailing winds—a kind of early air-conditioning. Apartment dwellers along these lanes still hang laundry off their balconies to let the wind do the drying.

Just behind and to the right of the city map, a small, brown *Porta Ossuna* sign marks the location of one of the original four city gates. Now all but one are gone—each torn down as the city outgrew its ancient dimensions. (We'll head through the lone surviving gate, Porta Pescara, later on this walk.)

• *Continue along on charming...*

Via Vittorio Emanuele

Enjoy strolling this street for a few blocks. You'll pass a series of water-view restaurants and wine bars *(enoteche)*. On the left, at #55, notice the massive old **grapevine** growing through the wall over the door. This thick vine taps into the underground Cefalino River, which has been providing spring water to Cefalù since ancient times...and still does. In fact, this source of fresh water was one of the attributes that originally attracted Greek settlers to Cefalù.

For another look at how locals have harnessed their river, walk a few feet farther and go through the gate on the left. Steps lead down to a **medieval laundry** *(lavatoio medievale)*. The smaller square pools were for scrubbing, and the wedge-shaped stones functioned as washboards. Water flowing from the stream to the little taps on the left created a rinsing zone, with the water passing into successive pools. Dirty water was continuously flushed from the basins out to sea. Women had few public social spaces in medieval times, so the laundry would have been a natural gathering place. Imagine the cacophony in this little courtyard: kids running around and women chatting while doing their washing. Believe it or not, this public laundry was used well into the 1970s.

Back on the street, continue the way you were headed. At #83 (on the left), you'll find a **fishing-net workshop.** Pop in and examine the fine craftsmanship of Salvatore Miceli, a retired fisherman with a passion for making fish traps and fishnets—some now creatively made into light fixtures.

• *Continue to #105, on the left, and turn into the archway.*

Porta Pescara

This is the last remaining gate of the old city—the Fisherman's Gate. Until the end of the 20th century, Cefalù's main industry was fishing, and this is where the catch of the day would be hauled in to market.

These days, the gate preserves the

memory of the town's fishy past with a small **clubhouse** (inside the gate, on the right). The wives of a few local fishermen meet here to embroider and weave scraps of fishing net with colorful fabrics to make clothing and scarves. They are the few women keeping this art form alive in Cefalù. Even if the club is closed, you can admire their work through the windows. On the wall is a portrait of "Il Presidente" Antonino Brocato, the former head of the local fishermen's union who spent his life fishing the seas around Cefalù.

• *Continue through the Porta Pescara.*

You'll emerge at the harbor. Walk a few steps to the right, where, behind a gate, you'll see a small display of traditional fishing gear. Notice the floating ring with the fat wick—a primitive lantern used to attract octopuses and anchovies at night.

• *Go down the steps onto the beach and wander out along...*

The Pier (Il Molo)

Strolling Cefalù's long breakwater pier rewards you with grand views of the town and beach. This is the old port of Cefalù, also known as *il porticciolo* ("the little port"). The harbor in front was the center of the fishing business for generations—but it's mostly quiet today, now that a modern port occupies the other side of La Rocca.

Facing town, look up to La Rocca looming overhead. It's worth the steep hike up La Rocca for its gobsmacking views (for details, see the listing under "Sights in Cefalù," later). Notice the crenellated wall that runs along the lower, flat layer of rock—offering strategic protection to the town below. The rock also shields the city center from strong winds. The summit is capped by the ruins of a Norman castle, and the hillside is home to a megalithic-era temple.

• *Follow the pier back toward town, circling around to the little square called...*

Piazza Marina

Movie buffs might find this square familiar. That's because it appears in the final scene of the classic 1988 movie *Cinema Paradiso* (in the Italian drama, flickering images are projected on the blank wall facing the sea). The movie, about a small-town projectionist-turned-filmmaker, was partially filmed here in Cefalù. This piazza is *the* place to be at sunset for a romantic picnic on its benches. The two archways facing the sea lead to a rocky coastal path that skirts

The Aeolian Islands

This remarkable little archipelago just off Sicily's northeast coast is made up of seven islands, formed by successive volcanic eruptions and easily visited as a day trip from Cefalù.

Lipari—the largest and most popular—is known for its pumice-stone beaches, scenic trails, bustling town center, and quaint villages, and has the most tourist services. Wild and rugged, **Vulcano** offers black sand beaches and active craters emitting sulfuric plume. While some visitors choose Vulcano for hiking—especially to summit the crater—others are turned off by the strong smell and prefer appreciating its beauty from a boat tour around its many coves. **Stromboli** is car-free and mystical, topped by a frequently erupting volcano and ringed by black sand beaches. Each evening, tour boats nestle offshore at Stromboli's *Sciara del Fuoco* (Path of Fire) to witness red lava spewing into the sea as the sun sets. The photogenic *Strombolicchio*, a sea stack off the north side of Stromboli, is another popular excursion by boat. **Salina**, known as the Green Island, is the second largest and has a handful of villages, lush vineyards, and fewer accessible beaches. The smallest island, **Panarea,** is frequented by celebrities and coveted for its privacy and seclusion. Rounding out the group, remote **Alicudi** and **Filicudi** are the least developed.

Aeolian Island Day Trips: In summer, several local outfits offer frequent day trips from Cefalù to the Aeolian Islands—a long, packed day, but doable. Tours range from €70-90. **Sicily Tours** (visitsicilytours.com) has several options, all starting with a one-hour bus ride to the port at Capo d'Orlando, where you'll meet your boat to the islands. **Barranco** (barrancoexcursions.it) instead goes by bus to the hydrofoil port at Milazzo, about 1.5 hours away. With more time it's possible to visit the Aeolian Islands on your own by **ferry** from the port at Milazzo (libertylines.it; Milazzo is a 2-hour train ride from Cefalù).

the north coast and leads out to the lighthouse on the other side of La Rocca.

• *With your back to the harbor, keep left to walk up the gentle slope of Via Carlo Ortolani di Bordonaro. This street is popular for its wine bars and restaurants with seaside terraces. If you're in the mood for gelato, stop at* **Squagghiò** *(on the right at #69) and try their signature flavor—a* combination of almond, sour cherry, and pistachio, often paired with mulberry or ricotta.

After two blocks, turn left onto narrow Piazza Francesco Crispi and head toward the water. Climb the staircase on the right up to the view terrace called...

Bastione di Capo Marchiafava

This terrace, part of a 17th-century fortification, takes in commanding views over the Tyrrhenian Sea. On a clear day, the westernmost islands of the Aeolian archipelago are visible on your right (for details on visiting these islands, see page 139). You can also see Cefalù's lighthouse perched on the point just below La Rocca.

The basin in the center of the terrace was used as a fountain. The decorative lions on its pedestal are in the Arab-Norman style, suggesting it could have been from the 1100s. The lion was the symbol of Roger II, who commissioned the cathedral and intended to make Cefalù the capital of his kingdom. Inside the cathedral you'll find a basin with a similar motif, used as a baptismal font.

• *Backtrack to Via Carlo Ortolani di Bordonaro and continue uphill. Take the first right onto Cefalù's bustling Corso Ruggero (my favorite place for a predinner* passeggiata*). A few blocks up, on the left, is...*

Piazza del Duomo

This central piazza is Cefalù's living room. Surrounded by palm trees, bars, and restaurants, this is the heart of the city—and it's always alive.

The focal point is the blocky Cefalù Cathedral. Its imposing scale dominates the town, as if it's on a stage with a rocky backdrop. Opposite the cathedral, the former Convent of St. Catherine has been converted into a stark white, minimalist Town Hall—with the flags of Sicily, Italy, and Europe flying under its concave eaves.

Find a seat and enjoy the scene from a bench at the bottom of the square or from a table at one of the restaurant patios—perfect for nursing a *granita* or a glass of wine. Take time here to do some people-watching as the locals go about their day.

• *Our walk is finished. From here, you could tour the cathedral, then explore the town or hit the beach. To the right of the cathedral, Via Bevilacqua Pittore (next to the Duomo Ristorante-Pizzeria) leads to the trailhead for the hike up La Rocca.*

Sights in Cefalù

▲▲Cefalù Cathedral (Cattedrale di Cefalù)

Despite its lazy beach-town ambience, Cefalù has one of Sicily's most interesting cathedrals—a classic Norman fortified church, with stout towers, narrow windows, and zipper-toothed crenellations. The stern-looking church (built between 1131 and 1240) hides an elegant surprise: inside is a monumental, glittering mosaic of Christ Pantocrator, considered the most elegant in Sicily.

Cost and Hours: Free to enter and walk down the nave to the transept; €10 "Blue" ticket includes up-close look at apse mosaics plus tower climb and south-side roof top; €10 "Green" ticket includes apse mosaics, sacristy, treasury, and Bishop's Chapel but no tower climb; €13 "Red" ticket covers everything. All three tickets include the so-called King Roger II's Palace. Open daily 9:00-13:00 & 15:30-18:30, shorter hours and closed midday Oct-March, +39 0921 926 366, duomocefalu.it.

Background: In 1131, Norman King Roger II was returning from Salerno when a violent storm caused his ship to run aground in the shallow waters off Cefalù—but he survived unharmed. To thank God for his survival, Roger commissioned this massive cathedral. His motives for the project were also political: He intended to make Cefalù his capital city. The Normans may have conquered Sicily, but fusing cultures on the island proved a challenge. Palermo was the Norman stronghold, but Byzantine Taormina remained sympathetic to the Greek Orthodox religion. By relocating his government to Cefalù, strategically located between the two centers of power, Roger would have asserted control over the entire island. But the king died before he could bring his government here, and the Norman capital remained in Palermo. Nonetheless, Roger left Cefalù with the beginnings of this oversized cathedral, which by the 13th century had become a grand monument to the capital that never was.

Visiting the Cathedral: The **exterior** is a textbook example of an *ecclesia munita*, a church-fortress. Notice the crenellations on top of the towers and, lower, the slit windows for archers' arrows (typical features of castles built in France around the same time). Imagine soldiers patrolling outside on the upper gallery while the sounds of Mass drifted out to the piazza. Decorations on the facade are few—most are the simple, geometric, zigzag patterns typical of Norman churches in France and England.

Inside, the long stone **nave** is characteristic of Norman simplicity, with ancient columns and capitals—scavenged from pagan Roman temples—supporting a parade of arches. High in the transept, pointed-arch windows hint at the new Gothic style emerging farther north. What makes the architecture here special is the fusion of French-Norman style and North African-Arab style. The Normans may have pushed Arab rule out of Sicily, but Arab citizens remained. Arab craftsmen working on the cathedral used their traditional design and engineering, which you can see in the high, near-horseshoe arches springing from the ancient Roman columns. This variety of architectural styles—Norman towers, Roman columns, Arab arches, and Byzantine mosaics—makes Cefalù Cathedral a unique, multicultural work of art.

The most recent addition to this patchwork interior is the collection of modern **stained-glass windows,** completed in 2003. They were installed with much controversy due to their stark contrast with the surrounding medieval architecture. The windows' abstract style makes it difficult to make out the biblical scenes, but you can give it a try. The panes in the central nave represent scenes from the Book of Genesis. Over the entry door, the large and colorful pane divided in four sections depicts the Last Judgement. In the aisles are panes inspired by the lives of St. Peter (left aisle) and St. Paul (right aisle).

Over the altar, the glittering **mosaic** of Christ Pantocrator ("All Powerful") makes eye contact and invites you to come closer. If you've paid for a ticket, you'll also see the cathedral's **apse and choir.** They are wallpapered with golden Byzantine-style mosaics (some of which predate those at Monreale) but the rest of the church was left unfinished. After Roger died, his successor focused his energy on projects in Palermo instead.

Christ Pantocrator watches over the faithful with his refined and elongated features and expressive eyes. The Bible he holds is open to John 8:12, with the first page written in Greek (είμαι το φως του κόσμου; "I am the light of the world"). Below

Sights in Cefalù

Christ, Mary greets you like a Byzantine empress, flanked by angels. In the lower sections, the Twelve Apostles complete the scene.

This cathedral, its mosaics, and Palermo's Palatine Chapel (with a similar Christ Pantocrator mosaic) were all initiated by King Roger II in the early 1100s. At Monreale Cathedral, however, constructed in the late 1100s by Roger's grandson, the Christ Pantocrator holds a Bible with the first page written not in Greek, but in Latin. This may seem a small detail, but the change in language parallels a major cultural shift away from Byzantine Greek Christianity and toward the Latin church.

Nearby: The **cloister** next to the cathedral can be visited only with a "Red" or "Green" ticket. You'll enter on the left as you face the cathedral's main stairs. It's ringed by columns with carved capitals, similar to those at Monreale, although most of these are worn down to almost nothing. Parts of the original cloister were damaged in a fire in 1809—that damage is finally being repaired all these years later. The cathedral's south side **rooftop** is accessible by climbing the church's towers ("Red or "Blue" ticket required). It's 80 steps with no elevator, but climbers are rewarded with amazing views. The 13th-century building built on the ruins of **King Roger II's Palace (Osterio Magno)** is several blocks down Corso Ruggero (show any cathedral ticket for free entry, otherwise €2).

▲Mandralisca Museum (Museo Mandralisca)

Cefalù's only museum hosts a delightful array of art that spans centuries. The collection, with minimal English information, fills a former nobleman's townhouse a block off Piazza del Duomo and is worthwhile if you're tired of the beach.

Cost and Hours: €8, daily 9:00-19:00, until later in summer, Via Mandralisca 13, +39 0921 421 547, fondazionemandralisca.it.

Visiting the Museum: The museum hosts the collection of the 19th-century art lover Baron Enrico Piraino, whose bust is on the first floor facing the entrance. The most interesting section is to the left, with a humble (but beautifully displayed) painting gallery and one of Sicily's best-preserved ancient kraters (wine-mixing urns). Piraino found this fourth-century Greek krater during an archaeological dig on the island of Lipari. Known as the "Krater of the Tuna Seller," it's decorated with a scene of a man at a fish market buying tuna. He has just one coin in his hand, and the tuna seller offers only the tail or the head of the tuna. Tuna was prepared and sold just like this on Cefalù from antiquity until very recently.

In a darkened room at the end of this hall is the highlight: *Portrait of a Man* (c. 1470), by Sicily's most famous Renaissance artist, Antonello da Messina (for more on Antonello, see the sidebar). The subject looks out slyly with an impish smirk in a three-quarter view. The juxtaposition of the dark background and brightly lit facial features demonstrates the then-developing technique called chiaroscuro, which literally means "light/dark." Piraino

found this painting on the island of Lipari, decorating a cabinet door in a friend's pharmacy. He asked the pharmacist if he could have it, and the naive friend agreed, likely not realizing the painting's significance. In the same room is *St. John the Baptist* by late-Renaissance Florentine painter Giovanni Antonio Sogliani.

A few steps up is the archaeology section, with an assortment of Greek and Roman artifacts and more kraters. On the second floor is a collection of ancient coins and gems, an extensive seashell collection, furniture, more paintings, and taxidermied local wildlife—mostly birds.

▲▲La Rocca

High above Cefalù soars a mighty rock, La Rocca, crowned at 885 feet by the ruins of a Norman castle. If you're up for a serious hike to grand views, summiting the rock is worth the effort. Or go halfway up to the megalithic "Temple of Diana," where you'll still get good views of the town below. Early settlers strategically built on this rock rather than on the less defensible harbor below.

Cost and Hours: €5, daily 8:00-20:00, Nov-Feb until 17:00, March-April 18:30, last entry one hour before closing. Exit times are strictly enforced—the only way out after the gates are locked is to call the police.

Planning Your Hike: It's best to go early or late in the day to avoid the midday heat. Give yourself plenty of time. People in great shape need at least two hours round-trip, not including time to linger and enjoy the views. For a shorter, easier hike, you'll find good

Antonello da Messina (c. 1430-1479)

The Renaissance didn't thrive in Sicily the way it did in the rest of Italy—so Sicily has few famous artists from the period. The one great exception is Antonello da Messina. A native of Messina, on Sicily's northeast coast, he studied in the court of the king of Naples and later in Milan, and he's thought to have learned the detailed techniques of Netherlandish oil painting from another court artist. Antonello also spent time in Venice, and some sources credit him with introducing oil painting to that city (it's more likely that he showed the Venetians how to make better use of the medium). The altarpiece Antonello painted there for the Church of San Cassiano, with its incipient mastery of perspective, would influence Giovanni Bellini and other Venetian masters. Antonello's portraits are prized for their detailed and expressive faces, and of his remaining works, *Portrait of a Man* (in Cefalù's Mandralisca Museum) is the most intriguing and irreverent.

city views halfway up, just below the temple. Fit hikers should allow at least an hour round-trip for this option.

Summiting La Rocca: The route up is on the zigzagging path called Salita dei Saraceni, which you can find by following brown *Tempio di Diana* signs in the center of the old town. The most straightforward route heads straight up from Piazza Garibaldi (on Via Giuseppe Fiore—find the signed steps tucked between two buildings); you can also head up from Corso Ruggero on little Vicolo Saraceni. From Piazza del Duomo, follow narrow Via Pittore Bevelacqua up.

Once you reach the **trailhead,** you'll buy a ticket and go through a turnstile. Confirm what time you'll need to be back down. Then wind your way steeply up well-marked stone steps and gravel paths, passing agave, cactus, and wildflowers. At the rock's plateau, you'll step through a stout stone gateway (with a door that locks at closing time). Just above that, signs point to your two options: left to the archaeological site or right to the *castello/*castle.

I'd head left to the best views first, while you're still fresh. This route takes you on a trail above the ruins of the Church of Sant'Anna—a small, single-nave chapel from the ninth or 10th century—a few brick ovens, and more building ruins (likely medieval military barracks). You'll then reach the ruins of the **Temple of Diana.** The ninth-century BC temple was built by the Sicani (or Sikans), an indigenous tribe who lived here before the arrival of the Greeks. The megalithic temple was made with large, stout blocks of local stone, perfectly aligned with the spring and fall equinoxes, and added on to by the Greeks in the fourth or fifth century BC. It's likely the temple was originally dedicated to an indigenous deity equivalent to Artemis for the Greeks (Diana for the Romans). While there's little to see today, the entrance portal has survived, and the structure is evocative.

From the temple, head down to the crenellated wall just below for stunning views over Cefalù's old and new towns and the nearby coastline.

To conquer the summit, head back past the Temple of Diana and follow signs to the *castello*. Here the trail becomes even steeper and the footing more challenging (a mix of rock and dirt). At the top, you'll find the ruins of a **Norman castle** from the time of King Roger II. From what's left—a few stretches of crenellated wall—you can see over the back side of La Rocca, with distant views of five of the seven islands of the Aeolian Archipelago and, on a clear day, even of Mount Etna.

From the castle, you could head back down the way you came or, to enjoy more scenery, turn your hike into a loop: Continue along the ridge toward the mainland, where you'll reach additional ruined fortifications. From there, hike steeply back down to the main gate.

Beaches

Cefalù has one of the largest sandy beaches in northern Sicily. Beach season starts after Easter and ends in October, depending on the weather. High season is in August, when Italian tourists flood the beach during *Ferragosto*, the August 15 national holiday.

For an easy spot with a decent handy restaurant, try the beach at **Lido Eolo** resort, in front of the recommended Hotel Villa Gaia (daily 8:00-19:00,

Lungomare Giuseppe Giardina 133, +39 338 523 7623). Locals prefer the quieter, far end of the beach, away from the historic center (about a 15-minute walk south). Italians prefer maintained beaches with rental chairs (see sidebar), but there are always slices of free sand to lie on—look for them in between resorts and at the ends of the beach.

Sicilian Beach Tips

Italians take their beach vacations seriously. While it's possible to flop a towel down on any stretch of empty beach, spending the money to go to the *spiaggia* like an Italian is a fun experience. Shop around and find the location and amenities that suit you.

All along the beach, seasonal restaurants and cabanas rent handy *lettini* (lounge chairs) sprawled along the prime real estate. (Vendors rent their stretch of beach from the city and charge admission.) A typical *lettino* with shade costs €15-25 per day. If you go late in the day, negotiate your chair price.

Some beach properties *(lidi)* also have changing rooms, toilets, restaurants, and cocktail bars with service to your chair. Many hotels have beach chairs reserved for their guests—ask your hotel before heading to the beach. Then settle in and listen for the call of the coconut vendors that roam the waterfront.

Nightlife in Cefalù

The early-evening action is centered on Piazza del Duomo and along Corso Ruggero. Locals come out for their evening *passeggiata,* kids play, and teenagers flirt. The bar scene on Via Carlo Ortolani di Bordonaro gets lively at dinnertime, and in summer the fun continues until late. **Piper** (at #56) serves beer and panini, offering a nice hangout vibe but no sea views. **Bordomari** (at #50, until 23:00) offers drinks on a deck with romantic sea views.

Disco: In the summer, the *lidi* (beach resorts) are at the center of evening fun. **Maljk Lido** hosts DJs and offers *apericena* deals—an *aperitivo* with generous snacks (open late May-Sept, Lungomare Giuseppe Giardina, maljk.it).

Sleeping in Cefalù

There are no big hotels in the historic area—only B&Bs—so if you need comforts like elevators and parking, plan to stay near the train station or along the beach. Prices soar in August, peaking around the *Ferragosto* holiday on August 15. Many B&Bs close from November through March.

OLD CENTER

€€€€ **Taliammari,** right in the thick of the action on Via Carlo Ortolani di Bordonaro, offers 17 rooms with a sleek, modern vibe and a welcoming breezy hall that leads straight to a deck bar overlooking the sea. Some rooms have sea views (air-con, rooftop terrace, Via Carlo Ortolani di Bordonaro 50, +39 0921 994 167, taliammari.it, taliammari@gmail.com, kind Lillo, Andrea, and Antonino).

€€€ **La Rosa dei Venti** has seven small apartments in the center of town. The modern, minimalist units have small living rooms, itty-bitty kitchens, and not much character. One room is on the ground floor, while the remaining rooms require navigating steep staircases (air-con, no breakfast, Via Gioeni 82, +39 0921 925 897, viaggiesapori.com/rosadeiventi, info@rosadeiventicefalu.it, Lara).

€€€ **Palazzo Raho,** well located on a side street in the historic center, has seven stately and tastefully decorated rooms (family rooms, air-con, +39 0921 571 227, Via XXV Novembre 47, palazzoraho.it, info@palazzoraho.it, Fabio and Sara).

€€ **Scirocco B&B** overlooks Piazza Garibaldi, with four tidy rooms in vivid colors. While the rooms are simple and the stairs never end, the panoramic terrace floating above the city is magical (air-con, Piazza Garibaldi 8, +39 392 644 4131, sciroccobeb.com, sciroccobeb@gmail.com, spunky Nicole).

ALONG THE BEACH

€€€€ **Hotel Villa Gaia** is a family-run place facing the beach about a 10-minute walk from the historic center. Its 12 rooms are basic and homey compared to the resort-like hotels surrounding it, but the place is far enough from the beach scene to be relatively quiet (air-con, no elevator, easy free parking, free beach chairs for guests, Via Maestro Pintorno 101, +39 0921 420 992, villagaiahotel.it, info@villagaiahotel.it).

€€€€ **Victoria Palace** gives you the four-star resort experience, with a pool, private beach (summer only), spa and gym (in their nearby sister hotel), and rooftop terrace with stunning views to the old town. The 30 rooms are polished and classy, with balconies so you can soak up the rays (parking, air-con, elevator, Lungomare Giuseppe Giardina, +39 0921 571 184, cefaluvictoriapalace.it, booking@victoriapalacecefalu.it).

OTHER ACCOMMODATIONS

In the New Town: Slightly out of the tourist fray, €€€ **B&B Bohémien** offers five modern, large, airy rooms and a good-quality, locally sourced breakfast (air-con, Via Umberto I 15c, +39 331 758 3397, bohemienbeb.it, booking@bohemienbeb.it, Mari).

Near Cefalù: About a 20-minute drive from Cefalù, €€€ **Abbazia Sant'Anastasia** is a peaceful hotel and winery within the walls of a medieval abbey. The property is set high above the sea among expansive vineyards, so while the rooms are nothing special, the pretty views and lovely pool area make it a nice alternative to busy Cefalù (family rooms, air-con, no elevator, good restaurant and wines, near

Castelbuono at Contrada Sant'Anastasia, two miles off SS-286—follow the signs, +39 0921 67 22 33, abbaziasantanastasia.com, relais@abbaziasantanastasia.com).

Eating in Cefalù

Cefalù is a touristy town filled with touristy restaurants. You'll pay a little more here—especially if you want to eat with a sea view or on Piazza del Duomo. Still, the seafood is enticing, and the service is generally good.

Supermarket: FoodSicily Market is the most central grocery (long hours daily, Via Archimede 9).

DINING WITH A SEA VIEW

If you're going to eat with a sea view anywhere in Sicily, make it here in Cefalù. Anticipating a warm evening, I'd take a few minutes at lunch to find a place that feels right and make a reservation for dinner. The beach promenade just south of the old center has a few options, but I prefer the places on Via Carlo Ortolani di Bordonaro (most have view terraces), where you'll see lots of  high-end choices mixed in with more rustic options. Simpler restaurants have antipasto buffet spreads with stools facing the sea; fancier places have terraces built out over the rocky shore (look for *terrazza sul mare*). More informal diners grab a bite to go and picnic on the beach, either at the west end of town or on a bench at Piazza Marina.

€€ **Al Porticciolo** is *the* place for a traditional and fancy seafood dinner on Via Carlo Ortolani di Bordonaro. Nicola and Paolo take pride in their fish and meat dishes, and traditional wood-fired oven pizza. The romantic seaside terrace is swoon-worthy at sunset (free welcome prosecco with this book, reservations smart, closed Wed and Dec-March, Via Carlo Ortolani di Bordonaro 66, +39 0921 921 981, alporticcioloristorante.com).

€€ **Al Gabbiano** is a popular choice among the several restaurants offering relaxing views along the beach. They serve pizza and fish in a vast interior, with a large, covered terrace and beachfront seating (daily until late, Lungomare Giardina 17, +39 0921 421 495).

€ **Antica Focacceria Sapori Siciliani,** steps from the sand in the old town, sells pizza and street food, including *arancine* and pasta dishes. Grab your lunch or dinner here for a picnic on the beach (closed Wed, Via Gioeni 87, +39 0921 820 393).

ON AND NEAR PIAZZA DEL DUOMO

The most central place in town is filled with tables, umbrellas, and people enjoying the delightful vibe. A meal here, while touristy, leaves you with fine memories. Your options range from basic bars to more elegant pizzerias and restaurants—but most are essentially interchangeable (all are typically open long hours daily in peak season).

€ **Bar Duomo** serves cheap and basic pizzas, *arancine*, sandwiches, gelato, and *granite* and spritz *aperitivi*, with lots of outdoor tables (long hours daily, Piazza del Duomo 24, +39 0921 421 164).

€€ **Duomo Ristorante-Pizzeria** has a classy custom-made double deck wooden dining room, and outdoor seating in the piazza with the first row facing the cathedral. Serves fish and meat courses for long hours (daily, Piazza del Duomo 19, +39 0921 421 164).

€€ **Passafiume Bistrot** flanks the cathedral with a dozen tables in a cozy space, plus a few outdoor tables. Francesco offers a small menu of creative cuisine and intriguing daily specials. Lino the bartender mixes up a range of fanciful drinks, including an orange-flower gin and tonic (closed Thu, Via Passafiume 6, +39 0921 820 404).

OTHER OPTIONS IN THE OLD TOWN

€€ **La Brace,** with a stylish red dining room reminiscent of a Parisian bistro, serves Sicilian dishes with French and Dutch influences. The menu is fresh and seasonal: If the daily catch isn't quality, you won't see it on the menu (reservations smart, open for dinner Tue-Sun, closed Mon, Via XXV Novembre 10, +39 0921 423 570).

€€€€ **Cortile Pepe** is a good choice for a stylish splurge in Cefalù. Rather than big, sloppy, tourist-pleasing plates of pasta and fish (as is often the local standard), here you'll enjoy delicately crafted, high-end Sicilian cooking. The interior is sophisticated and minimalist, and there are a few breezy tables out front (closed Wed, shorter hours off-season, Via Nicola Botta 15, +39 0921 421 630).

€€€€ **BIF** (Braceria Italiana Fuorimondo) specializes in meat, with modern-yet-warm interiors, tables outside in the quiet alley, and an extensive wine list. If a perfectly aged T-bone steak makes your mouth water, this is your place (daily, Via Madonna degli Angeli 12, +39 0921 421 164, bifbraceria.it, Pasquale).

€€ **Tinchitè** has a modern dining room and a long string of outdoor tables across the street. Kind chef Armando's traditional Sicilian recipes feature both fish and meat, and portions are large (in Sicilian, *a tinchitè* means "a lot"). Among his specialties are fish couscous and the very rich *pasta a tajano*—rigatoni pasta with shredded beef, fried eggplant, pecorino cheese, and fresh basil on top (daily, Via XXV Novembre 37, +39 0921 421 164).

Cefalù Connections

From Cefalù by Train to: Palermo (1-2/hour, 1 hour), **Messina** (hourly, 2 hours), **Agrigento** (hourly, 2.5 hours, change at Termini Imerese). To **Taormina, Catania, Siracusa,** or other east-coast destinations, you'll connect through Messina or Palermo.

Connecting Cefalù to Palermo Airport: Regular **trains** run 1-2 hour (2 hours with a change at Palermo's Stazione Centrale); **direct trains** run only on weekends (Cefalù Line, 2/day Sat, 4/day Sun, 1.5 hours). A **taxi** to or from the airport can be reasonable if shared with others (**Taxi Service Cefalù** offers the trip for €160, see contact info earlier under "Helpful Hints"; **Rosaria Lisuzzo** charges €140/up to 3 people, €180/up to 8 people, €30 supplement before 7:00, +39 370 156 0247, book two days in advance).

Route Tips for Drivers: Palermo is an easy, one-hour drive west on highway E-90. To reach **Catania** (2.5 hours), leave Cefalù in the direction of Palermo, then turn south on speedy A-19 to Catania. For **Agrigento** (2.5 hours), head west on E-90, then take A-19 toward Catania. At Caltanissetta, follow signs to *Agrigento* and head south on SS-640.

To reach **Taormina** (3 hours), head east out of Cefalù, following the seafront road before twisting up, up, up to get on the E-90 highway eastbound at Pollina-Castelbuono (toward Messina). Follow this highway along the coast, taking in the scenery of the Madonie Mountains, the Aeolian Islands, and the Strait of Messina. At Messina, head south on SS-114 to Taormina.

TRAPANI & THE WEST COAST

Trapani • Erice • Egadi Islands • Mozia Island • Selinunte

Sicily's west coast has a different flavor than the rest of the island. For one thing, it's a bit rainier—and therefore greener—than other parts of Sicily. Geographically and culturally, it's Sicily's closest point to Africa (Marsala is 90 miles from the northeast coast of Tunisia). The cuisine of the west-coast region feels exotic and vaguely African—this is the place to try couscous with fish broth.

The region is anchored by the port of Trapani, a salty, workaday town with a pleasant historic center that's perfectly situated for exploring the region. Trapani is about 65 miles, or 1.5 hours by car, from Palermo. Several worthwhile stops are within easy striking distance: the skyscraping hill town of Erice, the charming Egadi Islands just offshore, and the salt flats and scant Carthaginian ruins at Mozia Island. Temple lovers can venture farther afield to the Greek ruins at Selinunte (hit them on the way in or out of the region).

A visit to this charming and less touristed region nicely rounds out your look at Sicily.

PLANNING YOUR TIME

Trapani has no essential sights other than the enjoyable town itself—which can be experienced in a couple of hours in the early evening. But its good range of hotels and restaurants makes it an ideal home base. To thoroughly visit everything in this chapter, I'd spend two nights in Trapani. If driving from Palermo, see Segesta on the way in (see page 129), enjoy an easy evening in Trapani, side-trip to Mozia and the salt flats the next morning, then spend the late afternoon and early evening in Erice. With an extra day,

Trapani & the West Coast 153

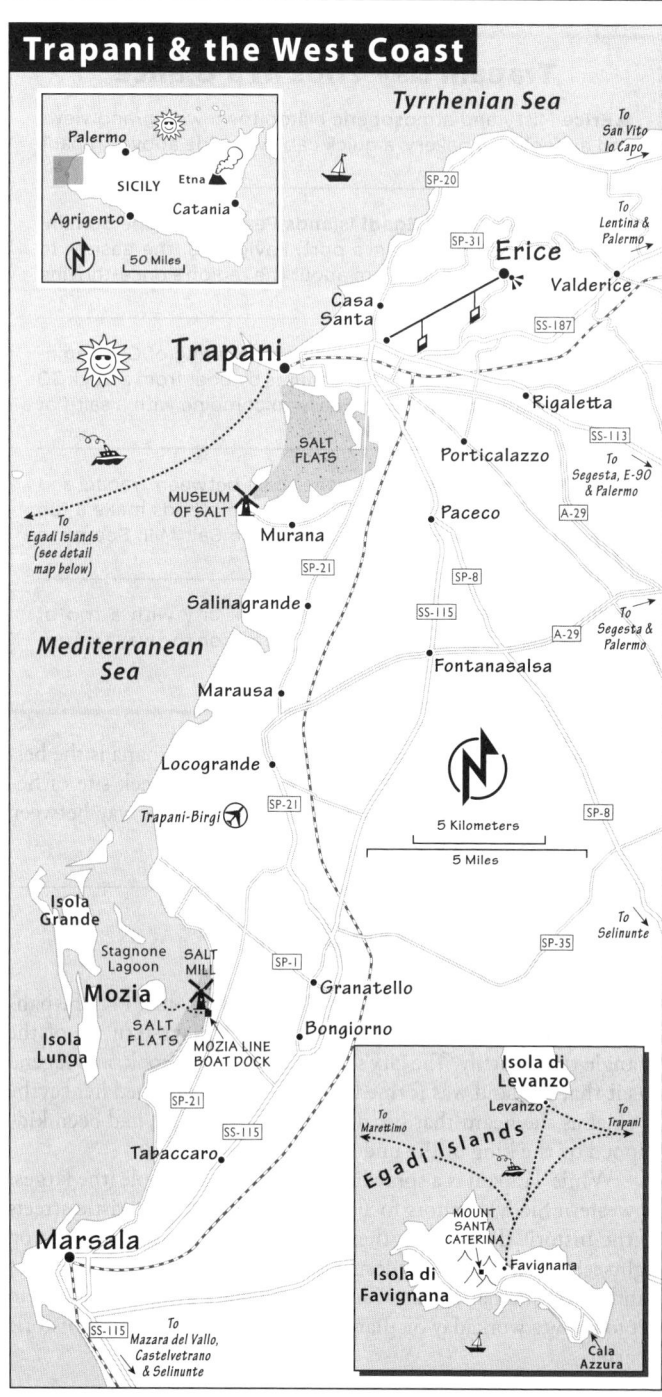

Trapani Day Trips at a Glance

▲**Erice** Misty and atmospheric hilltop town with grand views and a renowned bakery, a quick cableway ride above Trapani. See page 174.

▲**Favignana and the Egadi Islands** Peaceful escape 30 minutes by boat from Trapani's port. Favignana, the easiest to reach, hosts a good museum about the region's once-thriving tuna industry. See page 182.

▲**Mozia Island** Private island with a smattering of Carthaginian ruins and lots of nature, 10 minutes by boat from a dock 30 minutes south of Trapani and easy to combine with a salt-flat visit (see next). See page 186.

▲**Salt Flat Experiences** Along the coast between Trapani and Marsala, salt flats worked by traditional methods make a fun stop—particularly the Ettore and Infersa Salt Mill. See page 194.

▲**Selinunte** Picturesque toppled Greek city with a trio of temples, a 1.5-hour drive south of Trapani (on the way to Agrigento). See page 197.

hydrofoils can take you to the Egadi Islands (Favignana is the best quick look), or you can drive south to visit the Greek site of Selinunte. Selinunte also makes a natural stop on the way between Trapani and Agrigento.

Trapani

Dramatically stretching out into the sea, Trapani (TRAH-pah-nee) sits on a long, curved promontory at the western tip of the triangle that is Sicily. The city's shape resembles a hook, and legend has it that the land was formed when Demeter dropped her scythe in grief as she heard that her daughter, Persephone, had been kidnapped by the king of the underworld.

While Trapani is a sprawling city of 70,000 people (the largest in western Sicily), visitors focus on the lively, characteristic streets of the historic district—at the far end of the peninsula. Light on sightseeing, Trapani is a pedestrian-friendly pleasure with plenty of handy accommodations and fun places to eat, and offers a chance to get to know a workaday Sicilian port town with a charming historic quarter.

Orientation to Trapani

The old-town center lies west of the Villa Margherita public gardens, starting at Piazza Vittorio Veneto and the elegant pedestrian street of Via Garibaldi. The area around the intersection of the two main shopping streets, Via Torrearsa and Corso Vittorio Emanuele, is considered the heart of the old town, anchored by Palazzo Cavarretta. The functional, modern part of the city spreads east of the public gardens along Via Giovanni Battista Fardella for two miles, toward Erice.

TOURIST INFORMATION

The TI has info on Trapani and the west coast and is centrally located in Palazzo Cavarretta (Mon-Fri 9:00-14:00, Mon and Thu also 15:00-17:30, Sat 10:00-13:00, closed Sun, shorter hours and closed Sat off-season, Via Torrearsa, +39 0923 544 533, trapaniwelcome.it).

ARRIVAL IN TRAPANI

By Bus: Buses from Palermo arrive next to the hydrofoil terminal, along the south side of the peninsula on Via Ammiraglio Staiti. To reach the town center from here, walk a couple of blocks toward the tip of the peninsula (with the water on your left), then turn right (inland) on the Via Torrearsa shopping street. Buses from Agrigento arrive at the bus station in the new town, just south of the train station.

By Car: From the autostrada, drivers will arrive near the port on the south side of town. You may see a few pay spots along here, but most parking opportunities line the north coast. To get there, follow Via Ammiraglio Staiti along the port, turning inland just before Piazza Garibaldi at Via Turetta, and following the street until it turns right, onto Via Libertà. The road immediately curves left, then right onto Lungomare Dante Alighieri. Along here you'll find many pay spots (indicated by blue lines, enforced 8:00-13:30 & 15:30-24:00, Oct-May until 20:00; may be possible to pay and display at nearby machines, easier to use the EasyPark app; prepayment for the next day is OK—see machines). For free parking, continue along Lungomare Dante Alighieri all the way to the big parking lot at Piazza Vittorio Emanuele. Additional pay spaces can be found in the historic center, including in front of Piazza Garibaldi.

HELPFUL HINTS

Tap-Water Warning: Due to old pipes, it's not advisable to drink the tap water in Trapani. Stock up on bottled water.

Laundry: Trapani's new town—a longish walk from the historic

center—has several good launderettes, including self-service **Lavanderia La Casa del Pulito,** near the train station (daily 8:00-24:00, Via Vito Carrera 5, mobile +39 327 005 2420).

Thursday-Morning Market: Trapani's weekly market (in the New Town, near the main port and Trapani's sports arena) sells a little of everything—it's like a mobile Walmart (Thu 8:00-14:00, free shuttle bus #2 from intercity bus stop at the hydrofoil port along Via Ammiraglio Staiti; drivers can park in lot off Via Isola Zavorra—head east on Via Illio; lot is just past the roundabout where you turn right onto Via Isola Zavorra).

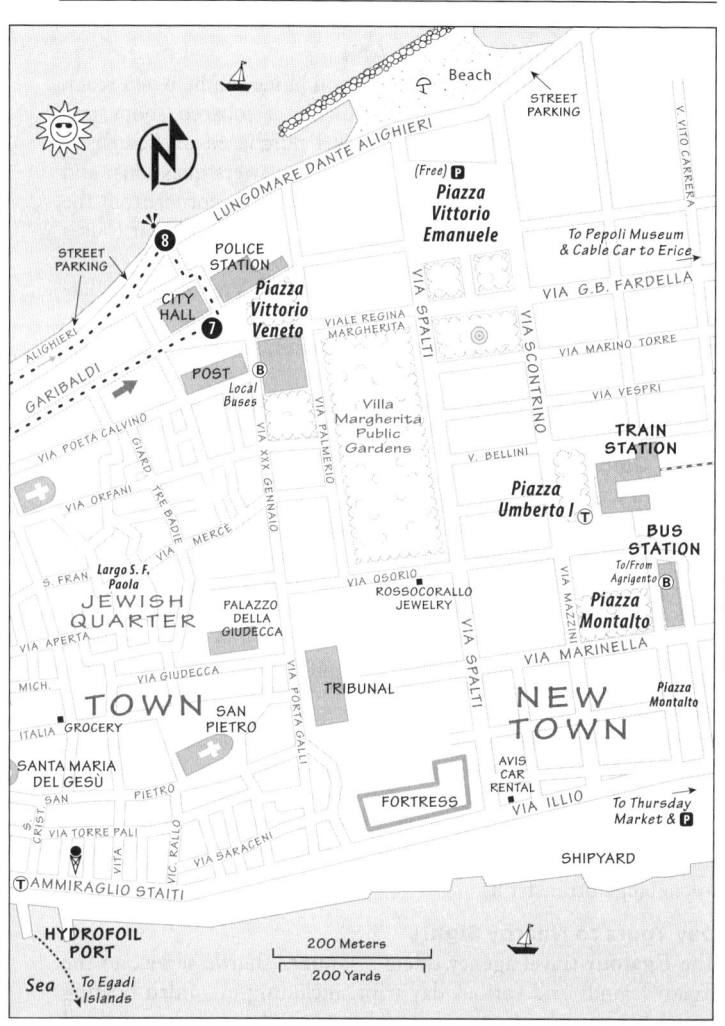

- **Beaches:** Several fine beaches stretch along Lungomare Dante Alighiere from the Piazza Mercato del Pesce all the way east to where Trapani becomes Erice. The small beach directly below Piazza Mercato del Pesce, known as **Spiaggia della Pescheria,** is an easy, free place to dip your feet in the sea. On nice days it's often packed with locals.
- **Car Rental: Avis** rents cars from a location facing the shipyard (Mon-Fri 9:00-13:00 & 15:30-18:30, Sat until 13:00, closed Sun, Via Avvocato Giuseppe Palmeri 3, +39 0923 872 848).

GETTING AROUND TRAPANI

Trapani's historic center is walkable, and buses can help you reach outlying sights. Bus tickets are available at tobacco shops and newsstands (€1.20/90 minutes, €1.50 if purchased on board). A custodian on each bus helps with tickets, answers questions, and will show you your stop. The bus stop around the corner from the post office on Via XXX Gennaio serves the Erice cable car (buses #21 and #23 to Cableway stop) and the Pepoli Museum (buses #25, #28, and #30 to Museo stop) making stops on Via Giovanni Battista Fardella along the way. Long-distance buses depart from the bus station on Piazza Montalto and from near the hydrofoil port.

Tours in and near Trapani

Local Guides

Azzurra Cusenza guides in Trapani and the surrounding areas. She has a gentle way and an interest in archaeology on the island of Mozia (€80/hour, 2-hour minimum, +39 340 252 7728, azzurra.cusenza@virgilio.it). **Elena Rutkowska Buscemi** puts her heart into shedding light on the mysteries of the Carthaginian civilization, and guides all over western Sicily (€190/4 hours, €300/8 hours, +39 389 055 9845, elenar.buscemi@gmail.com).

Driving Tours

Michelangelo Marchingiglio, a reliable English-speaking guide and driver, has an eight-seat van for short city trips or longer excursions in the countryside, such as Mozia or Selinunte (guided driving-€300/4 hours, €400/day; driving only-€200/4 hours; more for areas outside western Sicily, +39 335 822 5215, info@michelangelotransfer.it).

Day Tours to Nearby Sights

The **Egatour** travel agency offers a summer shuttle service to the Egadi Islands and various day trips, including unguided boating options to the islands for swimming and snorkeling. They also sell bus tickets for long-distance trips (office open Mon-Fri 6:00-20:00, Sat 7:00-18:30, Sun 9:00-12:00 & 16:00-20:00, Via Ammiraglio Staiti 13—across from the bus stop at the hydrofoil port, +39 092 321 754, egatourviaggi.it, info@egatourviaggi.it).

Trapani Town Walk

This one-hour walk will take you from the ferry port, through the historic center, to part of the modern town, and finish at the former fish market. It's ideal in the early evening, just before sunset—when the shops and churches are still open, and people are beginning to come out and stroll. To trace the route of this walk, see the "Trapani" map, earlier.

• *Start in Piazza Garibaldi, facing the busy port area, on the south shore of Trapani's peninsula.*

❶ Piazza Garibaldi

The statue on the big pedestal is **Giuseppe Garibaldi**—Italy's most famous and colorful revolutionary. Before becoming the leader of the military arm of the unification of the country, he was a jack-of-all-trades and an adventurer who lived in the US and South America. Standing here, he looks toward Marsala, where he landed with his troops in 1860 to begin the Risorgimento, that long and complicated political march that eventually led to unification and the establishment of modern Italy in 1861.

Along the waterfront is Trapani's hardworking port area. You'll see pleasure craft, public boats, and military ships. A few blocks to the left is the departure point for speedy hydrofoils to the Egadi Islands, just offshore (the best one is Favignana, described later in this chapter).

• *Circle around the statue and, with your back to Garibaldi, take the street on the left, Via Verdi, heading away from the water. After two short blocks, turn left. You'll see an ornate facade ahead on the left side of the street. Walk toward the...*

❷ Church of the Souls in Purgatory (Chiesa delle Anime Sante del Purgatorio)

This Baroque church has an interior that's unexceptional—except for the 20 sculpture groups you'll find displayed around its nave. These sculptures—illustrating the story of the Passion of Christ, collectively called *i Misteri*—play an integral role in Trapani's unique Easter celebrations and are a source of town pride year-round.

Cost and Hours: Pay the suggested €1 donation or languish in *purgatorio;* open Mon-Fri 7:45-12:00 & 16:00-19:00, Sat-Sun from 9:30; Via San Francesco 33, chiesamisteri.it.

Sicily: Jumping-Off Point for Conquest

For thousands of years, Sicily's excellent ports and central location have made it the perfect place to grab a foothold on the path to conquering other parts of the Mediterranean—which explains why the island has been conquered so many times by so many cultures (see the map on page 421). In ancient times, it was an ideal trade outpost, providing a connection between North Africa and northern Europe. Successive invaders enjoyed control of the shipping lanes around the island, controlling Mediterranean trade. And on the western tip of the island, near Trapani, the revolutionary Giuseppe Garibaldi and his thousand men landed in 1860 to start the reunification of Italy. Garibaldi captured the island, then continued on a march toward Rome and the final goal of establishing an Italian state.

In 1943, the Allies used a similar strategy to retake Europe from the Nazis. Operation Husky landed hundreds of thousands of troops on Sicily's southern shore in the first major offensive by the Allies, allowing them to use the island as a base of operations in the Mediterranean. (For more on Sicily in World War II, see page 433.)

More recently, Sicily has been used as a strategic, protected airbase with quick access to Europe and North Africa. The United States maintains a naval air station at Sigonella in southeastern Sicily, and NATO forces use the Birgi airport in Trapani for missions to Africa and the Middle East.

Among those in the long chain of sojourners using Sicily as a bridge to Europe are immigrants from Africa, often escaping bad conditions back home by rafting over to Sicilian shores. Most of these refugees use Sicily as a transition point for reaching more prosperous countries in northern Europe. Once registered with refugee status, they are allowed to move freely throughout the European Union.

Background: Every year on Good Friday, at 14:00, each of the church's statue groups is carried out on the backs of one to two dozen strong men, accompanied by a band playing Sicilian funeral dirges. The scenes make their way through town with a swaying and rhythmic gait. Participants are draped with jewelry, coral (symbolizing blood), flowers, and lights. The whole city turns out in mourning clothes to participate in the symbolic funeral for Christ. This particular Easter tradition is not native to Sicily but was brought by Spanish occupiers. Processions like this are common in Sicily—but this one lasts a full 24 hours.

Dating from the early 17th to 18th century, the statue groups are made of wood, cork, and other lightweight materials. The figures' dramatic drapery is made using fabric dipped in glue and plaster, and then molded and dried. Some of the characters are portraits of actual locals, and the role of the Roman centurions is played by Spanish soldiers (who were to Sicily what the Romans were to the Jews 2,000 years ago). Many of the villains—such as Pontius Pilate—are depicted as Ottomans.

Visiting the Church: Entering the church, turn right and follow the story of the Passion (signs in English describe each scene). Local guilds sponsor and maintain each statue group and have the honor of carrying their ensemble through the city every year on Good Friday; each base is decorated with the symbol of its sponsoring guild. (A video of the Good Friday procession may be playing in the left transept.)

As plain as the church interior is, notice that the left transept is particularly austere. In 1940, Trapani was the first Italian city bombed by the Allies, when French bombers based in Tunisia hit this church. Luckily, at the time, the *Misteri* were housed elsewhere. The bombing, on April 6, 1943, is still commemorated today.

• *Exit the church and turn left. At the first intersection, turn right up Via Generale Enrico Fardella. Go two blocks, then turn right again on Corso Vittorio Emanuele—the lively central spine of the old town.*

Immediately on your left, at #46, you'll find an old-fashioned cantina, **Tenute Adragna.** *If you're taking this walk in the evening, pop in for a glass of wine and make a memory: Starting at around 18:00, Gregorio entertains a very local crowd here, selling red* (rosso) *wine right out of the big casks as well as chilled white* (bianco) *wine—just specify sweet* (dolce) *or dry* (secco).

A block farther along Corso Vittorio Emanuele, on the left, you'll find the...

❸ Trapani Cathedral (Cattedrale di Trapani)

It's hard to get a good vantage point to take in this cathedral, which sits right on the main street rather than on a spacious piazza. Before entering (daily 8:00-12:00 & 16:00-20:00), check out the modern iron-and-bronze gate. On the right side of the gate, notice the grill—the symbol of St. Lawrence, the church's patron saint, who was martyred by being grilled alive.

The Baroque/Neoclassical interior wrestles with the vintage-1950s white marble canopy and altar. The left transept has a statue of the protector of sailors—the Madonna of Trapani—whom you'll see all over the city (you can spot her by her ornate crown). This particular Madonna is new, made from a scan of an older original and cut by lasers. The most precious work in the church is found in the fifth chapel on the right: a crucifixion painting attributed to Anthony van Dyck.

• *Head back out onto the main street and turn left. Two blocks up the street, the second ornate building on the left side of the street is the...*

❹ Church of the Jesuit College (Chiesa del Collegio dei Gesuiti)

This Jesuit church and convent has a fluffy pink Baroque interior. On the right side you'll find yet another statue of the Madonna of Trapani (gotta keep those sailors safe). Notice the statues in the upper niches—the fronts of their bodies have been shorn off. It seems that these saints went out of style and were hidden behind drywall for years (€1, generally Mon-Fri 9:00-12:00 & 16:00-20:00, Sat-Sun vary).

• *Exit the church and turn left. The street dead-ends at...*

❺ Palazzo Cavarretta

This centerpiece of historic Trapani was used until the 1920s as the Town Hall. Imagine the townsfolk gathering before its ornate balcony for grand pronouncements. This end of Corso Vittorio Emanuele was the closest thing old Trapani had to an official gathering place. The palazzo's government days are over, so now it mostly hosts exhibits. At the top of the facade, you'll see a clock and a calendar. Below them are St. John the Baptist,

St. Albert, and in the center—you guessed it—the Madonna of Trapani. Three flags wave over the entrance: the red-and-yellow Sicilian flag, the blue EU flag, and—above all, at the very top of the building—the green, white, and red Italian flag.

• *Turn left at Palazzo Cavarretta and head toward the arcade of Piazza Mercato del Pesce, the former fish market. Our walk will end there. But first, we'll take a peek at the modern side of Trapani. A block before the big arcade, turn right and head down the grand pedestrian boulevard called...*

❻ Via Garibaldi

In the evening, Via Garibaldi is a great street to join the Trapani *passeggiata* (Corso Vittorio Emanuele and Via Torrearsa are even better). Sicilians love socializing, and the evening stroll is a precious opportunity to meet friends, window-shop, and get some fresh air before dinner.

We'll stroll the length of Via Garibaldi. Along the way, you'll pass former noble palaces, such as the big, hulking building on the left at the start of the street (at #7)—**Palazzo Burgio** (now Unicredit Bank). The nearby salt flats made a few elite Trapani families rich, and they flaunted their wealth by building fancy palaces along this main street. As you continue down the street, you'll notice that some of these fancy townhouses came with faux-historical flourishes: The palace at #40, on the right, has Venetian Gothic balconies, even though it was built in the 1800s, well after the decline of Venice.

Notice the window displays. At #42 (on the right), the **Sicilia Bedda** shop shows off local produce and lots of gifty edibles. At #60 (on the right), **Gral** café is the local hotspot for taking in soccer games on an outdoor big screen.

Farther along, at #70, the big building on the right (flying Sicily, Italy, and EU flags) displays a major underwater discovery made off the coast of Trapani in the early 2000s. The two **bronze rostrums** (battering rams, usually attached to a ship's bow) in the window are from the third-century BC Battle of Egadi, which took place near the Egadi island of Levanzo. In what became the turning point of the First Punic War, Roman ships surprised the Carthaginians as they attacked Trapani, using battering rams like these to slam into and sink the enemy's fleet (you'll see more examples in Trapani's Pepoli Museum and on Favignana at the Stabilimento Florio museum).

Across the street, at #77 (left), look for **red flags** marked *CGIL*. This is the headquarters for one of Italy's labor unions. And just a few doors down, after the church, teens often loiter in front of #83, the **high school.** Sicilian kids choose their high school a bit like Americans choose colleges, based on areas of study such as arts or engineering. The students at this *liceo* are studying science.

As you walk, you'll also pass a few stretches of single-story buildings on the right. Due to its important port, Trapani was heavily bombed during World War II, and some areas were never fully rebuilt. At #122, in the second stretch of buildings, the original lower floor is being used for a small **fruit shop**—but the upper floors are only a jagged edge of broken stone.

• *When the street ends, you'll pop out into a big modern square...*

⑦ Piazza Vittorio Veneto (Piazza Municipio)

This piazza marks the end of the old town and the start of the new. The broad boulevard stretching ahead of you is Via Giovanni Battista Fardella, which runs two miles to the cable-car station for

> ## Trapani's Coral Business
>
> Coral was one of Trapani's major industries from the 16th to the 19th century. Believed to have protective powers, it was used for jewelry, decorative arts, and clothing. In Greek mythology, coral represents the blood of the snake-haired Medusa, who turned anyone who viewed her hideous face into stone. When she was beheaded by Perseus, her blood hit the seawater and petrified into coral. From the Middle Ages through Baroque times, coral took on a religious meaning as a symbol of the blood of Christ, and was worn as jewelry by women and children to protect them from danger. In the area around Naples, coral was fashioned into "horns"—a fertility symbol that also had protective powers. Today's Sicilians consider coral good luck, worn as protection from the curse of the evil eye.
>
> But because the coral reefs between Sicily and Tunisia were harvested for generations, the supply was depleted. Coral is no longer harvested in Sicily, but some artisans remain—making jewelry out of antique coral, coral paste, or even a salt paste dyed to look like coral. In Trapani, Platimiro Fiorenza is one of the last artists working in coral, a profession handed down from his father. His shop, **Rossocorallo,** sells antique and modern coral jewelry (just south of the Villa Margherita public gardens at Via Osorio 36; for location, see the "Trapani" map, earlier).

Erice. On the left side of the square are the City Hall *(municipio)* and the police station *(questura)*. On the right, the yellow building is marked *Posta* and *Telegrafi*— the post-and-telegraph office from 1927, a lovely example of the Liberty Style (what Italians call Art Nouveau). If it's open, step up to the door and admire the fine ironwork. Inside, the ceiling is a stained-glass work of art. Italian post offices are for more than sending mail: This is where people pay bills and parking tickets, receive pensions, and deal with bureaucracy.

• *Leave the piazza by walking toward the water, between the City Hall and the police station. Cross the street and walk straight up to the railing along...*

ⓧ Trapani's Embankment (Lungomare Dante Alighieri)

From here, you can see almost the entire city of Trapani. Looking right (as you face the water), you'll see the looming mountain, Monte San Giuliano, capped by Erice—accessible via cableway, and a great side-trip destination.

Trapani is a city of 70,000 but looks much bigger. That's because Erice blends into Trapani, with an additional 26,000 people living at the foot of the mountain, plus 230 full-time residents in the medieval village at the top. The two cities form a larger municipality and share services. For instance, the public-transit company is managed by Trapani but also serves Erice. The local hospital is in the jurisdiction of Erice, so all citizens of Trapani are technically born in Erice...but everyone ends their days in Trapani, as the public cemetery is here.

Now turn left; from this vantage you'll see how the historic center of Trapani is squeezed onto a long peninsula curving out into the Mediterranean. The waters off Trapani are quiet these days, but once pulsed with fishermen. Tuna fishing and coral collection were big industries, powering the local economy. Both have been curtailed, sending the economy of Trapani into a tailspin. These days, tourism is a new solution for job creation.

• *Stroll with the water on your right, enjoying the humid sea breeze for a few blocks. Stop when you reach the big, arcaded semicircular structure.*

❾ Piazza Mercato del Pesce

This elegant seaside arcade was the site of the old fish market and the center of the local agricultural economy. But when much of the old town was cleaned up and renovated in 2005, the daily market (along with its fishy, smelly transactions) was relocated to the far-western tip of the city. These days, the arcade is occasionally used for special events. In the center of the piazza, the statue of Venus is a reminder that Trapani was originally the port of the town of Erice, where the goddess was deeply venerated as a protector of sailors. Hmm...haven't we heard that story before?

• *Our walk is over. A small beach beckons just below the arcade. And we're just a few steps from the start of the lively Via Garibaldi* passeggiata *zone, where we strolled earlier. But if it's late afternoon, continue your walk straight along the seafront promenade, ideal at dusk to view Trapani's impressive sunset.*

Sights in Trapani

Pepoli Museum (Museo Regionale Agostino Pepoli)

Trapani's art and local history museum, housed in a former Carmelite monastery two miles west of the historic center, is home to a painting gallery and an eclectic assortment from the personal collection of Agostino Pepoli, a merchant who made a fortune in the salt industry. Modest and distant from the historic center, it's skippable for most visitors but makes a decent rainy-day activity.

Cost and Hours: €8, Tue-Sat 9:00-18:00, Sun until 12:00, closed Mon; east of the old town at Via Conte Agostino Pepoli 180—take bus #25, #28, or #30 to Museo stop; +39 0923 553 269.

Visiting the Museum: The museum is fronted by a public garden; cross through to find the entrance in the corner. On the ground floor, you'll find Renaissance sculptures. The Renaissance never really took off in Sicily, making these sculptures unique: The Gagini and Laurana families were some of the few locals who embraced the style. To the left of the entry, a room displays artifacts from revolutionary Giuseppe Garibaldi's landing in Marsala. You'll see a giant flag from his ship *Il Lombardo;* a uniform from his troops, nicknamed "The Red Shirts"; and an actual guillotine, complete with elevated platform and trapdoor. Upstairs, the painting gallery houses a work thought to be by Titian, *St. Francis with Stigmata.* The collection also includes a bronze rostrum (battering ram) and amphora dating from the First Punic War, majolica ceramics, nativity scenes, clothing, and jewelry made with local coral carved by monks.

Ligny Tower (Torre di Ligny)

About 15 minutes' walk from the historic center along Corso Vittorio Emanuele, at the far-western end of Trapani, you'll find this coastal-fortification tower from 1671. Today, it houses a museum with a lackluster hodge-podge of prehistoric artifacts and model ships, all described in Italian; the only reason to pay the entrance fee is to climb to the top for the panoramic view (€2, cash only, daily 10:00-13:00 & 17:00-19:30). The location is the real attraction: You're standing where the Mediterranean meets the Tyrrhenian Sea. Straight ahead, over the horizon, is Gibraltar. To the right lies Italy, and Europe. To the left, Tunisia, and Africa. This is Trapani's top sunset spot—it's so romantic, you might have to find someone to kiss.

Sleeping in Trapani

All of my recommended places have air-conditioning and, unless otherwise noted, an elevator.

€€€ **Badia Nuova** has 20 smartly appointed rooms and apartments, some with full kitchens. Each room category is styled slightly differently, but all follow a similar contemporary design and most come with a balcony or terrace (no breakfast, Via Badia Nuova 33, +39 0923 24054, badianuova.it, info@badianuova.it, Ida).

€€€ **Central Gallery Rooms** has a mix of 18 spacious rooms and studio apartments—some with leftover details from the palace it used to be. A few rooms have sea views, and the studios come with simple kitchens (two- or three-night minimum in summer, Via Giuseppe Garibaldi 67, +39 0923 198 6559, centralgalleryrooms.com, centralgalleryrooms@gmail.com).

€€ **Hotel San Michele,** hidden in the tangle of streets, rents 21 upscale rooms with beachy-boutique vibes clustered around an inner courtyard that preserves architectural elements of an old church (Via San Michele 16, +39 0923 23470, sanmicheletp.it, info@sanmicheletp.it, friendly Alessandro).

€€ **Residenza La Gancia** fills the old monastery of Santa Caterina with 20 comfortable, near-business-class rooms, each equipped with a small kitchenette. Their top-floor view terrace is a sunny and cheery breakfast room—a nice place to sunbathe, and a fine spot to watch the sunset (small gym, Piazza Mercato del Pesce, +39 0923 438 060, lagancia.com, booking@lagancia.com, Rosanna).

€€ **Gaura Apartments,** run by La Gancia, offers 11 seaview apartments with kitchenettes, all beautifully designed for maximum efficiency. Their penthouse apartment has a private terrace with a 360-degree view (no breakfast, Via Mura di Tramontana, enter along the promenade, it's the nondescript door on the all-white building, mobile +39 347 296 3479, gauraapartments.com, info@gauraapartments.com, Rosanna).

€ **Ai Lumi B&B,** run by friendly husband and wife Rizzo and Francesca, occupies two floors in an 18th-century historic building overlooking a quaint courtyard just off Corso Vittorio Emanuele. Their mix of 15 rustic and colorful accommodations includes standard rooms, studios, and two-room apartments (no elevator, Corso Vittorio Emanuele 71, +39 0923 540 922, ailumi.it, info@ailumi.it).

€ Albergo Russo is right on the Corso Vittorio Emanuele pedestrian drag. Its 25 rooms are slightly outdated and modest—some spacious, some tight—but all are comfy, and the price/value ratio hits a sweet spot (no breakfast, Via Tintori 4, +39 0923 22163, albergorusso.it, info@albergorusso.it).

¢ B&B Alla Marina is the home of Goffredo Adragna, whose family owns the local cantina on the main street. The top floor used to be his grandmother's apartment and has been carefully converted into an inexpensive B&B with four charming old-world rooms sharing a cozy common space with a view of the port (Viale Regina Elena 4, +39 0923 26401, info@beballamarina.it).

¢ Albergo Maccotta is a simple, family-run 26-room hotel on a quiet lane in the old center. Set your expectations appropriately: This place is basic, but rather than drab it's cheerful, clean, well run, and a fine value for a budget room (Via degli Argentieri 4, +39 0923 28418, albergomaccotta.it, albergomaccotta@virgilio.it, Valentina and Emanuele).

Eating in Trapani

Trapani is the best place to try Sicilian couscous—traditionally served with a side of fish broth to ladle over it. The local pasta specialty is *busiate*, a long, twisted noodle typically served with a red pesto made of almonds, garlic, tomatoes, and cheese. This town also does good pizza, with crispy crust and lots of cheese, cut into bite-size pieces. *Fornos* and *panificios*—rustic bakeries selling bread, pizza, focaccia, and other yummy oven-baked goodies, often focusing on local specialties—line Via Ammiraglio Staiti (near the hydrofoil port) and are scattered throughout the old town. They're good for quick, cheap stand-up or takeaway food. For a memorable full meal, stick to my recommendations below. Note that restaurants here sometimes close spontaneously from October through Easter and during bad weather.

IN THE HISTORIC CENTER

€€€ La Bettolaccia is a snazzy but unpretentious space tucked deep in the back streets of the old town. They have helpful service and a tempting menu, including the best fish couscous in town, and a good selection of wines (daily, Via Generale Enrico Fardella 23, +39 0923 25932).

€€€ Gli Archi di San Carlo, with an elevated menu of *busiate* pasta and primarily meat *secondi* (roasted lamb, veal), is a solid option for a classy dinner under vaulted ceilings (Thu-Tue dinner only, closed Wed, Via Serisso 47, +39 339 234 6579).

€€€ Osteria Il Moro is a serious, upscale, chef-run place with a cozy, earth-toned dining room. The creative menu boasts some unusual takes on local specialties, such as rabbit cacciatore and *pane e panelle,* a desert incorporating ice cream, hummus, and sweet chickpea fritters. The pricey tasting *menu*s are splurgeworthy (daily, no lunch Sun, Via Garibaldi 86, +39 0923 23194, osteriailmoro.it).

€€ **Osteria San Pietro** is a family-run osteria near the port. Its one long room feels tucked away from all the tourists and is filled with locals enjoying the catch of the day (closed Wed, Largo Porta Galli, +39 3311 273 747, osteriasanpietro.com).

€€ **Al Vicoletto,** tucked away on a little alley *(vicoletto),* has won a reputation for its artistry with seafood. The menu is short, almost entirely fish, and ranges from classic to creative preparations (Mon-Sat dinner only, closed Sun, Via Biscottai 6, +39 320 810 3689).

€€ **Amici Miei Pizzeria** is a big, clattery warehouse of dining along the waterfront, with a movie theme. The menu is mostly pizzas, with a few pastas and main courses mixed in. This is a good bet if you want your pizza with a sea view, as they have two large outdoor terraces just across the street from the seawall (Tue-Sat lunch and dinner, Sun dinner only, closed Mon, Lungomare Dante Alighieri 28, +39 0923 25907).

Pizza and Sandwiches: €€ **Pizzeria Calvino** serves precut pizza in a funky building that was a WWII bordello (look for peephole slits in the walls). The best pizza in town comes with snippy service—typical of proud Italian pizzerias—and the wait can be long. It's smart to reserve in person at 18:00, one hour before opening (Wed-Mon dinner only, closed Tue, Via Nunzio Nasi 71, +39 0923 21464).

€ **Mozzico** is a solid budget choice for a quick lunch—pull up a stool on the sidewalk patio or get it to take away. The small menu, written on a chalkboard, details their focaccia sandwiches, which are made with typical Trapanese (and some Roman) products. They're willing to assemble a custom sandwich using the ingredients in the display case (daily, Corso Vittorio Emanuele 91, +39 338 851 1121).

Craft Beer and Pub Grub: € **Il Barbagianni,** near the Villa Margherita public gardens at the edge of the new town, is a fun place to experiment with Italian craft beers. They have microbrews both on tap and by the bottle, along with burgers and sandwiches, in an easygoing, modern atmosphere (Tue-Sun dinner only, closed Mon, Via XXX Gennaio 15, +39 339 393 6060).

Wine Bar: Enoteca Versi di Rosso has a long list of local wines and light meals to match. Marco and his staff know their wines and can suggest something to suit your tastes (Tue-Sun from 18:00, closed Mon, Corso Vittorio Emanuele 63, +39 329 971 4370).

Trapani Hotels & Restaurants

Accommodations
1. Badia Nuova
2. Central Gallery Rooms
3. Hotel San Michele
4. Residenza La Gancia & Gaura Apartments
5. Ai Lumi B&B
6. Albergo Russo
7. B&B Alla Marina
8. Albergo Maccotta

Eateries & Other
9. La Bettolaccia
10. Gli Archi di San Carlo
11. Osteria Il Moro
12. Osteria San Pietro
13. Pizzeria Calvino
14. Al Vicoletto
15. Amici Miei Pizzeria
16. Mozzico
17. Il Barbagianni
18. Enoteca Versi di Rosso
19. Gelateria Meno Tredici
20. To Piazza Jolanda Eateries
21. Grocery
22. Launderette
23. Car Rental

Gelato: Locals love **Gelateria Meno Tredici** (near the hydrofoil port at Via Ammiraglio Saiti 61).

Supermarket: A handy **Conad** supermarket is at Corso Italia 35 (Mon-Sat 8:30-13:30 & 16:30-20:00, closed Sun).

ON AND NEAR PIAZZA JOLANDA

For a more local side of Trapani, walk west along Corso Vittorio Emanuele to Piazza Jolanda. This very Trapanese parking-lot square is ringed by restaurants where locals outnumber tourists.

€€ **Santa Chiara 19** is a snug, charming hole-in-the-wall serving reasonably priced local fare—mostly fish and seafood—to

Trapani

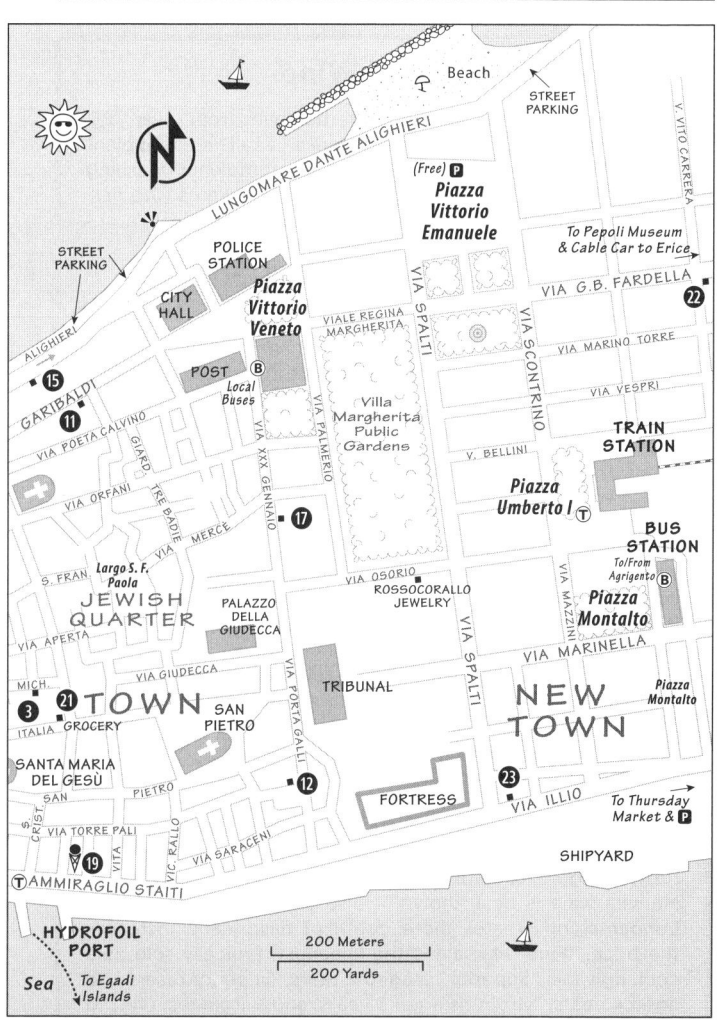

a younger-skewing crowd (Tue-Sat lunch and dinner, Sun lunch only, closed Mon, +39 366 229 9592).

€€€ Antichi Sapori, in the middle of the square, has a longer menu, a rustic interior under vaults, and a huge enclosed terrace (closed Tue, Corso Vittorio Emanuele 191, +39 0923 22866).

€€€ Salamureci, just a block away on the next square, is excellent, with quality local fare heavy on seafood (including higher-end options such as seafood couscous and a mixed grilled fish plate), a welcoming dining room, and deliberate service (closed Mon, Piazza Generale Scio 17, +39 0923 21728).

Marsala Wine

In 1773, John Woodhouse, a cloth merchant from Liverpool, came to western Sicily in search of *barilla*—a salt-resistant plant used in the production of soda ash (a key ingredient in washing powder). In Marsala, he tried a local wine known as *vino perpetuo* ("everlasting wine"). The wine had been aged for decades in wooden barrels in which a fraction of wine was evaporated and new wine continuously added.

Woodhouse grasped the sales potential of this wine as a competitor for Portuguese Madeira, which was very popular in England. He shipped 8,000 gallons from Marsala to Liverpool; to keep it from spoiling, he added brandy to the oak casks. When the wine arrived, it had taken on a new flavor, which became instantly successful in England. Later, when Madeira wine became scarce due to the Napoleonic Wars, Woodhouse signed an agreement with Lord Horatio Nelson to supply the British Navy with his fortified Marsala wine. Marsala took off after that, becoming a major business in Sicily.

Several other English families followed Woodhouse, including the Whitakers, and the Marsala-wine trade created strong financial ties between England and Sicily. (The Whitakers wound up purchasing the island now called Mozia as a retreat—you'll learn more about them if you visit there.)

Marsala wine is a blend with 15-20 percent alcohol, made with a combination of grapes typically including inzolia, catarratto, grillo, and damaschino. There are three colors: amber, ruby, and gold, each of which has its own flavor. While sweet Marsala wine is best known, it also can be dry or semidry. Longer aging creates more depth of flavor—and increases the price. "Fine" Marsala is the cheapest, typically sold as a cooking wine. "Superior" is aged 2 years, "superior reserve" is aged 4 years, "virgin" is aged 5 years, and "virgin reserve," 10 years. Marsala became the first Sicilian DOC *(denominazione di origine controllata)* wine in Italy, meaning that it is given a governmental seal of approval and must be made from grapes grown in the Marsala region.

Wine Bar in Trapani: Enoteca Versi di Rosso is a good spot to try local Marsala wine, paired with a cheese platter (closed Mon, Corso Vittorio Emanuele 63, +39 329 971 4370).

Marsala Winery Tour: Cantine Florio is a modern facility near Marsala, about 20 miles south of Trapani on the way to Selinunte, where you can see the winemaking process and learn about their company's history (€30, includes tour and tastes of three wines, reservations required, Via Vincenzo Florio 1, Marsala, +39 0923 781 307, cantineflorio.it, visitaflorio@duca.it).

Trapani Connections

BY PLANE

Trapani's **Birgi airport** (airport code: TPS, airgest.it) is a 15-minute drive south of the city. Buses wait just outside of the arrivals hall (hourly, 30 minutes). Taxis connect the airport and downtown Trapani (€35 fixed rate). Trapani's airport has few connections—you're more likely to use Palermo's, a 1.5-hour drive away.

BY PUBLIC TRANSPORTATION

Most buses leave from the port, near the hydrofoil port and across the street from the Egatour travel agency, at Via Staiti 13. Note that bus companies vary by destination, and few buses run on Sundays. Tickets are available at Egatour (daily 6:00-20:00, shorter hours on weekends, +39 092 321 754). Agrigento and Segesta buses depart from the bus station in Piazza Montalto (tickets sold at Bar Barraco, Via Virgilio 9).

From Trapani by Bus to: Birgi airport (roughly hourly, 30 minutes, AST, aziendasicilianatrasporti.it), **Erice** (6/day, 1 hour, AST—note that cable car takes just 10 minutes and is more enjoyable), **Segesta** (4/day, 40 minutes, Tarantola Cuffaro, tarantolacuffaro.it), **Palermo** (hourly, 2 hours, Segesta Autolinee, segesta.it), **Palermo airport** (hourly, 2 hours, Segesta Autolinee, segesta.it), **Agrigento** (3/day, 3 hours, Salvatore Lumia Bus, autolineelumia.it).

By Train to: Marsala (hourly, 30 minutes).

ROUTE TIPS FOR DRIVERS

To reach points south (such as **Selinunte** and **Agrigento**), hop on the autostrada east toward Palermo; soon after passing the Segesta turnoff, take the fork to the right toward *Mazara del Vallo* (autostrada E-90). This zips you south; exit at the olive-growing town of Castelvetrano. Soon after is the turnoff for the Selinunte ancient ruins. To proceed to Agrigento, turn east onto SS-115 (blue signs for *Agrigento*). You'll drive across long viaducts over bursting farm fields, then pass through the midsize town of Menfi; soon after, the landscape changes to rocky peaks, and you approach Agrigento. The drive from Trapani to Agrigento takes about 2.5 hours; Selinunte is a little over halfway.

Day Trips from Trapani

From your home base of Trapani, any of the destinations in this section make a fine day trip. To help decide which to visit, see "Planning Your Time," at the beginning of this chapter.

Erice

Atop a dramatic mountain overlooking the sea sits Erice (EH-ree-cheh), an ancient village often cloaked in sea mist, worth ▲. Erice is little and quite touristy. But its unusual church, grand views from its castle, easy proximity to Trapani (reachable in 14 minutes by cable car), and delicious sweets make the town a worthwhile 2-3-hour visit. Romantics like to spend the night—enjoying the spooky atmosphere as the tourists roll out and the mountain mist rolls in.

Erice's original settlers were the Elymians, who arrived around 1200 BC from Asia Minor. Unfortunately, little is known about them; they were displaced by the Carthaginians and later by the Romans. But we do know that all of these ancient cultures worshipped a similar goddess—one related to fertility. The Romans called her Venus Erycina, after Eryx, the ancient city name.

The cliff-capping position of Erice made it a desirable and defensible place to live in the Middle Ages; under the Normans, the city grew to the boundaries you see today. While the village these days is small compared to sprawling Trapani below, it was the opposite in the past: Erice was a thriving city and Trapani simply its port.

Getting to Erice: While you can drive to Erice, it may be easier to take the **cable car** from Trapani (€11 round-trip, Tue-Thu 8:30-20:00, Fri-Sun 10:00-23:00, Mon 14:00-20:00, closed Nov-March and during high winds; 14-minute ride, departs from station about 4 miles from central Trapani; funiviaerice.it). The cable car drops you a short walk below Erice's main gate (Porta Trapani).

To reach the center of town, cross the street and walk uphill past the parking lot, through the archway.

To reach the cable-car station in Trapani, you can take a **taxi,** or catch **bus** #21 or #23 at Via Giovanni Battista Fardella 14 (every 30 minutes, 15-minute ride). Bus #21 stops directly in front of the cable-car station, while #23 stops just around the corner on Via Cosenza.

Drivers can use the pay lots in front of the cable-car station. Or, if you enjoy white-knuckle drives, you can twist up the extremely scenic road from Trapani (SP-31, about 30 minutes)—less advisable in summer, when the road can be clogged and parking lots full. Once up top, follow signs for *Porta Trapani*, where you'll find a small pay lot; there are also a few spots at the far end of town, near the Castle of Venus. (You'll see other parking lots around town, but I find these the easiest.) The easier approach is simply to park at the lower cable-car station and ride up. Since the cable-car station is where the switchback road begins, you can decide when you get there. If you're arriving from the autostrada rather than Trapani, exit following signs for *Val d'Erice*.

Tourist Information: A small info kiosk is near the entrance to the city walls, across from the cable-car station (generally daily 10:00-18:00, closed Nov-March, +39 388 097 2089, prolocoerice.it).

Erice Town Walk

This walk introduces you to Erice in about an hour. It begins by sneaking around the back streets—to show you a slice of Erice most tourists miss—then plunges you right back down its touristy main drag to where you started. In this hilly burg, expect lots of up and down.

• *Begin your walk at the simple archway in the stone wall just above the cable-car station and parking lot.*

❶ Porta Trapani

This gate, at the western end of the triangular city, is one of the two entrances to the old city of Erice. Examine the lower, larger stones of the walls: These come from the time when the city was allied with the Carthaginians. The city later came under Norman rule, and the walls were fortified (the smaller stones date from this period). While the population in the past reached about

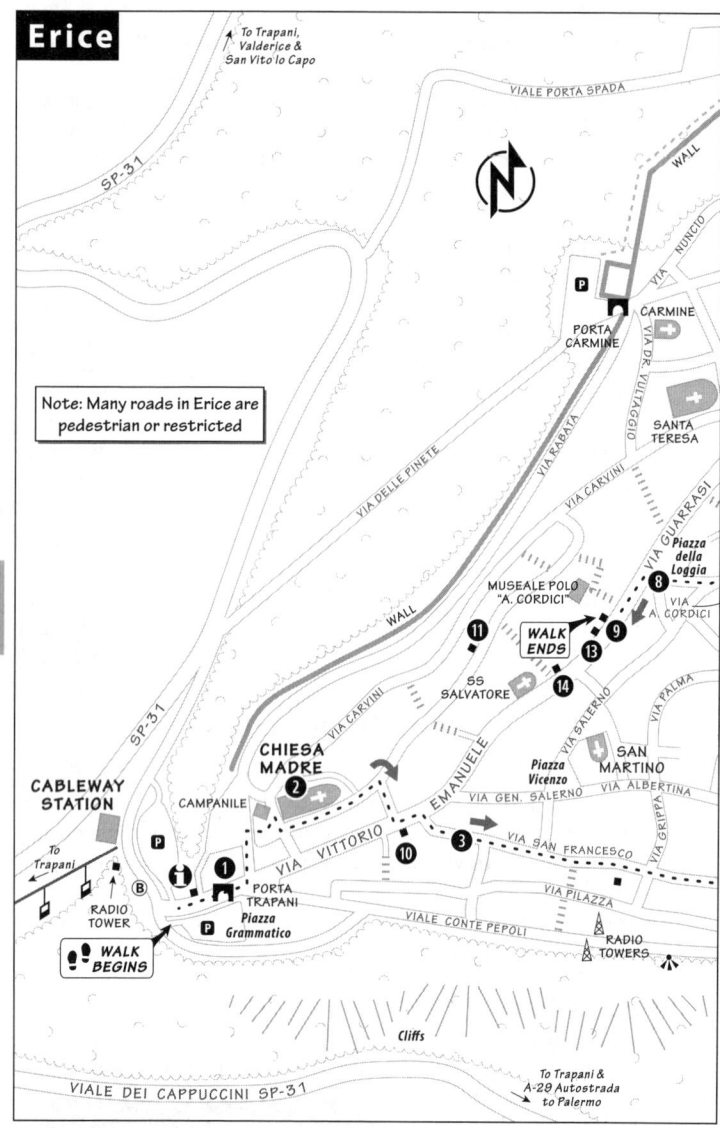

12,000, the city currently has only a few hundred year-round residents...and one priest.

• *Pass through the gate, take the first left, and walk toward the tower.*

❷ Chiesa Madre

The church is called Chiesa Madre—"mother church." Notice that it stands at the town entrance, rather than in the central piazza. The town's cult of Venus was strong, and its temple dedicated to the

Erice 177

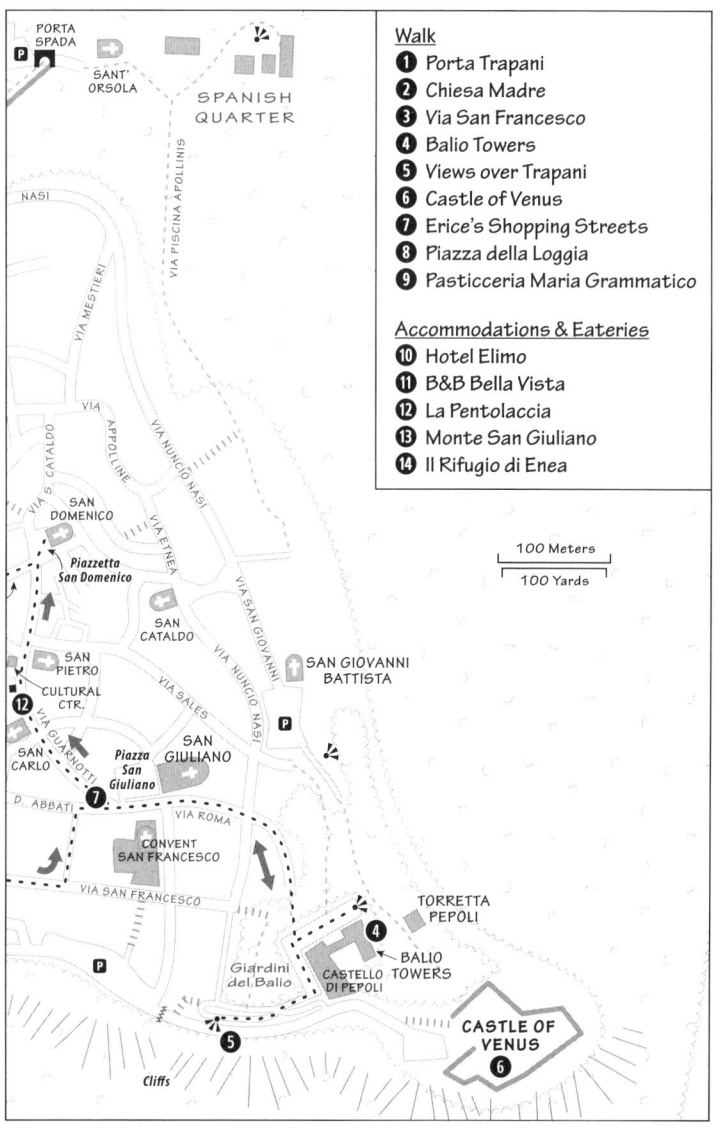

goddess could be seen for miles around. (We'll see the site of that temple later.) When paganism fell out of favor, this church—dedicated to a similar female divinity—was built on the opposite side of town, as a counterpoint to Venus.

Approach the church. Notice the large **covered porch**. Called the *gibbena*, this area was reserved for those who were not penitent (and therefore not allowed to enter the church).

Buy a ticket at the bell tower, then step inside the church (€2.50, daily 10:00-18:00; they also sell a handy town map). The unusual, undulating, stuccoed **ceiling** isn't as old as it seems. While the exterior of the church dates from the 1300s, the interior collapsed in the late 1800s and was rebuilt in a fanciful Neo-Gothic/Neo-Arabic fusion.

Step up to the **family crest** in the center of the floor near the entrance. It represents the House of Aragon from Spain, with red-and-yellow stripes. This church was built by the king of Spain, who also happened to rule Sicily at the time.

Turn to the left aisle and find the third chapel. The painting of the **Madonna of Custonaci** is a town treasure. Notice it's set in a special frame that can be carried on processions through the streets—during which townspeople ask for the Madonna's assistance. Just beyond, in the same aisle, find the plaque on the wall that lists the dates of processions held in times of desperate need: rain *(pioggia)*, war *(guerra)*, locusts *(cavallette)*, earthquake *(terremoto)*, and so on *(idem* means "ditto"). These parades were originally held at random in times of need, but the custom grew so popular it became an annual event each August.

To see a more austere original bit of the church from before the reconstruction—with simple stone arches and plain white vaults—go to the last large chapel on the left, which also houses the **treasury.** The Renaissance-era **main altarpiece,** a cascade of marble, is another piece from the older church.

• *Exit and turn left to walk alongside the church building. The nine crosses along the outer church wall are said to be recycled pieces from the original temple of Venus. Reaching the end of the church, continue uphill a few more paces and take the first right; after that, a quick left and a quick right will bring you to...*

❸ Via San Francesco

Follow this quiet lane several blocks gently uphill, nearly to the far end of town. The homes on this residential lane may look plain, but the austerity on the outside is an Arab-Sicilian tradition meant to hide the treasures inside. Look through the gates as you pass, and you'll see that many homes here have fine little courtyards.

Many of the houses here are not inhabited. Erice has become depopulated in recent years, with locals preferring to live down below in the modern suburbs of Trapani. Erice can be cold and windy in the winter, often wrapped in thick, misty clouds, so homes up here are now primarily used as summer retreats.

Continue your stroll, enjoying peekaboo views over the valley on your right. Look on the left (between #80 and #82) for a classic example of a *venula*—a passageway barely wide enough for a person. Erice has many of these passages, which were intended to provide ventilation for the homes around them.

• *Squeeze your way up to the top of this long, skinny venula. When you reach the end, turn right and carry on straight ahead, past the pinkish church, and up the lane until it dead-ends at a wall. Follow the ramp on your right, then curl your way up into the park, Giardino del Balio. Head for the tall, blocky, crenellated towers.*

❹ Balio Towers (Torri del Balio)

These towers still stand from the original medieval castle, some of which was torn down in the 19th century. The rest was refurbished as a classy retreat for the Pepoli clan. Salt was a valuable commodity in the past, and the Pepoli family made a fortune at the nearby salt flats in the 19th century. They restored part of the castle to live in and became patrons of the arts (their collection became  the foundation of the Pepoli Museum in Trapani).

Go to the left end of the towers and find the adorable little crenellated **lookout terrace.** Peer between the rocky teeth, over sweeping views of the Sicilian coastline, fertile farmlands, otherworldly Monte Cofano rocketing up at the far end of the bay, and—at your feet—the fanciful little tower called Torretta Pepoli, which was built as the library for the Pepoli family complex.

• *Facing the blocky towers, turn right and walk straight ahead through the gardens until you hit a railing with a* fantastico *view over the Trapani area. Turn right and walk about 50 yards for the best view (near the drink bar).*

❺ Views Over Trapani

This stunning view suggests why Erice was such a strategic location for centuries. Looking out to sea, you can see hook-shaped Trapani pointing out toward the Egadi Islands. The island on the left, Favignana, is easy to visit

by hydrofoil from Trapani. Notice the modern, concrete, high-rise sprawl between Trapani and Erice's mountain.

Just left of Trapani are the salt pans that put this region on the map economically and are still fun to visit. Now turn to see the historic castle perched on the hill beside you.

• *This is the...*

❻ Castle of Venus (Castello di Venere)

This rambling, cliff-capping complex is a Norman castle with layers of ruins inside. There are no real exhibits, but if it's open, scrambling over the ruins can provide a fun king-of-the-castle experience.

Survey the castle from afar and consider its epic story. It began as a **temple** to the Phoenician goddess Astarte, built in the seventh century BC, and was later converted into a Roman temple to Venus Erycina. Venus, the goddess of love—like Astarte before her—was important to sailors. Making a sacrifice to her could assure smoother seas: Venus had the power to send Cupid to plant an arrow in the heart of the sea god Neptune, enrapturing him so that the seas stayed peaceful. The (male) sailors came up with a creative way of, ahem, "venerating" the goddess—by paying a visit to the *ierodulai* (priestesses) in this temple. (Today the word *iarusa* means "prostitute" in Sicilian.) This "sacred prostitution" kept the sailors safe...or so they told their wives.

Whatever may have happened on the top of Mount Eryx, there is a special feeling up here—something mystical in the mists that often cover the city.

• *Go back through the park to Via Roma and retrace your steps down past the pinkish church. Just past the church, where the road forks, bear right to find...*

❼ Erice's Shopping Streets

After enjoying sleepy back streets and communing with the town goddess, we've finally found our way to Erice's tourist gauntlet. While some shops seem tacky, their wares go way back. The **tapestries** with the zigzag pattern are unique to Erice. The frugal women of

Erice used to recycle clothing and fabric scraps, weaving strips together to make sturdy floor coverings. These days, the woven rag rugs are made into artful purses and tapestries. Some of the shops in Erice have looms; ask for a demo if you see one.

Continue straight as Via Roma turns into Via Guarnotti. At #26 (on the left, just before the overhead passage), you'll pass the Centro di Cultura Scientifica e Marjorana, an important **cultural center** and think tank for physicists, established here by a Trapani-born physics professor in 1963.

Walk farther, until you reach the tiny square of **Piazzetta San Domenico,** one of the loveliest in Erice. Take a look down little Via Antonio Cordici, which veers off from where you enter the square. Some of the shops along the right side of this street (at #22, #10, and #6) show the city's ancient roots: The arrangement of the shop door connected to a window was typical of shops in many towns in antiquity.

• *Via Antonio Cordici leads you right into the main square...*

❽ Piazza della Loggia

The lack of real services on this square—banks, markets, or pharmacies—is a reminder that Erice is mostly a tourist town these days, though there is a sleepy Town Hall, a small tourist information kiosk, and a lonely ATM. Even so, the square is a pleasant place for a drink at an outdoor table, if the weather is fine. Hang on, though—you're just steps away from the sweetest part of Erice.

• *Walk straight to the bottom of the square, then turn left down Via Vittorio Emanuele, where you'll find two of my recommended restaurants nearby. But first, ruin your appetite by dropping in at #14...*

❾ Pasticceria Maria Grammatico

Maria's bakery is an Erice institution, and her almond-based sweets have become famous in Italy. As a child in the 1950s, Maria was sent to live in a convent, where she learned baking techniques from the nuns. She worked long hours in the kitchens, crushing almonds by hand and producing sweets to sell. When she was old enough to leave, she took the recipes she'd learned and opened her own pastry shop—a rare thing for a woman to do at the time. Specialties include *tette delle monache* ("nuns' breasts"), *genovesi* (pastries with custard or ricotta filling), and fresh cannoli. Maria and her assistants can assemble a sampler tray of indulgent sweets if you can't decide where to start (daily 9:00-23:00).

• *Your Erice walk is finished. Use your sugar high to continue downhill a few more blocks on Via Vittorio Emanuele. You'll wind up at the Porta Trapani, right where we began.*

Sleeping and Eating in Erice

Sleeping: Erice is jammed with day-trippers in high season, but spending the night on the mountain—when it's quiet and you have the place to yourself—can be unforgettable. Particularly off-season, evening mists swirl, providing a romantic atmosphere, just as Venus would have wanted.

€€€ **Hotel Elimo** offers 21 bright rooms in a homey palazzo at the bottom of the main drag (no air-con in 3 economy rooms, terrace, Via Vittorio Emanuele 75, +39 0923 869 377, hotelelimo.it, info@hotelelimo.it, Floriana and Erina).

€ **B&B Bella Vista** has nine rooms in two old but tastefully modernized houses on a quiet back street. Many of the rooms have small kitchens; a few come with views, and everyone gets to take in the panorama during breakfast on the rooftop terrace (no elevator, Via Chiaramonte 25, +39 0923 194 1528, bellavistaerice.it, info@bellavistaerice.it).

Eating: Since Erice caters to tourists, its restaurants do, too. Choose wisely. Many restaurants close Nov-Easter.

€€ **La Pentolaccia**, in a 17th-century convent where cloistered nuns used to make sweets, serves a specialty of fish ravioli with swordfish, caper, mint, and eggplant sauce (closed Tue, Via Gian Filippo Guarnotta 17, +39 0923 869 099).

€€€ **Monte San Giuliano** makes a variety of rich pastas, such as seafood *cacio e pepe* and their namesake *busiate giulianao* with tomatoes, almonds, potatoes, and eggplant (closed Mon, Vicolo San Rocco 7, +39 0923 869 595).

€€ **Il Rifugio di Enea** offers basic coffee and snacks—handy for a light lunch. They also have a €€€ sit-down restaurant area with table service and higher prices. This is an unusual Erice eatery that's open all year (closed Wed, Via Vittorio Emanuele 28, +39 0923 869 142).

Favignana and the Egadi Islands

Just a half hour by boat from Trapani, the quiet Egadi (EH-gah-dee) Islands are a peaceful escape. The trio of islets—Marettimo, Levanzo, and ▲ Favignana—have ancient roots. This was the site of a pivotal naval battle between the Romans and Carthaginians in 241 BC; the Romans prevailed and crushed the Carthaginian fleet, claiming victory in the First Punic War. More recently, the sleepy islands were bases for lucrative tuna fishing. Favignana (fah-veen-YAH-nah) is the easiest to reach and has a fun-to-explore town, a good museum about the local fishing industry, and a few nice beaches reachable by bike. It makes a fun getaway from Trapani.

GETTING THERE

The seasonal Liberty Lines **hydrofoil** departs Trapani for Favignana from the dock on Via Ammiraglio Staiti. It's fast and easy to buy tickets online—the process is essentially the same as buying at the terminal, where you'll probably have to wait in a long line. In high season, it's smart to get a round-trip ticket; you'll sacrifice some flexibility, but you're guaranteed a seat on the ride back (€12-16 each way, roughly hourly, 30 minutes, last boat in each direction between 20:00-21:00 in high season, libertylines.it). Avoid the larger ferries from the ferry terminal nearby—they take much longer. On Favignana, the hydrofoil docks at the small harbor, just in front of the town.

VISITING FAVIGNANA

When you get off the boat, notice the humble fishing fleet of blue-and-white dinghies. Nearby are piles of nets and canopy-covered, stainless-steel fish-processing tables. Now pan to the right, where—across the harbor—you'll see a sprawling industrial facility, with smokestacks and big "garage doors" for boats, from the heyday of Favignana's commercial fisheries. This is now the fine Stabilimento Florio museum (more on that later).

Towering high above the old factory is the nearly perfect, conical-shaped **Mount Santa Caterina.** A fortress has stood atop this imposing spot since at least the ninth century; the version you see today was cobbled together under Spanish rule, in the late 15th century. If you're fit, you could hike up there in about 45 minutes. While there's nothing left in the fortress, the views are stupendous.

• *Now continue up the ramp into town.*

Bike Rental: Passing through a gauntlet of peddlers who wait for day-trippers to disembark, you'll reach a long, orange building with a row of handy rental shops, where you can rent a **bike** or a scooter. If you're spending more than a couple of hours on the island, a bike is a great way to get beyond the main town. (Try **Noleggio Campo** at Scalo San Leonardo 3, +39 0923 921 599.) The is-

Tuna Fishing

Fishing has always been important in western Sicily, and the sea's top prize used to be bluefin tuna. There were 21 *tonnare* (tuna canneries) in the province of Trapani at the end of the 1800s, packing high-quality tuna in olive oil for export. Trapani depended heavily on the tuna business for decades.

It all came to an end in the 1980s, when Japanese fishermen came to the Mediterranean and began tracking and netting schools of tuna in the open seas using new technologies. Their methods took not only the mature tuna but also young offspring. Few fish reached the traditional nets of Trapanese fishermen, and the local tuna fishery collapsed. Florio, the last remaining cannery on Favignana (once known as the queen of the *tonnara*), closed for good in 2007. The large, ancient cannery warehouses dotting the coast were left idle and empty; some have lately gained new life as museums and hotels (the Florio cannery is now a museum).

Tuna is still occasionally caught by local fishermen—especially in May and June, when the tuna migrate past Sicily. Fresh-caught tuna is now considered a delicacy and is very expensive. There is just one remaining cannery in Trapani, processing tuna from other places.

---

land is dotted with ancient stone quarries and ringed by scenic cliffs and small beaches. Riding from town out to the **Cala Azzurra**—a beautiful beachy bay at the southeast corner of the island (follow the brown signs on Via Frascia)—takes about 30 minutes and gives a quick overview of the island. The ride is mostly flat and easy.

• *After the bike-rental shops, turn right and head into town.*

Palazzo Florio and TI: The grand building you'll pass on the right is the Palazzo Florio, built by Ignazio Florio—a wealthy industrialist who bought the entire island (and its fishing rights) in the late 19th century. Today, the palazzo is a civic building that houses the TI (daily 10:00-14:00, closed Nov-March, +39 0923 925 443).

Piazza Europa and Piazza Madrice: After passing the palazzo, bear left to pop into the inviting Piazza Europa (with the recommended **U Coppu** eatery). At the end of the square, turn up Via Vittorio Emanuele, which passes the recommended **Pescheria Stella Maris** and takes you up the heart of Favignana's charming, mostly pedestrianized town center, culminating at the main square, Piazza Madrice. Check out the little **Capricci del Tonno** shop, selling old-school tins of tuna—which used to be the island's lifeblood (it's on the corner where you enter the square).

• *From Piazza Madrice, follow brown* Stabilimento Florio *signs leading south around the bay (primarily on Via Armando Diaz and Via Amendola). In less than 10 minutes you'll reach the massive...*

Stabilimento Florio Museum: The only real "sight" in town, this museum housed in a former tuna-processing plant is worth ▲. While there's limited English posted, the free English audioguide app helps explain well-presented exhibits on both ancient nautical combat and (in greater depth) the crucial tuna-fishing industry of more recent times. Just strolling through the vast complex is impressive (€10; usually daily 10:00-14:00 in summer—check locally before making the trip, closed Nov-March; free English audioguide app; +39 338 536 5899). Your visit includes a tour, but it's usually in Italian only (try emailing ahead to request one in English, info@tonnarafloriofavignana.it).

The first exhibit (straight ahead from the entrance) explains the **warships** of the Carthaginians and Romans, who fought the Battle of the Egadi Islands in 241 BC, which ended the First Punic War. You'll see third-century BC bronze rostrums (battering rams) that were attached to the bows of these ships and used to slash and sink enemy vessels, and piles of amphorae, the ancient containers used for transporting olives and liquids.

Then explore the old **fishing factory** (through the courtyard to the right). You'll see the cannery *(casa dell'olio)*, where tin cans are neatly lined up on stone tables, and an industrial-sized row of giant kettles, heated by three smokestacks. (Tuna must be cooked before it's canned, and then the cans are heated to complete the preservation process.) A large, darkened hall has video clips of local old-timers describing the old fishing industry (unfortunately, in untranslated Italian).

The visit culminates in a giant hall with three dry docks, where you can see massive old **wooden boats** pulled up on ramps. Illustrations show how the nets could be spread out in this huge hall, and how they were used to block off the mouth of the bay and funnel tuna toward the fishermen's waiting boats.

Eating on Favignana: Prices are much higher here than in Trapani, but it's fun to have lunch on the island. For a fine fish meal, €€€€ **Quello che C'e C'e** has a friendly feel and good pasta in the town center (daily, from main drag head right down Via Garibaldi to #38, +39 923 567 699). A bit more affordable is €€ **Spaghetteria Pakkaro,** an unpretentious pasta shop tucked around the right side of the town church (daily, Piazza Madrice 26, +39 328 061 3380). €€ **Pescheria Stella Maris** is a third-generation seafood joint serving paper cones of fried ocean critters and appetizing panini. If the *Tuna Oggi* sign is hanging up, it means they're serving fresh tuna—a real treat (daily, Via Vittorio Emanuele 31, +39 320 284 7478, Campo family). For a quick bite on the go, try € **U Coppu,** near the port; they have deep-fried seafood, sandwiches, and other street food (daily, Piazza Europa 33, +39 328 907 2598).

Mozia Island and Salt Flats

The little island of Mozia, south of Trapani, once supported a trading post, one of a few Carthaginian settlements (including Palermo) on Sicily's west side. A town with defensive walls and a port prospered here for centuries—until Dionysius I of Siracusa sacked it in 397 BC. Now privately owned, pleasant Mozia (MOHT-zee-yah) is today little more than a picnic destination—but it's also home to a worthwhile small museum of Greek, Carthaginian, and Roman artifacts. And the salt flats *(saline)* in the shallow lagoon between the island and the mainland are some of Europe's oldest in continuous operation.

Planning Your Time: Mozia pairs perfectly with a trip to the salt flats. The island and the Ettore and Infersa Salt Mill (Mulinao delle Saline Ettore e Infersa) are about 30 minutes south of Trapani and can easily be combined in a day trip—the boat for the island departs directly from a pier near the salt mill/visitors center (see details later).

Mozia Island and Salt Flats

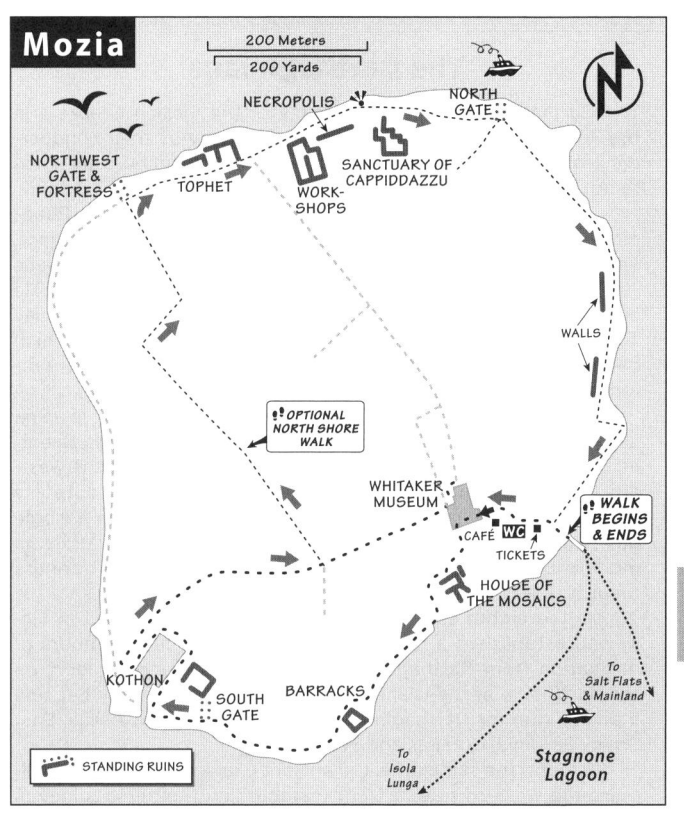

MOZIA ISLAND

Here, nature, birds, vineyards, archaeological digs of Carthaginian ruins, and a few fine ancient artifacts peacefully coexist. As ancient sites go, there's very little to see. But the boat ride to the island—through salt flats and the Stagnone lagoon marine park—is enjoyable, and the small museum is engaging. For those with an appetite to learn more about the Carthaginians, the trip to Mozia is worth ▲ and a few hours.

Getting There: Two different companies run boats to the island. I prefer the handy **Mozia Line,** which departs from a pier south of the town of Ettore Infersa, about a 30-minute drive from Trapani. The boat trip is quick (10 minutes), mellow, and scenic, though it can be canceled in bad weather (€5 round-trip; daily 9:15-18:30, Nov-March until 15:00, runs about every 30 minutes; €10 one-hour lagoon tour also available, +39 338 786 0474, mozialine.com, Mario). Buy your Mozia Line ticket from the kiosk; you'll buy another ticket on the island that entitles you to stroll around and visit the Whitaker Museum there.

The Carthaginians

The Carthaginians—the great enemy of the Sicilian Greeks and the Romans—were largely erased from history by their conquerors, leaving nothing written in their own words. But here are a few things we do know.

The Carthaginians were successors of the seafaring Phoenicians (themselves originally from today's Syria and Lebanon). The Phoenicians were great traders; their name roughly means "the purple people," as they were known for trading rare purple cloth. Around 1000 BC, the Phoenicians colonized modern-day Tunisia, founding a "New City"—Kart Hadascht (Carthage), which became a major trading center in the Mediterranean. History refers to these colonizers as the Carthaginians.

Their talented craftsmen specialized in textiles, jewelry, ivory, glazed majolica tiles, and glass. To trade their goods, talented Carthaginian navigators founded colonies all around the western Mediterranean, establishing a network of trading outposts every 25 nautical miles—the distance they could sail in a single day. They settled as far south as the Atlantic coast of Africa, in modern-day Mauritania. In order to keep track of their business records, they invented a phonetic alphabet with 22 letters.

In the eighth century BC, the Carthaginians arrived in Sicily and established a colony in Motya (Mozia)—just 24 hours of navigation from Carthage. They later founded another port on the north side of the island, Panormus (Palermo). Sicily became a pivotal hub for Carthaginian trade between North Africa, East Spain, Sardinia, Corsica, and West Italy.

Around the same time, the ancient Greeks also began to colonize the western side of Sicily (establishing their first colony in 734 BC—for details, see "The Greeks in Sicily," on page 303). The Carthaginians fought against their Greek neighbors for control of the island and the sea. They raided towns from their home base

To reach Mozia Line's boat dock by **car** from Trapani, leave town heading south on SP-21, following signs for *Marsala* and *Birgi* (Trapani's airport). After passing the airport and going through the village of Ettore Infersa, follow brown roundabout signs to *Mozia* and *Riserva Naturale dello Stagnone*. When you hit the T-intersection at the shoreline, turn left and drive toward the salt flats; watch for parking on the right. The ticket kiosk is in the parking lot, near the dock.

Without a car, you can take a **tour** from Trapani or hire your own **driver;** I like working with Michelangelo Marchingiglio (€150 round-trip transfer, €160 half-day guided tour of salt flats and Mozia, for contact information, see "Tours in and near Trapani," earlier).

Island/Museum Cost and Hours: €10, includes admission to

at Mozia, eventually establishing dominance over western Sicily. The Greeks took revenge by brutally sacking the large city of Selinunte in 409 BC and Akragas (Agrigento) in 403 BC—bringing forces of 100,000 men, incredible armies for the time.

A new power rising in the Mediterranean would be Carthage's greatest rival—the Romans. Three Punic Wars ("Punic" coming from "Phoenician") pitted the two great powers in a war of attrition (264-146 BC). The most famous conflict featured the Carthaginian general Hannibal, who marched against Rome with his army, mounted on elephants, traveling from Spain over the Alps.

Ultimately, Rome prevailed. Roman Senator Cato the Elder took to ending all of his public orations with an appeal: *Carthago delenda est*—"Carthage must be destroyed." And so it was. The Romans set about erasing the existence of Carthaginian culture—destroying their cities and wiping out their history. The only accounts of the Carthaginians are written not by their own scribes, but by their Greek and Roman contemporaries. Some archaeologists consider these accounts, which portray the Carthaginians as rootless pirates who engaged in human sacrifice, as unreliable propaganda intended to defame an enemy.

The complete truth of Carthaginian civilization may never be fully understood. The Phoenicians are credited with inventing an alphabet, but other than funeral inscriptions, there's nothing that records their grand past. We have no names of Carthaginian philosophers, writers, or historians. When visiting the archaeological area of Carthage, only Roman ruins are left—built over the remains of the razed city. Considering how very few remnants of the ancient Carthaginians survive, even the traces at the archaeological site of Mozia become remarkable.

---

the island and its Whitaker Museum; museum open daily 9:30-13:30 & 14:30-18:30, Nov-March 9:00-15:00; +39 349 625 6508, fondazionewhitaker.it.

Avoiding Bugs: Mozia is often full of mosquitoes. Apply bug repellent before your visit (buy it at a mainland pharmacy).

Eating: Near the mainland boat dock, the big **€€ Mamma Caura** restaurant overflows with gray tables and has pricey cocktails and decent, basic food with a great view over the salt pans (closed Tue). Over on Mozia Island, there's a fine little **€ café** with good sandwiches and pleasant, shady seating. Both are open basically whenever the boats are running.

Background

In the middle of the lagoon called Stagnone, Mozia is a private island purchased by Joseph "Pip" Whitaker in the late 19th century. Whitaker was part of a wealthy English family that came to Sicily to make their fortune in the Marsala-wine business (for more on that industry, see the "Marsala Wine" sidebar, earlier). Like other upper-class men of the time, he collected art and studied ancient cultures. Whitaker had an interest in archaeology and suspected that there were ruins of a lost Phoenician city hidden underground. He initiated archaeological digs and—sure enough—unearthed the Carthaginian colony of Motya. A gratified Whitaker rechristened the island with its historical name, Mozia.

Mozia Island Walk

Enjoy the boat ride over—first you'll cut through the middle of the salt pans, then ply the lagoon's shallow waters...just a few feet deep. On the way you'll see stacks of tiles lining the pans—these were, or will become, protective roofing for pyramids of salt. Notice the captain sighting poles to navigate around rocks. The island is tiny—less than a quarter of a square mile; you can walk from one end to the other in about 15 minutes, or follow my walking directions to circle the island.

• *As you exit the boat, walk uphill toward the island/museum ticket booth. Just past that, you'll reach some info boards. WCs are to the left; beyond the info boards, you'll find a café, and past that, the entrance to the...*

Whitaker Museum

This modest museum displays artifacts from the Whitaker archaeological digs on the island as well as from the area between Trapani Birgi (near the airport) and Marsala. Archaeology wasn't carried out in a professional, systematic way in Sicily until the 1920s; wealthy nobles studied ancient history for fun and did their own excavations as a hobby, often selling entire collections abroad. Since Whitaker owned the island, he excavated as he pleased—and collected his finds into this homegrown museum.

As you enter, grab a flyer with a map and basic information on the sights around the island. Later, as you explore the sights, you'll find signboards in English with more details.

Enter the room on the left. Use the **aerial photo** of Mozia to get familiar with island features you'll see during your visit. Nearby is a model of the rectangular Kothon, a sacred pool. To the right is a small model of the North Gate of ancient Motya. This gate—with its tall towers—suggests how the wall of the city might have looked.

Proceeding through the museum, you'll reach the exquisite (and mysterious) marble statue dubbed the **Youth of Motya,** from the fifth century BC. His identity is unknown, his posture enigmatic. Is he a role model of Greek beauty and harmony striking a pose? Is he a charioteer on parade after winning the Olympics? Is he a portrait of a long-forgotten VIP? What is known is that this Greek statue was found in a Carthaginian city, which means it was either purchased by a rich merchant or brought back from the conquest of a Greek city.

In the next room, pause at the glass case in the middle. The **seashells** displayed here contain a pigment used to dye textiles that made the Carthaginians famous in ancient times. To make just one gram of the precious purple pigment, 10,000 shells were needed—making the dye as valuable as gold. That's why purple was the color of emperors and kings in ancient times: It was so expensive that only the ruling class could afford it.

Continue into the room with a wall of **funeral stones.** These limestone *steles* were found in the *tophet* (burial ground) in the eastern part of Mozia (you'll see it later if you take the walk to the north shore). The slabs have symbols and writing in Phoenician.

Find the terra-cotta **mask** in the glass case on the opposite side of the room. It has sorrowful eyes but cheerful cheeks. Carthaginians are thought (by some) to have made human sacrifices to their gods in times of crisis. Because this mask was found in the *tophet*, a possible place of sacrifice, it's tempting to think the mask depicts the Carthaginian attitude toward human sacrifice: a smile for the good the offering might bring, but tears of sadness at the same time. But like so many ancient works, it is difficult to recapture what motivated the artist.

Now head in the direction the mask is looking. Pause at the partition with photographs of the **Whitaker family.** Look for Pip Whitaker and his two daughters, Norina and Delia. Norina married General Antonino di Giorgio, minister of war under Benito Mussolini. Before she died in 1971, Delia left instructions for the creation of the Fondazione Whitaker—a nonprofit foundation dedicated to the preservation and maintenance of Mozia, and research on the Carthaginian civilization.

Continue into the room on the other side of the partition, the **Pip Whitaker Room.** Objects here have been left as Pip planned, some still labeled with tags in his handwriting. In the first half of the room there are findings from the ancient Carthaginian city of Lilibeo (at modern-day Marsala): vases, terra-cotta statuettes, lamps, tiny glass jars, and containers. In the middle is a sculpture of two lions attacking a bull, with fragments of Mozia's fortifications—originally this stood on the upper part of the North Gate. On the far side of the room are fishing hooks, earrings, arrowheads in bronze, loom weights, and ostrich eggs used in burial rituals.

• *Exiting the museum, make a right. Near the end of the concrete patio, go left down a dirt path toward the sea. You'll soon come to an excavation, part of which has a little roof. This is the...*

House of the Mosaics (Casa dei Mosaici)

Survey these ruins to spot scant mosaics made with black and white pebbles. The mosaics depict animals, including lions, bulls, and a lion jumping on a bull. The complex mosaics of the Roman Empire have their roots in this simple type of stonework using cheap materials. This ruin was once a wealthy home with an enclosed courtyard.

• *Now head down to the water and continue along the peaceful southern shore of the island, with the lagoon on your left. As you stroll, you'll notice the city of Marsala coming into view on the horizon. Stay on the path and pause when you reach the ruins on your left.*

Barracks (Casermetta)

The island was heavily fortified with high walls and surrounded by a shallow lagoon. These ruins were probably military barracks or a watchtower, originally built near a tower in the walls. The Carthaginians carefully planned their settlements so each was within a day's sailing time, and any call for help could be answered quickly. The people must have felt very safe here, but the city came to a terrible end. The Syracusans surprised them with

an attack using mobile siege towers, which allowed the attackers to easily scale Mozia's walls. While the fight raged, the call for help was answered, but reinforcements were blocked by a Syracusan

fleet waiting in the open sea. Nobody arrived to save the citizens of Mozia, and the city was mercilessly crushed. The men who suffered the most were Greeks living in Mozia, who were considered traitors to their culture.
• *Continue along the coastal trail. Gradually, the long, skinny island called Isola Lunga comes into view. Mozia is just one of three islands in the lagoon; Isola Lunga acts as a barrier island, separating the open sea from brackish waters.*

Pause when you reach the big, rectangular pool on your left.

Kothon

This pool was originally thought to be a dry dock for ships. But a few years ago, the University of Rome excavated and drained the pool. They discovered that spring water was continuously refilling it, and they found a stone pedestal with fragments of feet that corresponded to a statue of a god unearthed nearby. This, along with recently excavated circular walls, made archaeologists change their minds: Now they believe the pool was used for sacred bathing and religious rituals.

• *Circle around the pool, cross the metal bridge, and head back uphill toward the museum, passing vineyards on your left, then on your right. From here, you have two choices: Return to the museum and grab a bite at the café or hop on the boat back to the mainland. Or, if you're intrigued by the Carthaginians and want to see more, turn left at the* Tophet/Necropolis *sign to extend your visit by about 20-30 minutes and walk to the island's north shore.*

Optional Detour: North Shore

The path takes you about 10 minutes across the middle of the island, through serene vineyards. Keep straight at the fork—you'll pop out at the scant remains of the **Northwest Gate and Fortress.** Continuing on the path from here, ahead on your left are the ruins of a *tophet*—a sanctuary and burial ground that scholars speculate may have been a site for human sacrifices; the funeral *steles* and the mask we saw in the museum were found here. The ruins just past the *tophet* housed **workshops** used for producing ceramics and textiles—including fabrics using the purple pigment from the seashells you saw in the museum.

Continuing along the north-shore path, you'll pass a **necropolis** with tombs dating as far back as the eighth century BC.

Look out over the water: On a sunny, windy day, you might spot kite-flyers and kite-surfers frolicking in the bay at the end of Isola Lunga. Erice looms over Trapani in the distance. You also may hear fighter jets screaming overhead: The mainland Birgi airport is used by NATO planes.

After a few minutes, you'll reach the **Sanctuary of Cappiddazzu,** the main temple of the city, used for rituals and animal sacrifices. First erected in eighth century BC on the highest point on the island, it began as little more than a field with an altar. A shrine was added in the sixth century BC, and the temple was reconstructed after Mozia was destroyed in 397 BC.

From here, veer left, following signs to the *Porta Nord*. Walk all the way to the water's edge and turn around to take in the twin, stubby bases of what was the **North Gate** of the island, with ruins of shops and a main street. This is where the Youth of Motya sculpture was found in 1979. At the shoreline, you'll find traces of a submerged road, which used to link the island to the mainland.

From here, continue strolling with the water on your left. This path will take you all the way back to the boat dock in just a few minutes, and along the way you'll see more fragments of the mighty **wall** that once defended Mozia.

As you walk, ponder this: Mozia is an area of 110 acres, but only a quarter of it has been excavated. Imagine what else could be found. For now, the Whitaker foundation has planted vineyards in the empty fields, allowing new vines to grow alongside the ruins.

SALT FLAT EXPERIENCES

Salt flats sprawl for several miles between Trapani and Marsala; you may see workers tending the salt pans in the shallow lagoon dotted with windmills. While visiting the salt flats, watch for flamingos, herons, egrets, and cormorants—the area is a protected reserve for the many bird species that migrate between Africa and Europe. The museums here dedicated to salt aren't standouts, but all in all visiting the flats is a unique experience worth ▲. For more on this industry, see the "Salt Harvesting" side-

Salt Harvesting

Carthaginians began harvesting salt in the area south of modern Trapani in the eighth century BC. They used the salt to  cure the fish they caught, mostly tuna. Salt remained a precious resource for more than three millennia—highly valued for its ability to preserve food (in an age before refrigeration). Throughout Europe, salt was worth its weight in gold. The ancient Romans paid their workers a *salario* (from *sale*, the Latin word for "salt"). To this day, when a Sicilian thinks something is too expensive, she might say *"salato!"* (meaning "salted").

Salt was also an important export, traded as far away as Norway for preserving cod for long sea voyages. The Norwegians sent back boatloads of the preserved cod, explaining why that cold-water fish is oddly popular in Sicily and the rest of Italy. Salt remained an important commodity through the late 19th century, when the Trapani area alone had about 40 salt flats. Nowadays, the number of active salt flats is fewer than 10.

The Trapani area is ideal for salt harvesting because of its breezy yet sunny climate and its very shallow, smooth, clay-lined seabed. Ocean water is moved through progressively shallower man-made pools over the course of the summer to evaporate the water and filter out impurities. The color of water in the basins—from blue to orange to pink to milky white—varies based on the depth and the salt concentration. The pink color results when the water becomes so concentrated with salt that the only thing surviving in it is an algae that produces beta carotene.

The antique windmills scattered in the flats—a unique feature of Trapani salt harvesting—powered an Archimedes screw that moved water from the sea into the starting basin. Wind power also drove the grindstones that reduced the coarse, chunky salt into a more useable powder.

Salt is harvested from June to September. While most production is now mechanized, the best-quality salt is harvested by hand—a labor-intensive practice. Imagine shoveling heavy loads of salt, in blazing heat, with the sun reflecting like a mirror off the water and salt. The salt is stacked in elongated pyramids to dry and covered over the winter with terra-cotta roof tiles to protect it from rain. The following spring, the previous season's harvest is ground, packaged, and shipped.

Traditional sea salt went through hard times, but it's newly en vogue with cooks and foodies. Most lucrative is *fiore di sale* (better known by its French name, *fleur de sel*). This is the first salt skimmed off the basin in July.

bar; for locations, see the "Trapani and the West Coast" map near the beginning of this chapter.

Salt Flat Options

There are two opportunities to get an up-close look at the salt pans, to learn about the salt-harvesting process, and to walk through a windmill. If you're **going to Mozia,** opt for the Ettore and Infersa Salt Mill, located on the pier where the ferry to the island docks. Overall it's a better, fuller experience than your second option, the Museum of Salt, which is just a 20-minute drive from Trapani, but only worthwhile if you're up for the lengthy guided tour.

Ettore and Infersa Salt Mill (Mulino delle Saline Ettore e Infersa)

Your visit starts with an interesting 10-minute film that explains (in English) the entire salt-harvesting process. Afterward, you'll explore meager exhibits with traditional tools and a few touchscreens, then walk up the tight, stone spiral stairs to the terrace with the windmill.

Cost and Hours: €8; daily 9:00-19:00, until 20:00 in summer, may close Jan-Feb; on pier by Mozia Line ferry, +39 0923 733 003, seisaline.it. They also organize guided one-hour visits to the salt flats (€16, in English and Italian, April-Oct usually daily at 12:00 and 17:00, more in summer).

Getting There: Follow the directions for Mozia Island on page 187.

Museum of Salt (Museo del Sale)

This family-owned salt-harvesting facility goes back generations. Under a classic old windmill, a dusty three-room museum displays traditional tools of the trade. What brings the place to life is the 75-minute tour led by a member of the family—it's really the only reason to come here. You can usually get an English tour just by asking at the entry, but it's a good idea to confirm by phone before making the trip. At the end of the visit, you can climb up onto the rooftop for a closer look at the 600-year-old windmill and views of the salt flats, the old town of Trapani, and Erice's mountain on the horizon.

Cost and Hours: €5, €3 extra to walk through the working salt pans out back, €16 tours run on demand daily 9:30-19:00; Via Chiusa, in the town of Nubia; mobile +39 320 657 5455, museodelsale.it. A €€ trattoria is on-site (July-Aug closed Sun, Sept-June closed Mon).

Getting There: Head south from Trapani's port on SP-21 and watch for the turnoff on the right to *Nubia*, then follow brown *Museo del Sale* signs.

Selinunte

Near the southwestern tip of Sicily, ▲ Selinunte (seh-lee-NOON-teh), a once-thriving Greek settlement, lies in ruins like a pile of Legos. The city once covered 250 acres, making the archaeological park a large, picturesque spot. Today it's an evocative collection of temples—one reconstructed, another partially intact, and the rest a heap of toppled columns—spread over two different areas. Agrigento's Valley of the Temples takes top billing among ancient sites in this part of Sicily, but Selinunte is a worthwhile stop, conveniently situated between Trapani and Agrigento.

Note that many of Seliunte's sculptures are displayed not on-site, but at the Salinas Regional Archaelogical Museum in Palermo.

GETTING THERE

Located on the southwestern coast, Selinunte is about an hour's drive from Trapani, or a 1.5-hour drive from Agrigento. From Trapani, take the main highway, SS-113, back toward Palermo. Just past Segesta, follow signs south to *Mazara del Vallo* on A-29. Exit the highway at Castelvetrano, take a left from the offramp, then the next left, following brown signs to *Selinunte*. The archaeological park is about 20 minutes down the road; park at the main entrance just past the concrete roundabout on the right.

PLANNING YOUR TIME

The site has two major sections, on adjacent hilltops overlooking the sea: the temples in the Eastern Agora (Agorà Orientale; also called the Eastern Hill or Collina Orientale) and the Acropolis. On a quick visit, the Eastern Agora temples are the priority—you can see them in under an hour. With another hour, walk over to the Acropolis. A third area—the Malophoros—is skippable.

Note that Selinunte sits just a 20-minute drive from the town of Castelvetrano, which is synonymous with its famous, plump ol-

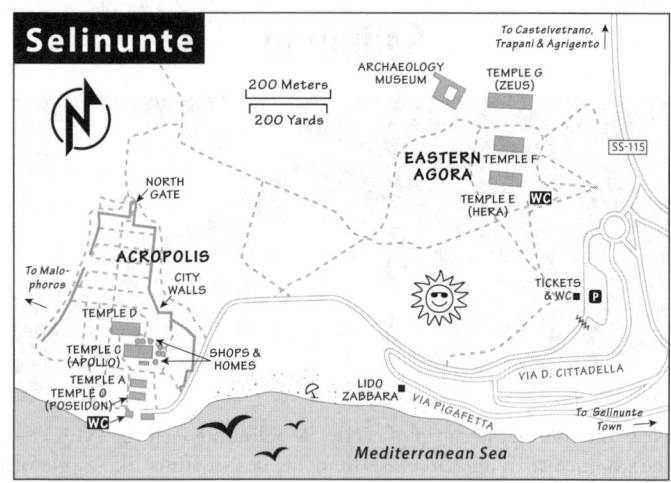

ives. While you might be tempted to explore the town, don't bother—it's pretty much the pits, and might spoil your affection for its famous product.

ORIENTATION TO SELINUNTE

Cost and Hours: €14; daily 9:00-20:00, Nov-Feb until 17:00, March until 18:00; last entry one hour before closing, audioguide-€5, +39 0924 46277, coopculture.it (search "Selinunte").

Getting Around the Site: A shuttle service runs from the Eastern Agora to the Acropolis and back to the entrance (€8, purchase at the entrance or from the archaeological museum). Walking the entire site is about three miles.

Services: In the Eastern Agora section, WCs are in a building just to the right of Temple E, and there's a decent café inside the archaeological museum. In the Acropolis, WCs and a small bar are near Temple O.

Eating Nearby (and at the beach): A few scruffy, touristy cafés face the parking lot; more are on nearby streets. In the warmer months, it's worth venturing to the nearby beachfront village of Selinunte, with a fun strip of eateries (to get there, as you exit the archeological site take the second right at the roundabout; head downhill and veer to the right when the road hits seashore). The most appealing of these—popular with tour groups—is the last one you'll reach: **€€ Lido Zabbara** offers a lunch buffet with a tempting table of regional specialties, plus other basic light meals à la carte. It's a rustic, boardwalky spot overlooking a private beach where you can pay to rent an umbrella and chairs, and swim with a temple view (buffet available March-Oct daily 11:30-16:30, beach open May-Oct, Via Pigafetta 1, +39 0924 46194).

BACKGROUND

Selinunte was established in 628 BC as a colony of Megara Hyblea, a Greek city on the eastern coast of Sicily. For two centuries, Selinunte grew and prospered. But this expansion caused friction with the city on its northern border, Segesta—an Elymian city under the protection of Carthage. (For more on Segesta, see page 129.)

The Greeks on the east and south coasts and the Carthaginians in the west were in constant conflict, fighting over control of Sicily. In 480 BC, the Sicilian Greeks—led by the tyrant of Syracuse—won a massive battle against the Carthaginians at Himera. The Segestans lost their powerful ally and needed a new protector. They called out to mighty Athens, the enemy of Sparta and Syracuse.

In 415-413 BC, the Athenians sent an expedition to battle Syracuse and lost. Four years later, the Carthaginians invaded in full force, and, after a nine-day siege, defeated Selinunte before help could arrive from Syracuse. The city was almost totally destroyed, but the Carthaginians decided to move in, inhabiting the Acropolis and setting up temples to their own gods.

Two centuries later, the Romans conquered Sicily, setting the stage for a new conflict with Carthage. The remaining Carthaginians at Selinunte moved to their stronghold at Lilibeo (modern Marsala), and Selinunte was abandoned for good.

VISITING THE SITE

Begin at the trio of temples of the Eastern Agora. After buying your ticket, go out back and head for the big temple. While a few info boards are posted around the site, most visitors simply treat Selinunte as one big toppled-column photo op.

Eastern Agora

The first temple you reach is the remarkably big and intact **Temple E.** There's just one problem: It's not original. This temple was reassembled in the 1950s—a practice that archaeologists today would never consider. (Reconstructing a temple willy-nilly and moving blocks around can change the interpretation of the site.) On the other hand, this is one of the few Greek temples in Sicily you can actually enter. Climb up the steps and walk around the interior. The peristyle (outer line of columns) is fairly intact, but the inner sanctum (cella) is just a footprint.

A Typical Greek Temple

Greek temples, built to house the cult image of a god, follow the same basic layout, with an inner chamber surrounded by a parade of columns. Important activities mostly took place outside, at an altar in front of the temple doors.

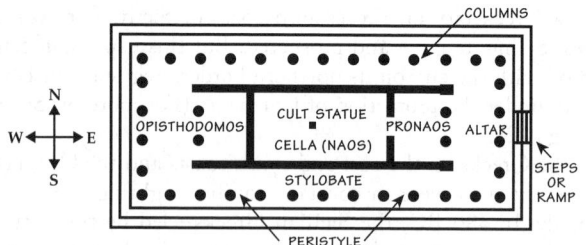

Pronaos: Small vestibule or porch, the entry to the cella

Cella (or Naos): The heart of the temple, where the cult image of the god was kept

Opisthodomos: Rear chamber, usually with no access to the cella and sometimes used as a treasury

Peristyle: Colonnade, the columns surrounding the cella

Stylobate: Platform on which the peristyle stands

Ponder what it might have taken to construct temples like these. It wasn't easy to transport such huge blocks of stone over large distances, but Greek ingenuity devised clever ways, such as affixing wheels to the ends of column pieces so that they could roll from the quarry to the building site.

Farther on is **Temple F,** about the same size as Temple E but still mostly ruined, with a half-dozen stubby columns poking up. A stroll around this temple offers a good look at toppled columns—like great towers of checkers knocked over by a giant toddler. You can see clearly the indentation in the center of each drum, where it was attached to the next one with pegs.

Next up is **Temple G,** a massive pile of monumental rubble. This was once set to be among the largest temples ever constructed in the Greek world. Measuring over 300 feet long and 150 feet wide, it would have

been as tall as a modern 10-story building. Only one lonely column remains standing. The temple, which should have been similar in size to the Temple of Olympian Zeus at Agrigento, was never completed. A nearby quarry, the Cava di Cusa, still holds cut blocks, waiting for delivery to the temple. It's worth walking all the way around Temple G, noticing the massive circumference of its toppled column drums compared to Temple F—big temple, big columns.

The building between Temple G and the sea houses a modest **archaeological museum,** called Baglio Florio. Despite displaying only scant artifacts, it does a semi-decent job re-creating what the sight would have looked like while it was inhabited. If you're short on time, or not particularly interested, it's skippable; the best finds from Selinunte are on display at Palermo's Salinas Regional Archaeological Museum (see page 60).

Looking out to sea, you'll spot a ruined colonnade on the adjacent hilltop—our next stop.

• *From here it's a 20-minute walk over to the second area of Selinunte. Head downhill from the museum on the paved lane; in the little valley, follow the first shortcut branching off left through the trees, then head right up another paved path toward the...*

Acropolis

Above the sea, to the west of the temples, is the city center at the Acropolis. Huffing up the road, notice the stout city walls of this fully enclosed, well-fortified city.

Past the two modern buildings, climb up the low stone stairs toward the still-standing colonnade of the Acropolis' centerpiece, **Temple C**—what's left of a temple to Apollo. Loop around this structure, surrounded by toppled columns and the remains of other temples.

Even more interesting, perhaps, are the foundations of **shops and homes** that surround the Temple C ruins. Explore, imagining what it was like when this was a thriving city. From the stony footprints, try to mentally resurrect the rubble: people scurrying to and fro, shopkeepers calling out their wares, and so on. A few doorstep mosaics still survive, which would have indicated what each shop sold. Facing Temple C after coming up the steps, look left along the lane, past the shade tree with the bench, to find a roped-off area displaying an example of one of the simple stone mosaics.

North from the Temple C ruins, just after the mosaic, a wide "street" leads through a part of the Acropolis that's unexcavated and overgrown with bushes—but you can clearly see where the city blocks once stood. At the far end of this drag, you'll come to the stout ruins of the city's **North Gate.**

• *When you're ready to return to the entrance you can either catch the shuttle or walk about 15 minutes. The quickest way on foot is to head down the paved road, follow signs to* Uscita *taking you up the hill, then take the first path on the left (near the top of the hill). Keep right, on the paved path. The first trail on the right leads directly back to the ticket office.*

AGRIGENTO & THE VALLEY OF THE TEMPLES

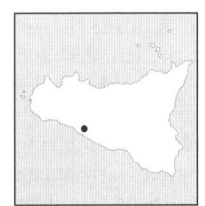

Of all the ancient sites in Sicily, the string of Greek temples on the southwest coast at Agrigento is the most impressive. In the fifth century BC, Agrigento had a population of 200,000 and was the third-largest city in the ancient Greek world (after Athens and Syracuse). To realize that 2,500 years ago two of the top three cities in the Greek world were in Sicily is another reminder of the often-underestimated importance of this island in ancient times.

Today, the modern city of Agrigento (pop. 60,000) fills a hillside above the Valley of the Temples—an ensemble of ancient temples unlike anything you'll see elsewhere. Visitors to the temples enjoy a long, scenic downhill stroll, with stops at some of the best surviving buildings from antiquity. Nearby, a fine museum filled with artifacts offers a glimpse into the culture of ancient Agrigento.

The Greeks began colonizing Sicily's eastern coast in the eighth century BC. About 150 years later, the now-Sicilian Greeks (Siceliots) established a colony here, calling it Akragas, which quickly became one of their wealthiest city-states. They displayed their prowess by building 15 grand temples in under 80 years, rivaling the great temples of Greece itself. Imagine the impression this must have made on sailors from all corners of the Mediterranean as they approached by sea. A destination for young aristocrats on their Grand Tour of continental Europe in the 18th century, this ancient ensemble stirred painters and poets of the Romantic Age—and has inspired visitors ever since.

PLANNING YOUR TIME

While most tourists come just for a few hours to see the ancient site, Agrigento is worth a full day. Those who stay the night can enjoy the modern city's historic center or the surrounding countryside. A good plan is to arrive by midday, tour the museum, then see the temples as it's cooling off and getting less crowded (the temples are open late and romantically illuminated after dark). If you're overnighting here, enjoy the *passeggiata* in the town center (see my Agrigento Town Walk, later), then settle into an in-town or countryside hotel before heading out the next morning.

How to structure your visit also depends on your transportation and the season. For drivers, the best plan is to see the archaeological museum first (setting the stage for the temples) and then visit the temple site. By bus/taxi, it's simpler to see the temples first, then the museum (note closing times). From May through September, it's smart to visit the air-conditioned museum during the blazing midday and see the temples before or after (early or late in the day). In the peak of summer (mid-July-mid-Sept), consider visiting the temples in the relative cool of the evening.

GETTING THERE

Agrigento is about a two-hour drive south of Palermo. It makes a good stop on any circuit of the island, whether traveling east from Trapani or west from Catania or Ragusa. Without a car, you can reach Agrigento by train or bus from Palermo or by bus from Trapani or Catania (see "Agrigento Connections" at the end of this chapter).

The Valley of the Temples Archaeological Park sits about 1.5 miles south of the modern town. (The moniker is something of a misnomer—although downhill from the city center, the temples string along a ridge rather than in a "valley.") The Pietro Griffo Archaeological Museum and half of my recommended hotels are between the temples and the modern town. The rest are in Agrigento or the countryside (within 20 minutes of the city).

By Car: To reach the **temples and museum** directly from Trapani and points west, as you approach on coastal road SS-115, you'll pass through congested Porto Empedocle. On the far side of Porto Empedocle, when the road forks, bear left to stay on the main road, signed *Caltanissetta, Palermo,* and *Siracusa*—don't turn off to the right for *Agrigento*. Continue on SS-115/SS-640 for about three miles, then take the exit (SP-4 north) to Agrigento. (If com-

Agrigento & the Valley of the Temples   205

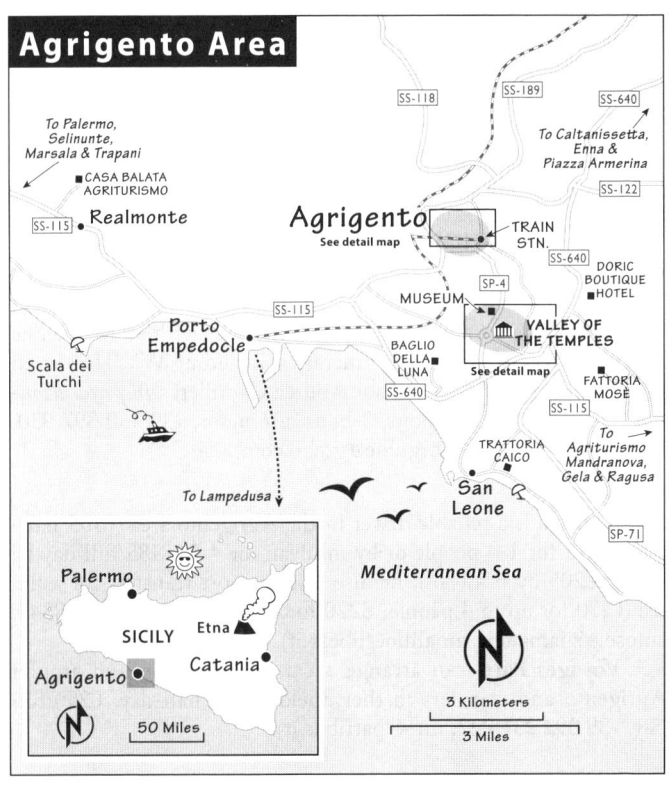

ing across the middle of the island from Palermo and points north, follow signs to *Valle dei Templi* to reach this same exit.)

At the big roundabout where SP-4 meets Via Giuseppe la Loggia, for the **museum,** continue straight (second exit), following blue signs to *Agrigento*. You'll drive under a pedestrian bridge and through the temple area, pass the museum on your left, and then turn into the easy-to-miss pay parking lot entrance (next to the gas station, beyond the museum on Via Passeggiata Archeologica).

For the **temples,** at the roundabout, take the third exit (heading west), following signs to *Villaseta* and *Valle dei Templi ingresso Porta V*. Look for the blue *P* signs to reach the **Porta V** pay parking lot and entrance (on your left).

By Taxi, by Bus, or on Foot: Taxis and city buses connect modern Agrigento's bus and train stations to the temples and museum (see "Getting Around the Valley of the Temples," later. It's about a 10-minute ride by **taxi** (€10-15—be clear on the price before you get in; Agrigento Taxi Coop, +39 327 496 4365). Buses make the trip roughly hourly and take about 10 minutes (€1.20, €1.70 if purchased on board, €3.40/24 hours).

It's also possible to **walk** from town to the archaeological park or museum in about 40 minutes. To reach the Temple of Juno entrance, take Via Francesco Crispi to Via Panoramica dei Templi. To reach the museum, take Via Francesco Crispi to Via Passeggiata Archeologica. Both destinations are downhill and the routes generally have sidewalks.

TOURS IN AGRIGENTO
Local Guide
Michele Gallo is a scholar of archaeology and leads an excellent tour of the temples and the museum. For those with more time, he offers a variety of interesting itineraries, including WWII-focused tours and one for fans of author Andrea Camilleri's *Inspector Montalbano* mysteries (€80/hour, 2-hour minimum, +39 360 397 930, sicilytravel.net, gallotourguide@gmail.com).

Local Drivers
Lillo Amato is a reliable driver in the Agrigento area (€165/half-day by car for 1-4 people or by minivan for 4-8; €185/full day by car or €205 by minivan); he also does airport transfers for a flat fee (€170 for up to 4 people, €220 for up to 8, +39 335 661 8345, autoserviziamato.it, amalillo@libero.it).

Voyages Patti can arrange a car and driver in and around Agrigento and transfers farther afield (€200/half-day, €250/full day, +39 092 231 222, info@pattibus.it).

Valley of the Temples

A complete visit to the Valley of the Temples has two main parts about a half-mile apart: the Valley of the Temples Archaeological Park and the Pietro Griffo Archaeological Museum. Allow about two hours for the archaeological park and one hour for the museum.

Getting Around the Valley of the Temples: The **archaeological park** has two entrances, reachable by car, bus, or taxi: The **Temple of Juno** entrance is at the eastern end, at the top of the hill (served by bus #2/); the **Porta V** (aka Porta Quinta) entrance is at the lower western end (served by bus #1). Regardless of where or how you arrive, the best way to visit the park is a one-way downhill walk, starting at the Temple of Juno and finishing at Porta V.

You can exit from either entry. You can also exit (but not enter) in the middle of the park, between the **Temple of Zeus** and the **Temple of Hercules** (labeled *Ercole* on signs)—this is the handiest place for nondrivers to exit, as **buses #1, #2, #2/, and #3/** all stop here on the way back up to the museum and Agrigento.

With a Car: Park at Porta V and take a five-minute shuttle taxi up to the Temple of Juno entrance (€3/person; look for the taxi shelter at the Porta V parking lot and ask for a ride), or enter here and walk uphill (15 minutes) inside the park to the Temple of Juno.

Without a Car: The easiest plan is to take a **taxi** or ride **bus #2/** from Agrigento to the Temple of Juno entrance. Once you're done with the park, exit from the Temple of Hercules, catching the first bus that passes by (every 15 minutes or so; all buses that stop here pass the museum on the way to Agrigento—tell the driver if you want to get off at the museum). You can also walk to the museum from here: Hike 15 to 20 minutes uphill, sticking to the left (west) side of the road, which has sidewalks.

If you exit at Porta V, you can connect to the museum or town by taxi or, if the timing works out, **bus #1** (keep in mind it only runs once per hour). After visiting the museum, catch any bus heading uphill to return to Agrigento (taxis do not wait at the museum, and walking back—uphill the entire way—would take more than 45 minutes).

VALLEY OF THE TEMPLES ARCHAEOLOGICAL PARK

A stroll through the ▲▲▲ Valley of the Temples is one of the great travel experiences of the Mediterranean. Along with the temples at Paestum, these are the best-preserved Greek temples in Italy—on par with anything you might find in Greece. Some are partially rebuilt, others are in poetic ruins, and one survives in pristine condition. Thirty thousand Carthaginian slaves built these temples during the fifth century BC. Each of the 15 Doric-style temples honored a different god. Because the various protections offered by these gods complemented each other, Agrigento had ancient visitors' religious needs fully covered. While most of the temples have been lost to time and recycling, the few that survive give a sense of the scale of ancient Agrigento and the importance of Magna

208 Rick Steves Sicily

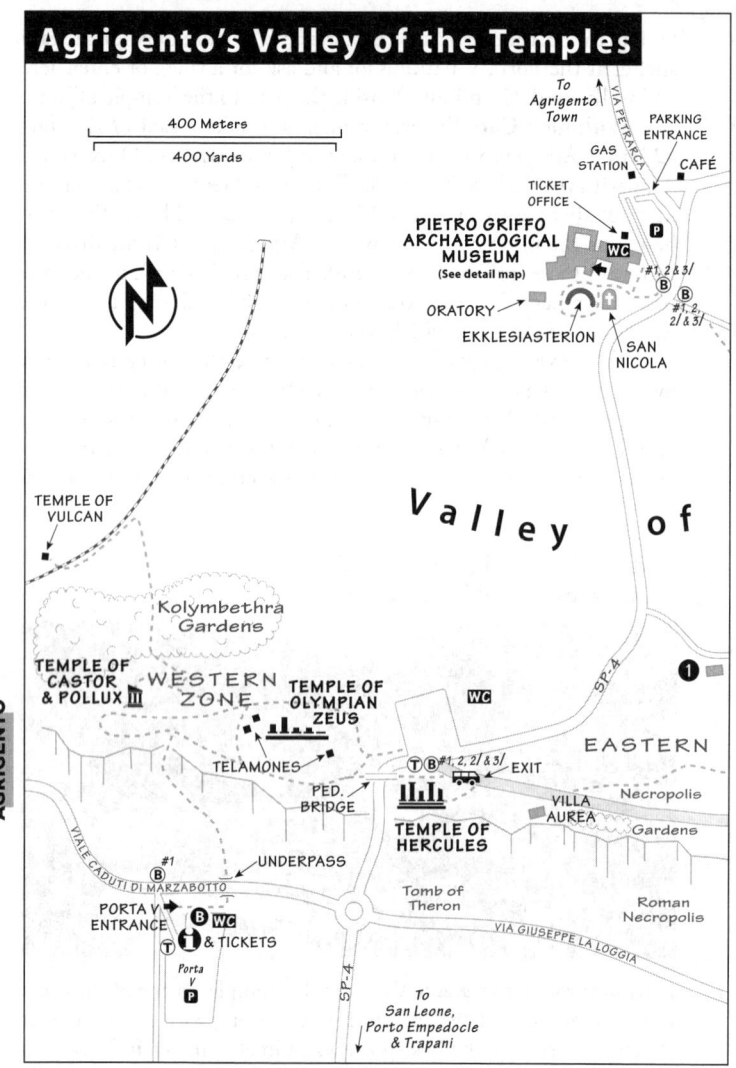

Agrigento's Valley of the Temples

Graecia ("Great Greece"), as the Greek colonies throughout the Mediterranean were known.

Cost: €17, €23 combo-ticket with museum; other options available. CoopCulture's **Agrigento Culture Pass** includes entrance to the temples and museum, plus a hop-on, hop-off electric minibus departing from Agrigento's train station with stops at the Temple of Juno, Temple of Hercules, and museum (€28, valid for one entrance to the temples and museum over the course of three days, buy online at coopculture.it/en/products/agrigento-culture-pass).

Valley of the Temples   209

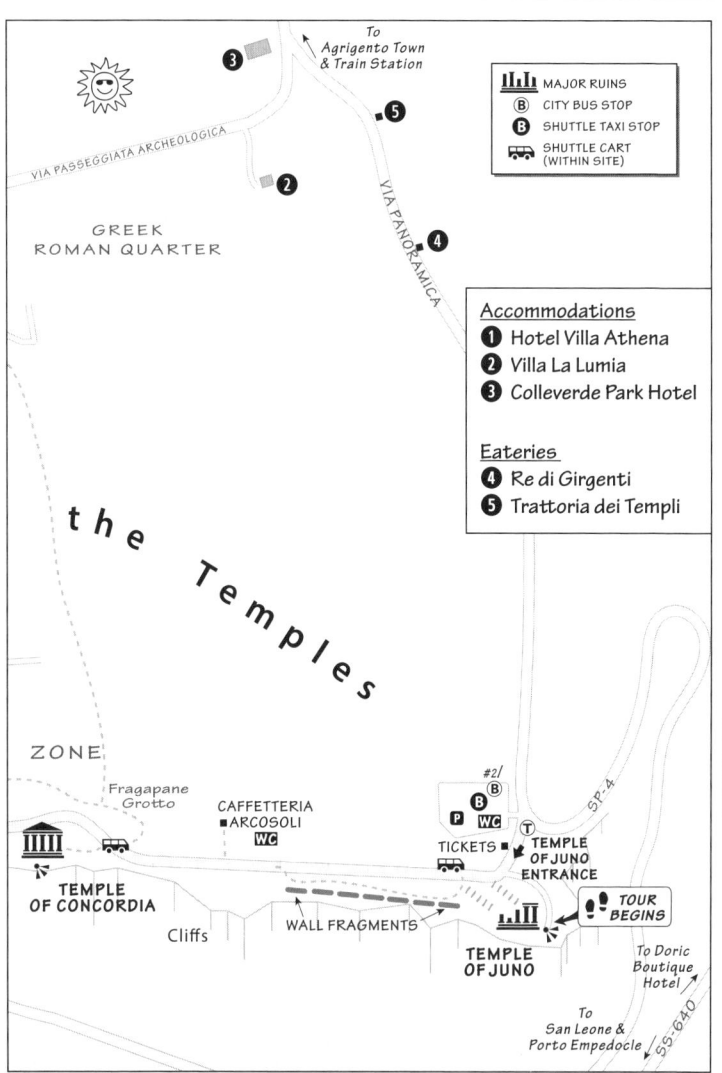

Hours: Open daily 8:30-20:00, mid-July–mid-Sept Mon-Fri until 23:00 and Sat-Sun until 24:00, last entry one hour before closing.

Information: +39 092 262 1611, coopculture.it (search for "Valley of the Temples").

Tours: Consider **Michele Gallo** (see "Tours in Agrigento," earlier), or an **audioguide** (€5, rent at Porta V entrance before taking shuttle taxi to the top of the site, leave photo ID, return it to the same office). Local guides hang around the entrance. In summer, guided **night tours** run each evening (€10, July-Sept daily at 18:30 from the Temple of Juno).

Kolymbethra Gardens: €7, included in the €23 combo-ticket, daily 10:00-18:00, shorter hours off-season (skippable for most visitors).

Visitor Services: There's usually a seasonal **TI** hut at the Porta V parking lot (daily 9:00-13:00, closed Nov-March). **WCs** are at both entrances (Porta V and Temple of Juno) and at Caffetteria Arcosoli. Unfortunately, there is no baggage storage at the Valley of the Temples or in Agrigento.

Getting Around the Park: Within the archaeological park, a shuttle cart is available to connect the Temple of Juno with the Temple of Hercules if needed (May-Oct, 4/hour, €4 one-way, buy on board). Note that this is different from the shuttle taxi service between the entrances.

Eating: Inside the park, between the Temples of Juno and Concordia, **€ Caffetteria Arcosoli** sells convenient (if overpriced) sandwiches, coffee, snacks, and gelato. Basic snack stands cluster just outside the Porta V entrance/exit. For more options (farther from the temples), see "Eating in Agrigento," later.

⊘ Self-Guided Tour

• *We'll start our tour at the eastern end—at the Temple of Juno entrance—and finish at the western end, a short walk from the Porta V entrance and Temple of Hercules exit (for tips, see the "Getting There" section, earlier). After the turnstile, head up the hill to the left to the...*

Temple of Juno (Tempio di Giunone)

Circle around to the left (east) side, which was the temple's entrance. From this windswept perch, survey the landscape of Agrigento. Rolling hills covered in almond, fig, agave, and cactus tumble into the aquamarine sea. Imagine this site 2,500 years ago when the temples were shiny and new—a line of mighty structures displaying the power of Greek culture.

Built in 460 BC, with six columns on each short side and 13 on each long side, the Temple of Juno was still intact in 1500, then crumbled due to earthquakes. In 1787, a local nobleman, inspired by the Enlightenment and the Neoclassical interest in antiquities, reassembled 30 columns and placed capitals atop 16. While this temple is named for Juno, it is not certain which god

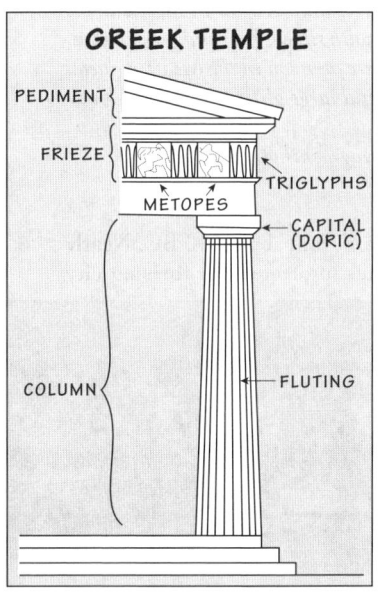

was worshipped here. (Its name, and those of most other temples here, is just a guess.)

This temple provides a fine opportunity for an architectural review: All Greek temples face east. (For reference, the modern city of Agrigento is north, and the sea is south.) Of the various temple designs, the most common is the peripteral style, with **columns** around the perimeter and on a stepped base. Within the colonnade is the inner **cella,** a room that enclosed the statue of the divinity. On the eastern side, out front, a raised **altar** was used for sacrificial ceremonies performed in public. Rites were celebrated at dawn, when the temple door would be open to allow the first sunbeams to light the statue of the god/goddess inside. Originally, simple **statues** of the gods were placed on the exterior altar, but as the statues became more elaborate and precious, they were moved inside the cella for protection. (For more on how Greek temples were laid out, see the sidebar on page 200.)

Move for a better look at the southeastern corner of the temple, and search for remnants of white stucco. Sicily's temples were built with local sandstone, and while sandstone is easy to quarry, it doesn't weather well. To prevent erosion from the sea winds (and imitate the look of marble), the stone was coated in stucco.

Imagine the process: The stone was quarried in a nearby hill (inland, toward the modern city). Each stone was cut to a prescribed dimension, as if part of a big jigsaw puzzle. Then the stones were rolled on a ramp over logs to the construction site. The massive slabs were hoisted up using pulleys powered by enslaved people on treadmills and lowered into place.

Columns were built with drums stacked atop each other, held in place by wooden pegs. Once assembled, they were fluted with elegant vertical grooves to hide the fact that they were not one giant monolith.

Finally, after finely carved decorations were applied, the temple was coated in stucco and painted in bold colors—very different from the classical white that we associate with ancient temples (or, in this case, golden yellow).

• *Circle around to the west (opposite) end, go down the stairs, and rejoin the path to begin the half-mile walk downhill. As you stroll, notice the almond and olive groves, interspersed with silver-gray and green agave, prickly pear, and myrtle. These species are common in the Mediterranean and grow well with little water. Several large olive trees dot the landscape, some more than 600 years old.*

On your left, keep an eye out for fragments of an...

Ancient Wall

The ruins of city walls on your left are from about 500 BC. Nearly seven miles of walls, with nine gates, protected the thriving city of 40,000. Ancient Akragas was large by the standard of the times; its agora (marketplace) was virtually the same size as the great market square of Athens. The ancient city spread from the temples across to where the modern city rises today. Work near the museum continues to unearth Akragas' remains—including a theater, right next to the museum.

The city wall is punctuated by occasional niches. In Christian times, niches in the wall were used for burials, which were not allowed inside the city. The niches, now eroded, have become peek-a-boo windows with sea views.

• *Keep following the path. On your right is Caffetteria Arcosoli, with WCs and overpriced snacks. Soon you approach the...*

Temple of Concordia (Tempio della Concordia)

Built in 435 BC, this is one of the best-preserved Greek temples in the world. Dedicated to an unknown god, archaeologists agreed that it should be called "Concordia" after an inscription found nearby.

In ancient Greece, religious rites were performed outside the temple, where the worshippers gathered around the altar. Only priests were allowed inside the temple itself, in the cella. The enclosed space of the cella was called *fanum*, and the area out front was called *profanum*, so anyone outside of the sacred space was considered "profane."

After Byzantine Emperor Theodosius declared an end to pagan religions in 597, many Greek temples were converted into Christian churches—including this one, which became the church

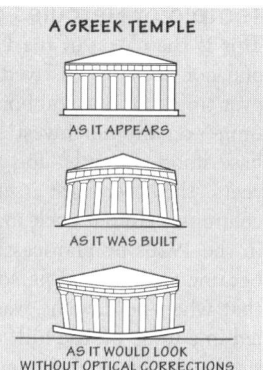

of Sts. Peter and Paul. The altar was moved indoors, the entrance was moved to the west side, and the temple was remodeled to create a large gathering space for the congregation. Gaps between the columns were filled in and the cella was opened up, with arches carved into its solid walls. The finished space had a central nave and two side aisles (which became the common design of most churches).

The temple was used as a church for almost 1,200 years. In 1788, at the peak of Neoclassical fashion (think Thomas Jefferson's Monticello), the building was stripped back to its original state and became appreciated as an ancient site.

This is the finest of the Agrigento temples and a great opportunity to understand and appreciate the sophistication of the ancient temple builders. The Greeks understood that viewing architecture from a distance would distort the proportion and symmetry, so they used optical illusion to correct the perspective.

Facing the temple, notice the columns on the sides—they slant very slightly inward. If not for this design, from a distance the two perfectly parallel columns would appear to lean out. The slant is nearly imperceptible, but if you were to extend the two corner columns up one mile, they would actually touch. Another challenge was the base. If built perfectly horizontal, the long base line would appear to sag in the middle. To compensate for this distortion, the stepped base bows up slightly in the middle—and you see a straight line.

• *Continue downhill past a garden and modern building on your left,* **Villa Aurea.** *This was the home of Alexander Hardcastle (1872-1933), an English nobleman who developed a passion for archaeology after visiting here. He moved to the site and poured his personal wealth into the reconstruction of the temples.*

The villa often hosts contemporary art exhibits. If its gardens are open, you can detour through them to see entrances of the Roman necropolis or **ipogei,** *caves used for Christian burial.*

Just after the villa, angle left to reach the...

Temple of Hercules (Tempio di Ercole)

This is the oldest of the Doric temples erected here and the only one not built by enslaved people. Most of the temple collapsed over time, but one stubborn column—on the northwest side—has stood proudly for 2,500 years. The other eight assembled columns were put back together in the 1920s by Hardcastle. He became such a local personality that when he died he was buried in a tomb on the hill, with a small window looking out over his beloved temple.

• *Walk toward the temple, then along its left side. At the far end, the path cuts through a pile of rubble. As you squeeze through, notice that some of the columns (and some toppled columns nearby) still have a thick layer of white stucco.*

Continue downhill, across the pedestrian bridge, to the ruined...

Temple of Olympian Zeus (Tempio di Zeus Olimpico)

The struggle between the Greeks and the Carthaginians for control of Sicily culminated in 480 BC at the Battle of Himera (near Cefalú, on Sicily's northern side). To thank the gods for the victory that led to Greek prosperity, this grand temple was built for Zeus, the king of the gods. Longer than a football field and taller than a 10-story building (185 feet wide, 370 feet long, and 108 feet tall), it was the largest Doric temple in the ancient world. A person could have hidden in one of the flutes of the massive columns, and the roof tiles were the size of pizza boxes.

The sacrificial altar in front of the temple's east end (which you approach first) was 40 by 180 feet, bigger than the footprint of the other temples. It had space to sacrifice hundreds of animals at once, with a few thousand worshippers gathered all around, waiting for a citywide barbecue after the slaughter.

This temple's architectural plan was unique. Rather than a line of open columns surrounding the cella, the temple had a solid outer wall with interlinked columns, which gave it the appearance of a massive block. The inner cella was roofless. The weight of the stone was immense, and underground foundations were built to disperse the load—something rarely seen in Greek temples. At most temples, the entrance door was centered beneath the facade, but here, due to the odd number of columns, the temple had twin entrances, one on either side.

Today, only 5 percent of the temple's original building material remains. The temple collapsed in 1401 and was almost completely recycled into other structures. As late as 1751, stones from the ruins were used by the Spanish to build a pier at the nearby town of Porto Empedocle.

• *Angle to the right and curl your way back "inside" the temple ruins.*

One of the defining features of the Temple of Olympian Zeus was its decoration. High above the ground, 38 giant telamon figures held up the massive roof. Imagine looking up at their toes, 40 feet above your head, between the towering pillars of the temple. The scant remains of three of these giants lie scattered around the site, like dissolving sugar-cube corpses. "Inside" the tem-

ple is a copy of the most intact giant (the original is now displayed in the archaeological museum). Keep an eye out for other telamon parts around the site.

Retrace your steps back out to the path and you'll see a giant column capital. The enormous scale of this temple is hard to grasp.

• *Loop around the left (north) side to see a mounted telamon giving you another sense of the temple's size, then carry on downhill past a field of rubble all the way to the...*

Temple of Castor and Pollux (Tempio dei Dioscuri)

Four lonely columns mark the final temple on our walk in the park. Not considered historically accurate, this imagined reconstruction consists of random pieces put together like Lego blocks. These days, archaeologists would never reconstruct a temple in this manner, which muddles the history of the building. Keeping the stones in a jumble on the ground is preferable. While the

building is said to have honored Zeus' twin sons Castor and Pollux, the site around the temple is known as the Sanctuary to Demeter and Persephone, mother and daughter goddesses who were protectors of fertility. Their cult was so important to this island in ancient times that Sicily was called "Zeus' wedding gift to Persephone."

Before you leave, take a moment to admire the landscape around you. Great civilizations rise, then disappear, leaving only traces of their former glory. Wandering through the plain of evocative rubble, you can only marvel at how wealthy and developed this mysterious Greek world was 2,500 years ago. Meanwhile, modern Agrigento perches on the ridge in front of you. Life goes on.

• *Our tour is over. If you have energy, you can extend your visit in the pleasant **Kolymbethra Gardens** (described next—look for the entrance immediately to the right as you face the Temple of Castor and Pollux). Beyond the gardens is the skippable Temple of Vulcan.*

*From here, it's a short downhill walk to the **Porta V** parking lot: Near the Temple of Castor and Pollux, look for the ramp that leads down to Parcheggio Porta V. You'll walk through an olive grove and an underpass and pop out near the WCs a short walk from the parking lot. **Taxis** wait in the parking lot to take visitors to the museum or back to town. To catch the city **bus** to the archaeological museum or back to the city center, you'll find buses #1, #2, #2/, or #3/ at the exit near the Temple of Hercules—only bus #1 runs from the Porta V parking lot (once an hour).*

Kolymbethra Gardens

This ravine alongside the temples was a water reservoir in Greek times, later drained by Arabs and turned into a lush garden, to which they introduced citrus varieties. The wind-sheltered position creates an ideal microclimate for cultivation of plants and vegetables. The gardens have a fragrant collection of 13 varieties of citrus (including orange, mandarin, lemon, tangerine, and citron) as well as almond and olive trees, all irrigated with ingenious water channels. A wander through the gardens' fragrant, shady paths can be a peaceful treat at the end of a walk through the valley, but it's skippable unless you're an avid horticulturalist.

PIETRO GRIFFO ARCHAEOLOGICAL MUSEUM

Built within the arches of a 14th-century Cistercian monastery, this ▲ museum (Museo Archeologico Regionale Pietro Griffo) helps visitors envision the civilization that created the Valley of the Temples. While 900,000 people visit the archaeological site annually, too few take advantage of the museum, which helps bring the temples to life. Its central room is built around

Valley of the Temples 217

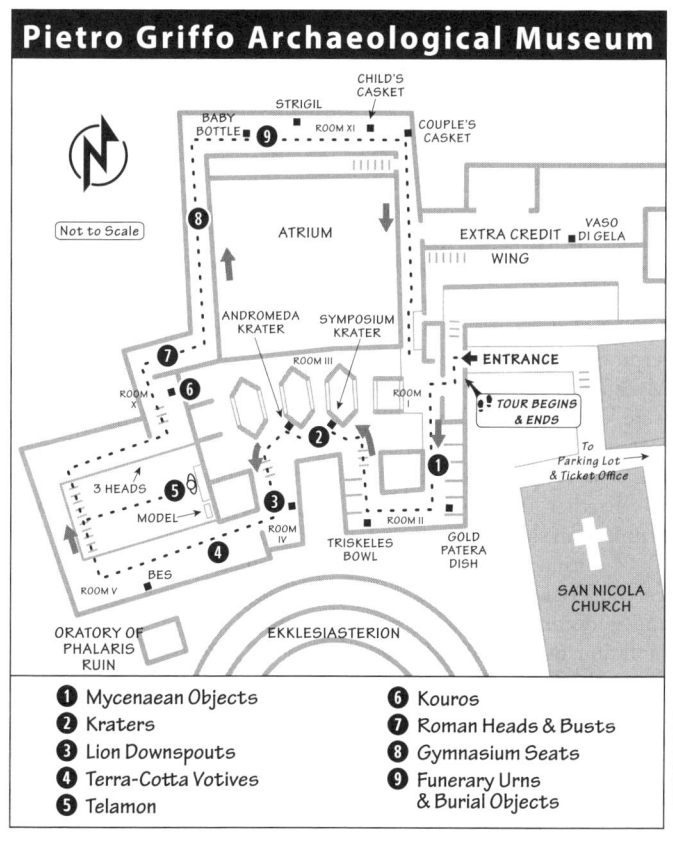

a telamon, a stone giant from the Temple of Olympian Zeus. The well-designed collection covers about 2,000 years of life on the shores of the Agrigento area. You'll see vases from Greek settlers of the sixth to third century BC, providing a fascinating glimpse into the fun and frolic of ancient times. With so many great Greek works found in Agrigento, it's clear that this important and wealthy city traded extensively with the wider Greek world.

Cost and Hours: €10, €23 combo-ticket with Valley of the Temples Archaeological Park, open daily 9:00-19:30.

Information: +39 092 240 1565, coopculture.it (search for "Pietro Griffo" or "Valley of the Temples").

Eating: The museum has a small café near the WCs. And just uphill from the museum, € **La Promenade** café offers a cold case of salads and pasta dishes—just point to assemble a plate—as well as sandwiches and desserts (open long hours daily). For more (and better) eateries a short drive away, see the "Eating in Agrigento" section, later.

◐ Self-Guided Tour

• *From the parking lot, follow* museo *signs inside to buy your ticket. Then head left into the exhibit. The one-way loop begins with Greek artifacts.*

❶ Mycenaean Objects

Long before the temples were built in Agrigento, earlier Greek people, the Mycenaeans, landed on the shores of Sicily and traded with the local tribes. (The Mycenaeans seemed as ancient and mysterious to the Golden Age Greeks as Socrates and Plato are to us.) This part of Sicily had deposits of sulfur and bitumen, a key waterproofing ingredient the Mycenaeans used in shipbuilding. The Mycenaean culture eventually died out, but traces of its influence were left on the local style of art. The first few cases display terra-cotta vessels, bronze spearheads, and—in the third display case—a *fibula* (safety pin) from more than 3,000 years ago.

Farther along is a replica of a **gold Patera dish.** Wine was drunk from shallow dishes like this in ancient times.

Continue around to the right, and in the second case, look for the **Triskeles Bowl.** This was made in the seventh century BC and is decorated with the earliest representation of the three-legged symbol of Sicily, the Trinacria. The legs likely represent the tips of the triangular island, and the face in the center is often identified as Medusa, possibly an allegory for Mount Etna—Medusa turned people into stone, while Etna created new stone. The symbol has been used on Sicilian flags since 1282. (For more about the Trinacria, see page 55).

• *Go up the stairs to a room with display cases featuring a variety of...*

❷ Kraters

These Greek terra-cotta urns were used as mixing bowls for wine. Greeks brewed up strong wine and, before serving it, mixed it with water in a krater. Depending on the time of day (or how drunk partygoers were), the host could secretly mix in more water to keep their guests' alcohol intake under control. Most of the kraters are decorated with scenes of fun-loving parties or wine-themed antics.

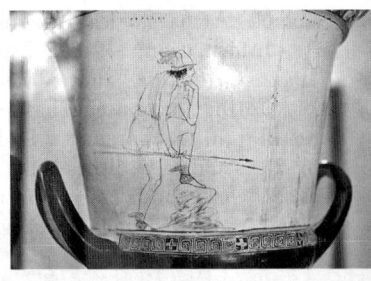

Examine the kraters in the

first case at the top of the stairs. These are the earliest in the collection, typical of the sixth century BC, with black figures on a red background. Later, in the fifth century BC, artists realized that if they reversed the technique—black backgrounds with figures in the red clay color—they could add more detail, movement, and skin tone to the figures.

In the lower-right corner of the second case, find the krater with a scene of a **symposium** (circle around the case to see both sides). While to us, "symposium" means a meeting for discussion, the original Greek word, *sumpótēs*, meant "drink together"—a drinking party for men. Around back, find the female figure playing a flute. The women featured in these scenes, called *hetairai*, were typically professional "entertainers" rather than partygoers. Similar to Japanese geishas, these women were educated in music and conversation, and artists such as Praxiteles used them as models. This krater shows a symposium nearing its end. When the wine was almost gone, the men would use the last drops for a target-practice game called *kottabos*. They would flick drops of wine at a target, and the man who got closest won a night with the lady in the scene. Some of the other kraters in these cases have similar symposium scenes.

In the fourth case of this section, look for the krater with a wide white band, with lower handles. This is one of two known ancient Greek vessels made from kaolin, a white clay used in making fine porcelain china. The illustration shows lovestruck Perseus liberating a handcuffed (and exhausted) **Andromeda.**

Stroll around to admire the variety of scenes and patterns on the kraters. Notice that some kraters devote more space to abstract patterns and less to decorative scenes. As time passed, Greek pottery was made in larger quantities, and it was quicker and cheaper to decorate in bold patterns.

Outside the nearby windows are terra-cotta amphorae, containers used to ship wine and olive oil. They were made long and slender, with a pointed bottom, so they could be sunk into the sand lining the cargo holds of ancient ships, preventing tilting and spilling. Amphorae and their contents would have been the typical Sicilian commodities traded to Greece for fine pottery like you see here.

• *Down the steps from the krater collection are...*

❸ Lion Downspouts

The cat faces hissing at you as you walk by were not just a decoration for the temples; they also served a practical purpose. These downspouts drained the temple roofs and warded off curses (similar to the French gargoyles on churches). Imagine these lions peering down at you in their original state, with brightly painted faces and gleaming white teeth.

• *The next hall is lined with several cases displaying...*

❹ Terra-Cotta Votives

These terra-cotta figures, in a variety of shapes and sizes, are votives—figures offered to the gods to ask for protection, healing, or the granting of a wish. Votives were made from various materials: marble or bronze for wealthy people, cheap terra-cotta for everyone else. They were sold in shops near the temples and brought to the altars, then left as an offering. The terra-cotta figures were produced in large quantities by using molds (some of which are displayed here). Women are common devotional figures, and a worshipper could buy a figure of the specific goddess from whom they were asking help.

About three-quarters along the way, at hip level, look for the mischievous, squatting creature. This little guy is **Bes,** a home protector and an ancient version of the common garden gnome. He was probably situated near the entry to the house and was believed to look out for all that was good in the home. He was also a protector of women and childbirth, which probably explains his funny posture.

• *Dominating this room—on the wall over your right shoulder—is the gigantic...*

❺ Telamon (Stone Giant)

The centerpiece of the museum is the larger-than-life figure of the telamon, a unique feature of the massive Temple of Olympian Zeus. This is the most complete survivor, and one of many that stood between its towering pillars.

• *Walk down the stairs to see him up close.*

Look for the cork **model** of the temple to get an idea of where the telamon once stood. This was the largest Doric temple ever constructed in the Greek world—as tall as a modern 10-story building. Imagine the overall scale of it, covering 370 feet in length (as large as a football field)—something, it must have seemed to the ancients, that only the gods could create.

This telamon was just one of 38 sandstone figures that decorated the sides of the supersized temple. The telamon has small feet compared with the rest of his body, but if you kneel below him and look up, you can understand why: He would have been displayed

Valley of the Temples 221

about 40 feet up, putting his small feet in proportion with his massive torso.

On the left, you'll see **three heads** from other telamon figures. Each reveals a different ethnicity. The Greek world was international, spread over three continents, and these figures represented the extent of the known world. Notice the white stucco on the lips on the left. The golden sandstone of the telamon was covered in stucco and then painted to make the creature more realistic.

• *Sit and admire the telamon or take a WC break. When you're ready, go up the staircase and continue circling your way around (past more cases of fragments) to the white statue opposite where you entered this room.*

❻ Kouros (Young Boy)

The Greeks were philosophers and mathematicians, and this statue is an example of their attention to the proportions of the ideal body. The Romans were obsessed with Greek works and reproduced them many times for their villas—so most marble sculptures you see in museums are Roman copies of Greek originals. This sculpture is precious because it is an original work from Greece, in the stiff "Severe" style influenced by Egyptian sculpture. It was found, with its legs shattered, at the bottom of a cistern—likely thrown away by Roman-era looters who regarded it as rather plain. If this was discarded, imagine what was taken.

• *Continue past the kouros, turning right into a section of Roman-era artifacts found in Agrigento. Along the left wall you'll find...*

❼ Roman Heads and Busts

Greek Sicily ended in 212 BC with the defeat of Syracuse. After that, all of Sicily became a Roman colony, and art drifted toward the new Roman style. Here you'll find a row of four Roman sculptures. Notice that the last one has a head that's not permanently attached to its shoulders. The Romans were practical: Generals and emperors came, saw, conquered...and went. So,

instead of creating new sculptures from scratch, only the heads were replaced—like ancient Photoshopping. This head, with its curly hair and beard, may depict Hadrian (the emperor who walled off Scotland)—or it may be a later VIP who simply imitated Hadrian's style.

• *Walk through the hallway with a wall of windows. On the right side, along the corridor, examine the...*

❽ Gymnasium Seats

This long row of weathered sandstone seats was once part of the local gymnasium, or sports complex. Fans sat on these seats to watch young men compete in running, fighting, and boxing. And as with stadiums today, patrons could pay for seat-naming rights. The Greek letters on the seats at the end of the hallway are part of a dedication by superfan Lucio, son of Lucius, to the gods Hermes and Heracles (Hercules).

• *The next hall is lined with several cases of...*

❾ Funerary Urns and Burial Objects

In Greek and Roman times, it was common for people to be buried with objects that held personal significance: women with jewelry or household objects, men with tools of their trade, warriors with armor, and children with toys.

In the third "room" of cases, find the curved metal object. This is a **strigil,** used in the baths as an exfoliator and commonly buried with men. Look into the case to your left and find the terra-cotta donkey, an ancient **baby bottle.** The donkey's fat body was easy for an infant to grip, the tail was the spout, and a small bead inside regulated the milk flow.

In the next "room," on the top shelf of the middle case, find two small bronze snakes curled up. These were decorations for women's hair, like ponytail holders. The small pots on either side would have held beauty products.

Notice the caskets lining the hall. Near the end of the hall (in the final "room" of cases) is an elaborately carved **small casket**—made for a wealthy family's child. Walk around the casket, and you'll see the story of the child's life. On one short end, the scene shows the baby being picked up while his mother looks on. On the opposite end, baby gets his first driving lesson from his dad and the used-sheep salesman. On the front—angled upward—the boy lies dying, with his sorrowful mother cupping his

chin. This was not an uncommon scene—the rate of infant mortality in the ancient world was more than 50 percent.

Compare this elegant example to the simpler **casket fragment** on the wall at the far end of the hall (with the wavy lines). A couple would have shared this casket; the gesture of the woman's hand suggests they were married. The faces on such mass-produced caskets would have been blank when purchased. A sculptor could later personalize the scene with the features of the deceased. This was an economical solution for middle-class Romans.

• *Continue down the hallway to the exit. Along the way, the (skippable) final rooms contain vases, plates, helmets, chest plates, and spearheads of Greek hoplite soldiers, and the* **Vaso di Gela,** *the largest Greek krater found in Sicily.*

Outside the main entrance gate, follow signs to the oratorio *for a short detour: You'll see the Oratory of Phalaris—the remains of a temple from the second century BC—as well as the* ekklesiasterion, *the amphitheater where Akragas held its popular assemblies, roughly analogous to a city council.*

For tips on linking the museum to the archaeological park, or returning to Agrigento, see "Getting Around the Valley of the Temples," earlier.

Agrigento Town

The modern city of Agrigento stretches east-west along a hillside, with the historical core in the center. In the middle—where you'll arrive by train, bus, or car—you'll find a tidy little park (near Piazza Vittorio Emanuele). The main drag—Via Atenea—leads from here toward the neighborhood up the hill known as the Kasbah. A **TI** kiosk with unpredictable hours is not far

from the train station, next to the park in Piazzale Vittorio Emanuele (theoretically Mon-Fri 8:30-14:00 & 14:30-19:00, Sat 8:30-13:00, closed Sun). Unfortunately, there's nowhere in town, or at the Valley of the Temples, to stow your bags for the day.

ARRIVAL IN AGRIGENTO
For directions on visiting the Valley of the Temples from Agrigento, see "Getting There" near the start of this chapter.

By Train: Trains from Palermo arrive at Agrigento Centrale station, a block below the city center (and about 1.5 miles above

224 Rick Steves Sicily

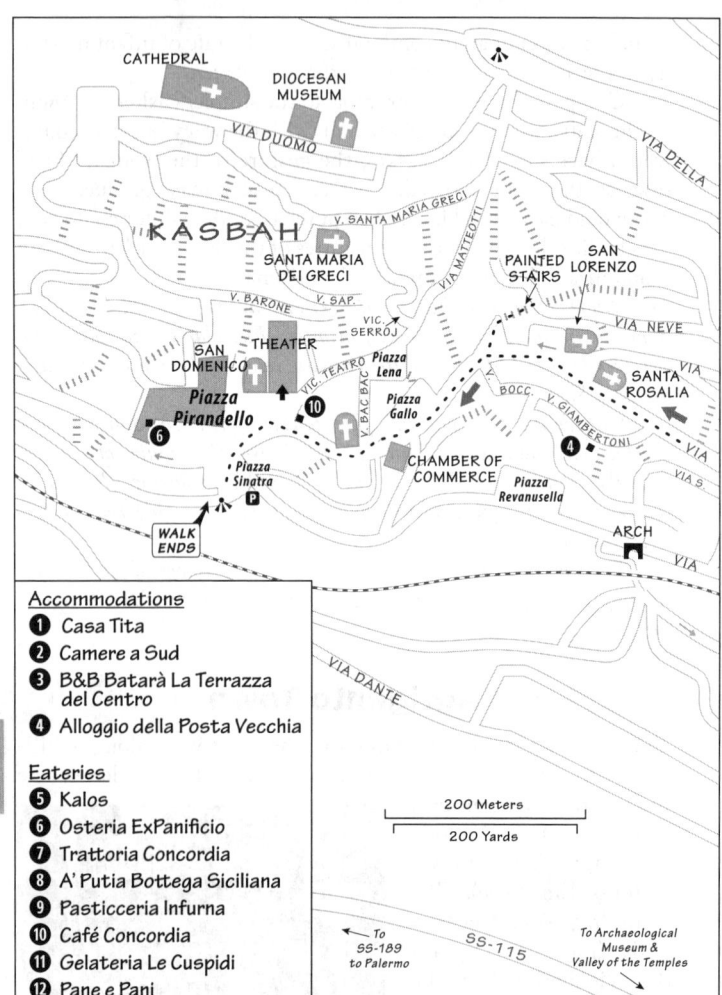

the temples). The historical center is a five-minute walk away. Turn left (uphill) at the stoplight in front of the station, then bear left through the park to find the main drag, Via Atenea.

By Bus: The main bus terminal is at Piazzale Rosselli, on the "back side" of the city's ridge. It's a five-minute walk to the historical center: Walk between the round fascist-era post office and the Cine Astor, carry on uphill to the park, and turn right to find Via Atenea.

By Car: To reach Agrigento's town center from the temple area, follow the road up past the archaeological museum and parking lot, taking the right fork for *Centro* onto Via Passeggiata Archeologica. Passing ancient ruins and winding up the hill, this road

Agrigento Town

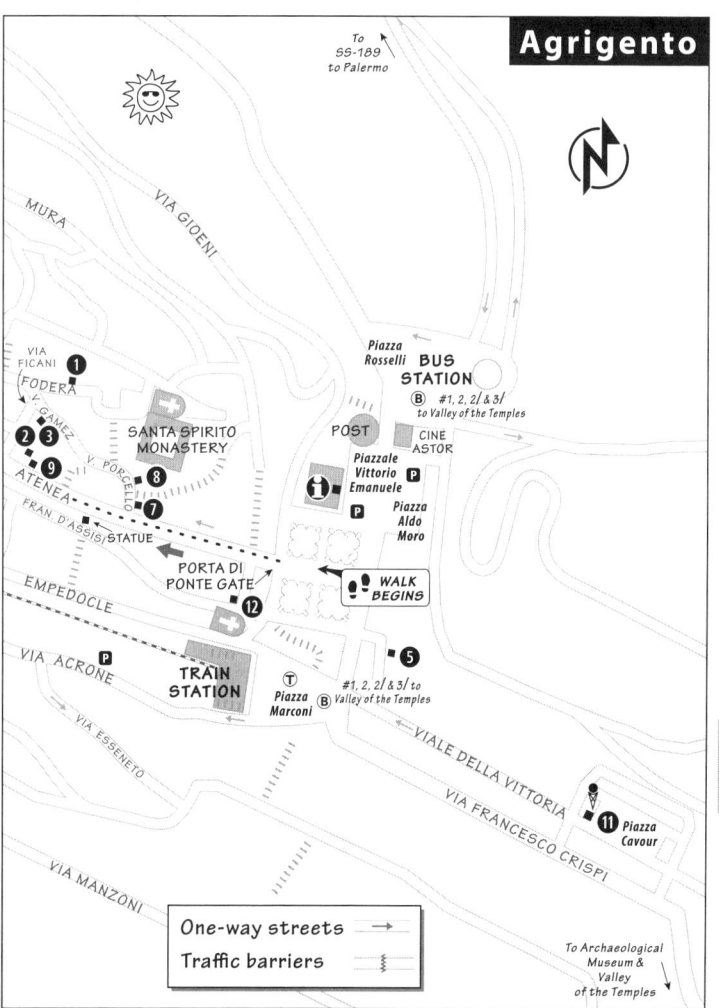

becomes Via Francesco Crispi, which leads to the train station. Take a right in front of the train station to find pay parking lots (coins only) just past the park at the entrance to town on Piazzale Vittorio Emanuele. Another coin-only parking lot lies beyond the train station, on Via Empedocle. On the south side of the train station, the expensive 24-hour Parcheggio Pirandello lot is open 24 hours and accepts credit cards (Via Acrone 5).

AGRIGENTO TOWN WALK

Most people who visit the magnificent temples near Agrigento never set foot in the modern city. While understandable, that's unfortunate. Those who do take a look find a pleasant workaday town—worth ▲—crammed with enticing eateries and a main drag that's well suited for a *passeggiata*. If time allows, let curiosity lure you into town for this half-hour stroll.

• *From the train station or nearby parking lots, head through the little park and turn onto Via Atenea, stopping at the…*

Porta di Ponte Gate: The Porta di Ponte is the gateway to a fun-to-stroll section of Via Atenea, lined with shops and tempting eateries. Stairstep lanes lure you up and down off this artery. Before passing through, look above at the niche on the left side of the street and notice the carving of three telamon giants, like the ones at the Temple of Olympian Zeus in the archaeological park. This is the symbol of the city of Agrigento.

• *Now walk down Via Atenea a couple of blocks into town, watching on the left for a small patio with the bronze statue of…*

Andrea Camilleri: One of Sicily's beloved writers, Camilleri was born and raised in nearby Porto Empedocle and attended school as a youth in the very place he now sits, with an empty chair waiting to be filled by you. The statue was erected in 2020, a year after his death, and has been the subject of several notable transgressions since—befitting of an author who wrote detective novels. (For more on him, see the "Sicilian Writers" sidebar, later.)

• *Ahead on the right is the recommended…*

Pasticceria Infurna: This classic shop (at #96) serves an excellent selection of pastries and unique sweets, such as almond "shells" stuffed with pistachio paste. Everything's made in the shop at this family-run spot, and they have good gelato in summer.

• *Continue along Via Atenea until you reach a pair of…*

Side-by-Side Churches: On the right is the clunky brick front of **Santa Rosalia,** whose Baroque facade was taken down in 1951 for repairs. The pieces were numbered for reassembly and… disappeared—possibly decorating a local convent's garden. The citizens have petitioned the city to reconstruct it, but no luck yet. Next door is **San Lorenzo,** a "Purgatorio" church where the faithful come to pray their naughty relatives out of purgatory.

• *A little farther down Via Atenea, where the street bends, watch for the small triangular square on the right. At the back of the square you'll see colorfully painted stairs luring you up…*

Via Neve: *Neve* means "snow" in Italian, and this street was once where ice collected in the nearby mountains was sold. The ice

> ## Sicilian Writers
>
> The area around Agrigento, on the southwest coast of Sicily, produced some of the best Italian authors of the 20th century. Their writings explored the Sicilian experience, where everything is either comedy or tragedy (and often both).
>
> **Luigi Pirandello** (1867-1936), from Agrigento, won the Nobel Prize in literature in 1934. He wrote about the human condition and how preposterous it can seem. His most famous work, the play *Six Characters in Search of an Author*, premiered in 1921 and became a classic of absurdist theater.
>
> **Leonardo Sciascia** (1921-1989), from Racalmuto, focused on the political and social situation in Sicily in the mid-1900s. His 1961 novella *The Day of the Owl* was a mesmerizing account of the Mafia's hold over Sicilian village life.
>
> **Andrea Camilleri** (1925-2019), from Porto Empedocle, created the character of Inspector Montalbano—a modern Sicilian version of Sherlock Holmes. His popular mystery series chronicled the detective's adventures in solving crimes while painting a picture of the quirks of Sicilian culture. For more on the series, see page 277.

sellers have since been replaced by artists—take a quick detour up the steps to enjoy the street-art scene.

• *Back on Via Atenea, ahead of you you'll see a frilly gray building with a bell tower and clock. This is the Neo-Gothic **chamber of commerce**, from 1871, which replaced an earlier City Hall building. Walk a little farther, circling around the church on your right, until you reach...*

Teatro Pirandello: Named after local boy Luigi Pirandello, who went on to win the Nobel Prize in literature, this impressive structure dates from 1880. If it's open, pop in to the theater's courtyard (the entrance is flanked by two fancy streetlamps). To the right as you enter is a picture of the opulent interior; in the left corner is a WWII Fiat bomber propeller recovered from the sea near Agrigento.

• *Teatro Pirandello anchors the...*

Piazza Pirandello: This piazza marks the end of Via Atenea. Here you could stop for coffee and a sweet at the nearby recommended Café Concordia—try their "ricottamisu," a delightful Sicilian take on tiramisu. Then walk downhill two minutes more to **Piazza Sinatra** and a terrace with a grand view overlooking the valley and the sea beyond. If you're in the mood for gourmet fare, sit down for a meal at the recommended Osteria ExPanificio.

• *Our walk is finished. But to explore a bit farther, from Piazza Pirandello, you could take a steep little hike up to the...*

Kasbah Neighborhood: In this crumbling, gritty (but safe) neighborhood you'll find the interesting **Santa Maria dei Greci** church (€3, daily 10:00-19:00, Nov-March closed Mon and afternoons). To reach it, just to the right of Teatro Pirandello, head up the stairs of Vicolo Teatro and jog right to continue up the final, painted set, then take the first branch left and follow the yellow sign to *Chiesa Cattedrale*—it's ahead on the right. This humble 12th-century church was built over the ruins of a Greek temple, which you can see through the glass panes in the floor. On the right are stone seats, where, back in the Middle Ages, cadavers were placed and drained of blood as part of a preservation process.

Exiting the church, find a passage on the right of the courtyard, labeled *crepidoma*. You can see the steps of the temple, used as a foundation for the church. The structure was about the same size as the Temple of Concordia in the Valley of the Temples. Ponder the fact that the original ancient city stretched from the top of this hill all the way out to the valley—with even more temples that are now long gone.

SLEEPING IN AND NEAR AGRIGENTO

For visitors with a car, the best hotel strategy is to stay close to the temples, preferably with a view, or in a countryside retreat. Most of these hotels are between the train station and the temples. Nondrivers (or those who enjoy hanging out in a lively city) can sleep in the modern town of Agrigento. Unless otherwise noted, these listings have air-conditioning but no elevator.

In Agrigento Town

For the locations of these hotels, see the "Agrigento" map, earlier.

€ Casa Tita is well tended by Fabio and Sandro, who make you feel at home in their petite and stylish B&B. It's up a lot of stairs from the Via Atenea main drag but has street parking above, nearby (Salita Franceso Sala 2, +39 392 103 8256, casatita.it, info@casatita.it).

€ Camere a Sud is a relaxing oasis filled with soft music, colorful tiles, and little added touches like a coffee corner, an honesty bar, and thoughtful recommendations from owner Elvira (who speaks excellent English)—it's no surprise this was one of Agrigento's first guesthouses. The family (and Lola, the golden retriever) rents five rooms that share a common space, small terrace, and kitchen, and they can arrange a permit allowing you to drive onto the street to unload luggage (no breakfast, tucked into a corner at Via Ficani 6, +39 349 638 4424, camereasud.it, info@camereasud.it).

€ B&B Batarà La Terrazza del Centro is the most basic of my listings. The eight rooms (six in the main building, plus two more across the street) are simple, bordering on slightly run-down, but spacious—and many come with stupendous views (no air-con, lots of stairs, Via Ficani 34, +39 349 278 7101, batarabeb@virgilio.it, Angela and Alfonso).

€ **Alloggio della Posta Vecchia** is a funky B&B over an art-house theater. The four rooms have frescoed ceilings and antique furniture; guests often include artists performing at the theater (Via Giambertoni 19, +39 092 266 0179, agrigento-templi.it, alloggiodellapostavecchia@gmail.com, Angela).

At the Archaeological Park

For the locations of these hotels, see the "Agrigento's Valley of the Temples" map, earlier. All offer parking.

€€€€ **Hotel Villa Athena** sits in a prized position, right in the middle of the archaeological park a few steps from the temples. The hotel is luxurious, with friendly, attentive staff, 27 marbled rooms with outrageous views—and prices to match (private entrance to the temples, elevator, view restaurant, spa, Via Passeggiata Archeologica 33, +39 092 259 6288, hotelvillaathena.it, reservations@hotelvillaathena.it, Boris).

€€€€ **Villa La Lumia,** set in a stunning countryside villa, is one of the few guesthouses inside the archaeological park. Their nine rooms are cozy, with view terraces overlooking the temples; it's a short walk from the archaeological museum (Via Passeggiata Archeologica 19, +39 320 632 5568, villalalumia.it, info@villalalumia.com).

€€ **Colleverde Park Hotel** is warmly run and popular with big tour groups, with 48 impersonal but pleasant rooms. The shady gardens with a temple view are ideal for contemplating Greek philosophy while sipping cold *limoncello* (elevator, Via Portulano 1, +39 092 229 555, colleverdehotel.it, mail@colleverdehotel.it).

In the Countryside

For the locations of these hotels, see the "Agrigento Area" map near the beginning of this chapter.

€€€€ **Doric Boutique Hotel** is a classy, eco-friendly resort and an architectural showpiece a 10-minute drive east of Agrigento. Many of the 25 rooms are their own villas with stunning views. Mediterranean plants and herbs abound on the grounds, and there's a sexy swimming pool and top-class restaurant. As a high-end oasis, it's hard to beat (Strada E. S. A. Mosé, San Biagio 20, +39 0922 180 8509, doric.it, booking@doric.it).

€€€€ **Casa Balata,** a luxurious *agriturismo* retreat, perches on a quiet, rocky ridge with grand views about a 20-minute drive west, near the village of Realmonte. The giant house has five rooms with all the modern comforts, a saltwater swimming pool, manicured gardens, great dinners, and sharp Daniela at the helm. If you want to splurge in stony elegance away from the chaos of Sicily, do it here (Contrada Rina Cannameli 47, +39 366 870 5567, casabalata.it, casabalata.ag@gmail.com). It's not well signed and is tricky to find, even with GPS—use the detailed directions Daniela is happy to provide.

€€€€ **Agriturismo Mandranova,** 20 minutes southeast of Agrigento, produces almonds and olive oil on their large working farm. Eleven posh rooms are housed in a cluster of elegantly restored farm buildings, and four country-style rooms fill a former train station (pool, cooking classes, upscale dinner-€40, SS-115 at signpost 216, Palma di Montechiaro, +39 393 986 2169, mandranova.com, booking@mandranova.com, hardworking Silvia and Giuseppe).

€€€€ **Baglio della Luna,** a manor house with a courtyard and an old Spanish watchtower, is a peaceful escape to the southwest of Agrigento. The panoramic views of the temples in the distance and the well-manicured garden offset the 23 bland rooms (Via Serafino Amabile Guastella 1c, +39 092 251 1061, bagliodellaluna.com, info@bagliodellaluna.com, Felicia).

€€ **Fattoria Mosè,** an *agriturismo*, is a working farm on a hill overlooking a valley. The serene estate is surrounded by ancient olive trees and animals and offers short walks around the property and a refreshing pool. Four old-fashioned rooms cluster around homey common spaces in the main building, with six apartments in an annex. Hardworking Chiara multitasks on the farm work while cooking (home-cooked dinner-€32, Via Mattia Pascal 4a, +39 092 260 6115, fattoriamose.com, info@fattoriamose.com).

EATING IN AGRIGENTO
In the Town Center

Strolling Via Atenea, you'll come across a variety of eateries, some more touristy than others. My recommendations emphasize quality over views. For locations, see the "Agrigento" map.

€€€ **Kalos** is an upscale but unfussy place with artful cooking by chef Antonio Cipolla—try his signature spaghetti with shrimp and pistachios. A short walk from one end of Via Atenea, the restaurant's terraces overlook the Piazzetta San Calogero (reservations smart, closed Mon, upstairs at Salita Filino 1, +39 092 226 389, ristorantekalos.it).

€€ **Osteria ExPanificio** is a bakery-turned-gourmet-restaurant showcasing seasonal ingredients, such as risotto with cantaloupe and smoked cured ham in summer. Eat in their cozy interior, decorated with baking implements, or in the breezy square out front (daily, Piazzetta Sinatra 16, +39 092 259 5399).

€€ **Trattoria Concordia,** off Via Atenea, is a bustling spot for a family dinner of homestyle Sicilian favorites. Arrive early or reserve—it's popular with locals and tourists alike (Mon-Fri lunch and dinner, Sat-Sun dinner only, Via Porcello 8, +39 092 222 668).

€ **A' Putia Bottega Siciliana** is a casual, modern place for a drink and light meal a few steps uphill from Via Atenea (just above Trattoria Concordia). They have a large selection of beer and wine with meat-and-cheese platters to match in a chatty, hip setting (Tue-Sun dinner only, closed Mon, Via Porcello 18, +39 092 220 743).

€ **Pasticceria Infurna** offers an excellent selection of pastries and unique marzipan sweets and pistachio treats. Davide and his family make everything on-site and change the front display depending on the season—chocolates in winter and gelato in summer (long hours daily, Via Atenea 96, +39 092 259 5959).

€ **Café Concordia** perches on a pleasant piazza and dishes up traditional Sicilian treats, plus a delicious Sicilian version of tiramisu called "ricottamisu" (closed Mon, Piazza Pirandello 36, +39 092 225 894).

For Dessert: Locals are more than happy to walk a few minutes beyond the train station on the level, esplanade-like Viale della Vittoria to reach **Gelateria Le Cuspidi,** allegedly the best gelato in the region—it's flavorful and decadent (daily, Piazza Cavour 19).

Bakery: Leave the sweet treats to the places listed above and join the schoolkids who queue up at **Pane e Pani** for the fresh, hot, takeaway focaccia (daily, Via Luigi Pirandello 2).

Near the Temples

For locations, see the "Agrigento's Valley of the Temples" map, earlier.

€€€ **Re di Girgenti** offers elegantly composed cuisine in a hip-feeling atmosphere, with stellar views of the temples from their roadside terrace. It feels like a sophisticated escape (reservations smart, closed Tue, small parking lot, Via Panoramica Valle dei Templi 51, +39 092 240 1388, ilredigirgenti.it).

€€€ **Trattoria dei Templi,** on a busy strip just above the temples, has a lovely, modern, comfortable ambience. The fare is traditional Sicilian fish and pasta dishes with new and interesting twists (Mon-Sat lunch and dinner, Sun lunch only, Via Panoramica Valle dei Templi 15, +39 092 240 3110).

In San Leone

If you want some sea to go along with your ruins, the easiest option is the sandy stretch running southeast from the town of San Leone, about a 15-minute drive from Agrigento (also reachable by bus #3/; for location, see the "Agrigento Area" map, near the beginning of this chapter).

€€€ **Trattoria Caico** is a local favorite for a fine fish dinner in beachside San Leone. Wine connoisseur Marco and his wife Patrizia preside over the cramped dining room and can help you select the perfect Sicilian wine to complement the catch of the day (daily, Via Nettuno 35, San Leone, +39 092 246 4820).

Agrigento Connections

BY PUBLIC TRANSPORTATION

From Agrigento by Bus to: Palermo (7/day, fewer on weekends and holidays, 2 hours, Cuffaro), **Catania** (about hourly, 3 hours, SAIS Trasporti), **Trapani** (including **Trapani Birgi Airport**) (3/day, 3 hours, Salvatore Lumia). Bus info: Cuffaro (cuffaro.info), SAIS Trasporti (saistrasporti.it), Salvatore Lumia (autolineelumia.com).

From Agrigento by Train to: Palermo (hourly, 2 hours), **Cefalù** (hourly, 2.5 hours, change in Termini Imerese).

ROUTE TIPS FOR DRIVERS

To reach **Trapani** or the **Palermo airport,** follow the coastal road west toward Mazara del Vallo, then take the fast E-90 north toward Alcamo—this allows you to bypass central Palermo traffic. If you have time to dawdle along the coast, the Torre Salsa Nature Reserve offers white cliffs, miles of strolling, and nary a cocktail bar in sight. It's a 40-minute drive from Agrigento, between Siculiana and Montallegro.

The highway heading north from Agrigento connects to the main Palermo-Catania autostrada, A-19, a few miles north of Caltanissetta—watch for green signs. To reach the **Villa Romana del Casale,** at Caltanissetta follow signs for *Pietraperzia*, then *Barrafranca*, then follow the brown signs to *Villa del Casale* (2 hours).

If you're headed to **Siracusa**—and not stopping at Villa Romana del Casale—you'll save at least a half-hour by cutting north to the A-19 autostrada and Catania, then south along the east coast (on A-18, 2.5 hours total).

To reach **Ragusa** (again, if you're not visiting Villa Romana del Casale), follow the SS-115 coastal road toward Gela. This road is one of the most scenic on the island; be sure to notice the WWII bunkers in the hills between Agrigento and Gela. Continue through Vittoria and look for the turnoff to Ragusa just past Comiso.

VILLA ROMANA DEL CASALE

Tucked away in what seems like the middle of Sicily's nowhere is one of the world's finest remnants of the Roman Empire. In about AD 300, when Rome was falling and elites were inclined to build their fabulous palaces away from impending chaos, a rich and powerful Roman built a sprawling villa here and ornamented it with 38,000 square feet of exquisite mosaics. The identity of the villa's owner remains uncertain, but based on the mosaic themes, he is thought to have been a Roman senator—or even an importer of exotic animals. Today, this villa offers an intimate peek into the lifestyle of ancient Rome's upper crust.

Villa Romana del Casale is special, as it's one of few surviving Roman sites in Sicily. Although Sicily was the first Roman province outside the Italian peninsula, little of that past remains, as centuries of invaders looted, destroyed, or recycled the works of the civilizations that came before them. Yet Villa del Casale's floors—the largest collection of Roman floor mosaics ever found in situ—survived, probably because of the villa's remote countryside location. And thanks to a landslide that sealed off the area in the late Middle Ages, the site remained hidden from looters and plunderers for several hundred years. When the villa was excavated in the 1930s, society was ready to appreciate ancient treasures, and the site was protected and restored for visitors. Touring the villa, you'll enjoy some of the best-preserved and most playful mosaics in the Mediterranean. The illustrations are simply a delight.

GETTING THERE

Villa Romana del Casale is nestled in a valley about three miles southwest of the nearest town, Piazza Armerina.

234 Rick Steves Sicily

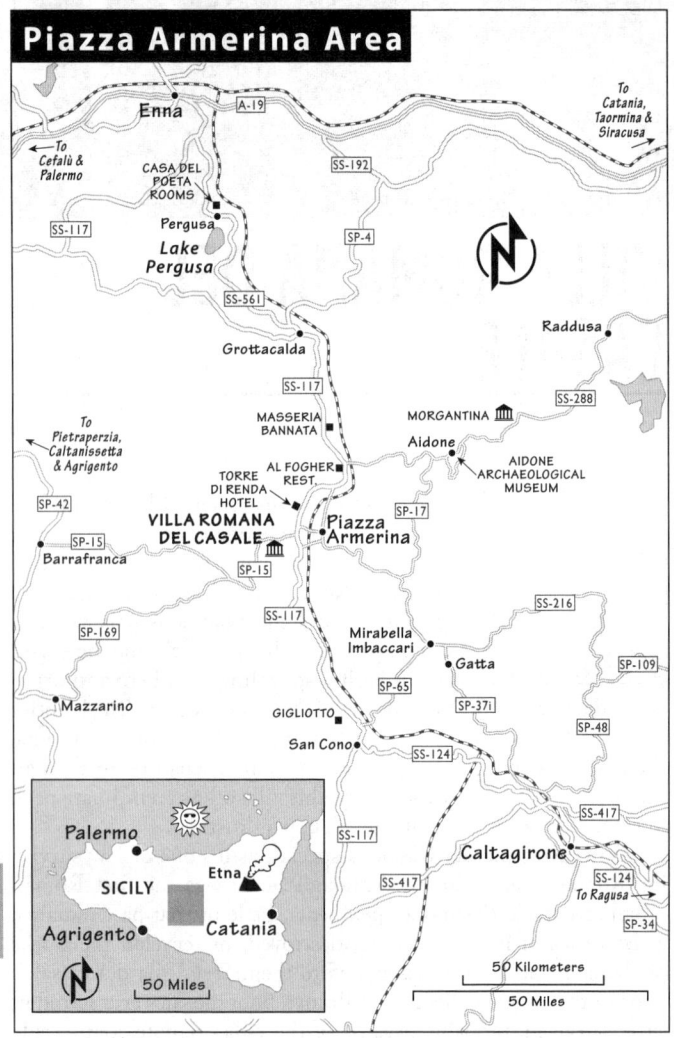

By Car: The villa is an efficient stop for drivers (1.5-2 hours from Agrigento, Catania, Siracusa, or Ragusa). To reach the villa from the main Palermo-Catania autostrada (A-19), head south near Enna in the direction of Caltagirone and Gela. Follow signs to *Piazza Armerina*, then look for brown signs pointing to *Villa Romana del Casale*. (If you're coming from Agrigento, see the "Route Tips for Drivers" at the end of that chapter.)

Villa Parking: Take a ticket as you enter the large parking lot at the villa; pay at the kiosk or nearby machines before you leave. To reach the villa from the parking lot, you'll walk about five minutes through a gauntlet of cafés and souvenir shops, then up the hill to the free WCs and ticket booth.

Returning to Ragusa or Siracusa: To Ragusa, drive south in the direction of Caltagirone. For Siracusa, it's best to return north to the A-19 autostrada, head toward Catania, then go south along the coast.

By Bus: While not ideal, it is possible to visit the site without a car. Buses run to the town of Piazza Armerina from **Palermo** (5/day Mon-Fri, less on Sat, not workable on Sun, 2 hours, SAIS, saisautolinee.it) and **Catania** (every 2 hours, 1.75 hours, Interbus/Etna Trasporti, interbus.it). Confirm schedules both ways before you commit.

Getting Between Piazza Armerina and the Villa: Buses arrive in the town of Piazza Armerina on the square called Piazza Senatore Marescalchi (aka "Piazza Stazione"), just north of the old-town center. From that square, **local buses** called "Villabus" depart sporadically to Villa del Casale, dropping off passengers along the road above the site (generally 6/day both ways, 20 minutes, €1.50, €1.70 if bought on board, €2.50 round-trip; scheduled departures from Piazza Armerina at 9:35, 10:30, and 12:30; from the site at 12:15, 14:15, 16:15, and 17:05).

You can also take a **taxi** to Villa del Casale (about 15 minutes). Taxis wait near where intercity buses arrive, at the corner of Piazza Senatore Marescalchi and Via Generale Muscarà. If no taxi is waiting, ask the staff at one of the bars on the square to call one for you. To return to the bus stop, ask the villa's parking lot attendant to call a taxi.

Local **drivers** Roberto Sapone and Giuseppe Lazzara offer transfers from Piazza Armerina to Villa del Casale (€5/person, €15 minimum; Roberto also available for longer trips and full-day excursions, +39 329 291 1435, robertosapone@hotmail.com; Giuseppe's mobile +39 333 202 7822).

PLANNING YOUR TIME

The speedy tourist can tackle Villa Romana del Casale as a strategic strike midway between Agrigento and Siracusa or Ragusa. To work a dose of hill towns, farm country, and wineries into your itinerary, stay in an *agriturismo*.

The actual visit takes about an hour, mostly walking along three-foot-wide metal catwalks designed to let visitors peer down at the precious mosaics without disturbing them. The villa is under a modern roof that protects sightseers from the brutal midday sun, though that's the most crowded time to visit.

ORIENTATION TO VILLA ROMANA DEL CASALE

Cost: €14, €24 combo-ticket with nearby site of Morgantina and museum in Aidone (described later).

Hours: Daily 9:00-19:00, may stay open later in summer; Nov-March daily until 17:00, last entry one hour before closing.

Information: +39 093 568 0036, villaromanadelcasale.it.

Crowd-Beating Tips: From mid-May to late September, visit before 10:00 or after 16:00 to avoid heat and crowds on the narrow catwalks (worst at midday). Outside of these peak months, crowds are usually no problem. If you find a bottleneck on the catwalks, use the Italian phrase *mi scusi, permesso* (mee SKOO-zee, pehr-MEH-soh) to ask other visitors to let you squeeze by.

Visitor Information: Good English-language info boards are posted throughout the site.

Tours: For a **guided tour**, consider the engaging guide team of Manuela Giadone and Sabrina Murgano (€70/hour, 2-hour minimum, they also guide in surrounding areas; Manuela: +39 333 861 5235, manugiadox@tiscali.it; Sabrina: +39 366 107 6957, murganos75@gmail.com). Other local guides hang around outside the guides' house past the shops, waiting to be hired. A two-hour tour costs €130. I'd skip the €6 **audioguide** that's advertised near the cafeteria.

Length of This Tour: One hour.

Services: Pay WCs are by the shops after the parking lot and at the cafeteria near the entrance (free with cafeteria purchase); free WCs are uphill to the left from the shops. There are no toilets inside the site.

Eating: A cluster of cafés sits at the edge of the parking lot. I like **€ Arione Café** (look for red *BAR* sign). They sell good sandwiches, sweets, coffee, and *granite*, and they have a few outdoor tables (daily, closed Jan-March). The **€ cafeteria** facing the ticket booth is dreary and overpriced, but convenient.

Starring: Elaborate and colorful mosaic floors with scenes of exotic beasts, wild parties, and the first bikinis.

◑ SELF-GUIDED TOUR

• *Just past the ticket booth, follow the path leading down to the site and pause when you reach the arch on your left. Take a moment to get oriented with this book's map, which helps you pinpoint where to stop for each description.*

Now turn your attention to the...

❶ Aqueduct

Masters of engineering, the Romans channeled water from the nearby Gela River into the villa with two aqueducts. The one on your left fed the baths, while the other served household needs.

Following the path downhill, on your left you'll pass the three furnaces of the baths (complete with their ranks of small terra-cotta steam pipes).

• *Rather than enter the site here, continue on the main stone pathway and circle around to the...*

❼ Monumental Entrance

Stand just outside of the patio surrounded by columns—which was the villa's "front door." Before you enter, imagine these ruined stumps extending up into a colorful triumphal arch. The villa was the centerpiece of a larger estate *(latifundium)*—a sprawling complex made up of living quarters, entertainment spaces, baths, and warehouses.

This landlocked villa, sitting on a hillside surrounded by thick woods, may seem randomly located. But it was strategically situated between Sicily's coasts and the two most important cities at the time, Akragas (Agrigento) and Katane (Catania). Some scholars theorize that the villa's owner was involved in the trade of exotic animals from North Africa and the Middle East. With access to ports, the location would have been practical for a trader in the ancient "stock" market, moving goods from the far reaches of the empire back to Rome.

From this grand entrance, a wall of frescoes on your right welcomed visitors. While it's mostly gone now, you might be able to make out the faded fragments of a horse's four hooves. Walk toward the entrance and notice the fresco fragment ahead (immediately right of the entry) that looks a bit like a vertical shish kebab. The Roman Empire was divided into four parts and ruled by four "tetrarchs"; this staff *(signum)* represented the tetrarchs who ruled the declining empire when this estate was built. This political symbol at the door announced the owner's importance and alliances. There is another one at the opposite end of the monumental entrance to your left.

Imagine approaching the entrance after a long, dusty journey on

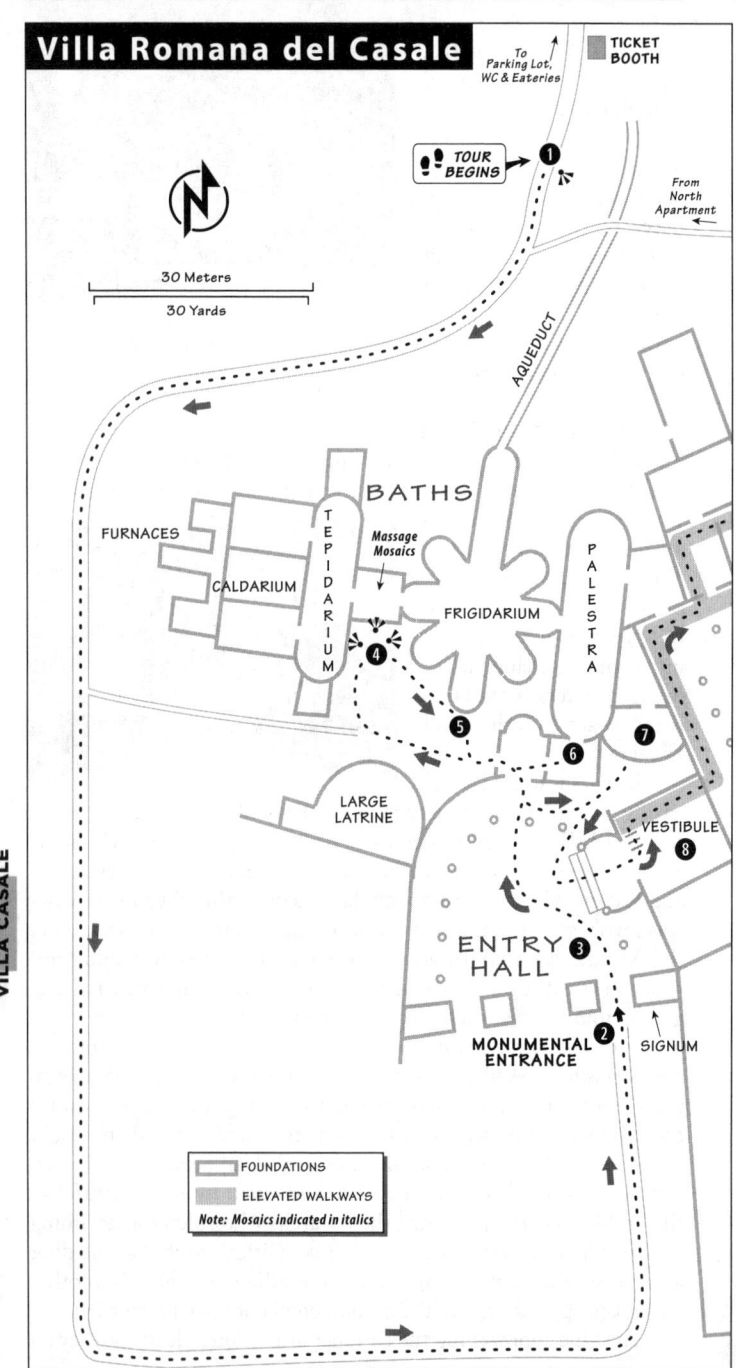

Villa Romana del Casale

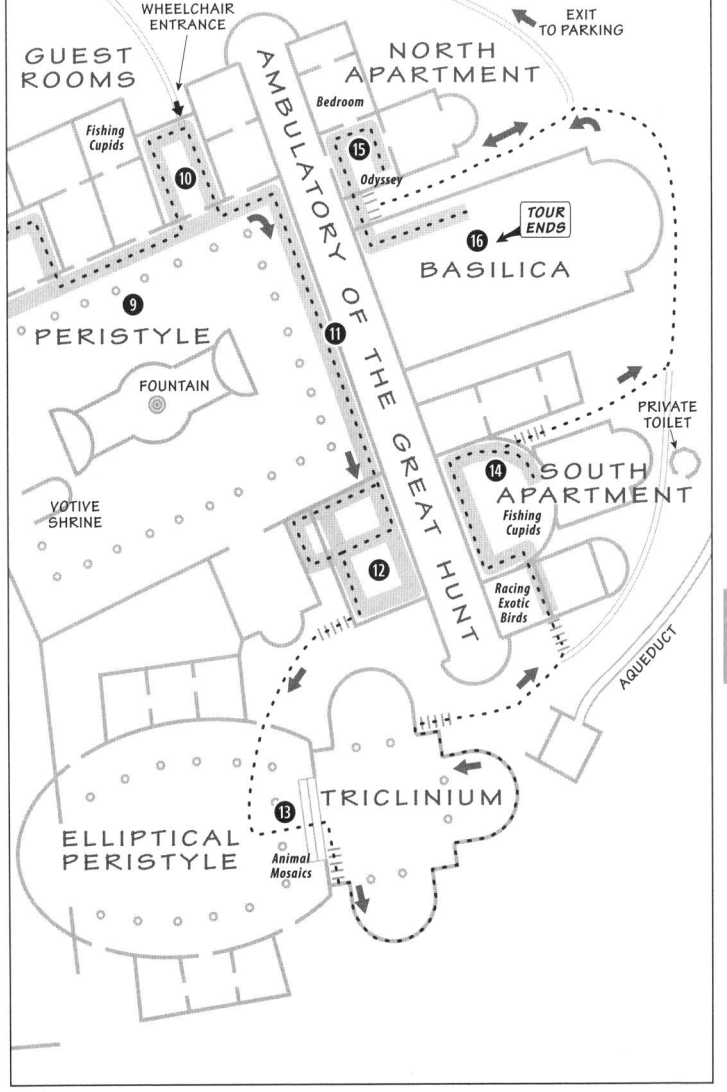

horseback. Just to the left is a trough decorated with mosaics of birds and foliage, where the horses could have a much-appreciated drink.
• *Now step inside.*

❸ Entry Hall

Just inside the wall, a small pool in the floor (at the base of the pillar) served to clean smelly feet, and the adjacent basin to refresh a dirty face.

Look around: You're standing in the entry hall, a semicircular covered portico supported by columns. In the middle, the *impluvium* (a basin where the roof drained) was a typical feature of entry halls in Roman homes. From this space, guests could spin off in different directions: toward the bath, the toilets, or the main house.
• *Head straight into the small glass-covered area, then angle left into the outdoor area. Straight ahead are the...*

❹ Baths *(Thermae)*

Romans bathed like we take coffee breaks. Baths were a daily social event—a ritual for the hygiene-obsessed ancients. Without soap, they used hot water to get clean. The bath process was similar to what you'd find in a fancy spa today. Bathers would go from room to room, slowly heating their bodies and opening pores in preparation for a massage and scrubbing.

From this point, you can see the long, pill-shaped **tepidarium,** a warm room with a double floor and double walls, and the **caldarium** beyond, where the sauna and the hot pools were.

Look through the net in the opening to the right of the tepidarium. This was the **massage room.** On the floor, you'll see a mosaic of barefoot masseuses ready to welcome guests. The bracelets on their right ankles might indicate that they were enslaved. The conical hat on one of the masseuses indicates his Persian origins, while his name, clearly written on his underpants, is Cassi. The masseuses would provide an aromatic-oil massage, then clean off the oil with a strigil—a curved metal scraper that would remove dead skin, dirt, and body hair all at the same time. The process, repeated daily, left Romans generally hairless. Imagine their surprise when they met hairy invaders with beards (*barba* in Italian), whom they called...barbarians. Here in the baths, the mosaic floors also served a practical purpose, providing a nonslip surface to walk on in the wet, steamy rooms.
• *Just to the right is the flower-shaped...*

❺ Frigidarium

The final bathing step: a cold-water shock to close pores in the cold room (frigidarium). Look for the deep soaking pool—covered with slabs of marble—that held tepid water. Beyond is a circulation space with a floor mosaic of sea gods. In the far wall, immediately in front of you between the two columns and past the arch, you can see an opening where cold water gushed out of the aqueduct into a frigid pool.

Take a moment to consider the excavations here. When the villa was discovered, the floors were preserved, but the roof and most of the walls had been destroyed by landslides and eroded by time. During the restoration (completed in 2012), archaeologists and architects took pains to enclose the mosaics to protect them from the elements. Using wood, plasterboard, and steel, the grand space of the original villa was re-created—but with the ambience of a barn rather than a palace. Traces of 1970s-era construction (with its sweat-inducing fiberglass and metal roofs) remain at the frigidarium, the palestra, and the triclinium.

• *Walk back up the four metal stairs; proceed straight ahead toward the wall and turn left to see the...*

❻ Palestra

Exercise was a part of the bath experience in Roman times, and this room served as a home gym. The shape of the room is similar to that of a chariot racetrack stadium *(circus),* perhaps providing competitive inspiration to the athletes. The mosaic floor decorations echo the shape of the room and show four teams with different colors racing around a central spine featuring an obelisk—

much like the Circus Maximus in Rome, à la *Ben-Hur*.

• *Head back up into the entry hall and take a sharp left into the little gap between the buildings.*

❼ Small Toilet

Imagine a whole team of athletes taking a communal bathroom break in this bathroom next to the gym—which could explain why Sicilians do not have a word for "privacy" (they just use ours and roll the *r*). Rather than flipping through a magazine on the throne, Sicilian ancients communally viewed a mosaic conversation piece—the animal-race scene on the floor—while sitting cheek-to-cheek. A steady stream of water meant things were constantly flushing.

And although the hygiene-conscious Romans didn't have toilet paper, they did have sticks equipped with a sea sponge at the end (the "business" ends of the sticks were then sanitized in vinegar).

• *Return one more time to the entry hall and U-turn left up the steps, entering the wood-covered area.*

❽ Adventus Vestibule

After cleaning up at the baths, a visitor was ready to meet the family. This grand vestibule is where the owner of the villa welcomed guests. Study what little remains of the mosaic. From the top of the metal staircase, you can look down to see how this mosaic is like a welcome mat: The noble family entourage awaits the arriving owner with ceremonial togas, laurel crowns, and a candle.

• *Turn left and continue around the catwalk, peering down into the large space just beyond, in the center of the villa.*

❾ Peristyle Courtyard

Roman villas were typically built as enclosed compounds facing an inner courtyard, a *peristylium*, with a fountain surrounded by a lush garden.

Some of the columns surrounding the peristyle are restored originals, some are reconstructed, and a few are still intact—either marble (with veins) or one-piece granite. All the capitals are original, in the Corinthian style (the Roman favorite).

The exotic animal heads in the floor design ringing the peristyle may have served as a catalog, illustrating which type of animals the villa owner sold.

Facing the inner courtyard are many rooms. As you continue from here, you'll pass over a series of service and guest rooms with floor mosaics showing geometric patterns and scenes of daily life. While I point out and describe my favorite scenes, take your time to enjoy the villa in general. It's mostly a one-way path (you'll go with the flow of the crowds). If a scene catches your interest, you'll generally find it described in English on a nearby info post. As a rule of thumb, rooms with geometric patterns rather than lively scenes were less important service rooms.

• *Near the far end of this side of the peristyle, pause at the...*

Roman Mosaics

Mosaics were a common way to cover floors in ancient Greece and Rome, particularly where they could add traction to the floors in wet areas such as baths. Ancient Romans also paved walls and ceilings with mosaics. The Romans learned their techniques from the Greeks: The earliest mosaics were made with pebbles pressed into wet plaster and initially were simple designs with geometric patterns. Later, as the art form advanced, they used finer materials, such as marble tiles, colored glass, or semiprecious stones. The Romans had the advantage of a large empire, so they could import stones of almost every color—giving their patterns more subtlety and their portraits more realism.

Mosaic tiles used in ancient times were usually about the size of a fingernail but could be as small as a pinhead. The Romans became masters of micromosaics, using such tiny pieces that the images look like photographs (they were so expensive that owners brought them along when moving to a new house). Mosaics are one of the finest art forms from ancient times because they're durable and their colors don't deteriorate as paint does on statues or frescoes.

This art form didn't die with the fall of Rome in the fifth century. It continued on in the Byzantine Empire, with craftsmen creating mosaics like the ones in Hagia Sophia in Istanbul, St. Mark's Basilica in Venice, Monreale Cathedral near Palermo, San Vitale and Mausoleo di Galla Placidia in Ravenna (in northern Italy), and many medieval basilicas in Rome.

⓾ Hall of the Small Hunt

A guest entering the villa would have been escorted to this side of the house, with a cluster of rooms facing the courtyard. This room, featuring a hunting scene, could have been the dining room. The floor mosaic depicts Roman techniques for capturing game; you can read it like a comic strip. Start on the bottom, where the hunt is in progress. In the middle, the hunters gather for an al fresco Thanksgiving dinner to enjoy their catch. The actual giving

of thanks takes place a level up, where the hunters burn incense for Diana, the goddess of the hunt.

Notice the fresco fragments on the walls. The Romans feared empty space, resulting in a decorating style that we might consider busy and over-the-top. Elaborate floors competed with Technicolor wall paintings, fancy furniture, and knickknacks.

As you circle the room, glance down to the left at the floor with cupids *(putti)* fishing. This was likely a room for children. The "V" symbols on the heads of the cupids could be the signature—like a trademark—of the North African mosaic masters who made them. But they're also possibly the tattoos that indicated Roman convict workers or enslaved people.

• *Circling around, at the far end of the peristyle, pass over the long...*

⓫ Ambulatory of the Great Hunt

This grand hall, the artistic highlight of the villa, showcases a 200-foot-long scene of an ancient safari, possibly depicting the owner's business in action. You'll see leopards, antelopes, cheetahs, Barbary lions (now extinct), tigers, elephants, ostriches, camels, water rhinoceroses, fish, dolphins, and many other species. As you stroll the length of this scene, note how the highly detailed animals are laid out—from one end of the corridor to the other, as if going west to east from Mauretania (today's Morocco) to India.

Stop and admire the accuracy of the animal bodies. The skin of the elephant looks scored and rough to the touch. The hunters demonstrate their creative techniques for capturing prey without killing them, leaving that work to the gladiators. Oxen and carts carry heavy wooden boxes containing wild animals, which are then loaded onto ships. Note the interesting clothing worn by the Romans from different parts of the empire, like an ancient fashion show.

• *Your tour of this long scene continues after a fun little detour. Follow the catwalks up a ramp, then look down to see...*

⓬ The Gymnasts

There really is nothing new under the sun—apparently, women in bikinis were popular even 2,000 years ago. While these figures are commonly called "the bikini girls," in reality they are serious athletes—lifting weights, running, discus throwing, and playing the first known game of beach volleyball.

Notice the realistic action poses and elegant hairstyles. The winner sports a palm frond (a symbol of victory) and a crown of roses. The woman in the golden gown on the far left, despite being more clothed than the rest, is suffering an unfortunate wardrobe malfunction.

In the top left corner, underneath the "bikini girls" mosaic, you'll see a fragment of the older floor mosaic with geometric patterns. Even the Romans enjoyed remodeling and home improvement, changing decor over time.

• *After the gymnasts, you'll reach the far end of the Ambulatory of the Great Hunt.*

End of the Hunt

Notice the tiger licking her cub. This is possibly illustrating a trick that hunters used to confuse and distract the animal: A mirrored orb fooled the tiger into thinking she saw her baby, but it actually showed her own reflection. To the left, a Roman on a white horse boards a ship with two cubs. Immediately behind the tiger, as we approach unknown territories, mythological figures appear. Notice the griffin hunched over a box. After the capture of so many animals, the final scene turns the tables on the human captors. You can barely make out a frightened human face peering out from inside the box (next to the griffin's paw). The hunt has been reversed, and the hunter has become the prey.

• *Stepping outside, go down some stairs to reach the...*

⓮ Elliptical Peristyle and Triclinium

Watch your step. This is the only section of the mosaic you can walk on. Along the flat side, find the lizard and the jackalope among the curly vines. The building on your left is the great dining hall, or triclinium. Here, the owner would have hosted lavish banquets, with guests comfortably lounging on

couches *(triclinia)* while eating, vomiting, and eating again. Its mosaic floors tell the myths of Hercules. The apse opposite the entrance features five Michelangelo-esque giants twisting in agony, struck by poisoned arrows fired by Hercules.

• *Continue around the far end of the triclinium and go in the door marked...*

⓮ Master's Southern Apartment

Based on its playful mosaics, this series of rooms may have been the apartments of the villa owner's children. Apparently, ancient Roman rich kids had some interesting hobbies—such as drag-racing chariots pulled by exotic birds.

In the semicircular portico nearby, chubby fishing cupids are pulling in today's catch. This space was a peaceful circulation hub for the private portions of the house, with a cool, burbling fountain coordinating with mosaics of aquatic scenes.

• *There are a few more mosaics at this end to peruse before you are routed back outside. As you exit, notice the small, octagonal foundation (on your right) of the private toilet for the owners, just steps from the main bedroom.*

Turn left and follow signs back inside and up the stairs to the...

⓯ Master's Northern Apartment

As these rooms were the living quarters for the owner of the villa, the majority have fine mosaics. Take your time to enjoy each one. As you enter, you'll find a famous episode from Homer's *Odyssey*, perhaps a representation of actors performing the myth on stage. The Cyclopes were described by Homer as one-eyed giants living in caves up on Mount Etna. Although Polyphemus, depicted here, has three eyes, those extra eyes don't seem to help. Mischievous Ulysses still tricks him with a cup of "grape juice." (Never trust Greeks bearing gifts...)

Over in the next room, the private bedroom of the *dominus* and his *domina*, the couple share figs and honey, the traditional diet of a newlywed couple. There's a full moon, and things are getting steamy...

Antiquity Smuggling

Museums around the world display Greek Sicilian works bought on the open market. Although legally any ancient artifacts of value found on private property belong to the Italian government—and it is a crime to remove them—pieces slip through the cracks with alarming regularity. Many of Sicily's archaeological sites are poorly guarded, lacking funds for proper maintenance. Grave robbers have been known to hop over fences and dig up precious works at night. Statues were purposely smashed and transported as rubble, then reassembled outside of Italy at black-market warehouses.

Although Italy has made a major effort to stop the theft—tasking a special police force with tracking and recovering stolen works—it's a challenge, especially when art dealers sell artifacts to prestigious museums, sometimes for millions of dollars.

For instance, in the 1980s, the J. Paul Getty Museum of Los Angeles purchased the seven-foot-tall *Venus of Malibu* for $18 million from an unscrupulous art dealer. The piece turned out to have been stolen from the Morgantina archaeological site, near Aidone. (One of the most heavily looted archaeological sites in Italy, it has lost unknown treasures to thieves.) The Italian government pursued the return of the goddess, and the Getty eventually signed an agreement in 2007 to return a number of works to Italy—including the statue that has since been rechristened *Goddess of Morgantina* (now in the Aidone Archaeological Museum—described later).

The looting continues, however. Major theft rings have been broken up as recently as 2017. The Italian government has a long way to go if they are ever to recover all their looted art.

• *Ahem! It's time to discreetly go back out the way you entered, then continue straight ahead, into the...*

⓰ Basilica

We usually think of a basilica as a Christian church. But the term dates from centuries before Christ: For the Romans, a basilica was a grand public meeting place, such as a hall of justice. And the Romans copied the basilica type of building straight from the Greeks. For the Greeks, it was the

formal hall where the governor *(basileus)* ran the administration of the territories.

Seated on the throne just below the apse of this hall, a wooden coffered ceiling overhead (like the replica you see today), the owner of this villa would have formally received guests and potential customers and managed the estate. This is the only room without any mosaics. Instead, the floors are covered in exotic and precious marble slabs that would have continued onto the walls. Since this was where business deals were struck, the intent of this room's decor was to impress and intimidate visitors.

Even today, with little more than its original footprint and tens of millions of mosaic chips (I counted them myself) decorating its many rooms, Villa del Casale—1,700 years later—may not intimidate, but it certainly does impress.

• *Our tour is finished. Head back outside and follow signs to the exit.*

SIGHTS NEAR VILLA ROMANA DEL CASALE
Piazza Armerina Town

The nearest town to Villa Romana del Casale—about a 15-minute drive away—is Piazza Armerina (pop. 20,000). This hill town, clustered along a ridge that runs roughly east-west, is crowned by a Baroque cathedral with a colorful tile dome. While there were settlements in the area for centuries, the city on the hill was started by the Normans in the 12th century, and most of the village that you see today was built from the 12th to 17th century.

There are no notable sights in Piazza Armerina, but a half-hour's climb up the narrow streets to the cathedral will take you through charming medieval back alleys of this workaday Sicilian village. At the top of town, you'll find a Spanish castle, a cathedral and its museum, and some views over the city. Drivers looking for views can follow the windy, uphill Via Giovanni Verga to the terrace near the sports stadium (Campo Sportivo).

Archaeological Sites near Aidone

For most visitors, seeing Villa Romana del Casale is plenty. But archaeology completists may want to drive about 30 minutes east to the pleasant, sleepy hill town of Aidone and its small museum, and about 15 minutes farther to the (scant) ruins of another ancient site, Morgantina, with an interesting main square and views.

Aidone Archaeological Museum: This small museum, filling a former monastery, houses an interesting collection of Greek and Roman artifacts found at the Morgantina archaeological area. The star of the museum is the *Goddess of Morgantina*—formerly known as the *Venus of Malibu* (see sidebar for details). This famous limestone-and-marble statue, dating from 420-410 BC, is incomplete—missing her hair and her left arm and foot. You'll also see several other finds from Morgantina and silver artifacts on permanent loan from the Metropolitan Museum of Art in New York City (€8, €13 combo-ticket with Morgantina site, €24 combo-ticket for both plus Villa del Casale, daily 9:00-17:00, May-Sept until 18:30, Largo Torres Truppia 1, Aidone, +39 093 587 307).

Morgantina: This archaeological site, just east of Aidone, has the remains of an ancient Sicel city that was later conquered by the Greeks and Romans. This is where the *Goddess of Morgantina* was originally found. There isn't much left, but it's interesting for its main square (agora) and sweeping territorial views (€8, see combo-ticket options above, daily 9:00-13:00, May-Sept until 16:00, +39 093 587 955).

SLEEPING NEAR VILLA ROMANA DEL CASALE

See the "Piazza Armerina Area" map at the beginning of this chapter for locations. Unless otherwise noted, these listings have air-conditioning but no elevator.

€€ Agriturismo Masseria Bannata, near Piazza Armerina, sits tucked into the side of a hill along the road north out of town. Signora Nietta has thoughtfully restored the six rooms on her family farm—some of them former chicken coops and feeding troughs—with quirky antiques and an eye for modern Italian design (family rooms, closed Nov-March, Contrada Bannata, on SS-117 at signpost 41, +39 328 298 8448, bannata.com, info@agriturismobannata.it).

€€ Casa del Poeta, run by Masseria Bannata, is a former hunting lodge near Lake Pergusa, a half-hour north of Piazza Armerina. The four rooms are artsy and modern, with a poetry theme—the poem of the day is available at the front desk (closed Nov-March, Via Diana, Pergusa, +39 328 298 8448, lacasadelpoetaenna.com, info@lacasadelpoeta.it).

€ Torre di Renda, a country hotel and recommended restaurant clinging to a cliff overlooking Piazza Armerina, rents 19 rooms with simple, modern charm set inside an old farmhouse (C. da Torre di Renda, +39 093 568 0208, torrerenda.it, info@torrerenda.it).

€ Gigliotto, an *agriturismo* and winery, is just off the highway 15 minutes south of Piazza Armerina. Although it's big and attracts groups for lunch, the views are postcard-worthy, and it's open year-round (no air-con; wine tastings—€25 and up; good restaurant, on SS-117 at signpost 60, San Michele di Ganzaria, +39 391 734 0376, gigliotto.com, gigliotto@gigliotto.com).

EATING NEAR VILLA ROMANA DEL CASALE

In addition to the places right at the villa itself, consider driving to these appealing countryside choices. Just above Piazza Armerina, the €€ **Torre di Renda** restaurant serves meals with a view (€30 fixed-price lunch/dinner, reserve ahead, daily, see contact details under hotel listing, earlier). €€€ **Ristorante Al Fogher** sits in a little cottage under the freeway a few miles north of Piazza Armerina. Affable Chef Angelo Treno uses quality local ingredients and creates modern dishes from old recipes. The €40 fixed-price lunch, a gourmet steal of four dishes, includes a goblet of wine and coffee (Tue-Sat open for lunch and dinner, Sun lunch only, closed Mon, closed Tue in off-season, reserve ahead for dinner, Viale Conte Ruggero—SS-117, +39 093 568 4123).

RAGUSA & THE SOUTHEAST

Ragusa • Southeast Countryside Drive • Noto

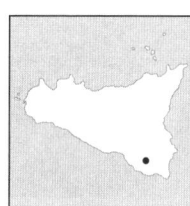

Sicily's southeast is charming, prosperous, and uncrowded—an ideal place for in-the-know travelers to relax for a day or two. With rolling green hills and low, stacked-stone walls, it looks almost like Ireland. Soaring hill towns (Ragusa) have their counterpoint in valley villages (Scicli). Small hamlets cluster along the sea, some with sandy beaches.

The fate of the entire region was altered by one massive event: the catastrophic earthquake of 1693. Villages with 2,000 years of history were flattened in an instant and later rebuilt in the Baroque style that was all the rage at the time. The town of Noto, reconstructed after the quake, is the jewel in the crown of Sicilian Baroque. (For more on Sicily's unique Baroque style, see the sidebar on page 66).

This region is one of Sicily's quietest and least touristed corners. Exploring here, you'll enjoy relatively affluent country towns and a relaxed pace. Ragusa—an easy-to-like hill town with a stunning setting—is an ideal home base, with more than its share of good hotels and restaurants.

PLANNING YOUR TIME

Ragusa can be seen in a day, but its lovely, quiet nature—combined with its easy access to nearby villages—makes it an ideal spot to linger for a couple of days.

Day 1: Explore Ragusa, starting with the steep climb from the lower town (Ragusa Ibla) to the upper town (Ragusa Superiore). Then head back to the lower town for your reward: a fancy lunch at the elegant Duomo restaurant. In the afternoon, follow my Ragusa Ibla Walk, drop in on vespers at the Church of San Giuseppe in the early evening, and enjoy a *granita* at Caffetteria Donnafugata. If you want to see some interesting interiors, make a reservation to tour Palazzo Arezzo di Trifiletti and/or sign up for one of Iblazon's tours (see "Tours in Ragusa," later).

Day 2: Follow my Southeast Countryside Drive, stopping for lunch on the coast or in Scicli. Finish your day with a relaxing dinner in Ragusa Ibla.

Ragusa

Built along a steep promontory and surrounded by a verdant gorge, Ragusa is a pleasant, sleepy place to catch your breath on a busy Sicily itinerary. It feels off the beaten path—a peaceful eddy all its own. It's low impact...except when you're negotiating its steep cityscape.

Ragusa (pop. 76,000) isn't a single town. It's two towns— each with its own character— connected by a wandering staircase. The original city, Ragusa Ibla, is on the smaller, lower hill. Ancient "Hybla" was almost entirely destroyed by the 1693 earthquake. Most of the town's wealthier families decided that it wasn't worth the effort to rebuild their broken homes and relocated to the higher hill and plain above. There they built Ragusa Superiore, anchored by a new, earthquake-fortified cathedral, with a grid street plan and room for expansion. Meanwhile, Ragusa Ibla was slowly rebuilt—in part by the people who could not afford to start over—keeping its medieval character of winding lanes and homes burrowed into the rock.

Today, the upper town bustles with modern shops and services, while the lower town is sleepy and residential, with pretty churches and great restaurants. Together, they make a perfect home base for your southeast Sicily visit.

Getting There: Ragusa is in a remote area of southeast Sicily without major highways, which means it takes a bit of time to get there. From Agrigento, the coastal route (SS-115) is best, cutting up near Gela (2.5 hours). From Siracusa, head south on E-45 past Avola, then head west through Noto and Modica—both great on-the-way stops (1.5 hours).

Orientation to Ragusa

Ragusa's two towns—the lower, ancient city of Ragusa Ibla and the upper, modern town of Ragusa Superiore—are set on adjacent hills. Most visitors concentrate their time in Ragusa Ibla (and should), but Ragusa Superiore can be worth a quick look.

The two hills are connected by a lower saddle of land, marked by Piazza della Repubblica (near a large parking lot). From here, a scenic and strenuous stair-and-hill climb heads up to Ragusa Superiore.

The heart of Ragusa Superiore is the Cathedral of San Giovanni Battista, surrounded by cafés, eateries, and shopping streets. The smaller, more modest center of Ibla is the piazza of the Cathedral of San Giorgio, from which Corso XXV Aprile runs down to the Ibleo public garden at the bottom edge of town. You can walk from one end of Ragusa Ibla to the other in about 15 minutes.

No matter where you walk, in either part of Ragusa, count on hills and stairs everywhere.

TOURIST INFORMATION

There are two helpful TIs, run by the same company: one in Piazza della Repubblica, which sits in the saddle between the two towns (daily, 10:00-13:00), and another in Ragusa Superiore on Piazza San Giovanni (Mon-Fri 9:00-19:00, may be open Sat-Sun in summer, +39 093 267 6550). The TI in Ragusa Ibla at Palazzo La Rocca, near the cathedral, is basically useless (Mon-Fri 9:00-19:00, closed Sat-Sun).

ARRIVAL IN RAGUSA

By Car: Ragusa Ibla has several options for parking. Pick a lot depending on where you're staying. Pay-and-display lots are just below Piazza della Repubblica, a manageable uphill walk (enter the lot from Via Avvocato Giovanni Ottaviano, the road that hugs the southern edge of Ragusa Ibla), and at the eastern end of Ragusa Ibla, near the Ibleo public garden. Closer to the center of Ibla, the Piazza Dottor Solarino lot is below the cathedral. Watch for the pedestrian-only ZTL signs at the center of Ragusa Ibla, and make sure not to drive in those areas (given how narrow some streets are, you won't want to drive in them anyway). You must have a permit or registered car before you can enter the ZTL, so if you plan on driving here, ask your hotel about this before your arrival.

If you're heading for Ragusa Superiore, an easy pay parking garage is under the post office (enter on Corso Italia). Throughout Ragusa, street parking within white lines is free; blue lines require a pay-and-display ticket (or look for signs for the EasyPark app).

By Bus or Train: Long-distance buses and trains arrive on the

254 Rick Steves Sicily

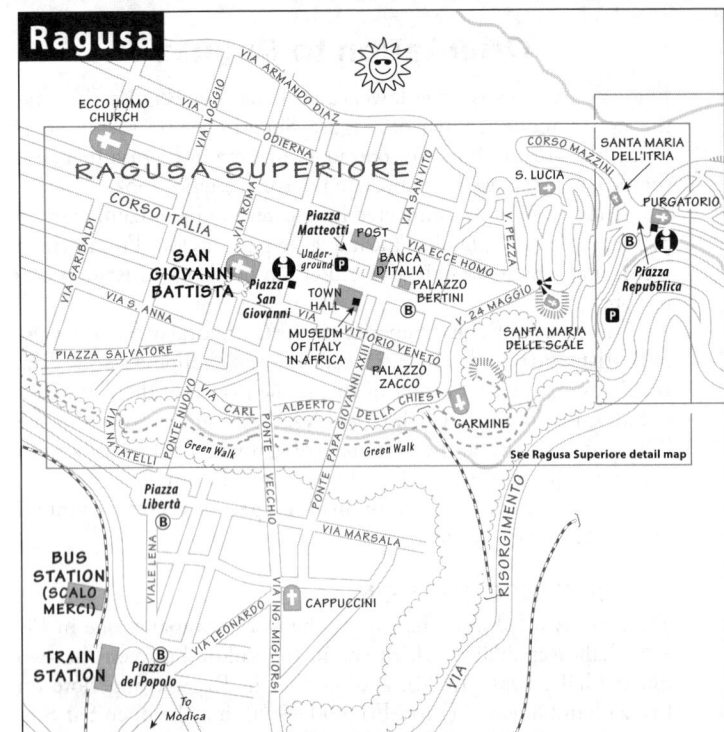

southwestern outskirts of Ragusa Superiore, a long walk from the cathedral and town center (too far to attempt on foot with luggage).

To reach Ragusa Ibla (and most of my recommended accommodations) from the train or bus station, it's easiest to take a **taxi** (€15-20). You can also take a **bus,** though they generally run just once an hour (buses #1 & #3 run daily, #2 Mon-Sat only; Etna Trasporti, etnatrasporti.it). Etna Trasporti also runs evening shuttles from Piazza del Popolo near the train station and Scalo Merci bus station to near the Ibleo public garden in Ragusa Ibla (€1, every 20 minutes; green line—May-Sept daily 18:00 until late, Oct-April Fri-Sun only; red line—June-Sept daily 19:15 until late, Oct-May Fri-Sun only).

HELPFUL HINTS

Market: A tiny weekly market takes place near the Ibleo public garden in Ragusa Ibla on Mondays until 13:00. Larger weekly markets are in Ragusa Superiore.

Festivals: San Giorgio, the patron saint of Ibla, is celebrated with processions at the end of May or early June.

Ferry to Malta: Ragusa Xpress runs a ferry that connects nearby Marina di Ragusa to Malta in about 40 minutes (typically 4/

Orientation to Ragusa

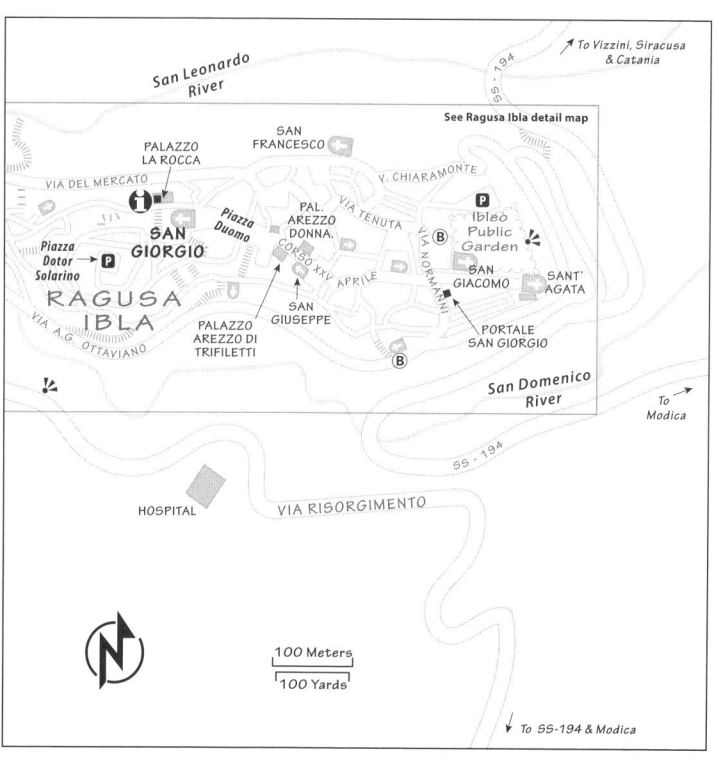

week, additional sailings in summer, check schedule online, ragusaxpress.com). Drivers can reach Marina di Ragusa directly in about 20 minutes (or indirectly as part of my Southeast Countryside Drive—see later in this chapter). Frequent buses also run to Marina di Ragusa (ask the TI or your hotel for details).

GETTING AROUND RAGUSA

By Bus: Ragusa's public buses, operated by Etna Trasporti, help connect its two towns, though the schedule is unpredictable and stops can be tricky to find. Bus #1 (runs daily) is generally better for getting from Ragusa Superiore to Ibla. It goes from Piazza del Popolo (near the Scalo Merci bus station and the train station) to near the cathedral in Superiore before switchbacking down to Piazza della Repubblica, looping around the base of Ragusa Ibla's ridge, and ending at the Ibleo public garden. Buses #2 and #3 are better for getting from Ibla to Superiore, going from the garden up to near the cathedral in Superiore (15 minutes between Ibla and Superiore, buses run about hourly; bus #3 daily, #2 Mon-Sat only; tickets are €1.20 if you buy at a tobacco shop or €1.50 on the bus).

By Taxi: Taxis charge €15 to travel between Ragusa Ibla and

Ragusa Superiore (fixed rates, depends on time of day). You may find them waiting in Ragusa Superiore at Piazza Zama and Piazza Libertà. There are not a lot of taxis in Ragusa Ibla (you may find them off Piazza Duomo or near the gardens). If you can't find one, call +39 0932 1832, or go into any bar and ask them to call for you.

Tours in Ragusa

Local Guide
Francesca Giovatto is an effervescent Ragusan who delights in showing the beauty of her city and region to visitors (€80/hour, 2-hour minimum, +39 339 137 5952, francescagiovatto@virgilio.it).

Walking Tours
A company called **Iblazon** offers tours with access to some interesting interiors. Their **Ibla 1860 tour** paints a picture of 19th-century aristocratic life. You'll go inside three spaces: the Circolo di Conversazione private club, the noble floor of Palazzo Arezzo di Trifiletti, and Cinabro Carrettieri, a Sicilian cart-painting workshop (€15, 3-4/week, 1.5 hours). Reserve a couple of weeks ahead, either via email or by sending a WhatsApp message to +39 366 319 4177, iblazonprivatetours.it, info@iblazonprivatetours.it).

Olive Oil Tasting
The region around Ragusa is known for its olive oil (thanks to a special olive called the Tonda Iblea), and you'll likely get to taste it at local restaurants. For a deeper dive, consider a tasting of several olive oils, which includes background information on the local olives and oil production, plus instructions on how to smell and taste olive oil. The experience is organized by Arturo in a special cellar at his guesthouse, where they also sell olive oil (€25/person, minimum two people, one hour, lunch tastings available, Via Capitano Bocchieri 46, reserve two weeks in advance by sending a WhatsApp message to +39 333 177 9430).

Tourist Train
A tourist train loops around Ragusa Ibla for a look at the old town (€5, departs hourly from Piazza Duomo, +39 0932 187 4135, treninobarocco.com).

Ragusa Ibla Walk

This walk takes you along the spine of the ancient city of Ragusa, from the cliffhanging Ibleo public garden to the cathedral square. While you could walk through the center of Ibla in 15 minutes, this stroll will take 30 minutes (or more if you set a leisurely pace and make a few stops). To trace the route of this walk, see the "Ragusa Ibla" map.

• *We'll begin at the ceremonial stone gateway of the Giardino Ibleo, Ragusa's public garden. To get there, simply walk downhill the length of Ragusa Ibla to its eastern tip.*

❶ Public Garden (Giardino Ibleo)

Step through the gateway and go for a little stroll clockwise through this delightful ▲▲ public park. The main path feels at once elegant and well used. Notice the Ragusans hanging out on benches, playing with their kids, catching up with neighbors, and so on.

As you walk, you'll pass a church on the left and come upon a convent (now a recommended hotel). Nearing the end of the path, bear left to reach a fine overlook into the ravine below. It's easy to imagine why a town would be built in this well-protected, strategic location.

• *Head back out the way you came in. From the garden gate, turn left and walk downhill about 30 yards. On your left, tucked back from the street, notice the...*

❷ Portale San Giorgio

Ragusa Ibla was a thriving city in the Middle Ages. But the 1693 earthquake virtually flattened the town—causing the townspeople to rebuild on the higher, flatter hilltop of Ragusa Superiore. The Gothic church that stood here from the 1300s collapsed in the quake, and this doorway is all that's left. It's among the oldest surviving architecture in Ragusa Ibla. Notice the lunette over the doorway: It's decorated with a sculpted relief of St. George (San Giorgio) slaying the dragon.

• *Backtrack up to the garden gate. With the garden at your back, walk straight ahead, through the piazza, and up...*

❸ Corso XXV Aprile

This is the main street of Ragusa Ibla, and it's filled with small

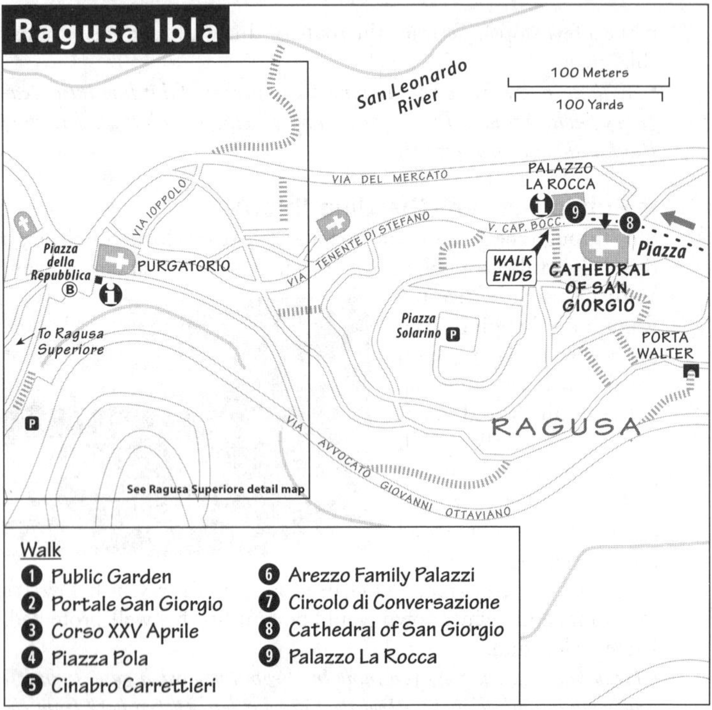

Ragusa Ibla

Walk
1. Public Garden
2. Portale San Giorgio
3. Corso XXV Aprile
4. Piazza Pola
5. Cinabro Carrettieri
6. Arezzo Family Palazzi
7. Circolo di Conversazione
8. Cathedral of San Giorgio
9. Palazzo La Rocca

shops, restaurants, and *gelaterie*. Walk up a few short blocks and jog left with the street. On your right, just after the jog, look for #41, with a door (usually open) at the base of a tower. Peeking in here, you'll see a candlelit shrine to the Virgin Mary. This tiny chapel is attached to the **Church of Santa Maria Maddalena.** Ragusans drop in as they pass by to pay their respects; some even cross themselves as they walk by on the street.

• *At the top of Corso XXV Aprile is the square called...*

❹ Piazza Pola

To your left is the Baroque **Church of San Giuseppe,** with its elaborate convex facade. Built in the late 18th century, this church serves a convent of cloistered Benedictine nuns whose once-large community has dwindled to only a few elderly nuns. You can join them in their lovely, small church for the saying of the rosary and the singing of vespers (generally Mon-Fri at 17:15; check schedule inside the door).

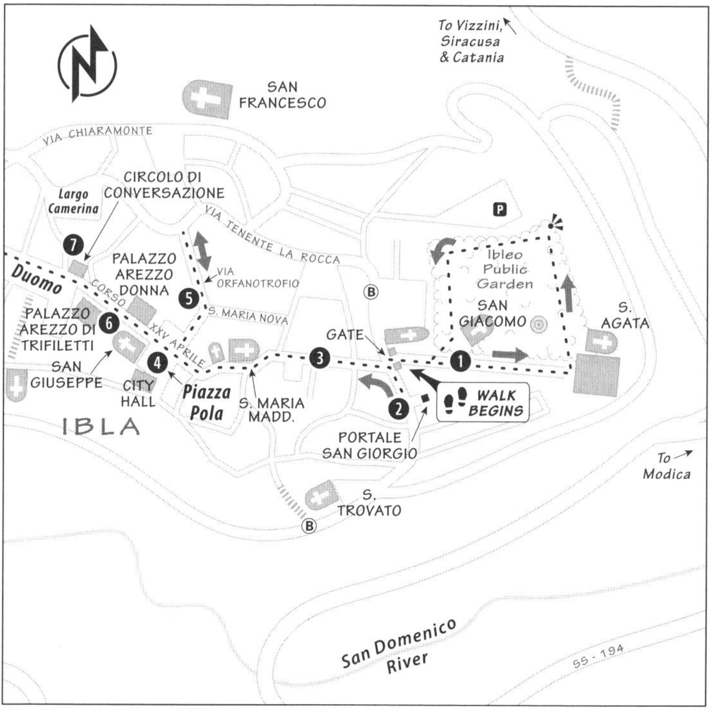

Ragusa Ibla Walk

• *From Piazza Pola, detour onto Via Orfanotrofio (the street to the right as you enter Piazza Pola from Corso XXV Aprile). Bear left at the fork and find #22, the home of...*

❺ Cinabro Carrettieri

This is the workshop of Biagio and Damiano, two of the final remaining artisans keeping alive the traditional Sicilian craft of painting and restoring carts. These colorful, elaborately carved carts were once used by traveling salesmen to tote their goods around Sicily. The carts also served as self-advertising—the better and more embellished, the more they stood out. Anyone can stop in for a closer look at the carts and to chat with the artists (ask to see a photo of their decorated Fiat 500, now in a museum). If you're interested in learning more, you can ask about a tour of their workshop in English (€6, +39 340 844 4804). The workshop tour is included in Iblazon's Ibla 1860 tour (see "Tours in Ragusa," earlier).

There are plenty of eating and drinking options around here. Next door to the cart workshop is **Lucernaio,** a microbrew pub serving an assortment of Italian craft beers on tap or by the bottle. And across the street, the recommended **I Banchi**—owned by a local celebrity chef—has an eatery with a takeaway counter, plus a sit-down restaurant in back. Or back on Piazza Pola, at the recommended **Caffetteria Donnafugata,** you can try a *granita*.

• *From Piazza Pola, continue uphill on Corso XXV Aprile, which becomes pedestrian only. Stop at #9.*

❻ Arezzo Family Palazzi

On opposite sides of the street, you'll see two palaces belonging to different members of the Arezzo family. These longtime aristocrats have been in Sicily since the 12th century and in Ragusa since the late 1700s. Keep an eye out for their coat of arms, decorated with four hedgehogs.

The larger palace on the right (at #9)—**Palazzo Arezzo di Donnafugata**—is owned by the branch of the family that built the countryside Donnafugata Castle and its extensive gardens (see the Southeast Countryside Drive, later in this chapter). This town palace has its own small, private theater, which was originally accessed only from the palace ballroom. But a later owner opened the theater to the public, converting former warehouse and storage areas into a foyer and lounges. The theater is adorably tiny, with just 120 seats, and regularly hosts classical concerts. For a peek inside and (pricey) private tours, reserve ahead, +39 334 220 8186, teatrodonnafugata.it.

On the other side of the street and down a bit (at #4) is the **Palazzo Arezzo di Trifiletti.** Members of the Arezzo family have lived in this beautiful Baroque palace, which includes a grand ballroom with a frescoed ceiling, since the mid-19th century. Domenico, the current owner's son, leads perfunctory 20-minute tours of the home in English. While the tour may be light on charm, the palazzo itself offers a unique behind-the-scenes

glimpse of historic and contemporary Italian aristocratic life (€6, reserve ahead by email or phone, +39 339 400 0013, palazzoarezzo.it, eventipalazzoarezzo@gmail.com). The palazzo is also viewable via Iblazon's Ibla 1860 tour.

• *At the next corner, admire the short but stately building on the right.*

❼ Circolo di Conversazione

Resembling a Greek temple, this "Conversation Circle" was founded in the mid-1800s by 18 elite local families as a private social club. Here they could enjoy one another's company without mixing with the rabble. A bit like a Lions Club, upper-class professional men gathered here for generations—and still do today—to chat in a fancy meeting room with velvet drapes and cushy chairs.  Women were finally admitted in 1973 (they have their own room). The building's facade almost feels like a stage set—designed specifically to evoke the classical "look" that was all the rage among Grand Tour travelers. It's worth going inside to see the convivial meeting rooms and the grand ballroom with red-silk walls and a frescoed ceiling (€6, open Tue-Sun 10:30-12:00, closed Mon, guided tours every 30 minutes; included on Iblazon's Ibla 1860 tour—see page 256).

• *Continue ahead to the long, sloping main square, crowned by the...*

❽ Cathedral of San Giorgio (Duomo di San Giorgio)

The centerpiece of Ragusa Ibla, this church was designed by the local architect Rosario Gagliardi, who kept busy after the earthquake designing churches for Ragusa Ibla, Modica, and his hometown of Noto. He admired the Baroque facades of churches in the German Rococo style, with a tall, central bell tower, and used optical illusions to add interest to his designs. For example, notice how the church's entry staircase veers to the left. To make sure that both the dome and the bell tower would be visible from the piazza, Gagliardi slightly skewed the orientation of the church so that it's not strictly aligned with the square. Find the repeating motif  of Saint George—San Giorgio—on a horse slaying a dragon in the exterior decoration: on the sides of the facade, on the stained-glass window, and even on the wrought-iron gate that surrounds the steps. At night, the church is floodlit, enhancing its Baroque drama.

To visit the interior, walk along the right side of the church to find a smaller, separate staircase that leads to the entrance (free, daily 10:00-12:30 & 16:00-18:30 except closed Tue morning, +39 093 222 0085).

• *Continue alongside the church on Via Capitano Bocchieri to #33 (on the right).*

❾ Palazzo La Rocca

Look up at the balconies on this late-Baroque palazzo. Peering down at you are masks, animals, and cherubs. Take a moment to identify some of the characters: musicians playing flute and lyre, a couple in an awkward embrace, a man with a barrel of wine, and more. Many of the Baroque *palazzi* of Ragusa have these creative flourishes. A TI is inside the palazzo.

Turn back the way you came to enjoy a picture-perfect view of the dome of San Giorgio. The church's architect wanted you not only to see the dome from the front but also to view it from the back side, so he carefully framed it here in this streetscape. This kind of dramatic staging is a typical, playful feature of Baroque architecture here in southeastern Sicily, taking inspiration from nature to give movement and interest to buildings. It's like a cross between architecture and opera—have fun with it.

• *Your stroll is over. From here, you can relax over a lavish lunch at the fancy, recommended Duomo restaurant (inside the Palazzo La Rocca).*

Or if you're feeling energetic, you can tackle a strenuous uphill climb to glorious views and the upper, modern part of the city. Continue along Via Capitano Bocchieri and work your way down to Piazza della Repubblica, in the little saddle between the two towns. That's where the next walk begins.

Hill Climb to Ragusa Superiore

The best sight in Ragusa is a view of the city itself. To get a sweeping panorama of Ragusa Ibla, tackle the ▲▲ scenic stair-and-hill climb between the upper and lower towns. It's a lot of climbing, but you'll be rewarded with pretty alleyways, stately *palazzi,* and colorful churches. (Entry is free to the several churches on this walk; most are closed at lunchtime.) To trace this route, see the "Ragusa Superiore" map.

A total of 248 steps—and an uphill walk—connect Ibla's Piazza della Repubblica to the Cathedral of San Giovanni Battista.

Without stopping, you can make the trek in about 15 minutes. With a slow pace and time for photos, allow at least 30 minutes. Taking this climb at sunrise or sunset is a treat for photographers.

• *Start in Piazza della Repubblica, the little square that sits on the western edge of Ragusa Ibla, in the gap between the upper and lower towns.*

❶ Piazza della Repubblica

Face the **Purgatorio Church** (Chiesa delle Anime Sante del Purgatorio), which overlooks this piazza. Above the entrance door, notice the inscription MISE-REMI-NI-MEI ("pity me"), carved just below poor souls writhing in flames. The concept of purgatory—the stopping-off point for unforgiven souls on the way to heaven—gained attention during the Counter-Reformation, and churches like this focused on departed loved ones who might need extra prayers to be purified of leftover sins. Purgatory churches are common in Sicily but not often found in mainland Italy.

Turning your back on purgatory, do not take the stairs directly in front of you; instead, take the street to the right of the café, where you'll see a stairway signed *Salita Commendatore*. Before you start climbing, look high on the corner above the stairs and find the monk holding a pole. This marks one end of **Palazzo Cosentini,** a noble 18th-century palazzo that—like many in Ragusa—has intricate wrought-iron balconies supported by elaborately carved decorations. Check out the supports on the upper level, which are in the shape of the grotesque figures traditionally thought to keep the evil eye away. Take a walk to the other end of the terra-cotta facade, enjoying the fanciful characters, including a "flashy" woman at the very end.

• *It's time to climb. Head up the stairs under the monk.*

❷ Stair Climb (Salita Commendatore)

Several stairs up, you reach a wide landing. On the right is the **Church of Santa Maria dell'Itria,** built in the early 17th century by the Knights of Malta. Its beautiful bell tower is tiled with blue majolica and floral motifs. (Keep in mind that you can duck into any open church for a bit of cool shade and a jolt of Baroque.)

Climbing the steps to the next landing, you'll find another Baroque gem, **Palazzo della Cancelleria,** with an unusually narrow facade and tunnel staircase passing through it.

• *Continue straight, up and up, passing beneath two modern roads. Just*

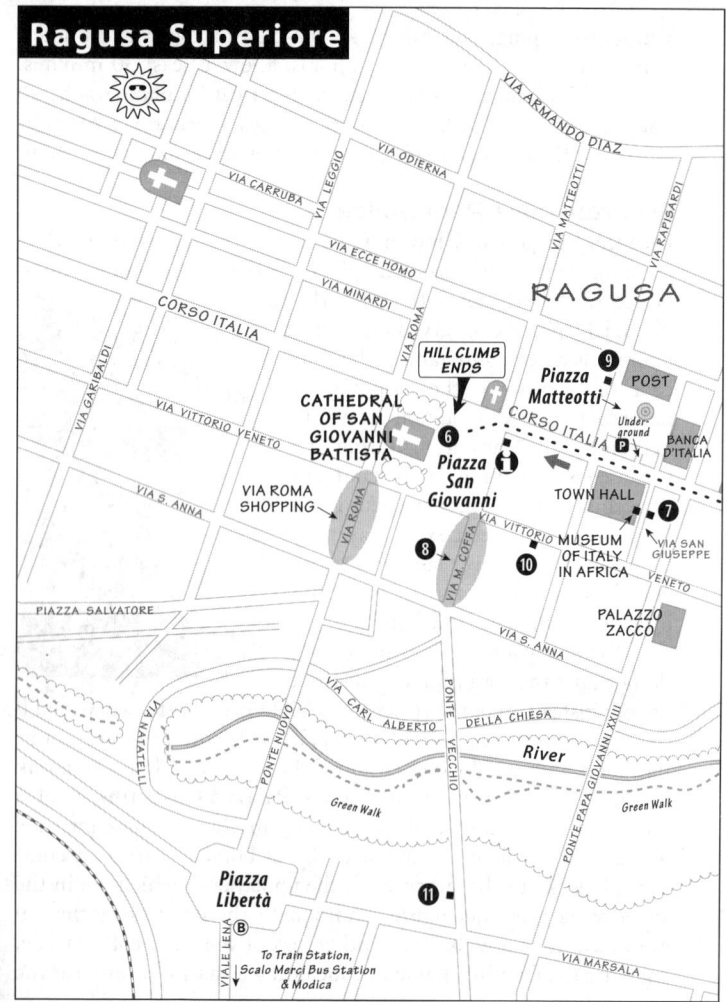

after the second underpass, follow the steps on the left. Cross the street to get your first glimpse back toward Ragusa Ibla, with the spire of Santa Maria dell'Itria on the left.

But we're not done climbing: Turn your back to the view and take the steps to the left, near where you just exited. You'll walk up, hugging the fronts of houses (and appreciating the grand views), then take the steps under the archway on your right, where you'll find your reward: a magnificent view of Ibla. This is also the location of a special church...

❸ Church of Santa Maria delle Scale (Chiesa di Santa Maria delle Scale)

This church dedicated to "Saint Mary of the Stairs" is the only one

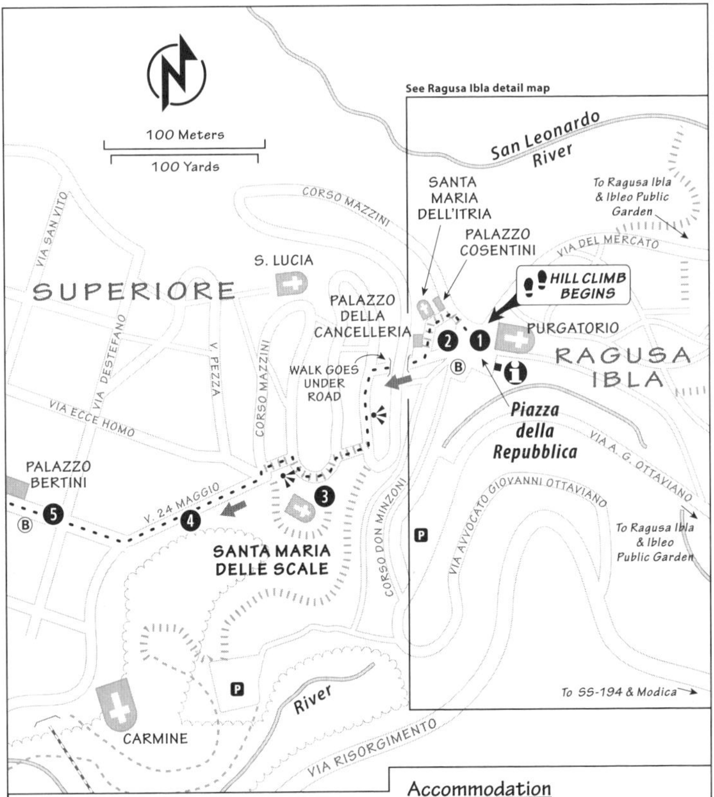

Hill Climb to Ragusa Superiore 265

Hill Climb
1. Piazza della Repubblica
2. Stair Climb
3. Church of Santa Maria delle Scale
4. Edge of Ragusa Superiore
5. Palazzo Bertini
6. Cathedral of San Giovanni Battista

Accommodation
7. Hotel Montreal

Eateries
8. Via Mariannina Coffa Eateries
9. Konza Pizzeria
10. Trattoria da Luigi
11. Panificio Giummarra

in Ragusa that predates the massive earthquake. It's partially remodeled in Baroque style, but not because of earthquake damage.

The church was enlarged in the 1700s, when a population boom demanded more worship space. These days, many churches, including some on this walk, have barely enough attendance to keep the doors open. In Italy, only about one-fourth of the population attends Mass regularly. Like many others on the island, this church still maintains a small but aging parish.

If it's open, step inside and look for fragments of the original church. A portal on the right side of the nave (straight ahead as you enter) is in the Catalan-Gothic style, from the period of Bourbon (Spanish) rule. Its elaborate carvings, like much of medieval church decoration, were once brightly painted (look closely to see remains of pigment). In the right aisle, find the exquisite 1538 terra-cotta relief depicting the Dormition of the Virgin.

• *Facing the church, take the steps to the right.*

As you ascend, you leave medieval Ragusa behind. Stop for a minute and look at the view over Ragusa Ibla framed by the church bell tower. Virtually everything you see was built after the 1693 earthquake, which so devastated the town that many people gave up and started over on the higher land here—with room for growth, a breeze, and no more dank houses. The population in Ibla dwindled, as most chose to move to the new town.

• *At the top of the steps, go straight onto Via 24 Maggio (the street directly in front of you). You're now at the...*

❹ Edge of Ragusa Superiore

The new, post-quake town of Ragusa, built in the 1700s, begins here. Both sides of the street are lined with large townhouses—a popular new style of home being constructed all over Europe at the time. Large families needed large homes. Even now, generations of families often live close to each other and spend time together. You'll find grandparents hanging the laundry out the window while grandkids play on the sidewalk.

Enjoy the relaxed vibe as you stroll uphill to the center, bearing right to stay on Corso Italia. Ragusa is a prosperous town and always has been. There's a feeling here that's different from other parts of Sicily. The streets are tidy, everyone knows everyone, kids wander freely, and doors are often left unlocked. The people take pride in their city and are curious about visitors. Be sure to say "*Salve!*" to greet residents as you pass.

As you walk up Corso Italia, townhouses give way to larger *palazzi* and modern apartment buildings. A few short blocks up on the right, you'll arrive at the 18th-century ❺ **Palazzo Bertini**, with its three curious *mascheroni* (masks) peering down at you. Its balconies used to be street-level doorways (before the roadway was lowered), and those faces once greeted visitors entering the palace.

Each face is said to represent a type of power. On the left, the grotesque caricature with a turban and a gnarled nose represents the power of money. The face in the center, wearing a plumed hat, is calm and sure, representing the power of nobility. And the grizzled face on the right is a reminder that the poor have perhaps the most daunting power of all: the power of nothing to lose.

Ahead on the left, you'll see the Town Hall—marked with the flags of Sicily, Italy, and the EU. In its basement (enter on Via San Giuseppe, the street to the left) is the curious little Museum of Italy in Africa (Museo Civico L'Italia in Africa). The museum is dedicated to Italy's colonial pursuits in Africa (Libya, Somalia, Ethiopia, and Eritrea) as told through a private collection of artifacts and uniforms. Signor Mario Nobile, who spent years assembling this collection, has a great passion for the subject and shares his knowledge (albeit one-sided) in Italian, occasionally with an assistant who speaks some English (free, generally Tue-Sat 9:00-13:00 plus Tue and Thu 15:00-17:00, closed Sun-Mon, try knocking anytime to see if someone is there, Via San Giuseppe 3).

Italy's foray into colonialism began in the 1800s, was key to Mussolini's fascist plans to expand the so-called Italian Empire in the 1930s, and came to an end with the Axis power's defeat in 1943. Some Italians look back at the colonial era with pride—having colonies put Italy on a par with other world leaders. Like many modern nations, Italy has yet to fully address the darker aspects of its colonial past.

Across the street from Town Hall, the square called Piazza Matteotti is surrounded by examples of bombastic, fascist architecture from the Mussolini era. The main post office sits in the square like a cathedral of civil service, and just to the right is the even more fascist Banca d'Italia building. The monument on the left side of the square honors postal workers who gave their lives for Italy.

• *Continuing uphill, you'll reach your final destination...*

⑥ Cathedral of San Giovanni Battista (Cattedrale di San Giovanni Battista)

This church, dedicated to St. John the Baptist, dominates Ragusa Superiore. Surrounded by lively cafés and shopping streets, it's the centerpiece of everyday life. It was built to replace the city's original cathedral in Ragusa Ibla, which was destroyed by the earthquake. To accommodate for the hilly terrain, this replacement was built on a unique platform that creates two piazzas, one in front of the church and one a level below, with cafés and shops tucked into its base.

From the piazza in front, notice a couple of details. The bell tower is rather squat, relatively short, and with thick walls. And on either end of the facade, the walls slope, as if this were a fortified bastion. After the quake, church architects were taking no chances; they overengineered the building inside and out with massive columns and thick outer walls.

• *Our hill climb is finished. (Phew!) Settle in with a drink at one of the cafés on the piazza or choose a restaurant nearby (see "Eating in Ragusa," later). Behind the church, you'll find Via Roma—the city's mostly pedestrianized shopping street.*

When you're ready to return to Ragusa Ibla, you can retrace your steps—the walk is much easier downhill, and you'll be facing the grand Ibla view the whole way down. Otherwise, you can take a taxi, or ride bus #1 from the stop at Corso Italia 26, just past Palazzo Bertini.

Sleeping in Ragusa Ibla

Most visitors sleep in the charming lower town of Ragusa Ibla, and you should too. If you have a car, email your hotel before you arrive to ask for parking advice. Note that many old Ragusa buildings are burrowed into cliffs, which means they can smell a bit dank and musty inside. All of my recommended places have air-conditioning and, unless otherwise noted, an elevator (or it's not necessary).

€€ San Giorgio Palace Hotel is dug into the side of Ragusa Ibla, with rooms stacked vertically from the road up to the old town. Their 32 rooms are sleek and Italian-modern—some higher rooms have views over the valley and others, lower down, have tidy garden patios. An internal elevator makes the trip from valley floor to the city a snap (RS%, terrace bar, free private parking, Via Avvocato G. Ottaviano, +39 093 268 6983, sangiorgiopalacehotel.it, info@sangiorgiopalacehotel.it, Erik).

€€ **Giardino sul Duomo** has 14 tidy, modern rooms at the tippy top of town, thoughtfully managed by Michele, who is happy to offer his help to guests. The quiet communal garden floats above the city, with a stellar view of Ibla and Superiore, and boasts the only swimming pool in the center (family rooms, ask about on-site cooking classes, Via Dottor Solarino 26A, +39 366 579 4027, giardinosulduomo.it, info@giardinosulduomo.it).

€€ **Epoca Camere con Stile** is your chance to feel what it's like to live in a palazzo. Sisters Costanza and Maria have turned their grandfather's home—part of a 300-year-old palazzo—into a guesthouse, with four elegant rooms furnished with period furniture belonging to their family. Each room is unique; the three main-level rooms are huge, while the lower-level room is smaller and opens to the street (but is less expensive). Beautiful, clean, and personal, it has a quiet courtyard and sun terrace (family rooms, Via Orfanotrofio 43, +39 347 549 3584, epoca-ibla.it, epoca.bb@gmail.com).

€€ **Hotel Antico Convento,** sitting within the peaceful Ibleo public garden, is a remodeled Capuchin convent with a hotel, restaurant, and cooking school. It has 16 small, modern rooms furnished with holy elegance and nun-sized doorways (Viale Margherita 41, +39 350 990 2487, anticoconventoibla.it, info@anticoconventoibla.it, Salvo).

€€ **Neropece** is a stylish five-room stay tucked just behind the cathedral. Set in a 19th-century building, it offers a tasteful mix of old stone walls and modern comforts. Rooms are tidy and thoughtfully furnished, some with views or private terrace (family room, no elevator, via Capitano Bocchieri 52, +39 392 276 7376, baroccoibleo.it, info.neropece@gmail.com, Cristina).

€ **B&B L'Orto Sul Tetto** feels like staying at an Italian friend's house. The three simply and tastefully decorated rooms fill a vertical townhouse, with a cute garden/eating terrace on the roof (no elevator, Via T. Distefano 56, +39 093 224 7785, lortosultetto.it, bubbly Rosita).

€ **B&B Terrazza dei Sogni** has six appealing Ikea-modern rooms in a lively area near the Ibleo public garden. The terrace on the roof, perfect at sunset, offers a happy hour (extra fee) and has lovely views of the city (no elevator, Vico Domenico Morelli 8, +39 333 493 9521, terrazzadeisogni.it, info@terrazzadeisogni.it, Emilio).

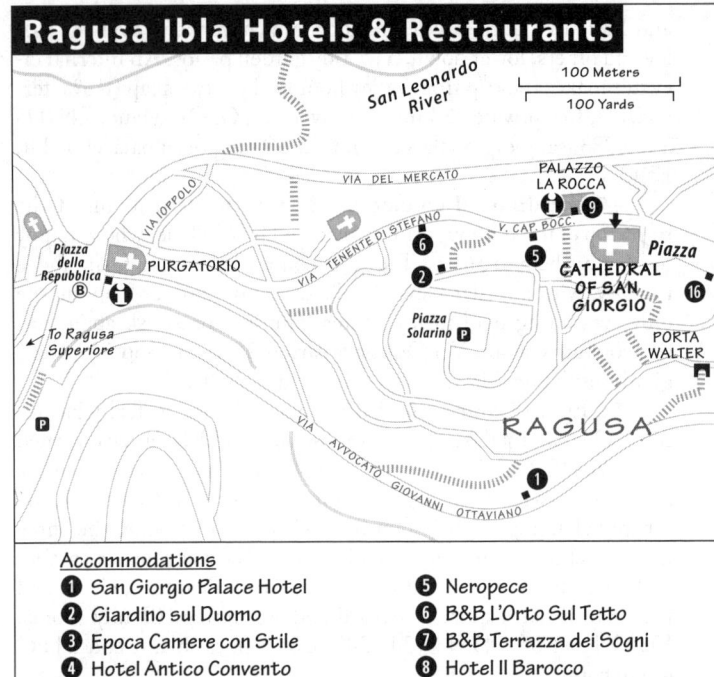

Ragusa Ibla Hotels & Restaurants

Accommodations
1. San Giorgio Palace Hotel
2. Giardino sul Duomo
3. Epoca Camere con Stile
4. Hotel Antico Convento
5. Neropece
6. B&B L'Orto Sul Tetto
7. B&B Terrazza dei Sogni
8. Hotel Il Barocco

€ **Hotel Il Barocco** rents 15 brightly colored rooms with old-fashioned furnishings. Although they don't have views, there's an inviting courtyard patio, and the location is convenient (family rooms, restaurant, Via Santa Maria la Nuova 1, +39 093 266 3105, ilbarocco.it, info@ilbarocco.it).

In Ragusa Superiore: While the upper town isn't as characteristic as Ibla, it has easy parking and is closer to the train and bus stations. € **Hotel Montreal** is a centrally located, family-run place, just steps downhill from the cathedral, facing the main post office. Their 50 rooms are standard business class (pay parking garage, Via San Giuseppe 14—see map on page 264, +39 093 262 1133, montrealhotel.it, info@montrealhotel.it).

Eating in Ragusa

The old town is crammed with appealing eateries ranging from traditional to trendy. There's no reason to go out of your way to dine in Ragusa Superiore, unless you need a bite while exploring there.

RAGUSA IBLA

€€€€ **Duomo,** located inside the Palazzo La Rocca, is *the* place for top-end elegance in Ragusa. Chef Ciccio Sultano is a local ce-

Eating in Ragusa 271

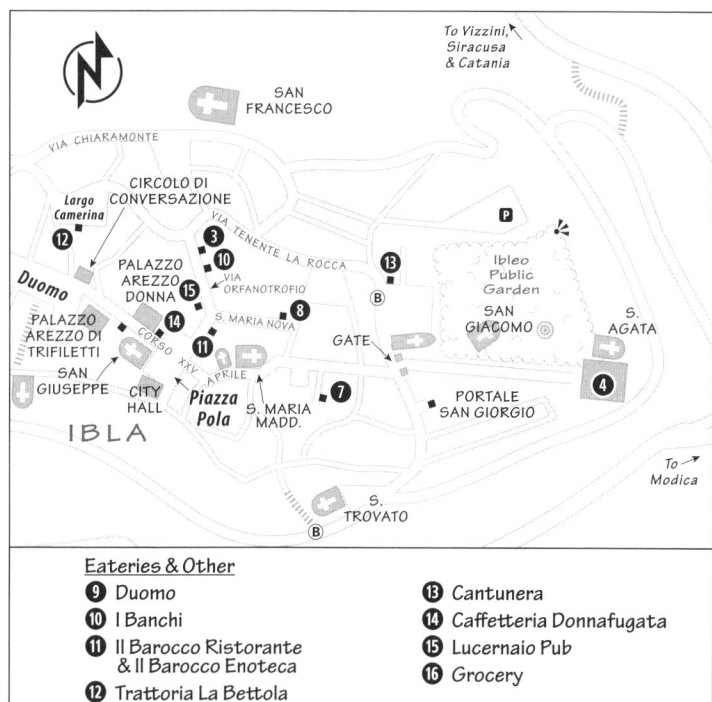

Eateries & Other
- 9 Duomo
- 10 I Banchi
- 11 Il Barocco Ristorante & Il Barocco Enoteca
- 12 Trattoria La Bettola
- 13 Cantunera
- 14 Caffetteria Donnafugata
- 15 Lucernaio Pub
- 16 Grocery

lebrity, with a reputation for creative and beautifully presented cuisine. While the dinner tasting *menu*s start at €198, there's usually a lunch deal (available Tue-Sat) starting at €75 (closed Sun-Mon, reservations required, Via Capitano Bocchieri 31, +39 093 265 1265, cicciosultano.it).

I Banchi is a food emporium owned by Chef Sultano from Duomo. Up front is a € **takeaway counter** and upscale bakery. They also have a slick boutique €€€ **restaurant** with a tempting à la carte menu as well as expensive fixed-price meals, which you can either enjoy at a table out on the sidewalk or under classy vaults (closed Sun, Via Orfanotrofio 39, +39 093 265 5000, ibanchiragusa.it).

€€ **Il Barocco Ristorante** has a long list of affordable pizzas, as well as a full menu of *primi, secondi,* and shareable antipasto platters, with ample outdoor seating (closed Wed, Via Orfanotrofio 27, +39 093 265 2397, ristoranteilbarocco.it). This is a separate restaurant from the enoteca next door of the same name (see next).

€€ **Il Barocco Enoteca** offers a taste of the region's wonderful food products, including olive oil and wine. Il Barocco's main offering is a special (and huge) antipasti platter filled with local cheeses, meats, olives, sundried tomatoes, jams, and more (€34 for two-person platter). They have just a few tables inside and a nice corner outdoor dining area on Piazza Pola; there's also a store where you can buy some of what you tasted (daily, Via Orfanotrofio 17, +39 0932 191 0697, enotecailbarocco.it, brothers Manolo and Carmelo).

€€ **Trattoria La Bettola,** tucked in a back street, is a charming, homey place for Sicilian cuisine, with lace curtains and checkered tablecloths. They have about 10 indoor tables (which can fill fast on chilly evenings) and a nice terrace in front (closed Mon, Largo Camerina 7, +39 342 759 9319).

€ **Cantunera** makes street food such as piping-hot *arancini* with tasty fillings or *crispelle*—fried dough stuffed with anchovies, cheese, or other savories—plus a selection of Sicilian microbrews. Eat at one of a few indoor or outdoor tables, or get your food to go and enjoy it in the sunny piazza out front or on a bench in the nearby Ibleo public garden (lunch daily, also open Fri-Sun for dinner, Largo San Domenico 18, +39 0932 185 7234).

€ **Caffetteria Donnafugata** serves up coffee, pastries, sandwiches, *granita,* and savory snacks, with streetside seating. Ask for a *granita* and a giant brioche for dipping—easily enough for two people (daily, Corso XXV Aprile 29, +39 093 265 3399).

Supermarket: A tiny **Despar** grocery can be found in Ibla at Piazza Duomo 6 (closed midday and on Sun).

RAGUSA SUPERIORE

If you need a spot to eat after a strenuous hill climb, these choices are close to the cathedral. For locations, see the "Ragusa Superiore" map, earlier.

Via Mariannina Coffa: This street leading downhill from the cathedral square is lined with enticing, modern, €-€€ eateries with outdoor terraces. You'll find traditional bars and trattorias as well as the creative **Konza** pizzeria at nearby Via Mario Rapisardi 87. It's sleepy at lunch (when many places are closed), but it's a great spot to browse if you find yourself here at dinnertime.

€€ **Trattoria da Luigi,** a block from the cathedral square, has a cozy, modern interior and a short-and-sweet menu with affordable prices (closed Thu, Corso Vittorio Veneto 96, +39 093 262 4016).

€ **Panificio Giummarra** is an old-school hole-in-the-wall bakery with sweets, savories, and bread (closed Sun, Via Traspontino 23).

Ragusa Connections

From Ragusa by Bus to: Catania (hourly, 2 hours, Interbus/Etna Trasporti), **Palermo** (4/day, 4 hours, AST), **Modica** (about hourly, 25 minutes, AST), **Scicli** (6/day, 2 hours, change in Modica, AST),

Noto (7/day, 2.5 hours, AST), **Siracusa** (6/day, 3 hours, AST). Most connections to other points in Sicily require a change in Catania. Bus info: AST (aziendasicilianatrasporti.it or download the "AST Ticketing" app), Interbus/Etna Trasporti (interbus.it).

By Train to: Siracusa (4/day, 2 hours).

Southeast Countryside Drive

RAGUSA LOOP

Sicily's southeast is a prosperous, mostly rural area with a relaxed vibe. Destroyed by the 1693 earthquake and reborn in Baroque style, the region's architecture is a festival of curlicue facades and undulating interiors, with a harmony not seen in other parts of the island. This lovely area and its trail of Baroque villages is worth ▲—or even more for Sicily aficionados who enjoy country joyrides. The beloved Italian TV show featuring the exploits of Inspector Montalbano was filmed in this area, making a visit particularly enjoyable for fans.

Using Ragusa as a home base, this loop drive links up a quartet of delightful stops—enough to fill a leisurely day and still make it back home to Ragusa in time for dinner. The highlights include a large valley town known for its chocolate factories (Modica), a smaller valley village with an interesting church and fun-to-stroll pedestrian zone (Scicli), a humble beachfront fishing village (Donnalucata), and the aristocratic country manor house of Donnafugata—the Donnafugata Castle.

Planning Your Drive: The stops on this drive (Modica, Scicli, Donnalucata, and Donnafugata Castle) form a handy loop starting and ending at Ragusa (about 50 miles and 2 hours of driving total). An easy day plan is to leave Ragusa around 9:00, stop in Modica to sample chocolates, continue to charming Scicli, and have lunch either there or on the coast in Donnalucata (both have good op-

274 Rick Steves Sicily

Southeast Countryside Drive

tions). In the afternoon, linger on the beach in Donnalucata and/or tour Donnafugata Castle and its aristocratic country gardens (allow 1.5-2 hours to tour the entire complex), then return to Ragusa for dinner. Note that the castle is closed on Mondays year-round.

Reversing the Loop: This drive is just as easy and satisfying in the other direction (Donnafugata Castle, Donnalucata, Scicli, and Modica). For this option, arrive at the castle by 9:30 or 10:00, then have lunch on the coast in Donnalucata or drive onward to Scicli. Explore Scicli, then head to Modica for chocolate sampling and perhaps dinner (chocolate shops along the main tourist strip generally stay open into early evening). This plan works well in the

From Ragusa to Modica

• *From Ragusa Ibla, take SS-115, following signs to* Modica *(set your GPS for Duomo di San Pietro in Modica; 20-minute drive). You'll twist up switchbacks, then drive through a lunar landscape above a dramatic, rocky ravine (SS-115 is also called SS-194 as you get closer to Modica). As you approach Modica, follow signs for* centro storico, *eventually ending up on Corso Umberto I. As you near the cathedral, start looking for pay-and-display street parking along Corso Umberto I (marked with blue lines).*

▲Modica

The city of Modica (pop. 54,000) fills a river valley a short drive from Ragusa. Although slightly smaller than Ragusa, the way it's situated—a wall of Baroque clambering up the steep cliffs of a ravine—makes it appear large and impressive.

While the city itself is appealing to stroll, visitors flock to Modica primarily to sample the local specialty, *cioccolato di Modica*. Sicily was under Spanish rule just as explorers were returning from the New World with exotic new foods, including tomatoes, corn... and cocoa beans. Modica mastered this new ingredient, crushing it on basalt plates *(metates)* and adding local sugar, creating an early version of chocolate bars. No visit to the town is complete without sampling the grainy texture and bittersweet taste of this old-style chocolate.

Visiting Modica: The city climbs up the hills on either side of its main street, Corso Umberto I. On a quick visit it's best to skip the upper town (Modica Alta) to focus on the lower town in the valley (Modica Bassa).

The lower town's main landmark is the **Cathedral of San Pietro,** with a grand staircase out front and a frilly interior. Near the cathedral, along the main drag, you'll find a **TI** (Mon-Sat 8:00-13:30 & 15:30-19:00, closed Sun, Corso Umberto I 141, +39 346 655 8227) and a chain of chocolate shops doling out samples.

Across from San Pietro, down a little alley, **Antica Dolceria Bonajuto** is the oldest and most famous of the chocolate shops. Browse the glass cases in this old-time, wood-paneled shop, and—just inside the entrance, on the floor—see the traditional grinding stone that was used to crush cocoa beans. The bustling kitchen in back turns out molten chocolate by the cup, as well as fancy local pastries. Ask for a sample and compare flavors like orange, spicy pepper, cinnamon, and about a dozen others. No fat is added to this style of chocolate, so it's practically a health food (daily 9:00-20:30, Corso Umberto I 159, +39 093 294 1225, bonajuto.it).

With more time, it's worth the 10-minute hike to Modica's other cathedral, the even-more-striking **Cathedral of San Giorgio.** To reach it, circle to the left of the Cathedral of San Pietro, then walk uphill along Corso Giuseppe Garibaldi. When you reach the big staircase on your right, head up the steps to reach the impressive cathedral. If it looks familiar, it's because it's by the same architect who designed the Cathedral of San Giorgio in Ragusa Ibla. Inside, you'll enjoy a grand Baroque space with massive stone columns.

As a reward for your climb, to the left of the cathedral is another popular chocolate shop, **Sabadì** (daily 9:30-20:00, Corso San Giorgio 103, +39 327 399 7711, sabadi.it).

Eating in Modica: The casual **€€ Osteria dei Sapori Perduti**, with a few sidewalk tables, serves up hearty bowls of pasta. It's about a five-minute walk from the lower cathedral and just below the upper cathedral (closed Tue and for dinner on Sun, Corso Umberto I 230, +39 093 294 4247, Federica and Fabrizio).

€ Mangiare di Casa is small and unfussy, with a few tables inside and noisy street tables outside. The pasta, meats, and salads are simple, fresh, and cheap (closed Mon, Corso Umberto I 261, +39 093 275 1132).

• *Next up: a 20-minute drive to Scicli (set your GPS destination as Piazza Italia in Scicli). Follow Corso Umberto I south to the main roundabout and take the third exit, toward Pozzallo (ignore the first exit that's signed for Scicli—though this would get you there, we're taking a more scenic route). Stay to the right to join Via Nazionale, which eventually puts you on road SP-42 (follow signs to Scicli).*

The final approach to Scicli is down a dramatic series of switchbacks, revealing more and more of the valley-filling town and the caves

Inspector Montalbano Mysteries

For fans of Inspector Montalbano, a fictional Sicilian detective, the areas around Agrigento, Ragusa, and Scicli might feel familiar. Sicilian author Andrea Camilleri's engaging mystery novels have been translated into English and inspired a popular TV series filmed in south and southeast Sicily.

Salvo Montalbano solves crimes large and small while navigating the everyday realities of Sicilian life. He runs into prostitution, drug crime, the Mafia, and murder, but he also deals with stubborn colleagues, nosy neighbors, and his on-again, off-again northern Italian girlfriend, Livia. Montalbano operates with panache, spot-on intuition, and a wicked sense of humor. Sicilian to the core, he always has time—even amid an intense investigation—to savor a wonderful Sicilian meal, preferably in silence. The plots are creative and ingenious but, above all, shine a light on the unique character of Sicilian culture.

Arguably one of Sicily's most famous writers, Camilleri (1925-2019) was a screenwriter and worked in television before he started writing the series in his 60s. He penned more than 20 books following Montalbano's adventures. The TV show *Inspector Montalbano* aired from 1999 to 2021 and spawned a spinoff prequel, *The Young Montalbano*. Fans flock to the locations seen in the series, including the Town Hall in Scicli (Montalbano's office), Ragusa Ibla (fictional town of Vigàta, where the detective works), Punta Secca (Marinella, his seaside home), Sampieri (coastal beach), and Donnafugata Castle (the lair of a mafioso nemesis).

and walls high on the cliffs above it. Dropping down to the main road, turn right onto Corso Umberto I to head into town, following signs for centro. Make a sharp left turn to stay on Corso Umberto I and another sharp left onto Corso Giuseppe Garibaldi, which leads you to the elongated main square, Piazza Italia. Look for pay-and-display parking (marked with blue lines) either along Piazza Italia or just beyond it along Via Nazionale.

▲Scicli

Scicli (SHEEK-lee, pop. 27,000)—also rebuilt after the earthquake of 1693—has small-town charm and a Baroque face. The hills surrounding the village are not just picturesque—they're pockmarked with caves where townspeople

lived until the 20th century. While there are no big-league sights here, Scicli is an enjoyable place to simply stroll, with a fine little pedestrian zone, a church with a fascinating statue and story, and a very good cannoli shop.

Visiting Scicli: Begin on the tree-lined **Piazza Italia.** Look up to the cliffs that hem in the town, and you'll see caves and walls embedded in the volcanic rock (called tuff, or *tufo*). The archaeological areas between Modica (Cava d'Ispica) and Scicli (Chiafura) are sprinkled with caves with a long history of human habitation (some as far back as the Bronze Age). Because tuff (volcanic ash that has compacted into rock) is easy to carve, these cliffs are ideal for burrowing into, with the added benefit that the caves stay cool in summer and warm in winter. In the past, caves were used for dwellings, and some functioned as tombs. The caves surrounding Scicli were inhabited from the Byzantine era (fifth century) until the 1950s, when the last residents moved out. These days, some of the caves are used for *presepe* displays (nativity scenes) during Christmastime.

On top of the cliffs sits the Castelluccio, which roughly translates to "big and broken-down castle." This fortification was central to the defense of this region until the earthquake, when it was damaged and abandoned.

On the main square, butted up against an eyesore modern building, is Scicli's main church, **Chiesa Madre di San Ignazio de Loyola.** Inside, on the left aisle, look for the side chapel with a fascinating statue called the *Madonna delle Milizie* (€1 to light it for three minutes). The Virgin Mary is depicted as a warrior-queen, sitting on a rearing white horse and brandishing a sword. According to local legend, the Normans and Saracens (North African Muslims) battled on the coast near here in 1091, and this "Militarized Madonna" appeared to help the Normans. Europe was under attack by the Ottoman Empire from the 16th to 18th century—so this statue and paintings served as emotion-stoking religious propaganda.

Notice that the Madonna's horse simultaneously tramples two types of "heathens": a dark-skinned African and a lighter-skinned Turk. If this strikes you as culturally insensitive—and it should—skip a visit here on the last Saturday in May, when this statue is paraded around town in an annual mock battle that commemorates the Virgin's appearance to the Normans. For the festivities, some locals dress up as, ahem, Saracens. The chatty custodian, who speaks only Italian (and doesn't care that you don't), loves to point out details of the statue: The Madonna is depicted not as a standard-issue brunette but with decidedly jet-black hair—like a good Sicilian. And the horse's belly is made with a wine barrel. The statue is flanked by two paintings showing the Madonna riding into battle.

Exit the church to the left and go left around the corner onto Via Nazionale. Walk two short blocks until you reach (on the left) the town's pedestrian zone, **Via Francesco M. Penna,** lined by stately civic buildings and fine churches. The start of this area is marked by a dignified municipal building and—attached to that—the lovely **San Giovanni Evangelista church.** Stop in to see its bright-blue-accented interior. Even in this land of dazzling Baroque, it's like stepping into a Fabergé egg.

As you stroll along Via Francesco M. Penna, you'll pass nice restaurants, trendy bars, and boutiques. Appreciate the frilly stone-and-metal balconies that jut out overhead. Via Francesco M. Penna is also home to several minor sights, which all charge a small admission fee (various configurations of combo-tickets are also offered). The **antique pharmacy** (#24), from 1902, gives you a quick glimpse of its Art Nouveau interior filled with medicine bottles, tincture jars, tools, and a poison cabinet. **Palazzo Spadaro** (#34) offers tours of its lovely period interior, used in the *Inspector Montalbano* TV series as the detective's office. At the end of the street, the deconsecrated **church of Saint Teresa** (now a museum) has an interesting display of detached frescoes in a fluffy Baroque interior.

Eating in Scicli: A two-minute walk from the pedestrian zone, €€€ **Baqqalà** serves up all fish, all the time, on its charming little urban terrace (daily, Piazza Ficili 3, +39 093 293 1028). With Via Francesco M. Penna at your back, cross Via Nazionale and bear right, then look for the restaurant on your left.

€€ **Prosit** is a Sicilian bistro in a loud, bustling cellar filled with locals and families. Their huge menu includes tons of starters, small bites, and salads, plus *primi* and *secondi* dishes (closed Thu, Via Dolomiti 6, +39 093 284 2028, prositsicilianbistrot.com).

€€€ **La Grotta,** serving high-end Sicilian cuisine, hunkers down in an atmospheric cavelike space carved into the rock (closed Mon, Via Dolomiti 62, +39 093 293 1363, lagrottascicli.it).

€ **Cannolia** serves standout cannoli. The portions are huge, the filling is light, the flavors are interesting (coffee, carob, and orange with ends dipped in sesame, etc.), and the shell is not only filled but also fried on the spot. Even if you have exceeded your cannoli limit, you must try it here (daily, Via San Bartolomeo 10, +39 351 762 3343, cannolia. it).

• *Our next stop is the coastal village of Donnalucata (enter Donnalucata beach in your GPS; 12-minute drive). From Piazza Italia, you'll get back on Corso Giuseppe Garibaldi going south; this eventually becomes Viale I Maggio/SP-39. Following signs for* Donnalucata, *you'll continue onto Via Sanremo, which turns into Via Miccichè. As you near the beach, look for street parking.*

Donnalucata

This little fishing village/beach resort is a scenic spot to take a lunch break and walk on the sand. This was the site of the 1091 battle between the Normans and the Saracens, when the Madonna legendarily appeared in battle armor to lead the Normans to victory (a moment commemorated by the statue you saw at the Chiesa Madre di San Ignazio de Loyola in Scicli). A monument to the battle eventually became the bell tower of the **Church of Santa Caterina da Siena**—and a village grew around it. Today the pretty little church (about two blocks north of the beach) has a simple, contemporary interior with gilded mosaics.

Besides seeing the church, you can walk or lounge on the sandy beach, which is short but broad and protected by a stout breakwater (Jammola, listed below, rents sunbeds and umbrellas); stroll the concrete waterfront promenade; and enjoy a seafood lunch.

Eating in Donnalucata: Eateries line the seafront promenade—look for one that appeals. Or consider the following places.

€€€ **Jammola,** with an indoor/outdoor beachfront restaurant and lounge bar, is a fine spot for drinks, fresh seafood, and overall relaxation. To rent sunbeds and an umbrella on their lido, it's best to reserve ahead in high season (long hours daily, closed off-season, Via Perello, +39 371 430 9149, jammola.com).

Just a block off the waterfront promenade, at the west end of town nearest the beach, popular €€€ **Ristorante Mezzaparola** offers a long list of changing specials, a case showing off their fresh fish, and a glassed-in terrace (closed Wed, Via Martiri d'Ungheria 2, +39 093 293 7474).

Other Beach Resorts: Several miles up the coast from Donnalucata are a couple of popular beach towns. **Marina di Ragusa** is extremely popular (and crowded) with locals, many of whom have summer homes here. It has a mile-long sandy beach, pleasant promenade, bustling old town center, and yacht-filled harbor. A 40-minute express ferry between Marina di Ragusa and Malta will likely be running by the time you read this (see page 254). Farther along the coast, **Punta Secca** is a fishing village that's famous as the fictional seaside town of Marinella in the *Inspector Montalbano* TV series.

• *From Donnalucata, it's a 30-minute drive to Donnafugata Castle. Head west on the waterfront Viale della Repubblica (SP-89), following signs for* Marina di Ragusa. *As you approach this large beach resort, you'll start heading inland (just follow signs for* Ragusa*). Eventually you'll turn left on SP-36, now following signs toward* Santa Croce Camerina. *After skirting around that town, follow signs to* Comiso *until you see the brown signs for* Castello di Donnafugata, *and follow them to the castle.*

▲Donnafugata Castle (Castello di Donnafugata)

Originally a farmhouse, this property was transformed in the 19th century into a Neo-Gothic castle by Baron Corrado Arezzo de Spuches, a journalist and influential politician of his day (he had enough clout to reroute train tracks to pass closer to his property). Corrado enjoyed traveling abroad and brought home architectural ideas to incorporate into his fanciful palace. What he  created is a textbook example of the mix-and-match Historicism of the Romantic Age. It's a big, blocky house anchored by medieval-style, round, crenellated towers, with faux-Venetian Gothic window frames. While Europe has plenty of country estates that are more impressive and more enjoyable to tour (this barely cracks the top 50), they're relatively rare in Sicily, making this a unique opportunity to get a taste of rural aristocratic life. You can also stroll the gardens in the 20-acre park and visit the interesting and well-explained costume museum (MU.DE.CO.).

Cost and Hours: €10 for entry to castle, park, and museum (individual tickets to each also available); open Tue-Sun 9:00-19:00, off-season until 16:00, closed Mon year-round; park on the street or in the private €2.50 lot, +39 093 267 6500, castellodonnafugata. org. There are a few eateries at the entrance to the complex.

Visiting Donnafugata Castle: The complex has three parts, all accessed from a central courtyard just beyond the ticket booth. If visiting all three sections, you'll be directed first to the costume museum (left side of the courtyard), then the castle (straight back from courtyard), and finally the gardens (enter from the right of the courtyard).

Costume Museum: Opened in 2020, the MU.DE.CO. (Museo del Costume) contains the personal collection of a modern Arezzo, Gabriele Arezzo di Trifiletti (1949-2022). Over his lifetime, Gabriele collected nearly 3,000 pieces of clothing, documenting the history of Sicilian dress from the 1700s to the 20th century. The beautifully displayed costumes are complemented by English info boards that take you through changing influences and styles, from more-is-more late Baroque (inspired by French fashion) to post-French Revolution Neoclassicism—a simpler style inspired by Greek classicism, and from 1800s Romanticism—a fusion of the two previous styles—to eclectic fin de siècle and Art Nouveau-inspired belle époque. You'll also see examples of fashion from the Roaring Twenties, Africa, and Asia.

Castle: Visitors tour 27 of the villa's 122 rooms, including the music hall, women's tearoom, billiard room, painting gallery, some private apartments, and a small-scale version of Versailles' Hall of Mirrors. Appreciate the original furniture, beautiful frescoes, silk-clad walls, and bright, cheery colors. In the Coat of Arms Hall, get a good look at the Arezzo family's seal (in the paintings): It's a shield with four hedgehogs. In Sicilian dialect, a hedgehog is *rizzo,* which sounds like Arezzo.

By the way, the name "Donnafugata"—meaning "fleeing woman"—connects the castle to a Sicilian fable of a queen who escaped imprisonment by an aged suitor. While it's fun to imagine that story at this romantic site, it actually happened at a different castle near Palermo.

Park: The 20 acre-park, with an informal English garden, formal French garden, stone labyrinth, circular temple, grotto, and more, is a lovely place to wander. Also look for the steps up to the terrace and turrets in front of the house, offering a good view of the eclectic architecture.

• *From Donnafugata Castle, it's 30 minutes back to Ragusa along SP-80 and SP-60 (follow signs to* Ragusa). *It's worth slowing down for the rolling countryside, striped with stone-walled farms. Linger, take pictures of the cows, and enjoy your drive in this beautiful, green part of the island.*

Noto

Nicknamed "the Garden in Stone," Noto (pop. 24,000, 20 miles southwest of Siracusa) may well be Sicily's most pristine small city. It's the capital of Sicilian Baroque (see the "Sicily's Unique Baroque" sidebar on page 66). Like neighboring cities, the ancient Noto Antica was destroyed by the earthquake of 1693. Besides some sections of town walls, little of the old city remains. Rather than rebuild in the same spot, residents moved five miles to the south. Starting with this blank slate, they designed the town in one fell swoop and built it according to a master plan—something rarely seen in Sicily before that time. The new city was planned on a regular grid with wide, straight streets and large squares. These gracious spaces were also functional: In case of another major earthquake, townspeople could easily find safe areas to gather. This new approach to urban planning and the unity of its single architectural style make Noto a visually striking place. A stroll through its elegant piazzas is like being immersed in a giant sculpture.

Tourist Information: The TI is along the main street, a few steps from the cathedral (daily 10:00-18:00, until later in summer, Corso Vittorio Emanuele 135, +39 339 481 6218).

Getting There: For drivers coming from Siracusa, follow

284 Rick Steves Sicily

Map labels:

Noto — 200 Meters / 200 Yards — One-way streets →

PALAZZO CASTELLUCIO, SAN DOMENICO, WALK ENDS, MONTEVERGINI, PALAZZO NICOLACI, Piazza XVI Maggio, VIA CAVOUR, SAN NICOLÒ, To Siracusa via SP-115 & A-45, CORSO V.C. NICOLACI, VIA GIO, SAN FRANCESCO, Piazza San Francesco all'Immacolata, VIA ANGELO CAVARRA, TEATRO TINA DI LORENZO, SAN CARLO, WC, Piazza Municipo, VITTORIO, CITY HALL, SANTA CHIARA, PORTA REALE, STADIUM, To Modica & Ragusa via SS-115, VIA DUCEZIO, EMANUELE, WALK BEGINS, Villa Comunale, STATUE, VIA AURISPA, VIA ROMA (SS-115), VIA PIOLA, VIA MAIORE, VIA PRINCIPE (SS-115), VIA NAPOLI, To Train Station, To Siracusa via SS-115 & E-45

Eateries
1. Caffè Sicilia
2. Caffè Costanzo
3. Sabbinirica
4. Anche Gli Angeli
5. To Mangiafico

E-45 south toward Avola and take the Noto exit. From Ragusa, it's an hour drive on country roads.

Arrival in Noto: The entrance of the town (and the start of my self-guided walk) is on its south side, at the ceremonial gateway called Porta Reale. Buses arrive just in front of the gate at the park. Drivers can find parking in two side-by-side pay lots near the town entrance, at the intersection of Via Cavour and Via Fabrizi. Driving toward Porta Reale, turn right on the narrow street just before the gate (Via Fabrizi). Make the first right off Via Fabrizi onto Via Cavour and enter one of the lots.

Noto Town Walk

This short walk is a straight shot through the heart of Noto. Along the way, you'll pass through the town's three main piazzas, designed as part of the rebuilt city. You can walk from one end to the other in 10 minutes if you don't stop—but you'll want to allow 30 minutes or more, especially if you plan to sample the town's gelato.

• *Start just outside the city on the south side, where a monumental gate faces the city park.*

Porta Reale

This royal gate welcomes you with the three symbols of the town: in the top center, a pelican (symbol of dedication to Ferdinand II, the Spanish/Bourbon king when the gate was built in 1838); on the left, a tower (symbol of strength); and on the right, a *cirneco* dog (an ancient local breed, representing fidelity—faith).

• *Walk through the gate and along...*

Corso Vittorio Emanuele

The architects who planned the new city after the great earthquake laid out a main axis that leads through three elegant piazzas—each one an outdoor living room. This traffic-free artery is a showcase of churches and monuments, but it's also alive with street vendor carts, shops, cafés, and world-famous *gelaterie*. While it may seem like the main street in any Sicilian town, pay attention to the architecture. The buildings are all the same color and style and are built on a similar scale. What sets Noto apart is the harmony of its design. As you walk, feel the flow from building to building.

In any other city in Sicily, you'll rarely find a grid of streets, much less any street that's straight for more than a few blocks. While the Romans appreciated the concept of urban planning, this wisdom was lost to the ages until the Renaissance. In Sicily, it was finally reapplied right here in Noto. For example, the city's main thoroughfare is rotated approximately 20 degrees from the east-west axis—an idea that originally came from the Roman architect and philosopher Vitruvius.

• *A few steps take you into Noto's first square...*

Piazza San Francesco all 'Immacolata

This unique, split-level square is divided in two: a lower square around a fountain, and an upper square around the statue of the Immacolata, the Virgin Mary. The wide staircase leading up to the Church of San Francesco unifies the two and offers a pleasant gathering space.

• *Continue straight ahead to the main square.*

Piazza Municipio

The oversized cathedral square, with its gracious steps creating a hangout zone for locals, is the centerpiece of the city.

Cathedral of San Nicolò: This church was nearly destroyed in 1996, when its dome collapsed due to lack of maintenance. The ensuing scandal focused a spotlight on the need to preserve the city, and funds were raised to reconstruct the church, which reopened with a shiny new dome in 2007.

Hike up the stairs and step inside if it's open. You'll know immediately that this is a new church, with stark and noticeably modern decor. As you enter, on the left at the base of the pillar, is the modern cross (marked *Croce Lignea*) made with pieces of wood from the shipwrecked boats of African refugees. (Other, similar crosses are displayed around the church.) The stained-glass windows in the central nave feature a mix of older and newer saints. Walk up to the front of the church, before the main altar, and look up. Under the cupola, the Virgin Mary leads apostles and local saints to the skies, with the Four Evangelists on the tops of the pillars just below.

• *As you exit the church, you're facing...*

City Hall (Palazzo Ducezio): This is yet another beautiful building, with a convex facade supported by 20 columned arches. The building is named for Ducezio, an ancient king of the Sicels, who founded the city and was one of the last to resist the Greek colonization of the island. Most of the building is off-limits to the public but you can pay a few euros to step into its Hall of Mirrors (Salone degli Specchi), with a ceiling fresco celebrating Ducezio (I'd skip it).

• *You're just a few steps from two opportunities to sample Noto's famous...*

Gelato

Noto has gained acclaim for its gelato artistry. **Caffè Sicilia**—a block past the cathedral, on the left at #125—prides itself on sourcing ingredients locally (daily, Corso Vittorio Emanuele 125, caffesicilia.it). Besides gelato, they make a wide range of Sicilian desserts. Is it the best in town? Only one way to find out...

To comparison-shop, head to **Caffè Costanzo,** another excellent *pasticceria* and *gelateria*. It's less famous, less crowded and, some believe, better. You'll find it just downhill from the cathedral, at the bottom of the square on the right side of City Hall (closed Wed, Via Silvio Spaventa 7). Their almond *granita* is delicious.

• *Just across from Caffè Sicilia is the street called...*

Via Corrado Nicolaci

On the third weekend of May, this street is transformed into a floral tapestry, decorated with millions of flower petals as part of a competition called Infiorata di Noto. Each participant is assigned a portion of the street on which to create a floral mosaic. Along this street are a palazzo and two churches worth a visit.

• *Up the hill on the left side of Via Corrado Nicolaci is...*

Palazzo Nicolaci: This aristocratic townhouse, built in 1737, has an exterior that demonstrates the delightfully whimsical decoration common to Sicily's Baroque architecture. You'll see carved lions, seahorses, and sirens (thought to protect households against *u malocchiu*—the evil eye). The interior may be open for tours, with 10 opulent rooms featuring colorfully  tiled floors, antique furniture, chandeliers, frescoed ceilings, and balconies with sweeping views over the city (check locally to see if there are any scheduled guided tours).

• *Via Nicolaci ends with the concave facade at the top of the street belonging to the...*

Church of Montevergini: If it's open, duck in to see a few costumes and banners used by the historical guilds of Noto for special occasions, such as Easter celebrations. For a few euros, you can climb the bell tower's spiral steps.

• *Return downhill to Corso Vittorio Emanuele.*

Church of San Carlo: This church is across from the bottom of Via Nicolaci. For a few euros, you can climb its 50 tiny and steep steps to a terrace with sprawling views down to the Ionian Sea.

Also on the terrace is a chunk of the old church's bell tower and bells.

• *Continue on the Corso, passing the recommended* **Sabbinirica** *sandwich shop (#93, on the left). Corso Vittorio Emanuele terminates at Noto's final square...*

Piazza XVI Maggio

This is the third and final "outdoor living room" in the town plan of Noto.

• *On the right is the...*

Church of San Domenico: This is where the main architect of Noto, Rosario Gagliardi, is buried (if open, take a look inside; generally May-Oct daily 10:00-20:00, Nov-April 9:30-14:30).

• *Opposite the church is...*

Teatro Tina di Lorenzo: This small but charming theater was built by local nobility in 1870. If open, it's worth paying the small fee to step inside and see the beautiful interior. Originally it had neither a royal box nor seats for commoners—just room for aristocrats. Commoners were welcome inside only if they were willing to stand. (More seats were added in 1920.) The theater—which still hosts performances from December through  May—was rechristened for a beloved actress who lived in Noto at the turn of the 20th century. Considering that the Baroque style is architectural theater, what more fitting way to end this walk than with a visit to a real theater?

Back out on the square, take a moment to appreciate the city as a whole. Unlike much of Sicily, with its jumble of styles from different periods, Noto is planned, with streets and buildings well thought out. It's a snapshot in time of architectural innovation in action.

• *Our walk is finished. Head back the way you came, perhaps browsing for lunch.*

Eating in Noto

If you want something beyond the gelato (and pastry) shops mentioned on the walk, here are a few recommendations.

€ Sabbinirica, a popular deli/sandwich shop with indoor and outdoor seating, is a great (if slow) spot to get a top-quality sandwich made with local produce (long hours, closed Mon, Corso Vittorio Emanuele 93).

€€ **Anche Gli Angeli** mixes Baroque charm with a modern flair. Part restaurant, part gallery, it serves creative Sicilian dishes in a one-of-a-kind space with high, vaulted ceilings and striking artwork (closed Wed, Via Arnaldo da Brescia 2, +39 093 157 6023).

€ **Mangiafico** is a bakery with light-meal options and a few streetside tables (daily, Via Ducezio 2—a couple of blocks past the theater, +39 093 158 7970).

Noto Connections

From Noto by Bus to: Ragusa (7/day, 2.5 hours, AST), **Siracusa** (8/day, 1 hour, AST; 4/day, 1 hour, Interbus/Etna Trasporti), **Catania** (7/day, 1.5 hours, Interbus/Etna Trasporti). Bus info: AST (aziendasicilianatrasporti.it), Interbus/Etna Trasporti (interbus.it).

From Noto by Train to: Siracusa (7/day, 35 minutes).

SIRACUSA

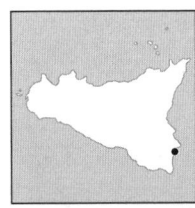

The bustling seafront city of Siracusa (sih-rah-KOOH-zah) mingles big-league ancient history, a charming old town squeezed onto an island, lively restaurants and hip bars, and equal parts serious sightseeing and lazy vacationing. All around, it's one of Sicily's most pleasing destinations.

Ancient Syracuse was a huge power in the Greek world—for a time even eclipsing its rival city-state, Athens; today, a rich trove of Greek (and Roman) ruins hints at the glory of what was one of the most important cities of Magna Graecia. The medieval-era town came tumbling down in the catastrophic earthquake of 1693 and was rebuilt in the Baroque fashion of the time.

The modern mainland city of Siracusa (pop. 115,000) huddles around its expansive bay, as if protecting the little island of Ortigia like a jewel. The once-fortified Ortigia (or-TEE-jah) is the ancient birthplace and contemporary heart of the city, with meandering lanes of eroding palaces and ruins side-by-side with thriving wine bars. Just a generation ago, Ortigia was mostly deserted. But in the last few decades, a new affluence has swept the island neighborhood, giving it a bohemian and trendy energy.

The modern mainland part of town is peppered with worthwhile sights: ancient ruins, an archaeological museum, catacombs, a modern church, and an old church with a Caravaggio painting. Spend your remaining time in the fascinating historic quarter filling the island of Ortigia. With its colorful market, lively main square, funky back alleys, and breezy sea views, Ortigia is, for me, the most enjoyable urban environment anywhere in Sicily.

PLANNING YOUR TIME

Siracusa demands at least one full day: a half-day for the important sights on the mainland and a half-day to explore the island of Ortigia. Ideally, visit the Neapolis Archaeological Park when it first opens to avoid tour groups and the midday heat. Ortigia is most enjoyable late in the afternoon and in the evening. With two days, devote one full day to just poking around Ortigia.

Here's an ambitious full-day plan:

8:30	On the mainland, hit the Neapolis right when it opens
10:00	Visit the Paolo Orsi Archaeological Museum
11:30	Tour the modern church across the street, the nearby catacombs, and/or the Basilica of Santa Lucia al Sepolcro
12:30	Head to the island of Ortigia to browse the market and grab lunch
14:00	Follow my Ortigia Walk, dropping into the cathedral and other sights that interest you
Late Afternoon/ Early Evening	Take in a puppet show
Evening	Stroll the harbor promenade and have dinner in Ortigia

Orientation to Siracusa

Siracusa is made up of two parts: the modern mainland city and the small, historic island of Ortigia at the center of the harbor. The mainland and Ortigia are connected by a pair of bridges: Ponte Santa Lucia and the older, stone Ponte Umberto I. Happily, Siracusa feels highly accessible to visitors yet not overrun with crowds.

The only reason to go to the **mainland** is to visit the important sights there: the Neapolis Archaeological Park, as well as the Paolo Orsi Archaeological Museum, the catacombs, and a couple of churches, all to the northwest of Ortigia.

Focus the rest of your visit on charming **Ortigia.** The main spine of the old town runs from the Temple of Apollo down Corso Giacomo Matteotti to Piazza Archimede, then to Piazza Duomo by way of Via Roma. The centerpiece of Ortigia is its lovely cathedral, surrounded by one of Sicily's finest squares.

TOURIST INFORMATION

Siracusa has two TIs, both near the cathedral in Ortigia. Each one is only marginally helpful and keeps unpredictable hours, but they're both good for city maps and other brochures (Via Roma 31—generally Mon-Fri 9:00-13:00, Wed also 15:00-17:30, closed Sat-Sun, +39 093 165 201; Via Maestranza 33—generally Mon-

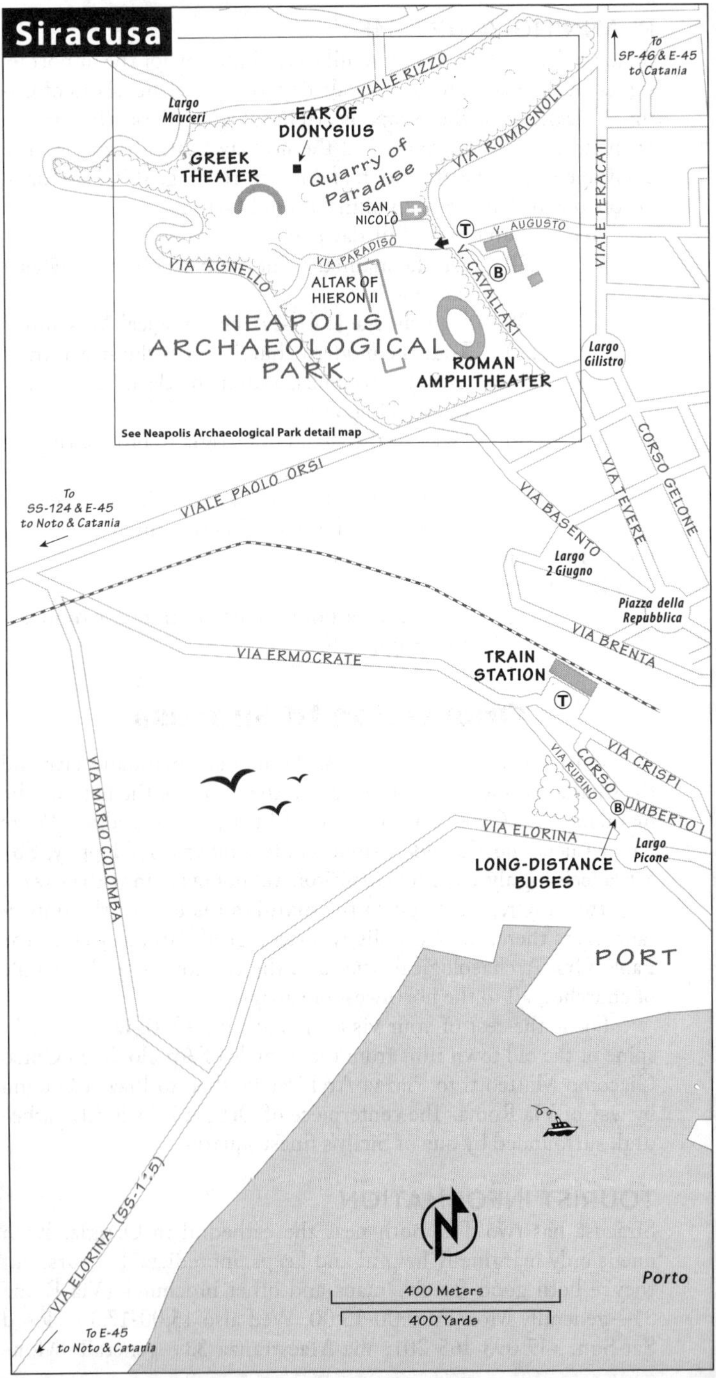

Siracusa

To SP-46 & E-45 to Catania

VIALE RIZZO

Largo Mauceri

EAR OF DIONYSIUS

VIA ROMAGNOLI

GREEK THEATER

Quarry of Paradise

SAN NICOLÒ

VIA PARADISO

V. AUGUSTO

VIA AGNELLO

V. CAVALLARI

VIALE TERACATI

ALTAR OF HIERON II

NEAPOLIS ARCHAEOLOGICAL PARK

ROMAN AMPHITHEATER

Largo Gilistro

See Neapolis Archaeological Park detail map

CORSO GELONE

To SS-124 & E-45 to Noto & Catania

VIALE PAOLO ORSI

VIA BASENTO

VIA TEVERE

Largo 2 Giugno

Piazza della Repubblica

VIA BRENTA

VIA ERMOCRATE

TRAIN STATION

VIA CRISPI

VIA RUBINO

CORSO UMBERTO I

VIA ELORINA

Largo Picone

LONG-DISTANCE BUSES

VIA MARIO COLOMBA

PORT

VIA ELORINA (SS-1.4.5)

To E-45 to Noto & Catania

400 Meters
400 Yards

Porto

SIRACUSA

Orientation to Siracusa 293

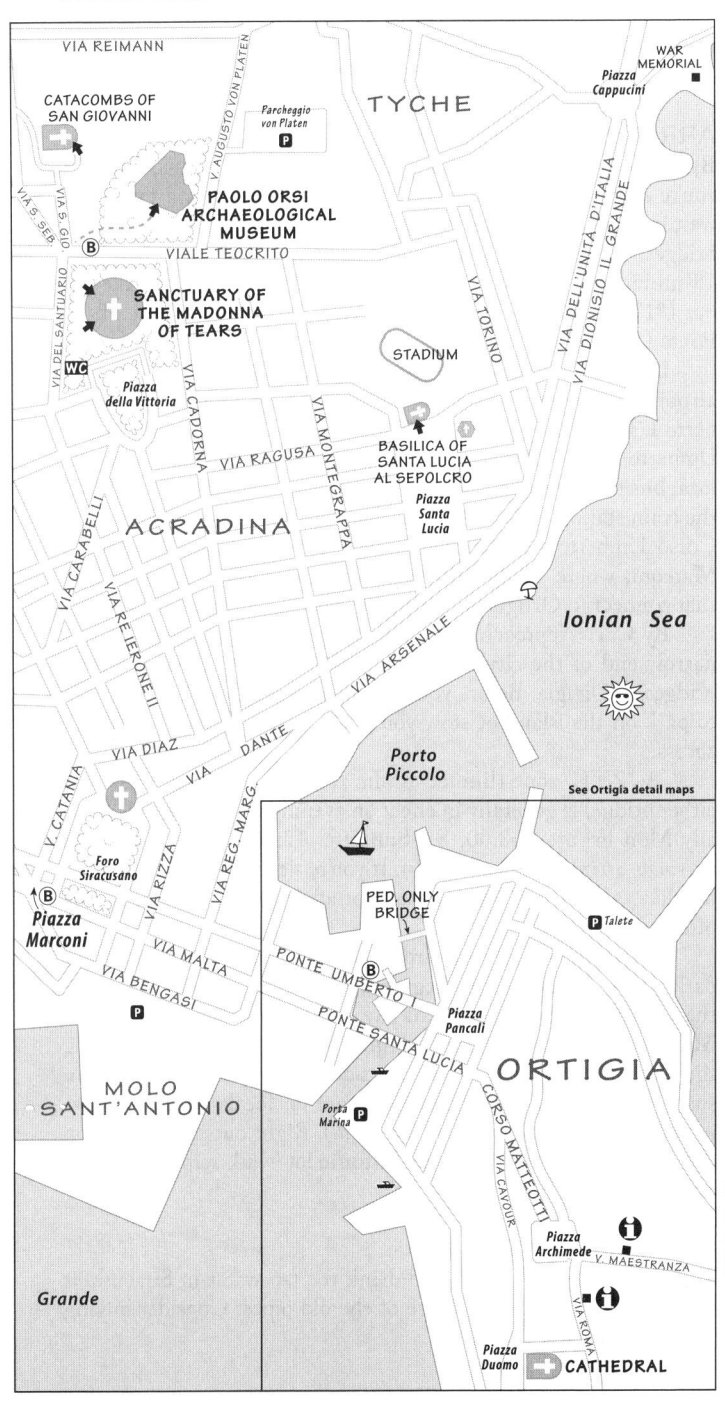

Fri 8:00-14:00, closed Sat-Sun, +39 092 146 4255; siracusaturismo.net).

ARRIVAL IN SIRACUSA

By Train: Trains arrive at Siracusa Centrale on the mainland. If you're staying in Ortigia, it's worth investing €20 for a **taxi** (they wait in front of the station). On foot, it's a 15-minute **walk** to the bridges that connect the mainland to Ortigia, then another 5- to 15-minute walk to my recommended hotels. Or you can take the bus (#106 runs from near the train station to the near side of the Ponte Umberto I bridge).

By Bus: Long-distance buses, including buses from Catania's airport, arrive one block from the train station along Corso Umberto I. From here, it's a 15-minute **walk** to Ortigia (follow Corso Umberto I, which leads straight to its bridge). Or you can take the local **bus** to the head of Ortigia from nearby Piazza Marconi. From the train station, exit to the left, then immediately bear right onto Corso Umberto I. Continue walking for five minutes to Piazza Marconi, where you'll find the bus terminal and several options that connect to Ortigia (see "Getting Around Siracusa," later).

By Car: Approaching Siracusa, you'll be funneled into the narrow end of the city's peninsula, eventually reaching the twin bridges to Ortigia. Before you get there, decide whether you want to park on the island or stow your car on the mainland and walk across.

A "ZTL" zone (limited traffic zone; begins when you cross either bridge) is generally in effect on evenings and weekends (usually Mon-Fri after 18:00, Sat-Sun after 12:00). If the ZTL sign says *non-attivo*, you can drive in. If you're sleeping in Ortigia, your hotelier can register your car; ask for advice about parking (some offer a valet service).

The most straightforward (and reasonable) long-term pay parking in Ortigia is **Parcheggio Talete,** to the left as you enter the island. There's also a small pay lot along the harbor at **Porta Marina,** as well as some free, unlimited-time parking spaces along the embankment road on the east side of the island. Park only in spaces with blue lines—yellow lines are for locals only (and towing cars is a favorite sport of the *vigili*). Right outside Ortigia on the mainland is the **Molo Sant'Antonio** lot (walk across the Ponte Santa Lucia to Ortigia).

HELPFUL HINTS

Tap Water: Though it's OK to drink the tap water in Siracusa, it doesn't taste good because of the old pipes. Consider buying bottled water.

ATMs: Avoid the numerous free-standing private ATMs in Ortigia, which charge hefty fees. Find a bank ATM.

Market: A bustling food market fills Ortigia's Via Emanuele de Benedictis, next to the Temple of Apollo (Mon-Sat 7:00-14:00, closed Sun).

Laundry: LaundryXpress offers self-service laundry in Ortigia, a block from Via Maestranza (long hours daily, Via dei Santi Coronati 36, +39 329 805 1549).

Spelling: Siracusa is also known internationally as "Syracuse," and Ortigia is often spelled "Ortygia" in English. I've used the Sicilian spellings, except when referring to the ancient city of Syracuse.

GETTING AROUND SIRACUSA

By Bus: The **Siracusa Open Tour** hop-on, hop-off bus is the best way to connect Ortigia and the mainland sights, including the archaeological museum and archaeological park. Stops in Ortigia include Piazza Archimede, the eastern end of Via della Maestranza where it meets Belvedere San Giacomo, the main parking lot (Talete), and possibly others. To find the nearest stop, use their online bus map (€20, pay driver, ticket good 24 hours, includes paltry headphone commentary; runs daily 9:00-19:30, every 20 minutes or so, less frequently off-season; +39 093 195 9912, siracusaopentour.com).

The small red SAIS buses #105 and #106 run from a stop just over the bridge from Ortigia (Porto Umberto I) to the archaeological museum, archaeological park, and Piazza Marconi (close to the train and long-distance bus stations). Bus #110 loops around Ortigia as well (€1.50; ticket good for 1.5 hours, buy on board or at a tobacco shop before boarding; runs roughly every 15 Sicilian minutes).

By Taxi: Taxis between Ortigia and the mainland sights cost about €15 (from Ortigia, catch one at Piazza Pancali, in front of the Temple of Apollo). You can also try booking a private driver (see "Tours in Siracusa," next).

Tours in Siracusa

Local Guides

Engaging and helpful **Liliana Rainieri** offers private tours of Siracusa, Noto, and the Ragusa area (€80/hour, two-hour minimum, +39 333 125 6596, lilianarainieri.it, liliana.rainieri@gmail.com).

Eva Greco leads insightful and fun private tours of Siracusa and nearby destinations (€80/hour, two-hour minimum, +39 338 755 8537, evatour1969@gmail.com).

Siracusa at a Glance

In Ortigia

▲▲**Siracusa Cathedral** Eclectic cathedral mirroring the patchwork of civilizations that built Siracusa. **Hours:** Mon-Sat 8:30-18:30, off-season 9:00-17:30, closed Sun except for Mass. See page 308.

▲**San Filippo Apostolo Underground** A look at 2,000 years of history below the church, with a crypt, WWII air-raid shelter, and Jewish bath. **Hours:** Mon-Sat 10:00-12:30 & 15:00-17:00, closed Sun and Nov-March. See page 310.

▲**Puppet Theater** Entertaining live shows of traditional stories performed with handcrafted puppets. **Hours:** Generally one show/day Mon-Sat, none Sun or late Nov, Jan, and Feb. See page 326.

In Mainland Siracusa

▲▲**Neapolis Archaeological Park** Remains from the ancient Greek city-state, plus a Roman theater. **Hours:** Daily 8:30-19:45, closes earlier mid-Sept-March. See page 313.

▲▲**Paolo Orsi Archaeological Museum** One of Sicily's top archaeology museums, with artifacts from prehistory to the Roman era. **Hours:** Tue-Sat 9:00-19:00, Sun until 14:00, closed Mon. See page 319.

▲**Sanctuary of the Madonna of Tears** Unexpectedly modern church dedicated to a weeping Madonna. **Hours:** Mon-Sat 7:30-12:30 & 15:30-19:30, Sun until 20:45. See page 318.

▲**Catacombs of San Giovanni** Best catacombs in Siracusa, below a ruined church. **Hours:** Daily 9:30-12:30 & 14:30-17:30, shorter hours and closed Mon in winter. See page 323.

▲**Basilica of Santa Lucia al Sepolcro** Norman church with an altarpiece painted by Caravaggio and the burial niche of Santa Lucia. **Hours:** Daily 9:00-12:45 & 15:30-19:00 except Thu from 11:00. See page 323.

Private Drivers

Paolo Gallo loves to share his country with travelers and can drive you anywhere in Sicily (€330/half-day, €620/full day, vehicles to accommodate any group size, +39 338 529 6915, sunnysicily.com, reservations@sunnysicily.com).

Salvatore Giurdanella drives within Siracusa and can connect to Catania or other cities in the region (one-way to Neapolis

Archaeological Park—€10/up to 4 people, €20/up to 8 people; to Catania airport—€60/up to 4, €80/up to 8; to Taormina—€110/up to 4, €150/up to 8, +39 339 221 8690).

Boat Tours
Blu Marlin offers scenic boat tours around Ortigia or along the mainland coast to see dramatic rock formations and small grottos (each tour €15, 50 minutes; €20 for combined 1.5-hour tour; English commentary; departs when a group forms). In summer, the boat stops in picturesque spots for passengers to take a quick dip. Kindly Carmelo and Ornella use glass-bottom boats in summer, and can also do tours off-season if you book in advance (+39 347 659 6900, or contact Ornella via WhatsApp at +39 327 573 9668, merlino.carmelo@alice.it).

Ortigia Walk

This hour-long walk leads you across the island of Ortigia, the heart of old Siracusa. We'll start at the historical beginning—the ancient Greek Temple of Apollo—then ramble through the side streets, unravel the architectural knot of the cathedral, and finish at a viewpoint on the far side of the island. This walk works well anytime; it's cool and mellow in the late afternoon, but note that the market will be dead then.

• *Begin on the mainland side of the two bridges that lead to and from Ortigia. Look for the giant anchor marking Ponte Santa Lucia (the bridge on the right) and cross partway over, pausing at the high point of the bridge for a look around.*

❶ Santa Lucia Bridge Spin-Tour

Two bridges link the mainland of Siracusa with the island of Ortigia. You're standing on Ponte Santa Lucia, named for the city's most famous saint.

Face the mainland. This modern part of Siracusa was built after the unification of Italy in the late 1800s, with a grid plan in the Liberty Style (Italy's version of Art Nouveau). Look left to find the big military-looking building, which houses the coast guard.

Spinning clockwise, look on the little piazza between the two bridges for the bronze statue of

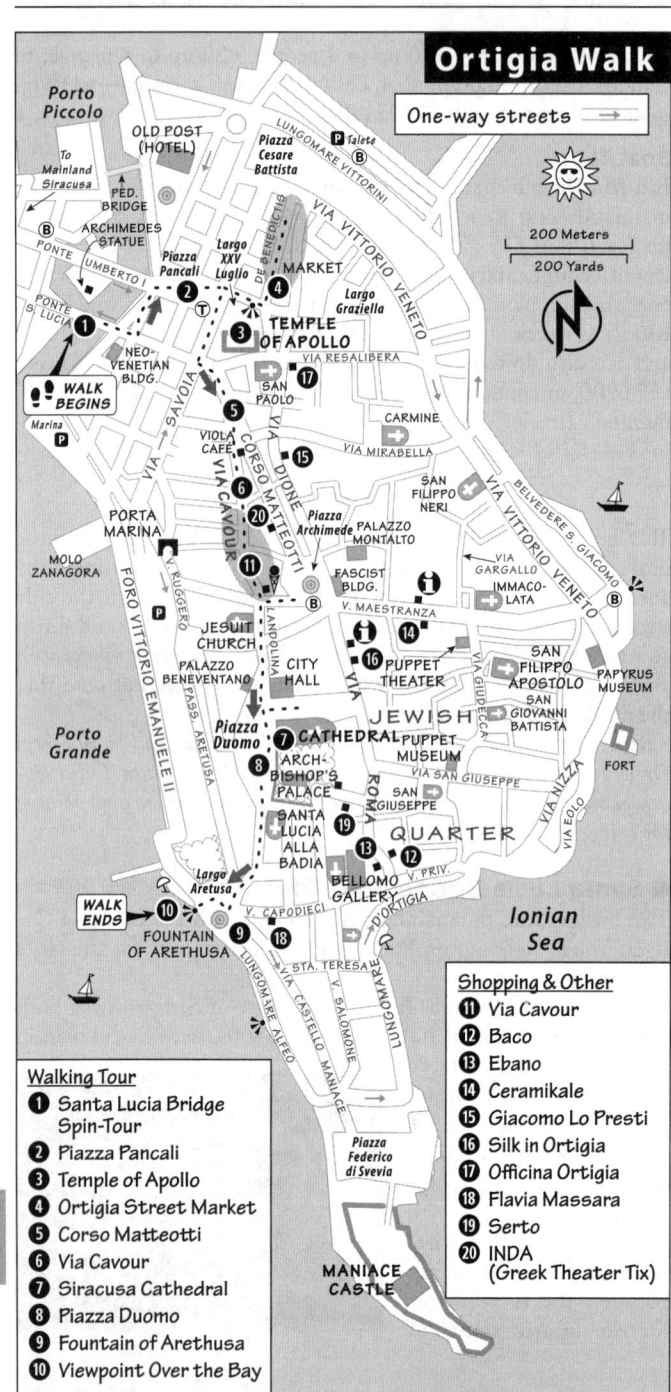

ancient Syracuse's most famous resident: the third-century-BC mathematician/physicist/genius, **Archimedes.**

The older, stone bridge just behind Archimedes—**Ponte Umberto I**—was built to celebrate the Risorgimento (unification of Italy), circa 1870. The little red public bus leaves from that bridge's far end.

The stately former **post office,** in the distance behind Archimedes, is an example of the bold infrastructure erected by Italy's 20th-century dictator Benito Mussolini and his fascist regime. These days, in the wave of gentrification, it's become a luxury hotel.

Now spin right and face the end of the bridge and Ortigia. The **Neo-Venetian building** on the right side of the bridge, with Gothic windows and a red hue, is a souvenir of the Romantic movement of the late 19th century.

The **harbor** all around you is home to a few fishing and sightseeing boats. But take a moment to look out and admire the bay where the ancient Greek Syracusans chained off their harbor and trapped enemy fleets. We'll get a better look at the full scope of this bay at the end of this walk.

Cross to the end of the bridge. Lashed to the railing on your left is a kayak-polo net—a reminder that Italy won the sport's world championship right here in 2016.

• *At the end of the bridge, turn left and walk along the embankment. When you reach the Umberto I bridge, turn right and jog slightly uphill to the leafy...*

❷ Piazza Pancali

This lively square—which feels more like a stunted boulevard—is where the gritty mainland meets the dreamy old town of Ortigia.

Consider hydrating at the **drink kiosk** in the meridian, with lots of fresh-squeezed juice options. For something simple yet refreshing, try a *seltz*—fresh-squeezed lemon, fizzy water, and a pinch of salt. For added sweetness, get it *con sciroppo* (with flavored syrup, like tangerine).

Beyond the drink kiosk is a **signboard** with funeral notices inviting the public to attend. Ortigia, like most of Sicily, is a tight-knit community, and the entire neighborhood is welcome to attend memorial services.

• *Walk to the top of the block and cross the street to a big open-air archaeological site. Walk around the left side of the site, pausing just before the little clump of palm trees, and look across the field of rubble.*

❸ Temple of Apollo

To the left of the wall, look for the two standing columns with the oversized capitals. These are the remains of the first Doric stone temple in Sicily, from about 580 BC. Notice the huge footprint of the temple. A long stretch of wall from the inner room (the cella) still stands. Short and stocky, this is one of the earliest stone temples, and it predates the Parthenon in Athens by 130 years.

The surviving columns are short and fat and closely spaced together. Each column is hewn from a single piece of stone, which is rare. (Later, to allow taller columns—and work with smaller and easier-to-move chunks of stone—columns would be made by stacking round drums connected by pins.) As builders became more sophisticated, the temples grew taller—with slender, refined columns spaced farther apart—and included more  detailed decoration. Everywhere you step in Ortigia, ancient history lies just underfoot.

• *With the temple ruins on your right, walk a few more steps up along the fence, then turn left on Via Emanuele de Benedictis. You've entered the...*

❹ Ortigia Street Market

This street hosts a lively market (Mon-Sat 7:00-14:00, closed Sun). If you're here when it's in action, venture down this main drag, then back up. Fish and produce are at the far end. At 13:00, the activity begins to die down, and by 14:00, the food vendors are gone. This was once a purely local scene, with lots of greengrocers. The big building on the left as you enter was the market hall. But today's locals are more likely to do their shopping  at suburban supermarkets. There aren't enough vendors to justify opening the market hall, and the outdoor stalls cater mostly to tourists.

There are lots of places along here to eat—either a meal at a fancy sit-down restaurant or a quick bite of street food. It's fun to comparison-shop these places for lunch; some are also open for dinner (see "Eating in Siracusa," later).

• *Returning to the Temple of Apollo, head right and walk along the ruins. When you reach the far side of the square, you'll get a closer look at*

Archimedes (c. 287-212 BC)

During ancient Syracuse's heyday as a leading city-state of the Greek world, no native son was more distinguished or influential than the scientist and mathematician Archimedes.

Some of Archimedes' inventions are still in use today—most notably the Archimedes screw, or screw pump. This simple yet ingenious device (essentially a very large screw set inside a cylinder) makes it possible to move water upward, against gravity—useful for pumping out the hold of a ship or for digging holes and draining water all at once.

Archimedes was well known for his brilliance in his time. Celebrated for great works of naval engineering that protected ancient Syracuse, he is said to have set fire to an entire Roman fleet with mirrors reflecting sunbeams. Archimedes famously discovered a way to measure the density of precious metals with water displacement while in a bathtub, and in his excitement ran through the city naked, yelling, "Eureka" ("I've found it"). He also wrote the mathematical law of the lever, prompting his other famous quote: "Give me a place to stand and I will move the Earth."

Perhaps Archimedes' most advanced work was in the field of calculus, developing methods to determine area and volume. His calculation of the ratio of a circle's circumference to its diameter is known today as the Archimedes Constant—or ϖ. According to legend, a symbol of his work—a sphere and cylinder of the same height and diameter—was carved on his tomb, although it has never been found.

The Romans would have liked to put Archimedes' genius to use. When they finally conquered Syracuse, they ordered his capture, unharmed. Unfortunately, a Roman legionary encountered the scientist, who was so deep in thought about mathematics he ignored the soldier. The soldier, infuriated, killed Archimedes for his insolence.

Today, Archimedes is immortalized in Ortigia with a memorial statue on Ponte Umberto I and a piazza in the heart of the island. Locals call him *il genio*—the genius.

---

some temple columns. Continue straight ahead, away from the square, pausing at the start of the big, modern street...

❺ Corso Giacomo Matteotti

In the 1920s, fascist dictator Mussolini cut the broadest boulevard in Ortigia right through the existing buildings, disregarding, as fascist dictators are wont to do, what was there before. This grand avenue has bold features—notice the stern balconies and cold uniformity, in keeping with fascist ideology. Originally named Via del Littorio—a fascist reference to banner carriers in ancient Rome—the street was later renamed for Giacomo Matteotti, an

Italian member of parliament (for the Socialist Party), patriot, and freedom fighter, who was killed by Mussolini's henchmen in 1924. Note also the name of the square you just left: Largo XXV Luglio—July 25, the date Mussolini was deposed and arrested in 1943.

Walk 50 yards uphill on Corso Giacomo Matteotti to the round, Art Deco café on the right (near the green pharmacy cross). The **Viola Café**, with its striking fascist design, has been a popular local meeting spot since the 1930s.

• *Head down the street to the right of Viola Café. This is Via Cavour, a narrow, colorful, characteristic lane crammed with shops and restaurants. It leads directly to the cathedral.*

❻ Via Cavour

Stroll Via Cavour, enjoying the renewed energy of old Siracusa. Survey the boutiques and souvenir stands, window-shop restaurants for your next meal, and notice the trendiness. Until the early 2000s, Ortigia was run down and seedy. Since then, a new interest in the island has started a regeneration and a surge in tourism.

Notice the long and narrow side lanes. Stop at an intersection and look up at the balconies often festooned with laundry—reminders that this is still a real neighborhood.

Via Cavour becomes increasingly more characteristic a couple of blocks in. As you stroll, drop into some of the fun shops. The **Fish House** gallery (at #29, on the right) sells all manner of fishy decor. **Tami'** (#27) is a design shop with a mix of Sicilian and international wares; their outpost for bags and sunglasses is at #14. You may see some artisans at work in front of their shops. Near the top of the street, at #2, is a popular *gelateria* (also sells cannoli).

From the *gelateria*, turn left and detour 50 yards to **Piazza Archimede** for a look at its fountain, dedicated to Artemis the huntress. As you enter the square, notice that the building straight ahead still sports its fascist-themed reliefs, celebrating employment. Mussolini came to power in 1922, in part because he promised good jobs. Each of these panels portrays a noble livelihood.

Return to Via Cavour, turn left, and continue on (the street's name changes to Via Landolina). On the right is the **Jesuit Church**—so crowded by the buildings that it's hard to appreciate its ornate facade…for that reason, the Jesuits never finished construction.

• *The street empties out into Piazza Duomo. On the left side of the square is the glorious…*

The Greeks in Sicily

Sicily is perhaps the most important place outside Greece when it comes to ancient Greek history. Ancient Syracuse briefly eclipsed Athens as the leading city-state of the civiliza-

tion. Many scholars maintain that the best-preserved ancient Greek buildings are not in Greece, but in Italy.

As Greece rose from 800 to 400 BC, its population exploded nearly tenfold, forcing a "go west, young man" mentality. The Greek version of manifest destiny began in Sicily, familiar to the Greeks because their Mycenaean ancestors had traded with local tribes.

The first settlers landed in 734 BC near modern Taormina and named their colony Naxos, after the Aegean island. Settlers from the Greek port of Corinth arrived in 732 BC and founded ancient Syracuse. Greek colonists soon flooded Sicily's shores, settling primarily in the east (closer to Greece) and on the southern coast (good trade routes). Sicily benefited greatly from access to markets in southern Italy, Africa, and Rome, and soon became an important part of the Magna Graecia ("Great Greece") empire.

Most Greek cities in Sicily had a theater, a market square, and temples built to mimic those at home. While all ethnically Greek, the colonial cities each had their own leadership, and rivalries imported from home kept the colonies in a state of constant discord and war. The Carthaginians controlled western Sicily from their base on Mozia island (see "The Carthaginians" sidebar on page 188). In a pivotal 480 BC battle, forces from Syracuse and Agrigento held off a Carthaginian invasion, securing (partial) Greek control of Sicily and spurring the rise of Athens—which now feared Carthage less.

Greek settlements in eastern Sicily, however, continued to squabble with the Carthaginians. They sought help from mighty Athens, which answered the call by invading the island in 413 BC. They sent 100 ships and 10,000 soldiers, but having underestimated their Sicilian cousins, the Athenian fleet was destroyed in Syracuse's harbor in a dramatic naval battle (bringing the Second Peloponnesian War to an end). Empowered Syracuse eclipsed Athens on the world stage, kicking off Sicily's own ancient golden age.

Then came the Romans. Sicily was one of Rome's first conquests (third century BC). Over the course of three Punic Wars (264-146 BC), Rome finally succeeded in defeating the troublesome Carthaginians, all but wiping their civilization from the historical record. The Roman conquest of Sicily also marked the end of ancient Greek Sicily.

⑦ Siracusa Cathedral

Siracusa's cathedral (Duomo di Siracusa) is a fine example of the city's 2,500 years of cultural influences: from Greek to Byzantine, to Arab, Norman, and Baroque.

The **facade** of the cathedral, from around 1750, is inspired by the great Baroque churches of Rome, but amped up with a Sicilian razzle-dazzle. Baroque architecture typically features lots of decoration in different planes, creating dramatic light-and-dark contrast. The apostles Peter (with his key) and Paul (with his sword) greet you at street level, while Mary hovers high above, in the middle. To the right of Mary is St. Lucia, the famous local saint who is celebrated throughout Europe with a festival of lights (see the sidebar, later). The cathedral **interior** holds some of her relics (and is worth touring—for details see the listing under "Sights in Siracusa").

But the surprise of this church is revealed on its side. Walk around the left side and look at the puzzle of stones that make up the **outer walls.** The church is like Sicily itself: a layer cake of civilizations. Studying the side of the church reveals the highlights of Sicilian history.

The structure was originally an ancient Greek temple, with six columns at the front and back, and 14 columns on the sides. It was built here at the highest point on the island to honor Athena, the goddess of war, after the defeat of Carthage in 480 BC. The original temple's steps are still visible along the base.

In the seventh century AD, under Byzantine rule, the temple was converted into a church. To create solid walls, the Byzantines simply filled in the spaces between the still-standing columns. Looking up, you can still see much of the ancient Doric **colonnade** built right into the church. Then, in 827, the Arabs crossed over from North Africa and turned the church into a mosque.

About a century later, the Normans conquered Sicily in a relatively short time (1061-1091). As they were busy converting new territories to Christianity, they had to economize on time and workforce. In their haste, they built a combo fortress/church (notice the **crenellations** they added along the top). The great quake of 1693 knocked down the Norman fortress-style facade and severely damaged the cathedral. It was later repaired (look at the columns farther away and note how the wall becomes thicker), and the facade was rebuilt in supercharged Baroque, making this cathedral a patchwork of the highlights of Sicilian architecture.

• *Return to the front of the cathedral and take in...*

❽ Piazza Duomo

This "square" serves as a delightful stage upon which the story of this community plays out. Designed in a graceful semicircle (a charming Baroque trick to heighten the community-theater feel), this is the living room of the island. Those who lived here even as recently as the 1990s remember the facade of the cathedral as blackened by time, and the square littered with cars and surrounded by dreary and depressed lanes. Now it's one of the most pleasant piazzas in Sicily.

The black lines in the pavement (just to the right of the cathedral steps) show where the earliest pre-Greek temple stood, built in the ninth century BC here, on the highest point of the island. Looking back to where you entered the square, you'll see two grand buildings. On the right is the **City Hall,** flying the flags of Sicily, Italy, and the EU. The bottom floor is a rare building that predates 1693; the upper floor—like most of post-quake southeastern Sicily—is Baroque.

Across from City Hall, on the left, is the **Palazzo Beneventano.** Study the powerful symmetry of the imposing Baroque facade of this grandiose townhouse, with the Beneventano family crest (two dancing wild boars) above the massive door. If the door is open, peek inside at the intriguing inner courtyard. Sometimes the shutters upstairs are open, affording an enticing peek at a glorious ceiling fresco.

Now turn to face the bottom of the square and start walking in that direction. First you'll pass the **archbishop's palace** (on the left, adjoining the cathedral). At the end of that building is the entrance to a vast **WWII-era bomb shelter** dug deep beneath this square; it offers little to see other than big caves and zigzag tunnels (if that interests you, stop by to see if it's open).

At the far end of the square is the Rococo facade marking the **Church of Santa Lucia alla Badia.** Above the doorway are

Santa Lucia

The patron saint of Siracusa, Santa Lucia (Italians say loo-CHEE-yah; English speakers know her as St. Lucy) was born here in AD 283, a time of Roman rule. She was a Christian during Diocletian's persecution of Christians, making her an oppressed minority.

Lucia's wealthy family had promised her in marriage to a non-Christian suitor. When her mother fell ill, Lucia brought her to visit the tomb of St. Agatha of Catania. During this visit, her mother was miraculously healed, and Lucia had a vision of St. Agatha. The young woman was so inspired that she canceled her impending nuptials and gave her dowry to the poor.

Lucia's angered fiancé alerted the authorities, and she was arrested and sentenced to be forced into prostitution. She refused to go. When the guards tried to physically remove her, they found that she could not be moved at all—not by pushing or pulling, nor even when she was harnessed to a team of oxen. They tried to burn her, but the wood refused to light. Some versions of the story say that they gouged out her eyes. Finally, they killed Lucia by stabbing her through the neck.

Lucia was buried in Siracusa (in the catacombs at the Basilica of Santa Lucia al Sepolcro), where her body remained for almost 700 years. In the meantime, she became one of the most widely popular of the early martyred saints. In the Middle Ages, during the Byzantine control of Siracusa, Lucia's bones were brought to the capital of Constantinople (today's Istanbul). The Venetian fleet sacked Constantinople in 1204 and brought most of those relics back to Venice—where they remain today. Siracusa's cathedral also has several relics of the beloved saint, including a piece of her arm and finger bones, which are venerated and paraded through town on holy days.

In art, St. Lucia is often represented as a beautiful, fair-skinned young lady—usually carrying her eyeballs on a plate. Thanks to the story of her blinding—and the root of her name (*lux*, Latin for "light")—Lucia is the patron saint of the blind.

Devotion to St. Lucia extends far beyond Sicilian shores. Because of her associations with light—and the proximity of her feast day (December 13) to the winter solstice—St. Lucia Day is often a festive celebration of light. In Scandinavian lands, schoolchildren parade through the streets, clad in white, carrying candles, and singing: "Sa-ahn-tah-ah Loo-oo-chee-ee-yah! San-TAH loo-chee-ee-yah!"

symbols of St. Lucia's martyrdom, including a sword, crown of virginity, and palm representing her sanctity. If it's open, step inside to see a 1574 painting representing the martyrdom of St. Lucia. (This church once held Caravaggio's *The Burial of Santa Lucia*, which is now located in the Basilica of Santa Lucia—described on page 323.)

• *Exit Piazza Duomo to the right of the church. Continue downhill a couple more blocks, looking up to notice the fine wrought-iron balconies (dating from the Spanish occupation), then angle right to reach the bay. Belly up to the railing overlooking a big pit filled with a pond and some plants.*

❾ Fountain of Arethusa

Most locals don't even know the formal name for this structure (Fonte Aretusa), which they call "fountain of the ducks." While just a pretty water feature today, this fountain was a big deal historically. This was the original freshwater spring that made the island a desirable place for settlement when the Greeks arrived in the eighth century BC from Corinth. The homesick

Greeks convinced themselves that the freshwater spring was connected to Greece by an underground river. Whether true or not, this spot was ideal: a big natural harbor, an easy-to-defend island, and plenty of fresh water bubbling up.

In more modern times, Jewish artisans used the fountain water to power nearby tanneries (the old Jewish quarter—called Giudecca—runs from here inland). After the Jews were ordered to leave in 1492 by Sicily's Spanish overlords, the fountain served as the community laundry until the 1800s.

You'll see papyrus here. Siracusa has a long tradition of making papyrus (in the style of the ancient Egyptians). You'll see fine paper sold in area stores, and a papyrus museum is on the opposite side of the island (at Via Nizza 14).

• *Walk 50 yards to the right, out to the far end of a terrace, for a...*

❿ Viewpoint Over the Bay

Here, at the end of your town walk, you can survey Siracusa's sweeping bay. This bay was a natural refuge, attracting sailors and traders since the time when the ancient Greeks arrived. Far to the left is the town fortress, reached by a pleasant harborside walk. Far to the right is the modern city (on the mainland), marked by the pointy peak of the modern Sanctuary of the Madonna of Tears, a church built in the 1950s to celebrate the miracle of the weeping Virgin Mary.

Ponder this: You are standing at one of Europe's most southern points. And had you stood here in 413 BC, in the middle of the Second Peloponnesian War, you would have had front-row seats to perhaps the most pivotal naval battle in Greek history—the Battle of Syracuse, which ended in the total defeat of the Athenian fleet.

• *Our walk is finished. Within a few minutes from here are several more sights: The Bellomo Palace Gallery is the town's top art gallery; beyond that are the Puppet Museum and Puppet Theater. And there's much to be seen elsewhere in Ortigia and on the mainland, too. These sights are all described in the next section (except the Puppet Theater, which is described on page 326).*

Sights in Siracusa

Sights are divided between Ortigia and the mainland, where you'll find the vast Neapolis Archaeological Park and a few other attractions. Another sightseeing option is to day-trip to the Baroque town of Noto (35 minutes by train; for details, see the end of the Ragusa and the Southeast chapter).

ORTIGIA

My self-guided town walk, earlier, connects several of Ortigia's top sights—including the cathedral.

▲▲Siracusa Cathedral (Duomo di Siracusa)

Siracusa's cathedral is a delightful and engaging potpourri of the civilizations that have called Ortigia—and Sicily—home. The exterior (including the stately Baroque facade and the ancient exoskeletal columns around the side) is described earlier, in the self-guided walk. The interior is well worth a visit for its surprising integration of architectural styles.

Cost and Hours: €2, Mon-Sat 8:30-18:30, off-season 9:00-17:30, closed Sun except for Mass, +39 389 550 3267.

Visiting the Cathedral: Upon entering, walk to the back of the **nave** and take in the history. You're standing in what was once the cella (inner chamber) of the original Temple of Athena, from 480 BC. The entrance would have been on the opposite side, where the altar now stands, as the temple would have faced east, in the direction the sun rises.

Up above, the lettering on the walls marks the top of the temple's inner cella wall, which was originally solid. In the seventh century, the Byzantines turned the temple into a church, closing off the colonnade by adding walls between the columns, opening up the cella wall with arches, and moving the entry to the west to make the point that religion had changed. The ancient roof would have been wooden, just like today. There's no transept, because the original temple didn't have one; you are essentially experiencing the harmonious architectural proportions of the Greeks. The inlaid marble floor dates from the 1500s, when Siracusa was under Spanish rule. The altar is Baroque, built after the church was damaged in the 1693 earthquake.

Now circle around the church, starting with the **left aisle** (the original temple's peristyle). The three statues along the aisle are St. Caterina, Madonna and Child, and St. Lucia. As you walk along the row of original 2,500-year-old Doric columns (which are also visible from the outside), notice how the sixth column nearly wobbled off its perch in the 1693 earthquake, while other columns lost their top halves altogether. The chapel to the left of the altar contains the statue *Madonna delle Neve (Our Lady of Snow)* by Antonello Gagini.

Now cross over to the **right aisle,** lined with chapels that generally take their dimensions from the spacing of the ancient columns. To the right of the altar is an exception: The Chapel of the Crucifix has more cohesive Baroque dimensions; it's dedicated to a 13th-century Byzantine-style crucifix. As you walk down the aisle, look high above at the fine workmanship of the exquisitely preserved capitals from ancient times. About halfway along, the Baroque decor of the Chapel of the Blessed Sacrament is more typically flamboyant than the rest of the otherwise tame interior. Just past it, the Chapel of St. Lucia contains the venerated relics of the saint. And finally, at the end of the aisle, the baptistery contains the baptismal font: a Greek krater on top of a Norman column capital, surrounded by bronze lions. Norman mosaics are displayed on the walls, and a tiny room next door shows video footage of the St. Lucia float on its procession through town during the Festival of St. Lucia.

Archbishop's Library (Biblioteca Arcivescovile): Exiting the cathedral to the left, look for the entrance to the Archbishop's Library, created by Bishop Giambattista Alagona in the late 18th century. Part of the Secreta Palatii (Secrets of the Palace) exhibition, this austere, dimly lit space inside the archbishop's palace offers a quiet step back in time, with more than 70,000 books dating as far back as the 16th century. To reach the main library hall, you'll walk down a corridor lined with ancient tomes and portraits of bishops (€2, Mon-Sat 10:00-18:00, closed Sun and Dec-March).

Bellomo Palace Gallery
(Galleria Regionale di Palazzo Bellomo)

This museum fills two floors of a noble mansion with paintings (15th-18th century)—including an important piece by Antonello da Messina—folk art, archaeological fragments, and religious artifacts, but there's very little written English information.

Cost and Hours: €10, Tue-Sat 9:00-19:00, Sun until 13:00, closed Mon, Via Capodieci 16, +39 093 169 511.

Visiting the Museum: The **ground floor** displays exquisite 15th-century altarpieces and stone carvings from churches. Circling around the courtyard, you'll see a collection of massive marble coats of arms taken from buildings, all hung here at eye level. The ground level also has several rooms displaying columns and capitals, stone carvings from churches and houses, religious polyptychs, an elaborate marble tomb, horse carriages, and more.

Climb up the stone staircase and loop around the **upper level,** starting with the 18th-century, wood-carved relief map of Ortigia. Next, in a darkened room, is the collection's prized possession: **Antonello da Messina's** *Annunciation* (1474). After a trip to the Italian mainland, Antonello brought to Sicily the technique of painting with oil, a mastery of depth, and a passion for detail he's thought to have picked up from Flemish painters that he met in his travels. Like Netherlandish painters of the age, Antonello has created a real world in which his subjects live:  Mary inhabits an authentic room with characteristic windows and ceiling beams, and the plant in a vase at the foot of her desk is as detailed as the subjects' faces. Appreciate the peaceful, enigmatic smile on Mary's face as she's greeted by the angel, arms crossed over her heart. Outside the window, a shooting star streaks the sky...and then appears *inside* the window, in the form of a ghostly dove—the Holy Spirit—heading straight for Mary (for more on Antonello, see page 145).

▲San Filippo Apostolo Underground

For a look at what hides beneath the streets of Ortigia, visit the Church of San Filippo Apostolo, where a 30-minute tour (usually in both Italian and English) takes you underground and uncovers three levels and over 2,000 years of history.

Cost and Hours: €5; tours depart every 30 minutes Mon-Sat

10:00-12:30 & 15:00-17:00, closed Sun and Nov-March; Piazza San Filippo, +39 366 357 0430.

Visiting the Underground: Your guide takes you steeply down the stairs, going deeper and deeper through three underground levels (ending 60 feet below the surface).

First is the circa-1700 church **crypt,** with tombs of aristocrats. Below that is a limestone quarry, in use since ancient Greek times. From here, tunnels burrow under the churches and squares of old Ortigia. During World War II, this space was converted into an **air-raid shelter.** Your guide will point out faint illustrations of Allied and Axis bomber planes and parachutes on the wall, as well as a Roman cistern that was used as an infirmary. Finally, you'll descend a spiral stone  staircase to a *mikveh*, a natural spring that was used as a purification bath by the local Jewish community going back to the 1200s. (The surrounding neighborhood, Giudecca, was the old Jewish quarter.) Heading back up all those stairs and squinting in the sunlight, you'll have a new appreciation for all that lies underfoot in Ortigia.

Maniace Castle (Castello Maniace)

On the very southern tip of Ortigia, Maniace Castle was built in the 13th century by Holy Roman Emperor Frederick II of Swabia to show his power and control over Siracusa. Throughout the centuries, it served not only as a fortress but also a royal residence and prison. Besides its stunning and prime defensive location, the castle is notable as being one of few structures from this period to remain standing after the 1693 earthquake.

Cost and Hours: €6; generally open Mon 8:30-13:30, Tue-Sun until 19:30 in peak season, shorter hours in off-season, last entry 45 minutes before closing; +39 093 145 0120.

Visiting the Castle: Visitors enter through a marble archway, with niches on either side that once contained bronze ram sculptures (reproductions of these statues are in the small museum near the castle entry). The core of the castle was built as a perfect square—167 feet per side—with cylindrical towers at each corner. The Sala Ipostila (central hall) is notable for its distinctive cross-vault ceiling—a mix of limestone and lava stone—supported by 36 limestone columns. Starting in the 16th century, the castle's defensive fortifications were beefed up, leading to the addition of the Vignazza fort, extending to the very tip of the peninsula like a diamond, with windows on both sides so the castle's cannons could be aimed in either direction.

Puppet Museum (Museo dei Pupi)

Members of the Mauceri family—who also operate nearly nightly puppet shows at their nearby theater (described later, under "Entertainment in Siracusa")—have been puppeteers for three generations. You can see their collection of traditional Sicilian puppets from past shows in a small museum, lovingly displayed and curated.

Cost and Hours: €3, €12 combo-ticket includes performance at nearby Puppet Theater; Mon-Sat 11:00-13:00 & 15:00-19:00, closed Sun; Via della Giudecca 78, +39 093 158 6360, teatrodeipupisiracusa.it.

MAINLAND SIRACUSA

Ancient Syracuse quickly outgrew the footprint of little Ortigia island and stretched out onto the mainland, and some impressive remains can be found about 1.5 miles from Ortigia at the Neapolis Archaeological Park. Nearby, you can also visit the Paolo Orsi Archaeological Museum, the modern Sanctuary of the Madonna of Tears, the evocative Catacombs of San Giovanni, and the Basilica of Santa Lucia (with a Caravaggio painting).

Getting There: To avoid a 30-minute walk to the mainland through dreary urban sprawl, opt for a taxi or the bus (hop-on, hop-off is easiest; for details, see "Getting Around Siracusa," earlier). The Paolo Orsi Archaeological Museum, the modern Sanctuary of the Madonna of Tears, and the Catacombs of San Giovanni are an unappealing 10-minute walk east of the archaeological park along Viale Teocrito, and the Basilica of Santa Lucia is a 10-minute walk from the Sanctuary of the Madonna of Tears. To link the sights by bus (and minimize walking), visit the Viale Teocrito sights first, since that bus stops here first. Then walk or hop back on the bus to the archaeological park.

Sightseeing Strategies: Because getting from Ortigia to these sights requires some effort, plan to visit all that interests you here in one trip. If you're getting an early start, do the archaeological park first, then the sights near Viale Teocrito.

To return to Ortigia, ride the hop-on, hop-off bus or take a taxi (you'll find them waiting across the street from the archaeological park entrance).

Sights in Siracusa

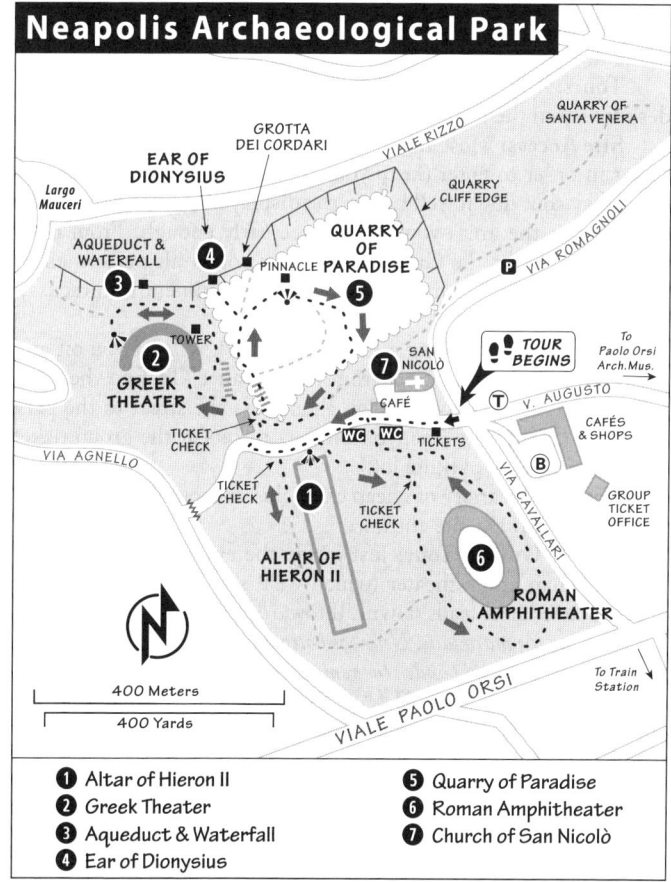

- ❶ Altar of Hieron II
- ❷ Greek Theater
- ❸ Aqueduct & Waterfall
- ❹ Ear of Dionysius
- ❺ Quarry of Paradise
- ❻ Roman Amphitheater
- ❼ Church of San Nicolò

▲▲Neapolis Archaeological Park
(Parco Archeologico della Neapolis)

At its peak in the fifth century BC, the city-state of Syracuse was the dominant military and economic power in the Greek world, with a population that rivaled Athens in size. While this city is long gone, wandering through its remains in this vast archaeological park gives you a sense of ancient Syracuse's immensity and power. You'll see a big Greek theater, the remains of a water system, the footprint of a sacrificial altar, a (later) Roman amphitheater, and the immense quarry where thousands of slaves cut the stone that made it all.

Cost and Hours: €14, €22 combo-ticket with Paolo Orsi Archaeological Museum is good for three days; open daily 8:30-19:45, closes earlier mid-Sept-March, last entry 1.25 hours before closing.

Information: +39 093 166 206, parchiarecheologici.regione.sicilia.it.

Tours: You can pay €13 for a guided tour (ask at the ticket desk for when the next English tour leaves).

Site Access: Most areas of the park require you to rescan your ticket in order to enter (keep your ticket handy). Note that some areas may shut down well before the displayed closing time, so be sure to visit the areas you want to see early enough. From mid-May to early July, the Greek theater hosts open-air performances and closes earlier, around 17:00 (see "Entertainment in Siracusa," later).

Getting In: If taking a bus to the site, it will let you off at a parking lot across the street from the entrance. To find the main ticket office, walk across the lot, then cross the street to the park entrance. (If there's a line, you can buy tickets at the group ticket office near the bus parking lot.)

Eating: A variety of cheap cafés cluster around the bus parking lot and near the site entrance.

◆ **Self-Guided Tour:** Just inside the entrance, on your left, is the Roman amphitheater (which we'll see last) and pay WCs. A long, paved lane leads downhill toward the huge Greek theater.

• *Walk along the main lane. Near the bottom of the lane, stop at the green railing on the left and ponder the remains of the...*

❶ **Altar of Hieron II** (Ara di Ierone II): Dating from the third century BC, this is the longest altar ever built in the Greek world. Scratch that: It wasn't built—it was chiseled, creating a mammoth monolithic altar. As long as a stadium, the altar was dedicated to Zeus and was used once a year for a grand festival that featured the sacrifice of 450 oxen (followed by the ancient world's longest lineup for barbecue). Sicilian Greeks had  the habit of supersizing everything they built, making sure their new community was more impressive than the homeland they'd left behind.

• *At the bottom of the paved lane, take a hairpin right turn, following signs to* Teatro Greco. *After the ticket check, you'll see a ramp (left) that leads up to the Greek theater, and stairs (right), which lead down to the quarry and Ear of Dionysius (we'll take this path later).*

For now, head left up the **ramp.** *Follow the path as it switchbacks up to the top of the hill and past a tower (about a five-minute walk; if the stairs are open, feel free to take them—they meet up with the path near the top). At the end of the path, stop for a fine view over the...*

Sights in Siracusa

❷ **Greek Theater** (Teatro Greco): The most important ancient monument here dates from 500 BC, back when a theater functioned like a church, teaching moral and religious principles. Most of the seats are carved directly from stone—etched into the hillside. (Because the theater could seat 15,000, archaeologists believe the total population of ancient Syracuse would have been

at least 150,000.) Of course, there was no amplification, so acoustics were important. A back wall helped to reflect the sound. The terrace above and behind the seats functioned as a grand lobby for the thousands attending performances; it was covered by a wooden roof and decorated with fine statues of heroes and gods filling the niches.

The theater is still used today, hosting performances of shows Greeks would have seen. During the summer outdoor theater season, protective wooden seats cover the original stone. Consider attending a performance—it's a magical experience for those who love ancient history, outdoor theater, or rowdy Sicilian school groups (see "Entertainment in Siracusa," later). Like theatergoers then and now, appreciate the grand view over Siracusa and its bay from the top of the theater.

• *Running along the very top of the theater's seats (above the waterfall) is the...*

❸ **Aqueduct** (Acquedotto): This waterfall *(nymphaeum)* is part of an aqueduct carved from the rock, allowing water to flow about 15 miles from a mountain spring into the city. Get up close and inspect the engineering. Imagine this cavern, decorated with statues of nymphs, gushing with life-giving water. When the Roman Empire fell in the fifth century, the theater was abandoned. Later, the Spanish redirected the aqueduct, carving a channel through the seats to power the grain mill where the stage is. The **tower** above the theater was built as a home and watchtower for the mill keeper.

• *Retrace your steps down the path back to the ticket checkpoint. As you walk, check out the view of the vast, lush quarry on your left—our next stop. At the bottom, take the stairs we bypassed before, then follow the path on the left. You'll walk through the jungle of vegetation that now fills the quarry. Follow the path deep into the jungle. Soon you'll hit a cliff face, where you'll see a tall, narrow cave.*

❹ **Ear of Dionysius** (Orecchio di Dionisio): This cave, which resembles a giant ear, was purportedly named by the painter Caravaggio for the city's ancient Greek dictator. Legend has it that the tyrannical ruler of Syracuse would employ the unusual acoustics of the cave to eavesdrop on the slaves below—often his political enemies.

See the chisel marks wallpapering the cave and imagine how blocks of stone were cut, over the generations, from the top down. Wooden pegs were placed in grooves carved a few inches deep then moistened with water. The pressure of the expanding wood would crack the stone into blocks.

Walk deeper in and clap or sing a few bars, sampling the acoustics. (Beware of the pigeons above you who call this cave home.)

• *From the Ear of Dionysius, head back the way you came and turn left at a side path (before you reach the break in the giant rock). Pass under an arch of trees to walk deeper into the quarry. At the end of the path, head left, then right; pause when you see a stony pinnacle sticking up amid the trees.*

❺ **Quarry of Paradise** (Latomia del Paradiso): Marveling at Syracuse's ancient temples and theaters, it's easy to forget that their construction was made possible by enslaved people, who labored to quarry, carry, and lay the stones until they died. Those enslaved people were often prisoners of war: About 7,000 Athenians were consigned to this quarry after being soundly defeated in the Second Peloponnesian War. The one tower of

stone still standing amid the vast green zone was a pillar supporting the roof of a giant cavern, which collapsed with the earthquake. Today, this verdant "Garden of Paradise" (an ironic name once you know its history) is overgrown with acanthus (whose jagged foliage inspired the Corinthian capital), oleander, bay leaf, bamboo, wild oranges, and mulberry.

• *Continue through the quarry; you'll eventually wind back up to this area's ticket check. Return to the main road and head back past the Altar of Hieron II, toward the main entry.*

At the WCs, turn down the path on the right leading downhill to another ticket check. After entering, circle around the...

❻ **Roman Amphitheater** (Anfiteatro Romano): The Romans may have conquered ancient Syracuse in 212 BC, but ultimately, they were conquered by Greek culture. This amphitheater, dating from the first century AD, is a fine example of Roman engineering. While Greeks would build into an existing hill, a Roman amphitheater is generally freestanding. In this case, the amphitheater combines techniques: It's partially carved, par-

tially built, and partially freestanding. The Romans put two theaters together and called it an amphitheater (from the Greek *amphi*, meaning "on both sides"). While Greek tragedies had their share of implied violence, those scenes always happened offstage. By contrast, the Romans shamelessly incorporated actual blood and gore into their entertainment. The amphitheater floor was layered with sand to soak up the blood. ("Arena" comes from the Latin word for sand.) Look for the archway, under which the losers of battle would be carted away.

The walkway is lined by stone sarcophagi, from a Greek necropolis discovered during the excavation of a nearby modern road. From above the theater, you can see a small pool in the center, which was likely used for gladiator fights using aquatic animals.

• *As you leave the amphitheater and head for the exit, notice the small Romanesque church across from the ticket desk.*

❼ **Church of San Nicolò:** The Normans invaded Sicily and ruled the island from 1060 to 1198, making their mark with a lot of fine Norman (Romanesque) architecture. This church of San Nicolò, from the 11th century, sits atop Piscina Romana, a first-century Roman cistern.

• *As you exit the park, look toward the spire of the modern church, the* ***Sanctuary of the Madonna of Tears****. When construction began on that church in the 1960s, layers and layers of Greek and Roman ruins were found. An entire ancient city lies beneath your feet...from here to the harbor at Ortigia.*

Other Mainland Sights

The first three sights cluster around Viale Teocrito within a few minutes' walk of the stop for the hop-on, hop-off bus and for buses #105 and #106. The Basilica of Santa Lucia is a 10-minute walk to the southeast. For locations, see the "Siracusa" map near the beginning of this chapter.

▲Sanctuary of the Madonna of Tears
(Santuario della Madonna delle Lacrime)

This giant, conical pilgrimage church rises like a massive spaceship in the middle of modern Siracusa—visible from just about every point in the city. The church was built to commemorate a 1953 miracle and is supposedly shaped like a teardrop *(lacrima)*. To me this modern church looks more like a super-sized lampshade...or like someone dropped a waffle cone, gelato-side down. It's worth stepping inside to appreciate the building's unusual architecture and the reverence with which the faithful venerate the miraculous Madonna.

Cost and Hours: Free, Mon-Sat 7:30-12:30 & 15:30-19:30, Sun until 20:45, Via del Sanctuario 33, madonnadellelacrime.it.

Background: In 1953, in the home of a humble Siracusa couple, a simple bas-relief of the Virgin Mary began weeping...and didn't stop for three days. The wife had been ill and had lost her vision but suddenly regained her sight as tears flowed down the Madonna's cheeks. Vatican investigators verified that the tears were indeed human and authenticated the miracle. The couple's house was suddenly on the pilgrimage trail, and the sculpture became the centerpiece of this striking, French-designed church, completed decades later.

Visiting the Church: At first, the **interior** has a stark and gloomy bomb-shelter ambience. But give it a chance to speak to you—it's really a sculpture of light, changing throughout the day. The entire top of the structure sits on 22 steel discs that keep the cone secure in an earthquake. Look up as you enter and see how the slits in the concrete cone create a halo of light.

The focal point of the church—near the main altar—is the case displaying the little **Madonna.** The inexpensive plaster sculpture is a stark contrast to the massive marble altar that protects it and the giant structure of the church. Go closer to the altar and wonder, how could liquid have flowed from this bust? The unlikely, modest miracle happened at a

time of turmoil in post-WWII Sicily and was an inspiration to the people of Siracusa. A **reliquary** holding the original tears cried by the Madonna in 1953 is often displayed here in the sanctuary.

Outside the church and to the left (counterclockwise), you'll find an entry to the sanctuary's **museum** (€1, contains jewels, relics, and items related to the miracle) and crypt.

▲▲Paolo Orsi Archaeological Museum
(Museo Archeologico Regionale Paolo Orsi)

Considered one of the finest archaeology museums in Sicily, this collection of artifacts from eastern Sicily spans from prehistory to Roman times. Located in a lush park, the museum can be challenging to visit thanks to its dense layout. But its highlights paint a vivid picture of ancient Syracuse and the rest of Sicily in antiquity. You'll see classical sculpture, everyday items, and an exquisitely carved, early Christian sarcophagus from the nearby Catacombs of San Giovanni.

Cost and Hours: €10, €22 combo-ticket with Neapolis Archaeological Park is good for three days; Tue-Sat 9:00-19:00, Sun until 14:00, closed Mon, last entry one hour before closing; Viale Teocrito 66, +39 093 148 9511, parchiarcheologici.regione.sicilia.it.

Visiting the Museum: From Viale Teocrito, enter the park and make your way to the blocky modern building at its center.

Inside, pick up a floor plan and wrap your head around the unusual layout: The two-floor museum is shaped like a honeycomb, with sectors based on topic. For the most part, we'll progress through the wings chronologically (they're lettered from A to F), but each wing is a maze in itself, and artifacts, while loosely organized by date, are crammed into overloaded glass cases. Just explore, look for the highlights below, and stop at anything that looks interesting (then find the English label).

• *Start with the coin collection (downstairs).*

Coin and Jewelry Collection: Inside a heavily fortified vault, display cases show off the coinage of various invaders, empires, and kingdoms that have ruled Sicily, as well as other civilizations the Sicilians have traded with. The coins are remarkably detailed (use the magnifying glasses to examine them) and well described in English.

Look for the beautiful collection of ancient Greek coins minted in Syracuse. Surveying coins from this era, notice how each city-state embossed its coins with its own unique symbology. For example, ancient Syracuse's coins typically had a chariot on the "tails" side and a profile of Arethusa, the nymph, on the "heads" side. In

Paolo Orsi Archaeological Museum

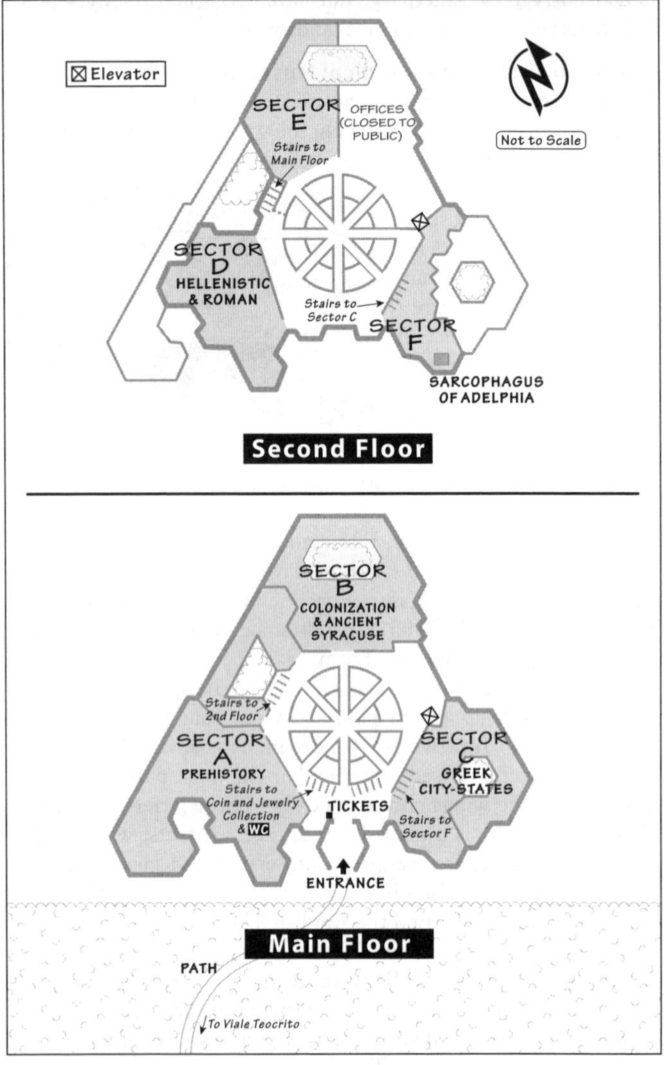

Second Floor

- Sector E
- Offices (Closed to Public)
- Elevator
- Stairs to Main Floor
- Sector D — Hellenistic & Roman
- Stairs to Sector C
- Sector F — Sarcophagus of Adelphia
- Not to Scale

Main Floor

- Sector B — Colonization & Ancient Syracuse
- Stairs to 2nd Floor
- Sector A — Prehistory
- Stairs to Coin and Jewelry Collection & WC
- Tickets
- Sector C — Greek City-States
- Stairs to Sector F
- Entrance
- Path
- To Viale Teocrito

the most ancient ones (seventh century BC) Arethusa is shown in profile with blunt, angular features; in later coins she has matured, with beautiful curly hair and a rounder face.

• *Back upstairs, circle around the rooms on this floor, starting with sector A, just left of the ticket desk.*

Prehistory (Sector A): In this section you'll find pottery and bones, including the skeletons of a pair of three-foot-tall **dwarf**

elephants, which lived on the island during the Pleistocene age. Notice that, with the sinus cavity exposed, the elephant skull looks like a fearsome one-eyed monster. Some believe these remains could be the origin of the Cyclops myth.

Colonization and Ancient Syracuse (Sector B): These rooms display the richest part of the collection—artifacts from the Greek era. The first section features exhibits about Greek colonies in eastern Sicily; the second section highlights objects uncovered from ancient Siracusa.

In the section on the ancient town of Lentini, founded in the seventh century, look for the painted **Lebes Gamikos vase** (fourth century BC, case 148). It features a female divinity, believed to be Persephone, and a handmaid in a temple. The vase is notable for its attempt to depict three dimensions, as in the three-legged stool. Nearby, the **Lentini Kouros** (early fifth century BC) is a classic example of a Greek Archaic *kouros* (young boy) statue (eyes closed; calm, neutral smile). It would take a couple of hundred years for this stiff Archaic sculptural style to relax into the realistic Classical style that Greek art is known for.

Other important artifacts in this section come from the settlement of Megara Hyblaea, about 12 miles up the coast from Siracusa. Look for the headless **Megara Kouros** (550 BC), found in the necropolis outside town and used as a funerary monument. The inscription on his right leg identifies him as "Sombrotidas, son of Mandrokles, doctor." Another headless statue, also discovered at the necropolis, is **Megara Kourotrophos.** Unlike the Megara Kouros, which was carved in marble, this was made with local Italian limestone and was pieced back together after being discovered in more than 900 shattered pieces. Depicting a mother feeding twins, her primitive toes poking out from her garment, Megara Kourotrophos conveys a sense of motherhood, fertility, and female divinity—important and symbolic to a country that's so intertwined with its rich and fertile land. You'll also see a **Greek theater mask** (late sixth century BC, case 154), with a big, wide-open mouth that was used to help magnify sound.

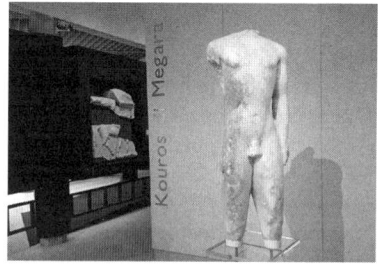

The second section of sector B contains important objects from ancient Siracusa. Find a case filled with rows of **female votives.** About 7,000 of these were discovered at Piazza della Vittoria, during a 1960s excavation to clear space for the construction of the Sanctuary of the Madonna of Tears. The sanctuary was built on the site of the Sanctuary of Demeter, and these clay votives of Demeter were used as offerings to the gods.

Look for a tiny, stylized **bronze horse** from ancient Corinth (c. 710 BC, case 188). Believed to have been a child's toy, it was found in a nearby necropolis and has become a symbol of both the museum and the city.

Finally, locate the section featuring **models of three major temples** that stood in ancient Syracuse. There's the Temple of Apollo (whose ruins you can still see in Ortigia), along with a pair of temples—one dedicated to Athena and the other to Artemis. While the Temple of Athena was integrated into Siracusa's cathedral, the Temple of Artemis was never finished, and eventually a building that now houses the city hall was constructed over it. Near the models, find several items from the **Temple of Athena,** including the striking plaque featuring a Gorgon (Medusa) holding Pegasus (possibly from a metope—a decorative panel from the exterior colonnade) and a marble torso of Nike from the temple pediment.

Syracuse Territory and Other Greek City-States (Sector C): Continue around to see pottery, architectural fragments, votives, spearheads, kraters (large vessels used to dilute wine), and so on—organized by the colonies where the items were found. Find *Dea di Grammichele*, a seated terra-cotta votive with an enigmatic, Archaic smile (fourth-fifth century BC).

• *From near the door you entered for sector C, find the stairs up to the second floor—and climb from BC to AD.*

Sarcophagus of Adelphia (Sector F): This area is devoted to sarcophagi found in the area, including the breathtaking Sarcophagus of Adelphia (late fourth century AD), from the nearby Catacombs of San Giovanni. Its incredibly detailed Old and New Testament scenes are worth lingering over. The inscription tells us it was carved for Adelphia, whom you can see in the center, alongside her husband, within a scallop-shell frame. We don't

know exactly who she was, but based on the quality of her monument, she was likely a Roman noblewoman. This carving was created just after the time of Constantine, when Rome became Christian; the figures are clumsy, signaling the beginning of the slow decline of Roman art.

- *Head back out the way you entered and go across to sector D.*

Hellenistic and Roman (Sectors D and E): Sector D proudly features **Priapus** (the god of fertility) at the entry. Farther in—deep in a maze of classical sculpture—find the famous **Venus Landolina,** a headless second-century-AD Roman copy of a second-century-BC Greek original. Roman sculptors were technically proficient but lacked the artistic mastery of their Greek predecessors—so replicas like this were common. Although headless, this Venus is admired for her beauty. If open, continue to sector E, with statues, reliefs, and architectural fragments from across central and eastern Sicily—including finds from once-prominent towns like Centuripe—offering a quiet glimpse into daily life and religion in the Greek and Roman eras. Look for a second Venus, a Medusa mask, and a relief of Demeter and Apollo.

▲Catacombs of San Giovanni (Catacombe di San Giovanni)

Below the ruins of the abandoned church of San Giovanni (which collapsed in the 1693 earthquake) is a series of hidden Christian tombs, providing a fascinating look at burial rituals from the fourth century AD. Visits here are by guided tour, which start with the ruins of the aboveground church and the early-Christian underground church of San Marciano—Siracusa's  *other* patron saint—decorated with evocative Byzantine-style frescoes. You'll then don a hard hat and enter the catacombs. Carved into the limestone, the catacombs are a complex network of large underground chambers. Some tombs are simple niches, others have large arches with fresco fragments, and others are carved out of old Roman cisterns. While this sounds spooky, most tombs are empty, and the long galleries of spacious, elegant rotundas make these catacombs less claustrophobic than some.

Cost and Hours: €10 for 30-minute guided tour; open daily 9:30-12:30 & 14:30-17:30, shorter hours and closed Mon in winter; these are last tour times—ask when the next English tour departs; €1 English pamphlet explains the highlights, Largo San Marciano 3, +39 093 164 694, info@kairos-web.com.

▲Basilica of Santa Lucia al Sepolcro

Located on Piazza Santa Lucia, this complex—including a basilica, an octagonal temple, and catacombs—marks the spot where Siracusa's patron, St. Lucia, was martyred in 304 AD. Today, it's worth a visit to see its altarpiece, *The Burial of Santa Lucia* by the Italian master Caravaggio, and the burial niche of Santa Lucia. For Lucia's whole story, see the sidebar earlier in this chapter.

Cost and Hours: Free, €1 to light the Caravaggio painting for four minutes; open daily 9:00-12:45 & 15:30-19:00 except Thu from 11:00; 10-minute walk southeast of the Sanctuary of the Madonna of Tears at Via Luigi Bignami 1, +39 093 167 946, basilicasantalucia.com.

Visiting the Basilica: Start at the main church, built in the 12th century by the Normans. Though later embellished with Baroque details in the 17th century, the church retains its Norman facade and interior layout. The wood ceiling, from the 16th century, features the coat of arms of the Aragonese crown.

The basilica's highlight hangs over the main altar. In 1608, Caravaggio painted *The Burial of Santa Lucia* for this spot (insert a coin to the left of the altar to light it). In Caravaggio's typical chiaroscuro style (with a deep contrast between light and dark), we see Lucia's body lying supine on the floor, a wound marking her throat. A Christian in the fiercely anti-Christian age of the Roman emperor Diocletian, Lucia rejected an arranged marriage, donated her wealth to the poor, and pledged herself to pious chastity. After resisting an attempt to force her into prostitution, Lucia was tortured and killed. Here Caravaggio depicts two burly brutes attempting to physically carry her away—but Lucia cannot be moved. The scene plays  out in front of a group of onlookers, including a Spanish soldier, a bishop with a miter, and several observers in despair (including, perhaps, Caravaggio himself—possibly the figure behind the hand of the bishop).

As dark and moody as his paintings, Caravaggio (1571-1610) was quarrelsome and violent. He'd had great success as a painter in Rome but fled the city after accidentally killing a man. He bounced from Naples to Malta to Sicily, where he spent a year. This piece, commissioned by the city's senate and facilitated by a friend, helped Caravaggio get back on his feet for a while. It's just one of three precious Caravaggio pieces in Sicily (the other two are in Messina). The backdrop of the painting—the tall brown walls—may represent the basilica's catacombs, where it is believed that Caravaggio took refuge (or it may depict the stone quarry at the Neapolis, by the Ear of Dionysius cave that Caravaggio named).

Once you're done studying the painting, look to the right,

where a column with a statue of Santa Lucia on top marks the spot of her martyrdom.

Other Basilica Sights: You may be able to tour the **catacombs** (€10, Mon-Sat 10:00-17:00, closed Sun and off-season). The octagonal **Temple of the Sepulcher,** down a set of stairs next to the basilica, was built in the 17th century around the tomb of Santa Lucia. Inside you'll see Santa Lucia's burial niche, adorned with a bas-relief of three animals that represent her character: courageous (lion), pure (dove), and incorruptible (griffin). A marble statue of Santa Lucia rests peacefully in a glass case in front of the tomb.

Shopping in Siracusa

For shopping, head to Ortigia. The island has an artsy soul. In recent years, artists and craftspeople have taken over dilapidated buildings and turned them into workshops for handmade goods. Note that shop hours and closed days can be fluid, and midday siesta closures are common.

Via Cavour, described in more detail on my self-guided Ortigia Walk earlier, is lined with shops and a good place to browse.

Via Roma also has some fine shops. At #101, **Baco** sells silver, bronze, and beaded handmade jewelry, all crafted by owners Marco and Simona. You can hang around and watch them work (daily, closed Tue off-season, +39 366 176 6111). At #154, **Ebano,** Giuliana sells her handmade handbags made of leather or canvas (both waterproof), as well as smaller accessories made from recycled inner tubes (daily, +39 324 605 9099, ebanostore.com).

Ceramics shops are scattered all around the island. **Ceramikale** is a tasteful shop with bowls, vases, ornaments, pine cones (a traditional Sicilian symbol of luck, fertility, and fortune), and more, all hand-painted in the back (daily, Via della Maestranza 70, +39 338 777 8402, ceramikale.it). **Giacomo Lo Presti** is a workaholic ceramist, making original creations with Sicilian themes in a hole-in-the-wall studio (daily, Via Dione 62, +39 339 213 4086).

Other interesting artisan shops include **Silk in Ortigia,** where Helene Moreau, who moved to Sicily from France, sells her hand-painted silk scarves (variable hours—feel free to call her if the shop is not open, Via Roma 27, +39 333 594 4518); **Officina Ortigia,** which sells a chaotic assortment of goods (jewelry, art, wovens, etc.) made both locally and elsewhere in Italy (daily, Via Resalibera 14); **Flavia Massara,** who creates unique paintings on papyrus, blending ancient Sicilian traditions with modern artistry (Mon-Sat 10:00-18:00, closed Sun, Via Capodieci 47); and **Serto,** where Giovanni makes bronze and silver jewelry in his nicely presented shop (daily, Via Giovanni Torres 15, +39 351 991 0597).

Entertainment in Siracusa

▲Puppet Theater (Teatro dei Pupi)

This charming 80-seat theater is run by the hardworking Mauceri family, who have a passion for this traditional art. Along with live performances, they also run the small Puppet Museum a few short blocks away (see "Sights in Siracusa," earlier). On most evenings, they perform an episode of a traditional saga, recounting the adventures of Charlemagne and the French knights. The stories are like old-time serial melodramas of good versus evil,

with superhero characters that captivate children. The play is in Italian, but they provide an English introduction. While the storylines can be complex, the presentation and effects are entertaining beyond any language barrier. The puppets, their shiny armor and helmets, and the props, scenery, and sets are all lovingly crafted with traditional methods by family members, who also perform live vocals and sound effects.

Cost and Hours: €11, €12 combo-ticket includes Puppet Museum; generally one show per day Mon-Sat, none on Sun or in late Nov, Jan, and Feb; buy tickets in advance or at the theater, advance tickets smart July-Aug; private tour of workshop, museum, or backstage available—see website; Via della Giudecca 22, +39 093 146 5540, teatrodeipupisiracusa.it.

Greek Theater in a Greek Theater

The Greek theater in the Neapolis Archaeological Park hosts a drama festival every summer, presenting famous Greek plays in Italian. Popular and lively, this is a fun way to experience an ancient site being used for its intended purpose. The cheapest seats are usually occupied by noisy student groups, so it's worth paying extra for a better seat. Performances typically begin in bright sunshine and end after sunset—be prepared for all the elements (from €35,

mid-May-early July, English-language pamphlets and headsets may be available for a fee—ask about the show you are seeing,

Sicilian Puppets

To understand puppets in Sicily, you have to start during the Middle Ages, when epic literary cycles were common, told by traveling troubadours recounting great adventures in faraway lands. Each country had its own version: In France, the stories were of Charlemagne and his knights; in England, King Arthur and the Knights of the Round Table; and in Arabia, the folk tales from *One Thousand and One Nights.*

In Italy in the 1500s, writers Ludovico Ariosto and Torquato Tasso recorded the French stories of Charlemagne and his chivalrous knights, writing the poems *Orlando Furioso* and *Gerusalemme Liberata.* In the 1860s, a poem called *The History of the French Knights* compiled earlier stories and was turned into traveling puppet shows in Naples and Sicily. Generations of *pupari,* or puppeteers, wrote their own plays and performed them in squares across southern Italy. Traditionally, the music was performed live by musicians, then later by a cylinder piano.

Puppets—*pupi* (POO-pee) in Italian—are heavier than marionettes and moved by one central rod in the head and

another controlling the right hand (used for sword fights). A string moves the less-mobile left arm. Sword fights are synchronized with wooden shoes worn by the puppeteers, who rhythmically tap the floor. Usually there are two puppeteers on an elevated backstage, but some shows require up to four. The stage and scenery are designed with optical illusions to make the puppets look much larger than they are. Nowadays, most music and sound effects are recordings, but voices of characters and some sound effects, like thunder or drums, are performed live. Building a puppet from scratch requires at least a full month of work, using wood, metal, fabric, and pigments.

The traditional main characters are the French knights Orlando (aka Roland) and his cousin, Rinaldo. Female characters are Angelica, a pagan princess from faraway Catai, and the sweet Fiordiligi. Each character has unique features to make them easily recognizable: Orlando has red plumage and shiny armor with an eagle on his chest plate and helmet. Blue-eyed, fair-haired Rinaldo has yellow plumage and a lion on his shield and helmet. Princess Angelica has big green eyes and a sultry voice and is usually involved in some sort of love triangle. Fiordiligi has dark hair, a simple dark dress, and no makeup. The fight scenes are the highlight of every play, sometimes involving dragons or giants, often resulting in a decapitation, and always with a high body count.

INDA Foundation ticket office is at Corso Matteotti 29, +39 093 148 7248, indafondazione.org/en).

Sleeping in Siracusa

My recommended accommodations are all in Ortigia. There's little reason to sleep on Siracusa's charmless mainland. All of these places have air-conditioning and, unless otherwise noted, an elevator (or it's not necessary).

€€€€ Algilà Ortigia Charme Hotel, tastefully renovated with all the luxuries, fills two buildings near the water. Its 54 rooms are sophisticated and modern while maintaining the elegance of the historic palaces they occupy. Although pricey, this can be a worthy splurge—or a bargain off-season (family rooms, restaurant serves dinner, Via Vittorio Veneto 93, +39 093 146 5186, algila.it, info@algila.it).

€€€€ Charme Hotel Henry's House is less hotel and more cozy home of a quirky art collector. Its 14 rooms cluster around a common seaview terrace, and each is decorated with funky antique furniture and modern art. Another terrace—on the roof—has views over the rooftops of Siracusa (family room, elevator to some rooms, pay valet parking, Via del Castello Maniace 68, +39 093 121 361, hotelhenryshouse.com, info@hotel3h.com).

€€€ Lanterne Magiche Ortigia is bright and modern, with 23 apartments in a rambling old palace. The rooms are spacious, each with a small kitchen, minibar, dining table, and coffeemaker (includes breakfast even though there are kitchenettes, family rooms, +39 0931 179 8038, Via G.B. Alagona 59, lanternemagicheortigia.com, info@lanternemagicheortigia.com, bubbly Domenico). Eight suites in a nearby building are also available (no kitchenettes and not all accessible with elevator).

€€€ Palazzo Alfeo offers six apartments on three floors right on the side of the sea where the sun sets. The apartments are simple and modern, with standout touches (such as refinished wood-door headboards and wardrobes). Most sleep up to four people (one bedroom, one bathroom, and a sofa bed in the living room), and all have sea views. It operates a bit more like a hotel, with daily cleaning service and breakfast delivered to your door for a fee (two-night minimum in summer, no elevator, pay valet parking, Via Lungomare Alfeo 18, +39 093 145 4632, palazzoalfeo.it, palazzoalfeo@gmail.com).

€€€ Domus Mariae Benessere and **Domus Mariae Albergo** are twin hotels that also serve as a convent and spa. In total they have 34 small, simple rooms. The sisters are often found gliding along the hallways. While the Albergo is a bit less convenient (no elevator, lots of stairs, and you eat across the street at Benessere),

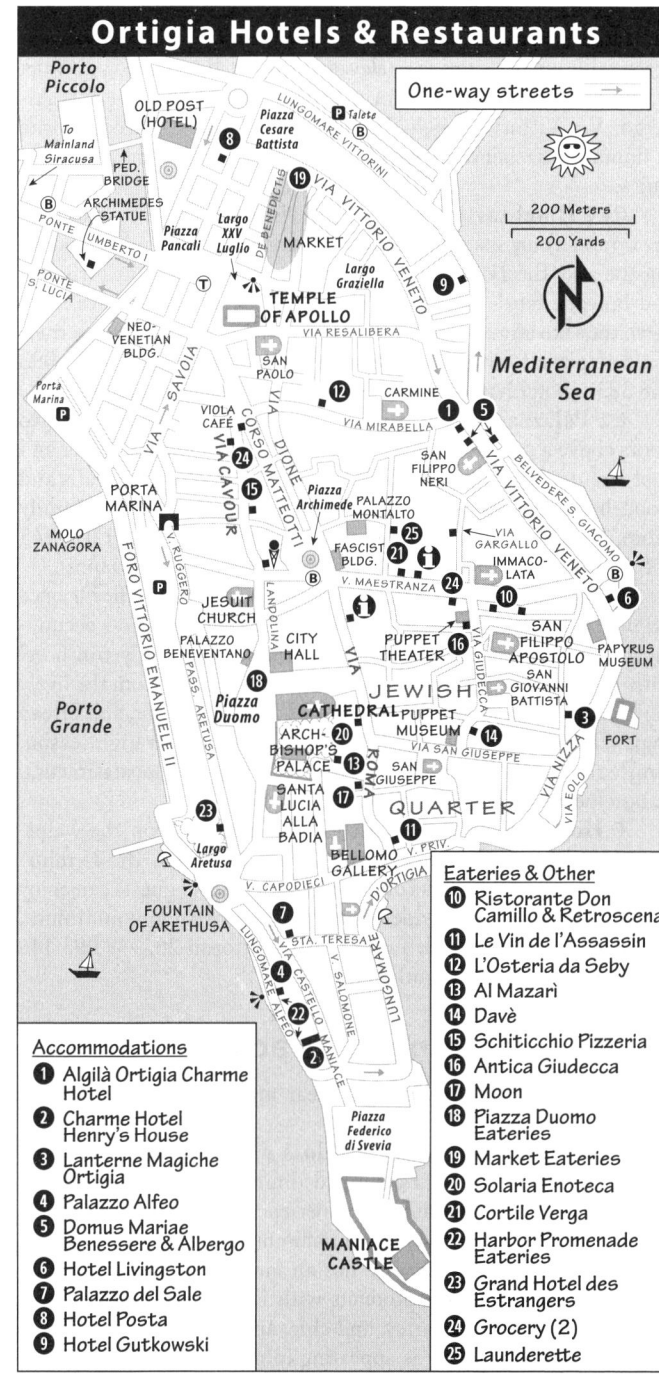

it's closer to the water and some of the rooms have balconies that practically open to the sea (elevator only at Benessere, pay valet parking; Benessere: Via Vittorio Veneto 89, +39 093 164 475; Albergo: Via Vittorio Veneto 76, +39 093 124 854; shared website at domusmariaebenessere.com, info@domusmariaebenessere.com, Luisa).

€€€ **Hotel Livingston,** which feels like it could be a stop on the Grand Tour, sits atop a cliff at the edge of the island, overlooking the sea. The 17 rooms have a regal feel, with elegant furniture and brocade fabric on the walls. While not all rooms have a sea view, they are large and have big windows. The rooftop view terrace is a fine place for breakfast (valet parking, Via Nizza 17, +39 093 146 3830, hotellivingston.com, booking@livingstonhotel.it).

€€ **Palazzo del Sale** offers six boutique-style rooms on two floors above a café. Rooms feature furniture by a local designer and cool architectural elements such as rock and brick in the walls and wood-beam ceilings (two-night minimum in high season, family room, no elevator, no breakfast, Via Santa Teresa 25, +39 093 165 958, palazzodelsale.com, info@palazzodelsale.com, Giovanni).

€ **Hotel Posta** takes its name from the old post office it once neighbored—not to be confused with the luxury hotel now occupying the historic building nearby. It is a colorful, family-run hotel with 17 tidy rooms at the edge of Ortigia, steps away from the lively daily market. An elevator gets you as far as the first floor, and fifteen steps take you to the second (two-night minimum in high season, family room, Via Trieste 33, +39 093 121 819, hotelpostasiracusa.it, hotelpostasiracusa.it, Willy).

€ **Hotel Gutkowski,** located in two buildings on the waterfront promenade, offers a very good value for Ortigia. The 25 minimalist rooms mix elements of modern and old, and guests can enjoy the hotel's terrace, with wide-open sea views (two-night minimum, restaurant, Lungomare di Levante Elio Vittorini 26, +39 093 146 5861, guthotel.it, info@guthotel.it).

Eating in Siracusa

These eateries are all in Ortigia, near my recommended accommodations.

€€€€ **Ristorante Don Camillo** is a local institution, serving fine cuisine since 1985 in a vaulted dining room. Their €80-100 tasting *menu*s are an indulgent experience (closed Sun, Via della Maestranza 96, +39 093 167 133, ristorantedoncamillosiracusa.it).

€€€ **Le Vin de l'Assassin** has an interesting French-Sicilian fusion menu, using local products with French preparations. The dining room is eclectic, artsy, and chic, and the outdoor seating—on a characteristic lane—is appealing (dinner only Tue-Sat, lunch and dinner on Sun, closed Mon in summer, reservations smart, Via Roma 115, +39 093 166 159).

€€€ L'Osteria da Seby is a warm and cozy place, where Seby and his crew serve a seafood-focused menu. While a bit old-school and well discovered by tourists, this is a reliable choice for a fancy fish dinner (closed Mon, Via Vincenzo Mirabella 21, +39 0931 181 5619, sebylosteria.it).

€€€ Al Mazarì, tucked away on a quiet lane near Piazza Duomo, is a family-run spot that brings the flavors of western Sicily—like couscous and tuna tartare—to the east coast. Meals are served in a cozy dining room or on the pleasant outdoor area (daily, closed Sun at dinner, Via Giovanni Torres 7/9, +39 093 148 3690, Ludovico).

€€€ Retroscena is a family operation (the husband, from Sicily, is the chef, while the wife, from Greece, hosts). They serve a seafood-focused menu of Sicilian dishes with Greek influence in an elegant space (dinner only, closed Sun, Via della Maestranza 108, +39 0931 185 4278).

€€€ Davè, a stylish and intimate spot in the heart of the Giudecca district, serves modern takes on Sicilian classics with creative flair. Dishes are elegantly plated and full of local flavor—think fresh seafood pastas and seasonal ingredients. With its quiet setting and polished service, it's a good choice for a more refined night out (open Wed-Mon for dinner, also open Fri-Sun for lunch, closed Tue, Via della Giudecca 75, +39 093 196 7821).

€ Schiticchio Pizzeria—a modern-feeling spot along atmospheric Via Cavour—has pizza and a range of good beers. But their specialty is burgers, which are enormous and made with local ingredients (daily, Via Cavour 30, +39 331 334 3721).

€ Antica Giudecca, near the Puppet Theater, is a neighborhood hangout with zero pretense. They sell pizza by the slice, calzone, *arancini*, and other *tavola calda* (buffet spread) items, all churned out nonstop by Signora Lucia and her husband. While most locals stop here for carryout, you can sit at one of the humble tables (closed Sun, Via della Giudecca 26, +39 093 144 9152).

Vegetarian: €€ Moon is a wildly creative eatery (its name stands for "Move Ortigia Out of Normality") with a big, minimalist, trendy interior and inviting outdoor tables. They serve up ambitious, hit-or-miss vegan food, with a fusion approach that incorporates Asian and African elements (open long hours, closed Tue, reservations smart, Via Roma 112, +39 093 144 9516, moonortigia.com).

Eating on Piazza Duomo: The glorious town living room that surrounds Ortigia's cathedral is one of Sicily's most inviting public spaces. A few eateries face this elegant square and are ideal for a scenic lunch or a romantic evening drink. While the food may be better in back-street restaurants, this location is hard to resist, and prices are reasonable. **€€ Gran Caffè del Duomo** has a predictable menu of pastas, pizzas, and main courses, as well as counters for gelato and takeaway street food (open long hours, closed Mon, at #18, +39 093 121 544).

Market Eateries: The main drag of Ortigia's outdoor market—Via Emanuele de Benedictis—is an entertaining place to browse for a meal (they're all open at lunch, and some are open for dinner; everything is closed Sun). Options range from sit-down *trattorie*, to high-end fish restaurants, to cheap-and-cheery fried street food. There's also a pair of very popular € deli/sandwich shops at the far end: **Caseificio Borderi** and its neighbor **La Salumeria Fratelli Burgio** are touristy but fun and good for grabbing a sandwich to go.

Wine and Cocktail Bars: €€ Solaria Enoteca, in an old-fashioned wine library, is run by Gianfilippo and Elisa. In addition to an extensive wine selection, they have a good menu of small bites to pair with your wine, including some creative bruschetta (closed Sun, Via Roma 86, +39 093 146 3007).

€€ Cortile Verga serves craft cocktails (one of their specialties is gin) in a palazzo courtyard full of ambience. The old-newsprint-style menu is a fun read, and the food selection is decent, including a good meat-and-cheese board (nightly from 17:30, Via Della Maestranza 33, +39 333 168 3212).

Along the Harbor Promenade: From the Fountain of Arethusa, you can stroll down to a delightful promenade that runs south along Ortigia's dreamy seafront—with views over the nearly 360-degree harbor. You'll pass a stretch of interchangeably romantic and overpriced €€€ fish restaurants—popular for a pricey meal or (better) a predinner cocktail. The food is forgettable, but the views are not.

For a particularly swanky experience, confidently walk into the Art Deco **Grand Hotel des Estrangers** and take the elevator to their top-floor bar (you may even be escorted there, as all are welcome). It's a nice place to watch the sunset with an overpriced drink (just behind the Fountain of Arethusa on Passeggio Adorno, privateluxuryproperties.com/clou).

Groceries: Both these supermarkets are open long hours except Sunday, when they close early. **Gusto Ortigia Market** is centrally located and has a deli (Via della Maestranza 80). A **Co op** grocery is at Via Cavour 71.

Siracusa Connections

BY PUBLIC TRANSPORTATION

From Siracusa by Bus to: Noto (8/day, 1 hour, AST; 4/day, 1 hour, Interbus/Etna Trasporti), **Ragusa** (5/day, 3 hours, AST), **Catania** (1-2/hour, 80 minutes, Interbus/Etna Trasporti), **Palermo** (3/day, 3.25 hours, Interbus/Etna Trasporti), **Taormina** (1/day direct, 2.5 hours, more with change in Catania, Interbus/Etna Trasporti). Bus info: AST (aziendasicilianatrasporti.it or download the "AST Ticketing" app), Interbus/Etna Trasporti (interbus.it).

From Siracusa by Train to: Noto (7/day, 35 minutes), **Catania** (hourly, 1.5 hours), **Taormina** (7/day direct, 2 hours, more with change in Catania), **Ragusa** (4/day, 2 hours), **Cefalù** (6/day, 5 hours, change in Messina), **Rome** (4/day, 12 hours).

ROUTE TIPS FOR DRIVERS

Siracusa is well connected to the rest of Sicily by the speedy E-45 expressway, which zips south to Noto in about 45 minutes, or north to Catania in about an hour. If you're connecting Siracusa to Ragusa, be sure to pause in Noto—it's a perfect lunch or gelato stop (see the Ragusa and the Southeast chapter).

CATANIA

Sitting at the foot of Mount Etna on the eastern shore of Sicily, the island's second largest city is an urban hub in a beautiful setting. Mamma Etna steams and sputters above, while the city below is made of her ashes: Most historic buildings are built with volcanic basalt trimmed in white limestone, giving the city a reverse-negative look.

With its handy airport and easy connections to sights on Sicily's eastern shores (Taormina, Mount Etna, Siracusa), many visitors simply pass through Catania en route to its more glamorous neighbors. While it's admittedly rough around the edges, those who spend some time in Catania will find a surprisingly genteel main square, wonderfully chaotic fish market, hidden Roman theater, and fascinating WWII museum.

Catania (pop. 315,000) was one of the first Greek settlements and came to prominence in Roman times, when it was likely the largest Roman city in Sicily. It had two large theaters and a smaller odeum, as well as a stadium only slightly smaller than the Circus Maximus in Rome. But time, invasion, and modern sprawl erased much of the ancient city, and today only scattered remnants can be found.

What remains of Catania from the Middle Ages is also scant. In 1693, an eruption of Mount Etna was followed by a major earthquake, destroying the city. It was rebuilt in Baroque style, following the architectural trend coming out of Rome. Later, in World War II, Catania was hit hard again, and some neighborhoods still bear the scars of war—with crumbling buildings and ugly, hastily built postwar apartments. But these days, the city is on the rise, and new initiatives are remaking the center into a lively, youthful hot spot.

I wouldn't go out of my way to visit Catania, but I wouldn't go out of my way to avoid it, either. While less appealing than some other Sicilian destinations, Catania warrants a half or full day. The city rewards travelers who enjoy the gritty energy of urban Sicily. It's easy to fly into or out of, and it can be a handy home base for those relying on public transit.

PLANNING YOUR TIME

Catania's airport makes it a common arrival or departure point on a Sicilian trip. The city is also a hub for trains and buses serving eastern Sicily. For a half-day of good sightseeing, follow my self-guided walk through town (which includes visiting the cathedral, exploring the fish market, and taking a peek at the Roman theater), then ride the Metro out to the city's fine WWII museum.

Travelers without a car can use Catania as a home base for exploring Mount Etna, Taormina, and Siracusa—all well connected from Catania by public transit.

Orientation to Catania

Catania (pop. 300,000) sprawls from the base of Mount Etna to the Ionian Sea. The main axis for visitors runs north from Porta Uzeda, near the fish market, through Piazza del Duomo (past the cathedral). From there, head up pedestrian-only Via Etnea, the main shopping street that stretches from Piazza Università, through Piazza Stesicoro (with a handy Metro stop), and on to the public gardens at Villa Bellini. With the exception of the WWII museum (near the train station), the main sights are within a few blocks of this axis.

TOURIST INFORMATION

The TI faces the side of the cathedral (Mon-Sat 8:00-19:00, Sun 8:30-13:30, Via Vittorio Emanuele II 172, +39 095 742 5573, comune.catania.it).

ARRIVAL IN CATANIA

By Train: Trains from Palermo, Messina, and Siracusa arrive at Catania Centrale train station, near the port. You'll exit toward a chaotic, giant roundabout called Piazza Giovanni XXIII. Note that the WWII museum is a five-minute walk away—see listing later, under "Sights in Catania."

Taxis are just outside the station (figure about €10 to the city center), and local **bus** stops line up directly ahead (#BRT5 takes

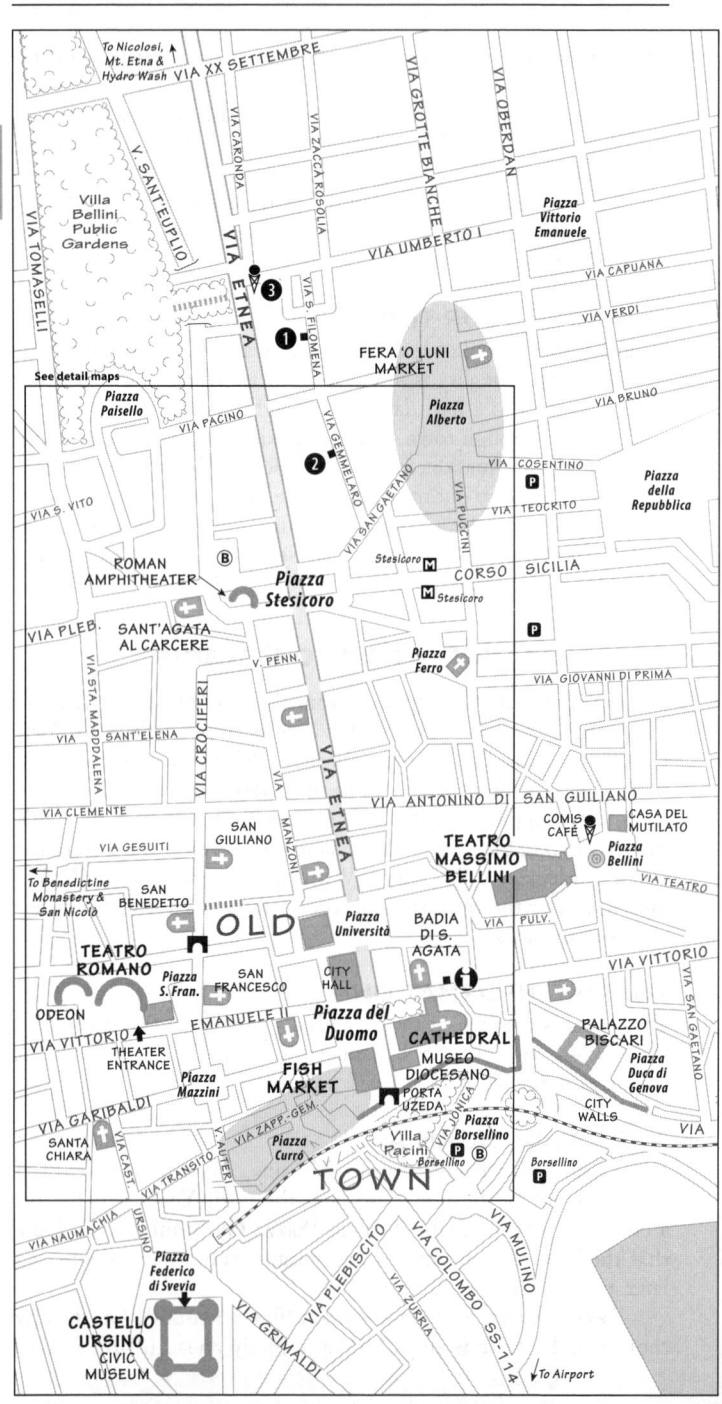

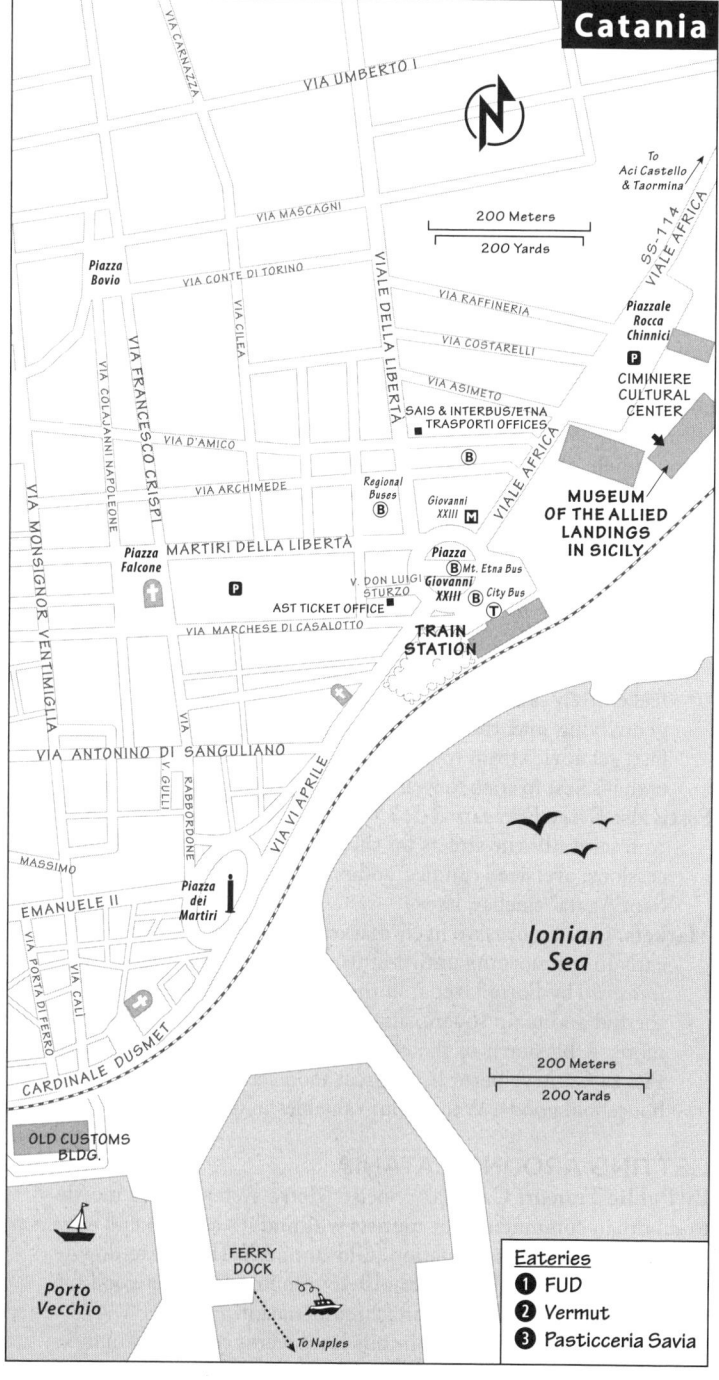

you to Piazza Stesicoro). It's a dreary 15-minute **walk** to the heart of the city.

It's easier and more appealing to hop on the **Metro**—the Giovanni XXIII station is directly in front of the train station (look for the red M signs) and take the train one stop to Stesicoro, the end of the line (for details on riding the Metro, see "Getting Around Catania—By Public Transit," later). You'll pop out at Piazza Stesicoro, in the middle of town.

By Bus: Regional and mainland Italy buses use several parking lots across the piazza from the train station, behind the Metro stop. From here, the **Metro** is the easiest way into town (see above).

By Car: Parking lots and pay street parking (look for blue lines) are all over the city. If you're staying overnight, ask your hotel about the best place to park. For a short visit, Parking Borsellino near Porta Uzeda (just off the roundabout at Via Jonica) is convenient. Lock your vehicle and put your belongings in the trunk.

By Plane: See "Catania Connections" at the end of this chapter.

HELPFUL HINTS

Safety: The areas I've described in this chapter get a fair amount of tourist traffic and are safe to explore. However, the center of Catania has some rougher neighborhoods that might not feel entirely safe, especially after dark. Since the city is quickly gentrifying and the character of neighborhoods can change fast, get advice from your hotelier about areas to avoid. In general, it's best to stick to well-lit major thoroughfares after dark.

Festivals: Every February 3-5, a festival celebrating the city's patron saint fills the streets for three days of madness, with processions, oversized candles, and fireworks. (See the "Festival of Sant'Agata" sidebar, later.)

Markets: Catania has two lively markets, both busy Mon-Sat from early in the morning until 14:00 (closed Sun). The **fish market** *(piscaria)* by Porta Uzeda, in the heart of the city near the cathedral and main square, also sells meat, cheese, veggies, and more. A bit north of the center, the **Fera 'O Luni** market at Piazza Carlo Alberto has a great food scene plus clothes and household goods. Watch your valuables in both markets.

GETTING AROUND CATANIA

By Public Transit: Catania's concise **Metro** system caters mostly to suburban commuters, but tourists will find it's a cheap and easy way to connect the train station (Giovanni XXIII stop) to downtown's Stesicoro stop (runs every 10-15 minutes, €1 ticket good for 90 minutes, €3/day). Metro info: circumetnea.it.

Catania's network of public **bus** lines seems constantly in flux.

On a short visit to the areas I describe, I'd generally stick to the Metro, walking, and occasional taxis, though it can be handy to hop on bus line #BRT1 to travel up and down Via Etnea (runs about every 15 minutes, €1 ticket good for 2 hours on both Metro and bus, €2.50/day, sold at newsstands and tobacco shops but not on board—look for AMT logo). Bus info: amt.ct.it.

By Taxi: Taxis wait at orange-signed taxi stands. Use only official taxis, and ask for an estimated price before you get in. Always use the meter unless you have agreed to a fixed price (+39 095 330 966, radiotaxicatania.org).

Tours in Catania

Local Guides and Drivers

Diana Mazza comes from a family of Sicilian guides. Besides tours of Catania, she also does Taormina and Siracusa walking tours (€80/hour, 2-hour minimum, +39 347 126 4530, trinacria2000@hotmail.com).

Giuseppe Leotta of Luxury Car Services offers day trips from Catania, including to Mount Etna (€180 for 4 hours, more for larger cars, +39 366 438 1797, luxurycarservices.it, info@luxurycarservices.it). He can also provide transfers from Catania Airport to Taormina (about €100).

Domenico Mannino of Sicily Transfer Taxi is a Catania-based driver who does trips to Mount Etna and elsewhere (€200 round-trip for 4 passengers, including 3 hours of waiting at Rifugio Sapienza at Mount Etna, more for larger car, +39 347 278 5999, sicilytransfertaxi.com, info@sicilytransfertaxi.com).

Food Tours

Streaty Tours runs fun, small-group street-food and market tours of Catania that include historical background, too, taking you to places you'd probably not go on your own (€64, 3-6/week at 11:00—check schedule and book ahead online, 3 hours, streaty.com). They also offer an evening food tour several times a week (€64, at 18:00, does not run in winter).

Bus Tours

Two hop-on, hop-off bus companies line up alongside the cathedral: **Katane Live** (yellow buses, +39 095 354 704, katanelive.it) and **Tourist Service** (red buses, +39 095 820 4281, touristservice2006.com). Both offer similar circuits, including a 1.5-hour route that circles around the center of Catania before heading north along the coast to Aci Castello and Aci Trezza (both cost €15 and run about hourly). Both also have an Etna tour that goes from central Catania to Rifugio Sapienza on Mount Etna (see page 366 for details). Check details and buy tickets online.

Catania City Walk

At first glance, Catania can feel a little intimidating and scruffy. But this 1.5-hour walk through its historic heart can help you get comfortable with the city's lively and warm soul. This walk is best in the morning, when the fish market is open.

• *Begin outside the city walls at the Porta Uzeda, just south of Piazza del Duomo. Stand facing the gate, with the railroad trestle and the park at your back.*

❶ City Walls

In the 1500s, during the time of Spanish rule, Catania's defenses were fortified with sloping basalt walls. These stout walls are a symbol of the city's resilience; even after the 1693 earthquake, they remained intact. Where you are standing used to be water, and the city gate of **Porta Uzeda** was literally a port where boats unloaded their cargo. The bad smell of the port offended the delicate noses of the nobles and the clergy living in palaces attached to the walls, so the harbor was filled in and the port moved eastward.

Looking to the left, you can see the **fish market** and produce stalls spilling out under the train bridge. (We'll enter the fish market later from the other side.) If you see smoke in that direction, it's usually vendors roasting stuffed artichokes or peppers. Immediately left of the gate, **Uzeda Café** can power you up for this walk.

Pass through Porta Uzeda. Soon after, on the right, is the **Diocesan Museum,** with a skippable ecclesiastical-art collection. Its highlight is the heavy float used for the celebrations of St. Agatha. Although rooftop access is available here, the views are better at Sant'Agata alla Badia, described later (€6 includes tower climb; Mon-Sat 9:00-13:00, Tue and Thu also open 15:00-18:00, closed Sun; Via Etnea 8, +39 095 281 635, museodiocesanocatania.com).

• *Continue on until you reach the fancy facade of the...*

❷ Catania Cathedral (Cattedrale di Sant'Agata)

As you approach the cathedral, you'll walk along a row of buildings displaying the defining building material of Catania: black volcanic basalt with white limestone trim. Catania is a child of Mount Etna, which, if it's clear, you can see up the broad main street ahead, Via Etnea.

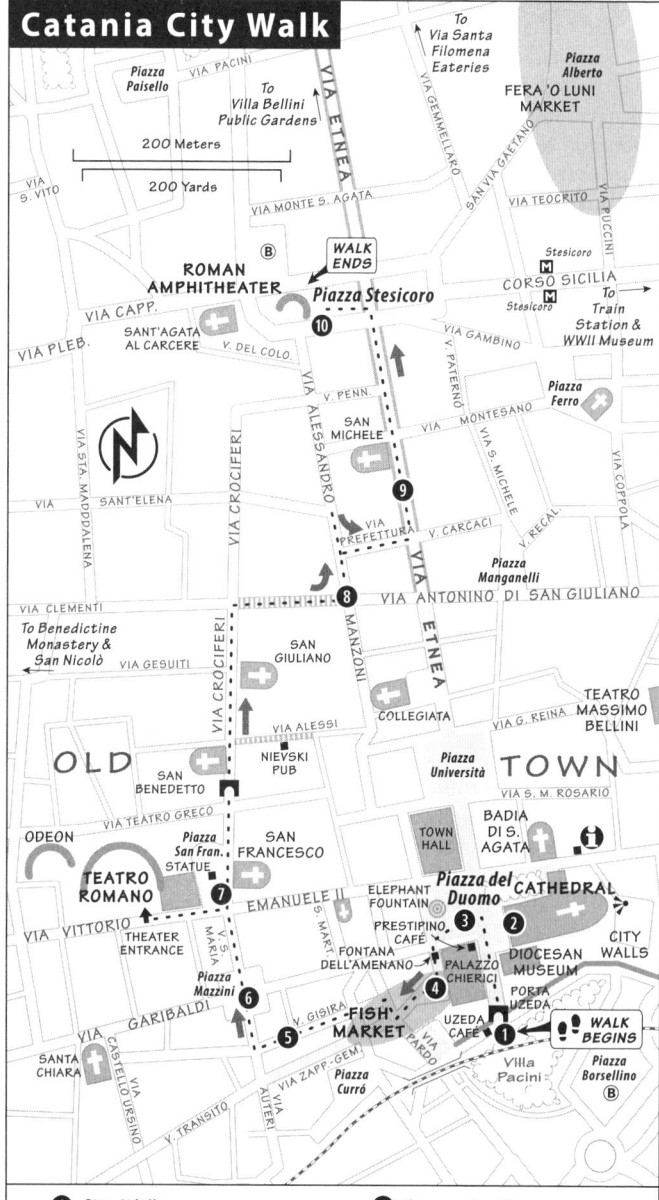

The cathedral is dedicated to **St. Agatha** (or *A Santuzza,* as the locals call her in adoration), the patron saint of the city. She is celebrated during an annual February festival with a wild procession through the city (see the sidebar for details).

This church sits over the ruins of an ancient Roman bath and was originally a Norman cathedral-fortress. You can see the surviving Norman apses around the back side of the church (head down Via Vittorio Emanuele II—the street to the left of the church—to #159). But most of the church came tumbling down in the 1693 earthquake and was rebuilt in the Baroque style. The columns decorating the facade were originally from Roman buildings in Catania, then repurposed as the columns for the nave of the church, and finally salvaged for the facade after the church collapsed.

Cost and Hours: Free, generally daily 7:15-12:30 & 16:00-19:00 but closes during services; inexpensive guided tours provide access to sacristy and other sections—check tour times at the front and ask about English tours; Via Vittorio Emanuele II 163, cattedralecatania.it.

Visiting the Church: Step inside and walk along the right aisle. Look for the sunken column bases from the old church and compare them to the thick columns alongside. After the earthquake, the new church was overbuilt for added stability. Farther up along the aisle is the glass casket of Cardinal Dusmet, a beloved local priest known for his devotion to the poor; beyond that (to the right of the altar) is the reliquary of St. Agatha. Standing in front of the altar, you can see the difference between the new, light Baroque nave and the old, heavy Norman apses with small windows.

In the left transept, the sacristy (only viewable via guided tour) contains a fresco that captures the close and at times dangerous relationship between Catania and Mount Etna. In 1669, a new vent opened on Etna and erupted for four long months—creating two craters that became known as the Monti della Ruina, "Mountains of Ruin." The initial lava flow destroyed several towns as it worked its way 10 miles south to Catania. After five weeks, the lava finally reached the stout city walls—which thankfully held, diverting the flow as it coursed around the town for another seven weeks. Catania was mostly unharmed, even as the lava flow extended the nearby coastline into the sea. The fresco, made not long after by an eyewitness, shows people boarding boats to escape the eruption, while practical women hang their laundry near the hot lava to dry.

Festival of Sant'Agata

A third-century Christian martyr, St. Agatha (Sant'Agata) is one of the most venerated saints in Sicily and southern Italy. Tradition says that when she was tortured for her faith, Agatha's breasts were cut off, which is why she's usually portrayed holding a plate with breasts on it. The patron saint of breast cancer, wet nurses, fire, and eruptions, she has many devoted followers.

The festival of Sant'Agata, held each February 3-5, is one of the largest religious celebrations in Italy. In Catania, more than 100,000 people attend, filling the historic center for three days of intense religious worship. Devotees dressed in white robes, gloves, and black hats are often escorted by their families. During the procession, it's a great honor to pull the float carrying the relics of St. Agatha, even for a few minutes. It can be dangerous, too, as the float weighs three tons and is moved by a crowd of men. Oversized candles accompany the float, coating the city streets in a thick layer of wax. Smaller floats provided by historic guilds follow Agatha's relics through the streets. The procession runs along Via Crociferi, and when it passes at dawn near the Benedictine convent, nuns gather on the bridge overhead to sing. The festival culminates in a fireworks display over the city. Every year on August 17, a smaller version of the procession takes place to commemorate the retrieval of Agatha's bones from Constantinople in 1126.

To better understand the fervor of this religious celebration, visit the courtyard of the Town Hall, where you can watch a video of previous years' celebrations. In the courtyard are two carriages used by the mayor and city authorities to open the festivities. The Museo Diocesiano (next to the cathedral) houses the main St. Agatha float, and the Church of San Francesco at the end of Via Crociferi has a collection of the smaller floats used during the procession.

Any time of year you can stop into a café in Catania to try *minnuzze di Sant'Agata* ("breasts of St. Agatha"). These rounded cakes, filled with ricotta, covered in icing and marzipan, and topped with cherries, represent the severed breasts of the city's beloved saint.

• *Exit the cathedral and walk to the center of the piazza, near the elephant fountain.*

❸ Piazza del Duomo

This main square is the heart of Catania. The little **elephant** in the center on the fountain is the symbol of the city—a Roman sculpture in Etna basalt with an Egyptian obelisk on its back.

From here, do a quick spin tour of the square. Starting with the cathedral and looking left, you'll see the big, stone dome of the church of **Sant'Agata alla Badia.** You can climb 170 steps to the rooftop terrace at the base of its dome for a grand view of the city and its smoldering volcano (€7, drop by to see if it's open).

Farther left, you'll see the beginning of Catania's main shopping street, **Via Etnea.** With limited traffic, this is an enjoyable artery to stroll and a lively spot in the evening. Just a block up the street is the pleasant Piazza Università, with the headquarters of the historic University of Catania.

To the left of Via Etnea is Catania's **Town Hall.** If you're curious about the city's St. Agatha celebrations, pop inside the doorway, where you can see a horse carriage and a Sicilian cart on display as well as a video loop showing footage of the annual event.

Turn to the opposite side of the square from Town Hall. The black building trimmed with white limestone is **Palazzo dei Chierici,** once a seminary and now a municipal building (when fascist dictator Mussolini visited Catania in 1937, he addressed a crowd from its balcony).

At the left corner of the palazzo is the recommended **Prestipino,** a classic spot for a special pastry, *minnuzze di Sant'Agata,* "breasts of St. Agatha": small, rounded cakes topped with a cherry.

Tucked away to the right of the palazzo is the shiny white **Fontana dell'Amenano.** At this fountain, you can get a peek at the underground Amenano River (which once ran above ground through Catania). This also serves as a gateway to the lively fish market.

• *Next to the Amenano fountain, squeeze through the passageway and go down the steps to the sunken plaza to find a raucous jumble of shoppers and makeshift sales kiosks at the fish market. (If the market isn't open, skip the next few stops by going to the far end of Piazza del Duomo and heading left on Via Vittorio Emanuele II to Piazza San Francesco. You'll rejoin the walk at stop #7.)*

❹ Fish Market *(Piscaria)*

Starting in the early hours of the morning, this fish market is one of the noisiest—you can hear the commotion from blocks around as the fishmongers shout and sing like auctioneers at a county fair (Mon-Sat until lunchtime, closed Sun). Fishermen have sold their catches here for over a thousand years. Their singsong vocalization comes from an Arab tradition, as the market was likely established under Arab rule. Walk down and take a lap around the tables, admiring the wide variety of fish, from swordfish to eel

to translucent heaps of baby fish used to make fish patties. For an in-depth tour of the fish market, see "Sights in Catania," later.

• *After exploring the lower area of the fish market, head back up to street level using the stairs opposite the ones you came down. From the top of the stairs, continue straight ahead on Via Zappalà-Gemelli to Piazza Santa Maria dell'Indirizzo, with a white church. Turn right at the church onto Via Riccioli, then left at...*

❺ Via Gisira

Along this street are market stalls and shops tempting you with very affordable produce, meat, and cheese. This is the real deal, a thriving market where locals shop. Thirty years ago, when there were no supermarkets, *fare la spesa* (doing the shopping) took hours, as each item had its own store: butcher, baker, pasta shop, and so on. The Sicilian way of life has become more contemporary, with big-box stores and shopping malls popping up where citrus groves used to be. But this market is one of the few that staunchly hangs on, with a real, untouristy vibrancy that few other Italian markets can match.

If you see them, try *fichi d'india* (prickly pears), which are loved by locals. Get the precut ones, and don't try to peel them yourself—or you'll be pulling little spines out of your fingers for the rest of your trip.

• *After half a block, turn right onto Via Auteri and you'll find...*

❻ Piazza Mazzini

After the 1693 earthquake, the city was not just rebuilt but also redesigned. Palaces rose on long, straight streets, and public piazzas like this one were constructed. The new geometric design served two purposes: to organize the city and make it more gracious, and to provide open spaces where it would be safe to gather during a major earthquake. The

portico of the piazza, meant to house a marketplace, has ancient Roman marble columns recycled from a church that collapsed in the earthquake.

• *Walk straight up to the next square, Piazza San Francesco. Note that from here, you can detour a half-block up Via Vittorio Emanuele II to the surprising* **Teatro Romano,** *hiding behind a plain gray facade (at #266, worth visiting, and described under "Sights in Catania," later). Opera lovers might also appreciate stopping by the Vincenzo Bellini Museum, housed in the composer's birthplace on the piazza.*

❼ Piazza San Francesco and Via Crociferi

On the right of the piazza is the **Church of San Francesco.** If it's open, go in to find some of the floats *(candelore)* used for the St. Agatha procession. Each of the city's guilds has a float that it brings out only for the big celebration. The big statue on the piazza is of Cardinal Dusmet, whose casket we saw earlier at the cathedral. Across from the church, the Bellini Museum—with modest multimedia installations—caters to music lovers, though it's skippable for most.

The street in front of the church (with the archway) is **Via Crociferi,** one of the prettiest in Catania and home to a cluster of lovely Baroque churches, palaces, and convents, including the Church of San Benedetto and the Church of San Giuliano. If you find any of these church doors open, go in for a look. The archway itself is connected to a convent of cloistered nuns, where the procession of St. Agatha ends.

• *Walk up Via Crociferi. If you need refreshment, take the staircase on the right (a bit past the arch) down to the colorful communist-themed pub,* **Nievski,** *on the landing below. Continue one long block on Via Crociferi, then turn right on the downhill, stepped, tree-lined Via Antonino di Sangiuliano. Then take the next left onto...*

❽ Via Alessandro Manzoni

Walk down this street a few blocks to find *mercerie*—stores selling fabric, yarn, and costumes. In medieval times, each street had shops specializing in similar services, such as shoemaking or stocking making. Catania still maintains some of the traditions that other Italian cities abandoned long ago, including this one.

• *When you're done browsing, head back the way you came, turning left on Via Prefettura, then left again onto...*

❾ Via Etnea

This main shopping street of Catania is always hopping. It's become mostly pedestrianized and has an elegant feel, with long views toward the cathedral to the south and Mount Etna to the north.

Stroll up the street for a few minutes. Soon you'll reach the long, rectangular **Piazza Stesicoro,** bordered by Baroque palaces. On the left side of the square, in the middle of the circus of whizzing Vespas and speeding cars, are ruins of an ancient ❿ **Roman Amphitheater,** excavated in the 18th century. Built with basalt, it may have seated 15,000 spectators. Catania, positioned between Africa and Rome, was along the trade route for wild game. Animal shipments often stopped in Catania, and it's likely that weak or dying animals were used in games here.

• *Our walk is finished, but there's more to explore. Here are some options:*

*For more **market action,** exit Piazza Stesicoro to the left on Via Etnea, then turn right on Via Pacini to reach the **Fera 'o Luni street market.***

*To zip out to Catania's **WWII museum,** ride the Metro: Find the red M signs at the opposite end of Piazza Stesicoro from the amphitheater ruins (down a block, along Corso Sicilia), buy a ticket, and take the Metro one stop to the Giovanni XXIII station. It's about a five-minute walk from there (see the listing under "Sights in Catania," later). Or to extend your stroll, continue straight up Via Etnea, browsing the shops until you reach the entrance to the public gardens at **Villa Bellini,** about a 10-minute walk. If you're ready for gelato, the recommended **Pasticceria Savia** is on the right side of Via Etnea (at #302), just across the street from the gardens.*

*For eating options, the charming **Via Santa Filomena**—with some recommended eateries—is five minutes away (see the "Catania" map, earlier).*

Sights in Catania

IN AND NEAR THE OLD TOWN
▲▲Fish Market Scavenger Hunt

Exploring a traditional street market—like Catania's fish market *(piscaria)* near Piazza del Duomo—is one of the liveliest, most genuinely local experiences you can have in Sicily. Shoppers have been wandering these market stalls for centuries, gathering the freshest ingredients for family feasts. From the cacophonous singsong of the fishmongers to the billowing smoke of grilling vegetables, this is Sicilian life at its least polished.

Dive into the action and toss aside your inhibitions (or fear of mysterious animal parts). Talk to the locals as best as you can: Ask for *un assaggio* (oon ah-SAH-joh)—a sample of whatever looks interesting. If you can't identify something, ask *"Che cos'è?"* (kay-kos-AY). Give each travel partner €5 and see what they come back with for an impromptu picnic.

Sicilian culture insists that you try to negotiate—it's considered a little pathetic to pay full price. Try saying, *"Ma è troppo caro"* (it's too expensive)—or, with a smile, *"Sconto?"* (discount?). If that doesn't work, offer to buy two items...if they'll give you a price break. The seller could refuse—but negotiating is an authentic market experience. Don't be shy and don't let language hold you back. Locals will appreciate your enthusiasm and interaction.

When to Go: The market is open Mon-Sat 7:00-lunchtime; get there early, since it's liveliest in the morning and most vendors are closing up shop by 13:00 (closed Sun). Keep an eye out for bloody fish guts and gills on the floor.

Fish of All Shapes and Sizes: Start just off Piazza del Duomo at the Fontana dell'Amenano fountain (described earlier, in my Catania City Walk) and head down the stairs into Piazza Alonzo di Benedetto—the beating heart of the fish-vending action. The selection changes every day and with the season. You might find seasonal specialties such as *spatola* (ribbon fish), *tonno* (tuna), *pesce spada* (swordfish), *neonata* (baby fish), *masculini* (small and lean anchovies), and so on. And there will be things you've never seen before. Early morning is best for variety and quality.

The vendors sing, yell, and chatter like auctioneers to get the attention of buyers. Ask someone to translate what the vendors are saying. Sometimes they're not just commenting on the fish but also on the people passing by.

Walk through the tunnel ahead to find the frozen-fish section—cheaper and more convenient, but not for gourmets. Go through the arch on the right to petite Piazza Pardo, and the fresh fish sections begin once again. Look for vendors selling little bites, such as anchovies on toast.

Near the train bridge in Piazza Pardo, find the drink kiosk where local shoppers refresh themselves with a brew called *seltz e limone* (*seltz*, for short)—fresh-squeezed lemon juice with seltzer water. They'll ask you *"sale?"* (SAH-lay?) to see if you want salt added. (It may sound strange, but a little salt makes this brew exceptionally thirst-quenching.) You may also see a barbecue roasting artichokes or peppers (just follow the smoke). If stuffed artichokes are in season, buy one to share—this is a truly local treat.

Meats, Cheese, and Produce: With the train bridge at your back, return through Piazza Pardo to the street on the left, Via Pardo. Walking up this street, you'll find butchers selling all kinds of cuts—from snout to tail and everything in between. Farther along are fruits, veggies, and dry goods, including the precious *pistacchio di Bronte*—the nuts the locals call "green gold."

When you reach Via Gisira, detour left to admire the stands

selling *formaggi e salumi* (cheese and cold cuts). Buy a few *etti* (1 *etto* = 3.5 ounces) of whatever looks good—perhaps *pecorino stagionato* (aged pecorino cheese)—and sample their delicious *olive condite* (dressed olives).

Return to Via Pardo and head left for more meats, some housewares, and produce. Count the types of citrus you pass—Sicily produces the largest variety in Italy (try some fresh-squeezed orange juice). In May and June, look for yellow *nespole* (loquats), a popular fruit treat. At the end of summer, you'll find another Sicilian favorite, *fichi d'india* (prickly pears). Let the vendor peel them for you or you'll be in for a prickly surprise. Locals like them chilled.

Café Break: At the end of the market stalls on Via Pardo, you'll hit the intersection with Via Garibaldi. Turn right to head back toward Piazza del Duomo and the cathedral. Consider a break at the recommended Prestipino café. This venerable watering hole sells coffee and street food day and night. Belly up to the bar and order a *granita* and brioche or a *cipollina*—one of many savory pastries this classic café offers.

▲Teatro Romano e Odeon (Roman Theater and Odeum)

There are plenty of ancient theaters in Sicily, but none is as surprising as this Roman one, which hides behind a plain, run-down facade. From the street, you'd never guess that an ancient theater has been incorporated into the newer surrounding buildings—structures that were lived in until the 1950s. Thought to be a Greek theater that was rebuilt in Roman times, this venue could have held up to 7,000 people.

Cost and Hours: €8, daily 9:00-19:00, possibly until later on Sun and in summer, Via Vittorio Emanuele II 266, +39 095 715 0508.

Visiting the Theater: Start with the small museum of artifacts found on-site. Upon leaving the museum, you'll enter the theater. Head all the way to the top for great views of the seats and surrounding buildings. The water in the orchestra pit comes from the underground Amenano River, which seeped into the theater as the ruins settled. Behind the Roman Theater, you can visit the smaller odeum, a more intimate performance space (at the top of the theater, to the left).

▲Palazzo Biscari

Taking up several city blocks near the cathedral, the sprawling Palazzo Biscari rises above the city walls. Built after the 1693 earthquake, this extravagant example of Sicilian Baroque is said to have 600 rooms. One of the heirs of the princes of Biscari, Ruggero Moncada sometimes welcomes visitors to his over-the-top palazzo via guided tour. You'll see portraits of the family, plus a string of state rooms, including a lavish ballroom and staircase that are reminiscent of Versailles. Guides tell the story of the family, bringing them to life via colorful tales. Of the private noble palaces to visit in Sicily, this is one of the most impressive and enjoyable.

Cost and Hours: €10 for 30-minute guided tour, email in advance as tours are sporadic and dependent on the season and private events. Private tours are possible and provide access to private apartments and secret courtyards (€60/1-4 people, €15/person after that, Via Museo Biscari 16, +39 320 211 4802, palazzobiscari.it, info@palazzobiscari.it).

▲Benedictine Monastery and Church of San Nicolò
(Monastero e Chiesa dei Benedettini di San Nicolò l'Arena)

Tucked just outside the noisy city center, this historic monastery and church complex seems a world apart—with quiet courtyards, gardens, and students from the University of Catania (which owns it) shuttling between classes. The outer courtyard, corridors, and back garden of the sprawling grounds are free to visit, and wandering the maze of halls is delightful. If you have the energy, climb the 132 steps up a spiral staircase to the rooftop terrace. For the full experience, join a guided tour.

Cost and Hours: Monastery guided tour—€10, tours run most days, at least one tour in English (usually at 13:00), more tours in Italian (ask for English text), check schedule and book ahead online, 75 minutes. If visiting on your own: monastery grounds—free, daily 9:30-17:00; church—€3, Mon-Sat 9:00-18:30, Sun until 12:30; +39 095 710 2767, monasterodeibenedettini.it.

Getting There: It's a 10-minute walk west of the city center at Piazza Dante 32. Take Via Gesuiti Clementi.

Background: The Benedictine order has had a presence on Mount Etna for centuries and moved to Catania in 1558. The monastery was destroyed twice—once by the 1669 Mount Etna eruption and then again in 1693 by the earthquake. After that, it was rebuilt on 10 acres—making it the third largest monastery in Europe and the largest in Italy. In 1866, the monks left the monastery, and the state took control of the complex, repurposing it as a military hospital with multiple schools. Finally, in 1977, it was given to the University of Catania, and today students here study liberal arts, philosophy, archaeology, history, and foreign languages.

Visiting the Monastery: While you can wander the grounds for free, certain areas can be visited only on a guided tour. The tour includes two exquisite cloisters—the Chiostro di Levante, with an elaborately decorated gazebo called the "caffehaus" by the monks, and the Chiostro di Ponente, with a Renaissance colonnade and fountain (rebuilt in the style of the original from 1558). You'll also see a room (in a university library) that was used by the monks to store food and wine and that later served as a bomb shelter during World War II. The tour also includes visits to the monastery's former kitchen, dining room, and large garden (built atop a lava flow), as well as Roman ruins underneath the monastery.

The enormous **church** attached to the monastery—with its imposing, clearly unfinished facade—is the largest in Sicily and yet only half the size originally intended. Construction began in the 1600s but was interrupted by the eruption and the earthquake, which made the heavy structure unstable and impossible to complete. Inside, on the floor, a meridian runs almost the entire width of the church, providing a daily calendar lit by a sunbeam.

Civic Museum (Museo Civico)

This eclectic city-history exhibit fills the **Castello Ursino,** a 13th-century fortress that's one of the few Catanian structures to survive the 1693 earthquake. The archaeological collection of the Biscari family is housed here, along with paintings, sculpture, and a coin collection.

Cost and Hours: May be closed for renovation when you visit; 10-minute walk from the fish market at Piazza Federico di Svevia—see the "Catania" map, earlier, +39 095 345 830.

Teatro Massimo Bellini

A few blocks east of Via Etnea, this ornate 19th-century opera house looms over an elegant square (close to streets often busy with sex workers, though the area is quickly gentrifying). While tours of the interior are sporadic, music lovers can try to catch a performance (Via Giuseppe Perrotta 12, +39 095 730 6111, teatromassimobellini.it). During the day, the Comis Café—facing the theater  on the piazza—is a fun place to enjoy a gelato or *granita*. Next door is the sternly fascist Casa del Mutilato, a stark contrast to the whimsy of the opera house.

NEAR THE PORT
▲▲Museum of the Allied Landings in Sicily
(Museo Storico dello Sbarco in Sicilia—1943)

Italy has few museums about World War II, but this well-presented exhibit helps remedy that. It focuses on Operation Husky, the 1943 Allied fight to gain a foothold in Italy through Sicily. While viewed from a distinctly Italian perspective (and with few English explanations), the powerful exhibits speak for themselves, as they tell the story of life before, during, and after the invasion. The museum's outlying location at Le Ciminiere (a former sulfur refinery) makes it optional for most, but it's well worth the trip for anyone interested in World War II.

Cost and Hours: €4; Tue-Sun 9:00-16:30, last entry at 15:00, closed Mon; Piazzale Rocco Chinnici, +39 095 401 1929. Consider the companion book for English explanations (€6).

Getting There: The museum is located outside the city center just past the Catania Centrale train station, in the Ciminiere cultural center. From downtown, either take a taxi (about €10) or ride the Metro (€1) one stop from the Piazza Stesicoro station to the Giovanni XXIII station, where you'll exit into the busy scene in front of the train station. With the train station and port at your back, angle to your left up the big street (Viale Africa) toward the old smokestacks. It's a five-minute walk to the museum, which is well signed within this converted industrial complex.

Background: Sicily saw lots of action in World War II. American, British, and Canadian forces under the command of US General George Patton and British General Bernard Montgomery invaded Sicily from Africa, landing at Gela and Siracusa on July 9, 1943. They fought a hard and bloody campaign against the Axis forces, and in just 39 days they'd taken all of Sicily—and were ready to cross over to the mainland to work their way  up the Italian peninsula. (For more on World War II in Sicily, see the "Sicily Goes to War" sidebar on page 433.)

Visiting the Museum: You'll begin by viewing a 12-minute film (with English subtitles) that sets the stage for Italy's role in World War II and the inception of Operation Husky. Then you'll step into a re-created Mussolini-era Sicilian piazza with fascist flags and slogans *(credere, obbedire, combattere*—"believe, obey, fight"). Poke into shops, read the latest newspaper headlines, and peer into a typical home with original artifacts. With the sound of approaching aircraft, run for cover in an air-raid shelter *(rifugio)*—

where you'll experience a simulated air raid, with shaking walls, screaming, and flashing lights. When the coast is clear, you'll step out to find the aftermath of the bombing—the same piazza is in rubble. A video screen shows historical footage of destroyed Sicilian cities.

From there, you'll follow a one-way route through a roughly chronological explanation of the Sicilian campaign. On the first floor, you'll see maps and models illustrating the Allied landings, then walk through display cases with original uniforms, weapons, equipment, and personal items from the Axis and Allied forces. At the end of the first floor is a pillbox bunker with mannequin soldiers operating a machine gun.

The top-floor exhibits outline more specifics from the landings and show off more weapons. You'll see life-size wax figures of Roosevelt, Churchill, Mussolini, Hitler, and King Victor Emmanuel III. The exhibit ends with the memorial to the unknown soldier, commemorating the 14,864 fallen troops of the Sicilian landing. A quote on the wall from Pope John XXIII sums it up: "Peace is the supreme good, to forget is pure folly."

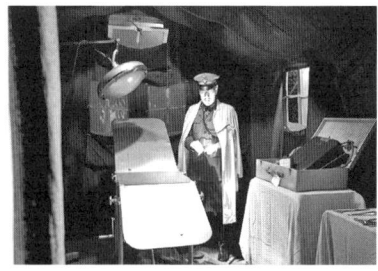

Back on the main floor, you'll find a case with WWII uniforms donated by visitors, an engine from a German Junkers Ju-88 bomber, a wheel from an American B-25 bomber, torpedoes, artillery, and miniature models. Before exiting, walk through the evocative collection of black-and-white photographs of soldiers in Sicily, taken by American war journalist Phil Stern.

Sleeping in Catania

Catania is busier, more chaotic, and less accustomed to tourism than other cities in Sicily. It's well worth the money to stay in a comfortable hotel in a better part of town. Stick close to Via Etnea or within a block of the cathedral—where you'll find my recommended hotels. If you have a car, consider staying in the seafront village of Aci Castello. All of my places have air-conditioning and, unless otherwise noted, an elevator (or it's not necessary).

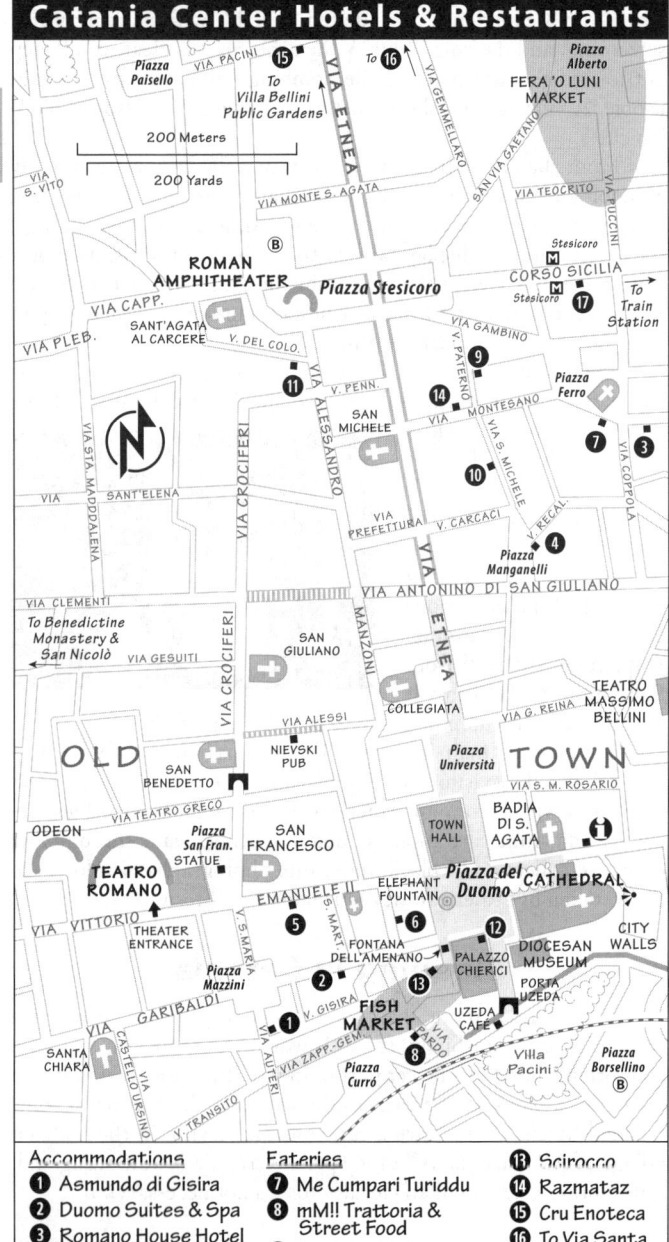

IN THE CITY

€€€€ Asmundo di Gisira, offering the full luxury experience, is like sleeping in a contemporary art installation with an Andy Warhol vibe. There are 13 rooms in two wings. On one floor, art rooms mix funky furniture with cool pieces, while on the second floor, the rooms are done up in Neoclassical Baroque decor (rooftop terrace, solarium, bookable private spa, ask about cooking classes and organized dinners, Via Gisira 40, +39 095 097 8894, asmundodigisira.com, info@asmundodigisira.com, Danila).

€€€€ Duomo Suites & Spa, in a tight, vertical building, has 13 colorful rooms—each with movie quotes from famous Sicilian films on the walls and graphic art (terrace, bookable private spa, private parking, Via Garibaldi 23, +39 095 288 3731, duomosuitesespa.it, info@duomosuitesespa.it).

€€ Romano House Hotel is a starkly modern hotel in the shell of an old palace a couple of blocks from Via Etnea (Via Giovanni di Prima 20, +39 095 352 0611, romanohouse.it, info@romanohouse.it).

€€ Manganelli Palace, on the fourth floor of Palazzo Manganelli, has a palatial air, with 20 aristocratic rooms and a private sun terrace (private parking, Via Recalcaccia 2, +39 095 715 1842, manganellipalace.it, info@manganellipalace.it).

€ Palazzo Bruca B&B has eight thoughtfully furnished, good-value rooms hidden in the large courtyard of a palace. Some rooms have a view of the Baroque churches on Via Croficeri, and a few have whirlpool baths (secure on-site pay parking, Via Vittorio Emanuele II 201, +39 095 587 4220, brucaroomhotelcatania.it, brucabeb@gmail.com).

€ Hotel Gorizia, a basic family-run hotel, has seven cheap and cheery rooms a block from Piazza del Duomo (no elevator, Via Spadaro Grassi 8, +39 095 715 0528, hotelgoriziacatania.it, albergo.gorizia@liberto.it).

NEAR CATANIA, IN ACI CASTELLO

Drivers who want to avoid Catania traffic and have easier access to parking can consider staying in the seafront village of Aci Castello, a few miles north of town and 30 minutes from the airport. If staying here, you can side-trip to Catania via bus or one of the sightseeing buses (see "Tours in Catania," earlier). Ask your hotel for advice.

Consider **€€€ Grand Hotel Baia Verde**, a massive old-time resort with 147 rooms and a swimming pool (Via Angelo Musco 8, +39 095 491 522, baiaverde.it, baiaverde@baiaverde.it). Or for something more personal, try **€ Villa Ortensia B&B.** With seven soft, calming rooms, a terrace, and a lush garden, this place feels like a welcoming relative's cozy house on the sea (Via Antonello da

Messina 93, +39 346 688 6040, bbvillaortensia.it, bbvillaortensia@gmail.com, kind Erminia).

Eating in Catania

Youthful and always busy, Catania has a thriving dining scene. I've focused my listings on and just off the central spine of Via Etnea, where most visitors spend their time.

€€€ **Me Cumpari Turiddu** mixes a nostalgic theme with a hipster atmosphere. Owner Roberta once was a lawyer in Milan, but seeing *Cinema Paradiso* inspired her to return to Sicily to follow her dream of opening a restaurant. This place is bright and sophisticated, and the produce comes from their own farm near Messina (dinner daily, lunch on Sat-Sun, Piazza Turi Ferro 36, +39 095 715 0142).

€€€ **mM!! Trattoria** serves *delizioso* fresh fish dishes right in the heart of the fish market (closed Sun for dinner and all day Mon, Via Pardo 34, +39 349 722 9801). Next door, €€ **mM!! Street Food** makes tuna burgers, *coppo fritto,* and *sarde beccafico* (stuffed fried sardines), matched with microbrews or local wine (closed Wed, Via Pardo 26, +39 342 057 5338).

€€ **Trattoria del Cavaliere** reflects Catania's affection for *carne di cavallo*—horse meat. (Even Garibaldi was advised to leave his horses outside the city.) Adventurous eaters enjoy atmosphere and service as old-school as the food (daily, Via Paternò 11, +39 095 310 491).

€€ **La Cucina dei Colori** is a convivial, vibrant restaurant with a daily changing menu of organic vegetarian and vegan food that focuses on what the markets offer that day. Pick some items from the counter (€12 for two, €14 for three) and join fellow diners at the community tables. At dinner there's also an à la carte menu (closed Mon, Via San Michele 9, +39 095 717 6146, lacucinadeicolori.it, Salvo).

€€ **Al Vicolo Pizza & Vino** serves enormous pizzas and oversized antipasto platters to hungry locals, with outdoor tables on a traffic-free street a block off Via Etnea (daily, Via del Colosseo 5, +39 095 836 0730, alvicologroup.com).

€ **Prestipino,** a historic family shop right on Piazza del Duomo, makes quality fare—from salty street-food snacks to decadent sweets—for takeaway or to eat at stay-awhile tables on the main square. Franca, the owner, is your long-lost chatty Sicilian auntie (daily, Piazza del Duomo 1, +39 095 320 840, prestipino.shop).

€ **Scirocco,** a hole-in-the-wall overlooking the fish market, turns out €7-8 fresh fried calamari and fish served in a paper cone. Order at the window and listen for your name. Eat standing or nibble while you stroll the market (daily, Piazza Alonzo di Benedetto 7, +39 095 836 5148).

Wine Bars: Sicily's top wine-growing area—Etna—is right at Catania's doorstep, and you'll find two popular wine bars in the city center. €€ **Razmataz** is always hopping, with a bustling scene filling a small square; they serve basic food (daily, Via Montesano 17). Those more serious about wine head a few blocks away to €€ **Cru Enoteca,** with a better variety, more knowledgeable staff, and a more tranquil, focus-on-the-wines approach; they also have boards of local meats, cheeses, and other nibbles to complement the wines (open long hours, closed Mon, just a few steps off Via Etnea at Via Pacini 8, +39 095 741 3807).

Supermarket: Grocery stores are abundant. You'll see a handy one near the Stesicoro Metro stop, just off Via Etnea (daily, Corso Sicilia 50).

On or near Via Santa Filomena

This fun little street, tucked a long block off the top of Via Etnea (a 10-15-minute walk from the cathedral area), is lined with appealing eateries with al fresco tables tumbling out onto the cobbles. It's a great street to simply stroll for a place that looks good—but here are some of my favorites. For locations, see the "Catania" map near the beginning of this chapter.

€€ **FUD** is the upscale Italian idea of what a burger should be: quality ingredients prepared well and presented artfully. In addition to beef and chicken, you could try donkey, buffalo, or horse—all washed down with a high-end craft beer (daily, Via Santa Filomena 35, +39 095 715 3518, fud.it).

€ **Vermut** is a lively, casual place on a pedestrian-only street, serving mixed plates of appetizers, salumi, and great drinks and cocktails—the bar's name derives from its quality selection of vermouth (daily, Via Gemmellaro 35-39, +39 347 600 1978).

Gelato: A block off Via Santa Filomena, **Pasticceria Savia** is the local favorite for gelato, *granite,* and a wide variety of delectable treats. Enjoy yours at a table out front, on a bench along nearby Via Etnea, or in the Villa Bellini park just across the street (closed Mon, Via Etnea 302, +39 095 322 335).

Catania Connections

BY PLANE

Catania's **Fontanarossa Airport,** located three miles south of the city, is small but busy (code: CTA, aeroporto.catania.it). You'll get a great view of Mount Etna as you take off or land.

Connecting the Airport and City Center: For the short drive into the city, **taxis** wait right outside the terminal (about €25, confirm price before departing).

The **Alibus airport shuttle bus** does a central city loop (buses are right outside the terminal—follow signs; €4, buy ticket at machine; runs every 25 minutes, daily 4:40-24:00; stops at the train station, Via Etnea, and more—see website for route map, amts.ct.it/alibus).

Connecting the Airport and Other Destinations: Long-distance buses line up near the terminal (exit to the right, ticket kiosks on sidewalk). You'll find direct buses to Taormina, Siracusa, Agrigento, and Palermo. See "By Bus," below, for details on bus companies, frequencies, and durations.

BY TRAIN

Catania is the main transportation hub for the eastern half of the island. Catania Centrale train station links the train system from Messina to Siracusa, but bus connections are often more reliable (see next).

From Catania by Train to: Taormina (1-2/hour, 1 hour), **Messina** (hourly, 2 hours), **Siracusa** (hourly, 1.5 hours), **Palermo** (7/day, 4 hours, 1-2 changes), **Naples** (3/day direct, 8 hours), **Rome** (4/day direct, 11 hours).

BY BUS

Across the piazza from the Catania Centrale train station are two large parking lots for buses. The main lot, for destinations across Sicily, is at the intersection of Viale della Libertà and Via Archimede (buses for Palermo, Ragusa, Siracusa, and Taormina). A secondary lot is across the street between Via D'Amico and Via Archimede (buses connecting with the mainland). Ticket offices for **SAIS** (serving Palermo—saisautolinee.it; and Agrigento—saistrasporti.it) and **Interbus/Etna Trasporti** (serving the other destinations, interbus.it) are across the street from the mainland-bus lot, on Via D'Amico.

From Catania by Bus to: Taormina (1-2/hour, 70 minutes, Interbus/Etna), **Siracusa** (1-2/hour, 80 minutes, Interbus/Etna), **Ragusa** (hourly, 2 hours, Interbus/Etna), Piazza Armerina near **Villa Romana del Casale** (every 2 hours, 1.75 hours, Interbus/Etna), **Agrigento** (about hourly, 3 hours, SAIS Trasporti), **Paler-

mo (hourly, 2.5 hours, SAIS Autolinee), **Naples** (1/day, 8.5 hours, SAIS Trasporti), **Rome** (1/day, 10.5 hours, SAIS Autolinee).

By Bus to Mount Etna: Rifugio Sapienza on Mount Etna is served by **AST** (aziendasicilianatrasporti.it or download the "AST Ticketing" app). The bus leaves from a lot on Piazza Giovanni XXIII (1/day, additional bus possible in summer, 2 hours, see page 366 for details).

MOUNT ETNA

Mount Etna Volcano Visit • Mount Etna Wine Country

Mount Etna, Europe's most active volcano, presides over her island like Mount Fuji presides over Japan. Mount Etna dominates the skyline of the east coast of Sicily, soaring to just over 11,000 feet. The area around the mountain is picturesque and diverse, with the busy city of Catania nestled into its southern flank. Wineries dot the north and east slopes (amid thick chestnut woods), quiet countryside scattered with pistachio groves lies to the west, and jagged cliffs stretch up the coast toward the Alcantara river, just before Taormina. The natural beauty of the region, the varied climate, and Etna's habit of frequent huffing and puffing make it one of the top sights in Sicily.

For the traveler, there are two reasons to visit Mount Etna: to experience the volcanic landscape (and perhaps even summit the rumbling giant), and to experience the wonderful wine country that those volcanic conditions sustain. Depending on your time and interests, you can choose to do one or the other, or a little of both.

PLANNING YOUR TIME

Mount Etna and its wine country are close to both Catania and Taormina—in just over an hour from either place, you can be climbing volcanic craters at altitude or sipping local vintages of Etna wine. But because these highlights are on different sides of the mountain (most volcano sights on the south slope, best wine and some summit hikes on the north slope), combining them into one day is ambitious.

Volcano Sights in a Day or Less

To experience the high-mountain volcanic side of Etna, you'll either head for a base camp called Rifugio Sapienza, on Etna's south flank (facing Catania) or Piano Provenzana, on the north (near Linguaglossa). Driving to either access point takes roughly an hour from Catania or Taormina.

For any Mount Etna adventure, it's best to get an early start, as the peak is most likely to be clear first thing in the morning (winter skies can be clearest). As the day goes on, evaporating moisture tends to cling to the mountain, often socking it in by midmorning, and the Rifugio Sapienza base camp tends to get more crowded as the day goes on, peaking around midday.

If you want to keep things short and simple, stick to the Rifugio Sapienza area and plan on about an hour to make the quick-but-rewarding hike around the lower-lying craters. If you want to head higher up the mountain, allow a half- to full day, depending on how high you go. Aim to take the cable car (which goes to a station at 8,200 feet) early, before it gets too busy—the first departure is at 8:30. From there you can take a 4x4 bus to a crater walk at 9,800 feet—allow 2-3 hours, including the cable car ride. Going even higher, to the summit, is a full-day commitment requiring a guide. For details, see "Higher-Altitude Activities," later.

Wine Country in a Day or Less

Quality wineries are scattered on Etna's easy-to-reach eastern and southeastern slopes (facing the sea), and on its northern slope (facing the Nebrodi mountain range). I particularly enjoy the northern slope, which is more scenic, less trampled by day trippers, and comes with its own dreamy culture. You could do a strategic strike at one winery, or settle in for a full day of scenery, wine

tastings, and stay-awhile meals at destination restaurants. Spending the night is a good option for wine lovers or anyone who enjoys lingering in the countryside.

Note that most of Etna's wineries expect you to book tours/tastings in advance—few let you drop in spontaneously. While this may seem like a hassle, it's well worth it for the personal attention you'll receive and the authenticity of the experience.

The Whole Shebang in One Day

Energetic, ambitious travelers who get a very early start can try

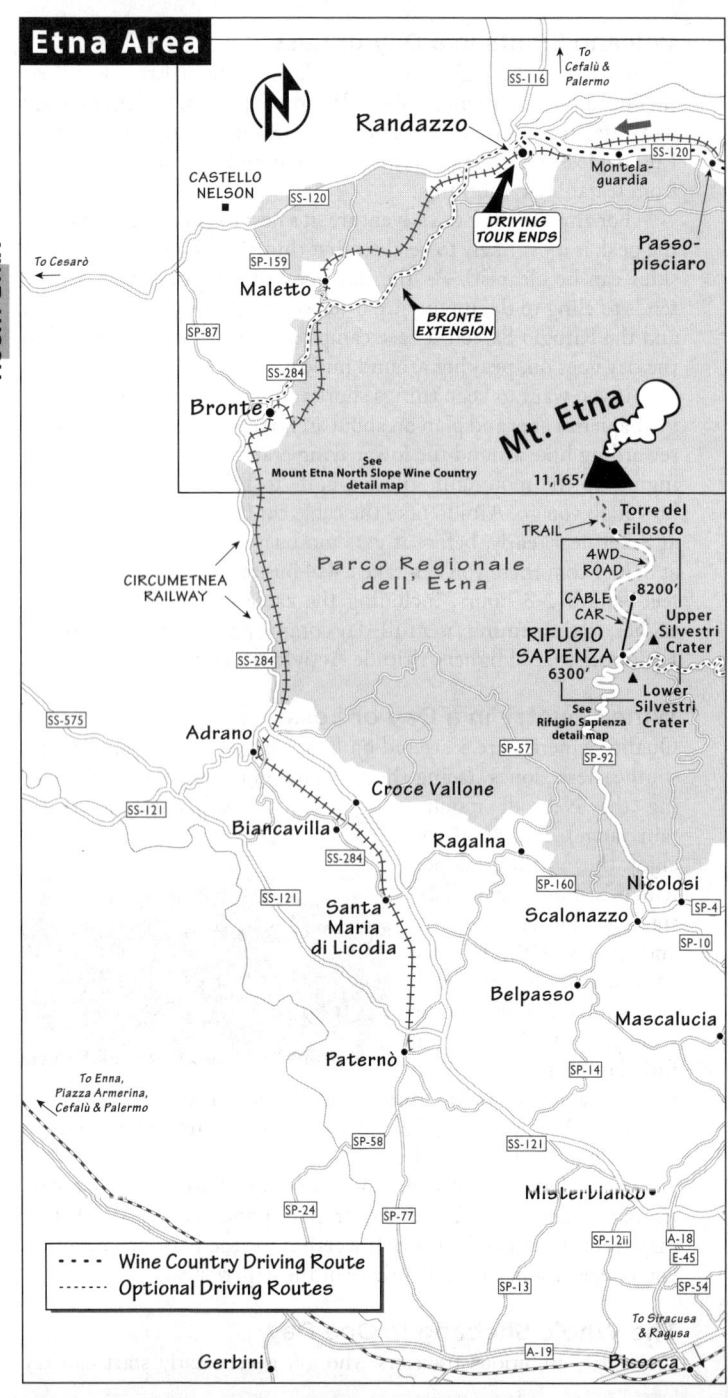

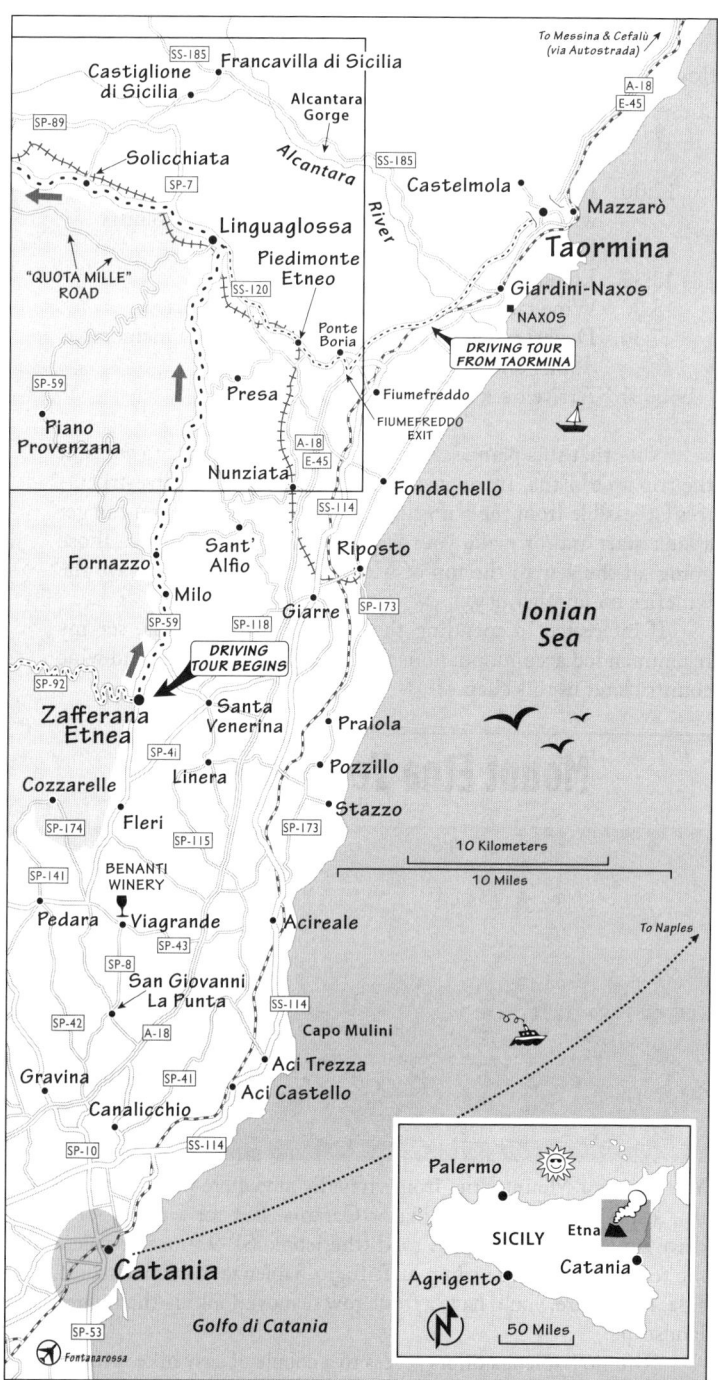

to squeeze both Etna experiences into one long day (side-tripping from Catania or Taormina, or en route between those destinations).

8:00	Hit the road (or start earlier)
9:00	Arrive at Rifugio Sapienza, take cable car and 4x4 bus to 9,800 feet, and walk around the crater
12:00	Descend, hop in your car, and drive around to the wineries following my North Slope Wine Country Drive
13:30	Lunch in wine country
15:00	Wine tastings, scenic drives, exploring villages
17:30	Depart wine country (or stick around for a memorable dinner and drive home late)
19:00ish	Arrive back at your home base

Note that this plan assumes good-enough weather to warrant the trip up to Etna. If you just do the easy hike at the Silvestri craters (accessible from the Rifugio Sapienza parking lot), you can get a later start and/or make your way to wine country earlier. Those going all the way to the top of Mount Etna will need to save the wineries for another day.

If interested in spending the night on Mount Etna, see my recommended accommodations for the Rifugio Sapienza and wine country later in this chapter.

Mount Etna Volcano Visit

You can spot Mount Etna from virtually anywhere in eastern Sicily—especially from Taormina or Catania. But for a closer look, drive up a twisty mountain road (the iconic SP-92) over a volcanic terrain to the base camp at Rifugio Sapienza, on Etna's south side. From here, you'll have a front-row seat overlooking the rugged landscape.

Rifugio Sapienza offers access to a couple of easy hikes around some extinct craters and is also the departure point for the cable car *(funivia)* that takes you higher up the mountain. You can explore the (boring) area around the upper cable car station on your own, but to go even higher, you'll need to join a guided tour (for details, see "Tours on Mount Etna" and "Mount Etna Activities," later).

Orientation to Rifugio Sapienza

The outpost at Rifugio Sapienza (6,300 feet)—carved into the bald, volcanic terrain—is the base for your Etna excursions on its southern flank. Clustered together are the base station of the cable car, a hotel, and the Guide Alpine Etna Sud office (where you can book excursions to the top); a five-minute walk away you'll find the Silvestri craters. Shops, eateries, and an info desk sprawl in the area between these two points.

GETTING THERE

The options outlined below are for getting to Rifugio Sapienza on your own. You can also go with a guided tour, which may include transfer options (see "Tours on Mount Etna," later).

By Car

The winding drive up to Rifugio Sapienza can be approached from two directions. From Catania and the south, you'll pass through the towns of Mascalucia and Nicolosi (the southern gateway to the mountain). From the north (Taormina or Messina), exit the E-45 highway at Giarre, heading toward Santa Venerina and then Zafferana Etnea. From Nicolosi or Zafferana Etnea, follow brown *Etna Sud* signs to reach Rifugio Sapienza on SP-92.

Parking is available at several lots near the lower cable car station and near the Silvestri craters. Most spaces are pay-and-display (blue lines). Buy a parking pass at one of the souvenir shops near the cable car station or at the visitor info desk, midway between the cable car and craters (€1.20/hour, €3.50/half-day, €6/day). There are some free spaces scattered around (white lines), though a "custodian" may ask for a donation to watch your car (€2 is enough). Note: Do not leave valuables in the car, and store anything that might be tempting to thieves in the trunk, out of sight.

By Public Bus

Each morning, an AST bus departs Catania for Rifugio Sapienza. The journey takes two hours with a pit stop partway up, in Nicolosi (departs at 8:15, possible additional bus Mon-Sat at 11:30 in summer, return bus departs Etna at 16:30, €6.60 round-trip, aziendasicilianatrasporti.it). Buy your ticket at the AST office in Catania (232 Via Don Luigi Sturzo); in peak season, it's best to do so the day before, or line up when the office opens at 7:30. The bus departs from the parking lot near the ticket office, on Piazza Giovanni XXIII (see the map on page 337 for ticket office and lot locations). Buying a ticket gets you a spot on the bus—but not an assigned seat.

By Excursion Bus

Excursion buses can take you to Etna with just enough time to explore the area around Rifugio Sapienza or ride the cable car.

From Catania: Tourist Service buses (with recorded commentary) stop at Rifugio Sapienza for three hours, with a short break in Nicolosi on the way (€35, book ahead online, departs daily at 11:30 from Piazza del Duomo, returns to Catania at 17:30, touristservice2006.com). **Katane Live** buses stop in Nicolosi, Rifugio Sapienza for three hours, and Zafferana Etnea (€30, departs daily at 11:30 from Piazza del Duomo, returns to Catania at 18:00, katanelive.it).

From Taormina: On Monday and Saturday only, **SAT** offers an Etna Basic tour to Rifugio Sapienza (€45, high point 6,300 feet, book online at least a day ahead, runs April-Oct—also available in the off-season with a minimum of 12 participants, departs Taormina at 8:30, returns around 16:00, +39 094 224 653, satexcursions. it). SAT also offers (on Wednesday and Friday) an Etna Round tour that includes the Alcantara River gorge, a stop in Randazzo with a Circumetnea train ride to Adrano (€60, high point 6,200 feet, departs Taormina at 7:30). Both tours offer an option to add on the cable car and 4x4 buses with a guide (€115, high point potentially 9,800 feet).

By Private Driver

If you don't want to drive but would like more flexibility than a bus, consider hiring a driver. Ask your hotelier to help you find one, or consider one of the following.

Catania-based drivers **Giuseppe Leotta** and **Domenico Mannino** can take you to and from Etna (see page 339 for prices and contact information). Taormina-based driver **Seby Melita** also does guided tours to Mount Etna and can pick up/drop off from Taormina or Catania (see page 392).

HELPFUL HINTS

Information: You can check the current volcanic activity on Etna at volcanodiscovery.com/etna/current-activity.html; weather information by elevation is available at mountain-forecast.com.

Extreme Weather Warning: Even though the mountain is on a Mediterranean island, the weather at the top is alpine. Things change fast. Rain clouds are attracted to Etna like magnets—and once they gather, they tend to stay put. Fierce winds can pick up without warning. The cable car doesn't run in strong winds, and excursions are canceled in bad weather. Use common sense and ask before venturing out if you're unsure of the conditions (note that very limited visibility can lead to a poor sense of direction). From November through March, the mountain can have deep snow even at lower levels.

What to Wear and Bring: Even if you just plan to stroll on the lower-lying Silvestri craters, wear solid shoes with good tread, as there are no groomed trails and you'll sometimes be walking on loose volcanic rock (called *lapilli*). Dress in layers; a waterproof jacket is always a good idea, as is a buff, such as a neck warmer, to shield you from wind and dust. The upper cable car station is at 8,200 feet, and the air is thin—so it's colder, and hiking is harder. If you're summiting Etna, bring a hat, gloves, and warm jacket—even in summer (also bring a packed lunch and water). Hiking poles are a good idea for longer treks. On

Mount Etna

Mount Etna, at 11,165 feet—give or take depending on the latest eruptions—is Sicily's grand summit and Europe's most active volcano. The mountain started as an underwater volcano a half-million years ago, and its summit remained below sea level for more than half of that time.

Geologically speaking, Sicily (like the rest of Italy), is positioned atop the slow-motion collision of the Eurasian and African tectonic plates. The force of that collision gave rise to the mountainous spines of mainland Italy and Sicily. Fissures between the plates, where magma escapes, created and feeds numerous volcanoes—including Vesuvius, Stromboli, and Etna.

With a circumference of roughly 100 miles, Mount Etna at its base covers an area comparable in size to London. Like a shield volcano formed by lava flows, Etna at first slopes up gently from its broad footing (such as Hawaii's Mauna Kea and Mount Kilauea), but then at the top it points up steeply, exhibiting the layered structure of a stratovolcano (such as Vesuvius near Naples, Krakatoa in Indonesia, and Mount Saint Helens in Washington state). While in recent years most of the volcanic activity at Etna has been at the summit (where there are four active craters), historically numerous "flank" eruptions occurred farther down the mountainside. As a result, more than 300 small lateral craters dot the volcano. Even though it's ringed by a belt of towns at about 2,000 feet, Etna rarely kills anyone. But should a lateral eruption persist, a lava flow could swallow a small town within a week.

Etna is called a "gentle giant" because the mountain typically just spews ash and occasionally oozes thick, slow-moving lava—but conditions can change rapidly. Even though the probability of a sudden violent eruption is low, the mountain is always active. Up to several hundred metric tons of vapor spew from the top craters every day. It's not unusual for the "black snow" of Etna to blanket much of the island.

Destructive as it can be, Mount Etna is also a major reason that the small island of Sicily can support so many people. The volcanic soil is particularly fertile, perfect for growing nearly everything—especially grapes, giving the area's wines their highly valued minerality. And in the seas around Sicily, Etna's ash fertilizes the phytoplankton—creating an underwater layer of "soil" that supports abundant sea life.

windy days, hikers will want sunglasses to protect eyes from blowing ash. Jacket and boot rentals are available at the upper cable car station for a few euros. If taking a guided tour, ask if hiking gear is provided.

Eating: The area near the lower cable car station has a variety of basic €-€€ eateries offering a quick bite. **Terrazza dell'Etna,** next to the parking lot below the guide hut, has a pleasant space and some good options at their counter. For something a little better, try the **Rifugio Sapienza** restaurant, at the lodge next to the cable car station; or **Bar Ristorante Crateri Silvestri** (next to the lower crater), with a coffee bar, good snacks, and a restaurant with outdoor seating and views of the craters. Basic food options are available at the upper cable car station.

Sleeping: € Rifugio Sapienza offers 24 simple, alpine-style rooms next to the lower cable car station (cable car discount for guests, +39 095 915 321, rifugiosapienza.com, info@rifugiosapienza.com).

Tours on Mount Etna

A number of companies offer guided tours up the northern and southern slopes of Mount Etna. Consider the following businesses. When looking at prices, take note of whether they include the pricey cable car and 4x4 transfer (some do, some don't).

Etna Unlimited runs several half- to full-day guided experiences on Mount Etna, including a 4x4 vehicle tour (also available with wine tasting), hikes of varying durations and difficulty levels, an e-bike tour, and a sunset tour (tours from €75, request RS%—10 percent; check their offerings and book ahead online; pickup in Catania or Taormina areas available for extra fee of €10, minimum 4 participants; +39 393 910 8061, etnaunlimited.com, info@etnaunlimited.com; Matteo, Guglielmo, and Roberto).

Guide Vulcanologiche Etna Nord, run by a group of professional volcanological guides, leads serious hikes on both the north and south slopes of the mountain. Check their calendar to see what trekking options are available when you're there (hikes from €30 on the north side, and €100 on the south, prices do not include mountain transportation, book ahead online, +39 345 574 1330, guidevulcanologicheetna.it, info@guidevulcanologicheetna.it). They don't do pick-ups in Catania or Taormina but can advise you on how to get to the meeting point, either via public transit or with a private driver.

AITNE, founded by cousins Marco and Davide Tomasello, offers informative summit hikes and e-bike tours of Etna. Their passionate guides do a good job explaining the landscape of the craters and volcanic activity (hikes range from "easy"—€50, 5

> ### Mount Etna in Myth
>
> The ancients relied on myths to explain powerful natural phenomena, such as lightning or storms—or volcanoes. The Aegean Greeks who arrived in Sicily knew of the massive eruption at Santorini from folk legend, but Mount Etna's ongoing belching and rumbling were something new.
>
> The Greeks came to identify Mount Etna, with its fiery eruptions, as the subterranean workshop of Hephaestus, god of fire and the maker of Zeus' thunderbolts. And the Greeks saw the volcano as home to other mythological creatures. The Cyclopes—one-eyed giants—lived in caves on the slopes of Etna, and the large rock formations off the coast near Catania (at Aci Trezza) were the work of the Cyclops Polyphemus, who threw stones from the mountain while Ulysses and his crew fled the island. Typhon, a monster confined under the volcano by Zeus, caused tremors whenever he turned over; his unhappy gasps were said to make the volcano erupt. And Cerberus, the three-headed dog of Hades (masterfully depicted by Gian Lorenzo Bernini's statue at Villa Borghese in Rome), lived on Etna.

hours from the south side—to an "expert"-level summit trek, €130, 8 hours, starting from the north side, extra fee for pickup/drop off in Catania, +39 339 480 2186, aitnmed.com, infotrek@aitnmed.com).

Mount Etna Activities

SILVESTRI CRATER HIKES

For an easy, quick, and free look at a volcanic landscape, choose one of these two hikes around the extinct craters at the eastern end of Rifugio Sapienza. The lower crater is an easy walk with little elevation gain; the upper crater is a steep climb with fewer people and better views. If you don't have the time or money to ascend the mountain by cable car, a hike around the Silvestri craters offers a satisfying Etna visit.

▲▲Lower Silvestri Crater (Easy)

On the left side of the Bar Ristorante Crateri Silvestri, a small trail leads up a short hill to the lip of the crater. This inactive crater, only 400 feet in diameter, is the result of a massive 1892 eruption.

Circling around the lip of the crater takes about 10 minutes with limited change in elevation, but watch your footing and the wind, which can be strong. About halfway around, turn back to face the mountain above you. Looming on the right is the climbable upper Silvestri crater (described next). Just to the left, notice how the cable car basically follows the path of a 2001-2002 eruption (it was rebuilt shortly thereafter). Spot the usually green "island" of vegetation at the top of the ridge that was not wiped out by the lava flow. This is called a *dagala*—from the Arabic "touched by Allah." Look down into the crater at your feet, where visitors have followed the old custom of stacking rocks into little towers.

Now turn 180 degrees and face out toward the sea, taking a few steps for a better look over the entire valley. This area is the most exposed to strong winds, so hold onto your hat—down below is a "hat cemetery." Visually trace the coastline to see the city of Catania, which starts at the corner of its big bay and sprawls up its valley. On the horizon, look for other small craters, or scoria cones. Mentally connect these and the one you're standing on: They form a chain of vents that line up along an underground channel known as a conduit. A vein of magma (superheated molten rock) can occasionally divert from the conduit and push through to the surface. You're seeing the evidence that Etna is not just one big crater but a cluster of hundreds of craters like this one—some dating back thousands of years, and some growing and changing right now. But scoria cones are almost never active twice.

▲▲Upper Silvestri Crater (Moderately Strenuous)

Just uphill from the lower crater, you'll see intrepid hikers summiting this much steeper option (total loop about 0.75 mile, 460-foot elevation gain, 30 minutes). There are two paths up—the one that swings left is easier, while the right fork is steeper and more direct, with lava fragments underfoot (remember the *lapilli?*) that are very slippery at this incline.

Both trails begin on the left side of the lava-buried Bar La Capannina. As you begin the ascent, notice that the restaurant is surrounded by lava—all the way up to the roof. Major eruptions and lava flows in 2001 and 2002 destroyed parts of the tourism infrastructure here, including the cable car. The lava passed around this restaurant but didn't destroy it; the owner says the buried window was "kissed by the lava flow."

Lava Rock

While visiting Etna—whether at high or low elevations—take a moment to appreciate the unique volcanic rock that makes up this giant, steaming mountain.

As Etna's lava flows slowly cool, they gradually solidify into a basaltic stone. The base color is dark, dense, and gray. Eruptions of the last century are richer in iron than those of earlier periods—which you'll notice in the rusty, reddish tone of the lava stones. Mixed in are shades of yellow (indicating the presence of sulfur) and even broken slabs of lemony sandstone—pushed all the way up from the seabed as Etna rose. You'll also see piles and piles of scree—small pebbles at the base of an eroded incline.

Large chunks of stone scattered around a crater are called "lava bombs"—masses of incandescent lava that shoot out of the crater during an eruption like giant hairballs.

Underfoot, the two main types of volcanic terrain have names of Hawaiian origin. Most of the Etna landscape consists of sharp, jagged a' ā (ah-ah)—allegedly named for the sensation of walking on the sharp rocks without shoes. A' ā occurs when a thick, sticky river of lava's upper layer rapidly cools while the layer below continues to flow. The friction between the two layers tears apart the upper layer, resulting in a rough surface. Much smoother is *pahoehoe* lava, created when a more fluid basaltic lava flow's surface cools while the molten layer below continues to flow. The resulting solidified surface looks like smooth, flat layers of petrified liquid.

On the drive up the mountain, you'll notice as the climate and the terrain changes—from subtropical near the bottom, to alpine near the top. Watch for lava tubes—natural tunnels that run under the volcanic rock. Historically, Sicilians used the tubes for storing ice. In the winter, they'd shovel snow into the caves and layer it with fern leaves to make it easier to divide into large chunks of ice. The high elevation and natural volcanic insulation kept the ice frozen through the summer—before refrigeration was available, the ice was chopped up and taken down to towns along the coast, for preserving fish and making cold drinks, even *granita*.

At the top of the crater, take in the color of the various lava fields—compare the darker stone around the bases of the posts supporting the cable car to the lighter-colored stone on which you are standing, which is over 120 years old. (For more on how to read geology into the various landscapes of Etna, see the sidebar.) Look around—from this perch, flows are visible from different centuries, like an open history book. Look down on the lower Silvestri crater to see its almost perfect cone shape.

HIGHER-ALTITUDE ACTIVITIES

At 6,300 feet, Rifugio Sapienza is the jumping-off point for trips higher on Mount Etna. There are three stages: A cable car takes you to 8,200 feet; from there you can go by 4x4 bus to 9,800 feet, where guided hikes then lead to the summit craters area, depending on conditions. Your guide can lead a hike as high as weather, volcanic activity, and local authorities will allow.

The cable car is not particularly satisfying as a standalone experience. There is nothing to do at the upper cable car station, and the hiking near it isn't that appealing, leaving you with a "halfway there" feeling. For a more complete Etna visit, continue to a higher crater in the 4x4 bus (the best choice for most travelers, including families); sturdy travelers can hike all the way to the summit with a guide. Summit trips are best from June to October, when there's no snow; the cable car and 4x4 bus run year-round.

▲Cable Car *(Funivia)* to 8,200 Feet

The cable car *(funivia)* whisks you partway up the side of the mountain in about 10 minutes. You can do the ride up and back, with a quick walk up top, in less than an hour. There's not much to do at the upper station—a couple of basic eateries, tacky souvenir stands, gear rental (jackets and hiking boots), and WCs—but you can scramble around on the rocky terrain, looking for different types of volcanic rock. A little pinnacle a few minutes' walk above the station offers nice views down over the valley and a good look at smooth fields of cooled lava *(sciara)*. You can walk up the hill following the 4x4 switchbacks for a ways (toward Torre del Filosofo), but note that hiking above 8,900 feet (2,700 meters) without an alpine guide is forbidden.

Cost and Hours: €52 round-trip, runs daily starting at 8:30, last descent at 17:15, in windy conditions they'll bus you to the upper station, +39 095 914 141, funiviaetna.com.

▲▲▲4x4 Bus and Crater Walk at 9,800 Feet

This option offers maximum volcano thrills with minimum time and exertion (allow 2-3 hours round-trip from the lower cable car station). You'll ride up the cable car, then hop on a 4x4 shuttle bus that takes you on a rough, rocky road to a crater formed during the 2002 eruption. An alpine guide will explain the geology while leading you on an easy, 45-minute walk around the crater's rim. From there, you'll be able to see the summit steaming just above.

Cost and Hours: €80 round-trip covers cable car and bus, last departure 1.5 hours before the cable car closes—arrive by 15:30, funiviaetna.com.

▲▲Guided Hike Near the Summit Area at 9,800 Feet

To hike along trails close to the summit craters you'll need to join a guided tour, either with the official Gruppo Guide Alpine Etna Sud or via an independent tour company, such as those listed earlier under "Tours on Mount Etna." Depending on the company, season, and current activity on Etna, you'll either meet in Piano Provenzana (in the north), or at Rifugio Sapienza (in the south). Approaching from either base camp, you'll use a 4x4 bus

to get to the trailhead, then begin a long, steep hike up (1,000 feet) leading close to the mountain's summit. On the way down you'll typically break for a quick lunch before continuing back to the trailhead. If starting from Rifugio Sapienza, you'll take the cable car up to meet a 4x4 bus, (which then heads to the 2002 crater described above) and return to the cable car station on foot, taking in more scenery on the way down (5-6 hours round-trip).

Cost and Hours: €130, meet 40 minutes before departure, includes loaner coat, hiking boots, socks and helmet, bring your own lunch, first hike departs at 9:30 and returns around 15:00, groups leave as max number is reached, last hike departs at 10:30, not available when the volcano is active, +39 095 791 4755, etnaguide.eu. It's best to reserve ahead online, but you can also book on-site,

Mount Etna Wine Country

While travelers flock to Etna's volcanic sights at Rifugio Sapienza, it'd be a shame to miss its lovely wine country. Grapes love this region's climate and unique volcanic soil, and Mount Etna has become synonymous with top-quality wines.

Wineries surround Etna to the east and north, but my favorite wine country anywhere in Sicily is along Etna's north flank, along the 12-mile stretch of rural road between the towns of Linguaglossa and Randazzo (outlined in the self-guided driving tour at the end of this chapter). This area boasts beautiful scenery, charming wineries, and world-class wines. Travelers with an affinity for good wine—or even just beautiful landscapes—should devote a half- to full day to this area; true wine aficionados won't regret spending the night.

Slow Train Around Wine Country: The historic, narrow-gauge **Circumetnea** ("Around Etna") railway begins in Paternò and trundles clockwise around the western and northern sides of Etna, with a stop in Bronte and a break in Randazzo, before picking up and continuing on to Linguaglossa and terminating on the eastern side by the sea, in Riposto (also runs the other way). Unfortunately, the train schedule is infrequent (2/day), most of the train cars are old and rickety, and it's a slow journey (1.5 hours from Paternò to Randazzo, break in Randazzo, then another 70 minutes to Riposto; schedule at circumetnea.it). Note that travelers from Catania must take a Ferrovia Circumetnea (FCE) bus from the Nesima Metro stop to the Paternò train station (3/day, 25 minutes, circumetnea.it).

Sleeping in Wine Country: There are a number of accommodation options in this area. One to consider is **€€ Parcostatella,** a rustic farmhouse off the main road near Randazzo. The rooms are classic Sicilian country, with knotty pine paneling and tile floors. You'll eat breakfast in the former horse's stable and cart depot (Via Montelaguardia 2, Randazzo, +39 095 92 4036, parcostatella.com, info@parcostatella.com).

Mount Etna Wineries

Scores of Etna wineries invite travelers for a taste and a tour. Visits usually include a walk through the vineyards, a look at a traditional *palmento* wine cellar/press, and a representative tasting of their wines, usually paired with some food. Wineries in Sicily generally require you to book ahead; very few offer drop-in tastings. For locations, see the "Etna Area" map at the beginning of this chapter.

Wine Tours: Etna Wine School offers educational tours of the Mount Etna wine region. Benjamin Spencer, an American wine consultant, educator, and author who moved to Etna to share his love of the region's wines, can tailor experiences to your interests and level of expertise (€140/person for half-day at one winery, €220/person for full day with two wineries; minimum two people, reserve in advance, experiences include wine and food; transportation and other experiences on Mount Etna can be added for an extra fee, etnawineschool.com, info@etnawineschool.com).

NORTH SLOPE WINERIES

These wineries are listed in the order you'd reach them coming from Taormina or Catania. For a suggested route, see the self-guided drive later in this chapter.

Emilio Sciacca

Opened in 2019 and located just two minutes outside of Linguaglossa, Emilio's winery is dedicated to the production of natural wines—a process that's sensitive to the elements and yields wines that can vary significantly from year to year. Tastings are held by sommelier Vincenzo in a restored and modernized *palmento* with a rooftop terrace (tastings from €24/person, see website for options, reservations preferred but not required—they'll take you if they have space, vineyard tour included with prebooked visits; open daily in season 10:00-16:30, last tasting at 15:30; Contrada Martinella, +39 347 662 0341, emiliosciaccaetnawine.it, info@emiliosciaccaetnawine.it). To get there from Linguaglossa, take Via Mareneve west and pass the Mareneve Resort. Take the first left and follow signs for *Enoturismo Emilio Sciacca*.

Tenuta di Fessina
With rustic antiques and designer fixtures, this place fills an old 17th-century depot where wine was once processed and loaded onto the train (you'll see the little Circumetnea train trundle through occasionally). Their informative tastings, well run by Jacopo and Daniele, start with a tour and are all paired with food (starts at €45/person for three wines, open daily in season, reserve at least one day in advance, Contrada Rovittello, SS-120, +39 094 239 5300, tenutadifessina.com, fessina@tenutadifessina.com).

Planeta Sciaranuova
This large, commercial winery—one of the first to open during the latest Etna wine renaissance—has estates all over Sicily. Feudo di Mezzo is their winery on Mount Etna, but visits take place at the Sciaranuova tasting room, in a restored *palmento*. They offer several different experiences, but most include a tour with food and tastings of both wine and olive oil, which they also produce (€60/person and up, see offerings and book ahead online, private tours and cooking classes also possible, closed Sun, Contrada Sciaranuova, SS-120, Passopisciaro, +39 0925 195 5460, planeta.it, reservation@planeta.it).

Filippo Grasso
Located on one of the most prestigious terroirs on the mountain, this no-frills wine producer offers the most personal of all my recommended wine experiences. Expressive Mariarita opens her home and shares her family's life with visitors. While her dad runs the vineyards and her brother makes the wine, Mariarita shows guests around and presents some of their excel-

lent, good-value wines, pairing them with a sampler platter of local products or with lunch, which she cooks herself (much of what

Etna Wines

Wine has been made in Sicily and in the Mount Etna area since antiquity. But an infestation of phylloxera aphids that damaged Sicilian vines in the late 1800s—combined with depopulation after World War II—caused many wineries to cease operation. In the 1970s and 1980s, new EU regulations (and funding) benefitted ambitious winemakers who could afford to implement them, while hampering traditional winemakers by prohibiting the use of old stone buildings, called *palmenti*. These were historically used for crushing and fermenting grapes into must, and then pressing the must into wine. You'll see many abandoned *palmenti* in the Etna region, though some have been repurposed into tasting rooms and for other uses.

Etna winemaking struggled along until the early 2000s, when a handful of well-established vintners from mainland Italy realized Etna would be an ideal place to make wine. These pioneers led a renaissance in high-quality Etna wines. Today, wine lovers and critics from around the globe are taking notice of this remote corner of Sicily.

Grape vines thrive in Etna's mineral-rich volcanic soil. Some vineyards are steeply angled, allowing the vines to catch the sun just so. Etna's north slope—at about 2,500 feet in elevation—means cooler temperatures than elsewhere on the island, causing grapes to ripen very slowly. The black soil retains the heat of the sun, keeping vines warm during particularly cold nights.

Etna wines, distinguished by their strong minerality, include white, rosé, red, and classic-method sparkling wines. Whites typically use the indigenous grape called carricante (meaning "overloaded," for its heavy yield), which results in savory (not fruity) flavors. The dominant red wine grapes are nerello mascalese and nerello cappuccio (the only Sicilian native red grapes that resisted the spread of the prolific Nero d'Avola, an intense red grape introduced under Greek colonization), with a pinot noir-like color and bouquet that have earned comparisons to Burgundy wines.

Fine Etna wines are expensive by Sicilian standards, but worthwhile when combined with a quality winery visit. Because the rejuvenated Etna winemaking scene is so new, experts are waiting to discover how well these wines will age—suggesting that the intense interest in Etna wines has only just begun.

Etna wine pilgrims should seek out Benjamin Spencer's book *The New Wines of Mount Etna,* which navigates this fast-evolving scene (Gemelli Press, 2020).

she serves comes from their garden). It's best to book ahead, but if you want to stop in last-minute, give it a shot—ideally send her an email or WhatsApp message that day, though you can try ringing the bell as the locals do, when they come for affordable *vino sfuso*, aka bulk wine (tastings from €35/person, up to €60 with lunch, closed Sun—but if it's the only day you'll be in the area, call ahead to double-check, Contrada Calderara, SP-89, +39 320 706 1375, filippograsso.it, info@filippograsso.it).

SOUTHEAST SLOPE WINERY
If you can't make it to the north slope, here's an option that's conveniently located between Catania and the volcanic sights at Rifugio Sapienza.

Benanti
About 10 miles north of Catania in Viagrande, Benanti prides itself on its boutique winery approach and has earned praise from wine critics and enthusiasts. The winery experience includes a vineyard tour (which climbs an extinct lateral crater) and a visit to their 18th-century *palmento*, as well as a guided tasting (tour and tasting of 4 wines paired with food starts at €60/person, RS%—20 percent discount, closed Mon, tours require minimum of 2 people and must be reserved at least 5 days in advance, +39 095 789 0928, benanti.it, info@benanti.it, Antonio and Salvino).

North Slope Wine Country Drive

The scenic north slope of Mount Etna warrants a drive—even if you're not into wine. You'll feel worlds away from the tourist crush... this is the lovely, rural, time-passed Sicily of romantic travel dreams. Along the way, you'll have several opportunities to visit a winery for a tour and tasting (book ahead), and some fine opportunities for a memorable meal. This self-guided drive is designed to follow a visit to Mount Etna's volcanic sights for a jam-packed, showstopper day. It's also possible to visit only the wineries, and/or add a visit to a nutty city (options outlined next). To trace the route of this drive, see the "Mount Etna North Slope Wine Country" map in this section; for a much broader view of the routes around Mount Etna, see the "Etna Area" map at the beginning of this chapter.

Wine and Volcano in One Day: This drive assumes you'll ap-

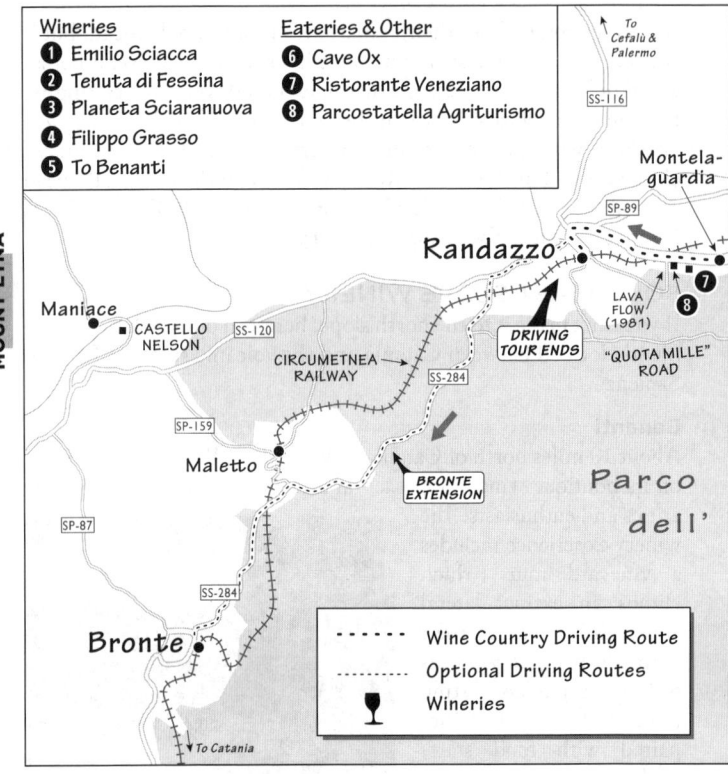

proach the north slope vineyards after the Mount Etna volcanic sights. Altogether it's 1.5 hours of driving (about 40 miles/60 km) to follow the route from the base camp at Rifugio Sapienza to the medieval village of Randazzo (not counting stops). The optional detour to Bronte (to sample pistachio goodies) adds another hour.

Wine-Tasting Only: Those who want a more leisurely day focused on wine can follow one of these route options. From **Catania,** head straight to Zafferana Etnea: Angle up through small towns, by way of Canalicchio, San Giovanni La Punta, and Fleri—passing the recommended Benanti winery in Viagrande (about 2 hours driving without stops; see the "Etna Area" map, earlier).

If coming from **Taormina,** skip Zafferana Etnea and jump straight ahead to Linguaglossa to get more quickly to the most beautiful stretch of wine country. Hop on expressway A-18 south (toward Catania), exit at Fiumefreddo, and twist up to Linguaglossa on SS-120 (about 1.5 hours driving without stops).

Bronte Extension: For most visitors, the wine road between Linguaglossa and Randazzo is the best look at this area. But foodies and pistachio addicts with time to spare can extend their trip to Bronte (30 minutes from Randazzo).

Mount Etna Wine Country 381

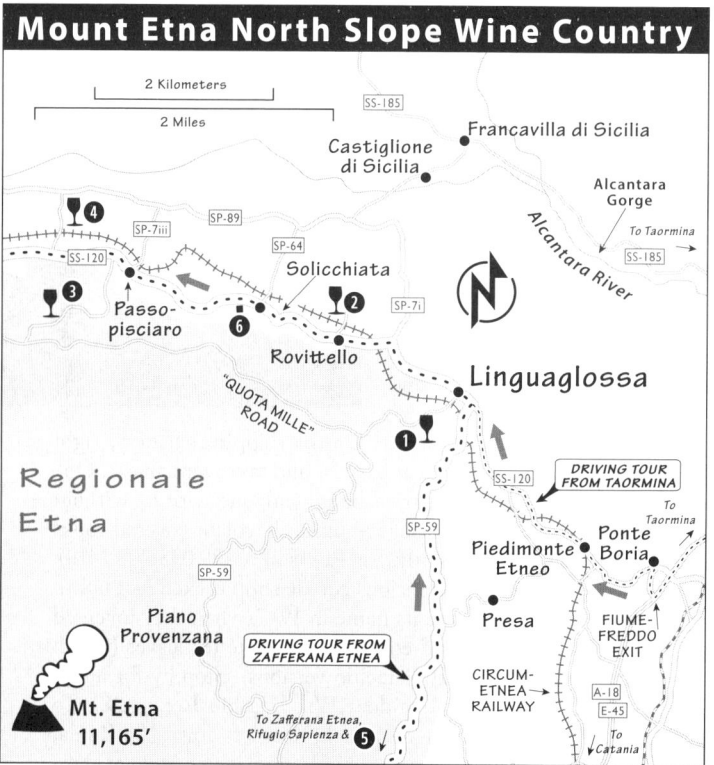

From Rifugio Sapienza to Zafferana Etnea
From Rifugio Sapienza, it's 30 minutes to the first stop, the village of Zafferana Etnea.
• *Head east from Rifugio Sapienza, passing the Silvestri craters. You'll drop down on the curvy SP-92 (following* Zafferana *signs) for 11 miles (18 km).*

Once in Zafferana, SP-92 comes to an angled T-intersection; turn right on Via San Giacomo and follow that street all the way down to the end. Turn left on Via Roma, where you'll come to the main church and square. Look for street parking near the main square—white lines indicate free parking for one hour, but you must set a cardboard clock (or leave a note) with your arrival time on the dashboard.

Zafferana Etnea
This town of 10,000 inhabitants is the closest to Etna's summit—which means it often deals with "black snow" from Etna's ash falls. In larger concentrations, the ash can be dangerous, and clean-up crews once bagged it as toxic waste. But now the usefulness of the ash is recognized in creating all kinds of products, including beauty

scrubs. Visitors stop in Zafferana to buy honey produced on the slopes of the mountain, and it's a good place to sample some local sweets. Every weekend in October, the town holds its Ottobrata Zafferanese—the Sicilian version of Oktoberfest. Here you'll find *vino rosso* instead of beer, home-made *salsiccia* instead of wurst, and pistachio-and-mushroom spread instead of kraut.

From the front steps of Zafferana's main church, a long, marbled, tree-lined belvedere reaches out toward the sea, filled with eateries, happy kids, and great views.

Sweets in Zafferana Etnea: Donna Peppina's bakery, right on the main square, serves local pastries and takeaway snacks. Options include the *siciliana,* a fried dough calzone with or without anchovies, and the *sciatore,* a sugar-bomb, chocolate-covered cookie that resembles an eclair (daily, Via Roma 220, +39 095 708 1410). **Dolceria Salemi,** an unpretentious cookie shop tucked just uphill from the main square, made its name in 1947, when they invented *foglie da té*—a crispy almond cookie shaped like tea leaves (which also comes in hazelnut and pistachio versions). Stop by for a free sample (closed Mon and at midday, Via Eusebio Longo 28). To find it, with the belvedere at your back, turn left down Via Roma, then take the first right up Via Eusebio Longo; it's a couple of short blocks up, on the right.

• *Leave Zafferana Etnea heading north on Via Roma (SP-59, tracking signs toward* Milo *and* Linguaglossa*) for the 45-minute drive to Linguaglossa.*

From Zafferana Etnea to Linguaglossa

This rural road—an appealing, upper alternative to the busy highway in the valley below—follows Etna's lower edge. As you drive through the towns of Milo and Fornazzo, enjoy the lush scenery. The vegetation here is almost subtropical in comparison to the barren, dry, rocky landscape of Etna's north and west slopes (where we're headed).

Keep an eye on your right for grand vistas; in some places, it's possible to see the toe of Italy and—on a clear day—even the Bay of Siracusa.

Dropping down into Linguaglossa, you'll cross over the 1895 narrow-gauge train tracks that once carried casks of wine to be shipped from the port of Riposto. Today, the Circumetnea ("Around Etna") train, which originates in Paternò, allows travelers a scenic (and slow) passage through Etna's bucolic wine country.

• *As SP-59 enters Linguaglossa (you'll see a faded* Benvenuti *sign), take the hairpin right turn onto Via Matteotti. At the end of this street, turn left onto Via Roma (SS-120).*

Linguaglossa

This sweet, inviting village has a funny name: "Tongue Tongue" (*lingua* is tongue in Latin, *glossa* is Greek)—maybe named for a giant lava flow that once licked the town. Notice the stately main street; historically, Linguaglossa was a prosperous burg. As the northern gateway to Etna wine country—and therefore a crossroads for trade—locals developed the gift of gab necessary for lengthy negotiations...perhaps a second meaning behind the town's name. Aside from its chatty natives, Linguaglossa is known for its *salsiccia a punta di coltello*—sausages made with local pork seasoned and chopped with a knife. Note that the recommended **Emilio Sciacca** winery is about two minutes southwest of town. (For driving directions, see the listing on page 376).

Eating in Linguaglossa: €€ In Cucina Dai Pennisi is the town's most respected butcher and cheese shop and also an upscale eatery, where you can choose your meat from the case and wait while they cook it. Watch the local sausage being mixed by hand behind the counter (closed Sun dinner and all day Mon, Via Umberto 9, +39 095 643 160, daipennisi.it).

• *Leaving Linguaglossa, continue west on SS-120 toward Randazzo (9 miles/15 km).*

Between Linguaglossa and Randazzo

This stretch is the gateway to Etna's north slope wine region. You'll pass through some of the loveliest wine country in Sicily and begin to see why so many wineries are taking advantage of the region's ideal volcanic soil. As you drive, enjoy glimpses of Etna's blackened slope and volcanic scoria cones mixed among olive groves and orchards.

About 10 minutes outside Linguaglossa is the recommended **Tenuta di Fessina** winery. (The turnoff is on the right—watch for it just after a church with a big clock, on the left side of the road.) About five minutes past Tenuta di Fessina, you'll pass through the village of **Solicchiata** (with the recommended Cave Ox restaurant). Another five minutes puts you in the humble town of **Passopisciaro,** a working-class hub for local vintners; you may see winemakers socializing in the shade of the trees on the main square.

Just beyond Passopisciaro are two more recommended wineries. The road to **Planeta Sciaranuova** is just past the train station (turn left at the *Etna* sign and wind your way up). Beyond that is the endearingly humble **Filippo Grasso** (turn right at the road just before Ristorante Da Antonio).

Driving onward, as you approach Randazzo, keep an eye out on the left for a 1981 lava flow (just past a big *Randazzo* sign). Look uphill to see the lava that coursed downhill.

Alternate Road—*Quota Mille*: As you drive along SS-120 from Linguaglossa to Randazzo, you'll see some side roads leading up (on your left) to the *Quota Mille* ("Altitude 1,000"—for its height in meters), the upper road that runs parallel to SS-120 around the northern base of Etna. From the Quota Mille, you'll see better views of the petrified lava flows, surviving WWII-era turrets (this area was fortified by Axis forces as a last line of defense against the Allies' advance during Operation Husky in 1943), and many *palmenti*. A feature of any Etna winery, a *palmento* is a traditional stone cellar where grapes were crushed, the resulting must fermented, and the red skins and stems pressed—before the EU outlawed them 30 years ago as being unsanitary. In recent years—with the renaissance in Etna wines—they are being restored and often converted into restaurants and tasting rooms (look for windows with cross-hatching on a building's lower level). Hardy travelers might consider returning on this upper road on their way back to civilization at the end of this drive. (But watch out for animals—cows and deer use this road, too.)

Eating Between Linguaglossa and Randazzo: The village of Solicchiata is home to €€ **Cave Ox,** a well-respected restaurant with a simple menu (pizzas and a few regional standards) and one of the region's best wine lists (closed Tue, on the main road at Via Nazionale Solicchiata 159, +39 094 298 6171, caveox.it).

On the outskirts of Randazzo, €€€ **Ristorante Veneziano** is a local favorite for a special-occasion splurge. The space is casual and unpretentious, and the menu highlights local mushrooms and other regional ingredients, such as Nebrodi pork and pasta with seasonal sauces. For high-end cuisine, the prices are reasonable (reservations smart on weekends, closed Sun for dinner and all day Mon, just east of Randazzo on SS-120, +39 095 799 1353, ristoranteveneziano.it). Don't confuse this restaurant—which is right along the main road—with a different Veneziano, which you may see signposted at the Parcostatella Agriturismo, nearby.

• *Continue straight on to...*

Randazzo

Randazzo (pop. 11,000)—the de facto capital of Etna's northern wine country—is a city made of the mountain. The medieval core of the town, as well as its main church and bell tower, are all built with black lava stone (basalt). You'll see basalt carved like fine marble, framing windows and decorating buildings. A wander through this very untouristy town takes you back to the late Middle Ages.

Mount Etna Wine Country

The city historically had three separate communities—Greeks, Latins, and Lombards (people from northern Italy)—each with their own traditions and languages. Each neighborhood had its own church: San Nicola for the Greeks, Santa Maria for the Latins, and San Martino for the Lombards. The churches are a patchwork of architectural styles, but they all feature blocks of the local Etna basalt.

Randazzo has the largest market in the area, filling the streets on Sunday mornings with vendors selling food, clothes, and household goods.

Eating in Randazzo: €€ San Giorgio e Il Drago sits deep in the town, tucked back by a deserted monastery. Inside it's a cozy, classic trattoria that's ideal for a home-cooked Sicilian meal. The *antipasti* are especially tempting, and they offer a good range of pasta dishes (closed Tue, Piazza San Giorgio 28, Randazzo, +39 095 923 972, ristorantesangiorgioeildrago.it).

€ Macelleria Sparta is a meat-and-cheese shop in the heart of town. Nunzio makes his own cheeses from sheep's milk and proudly displays beautiful lumps of pecorino and baked ricotta. For a few euros, he'll dish up a sampler platter of his cheeses and some of the house salami, including the *salsiccia muscia*—the still-soft, handmade sausage aged for 10 days (closes at midday, also closes early on Wed and Sun, Via Umberto 89, +39 095 921 045).

€€ Agorà Enoteca will transport you back in time with its medieval tavern location and interior. Their antipasto platter is a parade of interesting nibbles, and the main dishes use local Etna products (closed Wed, Via Tenente Francesco Fisauli 7, +39 329 072 5005).

Wine Shop: Il Buongustaio dell'Etna, in the heart of Randazzo, is a well-stocked wine shop and bar that also serves meats and cheeses and the owner *Pippo* (nickname for Giuseppe) can make you a delicious *panino*. While there's a bit of a language barrier, his son Giovanni *parla inglese*, and it is a great chance to peruse wines and select a glass without scheduling a win-

ery visit (long hours daily, Corso Umberto 8, +39 320 976 0623, buongustaiodelletna.com).

• *For most travelers, Randazzo is the natural end point of the Etna wine country drive. Retrace your steps toward Linguaglossa (or for different scenery, take the Quota Mille road—described earlier). From Linguaglossa, take SS-120 down to the hamlet of Ponte Boria, and follow signs to the A-18 expressway. Once on the A-18, it's just 20 minutes north to Taormina, or 30 minutes south to Catania.*

But if you'd like to explore further, consider extending your drive about 30 minutes southwest of Randazzo—beyond wine country and into pistachio country.

Optional Extension: Bronte and Pistachio Country

• *To reach Bronte from Randazzo, continue west on SP-120; about a half-mile out of town, take the left fork to continue south on SS-284, marked for* Maletto *and* Bronte.

In this area, farms dot the slopes of Etna, with some vineyards, olive groves, and wild fig trees. In spring and early summer, you'll likely see bright-yellow scotch broom (aka *ginestra*)—the first plant that populates a lava flow. After Maletto, you'll notice the landscape changing—becoming barren, with grand views of the mountain on the left. Soon you'll see pistachio groves and almond trees, and arrive in Bronte.

Visiting Bronte: This somewhat drab city (pop. 19,000) is the main population center for the west and north slopes of Etna—so close that it was named for one of the Cyclopes thought to live inside the volcano. Among travelers, it's famous as the center of production for high-quality pistachios—the town is surrounded by gnarled groves of ancient pistachio trees. While there's not much to see, Bronte pleases pistachio pilgrims.

Little Bronte produces about one percent of the world's pistachios. The combination of volcanic soil, a biennial harvest (to protect the trees), and natural irrigation produces smaller nuts than the more typical varieties from California, Iran, and Turkey. But Bronte pistachios have an intense color and taste that makes them sought after (and expensive) in the culinary market. Sicilians prize them so much that they've protected their nuts with a special DOP label, a sort of trademark for Italian foods.

By the way, the town is associated with England's greatest naval hero, Admiral Horatio Nelson. Some land in this area was turned into a duchy in 1799 and given to Nelson as thanks for the role he played in restoring King Ferdinand of the Kingdom of the Two Sicilies to his throne. Nelson intended to use his new castle (a former abbey nicknamed Castello Nelson) as a summer home—but died before he ever saw it. The castle now houses a museum, where visitors can learn about the history of the building and its key players through interactive multimedia exhibits (€5, Mon-Sat 9:00-13:00 & 14:00-17:00, Sun until 18:00, shorter hours off-season; +39 095 690 018, castellonelsondibronte.it).

The town's name is also linked to the English literary Brontë family. Patrick Brontë—father of Charlotte, Emily, and Anne—so admired Nelson that he is said to have adapted the spelling of his own name from Brunty to Brontë in recognition of the admiral's duchy.

Pistachio Shops: If you want to try some of the town's "green gold," head to the far end of town (along SS-284), where you'll find **Il Pistacchio.** Here, helpful owner Alfio offers free samples of pistachio products, including pastes and liqueurs. Ask to see samples of pistachios from other countries to understand the difference (closed Sat-Sun and midday, ring to be let in, Viale Catania 62, +39 095 692 946, ilpistacchio.it). If Il Pistacchio is closed, try **Mastro Pistacchio** across the street. Giancarlo is open daily and has longer hours (+39 328 117 1668, mastropistacchio.it).

Eating in Bronte: Near the pistachio shops, **€ Life Caffè** is an unpretentious roadside café serving good coffee, pastries, and gelato, all made with Bronte's signature pistachios. Try an *arancino* rice ball stuffed with pistachio pesto, prosciutto, and béchamel (closed Thu, Viale Catania 10, +39 095 692 252).

• *After Bronte, you can head back the way you came, via Randazzo and Linguaglossa, to the A-18 expressway. Or, if you're headed south to Catania, take the more direct route around the back side of Etna: Simply carry on south from Bronte on SS-284, then follow SS-121 to Catania (about one hour).*

TAORMINA

Clinging to a seaside cliff within view of smoldering Mount Etna, Taormina is Sicily's classic resort town. Saturated with languid echoes of 19th-century Grand Tour elegance, this tidy town has a too-perfect feel, but starry-eyed cruise-ship visitors and honeymooners don't seem to notice. Aside from its one must-see sight—the Greek-Roman Theater—Taormina is a good place to take a breather from sightseeing and relax, sip a glass of sparkling Mount Etna wine, and watch the crowds waltz by.

Taormina makes a workable springboard for day trips to Mount Etna, Catania, and even to Siracusa, Ragusa, or Villa Romana del Casale. It's also a good alternative to gritty, intense Catania, and is within an hour's drive of Catania's international airport.

While some see Taormina as a high-end "vacation from your vacation," for a more authentically Sicilian beach break, I prefer Cefalù. Taormina felt overly touristy even before it served as an idyllic setting for a season of HBO's *The White Lotus*. After dark, the town turns into one sprawling, posh cocktail party.

PLANNING YOUR TIME

Taormina has only one important sight, its Greek-Roman Theater, and you can see everything there is to see in one simple stroll. A single day is plenty to experience the town.

If visiting in high season, begin with the Greek-Roman The-

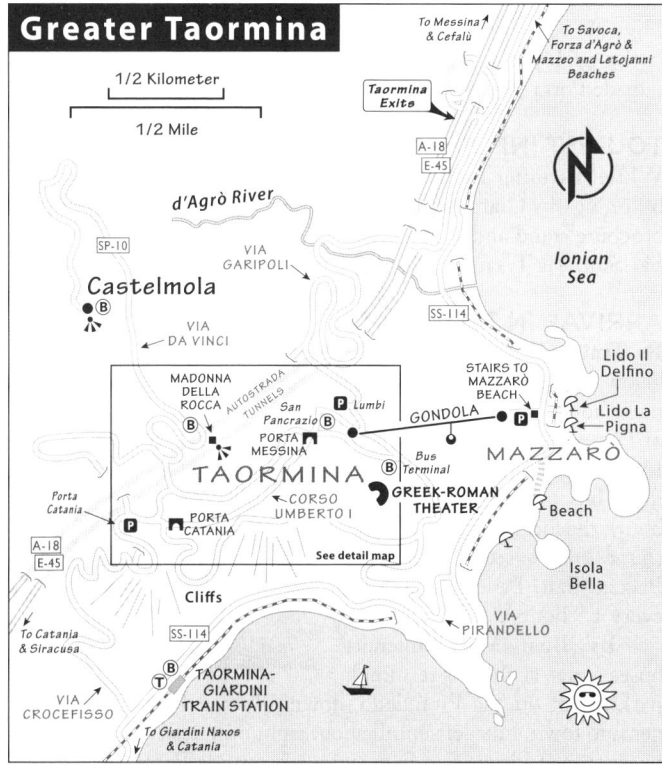

Greater Taormina

ater first thing in the morning to avoid crowds and heat, then do my self-guided walk through town (or start your day with the walk and save the theater for the late afternoon). Other than that, simply enjoy the town and its views, or consider going down to Isola Bella and its beach or up to Castelmola's scenic perch, or side-trip into the Mount Etna wine region (described in the previous chapter).

Orientation to Taormina

Taormina (pop. 11,000) sits halfway up the side of Mount Tauro, overlooking the Ionian Sea. While the townscape is steep (expect lots of stairs and hills), most of the action is clustered around the level main drag of Corso Umberto I. This street stretches between the two city gates, Porta Catania (west end of town) and Porta Messina (east end of town). You can walk the entire length of Corso Umberto I in about 10 minutes (but when the crowds roll in, it will take you twice that time).

The streets that tumble downhill below Corso Umberto I are filled with hotels, colorful shops, and a public garden with views.

High above Taormina is the scenic village of Castelmola; far below is the pebbly beach at Isola Bella. Most public transit stops just outside Porta Messina.

TOURIST INFORMATION

While charming Taormina surprisingly lacks a tourist information office, nearby Giardini Naxos offers one—but it's little more than a brochure stand and a shrug (generally Mon-Fri 9:00-13:00, closed Sat-Sun; Via Tysandros 54; +39 094 251 010; strgiardini.it).

ARRIVAL IN TAORMINA

By Train: Trains arrive at the Taormina-Giardini train station below town. Taxis wait just outside the train station (about €15 to most hotels). There are a couple of bus options: The bright blue Interbus goes to the Via Pirandello bus terminal (€1.90, 1-2/hour); the local orange ASM bus (*linea verde*—green line) goes to Piazza San Pancrazio (€1.10, every 1.5 hours).

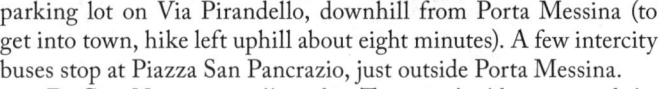

By Bus: Most intercity buses arrive at the bus terminal/parking lot on Via Pirandello, downhill from Porta Messina (to get into town, hike left uphill about eight minutes). A few intercity buses stop at Piazza San Pancrazio, just outside Porta Messina.

By Car: No cars are allowed in Taormina's old center, and the city is surrounded by a confusing one-way loop road that twists back on itself again and again. Approaching town on the E-45 expressway from Catania and the south, take the Taormina exit (be ready for it, just after a long tunnel). Continue straight, following signs to *Taormina/Castelmola*. You'll then twist along a serpentine road up into town...stay the course. Check with your hotel before you arrive—some have on-site or valet parking, and some may encourage you to drop off your bag before driving to one of Taormina's two parking garages.

The garages, at opposite ends of town, are signposted along the road into town; signs show the number of available spaces (about €28/24 hours). **Parcheggio Porta Catania,** a five-minute uphill walk to Porta Catania at the western end of town, is convenient to most accommodations. **Parcheggio Lumbi** is handier for places at the east end of town (a free shuttle bus takes you to Piazza San Pancrazio). To return to your car, wait for the shuttle bus at Piazza San Pancrazio (runs every 15 minutes or so).

By Plane: The nearest international airport is at Catania (described at the end of the Catania chapter), 40 miles from Taormina and about a one-hour drive in good traffic. Taxis from Catania airport to Taormina run about €100. Airport buses connect Catania with Taormina's bus terminal (€7, 1-2/hour, 1.5 hours, interbus. it). You can also book a private transfer with Giuseppe Leotta at Luxury Car Services (see page 339).

HELPFUL HINTS

Crowds and Seasons: Expect Taormina to be very crowded in summer. Unlike other parts of Italy, Taormina's busiest month is August, when it seems like the whole of the Mediterranean descends here for vacation. In winter (Nov-March), some hotels, restaurants, and tourist activities shut down.

Markets: A produce market bustles every day near Porta Messina until about 14:00 (see the "Taormina" map).

Laundry: Do it yourself at **Lavanderia Self-Service,** or use their drop-off option, which takes about two hours (daily, 8:00-20:00, Via Dionisio I 18B, +39 339 564 9988). For location, see the "Taormina Hotels and Restaurants" map, later.

Festivals: In April, Taormina hosts a balcony-decorating competition: **Vetrine e Balconi in Fiore** ("windows and balconies in bloom"). In preparation, from late March onward, residents ornament their town with flowers and colorful decorations. In summer (late June/early July), Taormina hosts an important **film festival** with showings at the Greek theater. Every July 9, locals honor their patron saint, **San Pancrazio,** with religious processions throughout the city.

GETTING AROUND TAORMINA

By Bus: Local buses are operated by two companies: ASM (orange buses) and Interbus (blue buses). There are also hop-on, hop-off buses (details under "Tours in Taormina," later).

ASM buses have limited frequency but can be useful for reaching sights outside the city center. The ASM bus hub is at Piazza San Pancrazio, just outside Porta Messina; look for the blue *fermata* sign on the left (on a building), just beyond and across from the taxi stand.

Line names are displayed on bus windshields (€1.10/ride—pay driver, asmtaormina.com). The **green line** *(linea verde)* goes down to Isola Bella and the train station and up to the Sanctuary of Madonna della Rocca (runs about every 1.5 hours). The **red line** *(circolare rossa)* does a loop around Taormina (every 45 minutes, stops at a few handy places, including Via Leonardo da Vinci and Porta Catania). The **blue line** *(linea blu/beachbus)* heads to beaches north of town, at Mazzeo and Letojanni (7/day).

Interbus uses the bus terminal on Via Pirandello. Its bright blue buses run throughout Taormina and to a few destinations beyond, including the Taormina-Giardini train station and the villages of Castelmola and Giardini Naxos (€1.90; confirm line, check schedules, and buy tickets at the bus terminal office).

By Taxi: There's a taxi stand on Piazza Vittorio Emanuele, near Palazzo Corvaja; taxis also wait just outside Porta Messina (on Piazza San Pancrazio) and Porta Catania.

Tours in Taormina

Local Guides

Franco D'Angelo does an interesting walk through Taormina's back streets, lesser-known corners, and the Greek-Roman Theater (€80/hour, 2-hour minimum, +39 349 283 1679, franz.tourguide@gmail.com).

Tommaso Pante, a proud Sicilian based near Messina, leads tours of Taormina and Messina. He also offers tours of *Godfather* locations, wine tasting on Mount Etna, and Sicilian genealogy research (€70/hour, 2-hour minimum, +39 347 185 6950, sunway.it, tpante@gmail.com).

Driver: English-speaking **Seby Melita** offers regional day trips and transfers (half-day excursion to Etna or Siracusa from €250, Catania airport transfer €120, transfer from Messina cruise port (up to 8 people) from €110, +39 346 371 8757, sicilywithsebastian.com, sicilywithsebastian@gmail.com).

Bus Tours

Details for the following buses are always in flux—confirm everything locally (look for brochures or ticket sellers). Sightseeing buses typically only run in peak season (April-Oct).

Interbus runs a hop-on, hop-off bus with a €15 one-day ticket that covers several different loops. The Full Tour (red line) stops at Giardini Naxos; Taormina bus terminal; Madonna della Rocca; Castelmola; the beaches of Letojanni, Mazzarò, and Isola Bella; and Alcantara Gorge. The blue line does a smaller loop that includes just Taormina, Madonna della Rocca, Castelmola, and the beaches; the orange line does a panoramic tour of Taormina from the bus terminal up to Madonna della Rocca, Castelmola, and back; and the green line goes to the *Godfather* towns of Savoca and Forza d'Agrò (buses run every two hours, ticket also good on local Interbus and Etna Trasporti buses, +39 094 262 5301, interbus.it/hopon-hopoff).

City by See runs several routes on an open-top bus, including a red route (Giardini Naxos, Taormina bus terminal, Letojanni, and Isola Bella) and a blue route that connects Taormina bus terminal with Madonna della Rocca and Castelmola (€20 for one-day ticket, hourly, +39 090 213 5672, citybysee.com). They also have buses that go to the *Godfather* towns and to Alcantara Gorge.

SAT also may offer a hop-on, hop-off route that stops at most points of interest (ask locally if they're running, taorminahop.it; see contact info below).

Excursions from Taormina
SAT offers a rotating schedule of day trips from Taormina to destinations across Sicily. There's a full-day basic Etna tour (see page 366), as well as Etna tours that also stop at the Alcantara Gorge. Other excursions include Siracusa, Palermo and Cefalù, Agrigento and Villa Romana del Casale, and the Aeolian Islands. They also do cooking classes and a boat ride along the Taormina coastline (see website for details, book at least a day ahead, Corso Umberto I 73, +39 094 224 653, satexcursions.it, booking@satgroup.it).

Boat Tours
VIP Sailing Taormina, departing from Giardini Naxos and led by Captain Enzo, offers coastal cruises with swimming stops, Sicilian snacks, and prosecco. The crew is friendly, and the atmosphere is festive, though it can get crowded in high season (+39 393 032 1686, vipsailingtaormina.com).

Taormina Town Walk

This lazy, self-guided walk will take you along Taormina's convivial Corso Umberto I, through grand Piazza IX Aprile, and to the doorstep of the impressive Greek-Roman Theater—connecting all the important landmarks and best panoramic views. Along the way, we'll squeeze in a little town history. To trace the route, see the "Taormina" map.

• *Begin at the west end of town, just outside Porta Catania, on the little square called Piazza Sant'Antonio Abate.*

❶ Porta Catania
The road you're standing on was once a major thoroughfare that connected the larger cities of Catania and Messina.

Walk a few steps downhill to the small park with several huge palm trees and look out over the water. What a lovely location for a town! This area was first populated by the Sicels—an ancient people who predated the island's Greek colonizers by hundreds of years. When Greek seafarers arrived around 734 BC, they founded Naxos (likely named for their home island)—the little village you see clinging to the peninsula below. The oldest known Greek settlement on Sicily, it's known today as Giardini Naxos. Ancient Greece was overcrowded, and many city-states chose to send citizens out to find fortune and more fertile land in the west. The colo-

394 Rick Steves Sicily

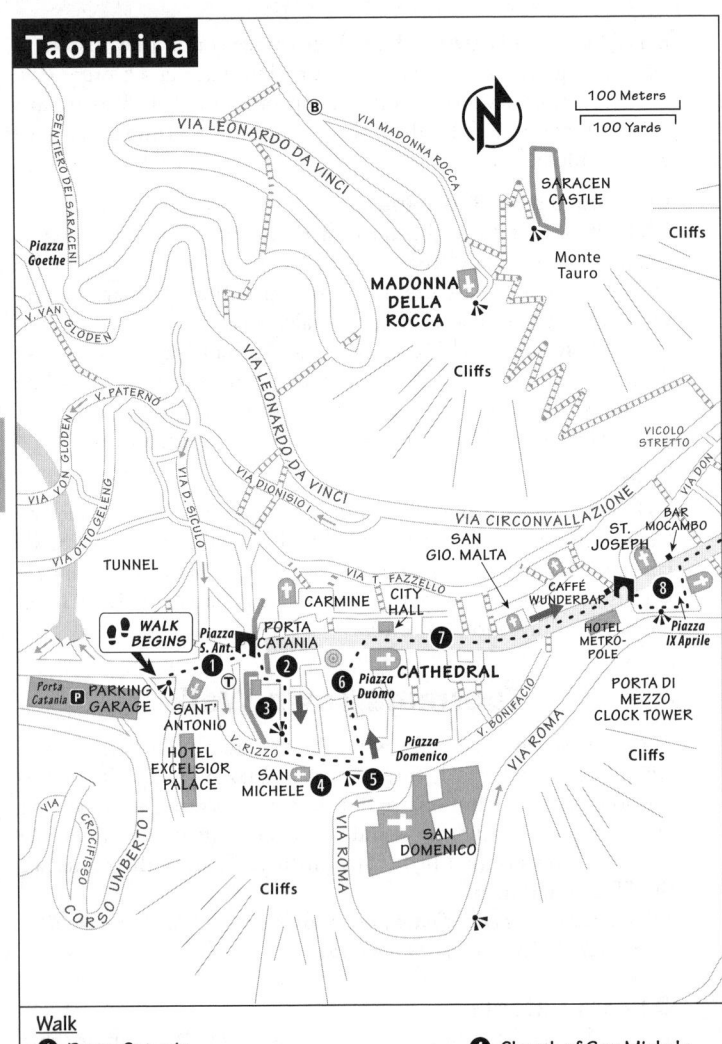

Walk
1. Porta Catania
2. Via del Ghetto
3. View of Palazzo Duchi di Santo Stefano
4. Church of San Michele
5. View of San Domenico Convent

nists who came to the east coast of Sicily imported more than just Greek culture: They also brought rivalries from their home cities and were at near-constant war with their neighbors in Sicily. In 403 BC, the powerful Greek city of Syracuse crushed little Naxos, sending the survivors to seek shelter on higher ground. They established a more defensible hillside city called Tauromenion, "the mountain shaped like a bull."

Notice that today's Taormina has two parts: the Greek city,

Taormina Town Walk 395

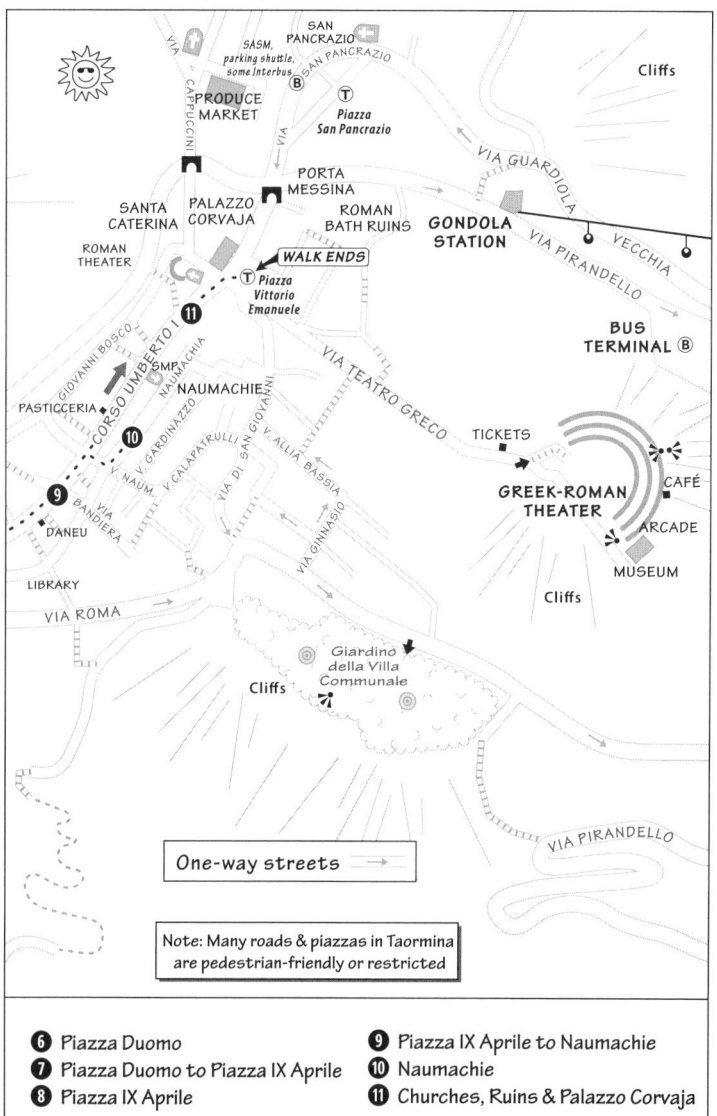

- ⑥ Piazza Duomo
- ⑦ Piazza Duomo to Piazza IX Aprile
- ⑧ Piazza IX Aprile
- ⑨ Piazza IX Aprile to Naumachie
- ⑩ Naumachie
- ⑪ Churches, Ruins & Palazzo Corvaja

which runs from the Greek-Roman Theater to the clock tower on Piazza IX Aprile, and the medieval Norman city that stretches from there to Porta Catania. We'll enter through the newer (Norman) part of town, built as the city expanded during the Middle Ages.

As you look out from the viewpoint, on your left is the **Hotel Excelsior Palace,** a reminder of another important epoch in the town's history. Some 2,500 years after the Greeks arrived here, Taormina became an important stop on the Grand Tour itineraries of wealthy northern Europeans seeking out great artifacts of the ancient world (see the sidebar). German author Johann Wolfgang von Goethe arrived in 1786 and praised Taormina in his writing; a century later, Friedrich Nietzsche authored portions of his seminal *Thus Spoke Zarathustra* (introducing his notion that "God is dead") right here. Taormina's legacy as a major hot spot for high-end tourism left it with many grand hotels; this one was a later addition, built in 1904 in a Neo-Moorish style, but it still evokes the elegance of the Grand Tour era. Now pan to the right, where you'll see a huge, concrete square just below you—the rooftop of the big Porta Catania parking garage, which injects a steady flow of latter-day Grand Tourists into town.

Head a few steps back up to the little chapel of **Sant'Antonio Abate,** which faces the square where you began. If it's open, step inside to see a remarkable example of the southern Italian and Sicilian custom of *presepi*—elaborate nativity scenes that sprawl into complete miniature villages. This one, not surprisingly, shows a village set in a dramatic cliff-hanging location.

Exiting the chapel, walk up to the old entry into the city walls. This is **Porta Catania,** which marks the city limits about 500 years ago. Taormina long ago outgrew its fortifications, incorporating the walls into the fabric of the city. Look left, up the street, to see a modern building supported by the town wall. Though the wall looks plain now, parts of it were originally decorated. As you step through the gate, look overhead to see fresco fragments from the ninth century.

• *Once through the gate, take an immediate right and walk along the wall down the lane called Vico de Spuches. Follow it downhill as it bends around and changes names to...*

❷ Via del Ghetto

As the name implies, this area was once Taormina's Jewish quarter, when it was home not only to a synagogue but also to a mosque. Six centuries ago, Christians, Jews, and Muslims lived side-by-side in a tolerant community. But when Sicily's 15th-century Spanish overlords began pursuing their Inquisition, the era of tolerance ended. Beginning in 1493, all non-Christian communities faced persecution or expulsion. Many Muslims left for North Africa, while the Jewish population either left Sicily or converted to Christianity, taking on new last names to conceal their past.

• *Walking down Via del Ghetto, follow the fenced garden of a fine palace.*

The Grand Tour

In the 1500s, the Vatican sponsored excavations throughout Italy to rediscover and inspire interest in Europe's antiquity. By the 17th century, the history of Greece and Rome and their influence across Europe became fashionable topics. This Neoclassical movement flourished well into the 19th century. Young wealthy noblemen and women from England and northern Europe traveled through the Continent, accompanied by a chaperone and guide, to witness the great artistic, architectural, and cultural treasures from past civilizations. For the rich, the Grand Tour was a rite of passage and an extension of one's education; the journey could take from a few months to several years. Travelers would take up residence in cities across Italy, using their days to contemplate art, to paint, and to write. Sicily was an important part of the Grand Tour; explorers here included Oscar Wilde, Richard Strauss, Richard Wagner, Johann Wolfgang von Goethe, and Florence Trevelyan, who built the villa on Taormina's Isola Bella. Their travels inspired others to do the same, and many Grand Tour destinations—including Taormina, Sorrento, and Florence—are still top tourism spots today. The romantic accounts of the Grand Tour still linger in the cultural memory of Europe, and modern tourism is a direct consequence of those elegant times.

When you reach the bottom of the street, look up (over your right shoulder) for a great view of...

❸ Palazzo Duchi di Santo Stefano (Fondazione Mazzullo)

Once the home of a noble family, this palace now houses modern-art exhibits. Notice the building's different architectural styles: The lower floor dates from the 1100s, during a period of Norman rule. The upper floor was added 400 years later in imitation of the earlier style, but with exaggerated Neo-Norman flourishes. You'll see over-the-top window designs: Gothic pointed-arch windows on the upper floor, with six-pointed stars. To finish it off, the roofline is more decorative than defensive, with geometric embellishments made of local lava stone. Notice how the palace also incorporates a stretch of the town wall into its structure.

• *Now, facing the sea, look for the small stone church across the street.*

❹ Church of San Michele (Chiesa di San Michele)

Approaching the church from the side, you'll see that the road covers the bottom part of a doorway on the long side. This illustrates how, as the city grew, the street level changed. Now circle around to the front door to see evidence of what was likely once a synagogue. After the expulsion of the Jewish community at the end of the 15th century, this building sat unused for 300 years, until it was turned into a church.

• *Now look out to sea. Head to your left, where you have a view of a larger church and bell tower. These are part of the...*

❺ San Domenico Convent (aka Four Seasons San Domenico Palace)

Taormina has always attracted famous visitors, and this one-time convent has been the backdrop for many Italian movies (and for the HBO series *The White Lotus*). It  also played host to an infamous visitor: Nazi General Field Marshal Albert Kesselring. He took over this complex as the headquarters for the German command of Sicily in World War II. This part of Taormina was heavily bombed during the Allied invasion of the island, and much of the area was rebuilt after the war. Today, the reconstructed convent is a Four Seasons hotel—one of the fanciest in the city (entry possible only with a reservation at one of their bars or restaurants).

• *Walk a few steps downhill, keeping an eye on the left for the street marked by a traffic barrier (Via Strabone). Turn up this street, which runs into a good spot for cheap eats, the recommended Da Cristina pizzeria. Take the stairs up alongside the pizza shop and you'll pop out at...*

❻ Piazza Duomo

In most Italian cities, the main cathedral sits in the heart of town on the central square, but Taormina's is well off-center, closer to the western gate. Since this end of town is newer—built during the Middle Ages as Taormina expanded from its original Greek core—it was considered more desirable.

Look up at the small **cathedral** (Duomo). Although it resembles a tiny Norman *ecclesia munita* (church-fortress), it was built in the 13th century—a century after Norman rule. It incorporates several architectural styles, with a blocky exterior, defensive-looking crenellations along the roofline, a delicate rose window, and a Baroque, marble-capped doorway (rebuilt in the 17th century). Inside, the central nave is dominated by six monolithic pink marble columns, possibly taken from the Greek-Roman Theater.

The **fountain** in the center of the piazza was built under Spanish rule in 1635. This patchwork of statues is a symbol of ancient Tauromenion: the city on the "bull-shaped mountain." The figure on top was originally a minotaur (half-man, half-bull), but the front hooves have been chiseled off. The bust of a crowned woman was added on top. She holds two symbols of power: a globe with a cross in one hand and a scepter in the other. The statue—known by locals as *Centauressa*—is featured on the town's coat-of-arms.

• *Now let's head along Taormina's main street, Corso Umberto I.*

❼ Piazza Duomo to Piazza IX Aprile

Corso Umberto I connects Porta Catania (where we began, behind you) to Porta Messina. This street is what put the city on the map, as it was the only route along the coast in the Middle Ages.

The pink building on the left side of the street (across from the cathedral) is **City Hall.** On the facade, notice three Stars of David. After the bombings of World War II, rubble revealed evidence of the Jewish neighborhood that once thrived nearby. These stars were added as a memorial to the neighborhood that no longer exists.

Stroll along this strip brimming with some of Sicily's most overpriced souvenirs. Keep an eye out for ceramic "head of the Moor" planters, shaped like the head of a woman or Arab man. For the whole story on these popular (if problematic) Sicilian fixtures, see the sidebar.

A few short blocks down on the right, at #190, notice the wide, low **arch** over the doorway. This is a feature of Catalan-Gothic architecture common from the 13th through 15th century, when Spanish nobles living in Taormina brought architects here to replicate the style of their homeland. Watch for more arches in this style farther along this street (including at #176, #174, and #172).

Down a bit and on the left, at #185, is the tiny former church of **San Giovanni dei Cavalieri di Malta,** built in 1533. The large blocks at the base of the church were taken from ancient Greek buildings nearby. Today the building is used as a memorial for the

The Head of the Moor

Across Sicily, you'll find planters on balconies and doorsteps—and in souvenir shops—shaped like two heads: a man with Arab features, and a fair-skinned woman. Several folk tales dating back a thousand years attempt to explain the origin of these heads.

In one version, set during the Arab domination of Sicily, a beautiful young woman was watering plants in her garden. An Arab stranger passed her garden, fell in love, and successfully wooed her. His secret, however, was that he was already married back home. When the woman found out, she devised a plan to ensure he could never leave her: She chopped off his head, put it in her garden, and planted seeds of basil in it. She watered it daily with her tears, and the plant grew lush and vigorous. Passersby thought the unusual pot must be the reason for the beautiful plant, so they created Moor-head planters of their own.

A similar story recounts a love affair between a French noblewoman and an Arab—a forbidden romance in Norman Sicily. After the woman's father discovered their affair, both were decapitated, and their heads were set on the castle walls as a warning.

Origin story aside, the planters became popular only in the past few decades. As tone-deaf as the caricatured faces may seem, Sicilians proudly sell all kinds of souvenirs (including jewelry and clothing) featuring the famous heads.

20th century's world wars. It's occasionally opened by a retired *carabiniere* (police officer).

• *Continue window-shopping along Corso Umberto I until you walk through the tall, stone gate (Porta di Mezzo) at the end of the street. You'll emerge at...*

❽ Piazza IX Aprile

This piazza marks the end of Taormina's medieval westward "expansion." You're now crossing into the historic core of Greek Tauromenion—the city's living room. This piazza is supposedly named for the day in April 1860 when word arrived in Taormina that Giuseppe Garibaldi had landed across the island at Marsala, with the intent to unify Italy. The news of the alleged landing ignited a revolt in town against the island's Bourbon rulers. In reality,

Garibaldi arrived a month later, on May 11—but the locals proudly named the piazza to commemorate their early revolution.

Walk across the broad, checkerboard view terrace and belly up to the railing. Survey the scene with a quick spin-tour, starting by looking out to sea.

First, look southeast (right), toward Greece. The green promontory at the end of the bay is where those first Greek settlers founded Naxos in the eighth century BC. Farther right, on the horizon, Mount Etna smolders, as it has done for eons.

Now bring your eyes back to the piazza. Just to the right of Mount Etna is the faded red **Hotel Metropole,** which was a popular spot for poets and artists visiting during the Grand Tour. To the right of the hotel is the **Porta di Mezzo** gate, topped by the clock tower *(torre dell'orologio).* The original 16th-century clock was replaced by this one in the 1900s.

On the other side of the gate (with tables spilling into the square) is the pricey and venerable **Caffé Wunderbar,** a hit with celebrities following World War II (Elizabeth Taylor, Greta Garbo, Tennessee Williams, etc.). A staircase to the right of Wunderbar leads to a sanctuary high above the city, the Madonna della Rocca (look for its cross poking out above the rocks; see "Sights in Taormina," later). Another once-beloved local hangout, Bar Mocambo, is now **DG Mocambo** (a couple of buildings to the right of Wunderbar); step inside to see a mural showing 1950s and '60s high society at the café—it's still serving drinks, though part of the building now houses a sleek Dolce & Gabbana boutique.

Facing the piazza is the Baroque **Church of St. Joseph** (San Giuseppe), often called the Purgatory Church. Notice its grim imagery: skull and crossbones over the door and at the peak of the facade, and flames at the base of the steeple. This was the town ossuary and the place to come pray your relatives out of purgatory. Attached to the right is a church-run community center for kids (Salesiani Don Bosco).

Across the street to the right of that, jutting out into the square, is another church—though this one has been converted into the town library. Farther to the right, you can see the top edge of the Greek-Roman Theater. The swath of green below is part of the public gardens. And down at sea level, the rocky point is called Capo Taormina.

• *Return to Corso Umberto I and continue in the direction you were headed.*

⑨ Piazza IX Aprile to Naumachie

As you stroll, look up and admire the balconies projecting over the street, adorned with cascading plants and flower baskets, including "head of the Moor" planters (see sidebar). This street ramps up its decorative flair every March and April for the city's annual balcony-decorating competition, when shop owners and residents try to outdo each other with elaborate displays.

The cheerful pink store on the right at #126 is **Daneu**, one of the oldest shops in the city. Signora Adriana's family emigrated from Slovenia to Sicily; they've been here since 1885 selling Sicilian ceramics and Italian linens.

• *Continue a bit farther along Corso Umberto I, then turn right on Via Naumachia and walk down the steps on the left. Look for an arch on the left to find the massive wall, known as Naumachie.*

⑩ Naumachie

This 400-foot-long wall was built by the Romans in the first or second century AD as a supporting structure for a large water reservoir. The word *naumachie* refers to the grand mock naval battles held by the Romans to celebrate their victories at sea. Although this structure would have been large enough to host such reenactments in the reservoir, there's no evidence that any battles were staged here. The wall, uncovered after the WWII bombings of 1943, is now the foundation for modern apartments above. The courtyard before you is covered in basalt slabs and was used as a Roman gymnasium. The 18 niches in the wall were filled with sculptures overlooking the athletes.

• *Retrace your steps back to Corso Umberto I and continue to the right. For a delicious fresh cannoli or other sweet treat, stop in at **Laboratorio Pasticceria Roberto** (#87, on the left).*

⑪ Churches, Ruins, and Palazzo Corvaja

At #42 (on the right) is the facade of the **Church of Santa Maria del Piliere**—or what's left of it. The church was named after Il Piliere, the admiral of Italy for the Knights of Malta. Built around 1530, it still features some original Renaissance details: the portal in pink marble, the wooden door, and the rose window above. It was used as a church until the 1800s but was later repurposed into a cocktail bar and restaurant.

Farther down Corso Umberto I, where the street widens, is the **Church of Santa Caterina of Alexandria,** built in the 1600s on top of a small Greek temple. Inside the church, on the floor on the right side, you can see traces of the Greek ruins underneath. Behind the church (take a left on Via Teatrino Romano) are ruins of a **Roman theater,** or odeum. The architecture  of the odeum is similar to that of the more famous Greek-Roman Theater, but on a smaller scale. This one was covered by a roof and used for more intimate performances.

The large palace to the right of Santa Caterina is the handsome **Palazzo Corvaja.** The Arabs originally built on top of a Roman forum here (10th-11th century) to create a defensive tower (hence the crenellated roof). The Spanish enlarged it during their occupation (15th century), and for a time the Sicilian parliament met here, presided over by the Spanish queen. Today, the palace houses special exhibits.

• *Our walk is finished. You have several options:*

From the little tree- and taxi-lined square adjacent to Palazzo Corvaja, it's a short walk to Taormina's top sight, the **Greek-Roman Theater:** *Go past the trees (on the upper street), following signs to* Teatro Antico *(on Via Teatro Greco); you'll arrive at the theater ticket desk in five minutes.*

The street's lower fork leads steeply downhill on Via Giovanni di Giovanni, past the recommended Bam Bar, to the leafy **public gardens.**

Corso Umberto I itself continues straight on to **Porta Messina.** *Beyond the gate, the street in front of you leads down the hill on the left to Piazza San Pancrazio, a handy transportation hub (see "Getting Around Taormina," earlier). The street immediately to the right is Via Pirandello, which leads to the gondola to Isola Bella.*

Or you could simply find an inviting café—perhaps back at glorious Piazza IX Aprile—and order a drink, then do what the leisure class did in the 19th century: Breathe the perfumed air, marvel at the beauty of Taormina, and reflect on your own Grand Tour around Sicily.

Sights in Taormina

IN AND BELOW TOWN

▲▲Greek-Roman Theater (Teatro Antico)

Sicily is home to many Greek theater ruins, but none has a setting quite like Taormina's: hanging off the edge of a cliff with expansive views of Mount Etna and the Ionian Sea. The original theater was built by the Greeks in the third century BC, but much of what is visible today is a Roman remodel, hence its unusual hybrid appearance and name. (For background on Greek and Roman theaters, see the sidebar on page 406).

Cost and Hours: €14; daily 9:00-19:00, April and early Sept until 18:30, late Sept until 18:00, shorter hours Oct-March; Via Teatro Greco 40, +39 094 251 001.

Crowd-Beating Tips: Cruise crowds flood the theater from roughly 10:00 to 14:00. It's best to arrive at 9:00 to avoid the crowds and the heat—and get the best light for taking photos. If you can't get there when the theater opens, go late in the afternoon, about an hour before it closes. It's not necessary, but tickets are sold online up to a day in advance at aditusculture.com (select "Museums & Parks" and find the Taormina Ancient Theater); with your electronic ticket, go straight to the gate.

Tours: Audioguide-€5, guided tours in English depart about hourly—ask at audioguide desk (€12).

Eating: A € café at the top of the theater offers street food, good pastries, coffee drinks, a cocktail bar, and a few outdoor tables on a view terrace.

Performances: The theater hosts famous musicians and shows throughout the summer. Check the schedule at ticketone.it; search for Teatro Antico di Taormina.

Visiting the Theater: For today's visitors, the most striking feature of this theater is how its **stage** frames the view of Mount Etna. Greek theatergoers, however, didn't see that grand vista: They would have looked out upon a solid backdrop. But the theater's scenic location was chosen deliberately. It perfectly combines the four elements important to ancient Greek thought: The theater sits atop a rocky hill (earth), overlooking the sea (water), with a gentle salty breeze (air), and a smoldering volcano in the distance (fire).

The semicircular rows of **seats** are arranged to give everyone an equally good view of the performers and to enhance the acoustics. Greek plays relied on dialogue to create action and tension, and scenes of violence were performed offstage and conveyed only through sound. So it was important that the audience ("those who hear") didn't miss a thing. Look at the red wall on the top level above the seats: **Niches** in this wall held marble statues and bronze urns, reflecting and amplifying sound.

The Romans had a different idea: The people in the theater were spectators ("those who watch"). The Romans remodeled the theater to suit Roman tastes and accommodate performances with visually captivating action, such as gladiator games. Since the site is bound by rocky cliffs, building a true, round amphitheater was impossible here. Instead, the Romans removed the first 10 rows of seats to create an area large enough for gladiator battles (the large **orchestra** in front of the stage). They also added a wall to protect spectators from the wild beasts used in the games.

Head to the top and stroll along the **walkway** above the last row of seats—passing a portion of reconstructed arcade, with efficient passageways for entering and leaving this huge theater. Gaze out over the Ionian Sea. To the north is a string of beach towns, starting with Letojanni.

Remarkably, the theater is still used today. Every summer, musicians from all over the world perform here, with the spectacular backdrop of the sea, sunset, and Mount Etna.

The small house perched on the hill overlooking the theater hosts a petite bookshop and modest **museum** holding artifacts—stone slabs with Greek inscriptions, a few mosaic floor fragments, and a carved, child-sized marble sarcophagus.

The little **terrace** next to the museum has a café and boasts the best views over town. The lush public gardens (described next) are just below, inviting you for a shady stroll. Scanning the cliffs above Taormina, notice the three skyscraping landmarks along the peaks above town (from left to right): the Sanctuary of Madonna della Rocca, Saracen Castle, and the hill town of Castelmola. Before leaving the theater, head down to the **stage level,** where you can walk around the vast vaulted side wings.

Public Gardens (Giardini della Villa Comunale)

This lovely green area just below the Greek-Roman Theater was originally the private garden of Florence Trevelyan—a 19th-century English noblewoman who also built a villa on Isola Bella. Lady Trevelyan (1852-1907) fell in love with Sicily while on her Grand Tour and never returned to England. Today, her garden and home (see next) are open to the public.

Nicely groomed terraces are sprinkled with statues and fantastical faux-ancient buildings (a uniquely British custom: a gigantic lawn with garden ornaments, called "follies"). Lady Trevelyan was

Greek vs. Roman Theaters

Sicily sparkles with ancient theaters from the Greek and Roman eras—impressive structures perched on hillsides, with dramatic views, harmonious proportions, and perfect acoustics.

Because the Greeks (734-264 BC) and Romans (264 BC-AD 410) were quite different people, their theaters—and the performances they housed—were also distinct. Where the Greeks preferred serious plays in simple surroundings, the Romans favored more spectacle on bigger stages.

The earliest Greek theaters were nestled amid the wonders of nature. The semicircular rows of seats were etched into the natural slope of the hillside, with mountains or seascapes in the distance. The "stage" was little more than a round space on ground level, perhaps with a small building as a backdrop. Sets were minimal. Actors wore stylized masks with wide mouths (like the classic masks of Tragedy and Comedy).

When the Romans came along, they inherited Greek hillside theaters and expanded them. Or they built theaters from scratch—free-standing, colossal, and built within a city. Most of Sicily's theaters are Greek-Roman hybrids.

---

an expert gardener: As on Isola Bella, she used this space to cultivate her collection of exotic plants. Green thumbs will delight in exploring the mishmash of species. As this is the city's main park, you'll find kids playing and families chatting on shady benches, making this an inviting spot for a stroll after a hot hike up to the theater (free, daily 8:00-18:00, possibly later in summer).

▲Isola Bella Beach and Island

Tucked along the craggy shoreline below Taormina is Isola Bella—a "beautiful island" tethered to its mainland beach by a pebbly isthmus just a couple of feet wide. The now-deserted villa on the islet was built by Lady Trevelyan (see previous listing). Even when the villa is closed, the beach and islet at Isola Bella are worth a visit for their natural beauty, a fun gondola ride, and plenty of things to do, including a boat

> The Romans' major innovation was a raised stage backed with a huge multistory facade. This *scaenae frons* was decorated with columns and statues like a palace entrance. It served as an eye-pleasing backdrop, a dressing room, and a framework on which to hang panels of painted scenery. Best of all, it gave actors an expanded playing area. Now characters could mount the stage to speak, pose between the columns, or emerge from doorways or balconies.
>
> Both the Greeks and Romans enjoyed plays where gods, mythological heroes, and everyday mortals mingled, while a chorus commented on the action. Musicians strummed harps and characters broke into song. The more austere Greeks preferred poetic plays that emphasized moral values. ("Why chase Ambition?" asks a Euripides heroine. "Better to praise Equality, which forever joins city to city and friend to friend.") Greek actors stood and delivered with a few stylized gestures. The Romans preferred lowbrow comedies and violent action plays. The sets were glitzier, and actors moved around miming the action.
>
> Besides theaters, there were other venues: odeums (for concerts), stadiums (for races), *ekklesiasterions* (city council meetings), and the largest of all—huge amphitheaters for gladiator and wild animal fights.
>
> Two thousand years on, these Greek and Roman structures still stand. And visitors today can enjoy performances as the ancients did—in the open air, surrounded by nature, in a magical atmosphere where gods and mortals mingle.

ride along the coast, eating at one of the restaurants, or swimming in the crystal-clear waters (bring water shoes, as it's rocky). For general locations, see the "Greater Taormina" map at the beginning of this chapter.

Getting There: Choose from one of the following ways to reach Isola Bella. You can also mix and match (for instance, walking down and taking the gondola back up).

By Gondola: An enjoyable way to reach Isola Bella is to take the gondola (€6 one-way, 5-minute ride departs every 15 minutes, daily 8:00 until late, shorter hours off-season, +39 094 268 1493, taorminaservizipubblici.it). The upper gondola station is just outside Porta Messina, about 200 yards ahead (on the left) on Via Pirandello. The gondola takes you to the Mazzarò station at the bottom. Exiting the station, walk through the parking lot toward the water. From here, Mazzarò beach is down the stairs in front of you, and Isola Bella is a 10-minute walk to the right (head along the main road, Via Nazionale, and continue uphill for about 200 yards; just after rounding the bend, watch for stairs on the left that lead down).

By Bus: You can reach Isola Bella via ASM's *linea verde* bus, Interbus (10/day; see "Getting Around Taormina," earlier), or hop-on, hop off bus (listed earlier, under "Tours in Taormina").

On Foot: It's a pretty 30-minute walk down to Isola Bella from the center of Taormina. Make your way to the belvedere off Via Pirandello (below Taormina) and take the path to the left of the belvedere down to Isola Bella.

Visiting Isola Bella: At Isola Bella, you can explore the villa and grounds on the islet, take a boat ride, lounge and swim, and eat at one of the restaurants.

Upon arriving at the **beach,** you'll find bar-restaurants in either direction. To the right, a narrow, walkable isthmus connects the beach to the tiny **Isola Bella islet and villa** (at certain times of year, you may need to take off your shoes and roll up your pants to cross the isthmus). Isola Bella was bought by Lady Trevelyan in 1890 and left to the city upon her death. You can pay to scramble across its rocky paths, but although the island is an extremely scenic backdrop, there's not much to see on the grounds. Several buildings and pathways are closed, and all that's left of the villa are a few run-down rooms burrowed into the rock (€4; when open, hours are generally daily 9:00 until about an hour before sunset, parconaxostaormina.com).

In nice weather, a **boat tour** is a fine way to see Isola Bella, Capo Taormina, Mazzarò Bay, and other parts of the coast, though you may have better luck with **VIP Sailing Taormina** based in Giardini Naxos as trips out of Isola Bella can be pricier (see "Tours in Taormina," earlier). **Pizzichella,** the restaurant to your left when you reach Isola Bella, offers several boat excursions (call or send WhatsApp message to +39 338 658 1525, escursionipizzichella.com). In high season, it's best to book ahead (you can also ask your hotelier for help).

For **lounging and eating** at Isola Bella, **Mendolia** serves food and drinks and rents sunbeds and umbrellas (to the right as you enter the beach). In high season it's smart to reserve a spot (ask your hotelier to call for you) or arrive before 10:30 (€10-30/person depending on season, includes umbrella, sunbed, shower, and changing room; generally open daily 8:00-19:00 in good weather, +39 094 262 5258). The other eating option at Isola Bella is **Pizzichella,** described above.

Mazzarò Beach

The beach directly across from the gondola station has several restaurants that rent sunbeds and umbrellas, including **Lido Il Delfino** (to the left when you reach the beach; +39 339 898 1289,

Sights in Taormina

lidoildelfino.it) and **Lido La Pigna** (lidolapigna.com). Boat trips are also available at Mazzarò beach, at **Lido Il Delfino** (book ahead).

SIGHTS ABOVE TAORMINA

The hill-topping village of **Castelmola** and the intimate **Sanctuary of Madonna della Rocca** (a church built into the rock) are along the same road above Taormina. Both have stunning settings, are well worth a visit, and are easy to combine into one trip (see below for options and advice). For general locations, see the "Greater Taormina" map at the beginning of this chapter.

Planning Your Time and Getting There: Madonna della Rocca is a steep half-mile above Taormina, and Castelmola is about 1.5 miles up. Plan on spending about 10 minutes at Madonna della Rocca and an hour at Castelmola.

You have several options for reaching these, but you need to be strategic. If driving or taking a bus, it's best to visit Castelmola first: For drivers, the turn-off to Madonna della Rocca is much easier to spot on the way down from Castelmola. And bus riders who start at Castelmola can visit Madonna della Rocca on the way down, then easily walk back to Taormina.

By Bus: The local **Interbus** line stops at Madonna della Rocca and Castelmola (6/day). In peak season, you can also take a **hop-on, hop-off** bus up to both (see "Tours in Taormina," earlier). Madonna della Rocca is also a stop on the *linea verde* of the local **ASM bus** (see "Getting Around Taormina," earlier). By bus, it's about 10 minutes to the sanctuary and 20 minutes to Castelmola.

On Foot: The hike up from Taormina's main square to Madonna della Rocca is steep but very doable: about a half-mile of walking up stairs, with an elevation gain of more than 300 feet. Find the Salita Castello trail (look for *Casteltaormina* signs off Via Circonvallazione, above town) and hike up about 15 minutes.

The trek up to Castelmola is for fit adventurers only—though it's just over 1.5 miles, it's virtually straight up—with an elevation gain of nearly 1,200 feet. If you choose to hike to Castelmola (about 45 minutes), get advice from your hotelier on which path to take, and don't underestimate the Sicilian heat. An easier option (if you have strong knees) is to bus or taxi up to Castelmola and walk back down.

By Taxi: Taxis from Taormina charge a flat fee that includes a round-trip ride to Castelmola, about an hour in the village, and a quick stop at Madonna della Rocca (expect to pay €60-70). For just a one-way trip to Castelmola, it's about €30, but note that it's difficult to find a return taxi from Castelmola (you can either bus or walk back down).

By Car: Driving up to Castelmola is simple and lets you be flexible with your timing. To reach the village, leave Taormina just past the Porta Catania parking garage and follow signs to *Castelmola* (10-minute drive). As you enter Castelmola, look for the big pay-and-display garage below the town center (easiest option; about 75 steps up to the center). If you drive past this lot, there's a smaller pay lot (with fewer steps to climb) along the main road under the overpass on the right (note that you will drive past a ZTL limited traffic zone warning sign, but it's OK to park in this lot).

If stopping at Madonna della Rocca on your way back down from Castelmola, here's what to look for: About five minutes down the hill, just past Villa Ducale (on your right), slow down and keep a sharp eye out for a road that splits off to the left. Take this street (Via Madonna della Rocca); the sanctuary is at the end of the street (park along here anywhere you can).

▲Castelmola

High on the rock above Taormina, the small, remarkably scenic village of Castelmola offers commanding views of Mount Etna, Taormina, and the Ionian Sea. With twisting alleyways and medieval charm, Castelmola is understandably touristy, but it's worth a visit to wander the medieval streets, try the local almond wine, and experience that top-of-the-world feeling.

During Greek and Roman times, Castelmola may have served as the higher of two acropolises for the ancient city of Tauromenion (the other was La Rocca del Tauro, where Saracen Castle now stands). Throughout the centuries, Castelmola was settled by various populations, including the Normans, who built the castle that still stands in ruins on top of the hill at the center of the village. Attacks by the Saracens in the 10th century destroyed the village, except parts of the castle.

Visiting the Village: The main square is elegant **Piazza Sant'Antonio,** laden with black-and-white basalt mosaics. With your back to the sea, find the stone archway to the right, above the wall. This is the **Porta di Mola,** the original entrance to the town; the keystone features an engraving of the castle with three towers.

Directly uphill from the square are the ruins of the **Norman castle** (head up the stairs to the right, following *Castello* signs). Little is known about the castle. It's believed that it dates from Roman times, but all that remains are the Norman walls. In the 14th century, the castle was enclosed and used for defensive purposes and as a prison.

Sights in Taormina

Return to the main square. Just downhill from the square is the small **Church of San Giorgio** (with your back to the sea, head left, down the stairs). A tight spiral staircase at the back of the church leads down to a terrace with more views over Taormina (follow *Belvedere* signs). From this point, you have an aerial view of three landmarks: from left to right, you can see the Greek-Roman Theater in Taormina, Saracen Castle, and Madonna della Rocca (white cross).

Back on Piazza Sant'Antonio, **Antico Caffè San Giorgio** is historic for being the first bar here to introduce almond wine *(vino alla mandorla)*, a local specialty. The heart of the village is straight ahead, along Via Alcide de Gasperi. Enjoy exploring the shop- and café-lined streets and strolling past tall, skinny houses with petite balconies. From Via Alcide de Gasperi, take the first left (Via Papa Pio IX), then a right to reach **Bar Turrisi**—a town institution famous for its phallic-themed decor. If the decoration is too much for you, for heaven's sake, don't flip through the guestbook. While the erotic furnishings may be a gimmick, locals claim there's a story behind them. Supposedly, Castelmola needed 1,000 residents in order to gain independence from Taormina. Determined to achieve their goal, the locals got "busy," and within a short time, 1,000 Castelmolans declared their autonomy. As the story goes, these phallic symbols are a tribute to Castelmola's civic-minded determination. Though the bar is as touristy and overpriced as you'd expect, the place is entertaining, and several balconies spread over four levels promise great views. Try some almond wine, served, of course, in phallic shot glasses.

Just below Bar Turrisi is inviting **Piazza Chiesa Madre** (facing the Church of San Nicolò di Bari), ringed by pleasant outdoor eateries.

▲Sanctuary of Madonna della Rocca

Perched on a peak above Taormina is this little 17th-century church carved into the rock. The interior is rustic and serene, with the stony roof of the grotto forming the low ceiling of the church. A statue of the Madonna sits next to the altar. Outside, the terrace offers good views of the Greek-Roman Theater. Next to the church is an abandoned monastery, and looming above it is the large concrete cross (the one you see from afar), built in 1930 during a mission by the Redemptorist Fathers.

Cost and Hours: Free, hours vary but generally daily 8:00-18:00, shorter hours off-season, +39 338 803 3448. See "Planning Your Time and Getting There," earlier.

Nearby: Hovering just above the sanctuary, and accessible via a staircase, is **Saracen Castle** (Castello Saraceno or Castello di Taormina). This was likely the site of the acropolis of ancient Tauromenion, though much of what you see today was built in the 10th century under Arab rule (hence the castle's name), with later Norman modifications. While the hike offers impressive views and a glimpse of history, the castle itself is lackluster. Start at the Madonna della Rocca church on Via Madonna della Rocca and follow the staircase up Mount Tauro for about 30–45 minutes. The rocky path requires sturdy shoes (€10, daily 10:00-19:00).

SIGHTS ALONG THE COAST

Giardini Naxos

The little coastal town of Giardini Naxos, about four miles south of Taormina, stretches along a **sandy beach** popular with sun worshippers. But this area is also an important **archaeological site.** The very first Greek settlers in Sicily landed here and colonized what they called Naxos in 734 BC. The city was destroyed 300 years later by neighboring Syracuse. Survivors pursued a safer location, establishing Taormina on the cliff (and displacing the  indigenous Sicels). This former settlement has only a few scattered ruins, but the small **museum** and park around it, with lovely views of Etna, make Giardini Naxos a peaceful getaway from the tourist crowds (museum and archaeological area-€6, daily 9:00-19:00, shorter hours off-season, Lungomare Schiso, +39 094 251 001, parconaxostaormina.com).

Getting There: Take the local Interbus line (direction: Catania/CTA airport, confirm your stop at the ticket desk; see "Getting Around Taormina," earlier). The hop-on, hop-off buses listed earlier also stop in Giardini Naxos.

Other Beaches Outside Taormina

For beaches beyond Isola Bella and Giardini Naxos, head for **Mazzeo** or **Letojanni,** about a 15-minute drive north of Taormina on SS-114. You can also take ASM's *linea blu/beachbus* or Interbus (see "Getting Around Taormina," earlier). Some of the best beaches are private; you'll pay about €25 for a lounge chair and umbrella.

DAY TRIPS FROM TAORMINA

You can easily day-trip to Mount Etna from Taormina, especially to the north slope wine country (see the Mount Etna chapter for details). Another option is to sign up for an excursion with SAT, which offers tours to destinations across the island (see "Tours in Taormina," earlier). Or consider the following.

Alcantara Gorge Botanical and Geological Park (Gole Alcantara Parco Botanico e Geologico)

A one-hour drive inland from Taormina, this place is popular for hiking and swimming in a flooded volcanic gorge with peculiar rock formations. Formed by lava flows, the gorge cuts between Mount Etna and the Nebrodi Mountains. Steep basalt rock formations on either side (as high as 160 feet) swoop and curve with the Alcantara River, creating a stunning natural landscape.

There are various ticket options at the gorge. A walking ticket gives you access to several hiking trails, including a path above the gorge (about a mile each way, 45 minutes total). The most popular option is to hike through the gorge itself, partly submerged (depending on water levels, you can hike about a half-mile into the gorge; ticket includes the elevator ride down to the river). Or you can pay for a guided river excursion, where you put on hip waders and head a little deeper into the gorge (only possible in summer). A cheesy theme-park picnic area surrounds the gorge (for park details, visit goleaIcantara.it).

To get to the gorge from Taormina, drive west on SS-185. It's also accessible via hop-on, hop-off bus (see "Tours in Taormina," earlier).

Godfather Filming Locations

Touristy **Savoca** and **Forza d'Agrò** were major filming locations for the *Godfather* series, standing in for the town of "Corleone" on screen. The towns are a 30-40-minute drive north of Taormina on SS-114. You can also reach the towns via the hop-on, hop-off buses described earlier under "Tours in Taormina."

Aeolian Islands

This stunning little archipelago just off Sicily's northeast coast is made up of seven volcanic islets, each with its own personality. It's a long, packed day trip from Taormina, but doable. For the most efficient visit, book an excursion package or a tour with a local guide (see "Tours in Taormina," earlier for options). For more about the islands, see the sidebar on page 139.

Sleeping in Taormina

Unlike many places in Sicily where prices dip in the off-season, Taormina's setting and cachet make it expensive year-round, especially in summer. While prices are high, Taormina serves up a blend of sultry beach days, luxe nightlife, and energetic side-tripping that's especially attractive to those on a modern-day Grand Tour with the budget to match. Yet a few moderately priced choices exist, too.

All of my recommended places have air-conditioning and, unless otherwise noted, an elevator (or it's not necessary).

€€€€ **The Ashbee** fills a historic, cliffside mansion just outside Porta Messina. The property has an air of exclusivity, with jasmine-scented gardens, a grand circular driveway, a good restaurant, and a pool with a panoramic view that seems a world away from busy Taormina. The 24 quiet rooms are spacious and come with all the extra touches, making this place perfect for a honeymoon or elegant splurge (pay parking, closed Nov-March, Via San Pancrazio 46, +39 094 223 537, theashbeehotel.com, info@theashbeehotel.com).

€€€€ **La Malandrina** has five upscale apartments with kitchenettes, lots of space, and fun pops of color (some have terraces with amazing views). They also have two suites with private terraces. The location is just above town, so the neighborhood feels quiet (family apartments, no elevator, valet parking, Via Dionisio I 2E, +39 094 223 310, lamalandrina.it, info@lamalandrina.it).

€€€€ **Hotel Villa Belvedere** is a large, old-time resort clinging to the edge of Taormina, next to the public gardens. The 43 rooms are elegant and comfortable, but the star of the property is the garden and swimming pool, where you can have lunch with glorious sea views. They also offer suites and apartments (hotel closed in winter, Via Bagnoli Croce 79, +39 094 223 791, villabelvedere.it, info@villabelvedere.it, Valerio).

€€€ **Hotel Continental** is a big, well-run hotel with friendly, professional staff and a terrace that is *indimenticabile* (unforgettable). It's conveniently located at the top of the steps above Piazza Duomo and Porta Catania. The 34 rooms are tidy and modern, most with small patios and some with views. The grand terrace—a delight both early and late—lets you eat breakfast or have drinks while watching Etna steam (RS%—use code "RICK-

STEVES," Via Dionisio I 2a, +39 094 223 805, continentaltaormina. com, info@continentaltaormina.com, Stefano).

€€€ **Hotel Casa Adele** is a thoughtfully run family place just outside Porta Catania. About half of the nine rooms have balconies with town views; the rest around back are bigger and quieter but don't have balconies or views. The beautiful rooftop terrace, with sunbeds and a shower, is a fine place to enjoy cocktails from the hotel's small bar (family rooms, includes cooked breakfast with buffet, pay garage parking, Viale Apollo Arcageta 16, +39 094 238 8739, hotelcasadele.com, info@hotelcasadele.com).

€€€ **Hotel Bel Soggiorno** has a stunning location on the side of a hill below the public gardens, about a 15-minute uphill walk to the center. There are 34 rooms with Old World furnishings—most have balconies or terraces with brilliant sea views—along with a large common lounge and nice sun room (family rooms, elevator serves two of the three floors, pay parking on property, Via Luigi Pirandello 60, +39 094 223 342, belsoggiorno.com, info@belsoggiorno.com, Carlo).

€€ **Casa Turrisi** has five good-value, chic, and modern rooms with fun painted-ceramic bathroom fixtures shoehorned into an old house. The location, down a charming street below the tourist action at the Greek-Roman Theater, is central but has a calm neighborhood feel (family rooms, terrace, no elevator, Via Giovanni di Giovanni 43, +39 094 262 6172, casaturrisi.com, casaturrisi@gmail.com, Eleonora).

Short Term Rentals: A private apartment can be a more practical, less expensive alternative in Taormina, especially for families or in high season. You'll find many choices through online booking sites. A couple of good options include €€ **Domus Enea,** a modern one-bedroom, one-bathroom place that can sleep up to four (booking.com/hotel/it/domus-enea.it, domuseneataormina@gmail.com), and €€ **Taormina House,** a vertical apartment for two people, with one bedroom and a roof terrace (taorminahouse.com, bookingtaorminahouse@gmail.com). Both offer an RS% discount and breakfast at the nearby Hotel Continental (request by emailing directly).

Eating in Taormina

For the following places, assume reservations are smart on weekends year-round and on any evening in high season. Some of these restaurants may close in the winter.

€€€€ **Osteria RossoDiVino** specializes in fresh-as-can-be fish. They work with a local fish shop in Naxos to offer the latest catch, presented on a tray for you to make your choice. Indoor and outdoor tables are in a quiet setting near Porta Catania. It's super

Taormina Hotels & Restaurants

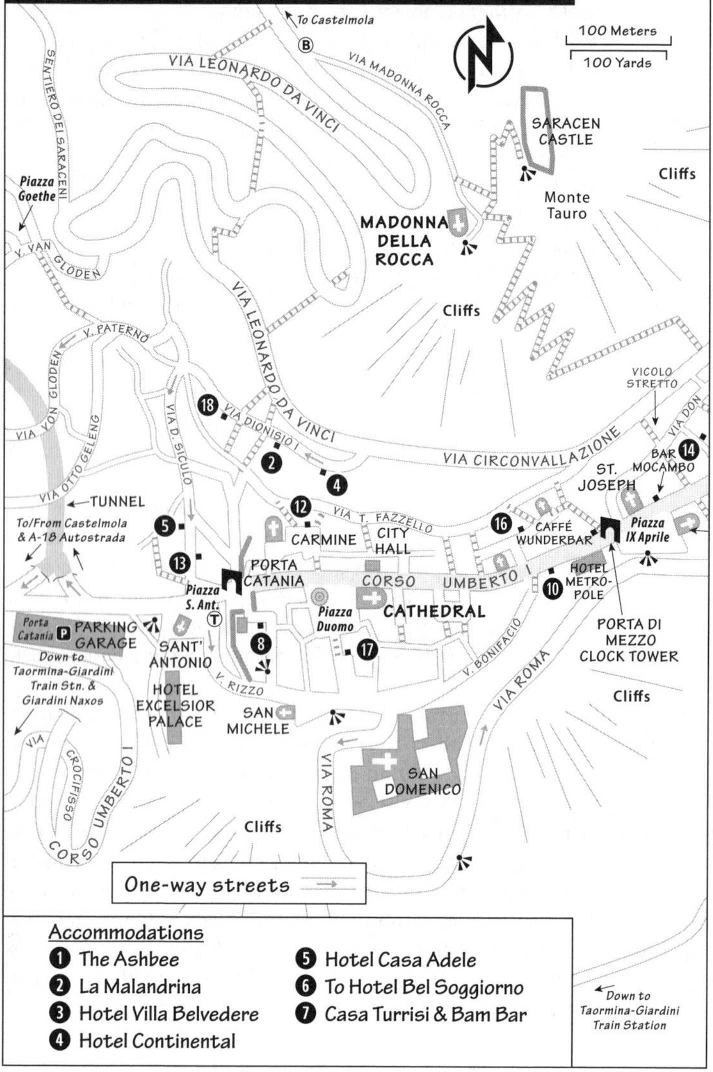

Accommodations
1. The Ashbee
2. La Malandrina
3. Hotel Villa Belvedere
4. Hotel Continental
5. Hotel Casa Adele
6. To Hotel Bel Soggiorno
7. Casa Turrisi & Bam Bar

pricey and worth it (closed Tue, Vico de Spuches 8, +39 094 262 8653).

€€€ Rosmarino, a stylish spot just off the tourist track, serves Sicilian classics with an international twist. Highlights include *pasta con polpette* (topped with tender beef meatballs) and a clever tuna carbonara. The small dining room and leafy terrace offer a relaxed, intimate setting (closed Thu, via Bagnoli Croci 88/B, +39 335 647 2883, rosmarinotaormina.com, Rita).

Eating in Taormina

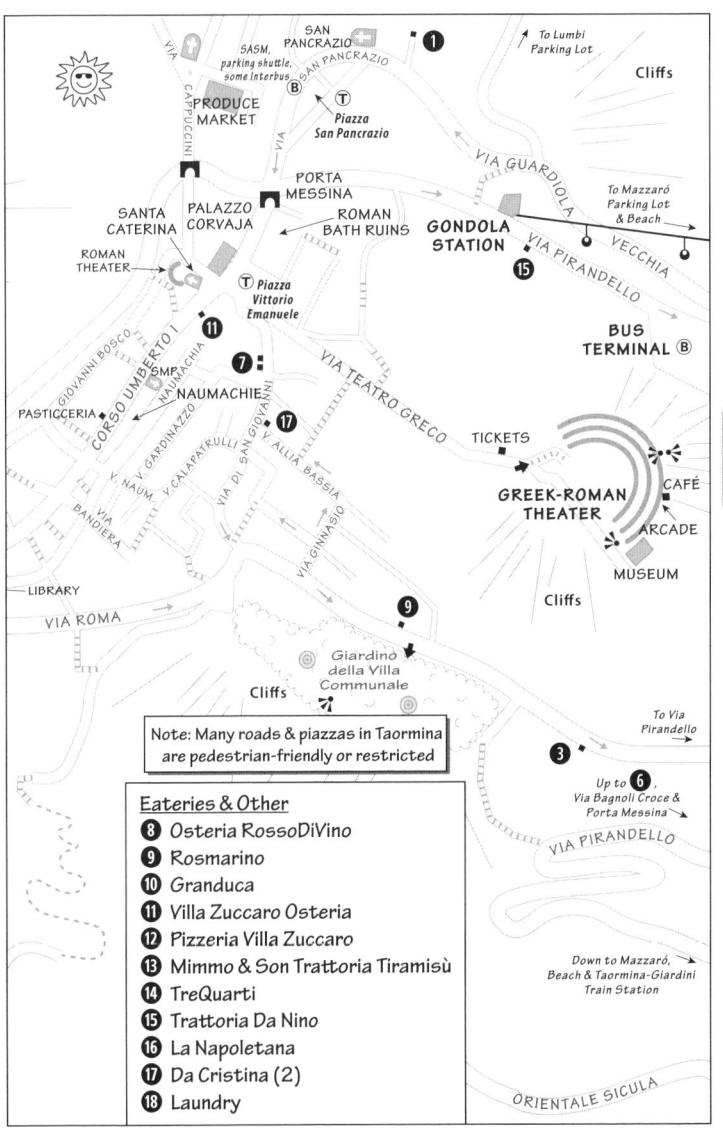

Eateries & Other
8. Osteria RossoDiVino
9. Rosmarino
10. Granduca
11. Villa Zuccaro Osteria
12. Pizzeria Villa Zuccaro
13. Mimmo & Son Trattoria Tiramisù
14. TreQuarti
15. Trattoria Da Nino
16. La Napoletana
17. Da Cristina (2)
18. Laundry

€€€ **Granduca** feels a little touristy but has a good menu with a variety of pizzas, pastas, and meat/seafood dishes. The food takes a backseat to the stunning panoramic views from the dining room balcony—some of the best in the city (daily, Corso Umberto I 172, +39 094 224 983, ristorantegranduca.it).

€€€ **Villa Zuccaro Osteria** is a welcoming restaurant specializing in quality, fresh ingredients. You can dine in the simple modern interior or out on one of their two terraces, one of which has views over the ancient Roman wall, the Naumachie (daily, Corso Umberto I 38, +39 094 261 5056, villazuccaro.com).

€€ **Pizzeria Villa Zuccaro** is the place for a quality Sicilian-style pizza in a peaceful garden setting. They fire up a crust that's crisp on the outside and soft on the inside. The pizza variety is huge, and the sauce and topping combos are beyond anything you've seen at your hometown pizzeria (daily, closed for lunch on Wed, Piazza Carmine 5, +39 094 262 8018).

€€€ **Mimmo & Son Trattoria Tiramisù** serves a nice Sicilian seafood menu in a cozy space with friendly service. Close to Porta Catania, this spot has a few outdoor tables (closed Mon, Viale Apollo Arcageta 9, +39 094 238 8741, trattoriatiramisu.it).

€€€ **TreQuarti** is a family-run restaurant serving delicious contemporary Sicilian food a few steps from Corso Umberto I. Their three-course tasting *menu*s (several choices, about €30) are a good way to sample the fare (closed Tue and in winter, Salita Guglielmo Melivia 7, +39 351 287 4780).

€€€ **Trattoria Da Nino,** a local favorite for over 50 years, is a family-run trattoria serving authentic dishes in a casual yet charming setting. Their *crudi di pesce*—a selection of fresh, raw seafood—makes a standout start. Reservations are smart, especially in high season (daily, Via Luigi Pirandello 37/A, +39 094 221 265, trattoriadaninotaormina.com, Gianluca).

€€ **La Napoletana** offers a simple menu of salads and Naples-style pizza. They cook their pies quickly at a high temperature in a state-of-the-art pizza oven, and the result is a soft, light, and chewy crust. The outdoor seating fills a street just off Corso Umberto I and seems far from the crowds (daily, Piazza Varò, +39 094 262 8049).

€ **Da Cristina,** below Piazza Duomo, serves quality takeaway at low prices. Choose from a dozen kinds of rustic pizza by the slice, *schiacciate* (stuffed pizza), or piping hot *arancini* deep fried on the spot. Cristina's small cafeteria next door offers more selection and basement seating (closed Wed, Via Strabone 2, +39 094 221 171). A second location, serving a similar selection plus a few heartier dishes, is near the Greek-Roman Theater (closed Thu, Via Giovanni di Giovanni 28).

€ **Bam Bar,** next to the recommended Casa Turrisi hotel, specializes in *granite* and serves a dozen seasonal flavors on a picturesque street near the Greek-Roman Theater. Try layering two *granita* flavors, top them with *panna* (whipped cream), and eat with a warm brioche bun. *Attenzione! Limone*

does not go with *cioccolata* (long hours, closed Mon, Via Giovanni di Giovanni 45, +39 094 224 355).

Taormina Connections

BY PUBLIC TRANSPORTATION

From Taormina by Train to: Palermo (hourly, 4.5 hours, change in Messina), **Cefalù** (hourly, 3-4 hours, change in Messina), **Catania** (1-2/hour, 1 hour), **Siracusa** (7/day direct, 2 hours, more with change in Catania).

From Taormina by Bus: Intercity buses are operated by Interbus/Etna Trasporti and usually depart from the bus terminal on Via Pirandello (a few routes depart from nearby Piazza San Pancrazio—confirm when you buy your ticket). Connections include **Messina** (3/day, 1-1.75 hours), **Catania**'s airport and downtown (1-2/hour, 70 minutes), and **Siracusa** (1/day direct, 2.5 hours, more with change in Catania). To get to Ragusa, Palermo, and elsewhere, you'll go to Catania and transfer (sometimes to a different bus line). Bus info: interbus.it.

ROUTE TIPS FOR DRIVERS

Taormina sits along the E-45 expressway, which follows Sicily's east coast between Catania and Messina.

If you're heading to **Cefalù** (about 3 hours from Taormina), you could zip down to Catania on E-45, then cut through the middle of Sicily on the A-19 expressway. But it's approximately the same amount of time, and far more scenic, to take the northern coastal route: Head north on E-45 toward Messina—with great views over the Strait of Messina. As you pass above Messina, carry on toward Palermo, staying on E-90 past Milazzo and along the north coast—with views of the Aeolian Islands just offshore. Approaching Cefalù, you'll exit at Pollina-Castelbuono, wind down to the seashore, and carry on the rest of the way into town. (Coming from this direction, using the Cefalù exit—farther along—will overshoot your goal and waste some time.)

SICILIAN HISTORY

Three Millennia at a Glance

HISTORY IN A HURRY

Sicily's history is about settlers and invaders (see map). Three thousand years ago, three tribes lived on the island: the Sicels, the Sicani, and the Elymi. They were joined by Carthaginians (Phoenicians) and, starting around 734 BC, Greeks. Later, the Romans invaded and defeated the Greeks, and eventually the Carthaginians, establishing Roman rule until the fall of the empire.

So-called "barbarians" ruled for a short period, replaced by the Byzantines. The Arabs arrived and modernized the island, bringing an age of prosperity. In 1060, the Normans conquered the island, creating a peaceful golden age. After the Norman line ended, the island was ruled by foreign powers from afar—the German Hohenstaufen dynasty, then the French Angevins, then a centuries-long succession of Spanish rulers. In 1860, Sicily was folded into the new Italian state, but the lack of a stable government gave rise to the Mafia, a problem that persisted through fascism, worsened with World War II, and marked much of the 20th century. The 21st century has seen Sicily in renewal, with cities remodeled and cleaned up, better industry and infrastructure, and a global outlook that welcomes visitors.

PREHISTORIC SICILY (2000-750 BC)

Ancient Sicily had two native peoples: in the east, the Sicels (or Siculi, for whom the island is named), and in the west, the Sicani (or Sikans). Around 1200 BC, a new group, the Elymi (or Elymians), arrived from Asia Minor (claiming to have escaped from Troy) and settled in the west, scattered on a few fortified hilltop

Sicilian History 421

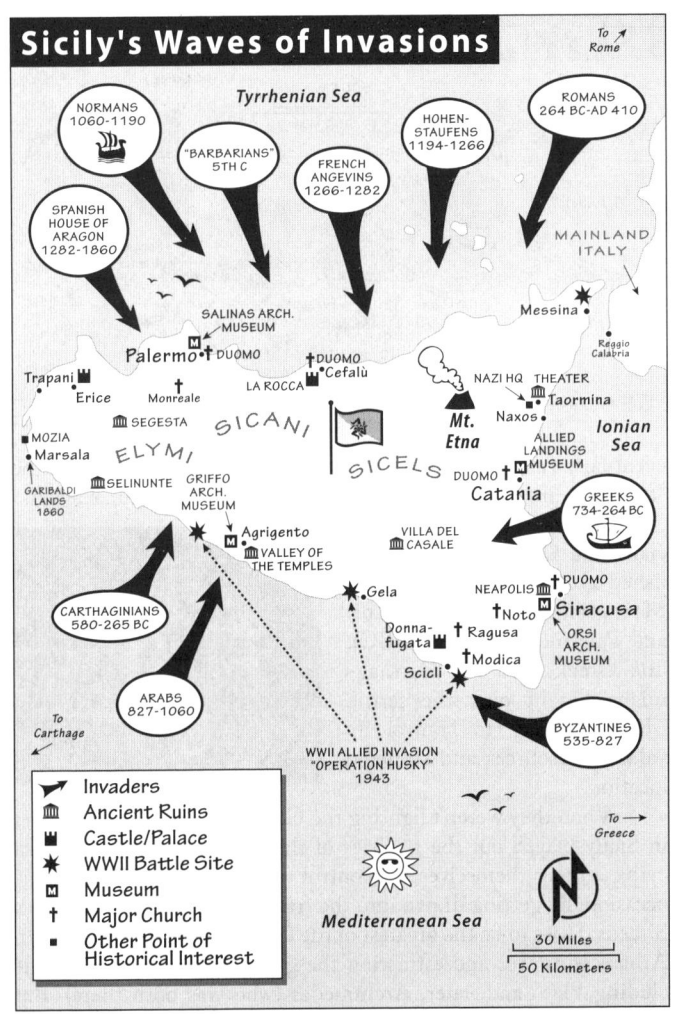

towns. Mycenaeans from Greece also visited the island and traded with the native people.

ANCIENT COLONIES (734-264 BC)

In their ancient version of "westward expansion," the Greeks began to seek more land and resources. They sent settlers to establish colonies in fertile Sicily—first arriving on the eastern shore, where they established Naxos (734 BC), near present-day Taormina. Collectively, the Greek cities in Sicily were part of Magna Graecia, or "Great Greece" (the southern Italian colonies of Greece) and were

eventually ruled as city-states by what the locals considered to be "tyrants"—illegitimate rulers who seized power in popular revolts.

Meanwhile, the Phoenicians and Carthaginians established colonies in the west, at Mozia (south of today's Trapani) and Palermo (around 800 BC). The Greeks and the Carthaginians fought over the fertile island, looking to control its valuable resources and strategic location.

When they weren't fighting the Carthaginians, Greek settlers in Sicily played out the rivalries of their home city-states—jockeying among themselves for control of the island—with Athens occasionally getting drawn into the fray. Ancient Syracuse (today's Siracusa) rose to be the greatest of the Greek cities, surpassing even Athens in power and attracting the great minds of the age—including Plato and, later, Archimedes (who was born there). But soon, a third power emerging in the Mediterranean set its eyes on Sicily: the Romans.

For more on Sicily's Greek age, see the sidebar on page 303; for the Carthaginians, see page 188.

Sights
- Archaeological Park and Museum of Giardini Naxos (near Taormina)
- Mozia Island (near Trapani)
- Salinas Regional Archaeological Museum (Palermo)
- Segesta
- Selinunte

Sicilian History

- Valley of the Temples Archaeological Park and Pietro Griffo Archaeological Museum (Agrigento)
- Neapolis Archaeological Park and Paolo Orsi Archaeological Museum (Siracusa)
- Cathedral of Siracusa

ROMAN DOMINATION (264 BC-AD 410)

The expanding Roman Republic eventually turned its attention to Sicily, eyeing its strategic location: Conquering Sicily would cripple the Romans' greatest rival—Carthage—and help them gain control of the Mediterranean. After three long wars where they defeated great Carthaginian generals (such as Hannibal) and conquered powerful Greek colonies (such as Syracuse), Sicily became a Roman province. And Rome became master of the Mediterranean. They called it *Mare Nostrum* ("Our Sea"); soon, booty and slaves from vanquished lands poured into the Republic.

The Romans bickered among themselves over their slice of the pie, pitting wealthy landowners (the ruling Senate) against the working class (plebs) and the rebellious slaves (Spartacus' revolt, 73 BC). In the chaos, charismatic generals like Julius Caesar, who could provide wealth and security, tried to seize power as dictators. The republic fell; in its place an empire was formed, with the new emperor, Augustus, establishing a period of peace (Pax Romana) and expansion.

Though Rome conquered Greece, it adopted Greek culture. From hairstyles to statues to temples to the evening's entertainment, Rome was forever "Hellenized," becoming the curators of Greek culture, passing it down to future generations. In some cases, Greek structures in Sicily were retrofitted to Roman specifications, best embodied by the Greek-Roman Theater in Taormina.

In Sicily, large estates were formed and given to Roman patricians. Few survive today, but the Villa Romana del Casale is a particularly well-preserved example. Sicily's forests were sacrificed to supply timber for the Roman fleet, and the island became the breadbasket of the empire, producing grain and little else. The Sicilians were left to farm the land, take on Roman ways, and pay taxes.

Before Christianity was legalized (AD 313), Christians in Sicily were persecuted. This produced two important Christian mar-

> ## Sicily Almanac
>
> **Official Name:** Regione Sicilia, but locals just call it "Sicilia."
>
> **Population:** About 4.8 million.
>
> **Latitude and Longitude:** 37° N and 14° E (latitude similar to San Francisco).
>
> **Area:** 9,927 square miles, including the three archipelagos of Aeolian Islands, Egadi Islands, and Pelagie Islands, and other minor islands.
>
> **Geography:** Sicily is shaped like an arrowhead, with its tip pointing west, toward Spain. About 150 miles from east to west, with more than 700 miles of coastline, Sicily is the biggest island in the Mediterranean. The terrain is generally mountainous or hilly; the mountains along the north coast are a continuation of Italy's Apennine Mountains. The highest point is Mount Etna (11,165 feet)—the tallest active volcano in Europe. Sicily's central location—just 90 miles from the African coast and two miles from the Italian peninsula—has long made it a natural stepping stone between Africa and Europe.
>
> **Biggest Cities:** Palermo (the capital, 680,000), Catania (315,000), and Messina (220,000).
>
> **Climate:** Sicily has a Mediterranean climate, with mild, wet winters and hot, dry summers. Sicily is also affected by sea currents from nearby Africa and often receives strong Saharan winds in summer. In winter, many interior mountain ranges are snowcapped.
>
> **Language:** The official language is Italian, but most people on

tyrs who are still highly revered today: St. Agatha of Catania (see page 343) and St. Lucia of Siracusa (see page 306).

Sights
- Villa Romana del Casale
- Greek-Roman Theater (Taormina)
- Roman Theater and Odeum (Catania)
- Catacombs of San Giovanni and Church of San Filippo Apostolo (Siracusa)

"BARBARIANS" AND BYZANTINES (AD 410-827)

The Visigoths sacked Rome in AD 410—but by then the Roman Empire was already effectively over. Constantine the Great had transferred the center of his new "Byzantine" empire to Constantinople in AD 330. As Rome fell, waves of "barbarian" tribes poured into Italy, and the Vandals took over Sicily. Byzantine Emperor Justinian sent his best general, Belisarius, to reassert control over the island. Belisarius succeeded, and the Byzantines ruled the is-the island also speak Sicilian (especially among close friends and family). Although it is a Romance language, Sicilian also draws heavily from Greek and Arabic; the differences are great enough that Italian and Sicilian are not mutually intelligible.

Economy: Sicily's gross domestic product is $110 billion; the GDP per capita is $22,000. About 68 percent of the economy consists of service jobs (especially tourism), 8 percent is industry (textiles, construction, chemicals), and 4 percent is agriculture (fruit, vegetables, olives, wine, fishing). The island has about 860 miles of train lines (mostly government-run and not all connected) and over 450 miles of expressway (autostrada).

Government: Sicily is the largest of Italy's 20 regions, and one of five with semi-autonomous powers, including its own parliament and president. Sicily itself is divided into nine provinces (Palermo, Trapani, Agrigento, Caltanissetta, Enna, Ragusa, Siracusa, Catania, and Messina) and 390 "communes," each with a community council and mayor.

Flag: Diagonally divided in red and yellow with the Trinacria symbol in the center (head of a Medusa with three dislocated legs and three ears of wheat).

Notable Sicilians: Archimedes, Empedocles, St. Lucia, painter Antonello da Messina, composer Vincenzo Bellini, playwright Luigi Pirandello, painter Renato Guttuso, writer Andrea Camilleri, Italian-American filmmakers Frank Capra and Martin Scorsese—and fictional gangster Vito Corleone.

---

land for almost 300 years (535-827), with one emperor even choosing to move his capital to Siracusa.

ARAB SICILY (827-1060)

As Islam expanded beyond the Middle East, Arabs (sometimes referred to as "Moors") spread throughout North Africa and began trading with Sicily. From nearby Tunisia they conquered the town of Mazara in 827, then Palermo, with its excellent port, and later established a capital there. Arab rule spread across the island, eventually bringing the Greek-Byzantine capital of Siracusa under its control. The Arabs brought mathematics, engineering, and advances in agriculture to the island. Palermo was laid out and developed as the center of the emirate. For more on this period, see the sidebar on page 53.

While little architecture survives from this period, Arab culture still permeates Sicily—perhaps most noticeably in its cuisine (with its sweet-and-sour *agrodolce* sauces) and in its thriving markets, where vendors still advertise their wares with an almost Arabic-sounding cadence. Arab design and architectural flourishes

Typical Church Architecture

History comes to life when you visit a centuries-old church. Even if you wouldn't know your apse from a hole in the ground, learning a few simple terms will enrich your experience. Note that not every church has every feature, and a "cathedral" isn't a type of church architecture, but rather a designation for a church that's a governing center for a local bishop.

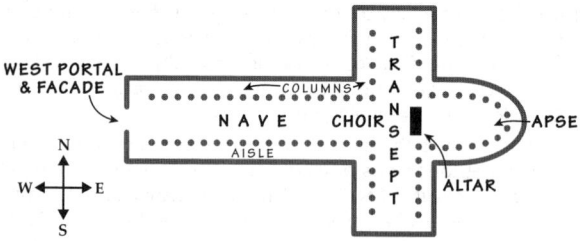

Aisles: Long, generally low-ceilinged arcades that flank the nave

Altar: Raised area with a ceremonial table (often adorned with candles or a crucifix), where the priest prepares and serves the bread and wine for Communion

Apse: Space behind the altar, sometimes bordered with small chapels

Barrel Vault: Continuous round-arched ceiling that resembles an extended upside-down U

Choir: Intimate space reserved for clergy and choir, located within the nave near the high altar and often screened off

Cloister: Covered hallways bordering a square or rectangular open-air courtyard, traditionally where monks and nuns got fresh air

Facade: Exterior of the church's main (west) entrance, usually highly decorated

Groin Vault: Arched ceiling formed where two equal barrel vaults meet at right angles

Narthex: Area (portico or foyer) between the main entry and the nave

Nave: Long central section of the church (running west to east, from the entrance to the altar) where the congregation sits or stands during the service

Transept: One of the two parts forming the "arms" of the cross in a traditional cross-shaped floor plan; runs north-south, perpendicularly crossing the east-west nave

West Portal: Main entry to the church (on the west end, opposite the main altar)

were also highly influential in Sicily's later Norman period, while major Palermo landmarks like the cathedral and the Norman Palace were built by skilled Arab craftsmen.

Sights
- Ballarò and Capo markets (Palermo)
- Fish market in Catania
- Palermo Cathedral
- Norman Palace (Palermo)
- Kolymbethra Gardens (Agrigento)

THE NORMAN KINGDOM OF SICILY (1060-1198)

Normans—Vikings (Norsemen) who settled in France—went on expeditions to England (Battle of Hastings, 1066) and to southern Italy and Sicily. By 1090, they dominated most of the island and conquered it from Arab rule (with the support of the pope). Under the first Norman king, Roger II, the island was united. A policy of religious tolerance allowed the kingdom to flourish, taking advantage of each group's skills to create a fusion of styles in art and architecture. Roger's nephew (the last Norman king, William II) turned Sicily into the most prosperous, important kingdom of Europe, building Monreale Cathedral—but he died young and without an heir. Roger's daughter, Constance I, was the natural successor, but Sicilians were suspicious of her marriage to foreigner Henry VI of Swabia, part of the Hohenstaufen dynasty and heir to the Holy Roman Empire. Nevertheless, after a brief period of instability and rule by a hostile cousin, Constance and Henry VI became queen and king of Sicily.

Sights
- Monreale Cathedral (outside Palermo)
- Church of La Martorana (Palermo)
- Cefalù Cathedral
- Palatine Chapel and Norman Palace (Palermo)
- Catania Cathedral

GERMAN HOHENSTAUFEN DYNASTY AND FRENCH ANGEVINS (1198-1282)

Following the deaths of both Henry VI (in 1197) and Constance (in 1198), Sicily passed to Constance and Henry's son, the young Swabian duke Frederick II, who was half German and half Sicilian-Norman. The ambitious new ruler united his kingdoms—becoming Holy Roman Emperor (1220) and adding Jerusalem, to boot (1225). He based his court mostly in Sicily and southern Italy; the people loved him because he grew up in Palermo and spoke fluent Sicilian and Arabic (and five other languages). His fans called

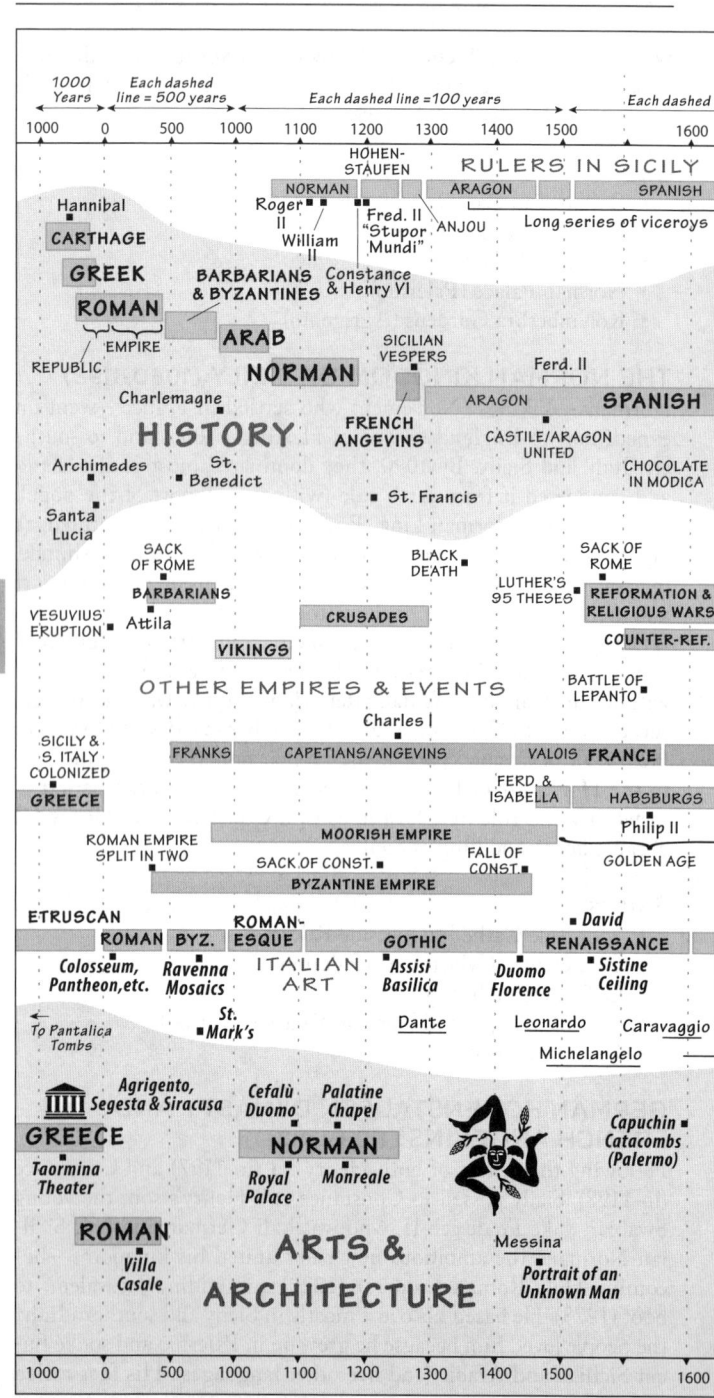

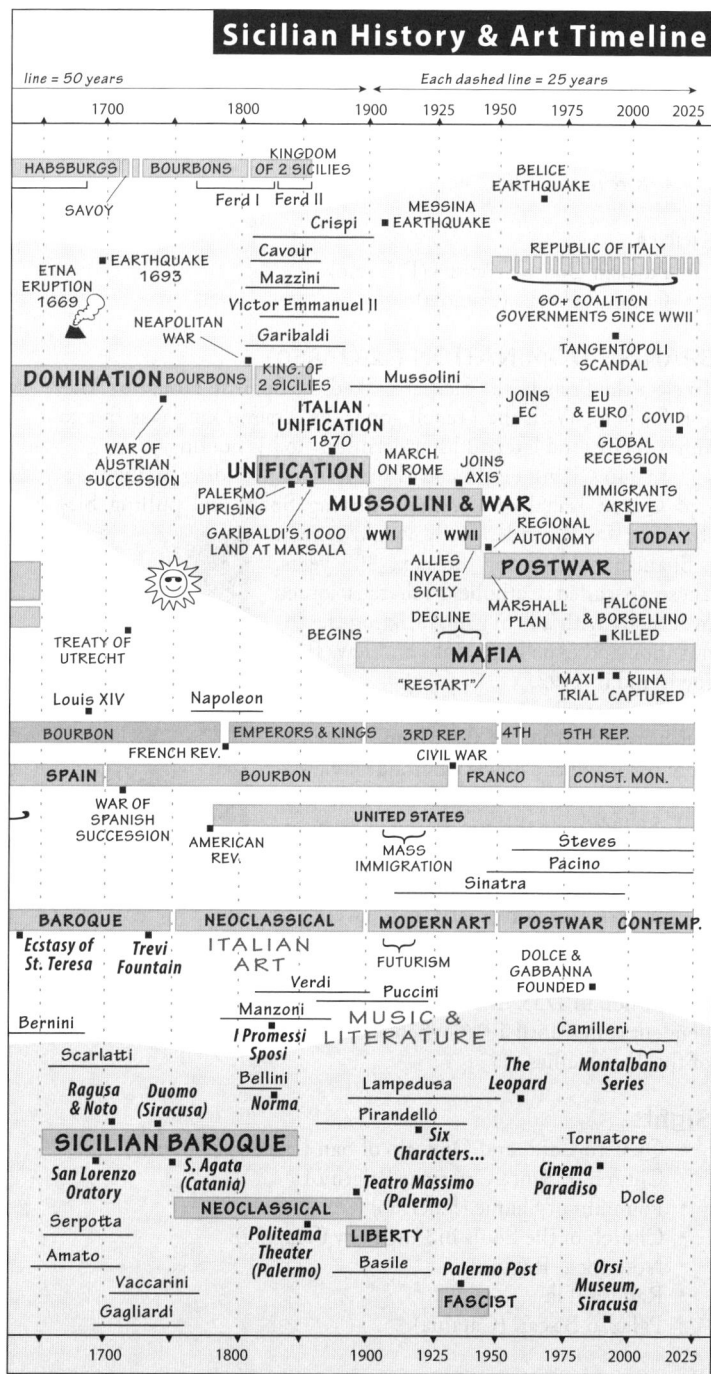

him "Stupor Mundi" (wonder of the world) for his charisma and freethinking ways, although Pope Gregory IX called him an antichrist and excommunicated him not once but twice. After his death in 1250, a chaotic power grab left the French Angevins holding the throne. Their rule of Sicily was short and ugly, ending with a bloody revolt in 1282.

Sights
- Palazzo Conte Federico (Palermo)
- Castello Ursino (Catania)

SPANISH DOMINATION (1282-1860)

To eject the French, the Sicilians asked the Spanish House of Aragon for help. With the French gone, the Aragon king was free to annex Sicily (and later add southern Italy to his holdings).

In 1469, King Ferdinand II of Aragon (including Sicily) married Queen Isabel of Castile—unifying Spain and pulling Sicily along for the ride. Sicily would remain a Spanish holding for the next 300 years. These so-called Catholic Monarchs lorded over Sicily with a firm grip, bringing the Inquisition and expelling Arabs and Jews from the island in 1492.

An earthquake in 1693 devastated the southeastern corner of the island, and cities were reborn in the flowery Baroque style imposed by the Counter-Reformation. In general, Sicily's over-the-top Baroque architecture and dramatic religious processions are the most visible legacies of Spanish rule.

A series of diplomatic maneuvers put Sicily briefly under the control of the House of Savoy in 1713, followed by the Austrian Habsburgs in 1720 and the Spanish House of Bourbon in 1735. The Bourbons ruled Sicily and Naples as independent states until 1816, when they were united as the Kingdom of the Two Sicilies.

Sights
- Quattro Canti and Oratorio of San Lorenzo (Palermo)
- Church of Santa Caterina (Palermo)
- Fountain of Shame (Palermo)
- Church of the Souls in Purgatory (Trapani)
- Noto (near Ragusa)
- Ragusa Ibla
- Palazzo Biscari (Catania)

Sicilian Emigration

The 19th century saw massive political and social upheaval in Sicily. The Spanish nobility was deposed in the 1860s, when Italy unified, but instability reigned for the remainder of the century.

While the south and north of Italy were relatively equal in terms of wealth at the beginning of the 19th century, the fate of the Sicilians changed under Italy's new monarchy. The ruling Savoy family was from Piedmont, in northern Italy. They exploited Sicilian resources and levied high taxes. Sicilian industries such as silk production declined, as the northern king invested in factories closer to home. Sicilians became poorer and disillusioned. At the same time, a pest called phylloxera decimated vineyards and winemaking, and the lucrative sulfur industry collapsed due to competition from the US.

As the economy suffered, desperate peasants looked for better fortunes abroad—some villages in central Sicily were completely abandoned. Men would leave first, establishing themselves in a new home, most returning to bring their families with them. A few started over completely, abandoning their wives and families—and never returning. Historians estimate that between 1880 and 1920, more than a million people left Sicily, many heading for the US (until nativist laws passed in the 1920s made it more difficult to immigrate). Today, more than 20 million people in the United States can claim Sicilian heritage.

Sicilian-Americans looking to connect with their homeland can find traces of their past with some research or the help of a genealogist. Birth certificates or emigration records can offer clues, and travelers can visit any town's City Hall or main church for birth and death records. To get started, check out the Statue of Liberty-Ellis Island Foundation (libertyellisfoundation.org) for searchable ship manifests with hometown information. Cognomix—another genealogy site—lets you find the origin and concentrations of Italian families (website mostly in Italian, cognomix.it).

KINGS AND DICTATORS (1860-1945)

In 1860, the Italian revolutionary Giuseppe Garibaldi landed on the west coast of Sicily (at Marsala) in a campaign that would eventually lead to the Risorgimento—the unification of Italy after centuries of being divided and ruled by foreigners. In the process, Sicily's entrenched noble families lost much of their land, and the aristocratic social order was swept away. The new kingdom of Italy joined Sicily to the mainland under King Victor Emmanuel II. As throughout Italy, the Risorgimento came with a boost in local pride, coinciding with the construction of grand opera houses in Palermo and Catania.

Although the Risorgimento was, at first, a positive development for Sicily, the faraway Savoy king both ignored Sicily and southern Italy...and raided their assets. Religious orders were abolished, and private land was turned over to the monarchy. Industry in the north was modernized and developed, while the south was left mostly agricultural. Poor and corrupt management under the new government gave rise to crime syndicates, which later became known as the Mafia. Many Sicilians and other southern Italians chose to seek better fortunes in North and South America (see the sidebar, earlier).

In 1922, Benito Mussolini seized the Italian government, ruling as prime minister, then dictator for the next two decades with the king as a figurehead. Mussolini responded to the Great Depression (1930s) with big public-works projects, government investment in industry, and an expanded army. But he also allied his country with Hitler's Nazi regime, drawing an unprepared Italy into World War II (1940).

In 1943, Sicily took center stage in the war when the Allies invaded the island to free Italy from the Germans (see the sidebar). After Sicily was liberated, Mussolini was toppled by his own citizens and Italy declared a surrender (September 3, 1943). But Italy couldn't exit the war that easily. The Germans reinstalled Mussolini and occupied the country. It wasn't until May 1945 that Mussolini could be ousted again and the Nazis driven out, thus ending the war.

Unfortunately, when it came time to reestablish local Sicilian rule, US forces made the mistake of enlisting help from well-connected Sicilian-American families—and the Mafia filled the vacuum left by Mussolini's strong-arm rule.

Sights

- Garibaldi statue (Trapani)
- Teatro Massimo (Palermo)
- Teatro Massimo Bellini (Catania)
- Museum of the Allied Landings in Sicily (Catania)

Sicily Goes to War

The sleepy isle of Sicily is where the course of World War II—and history itself—turned. Its liberation by American, British, and Canadian troops tipped the balance, hastening the end of the war.

It was the summer of 1943. The entire European continent was still in the grip of Nazi/Fascist control. The Allies hatched a bold plan ("Operation Husky") to use Sicily as a stepping stone from their base in North Africa to fascist-held Italy.

On July 10, Allied ships stormed the beaches of Sicily's southern coast. From there, soldiers marched north in a two-pronged attack. The Americans (under General George S. Patton) headed up the west coast, the Brits and Canadians (under British Field Marshall "Monty" Montgomery) up the east. Their goal? The port of Messina, from where they could launch a direct attack on the Italian mainland.

For the next 39 days, Sicily was a battlefield. Allied planes bombed towns to smithereens. Terrified villagers huddled in wine cellars. Allied foot soldiers battled fierce German troops and less fierce Italians. Some 15,000 Allied and Axis soldiers and an estimated 6,000 civilians died.

On their "Race to Messina," the Allies covered ground familiar to tourists today. Patton's Americans marched through historic Agrigento, medieval Monreale, strategic Palermo, and beachside Cefalù. Meanwhile, Monty took the vital ports of Siracusa and Catania, the rugged hills of Mount Etna, and the Nazi HQ at Taormina. On August 10, Messina fell to the Americans—winning the friendly rival "race" and the battle for Sicily.

The next dominoes fell swiftly. The Allied victory at Messina so demoralized the Italians that within weeks they toppled Mussolini and surrendered. Hitler had to divert valuable resources to slow the Allied advance across Italy. Soon, the Allies would launch the massive amphibious D-Day assault at Normandy in France (patterned after the Sicily invasion), bringing the war to an end.

The war years had a lasting impact on Sicily. There's the legacy of Mussolini's monumental fascist architecture. Once-grand neighborhoods devastated in the bombing were hastily rebuilt with cheap apartments. Sicily's social infrastructure was demolished too, leaving the island stuck in old feudal ways and Mafioso corruption.

Sicily is catching up, but visitors will still see remnants of the war. There's Catania's powerful WWII museum (see page 352) and Taormina's former Nazi HQ (page 398), plus ruined buildings, bunkers, gun turrets, and makeshift bomb shelters (page 351).

The one positive legacy is that, because the war slowed Sicily's modernization, tourists visiting today enjoy a more pastoral Italy from a bygone age.

MODERN SICILY (1946-today)

At war's end, Italy was physically ruined and extremely poor. The nation rebuilt in the 1950s and 1960s with Marshall Plan aid from the United States. Being a founding member of what would become the European Union was also a boost.

However, Italy's national government remained weak, changing on average once a year, shifting from right to left to centrist coalitions (Italy has had 65 governments since World War II). The country remained sharply divided between the rich industrial north and the poor rural south. Many Sicilian men moved to northern Europe to find work; many others left farms and flocked to the cities.

In Sicily, postwar rebuilding was often quick and dirty, without a master plan and with little concern for the island's historic character. Concrete suburbs and unsightly industrial areas proliferated. Inner cities were left in rubble, and some areas, particularly in Palermo, waited decades for reconstruction.

The flow of reconstruction funds fell into the hands of corrupt politicians, multinational corporations, and organized crime. Sicilian Mafia influence reached new heights in 1982, with the assassination of Carlo Alberto Dalla Chiesa, a general sent from Rome to deal with the mob problem in Sicily. The Mafia's rise culminated in 1992 with the assassinations of two prestigious anti-Mafia prosecutors—Giovanni Falcone and Paolo Borsellino—who were leading investigations against organized crime. But rather than discourage prosecution, the tide turned, and hundreds of Mafia bosses were convicted.

After surviving the government-a-year turbulence and Mafia-tainted corruption of the postwar years, Sicily today is more stable and organized. Pollution and corruption are waning, and the 21st century has seen renewed investment in cities across the island. Former slums in Palermo, Catania, and Siracusa now house chic boutiques. Rustic fishing villages are becoming vacation destinations, dusty fields now host wind turbines, and new highways zip across the island. Tourism is a burgeoning industry, with hotel owners jump-starting a revitalized business climate.

As you travel through Sicily today, you'll encounter a fascinating region with a rich history and an up-and-coming economy. While Sicily has been dominated for centuries by invaders, now it's ready for a new wave of foreigners—tourists, travelers, and you—to come and make your own history.

PRACTICALITIES

Travel Tips	435
Resources from Rick Steves	436
Money	440
Staying Connected	445
Sightseeing	448
Sleeping	451
Eating	460
Transportation	481
Conversions	496
Packing Checklist	498
Italian Survival Phrases	499

This chapter covers the practical skills of European travel: how to pay for things, sightsee efficiently, find good-value accommodations, eat affordably but well, use technology wisely, and get between destinations smoothly. For even more in-depth information on these topics, see rickssteves.com/travel-tips. And for a full run-down of the wealth of free trip-planning content and resources available on my website, see the sidebar on page 436. You can also follow me on Facebook, Instagram, and other social media channels.

Travel Tips

Entry Requirements: Before traveling, check the latest entry requirements and any advisories for your destination at travel.state.gov (US State Department travel pages). The US embassy website for **Italy** is another good source of information (see later).

Resources from Rick Steves

I've always measured "profit" not in dollars but in trips impacted. That's why my company offers a world of free and practical information to help travelers have fun and meaningful trips.

Begin Your Trip at Ricksteves.com

My expansive **website** is *the* place to explore Europe in preparation for your trip. Here you'll find a mountain of free content—video, audio, articles, travel news and insights, itinerary and planning advice, guidebook updates (ricksteves.com/update), and more—all uncluttered by advertising and available without a subscription.

Explore Europe: Our extensive online content is organized by country, including recommended itineraries and hundreds of inspiring travel articles. Find your destination at ricksteves.com/europe.

Travel Forum: On a well-groomed collection of message boards, our travel-savvy community answers questions and shares their personal travel experiences—and our well-traveled staff chimes in when they can be helpful (ricksteves.com/forums).

TV Shows and Video Library: My public-television series, *Rick Steves' Europe,* covers Europe from top to bottom with more than 100 half-hour episodes—and we're working on new shows every year. Watch full episodes for free (ricksteves.com/tv). My free online video library, **Rick Steves Classroom Europe,** offers a searchable database of short video clips on European history, culture, and geography (classroom.ricksteves.com).

Monday Night Travel Talks: To raise your travel IQ, join our virtual party every Monday, featuring experts discussing European destinations, art, culture, food, tips, and more. Stream the live events or watch the video recordings (ricksteves.com/mnt).

Audio Tours on My Free App: I've produced more than 60 free, self-guided audio tours of the top sights in Europe. For those tours and other audio content, get my free **Rick Steves Audio Europe app,** an extensive online library organized by destination. For more on my app, visit ricksteves.com/audioeurope.

In addition to your **passport,** US and Canadian citizens may be required to register online with the European Travel Info and Authorization System **(ETIAS)** before entering Italy and other Schengen Zone countries (travel-europe.europa.eu/etias). If your travel plans include the United Kingdom (England, Scotland, Wales, Northern Ireland), you'll need an Electronic Travel Autho-

Radio: My weekly public-radio show, *Travel with Rick Steves,* features interviews with travel experts from around the world. It airs on 500 US public radio stations. An archive of programs is available at ricksteves.com/radio.

Podcasts: You can enjoy my travel content via three free podcasts. The podcast version of my radio show brings you a weekly, hour-long travel conversation. My other podcasts include a selection of video clips from my public television show and video recordings of my travel classes (ricksteves.com/podcasts).

Recommended Books, Films, and TV: To add context to your trip, we've compiled a list of recommended books, films, and TV shows that feature Italy. See ricksteves.com/travelreading.

Also on Ricksteves.com

Rail Passes: Our website can help you find the perfect **rail pass** for your itinerary and your budget, with easy, one-stop shopping for rail passes, seat reservations, and point-to-point tickets (ricksteves.com/rail).

Travel Guidebooks: This book is just one of over 80 titles in my best-selling series on European travel. These include full-coverage country and city guidebooks, "Best Of" guidebooks (condensed, full-color country guides), Pockets (full-color little books on big cities), Snapshots (excerpted chapters from bigger guides), and my travel skills handbook, *Rick Steves Europe Through the Back Door*. A complete list of my titles—including phrase books and travelogues on European art, history, and culture—appears near the end of this book.

Travel Gear: We offer **bags and accessories** custom-designed to help you travel smarter and lighter, including my popular carry-on bags (which I live out of four months a year), money belts, totes, toiletries kits, adapters, guidebooks, and planning maps (ricksteves.com/shop).

Small-Group Tours: Want to travel with greater efficiency and less stress? Each year about 30,000 travelers join our expert guides on a Rick Steves bus tour. We offer more than 40 itineraries reaching the best destinations in this book...and beyond. You'll enjoy great guides and a fun bunch of travel partners, with small groups of 24 to 28 travelers (+1 425 771 8303, ricksteves.com/tours). And even independent travelers can learn from the day-to-day descriptions in our smartly designed itineraries.

rization **(ETA).** It's wise to take care of this minor bureaucratic hassle a week or two before your trip (required for all ages, gov.uk/visas-immigration).

Tourist Information: Before your trip, scan the website of the Italian national tourist office (italia.it) for a wealth of travel information. If you have a specific question, try contacting one of their US offices (New York: +1 212 245 5618, newyork@enit.it; Los Angeles: +1 310 820 1898, losangeles@enit.it).

Local tourist information offices (abbreviated **TI** in this book) are hit or miss. Their advice can be influenced by partnerships with local businesses, but they're still a handy place to pick up maps, browse brochures, and ask basic questions. If the TI falls short, you can often get local information from your hotelier, or even staff at sights and other businesses.

Be wary of travel agencies or information services that masquerade as TIs but serve fancy hotels and tour companies. They're selling things you don't need, often at a markup.

Holidays and Festivals: For a list of festivals and national holidays observed throughout Italy, see ricksteves.com/festivals. Before planning a trip around a festival, verify the dates with the festival website or the national tourist office.

In deeply Catholic Sicily, a region where everything is either a drama or a comedy, every town has a festival celebrating its patron saint (even more exuberantly than on the mainland). If you happen to be here on a feast day, you'll see the town taken over by processions, Masses, street fairs, festive lights, random fireworks, and devotees hauling huge candles, along with effigies of the saint. Celebrations are open to all, so feel free to jump in.

Hotels get booked up on Easter weekend, as well as on Liberation Day and Labor Day—especially when these two holidays fall close to a weekend. In beach destinations, August is flooded with vacationing Italians and Europeans, particularly around the Feast of the Assumption.

Emergency and Medical Help: For any emergency service—ambulance, police, or fire—call **112** (operators typically speak English). If you get sick, do as the locals do and go to a pharmacy for advice. Or ask at your hotel for help—they'll know the nearest medical and emergency services.

Theft or Loss: To replace a passport, you'll need to go in person to an embassy (see next). If your credit and debit cards disappear, cancel and replace them (see "Damage Control for Lost Cards" on page 443). File a police report, either on the spot or within a day or two; you'll need it to submit an insurance claim, and it can help with replacing your passport. For help with a lost phone, see "Damage Control for Lost Phones" on page 447. For more information, see ricksteves.com/help.

US Embassies and Consulates: Consular agency in **Palermo** +39 091 385 057 (Via Vaccarini 1). Embassy in **Rome** +39 06 46741, passport and nonemergency consular services, by appointment only (Via Vittorio Veneto 121). Consulates in **Milan** +39 02 290 351 (Via Principe Amedeo 2/10); **Florence** +39 055 266 951 (Lungarno

Vespucci 38); and **Naples** +39 081 583 8111 (Piazza della Repubblica). For all, see it.usembassy.gov.

Canadian Embassies: Rome +39 06 854 442 911 (Via Zara 30); **Milan** +39 02 626 94238 (Piazza Cavour 3). For both, see international.gc.ca/country-pays/italy-italie. After-hours emergency in Ottawa +1 613 996 8885.

Avoiding Theft and Scams: While most travelers visit Sicily safely, petty theft is a possibility at popular sights and anywhere there's a crowd. Pickpockets don't want to hurt you—they usually just want your money and gadgets. Consider any jostle or commotion a possible smokescreen for thieves. Wear a money belt, and keep valuables buttoned or zipped up.

Sneaky thieves pretend to be teenagers on holiday, well-dressed businessmen, or tourists wearing fanny packs and even toting Rick Steves guidebooks. Be on guard while boarding and leaving buses and trams, at heavily touristed sights, and while shopping at bustling street markets. In a crowd, hold your bags in front. If you wouldn't walk down a dark and deserted street at home, don't do it in Europe.

Green or sloppy tourists are more likely to fall victim to scams. Be wise to overly kind strangers offering too-good-to-be-true deals. Insist on clear and itemized bills. When paying in cash, know how much you're handing over, and count your change. Be confident and aware, and you'll be fine.

Time Zones: Italy, like most of continental Europe, is generally six/nine hours ahead of the East/West Coasts of the US. For a handy time converter, use the world clock app on your phone.

Business Hours: "Siesta" hours (with a midday closure) are no longer required by law in Italy, so many shops stay open through lunch or later into the evening, especially larger stores in tourist areas. Sicily sticks to the old ways more than the mainland though, and the siesta is often still in effect, even in larger cities, especially during summer. Midday closures are common at stores and even at sights. Smaller stores are often closed on Sunday and sometimes also Monday.

Websites: Some Italian websites ending in *.it* only operate while the sight itself is open. This means you may need to stay up late (or get up early) to access them.

Watt's up? Europe's electrical system is 220 volts, instead of North America's 110 volts. All electronics and most appliances (hair dryers, CPAP machines) convert automatically, so you won't need a converter, but you will need an adapter plug with two round prongs, sold inexpensively at travel stores in the US.

Tobacco Shops: Known as *tabacchi* (often indicated with a big *T* sign), these Italian-style minimarts are ubiquitous across the country. They're handy places to purchase tickets for city buses and subways and sometimes postage. If you aren't sure where to buy something, a *tabacchi* is a good place to start.

Online Translation Tips: Google's Chrome browser instantly translates websites. The Google Translate app converts spoken or typed English into most European languages (and vice versa) and can also translate text it "reads" with your smartphone's camera. Before your trip, it's a good idea to download the Italian dictionary in the app so it can translate even if you're offline.

Going Green: There's plenty you can do to reduce your environmental footprint while traveling. When practical, take a train instead of a flight within Europe, and use public transportation within cities. In hotels, use the "Do Not Disturb" sign to avoid daily linen and towel changes (or hang up your towels to signal you'll reuse them) and turn the air-conditioning off when you leave the room. Bring a reusable shopping tote and refillable water bottle (most of Sicily's tap water is safe to drink—ask your hotelier). Skip printed materials that you don't plan to keep—get your info online instead. To find out how Rick Steves' Europe is offsetting carbon emissions with a self-imposed carbon tax, see ricksteves.com/about-us/climate-smart.

Money

Here's my basic strategy for using money wisely in Europe. I pack the following:

Credit Card: You'll use your credit card for purchases both big and small. Some European businesses have gone cashless, making a card your only payment option.

Debit Card: Use this at ATMs to withdraw a small amount of local cash. Wait until you arrive to get euros (Italian cities have plenty of ATMs); if you buy euros before your trip, you'll likely pay bad stateside exchange rates. While many transactions are by card these days, cash can help you out of a jam if your card randomly doesn't work, and can be useful to pay for things like street food, incidentals, tips, and local guides.

Backup Card: Some travelers carry a third card (debit or credit; ideally from a different bank) in case one gets lost or simply doesn't work.

Stash of Cash: I carry $100-200 in US dollars as a cash backup, which comes in handy in an emergency.

BEFORE YOU GO

Know your cards. In Europe, Visa and Mastercard credit cards are universal, while American Express and Discover are less common. Most credit cards are enabled for "contactless" payments (look for

> ## Travel Insurance
>
> Travel insurance can minimize the considerable financial risks of traveling: accidents, illness, missed flights, canceled tours, lost baggage, theft, terrorism, travel-company bankruptcies, natural disasters, emergency evacuation, and getting your body home if you die. The decision to buy travel insurance (and how much) depends on your situation. First determine what coverage you already have; some premium credit cards include generous coverage, and other expenses may be covered through your health, homeowners, or renters insurance. Then consider how likely it is that you'll need to change or cancel (for example, if you or a loved one is in frail health), how much of your prepaid trip costs are nonrefundable, and your risk tolerance.
>
> It costs money to buy away the financial risk of travel. But if insurance adds 10 percent to your total trip cost, that may be a small price to pay—and worth the peace of mind—compared to the potential loss in the event of something catastrophic. You can compare insurance policies and costs at insuremytrip.com.

the tap-to-pay symbol—four curvy lines). Debit cards with a Visa or Mastercard logo will work in any European ATM.

Set up a payment app. To tap-to-pay with your smartphone or smartwatch, link a credit card to an app such as Apple Pay or Google Pay. If you've arrived in Europe without a tap-to-pay card, you can easily set up your phone with a payment app.

Know your PIN. Make sure you know the numeric PIN for each of your cards, both debit and credit. Request it if you don't have one, as it may be required for some purchases. Allow time to receive the information by mail—it's not always possible to obtain your PIN online or by phone.

Report your travel dates. Some banks want to know that you'll be using your cards overseas, specifically when and where you're headed. Depending on your bank, you can do this either online or over the phone.

Check your ATM withdrawal limit. Find out how much you can withdraw daily and ask for a higher limit if you want to get more cash at once. Note that European ATMs will withdraw funds only from checking accounts, not from savings accounts.

Find out about fees. For any purchase or withdrawal made with a card, you may be charged a foreign transaction fee (1-3 percent). Shop around; you can compare credit cards on bankrate.com. Some cards offer lower international fees than others—and some don't charge any at all. Most credit unions and some loyalty or rewards cards have low or no foreign transaction fees.

> ## Exchange Rate
>
> For this book, I've used the following conversion (but check xe.com for the latest rates):
>
> **1 euro (€) = about $1.10**
>
> To convert prices in euros to dollars, add about 10 percent: €20 = about $22, €50 = about $55. Like the dollar, one euro is broken into 100 cents. Coins range from €0.01 to €2, and bills from €5 to €200 (bills over €50 are rarely used).

IN EUROPE
Using Credit Cards and Payment Apps

Tap-to-Pay Cards and Apps: Simply tap your contactless card or smartphone/watch against a contactless reader to make a purchase. A PIN is generally required only as a security measure for larger purchases. This is by far the easiest way to pay and is available in much of Europe.

Payment Problems: Rarely, a vendor or self-service payment machine (such as a transit-ticket kiosk, toll-booth, or fuel pump) may not accept older credit cards. Have some cash handy or look for a cashier who can process your payment manually. When approaching a toll plaza or ferry-ticket line, use the "cash" lane.

Always choose to pay in the local currency. During a credit-card transaction, the payment terminal may ask whether you want to pay in US dollars or in the local currency. Always refuse the conversion and *choose the local currency.* While this "service"—called Dynamic Currency Conversion (DCC)—offers the illusion of convenience, it comes with a poor exchange rate and/or higher fees, and you'll wind up losing money.

Using Cash

ATMs: European ATMs work just like they do at home—except they spit out local currency instead of dollars. In Europe, the universal term for an ATM is "bankomat"; in Italy, you'll see it as *bancomat*. Look for an ATM operated by a local bank, ideally one just outside a brick-and-mortar bank (in the rare event that you have any issues).

Beware of ATMs run by exchange or money-transfer companies, which have less-favorable rates and higher fees than banks. These can be marked Euronet, Travelex, Your Cash, or Cashzone—or simply marked generically as "bankomat" or "ATM." Rip-off exchange ATMs are often the only option at airports and train stations: On arrival, consider using a credit card to get downtown, then find a bank's ATM near your hotel.

If your debit card doesn't work, try a lower amount—your request may have exceeded your withdrawal limit or the ATM's limit. If you still have a problem, try a different ATM or come back later. When offered the choice to process your transaction in US dollars or the local currency, always choose the local currency.

Exchanging Cash: Minimize exchanging money in Europe; it's expensive (you'll generally lose 5-10 percent). In a pinch you can find exchange desks at major train stations or airports. Banks generally do not exchange money unless you have an account with them.

Security Tips

Pickpockets target tourists. Keep your passport and backup cash and cards secure in your money belt (or your hotel-room safe) and carry only a day's spending money and one card in your wallet.

Before inserting your card into an ATM, inspect the front of the machine. If anything looks crooked, loose, or damaged, it could be a sign of a card-skimming device.

Don't use a debit card for purchases. Because a debit card pulls funds directly from your bank account, potential charges incurred by a thief will stay on your account while your bank investigates.

If accessing your accounts online while traveling, be sure to use a secure connection (see the "Tips on Internet Security" sidebar, later).

Damage Control for Lost Cards

Report the loss of a credit or debit card immediately to your bank (using a secure app) or the following global customer-assistance centers: Visa (+1 303 967 1096), Mastercard (+1 636 722 7111), and American Express (+1 336 393 1111).

You'll need to provide the primary cardholder's identification-verification details (such as birth date, mother's maiden name, or Social Security number). You can generally receive a temporary card within two or three business days in Europe (see ricksteves.com/help for more).

If you report your loss within two days, you typically won't be responsible for unauthorized transactions on your account, although many banks charge a liability fee.

TIPPING

Tipping in Sicily isn't as automatic and generous as it is in the US. In general, if someone in the tourism or service industry does a good job for you, a small tip of a euro or two is appropriate...but not required.

Restaurants: In Sicily, a service charge *(servizio)* is usually built into your check (look at the menu carefully). If it's not included, you can tip by rounding up the bill (or about 5-10 percent is plenty). European credit card receipts typically do not have a tip line—request to add a tip before they run your card, or leave a tip in cash. For more details on restaurant tipping, see page 463.

Taxis: For a typical ride, round up your fare a bit (for instance, if the fare is €13.50, pay €15). If the cabbie hauls your bags and zips you to the airport to help you catch your flight, you might want to give a little more.

Services: For local guides, private drivers, or others who spend several hours with you—and significantly improve the quality of your trip—a healthy tip (of around 10 percent) is not extravagant. In hotel rooms, leaving a tip of €1-3 per night is standard. If you're not sure whether (or how much) to tip, ask a local for advice.

GETTING A VAT REFUND

Wrapped into the purchase price of your Sicilian souvenirs is a value-added tax (VAT) of about 22 percent. You're entitled to get most of that tax back if you purchase more than €70 worth of goods at a store that participates in the VAT-refund scheme. Typically, you must ring up the minimum at a single retailer—you can't add up your purchases from various shops to reach the required amount. (If the store ships the goods to your US home, VAT is not assessed.)

Getting your refund is straightforward...and worthwhile if you spend a significant amount.

At the Merchant: Have the merchant completely fill out the refund document (they'll ask for your passport; a photo of your passport usually works). Keep track of the paperwork and your original sales receipt. Note that you're not supposed to use your purchased goods before you leave Europe.

At the Border or Airport: Process your VAT document at your last stop in the European Union (such as the airport; allow plenty of extra time for this process and have your purchased items easily accessible for inspection). At some airports, you'll go to a customs office to get your documents stamped and then to a separate VAT-refund service (such as Forexchange, Global Blue, or Planet) to process the refund. Elsewhere, a single VAT desk handles the whole thing, or you may be able to do it at a self-validation kiosk. (Note that refund services typically extract a 4 percent fee, but you're paying for the convenience of receiving your money in cash immediately or as a credit to your card.) Otherwise, you'll need to mail the stamped refund documents to the address given by the merchant.

CUSTOMS FOR AMERICAN SHOPPERS

You can take home $800 worth of items per person duty-free, once every 31 days. Many processed and packaged foods are allowed, including cheeses, dried herbs, jams, baked goods, candy, oil, vinegar, condiments, and honey. Fresh fruits and vegetables and most meats are not allowed, with exceptions for some canned items. As for alcohol, you can bring in one liter duty-free (it can be packed securely in your checked luggage, along with any other liquid-containing items).

To bring alcohol (or liquid-packed foods) in your carry-on bag on your flight home, buy it at a duty-free shop at the airport. You'll increase your odds of getting it onto a connecting flight if it's packaged in a "STEB"—a secure, tamper-evident bag. But stay away from liquids in opaque, ceramic, or metallic containers, which usually cannot be successfully screened (STEB or no STEB).

For details on allowable goods, customs rules, and duty rates, visit help.cbp.gov.

Staying Connected

Your phone is an indispensable tool for efficient travel. Fortunately, staying connected in Europe gets easier each year. You can use your devices much like you do at home, either by getting an international plan or connecting to free Wi-Fi whenever possible. Another option is to buy a European SIM or eSIM card for your phone. More details are at ricksteves.com/phoning.

USING YOUR PHONE IN EUROPE

Prepare your phone. Before your trip, stock your device with any content or apps you'll want on the road. Helpful tools include Google Translate, your airline's app, public transit apps for your destinations, and sight-specific apps (such as museum audioguides). Also download maps if you plan to use offline navigation, and TV shows or movies to watch on the plane or during downtime.

Sign up for an international plan. Most providers offer a simple bundle that includes calling, messaging, and data. Your normal plan may already include international coverage (for example, T-Mobile's covers unlimited text and low-speed data, plus reasonable per-minute voice calls).

Use free Wi-Fi whenever possible. In Europe, look for and use Wi-Fi for most online tasks. Most accommodations offer free Wi-Fi. Many cafés offer hotspots for customers; ask for the password when you buy something. You may also find Wi-Fi at TIs,

> ## Tips on Internet Security
>
> Whether using a laptop or phone on the road, make sure it's running the latest versions of its operating system, security software, and apps. Ensure that your device and apps are password-protected (enable facial recognition where possible). If two-factor authentication is an option, activate it.
>
> Use only secure, password-protected Wi-Fi. Ask the hotel or café staff for the specific name of their network, and make sure you log on to that exact one.
>
> To access sensitive information (such as bank accounts), use a dedicated app, and ideally a cellular connection, which is more secure than a shared Wi-Fi network. Or consider subscribing to a VPN (virtual private network). If you're using the Safari browser on an Apple device, an encryption feature called "Private Relay" works in a similar way.

city squares, major museums, public transit hubs, and airports, and aboard trains and buses—though these can be hit or miss.

Minimize the use of your cellular network. The best way to make sure you're not accidentally burning through data is to put your device in "airplane" mode (which also disables phone calls and texts), then turn on Wi-Fi and connect as needed. Turn on your cellular network (or turn off airplane mode) only when you can't find Wi-Fi.

Save large-data tasks for Wi-Fi. If your included data is slow, limited, or expensive, wait until you're on Wi-Fi to make video calls, download audio tours or apps, stream videos, or do other megabyte-greedy tasks. Navigation apps such as Google Maps require lots of data; download maps when you're on Wi-Fi, then use the app offline.

Limit automatic updates and uploads. By default, your device constantly checks for a data connection to update app content or back up photos and videos to the cloud. Adjust your settings so this happens only when you're on Wi-Fi—not when using cellular data.

Use Wi-Fi calling and messaging apps. WhatsApp, FaceTime, and Google Meet are great for making free or low-cost calls or sending texts over Wi-Fi worldwide. WhatsApp is especially popular throughout Europe and is often the easiest way to communicate with guides, drivers, or other local contacts.

Consider buying a European SIM or eSIM card. Both give you a European phone number and access to local calling and data rates; if you're traveling to other countries within the EU, there are no additional roaming fees. Physical SIM cards can be purchased at mobile-phone shops and inserted into your (unlocked) phone,

How to Dial

Here's how to dial from anywhere in the US or Europe, using the phone number of one of my recommended Palermo hotels as an example (091 616 6881). If a non-Italian number starts with 0, drop it when dialing internationally.

From a US Mobile Phone
Phone numbers in this book are presented exactly as you would dial them from a US mobile phone. For international access, press and hold the 0 (zero) to get a + sign, then dial the country code (39 for Italy) and phone number.

▶ To call the Palermo hotel from any location, dial +39 091 616 6881.

From a US Landline
Replace + with 011 (US/Canada access code), then dial the country code (39 for Italy) and phone number.

▶ To call the Palermo hotel from your home landline, dial 011 39 091 616 6881.

From a European Landline
Replace + with 00 (Europe access code), then dial the country code (39 for Italy, 1 for the US) and phone number.

▶ To call the Palermo hotel from a French landline, dial 00 39 091 616 6881.
▶ To call my US office from an Italian landline, dial 00 1 425 771 8303.

From One Italian Phone to Another
To place a domestic call (from an Italian landline or mobile), drop +39 and dial the phone number.

▶ To call the Palermo hotel from Siracusa, dial 091 616 6881.

More Dialing Tips
Local Numbers: European phone numbers and area codes can vary in length and spacing, even within the same country. Mobile phones use separate prefixes (for instance, in Italy, landlines begin with 0, and mobile numbers begin with 3).

Toll and Toll-Free Calls: It's generally not possible to dial European toll or toll-free numbers from a US mobile or landline. Look for a direct-dial number instead.

Calling the US from a US Mobile Phone, While Abroad: Dial +1, area code, and number.

More Phoning Help: See howtocallabroad.com.

---

although some newer US phones may not accept physical SIM cards. Electronic SIM cards (or eSIMs) can be purchased online and downloaded. In Italy, you'll be required to register the SIM card with your passport as an antiterrorism measure.

Damage Control for Lost Phones: Losing your phone can be a significant inconvenience. Before you leave home, make sure your device is set up for automatic cloud backups, and enable the "find my phone" feature (make sure you have access to it from another device, like your travel partner's phone or a laptop). Familiarize

> ## Hurdling the Language Barrier
>
> Many Sicilians—especially those in the tourist trade and in big cities—speak English. And all Sicilians speak both Italian and Sicilian.
>
> In smaller, nontouristy towns, Sicilian and Italian are the norm. The two languages have a lot in common, but some words are very different. For example, a cup of coffee is *tazzina da caffé* in Italian but *cichira* in Sicilian (likely borrowed from the Portuguese *xicara*).
>
> Sicilian is more than a dialect; it's actually an older language than Italian. It descended from the Latin spoken by Roman conquerors and has elements of Greek, Arabic, French, Catalan, and Spanish—the legacy of years of foreign influence, trade, and occupation. Sicilian is not an active language, as new words are not being created.
>
> During the early 20th century, the government enforced Italian as the national language, bringing Sicilian to the verge of extinction. However, Sicilian is now making a comeback, as it is being reintroduced and taught in schools.
>
> While you can communicate with Sicilians in Italian, you will commonly hear them conversing in Sicilian. Like many Italians, Sicilians have an endearing habit of talking to you even if they know you don't speak their language. And yet, thanks to gestures and thoughtfully simplified words, it somehow works—just go along for the ride.
>
> Locals visibly brighten when you use some Italian or Sicilian pleasantries. Give it your best shot. You'll find that doors open more quickly...and with more smiles.

yourself with your phone's "lost and lock" mode, which you can enable from another device if your phone goes missing. Report the loss to your mobile carrier; if your phone remains lost, use the "wipe" feature to erase its data.

Sightseeing

Sightseeing can be hard work. Use these tips to make your visits to Sicily's finest sights meaningful, fun, efficient, and painless.

MAPS AND NAVIGATION TOOLS

Your best navigation tool is the mapping app on your phone. In addition to driving and walking directions, **Google Maps** (and similar apps) offers detailed public transit instructions—in most cities you can simply plug in a destination and get details on reaching it by subway, bus, or tram.

To conserve data, most mapping apps let you download maps in advance (do this when you're on strong Wi-Fi). However,

Sicilian for Beginners

English	Italian	Sicilian
Good day.	Buon giorno.	Bon jornu.
Hello. (informal)	Ciao.	Salve.
Please.	Per favore.	Pi fauri.
Thank you.	Grazie.	Ringraziamu.
Let's go.	Andiamo.	Amuninni.
How much is it?	Quanto costa?	Quantu veni?
It costs too much!	E' troppo caro!	Chi??? Nonzi! Iè troppu caru!
Where is…?	Dov'e?	Unn'è?
You are beautiful.	Tu sei bella.	Tu si bedda.
My grandpa was Sicilian!	Mio nonno era Siciliano!	Me navodannu iera di cà, paesano!

Note that Italian is pronounced much like English, with a few exceptions: *c* followed by *e* or *i* is pronounced *ch* (to ask, *"Per centro?"*—"To the center?"—you say, pehr CHEHN-troh). In Italian, *ch* followed by *e* or *i* is pronounced like the hard *c* in Chianti (*chiesa*—church—is pronounced kee-AY-zah). Adding a vowel to the English word often gets you close to the Italian one.

For more Italian survival phrases, see page 499, and consider the *Rick Steves Italian Phrase Book* (available at ricksteves.com).

---

offline maps may not include every feature, such as real-time traffic updates and journey planning on public transit. For more on using your phone during your trip, see page 445.

The **maps in this book** are concise and simple, designed to help you locate recommended destinations, sights, hotels, and restaurants. Simple **paper maps** are generally free at TIs and hotels; maps with more detail are sold at newsstands and bookstores.

PLAN AHEAD

Set up an itinerary that allows you to fit in all your must-see sights. For a one-stop look at opening hours, see the "At a Glance" sidebars for Palermo, Trapani Day Trips, and Siracusa.

Note that hours in Sicily can be unpredictable (see "Hours and Closures," later). In the off-season (Nov-March), many Sicilian sights have limited hours and may be open only in the mornings.

While you won't find the crowds typical in Italy's big, mainland cities, a few of Sicily's major sights—such as Villa Romana del Casale, Taormina's Greek-Roman Theater, and the Palatine Chapel in Palermo's Norman Palace—can be very busy at peak times, especially when a cruise ship is in town. Going first thing in the morning or at the end of the day usually makes for a smoother visit. Late-day visits (when possible) are usually peaceful, with fewer crowds (but don't cut it too close to closing time, as some sights sometimes start shutting down early).

Don't put off visiting a must-see sight—you never know when a place will close unexpectedly for a holiday, strike, or restoration.

Many museums are closed or have reduced hours at least a few days a year, especially on major holidays (see ricksteves.com/festivals for a list of European holidays). In summer, some sights may stay open late. Off-season hours may be shorter.

When visiting a popular cruise destination (such as Taormina), you can use cruisemapper.com to look up any scheduled cruise arrivals—how many ships are coming, how big, and at what time—to be prepared for (and avoid) the worst of the cruise crowds. For example, if multiple ships are staying late into the evening, you'll want to book ahead for dinner (or eat outside the town center).

If you plan to hire a local guide, reserve ahead by email. Popular guides can get booked up.

Study up. To get the most out of the self-guided tours and sight descriptions in this book, read them before you visit.

AT SIGHTS

Every sight or museum offers more than what is covered in this book. Use the information I provide as an introduction—not the final word. Here's what you can typically expect at sights:

Hours and Closures: Except at major sights, in Sicily expect posted hours to be more of a guideline than a rule—places might close earlier than stated or may not open at all. I've listed official opening times, but in practice these can change with the day, the season, or for no perceptible reason. Hours listed online are often just plain wrong. The only way to be sure is to check hours locally. Call or drop by and ask: *Aperto oggi?* (ah-PER-toh OH-jee; Are you open today?) and *A che ora chiude?* (ah kay OH-rah kee-OO-day; What time do you close?).

Discounts: Discounts for sights are generally not listed in this book. However, youths under 18 and students and teachers with proper identification cards (obtain from isic.org) can get discounts at many sights—always ask. Italy's national museums generally offer free admission to children under 18, but some discounts are available only for citizens of the European Union (EU).

Entering: You may not be allowed to enter if you arrive too close to closing time. And guards start ushering people out well before the actual closing time, so don't save the best for last.

Security Check: Allow extra time for security lines. At some sights, you may need to pass through a metal detector and put your bag through a scanner. Some sights require you to check day packs and coats. (If you'd rather not check your day pack, try carrying it tucked under your arm as you enter.)

Photography: If the museum's photo policy isn't clearly posted, ask a guard. Generally, taking photos without a flash or tripod is allowed. Some sights ban selfie sticks; others ban photos altogether.

Audioguides and Apps: Some sights offer audioguides in English (which can vary in quality). Often museums post QR codes that allow you to access the tour on your phone (using free—if spotty—Wi-Fi, or your own data plan). A+ students can check ahead and download audioguides before their trip. Less frequently you'll borrow or rent a device preloaded with the audio content.

Expect Changes: Artwork can be on tour, on loan, out sick, or shifted at the whim of the curator. Pick up a floor plan as you enter and ask the museum staff if you can't find a particular item. Say the title or artist's name, or point to the photograph in this book and ask, *"Dov'è?"* (doh-VEH, meaning "Where is?").

Services: Important sights usually have a reasonably priced on-site café or cafeteria (handy air-conditioned places to rejuvenate during a long visit). The WCs at sights are free and generally clean but often out of toilet paper—carry tissues.

FIND RELIGION

Churches offer some amazing art (usually free), a cool respite from heat, and a welcome seat.

A modest dress code—no bare shoulders or shorts for anyone, even kids—is enforced at larger churches (such as the cathedrals in Siracusa and Monreale) but might be overlooked elsewhere. Sicily is more conservative than mainland Italy, though, and it's best to err on the side of respectful dress at religious sites. (I wear a super-lightweight pair of long pants rather than shorts for my hot and muggy Italian sightseeing.)

Some churches have coin-operated boxes that trigger lights to illuminate works of art. I pop in a coin whenever I can, to improve my experience (and photos), as a small contribution to that church, and as a courtesy to other visitors enjoying this great art. Whenever possible, let there be light.

Sleeping

One of my joys as a guidebook writer is connecting my readers with the small-hotel owners I've come to know over the years. Even if you're willing to spend more, you'll have a far richer trip if you stay in places with a strong sense of local character.

> ## Sleep Code
>
> Hotels in this book are categorized according to the average price of a standard double room with breakfast in high season. These ranges apply to cities; you may pay less in towns.
>
> | | | |
> |---|---|---|
> | €€€€ | **Splurge:** | Most rooms over €250 |
> | €€€ | **Pricier:** | €175-250 |
> | €€ | **Moderate:** | €125-175 |
> | € | **Budget:** | €75-125 |
> | ¢ | **Backpacker:** | Under €75 |
> | **RS%** | Ask about Rick Steves discount | |
>
> Unless otherwise noted, credit cards are accepted and hotel staff speak basic English. For the best deal, *book directly with the hotel.*

My best tips for booking rooms: Book direct and book early. While third-party sites and room-booking services may seem convenient, booking directly with my recommended hotels puts you in contact with your host and can sometimes save you (and them) money.

Reserve your accommodations as soon as your itinerary is set, especially if you want to stay at one of my top listings or if you'll be traveling during busy times. See rocksteves.com/festivals for a list of major holidays and festivals in Italy.

USING MY RECOMMENDATIONS

Curated and opinionated listings of good-value rooms are a major feature of this book's Sleeping sections. Rather than list accommodations scattered throughout a town, I choose hotels in my favorite neighborhoods that are convenient to sights.

My recommendations run the gamut, from dorm beds to luxurious rooms with all the comforts. I like places that are clean, central, relatively quiet at night, reasonably priced, friendly, small enough to have a hands-on owner or manager, and run with a respect for Italian traditions. I'm more impressed by a handy location and fun-loving philosophy than oversized TVs and a fancy gym. Most of my recommendations fall short of perfection. But if I can find a place with most of these features, it's a keeper.

RATES AND DEALS

I've categorized my recommended accommodations based on price, indicated with a euro-sign rating (see sidebar). Room prices can fluctuate significantly with demand and amenities (size, views, and so on), but relative price categories remain constant. Taormina tends to be more expensive than the rest of Sicily (and rates in popular places like Taormina and Siracusa can soar in high season).

City taxes, which can vary from place to place, are generally insignificant (a few dollars per person, per night).

Booking Direct: Once your dates are set, compare features and prices at several hotels. Start with the recommendations in this book, then use hotel websites, booking sites such as Booking.com, and user-review sites such as TripAdvisor to narrow down your options.

After you've zeroed in on your choice, it's best to **book directly with the hotel itself**—on the hotel's website or by email or phone. If paying through the hotel's website, make sure the final price is listed in euros, not dollars, to avoid an unfavorable exchange rate (see page 442).

While big booking sites are convenient for travelers, they can be a curse for small, independent, family-run hotels. Without a presence on these sites, small hotels become almost invisible. But to be listed, they must pay a big commission...and promise that their own website won't undercut the price on the booking-service site. When you book directly with the hotel, the price may be the same as via a booking site, but more of your money goes to the hotel. In exchange, they may offer you a nicer room or a free breakfast (if it's not already included). Booking direct also increases the chances that your hotelier will be able to accommodate special needs or requests (such as shifting your reservation).

Getting a Discount: Some hotels extend a discount to those who pay cash or stay longer than three nights. And some accommodations offer a special discount for Rick Steves readers, indicated in this book by the abbreviation **"RS%."** Discounts vary: Ask for details when you reserve. Generally, to qualify for this discount, you must book direct (not through a booking site), mention this book when you reserve and show it upon arrival, and sometimes pay cash or stay a certain number of nights. In some cases, you may need to enter a discount code (which I've provided in the listing) in the booking form on the hotel's website. Understandably, discounts do not apply to promotional rates.

TYPES OF ACCOMMODATIONS
Hotels

Double rooms listed in this book range from about €50 (very simple, toilet and shower down the hall) to €450 (maximum plumbing and more), with most clustered around €175-200 (with private bathrooms). Prices are higher in big or heavily touristed cities, and lower off the beaten path. Traveling alone can be expensive: A *camera singola* is often only 25 percent less than a *camera doppia*.

Some hotels can add an extra bed (for a small charge) to a double; some offer larger rooms for four or more people (I call these "family rooms" in the listings) or have connecting double rooms.

The Pros and Cons of Short-Term Rentals

Short-term rental services like Airbnb are having a big impact in Europe. As hotels have become more expensive and less personal—especially in big cities—short-term rentals have filled the gap.

An apartment or house can provide more space and amenities than a cookie-cutter hotel (and is an especially good value for stays longer than a few days). Having your own kitchen can save on restaurant costs; a washer-dryer can spare you a trip to the launderette; and families who want to spread out get better value renting an apartment rather than multiple hotel rooms. Airbnb fans appreciate feeling part of a neighborhood and getting into a daily routine as "temporary Europeans." Some places are run by thoughtful hosts, allowing you to get to know a local and keep your money in the community.

Other places are impersonally managed by large agencies, with self check-in and minimal contact. Critics of Airbnb see it as a threat to "traditional Europe." Absentee landlords can make more money renting to short-stay travelers, driving rents up—and local residents out. Traditional businesses are replaced by ones that cater to tourists. And the character and charm that made those neighborhoods desirable to tourists in the first place goes too. Some cities have cracked down, imposing limits or banning short-term rentals altogether.

As a lover of Europe, I share the worry of those who see residents nudged aside by tourists. I've witnessed some of my favorite charming old neighborhoods sell out to the tourist dollar. Locals are left feeling like strangers, no longer able to identify with their temporary neighbors.

As an advocate for travelers, I appreciate the value short-term rentals provide in offering the chance to stay in a local building or neighborhood with potentially fewer tourists, and the convenience for families. But before searching on a short-term rental site, consider staying in a small, family-run hotel, to help preserve the culture you are traveling so far to see.

Arrival and Check-In: Hotels and B&Bs are sometimes located on the higher floors of a multipurpose building with a secured door. In that case, look for your hotel's name on the buttons by the main entrance and ring the bell.

Hotel elevators are common, though small, and some older buildings still lack them. If stairs are unavoidable, ask the front desk for help carrying your bags up.

Most European countries require hotels to collect your passport details. At check-in, the receptionist might ask for your passport to scan or photocopy, or they may keep it briefly to copy down

> ## Keep Cool
>
> If you're visiting Italy in the summer, you'll want an air-conditioned room. Most hotel air-conditioners come with a remote control that generally has similar symbols and features: fan icon (toggle through wind power, from light to gale); temperature (20 degrees Celsius—about 68 Fahrenheit—is comfortable); louver icon (steady airflow or waves); snowflake and sunshine icons (cold air or heat); and clock ("O" setting: run X hours before turning off; "I" setting: wait X hours to start). You may also see a "Powerful" button (or an outline of a person flexing their bicep), which boosts the fan temporarily to quickly cool off a hot room. When you leave your room, do as the environmentally conscious Europeans do and turn off the air-conditioning.

the information they need. If you're not comfortable leaving your passport at the desk, bring a copy to hand over instead.

If you're arriving in the morning, your room probably won't be ready. Check your bag safely at the hotel and dive right into sightseeing.

Some hotels offer self check-in. You'll receive instructions before you arrive with a code for your room (and sometimes for the building's front door).

In Your Room: Pricier hotels usually come with a small fridge stocked with beverages, called a *frigo bar* (FREE-goh bar; pay for what you use). Nearly all places offer private bathrooms, which have a tub or shower, a toilet, and a bidet (which Italians use for quick sponge baths). Some rooms come with a safe, and other hotels have safes at the front desk.

Double beds are called *matrimoniali*, even though hotels aren't interested in your marital status. Twins are *due letti singoli*. Convents offer cheap accommodation but have more *letti singoli* than *matrimoniali*.

Breakfast and Meals: Italian hotels typically include a satisfying breakfast in their room prices (for details, see page 461). For hotels in this book that don't include breakfast, it's sometimes offered as an optional add-on cost when you book online.

Hotels in resort areas may charge you for half-pension, called *mezza pensione*, during peak season. Half-pension means that you pay for one meal per day per person (lunch or dinner). Sometimes half-pension is required; even when optional, it can be worth considering, especially if the per-meal charge is less than you've been paying for an average restaurant meal (and provided the chef is good).

Hotelier Help: Hoteliers can be a good source of advice. Most

> ## Making Hotel Reservations
>
> Reserve your rooms as soon as you've pinned down your travel dates. For busy national holidays, it's wise to reserve far in advance (see ricksteves.com/festivals).
>
> **Requesting a Reservation:** Book directly with the hotel (not through a third-party booking site). Even small, family-run places typically have websites that offer online bookings. If not, book your room directly via email or phone.
>
> Here's what the hotelier wants to know:
> - Type(s) of room(s) you want and number of guests
> - Number of nights you'll stay
> - Arrival and departure dates, written European-style as day/month (for example, 18/06 or 18 June)
> - Special requests (en suite bathroom, cheapest room, twin beds vs. double bed, quiet room)
> - Applicable discounts (such as a Rick Steves discount, cash discount, or promotional rate)
>
> **Confirming a Reservation:** Most places will request a credit-card number to hold your room. If the hotel's website doesn't have a secure form where you can enter the number, share this info by phone.
>
> **Canceling a Reservation:** If you must cancel, it's courteous—and smart—to do so with as much notice as possible, especially for smaller family-run places. Cancellation policies can be strict; read

know their city well and can assist you with everything from public transit and airport connections to finding a good restaurant, the nearest launderette, or a late-night pharmacy.

Hotel Hassles: Even at the best places, mechanical breakdowns occur: Sinks leak, hot water turns cold, toilets may gurgle or smell, the Wi-Fi goes out, or the air-conditioning dies when you need it most. Report your concerns clearly and calmly at the front desk. In Sicily, a few towns (including Trapani and Siracusa) have old pipes; it's not advisable to drink the tap water. In these places, if you see an extra wastebasket next to the toilet, it means they'd rather you not flush toilet paper.

If you anticipate night noise being a problem, request a quiet room when you book (it may not be possible to change rooms if you discover this on arrival).

For more complicated problems, don't expect instant results. Above all, keep a positive attitude. If your hotel is a disappointment, spend more time out enjoying the place you came to see.

Bed-and-Breakfasts

B&Bs can offer good-value accommodations in excellent locations.

> From: rick@ricksteves.com
> Sent: Today
> To: info@hotelcentral.com
> Subject: Reservation request for 19-22 July
>
> Dear Hotel Central,
>
> I would like to stay at your hotel. Please let me know if you have a room available and the price for:
> - 2 people
> - Double bed and en suite bathroom in a quiet room
> - Arriving 19 July, departing 22 July (3 nights)
>
> Thank you!
> Rick Steves

the fine print before you book. Many discount deals require prepayment and can be expensive to change or cancel.

Reconfirming a Reservation: Always call or email to reconfirm your room reservation a few days in advance. For B&Bs or very small hotels, I call again on my arrival day to tell my host what time to expect me (especially important if arriving after 17:00).

Phoning: For tips on calling hotels overseas, see page 447.

Usually converted family homes or apartments, they can range from humble rooms with communal kitchens to high-end boutique accommodations with extra amenities. Boutique B&Bs can be an especially good option, as they are typically less expensive than a big hotel, but often newer and nicer, with more personal service.

Short-Term Rentals

Short-term vacation rentals offered through Airbnb and other booking sites can be cost-effective, especially for groups or if you're settling in one location for several nights. Keep in mind that European apartments, like hotel rooms, tend to be small by US standards. But they often come with laundry facilities and small, equipped kitchens, making it easier and cheaper to dine in.

Many places require a minimum stay, have strict cancellation policies, and levy a hefty one-time cleaning or service fee. And you're generally on your own: There's no reception desk, breakfast, or daily cleaning service.

Finding Accommodations: Websites such as Airbnb, Booking.com, and Vrbo let you browse a wide range of properties. Alternatively, rental agencies such as interhome.com or rentavilla.

com can provide a more personalized service (their curated listings are also more expensive).

Before you commit, be clear on the location. I like to virtually "explore" the neighborhood using Google Street View. Consider the proximity to public transportation and amenities that are important to you (elevator, air-con, laundry, parking, etc.). Reviews from previous guests can help identify trouble spots.

Think about the kind of experience you want: just a key and an affordable bed...or a chance to get to know a local? Some hosts offer self check-in and minimal contact; others enjoy interacting with you. Read the description and reviews to help shape your decision.

Confirming and Paying: Many places require payment in full before your trip, usually through the listing site. Be wary of owners who want to take your transaction offline or ask you to wire money, which can be indicators of fraud.

Rooms in Private Homes: In small towns, there may be few hotels or apartments but an abundance of Airbnb rentals and some *affittacamere* (rental rooms). These can be anything from a set of keys and a basic bed to a cozy B&B with your own Sicilian grandmother. Renting a room in someone's home is a good option for those traveling alone, as you're more likely to find true single rooms—with just one single bed, and a price to match. These can range from air-mattress-in-living-room basic to plush-B&B-suite posh. While you can't expect your host to also be your tour guide—or even to provide you with much info—some are interested in getting to know the travelers who pass through their home.

Agriturismi

Agriturismi—working farms that double as countryside B&Bs—began cropping up in the 1980s to allow small family farms to survive (as in the US, many have been squeezed out by giant agribusinesses). By renting rooms to travelers, farmers receive generous tax breaks that allow them to remain on their land and continue to grow food crops. These B&Bs make a peaceful home base for those exploring rural Sicily and are ideal for those traveling by car—especially families.

It's wise to book several months in advance for high season (late May-mid-Oct). July and August are jammed with Italians and other European vacationers; in spring and fall, it's mostly foreigners. Weeklong stays (typically Saturday to Saturday) are preferred at busy times, but shorter stays are possible off-season. To sleep

> ## Crowd-Sourcing vs. Guidebooks
>
> User-generated reviews on platforms such as TripAdvisor, Yelp, and Booking.com can give you a consensus of opinions about everything from hotels and restaurants to sights and nightlife.
>
> I find online reviews more reliable for accommodations and sightseeing experiences than for restaurants (which tend to favor touristy options over local gems). When scanning reviews, I look for patterns: repeated complaints about bad service, a problematic location, or nighttime noise. I take one-off complaints with a grain of salt: Even the most expertly run business can have a bad day...or a cranky guest.
>
> As a guidebook writer, my sense is that there's a big difference between the uncurated information on a review site and the vetted listings in a guidebook. A user review is based on the limited experience of one person, who stayed at just one hotel in a given city and ate at a few restaurants there. A guidebook is the work of a trained researcher who forms a well-developed basis for comparison by visiting many restaurants and hotels year after year.
>
> Both types of information have their place, and in many ways, they're complementary. If something is recommended in a guidebook and also gets good online reviews, it's likely a winner.

cheaper, try early spring and late fall. Most places are closed in winter (about Nov-Easter).

As the name implies, *agriturismi* are in the countryside, although some are located on the outskirts of a large town or city. Most are family-run. *Agriturismi* vary dramatically in quality—some properties are rustic, while others are downright luxurious, offering amenities such as swimming pools and riding stables. The rooms are usually clean and comfortable. Breakfast is often included, and *mezza pensione* (half-pension, which in this case means a home-cooked dinner) might be built into the price whether you want it or not. Most places serve tasty homegrown food; some are vegetarian or organic, others are gourmet. Kitchenettes are often available to cook up your own feast.

To qualify officially as an *agriturismo*, the farm must still generate more money from its farm activities, thereby ensuring that the land is worked and preserved. Some farmhouse B&Bs aren't working farms, but are still fine places to stay. Some travelers who are enticed by romanticized dreams of *agriturismi* are turned off when they arrive to actual farm smells and sounds. These folks would be more comfortable with a countryside B&B or villa that offers a bit more upscale comfort. In this book, I've listed both types of rural accommodations; if you want the real thing, make sure the owners call their place an *agriturismo*.

In addition to my listings, local TI websites sometimes have a list of places in their area. For a sampling, visit agriturismoitaly.it/ or search online for *agriturismo*.

Hostels

A hostel provides cheap beds in dorms where you sleep alongside strangers. Travelers of any age are welcome, and family and private rooms are often available. Most hostels offer kitchen facilities and a self-service laundry. Hostels almost always provide bedding, but some charge to rent towels.

Independent hostels tend to be easygoing, colorful, and informal (no membership required; hostelworld.com). You may pay slightly less by booking directly with the hostel. **Official hostels** are part of Hostelling International (HI) and share a booking site (hihostels.com). HI hostels typically require that you be a member or else pay a bit more per night.

Eating

The Italians are masters of the art of fine living. That means eating long and well. Lengthy, multicourse meals and endless hours sitting in outdoor cafés are the norm. Americans eat on their way to an evening event and complain if the check is slow in coming. For Italians, the meal is an end in itself, and only rude servers rush you.

I've written an entire book (with co-author Fred Plotkin) on the subject: *Rick Steves Italy for Food Lovers*, a region-by-region handbook on how to appreciate Italian cuisine like an Italian. This section condenses that book's most valuable tips and insights.

A highlight of your Sicilian adventure will be this island's cafés, cuisine, and wines. Trust me: This is sightseeing for your palate. Even if you liked dorm food and are sleeping in cheap hotels, your taste buds will relish an occasional first-class splurge. You can eat well without going broke. But be careful: You're just as likely to blow a small fortune on a disappointing meal as you are to dine wonderfully for €25. Rely on my recommendations in the various Eating sections throughout this book.

Traditionally, lunch *(pranzo)* was the largest meal of the Italian day, eaten at home between 13:00 and 14:30 (earlier in northern Italy, later in the south). Dinner *(cena)* was a lighter affair, often just soup with cold cuts, eaten around 20:00 or 21:00 (maybe earlier in winter).

However, as times have changed, so have eating habits. So, while some Italian families still have a big lunch and a small dinner, others do the reverse. Many Italian urbanites grab a quick

> ## Restaurant Code
>
> Eateries in this book are categorized according to the average cost of a higher-end pasta or typical main course. Drinks, desserts, and splurge items can raise the price considerably.
>
> €€€€ **Splurge:** Most main courses over €25
> €€€ **Pricier:** €20-25
> €€ **Moderate:** €15-20
> € **Budget:** Under €15
>
> Pizza by the slice and other takeaway food is **€,** a basic trattoria or sit-down pizzeria is **€€,** a casual but more upscale restaurant is **€€€,** and a swanky splurge is **€€€€.**

lunch in a *tavola calda* bar (cafeteria) or buy a *panino* or *tramezzino* (sandwich). To bridge the gap until dinner, people drop into a bar in the late afternoon for a cocktail *(aperitivo),* often served with snacks.

RESTAURANT PRICING AND HOURS

I've categorized my recommended eateries based on the average price of a typical main course, indicated with a euro-sign rating (see sidebar).

The categories also indicate the personality of a place: **Budget** eateries include street food, takeaway, order-at-the-counter shops, basic cafeterias, and bakeries. **Moderate** eateries are nice (but not fancy) sit-down restaurants, ideal for a pleasant meal with good-quality food. Listings that fall in this category are great for a taste of the local cuisine at a reasonable price.

Pricier eateries are a notch up, with more attention paid to the setting, presentation, and (often inventive) cuisine. **Splurge** eateries typically come with an elegant setting, polished service, and pricey and refined cuisine.

Most of my recommended restaurants are open daily for lunch and dinner; I've noted exceptions in the listings.

BREAKFAST

Italian breakfasts, like Italian bath towels, used to be small. But many Italian hotels now offer generous buffet breakfasts. In Sicily, these buffets usually include cold cuts, cheese, croissants, and some sweet items (such as pastries, cakes, cannoli, or cookies), along with yogurt, fruit, sometimes cereal, juice (the delicious red orange juice—*spremuta d'arancia rossa*—made from Sicilian blood oranges), and coffee. A few places may serve eggs (typically hard-boiled; scrambled or fried eggs are less common).

If you want to skip your hotel breakfast (or if it's not included with your room), consider browsing for a morning picnic at a local open-air market. Or do as the Italians do: Step into a bar or café to drink a cappuccino and munch a *cornetto* (croissant) while standing at the counter. While the *cornetto* is the most common pastry, you'll find a range of *pasticcini* (pastries, sometimes called *dolci*). Look for *otto* (an 8-shaped pastry, often filled with custard, jam, or chocolate), *sfoglia* (filo-dough crust that's fruit-filled, like a turnover), or *ciambella* (doughnut filled with custard or chocolate).

In the hot summer months, many Sicilians opt for *granita* at breakfast time. This frozen slush, made with blended fruit or milk, comes in flavors such as coffee, almond, or lemon, and can be topped with whipped cream. To make your order authentic, ask for a warm brioche to dip into your *granita* (or use it as a scoop).

ITALIAN RESTAURANTS

In Italy, a **ristorante** typically means a high-end, sit-down restaurant. A **trattoria** is a notch below a *ristorante* in price, but the food is often just as good, if not better. An **osteria**, which originated as a place to drink wine accompanied by food, is similar. *Trattorie* and *osterie* are generally family-owned and serve home-cooked meals at moderate prices. A *locanda* is an inn, a *cantina* is a wine cellar, and a *birreria* is a brewpub. *Pizzerie*, *rosticcerie* (delis), *tavola calda* ("hot table") bars, *enoteche* (wine bars), and other alternatives are explained later.

I look for restaurants that are convenient to your hotel and sightseeing. When restaurant hunting, choose a spot filled with locals, not tourists. Restaurants parked on famous squares generally serve bad food at high prices to tourists. Venturing even a block or two off the main drag leads to higher-quality food for a better price. Locals eat better at lower-rent locales. Family-run places operate without hired help and can offer cheaper meals.

Most restaurant kitchens close between their lunch and dinner service. Good restaurants don't reopen for dinner before 19:00. If you arrive at opening time, most restaurants will be empty and available—the main push of customers arrives later. Small restaurants with a full slate of reservations for 20:30 or 21:00 often will accommodate walk-in diners willing to eat a quick, early meal, but you aren't expected to linger.

When you want the bill, mime-scribble on your raised palm or request it: *"Il conto, per favore."* You may have to ask more than once. If you're in a hurry, request the check when you receive the last item you order. At more casual places, you can usually skip asking for *il conto* and just walk up to the register and pay.

Cover and Tipping

Avoid surprises when eating out by familiarizing yourself with two common Italian restaurant charges: *coperto* and *servizio*. You won't encounter them in all restaurants, but both charges, if assessed, by law must be listed on the menu.

The ***coperto*** (cover) is a minor fee (€1.50-3/person) covering the cost of the linens, cutlery, and typical basket of bread found on your table. (It's sometimes called *pane e coperto*—"bread and cover.") It's not negotiable, even if you don't eat the bread. And it's not a tip. Think of it as a fee paid to the owner entitling you to use the table for as long as you like.

The ***servizio*** is a 10-15 percent "service" charge that goes to the server (similar to the mandatory gratuity that American restaurants often add for groups of six or more). These days, most Italian restaurants don't charge this separately; rather, they include service in their prices—you'll see *servizio compreso* or *servizio incluso* on the menu. (At places that do levy a separate *servizio* charge, you don't need to leave an additional tip.)

Italian servers are well paid and are not as reliant on additional **tips** as servers are back home. Even so, if you're pleased with the service, it's polite to add a small tip *(una mancia)*. At a simple restaurant or pizzeria, figure on €1 per person (or simply round up the bill); at a finer restaurant, figure a few euros per person. If paying with a credit card, ask to add the tip before they run your card, or tip separately with cash or coins. (Credit card receipts don't come with a "tip line" to fill in.) If paying with cash, it's classy to simply round up the bill when paying. (For instance, if the bill is €46, hand the server €50 and tell them to keep the change.)

Italian Menu Courses

A full Italian meal consists of multiple courses. On some menus, you'll see a few numbers—such as 1, 3, 7—listed after each dish (not the price); these correspond to allergens (ask the restaurant for a decoder list if it's not at the bottom of the menu).

Antipasto: An appetizer such as *salumi* (cured meats, including salami and prosciutto), cheeses, bruschetta, grilled veggies, or deep-fried tasties. To get a sampler plate of *salumi* and cheeses, look for *affettato misto* (mixed *salumi*), *antipasto misto* (*salumi*, cheeses, and marinated vegetables), or *tagliere* (a sampler "board").

Primo piatto: A "first dish" generally consisting of pasta, soup, rice (usually risotto), or polenta

Secondo piatto: A "second dish" of meat or fish/seafood

Contorno: A vegetable side dish that may come with the *sec-*

ondo but more often must be ordered separately. Typical *contorni* are *insalata mista* (mixed salad), spinach, roasted potatoes, or grilled veggies. Vegetarians can skip the *secondo* and order several *contorni* to make a meal.

Dolce: No meal is complete without a sweet. On most menus, you'll find typical Italian desserts such as tiramisu and *panna cotta*, or other local favorites (for a rundown of Sicily's dessert specialties, see page 7). Servers are accustomed to diners splitting a single dessert—just ask for extra forks. Fruit *(frutta)* is often eaten as a dessert, often in the form of *macedonia* (a mixed-fruit salad). A shot of espresso *(un caffè)* is typically served after dessert. (Or skip the restaurant dessert and wander around licking a cone of gelato.)

Ordering Tips

For most travelers, a complete, multicourse meal is simply too much food—and the euros can add up in a hurry. To avoid overeating (and to stretch your budget), share dishes. A good rule of thumb is for each person to order two courses. For example, a couple can order and share one *antipasto*, one *primo*, one *secondo*, and one dessert; or two *antipasti* and two *primi;* or whatever combination appeals. Small groups can mix *antipasti* and *primi* family-style (skipping *secondi*).

It can be worth paying a little more for an inventive fixed-price meal that shows off the chef's creativity. A *menù turistico* is a made-for-tourists plate of Italian food clichés for one fixed price. But locals have their own, typically more interesting version, usually called a *prezzo fisso* or sometimes *menù del giorno* (menu of the day). For a smaller appetite, some restaurants serve a *piatto unico*, with smaller portions of each course on one plate (for instance, a meat, starch, and vegetable).

Seafood and steak may be sold by weight and priced by the *etto* (100 grams, 3.5 ounces) or the kilo (1,000 grams, 2.2 pounds). The abbreviation *s.q. (secondo quantità)* indicates an item is priced by weight (often used at antipasto buffets). Unless the menu indicates a fillet *(filetto)*, fish is usually served whole with the head and tail. You can always ask your server to select a small fish and fillet it for you. Sometimes, especially for steak, restaurants require a minimum order of four or five *etti* (which diners can share). Make sure you're clear on the price before ordering.

Some dishes come in larger quantities meant to be shared by two people. The shorthand way of showing this on a menu is "X2" (for two), but the price listed could indicate the cost per person.

If you order only a pasta and a salad, the server may bring them in that order, which is the opposite of what you might expect; astute servers ask if you want it *insieme* (een-see-EH-meh; together).

Because pasta and bread are both starches, Italians consider them redundant. If you order only a pasta dish, bread may not come with it; you can request it, but you may be charged extra. On the other hand, if you order a vegetable antipasto or a meat *secondo*, bread is often provided to balance the ingredients.

At places with counter service—such as at a bar or a freeway rest-stop diner—you'll first order and pay at the *cassa* (cashier). Then take your receipt to the counter to claim your food.

When going to an especially good restaurant with an approachable staff, I like to find out what they're eager to serve. Sometimes I'll simply say, "Make me happy"...and set a price limit.

BUDGET EATING

Italy offers many budget options for hungry travelers. Self-service cafeterias provide the basics without add-on charges. Travelers on a hard-core budget equip their room with a pantry stocked at the market (fruits and veggies are remarkably cheap), or pick up a sandwich or a kebab, then dine in at picnic prices. Bars and cafés are also good places to grab a meal on the go. In Sicily, cheap and tasty street food can be found in almost every city, either at the markets or in any bar.

Pizzerias

Italians head to a pizzeria at dinnertime to order a one-person pie. Some shops sell *pizza rustica* (also called *pizza al taglio* or *pizza al trancio*)—thick pizza baked in a large rectangular pan and sold by weight. If you simply ask for a piece, you may wind up with a gigantic slab. Instead, clearly indicate how much you want: *un etto*—100 grams—is a hot and cheap snack; *due etti*—200 grams—makes a light meal. Or show the size with your hands: *tanto così* (TAHN-toh koh-ZEE; this much). They may ask if you want it *riscaldata* (ree-skahl-DAH-tah; heated up). The correct answer is *sì*. For a rundown of common types of pizza, see that section, later.

Bars/Cafés

An Italian bar isn't so much a tavern as an inexpensive café. These neighborhood hangouts serve coffee, light food, and drinks from the cooler. This is where locals go for a breakfast of cappuccino and *cornetto* (croissant). Throughout the day, bars are the place to drop in for a coffee or another drink.

Many bars are small—if you can't find a table, you'll need to stand or find a ledge to sit on outside. Most charge extra for table service. To get food to go, say, *"da portar via"* (for the road). Most bars have a WC *(toilette, bagno)* in the back, available to customers...and the discreet public.

Food: To save time for sightseeing, stop by a bar for a light lunch. For quick meals, bars usually have trays of cheap, premade sandwiches (panini, on a baguette; *piadine,* on flatbread; *tramezzini,* on crustless white bread; or *toast*s, on, well, toast)—some are delightfully grilled. They'll sometimes have a variety of salads ready to serve up from under the glass counter.

Ordering: If the bar isn't busy, you can probably just order and pay when you leave. Otherwise, there's a particular procedure: First look around to decide what you want, then go to the cashier *(la cassa)* to order and pay. Often, a list with two sets of prices is posted near the cashier: *al banco* (standing at the bar) or *al tavolo* (seated). Unless you really plan to settle in and watch the world go by, have your drink at the bar. If you're not sure, you can ask, "Same price if I sit or stand?": *"Costa uguale al tavolo o al banco?"* (KOH-stah oo-GWAH-lay ahl TAH-voh-loh oh ahl BAHN-koh).

Upon paying, you're handed a receipt *(scontrino).* Take that to the bartender (whose clean fingers handle no dirty euros) and say what you want. It's customary to set a small coin or two on the bar, as a tip, when you place your order. Throughout Italy, you can get cheap coffee at the bar of any establishment, no matter how fancy, and pay the same low, government-regulated price (generally about a euro if you stand).

Tavola Calda Bars and *Rosticcerie*

For a fast and cheap lunch, find an Italian variation on the corner deli: a *rosticceria* ("roasting place," specializing in roasted meats and accompanying sides, such as roasted potatoes or sautéed greens) or a *tavola calda* bar (a "hot table" point-and-shoot cafeteria with a buffet spread of meat and vegetables; sometimes called *tavola fredda*). For a healthy light meal, ask for a mixed plate of vegetables with a hunk of mozzarella *(piatto misto di verdure con mozzarella;* pee-AH-toh MEE-stoh dee vehr-DOO-ray). Don't be limited by what's displayed. If you'd like a salad with a slice of cantaloupe and some cheese, they'll whip that up for you. With a pointing finger, you can assemble a fine meal. If something's a mystery, ask for *un assaggio* (oon ah-SAH-joh) to get a little taste. To have your choices warmed up, ask for them to be heated *(riscaldata;* ree-skahl-DAH-tah).

Wine Bars

Wine bars *(enoteche)* are a popular, fast, and generally inexpensive option for lunch. Meaning "wine library," an *enoteca* is usually a bar highlighting local wines, accompanied with well-paired light food (such as *salumi* and cheese, a salad, or simple seasonal dishes). A good *enoteca* aims to impress visitors with its wine—look for a blackboard listing today's selection and price per glass. The food prices can add up—be careful with your ordering to keep this a budget choice. For more on Italian cocktails and wines, see page 478.

Aperitivo Snacks *("Apericena")*

The Italian term *aperitivo* means a predinner drink, but it's also used to describe their version of what we might call happy hour: a few light snacks served with the order of a drink during the predinner hours (typically around 18:00 or 19:00 until 21:00). Some places offer a buffet of light bites (though these are becoming less common). The drink itself may not be cheap (typically around €8-12), but some bars offer an enticing array of *salumi*, cheeses, grilled vegetables, and other *antipasti*-type dishes.

Really good spreads earn the nickname *"apericena"*—a pun combining *aperitivo* and *cena* (dinner). It's intended as an appetizer course before heading out for dinner. For light eaters who've had a too-big lunch, this could wind up being enough to skip dinner. Drop by a few bars to scope out their *apericena* before choosing. Or opt for a place with a big view and simpler snacks—either way, you'll get your money's worth.

Markets, Groceries, and Delis: Assembling a Picnic

Picnicking saves lots of euros and is a great way to sample regional specialties. Try the fresh ricotta, *presto* pesto, shriveled olives, and anything else locals are excited about.

Markets: For the most colorful experience, gather your ingredients in the morning at a produce market. Towns big and small have markets selling everything imaginable for a fantastic picnic, including cheese, meat, bread, sweets, and prepared foods (Palermo, Catania, and Siracusa have excellent markets). You'll often find street-food stalls tucked into the marketplace as well (note that many markets close in the early afternoon).

Groceries and Delis: Another budget option is to visit a supermarket (look for the Conad, Carrefour, and Co-op chains), *alimentari* (neighborhood grocery), or *salumeria* (delicatessen) to pick up *salumi,* cheeses, and other picnic supplies. Some grocery stores, *salumerie,* and any *paninoteca* or *focacceria* (sandwich shop) can make a sandwich to order. Just point to what you want, and they'll stuff it into a *panino.* Almost every grocery store has a deli case with prepared items like stuffed peppers, marinated olives, lasagna, and chicken, all usually sold by weight; if you want it reheated, remember the word *riscaldata.* And *rosticcerie* sell cheap food to go—you'll find options such as lasagna, rotisserie chicken, and sides, including roasted potatoes and spinach. For more on *salumi* and cheeses, see those sections, later.

Ordering: A typical picnic for two might be fresh rolls, *un etto* (3.5 ounces) of cheese, and *un etto* of meat (sometimes ordered by the slice—*fetta*—or piece—*pezzo*). For two people, I might get *un etto* of prosciutto and *due pezzi* of bread. Add some fruit and veggies, yogurt, and juice. Total: about €10.

If ordering *antipasti* (such as grilled or marinated veggies) at a deli counter, you can ask for *una porzione* in a takeaway container *(contenitore).* Use gestures to show exactly how much you want. To set a price limit of €5 or €10 on what you order, say *"Da [cinque/dieci] euro, per favore."* The word *basta* (BAH-stah; enough) works as a question or as a statement.

Shopkeepers are happy to sell small quantities of produce, but it's customary to let the merchant choose for you. Say *"per oggi"* (pehr OH-jee; for today) and he or she will grab you something ready to eat. To avoid being overcharged, know the cost per kilo, study the weighing procedure, and do the math. Remember that a kilo is 2.2 pounds.

ITALIAN CUISINE STAPLES

Much of your Italian eating experience will likely involve the big five: pizza, pasta, *salumi,* cheese, and gelato. Here's a rundown on what you might find on menus and in stores. I've included specifics on regional cuisine throughout this book. For more food help, consider *Rick Steves Italy for Food Lovers* or the *Rick Steves Italian Phrase Book & Dictionary,* both of which have menu decoders and plenty of useful phrases for navigating the culinary scene.

Pizza

Here are some of the pizzas you might see at restaurants or at a pizzeria. Note that if you ask for pepperoni on your pizza, you'll get *peperoni* (green or red peppers); instead, try requesting *salsiccia piccante* (spicy sausage) or *salame piccante* (spicy salami).

Bianca: White pizza with no tomatoes

Capricciosa: Prosciutto, mushrooms, olives, artichokes, and hard-boiled eggs—literally the chef's "caprice"

Carciofi: Artichokes

Diavola: Spicy hot

Funghi: Mushrooms

Margherita: Tomato sauce, mozzarella, and basil—the red, white, and green of the Italian flag

Marinara: Tomato sauce, oregano, garlic, no cheese

Napoletana: "Naples style"—mozzarella, anchovies, and tomato sauce

Ortolana or ***vegetariana:*** "Greengrocer-style," with vegetables

Quattro formaggi: Four different cheeses

Quattro stagioni: "Four seasons," with tomato, mozzarella, and usually one-quarter each of ham, mushrooms, artichokes, and olives

Salsiccia: Sausage

Siciliana: Capers, olives, and often anchovies

Pasta

In Italy, pasta is considered a *primo piatto*—a first course. There are hundreds of varieties of Italian pasta, each used to highlight a certain sauce, meat, or regional ingredient. *Pastasciutta* is dry-stored pasta, which is boiled until *al dente* (chewy, "to the tooth") and tossed with a sauce. *Pasta fresca* is fresh pasta cut into noodles and served with sauce, or cut into sheets *(sfoglie),* filled with different ingredients, folded, cooked, and then covered lightly with butter, cream, or broth.

Don't assume that dry pasta is inferior to fresh. If prepared well, it can be just as satisfying. There are two general types of dry pasta. *Pasta lunga* (long pasta) is long enough to twist around a fork: think spaghetti, linguine, and fettuccine. The noodles can be round, such as *capellini* (thin "little hairs"), *vermicelli* ("little worms"), and *bucatini* (long and hollow); or flat, such as *tagliatelle* (flat and wide) and *pappardelle* (very wide, best with meat sauces).

Pasta corta (short pasta) is smaller and in shapes that can be scooped or speared with a fork, such as penne or macaroni. It goes well with creamy sauces and chunkier meat sauces. Tubular pastas come either *lisce* (smooth) or *rigate* (grooved—so sauce clings better). Many short pastas are named for their shapes, such as *conchiglie* (shells), *farfalle* (butterflies), or *cavatappi* (corkscrews).

Here's a list of common pasta toppings and sauces. On a menu, these terms are usually preceded by *alla* (in the style of) or *in* (in):

Aglio e olio: Garlic and olive oil

Sicilian Food

Like all things Sicilian, the local cuisine resembles Italy's, but it's decidedly its own thing. The Sicilian diet relies on Italian staples such as pastas, olives, savory breads, and tomatoes, but gives them a local twist. The island's warm temperatures and fertile volcanic soil mean that the best possible ingredients are available home-grown in Sicily.

Thanks to centuries of North African and Middle Eastern influences, Sicilian cuisine includes distinctive ingredients such as couscous, almonds, ginger, apricots, cinnamon, and lots of citrus. The Arabs popularized fried foods, which is why so many Sicilian street-food classics—and even some pastas—are deep-fried. Sicilian cooking also comes with Greek and Spanish touches. Choosing between fish couscous and spaghetti Bolognese on the same menu, you know you're at a crossroads of cultures.

Sicilian Staples

Seafood is abundant in Sicily: all kinds of fish (swordfish is popular), octopus, squid (cuttlefish), shrimp, and on and on. The real prize is tuna, which is caught wild in the early summer—if it's available fresh, try some. Seafood is commonly served with some combination of pine nuts, pistachios, raisins, and breadcrumbs. Octopus *(polpo)* is often served as a salad with celery and olive oil, or simply boiled, chopped, and accompanied by a wedge of lemon.

Citrus abounds—especially around Etna. Deep-red blood oranges are especially prevalent. Dishes scented with orange and lemon are common, and you'll see tempting juice kiosks offering fresh-squeezed O.J. or a thirst-quenching *seltz*—fresh-squeezed lemon juice, a pinch of salt, and fizzy water (no added sugar).

Pistachios are another Sicilian staple. The best-quality pistachios are grown on the northwestern slopes of Mount Etna, near the town of Bronte. You'll notice pistachios liberally used in cooking (for example, crushed up and sprinkled on pasta).

Oversized **olives** from Castelvetrano are the local answer to Greek Kalamata olives. **Sundried tomatoes** *(pomodori secchi)* are still traditionally made by drying tomatoes on wooden planks on sunny days. Olive oil is a specialty around Mount Etna and in southeastern Sicily, near Ragusa.

Sicily's **cheese** staple is sheep's-milk ricotta. It's used liberally, including sweetened as a filling for cannoli. Another standby is *pecorino*—a semi-hard sheep's-milk cheese that ages well. Pecorino is common in other parts of Italy; the local version is *pecorino siciliano*. *Caciocavallo* is the Sicilian version of parmesan—a dry, crumbly, salty, grateable cow's-milk cheese.

Street Food

Sicily is Italy's street-food mecca. In the hardscrabble markets of Palermo and Catania, locals seek out deep-fried rice balls (*arancine*), chickpea fritters (*panelle*), onion turnovers (*cipollina*), "Sicilian pizza" (*sfincione*), potato croquettes (*cazzilli*), boiled octopus (*polpo bollito*), and the notorious spleen sandwich (*pane con milza*, or *pani c'a meusa*). While these dishes are most authentic in the urban markets of Palermo, Sicilian street food sometimes appears on menus at sit-down restaurants in other parts of Sicily and on the mainland. For a full primer on street food, see page 98.

Sicilian Specialties

Consider trying one of these regional dishes. For local pasta specialties, see "Sicilian Pasta Dishes."

Caponata: Simple yet luxurious sweet-and-sour eggplant stew, served both hot and cold, as a starter or as a side

Couscous al pesce: Couscous served with a side of fish broth, which you ladle on to taste. Fancier variations are topped with a more elaborate array of shellfish and other seafood (*couscous ai frutti di mare*).

Insalata pantesca: A salad made with tender potatoes, tomatoes, onions, and capers

Insalata siciliana (or *insalata di arance*): A popular springtime salad, both delicious and refreshing, made with juicy chunks of orange, chopped wild fennel, and raw onions. You'll never see this prepared the same way twice.

Nero dei Nebrodi: High-end restaurants brag about their "black pork from Nebrodi"—meat from small free-range black pigs raised in the Nebrodi Mountains of northeast Sicily. The pigs, originally brought here under Spanish rule, are the same breed that produces the most expensive Spanish *ibérico* ham.

Parmigiana di melanzane: Eggplant parmesan—fried eggplant layered with tomato sauce and cheese—is a classic that, Sicilians claim, originated on the island.

Polpette: Meat rolls or meatballs made with mixed meat, fish, or even veggies. Real Sicilian meatballs combine beef, veal, and pork.

Polpettone: A traditional meatloaf; its core is filled with spinach, carrots, and cheese

Sarde a beccafico: Rolled-up sardines sprinkled with raisins, pine nuts, and breadcrumbs

Sarde beccafico alla Catanese: Breaded and fried sardines

Eating with the Seasons

Italian cooks love to serve fresh produce and seafood at its tastiest. You'll see Sicily's seasonal specialties displayed in open-air markets throughout the island. To get a plate of the freshest veggies at a fine restaurant, request *"Un piatto di verdure della stagione, per favore."* ("A plate of seasonal vegetables, please."). Italians take fresh, seasonal ingredients so seriously that a restaurant cooking with frozen ingredients *(congelato)* must note it on the menu. Here are a few examples of what's fresh when:

March-May: Calamari, *romanesco* (similar to cauliflower), fava beans, green beans, asparagus, artichokes, wild fennel, citrus

April-June: Asparagus, zucchini flowers, zucchini

May-June: Tuna, mussels, cantaloupe, loquats, strawberries

May-Aug: Eggplant, clams, watermelon, mulberry

July-Sept: Figs, *fichi d'india* (prickly pears), grapes

Oct-Nov: Mushrooms, persimmons, nuts (pistachio, hazelnuts, walnuts)

Nov-Feb: Radicchio, cardoon (wild artichoke)

Alfredo: Sweet butter and heaps of Parmigiano-Reggiano cheese

Amatriciana: Guanciale (pork cheek), tomatoes, *pecorino romano* cheese, and chili peppers

Arrabbiata: "Angry," spicy tomato sauce with chili peppers

Bolognese: "Bologna-style" meat-and-tomato sauce

Boscaiola: "Woodsman-style," with mushrooms and sausage or ham

Brodo: Broth (typical for filled pastas)

Burro e salvia: Butter and sage

Cacio e pepe: Pecorino romano cheese and fresh-ground pepper

Carbonara: Raw egg, *guanciale* (pork cheek), *pecorino romano* cheese, and fresh-ground pepper

Carrettiera: Spicy and garlicky, with olive oil and little tomatoes

Diavola: "Devil-style," spicy hot

Frutti di mare: Seafood

Genovese: Basil ground with Parmigiano-Reggiano cheese, garlic, pine nuts, and olive oil; aka pesto

Gricia: Cured pork cheek and *pecorino romano* cheese

Marinara: Usually tomato, often with garlic and onions, but can also be a seafood sauce ("sailor's style")

Mollicata: Simple sauce of tomato, onion, red wine, breadcrumbs, and sometimes anchovy

Pescatora: Seafood ("fisherman style")

Pomodoro: Tomato only

Puttanesca: Tomato sauce with anchovies and/or tuna, olives, capers, and garlic

Scoglio: Mussels, clams, and tomatoes

Sorrentina: "Sorrento-style," with tomatoes, basil, and mozzarella (usually over gnocchi)

Sugo di lepre: Rich sauce made of wild hare

Tartufi: Truffles (also called *tartufate*)

Vongole: Clams and spices

Sicilian Pasta Dishes

Rather than defaulting to the clichéd *spaghetti carbonara* or *Bolognese*, try some uniquely Sicilian pasta dishes.

Anelletti al forno: Ring-shaped pasta, originating in Palermo, baked with tomatoes, meat, eggplants, and cheese

Busiate alla Trapanese: A twisty noodle, similar to fusilli, topped with red pesto made from almonds, tomatoes, garlic, and cheese

Norma: Tomato, eggplant, basil, and *ricotta salata*

Pasta alla botarga: Dried tuna roe—very salty and very fishy

Pasta con le sarde: Topped with sardines and anchovies. The similar *pasta alla Palermitana* includes sardines, fennel, pine nuts, and breadcrumbs.

Pasta cu maccu: A stick-to-your-ribs fava-bean stew with pasta—once eaten by famished peasants

Spaghetti ai ricci: Spaghetti topped with sea urchin, a top-end choice for eaters who enjoy a taste of the sea

Salumi

Salumi (cured meats)—sometimes called *affettati*—are an Italian staple. While most American cold cuts are cooked, in Italy they're far more commonly cured by air-drying, salting, and smoking. While called "raw"—*crudo*—these are perfectly safe to eat.

The two most familiar types of *salumi* are *salame* and *prosciutto*. *Salame* is an air-dried, sometimes-spicy sausage that comes in many varieties. When Italians say *"prosciutto,"* they usually mean *prosciutto crudo*—the raw ham that air-cures on the hock and is then thinly sliced. Produced mainly in northern Italy, *prosciutto* can be either *dolce* (sweet) or *salato* (salty). Purists say the best is *prosciutto di Parma*. Squeamish eaters should avoid *testa in cassetta* (headcheese—organs in aspic) and *lampredotto* (cow stomach).

> ### *Arancina* vs. *Arancino*
>
> Sicily's most popular street food is a deep-fried rice ball with *ragù* (meat sauce) inside—but what you get varies, depending on where you are on the island. In Palermo and the west, where the rice balls originated in the 10th century, they're called *arancina* (fem., pl. *arancine*). In Catania and the east, they're called *arancino* (masc., pl. *arancini*). Classic western *arancine* are round, flavored with saffron, and contain no tomatoes. Traditional eastern *arancini* are pointy and usually contain tomatoes but rarely have saffron. The pointed shape resembles the profile of Mount Etna, and the molten *ragù* inside echoes the volcano's hot lava.
>
> In either city, you'll find variations in shapes and fillings. Sometimes the shape indicates what's inside. Look for these at bars and pizza shops: butter and ham (spherical), eggplant (oval, darker crust), pistachio cream (oval), and *alla Palermitana*—with sardines, wild fennel, pine nuts, and pecorino cheese (oval).
>
> No matter which one you pick, watch your language: Never call it *arancino* in the west, or *arancina* in the east. Just... don't.

Other *salumi* may be less familiar, but no less worth trying:

Bresaola: Air-cured beef
Capocollo: Peppery pork shoulder (also called *coppa*)
Culatello: High-quality, slow-cured prosciutto
Finocchiona: *Salame* with fennel seeds
Guanciale (or **quanciale**): Tender pork cheek
Lardo: Pork lard made fragrant with herbs and spices; the best is *lardo di Colonnata*
Lonzino: Cured pork loin
Mortadella: A finely ground pork loaf, similar to our bologna
'Nduja: Super-spicy, smoky, soft, spreadable pork sausage that's bright red and with a texture like pâté
Pancetta: Salt-cured, peppery pork-belly meat, similar to bacon
Salame di Sant'Olcese: What we'd call "Genoa salami"
Salame piccante: Spicy hot, similar to pepperoni
Soppressata: A simple dry *salame* that has some kick, common in the south
Speck: Smoked pork shoulder

Cheese

When it comes to cheese (*formaggio* or *cacio*), you're probably already familiar with most of these Italian favorites:

Asiago: Hard cow cheese that comes either *mezzano* (young and firm) or *stravecchio* (aged and pungent)

Burrata: Ball of mozzarella wrapped around a buttery center

Caciocavallo: Depending on its age, a mild to sharp cow's-milk cheese shaped like a pear

Fontina and **Montasio:** Semihard, nutty, Gruyère-style mountain cheeses

Gorgonzola: Pungent, blue-veined cheese, either *dolce* (creamy) or *piccante* (aged and sharp)

Grana or **Grana padano:** Hard, nutty cheese used for grating; a less expensive alternative to Parmigiano-Reggiano

Mascarpone: Sweet, buttery, spreadable dessert cheese

Mozzarella di bufala: Made from the milk of water buffaloes

Parmigiano-Reggiano: Hard and nutty cow cheese, ideal for grating over pasta

Pecorino: Sheep's cheese, either *fresco* (fresh and soft) or *stagionato* (aged, sometimes called *pecorino romano* and popular for grating)

Provolone: Rich, firm, aged cow cheese

Ricotta: Soft and creamy, made by "recooking" cheese curds a second time; ***ricotta salata*** ("salted") is hard and used for grating

Scamorza: Similar to mozzarella, but often smoked

Gelato

American and Italian ice cream are similar but decidedly not the same. Italy's gelato is denser and creamier (even though it has less butterfat than ice cream) than American versions, and connoisseurs swear it's more flavorful.

A key to gelato appreciation is sampling liberally and choosing flavors that go well together. At a *gelateria*, ask, as Italians do, for a taste: *"Un assaggio, per favore?"* (oon ah-SAH-joh pehr fah-VOH-ray).

Most *gelaterie* clearly display prices and sizes. Point to the price or say what you want—for instance, for a €3 cup, say: *"Una coppetta da tre euro"* (OO-nah koh-PEH-tah dah tray eh-OO-roh).

The best *gelaterie* display signs reading *artigianale, nostra produzione,* or *produzione propria,* indicating that the gelato is made on the premises. Seasonal flavors are also a good sign, as are mellow hues (avoid colors that don't appear in nature). Gelato stored in covered metal tins (rather than white plastic) is more likely to be homemade.

Other Italian frozen treats include *sorbetto* (sorbet—made with fruit, but no milk or eggs), *granita,* and *cremolata* (a gelato-*granita* float). *Caffè affogato* is a scoop of gelato "drowned" in a shot of hot espresso.

Classic gelato flavors include:

Bacio: Chocolate hazelnut, named for Italy's popular "kiss" candies

Caffè: Coffee

Cassata: With dried fruits
Ciliegia: Cherry
Cioccolato: Chocolate
Crema: Plain (similar to vanilla)
Croccantino: "Crunchy," with toasted nut bits
Fior di latte: Creamy milk
Fragola: Strawberry
Frutti di bosco: Mixed berries
Gianduia (or *gianduja*): Chocolate-hazelnut
Lampone: Raspberry
Limone: Lemon
Macedonia: Mixed fruits
Malaga: Similar to rum raisin
Menta (or *cioccomenta*): Mint or mint-chocolate
Nocciola: Hazelnut
Noce: Walnut
Pistacchio: Pistachio
Riso: With actual bits of rice mixed in
Stracciatella: Vanilla with chocolate shreds
Tartufo: Super chocolate
Zabaione: Named for the dessert of egg yolk and Marsala wine
Zuppa inglese: Sponge cake, custard, chocolate, and cream

BEVERAGES

Italian bars serve great drinks—hot, cold, sweet, caffeinated, or alcoholic.

Water, Juice, and Other Drinks

Italians are notorious water snobs. At restaurants, it's customary and never expensive to order a *litro* or *mezzo litro* (half-liter) of bottled water. Ask for *con gas* if you want fizzy water and *senza gas* if you prefer still water. You can try asking for *acqua del rubinetto* (tap water), but your server may give you a funny look—they just can't understand why you wouldn't want good water to go with your good food. Water is rarely served with ice; Italians are adamant that ice-cold drinks are bad for digestion. If you request ice, you'll likely be given a few cubes on a little saucer.

Chilled bottled water—still *(naturale)* or carbonated *(frizzante)*—is sold cheaply in stores. Half-liter bottles of mineral water are available everywhere for about €1.

Juice is *succo,* and *spremuta* means freshly squeezed. Order *una spremuta* (don't confuse it with *spumante,* sparkling wine)—it's usually orange juice *(arancia),* and from February through April it can be made from Sicilian blood oranges *(arance rosse).* Stands selling *spremuta* are all over the island, and many will mix different juices to make fresh-squeezed concoctions.

In grocery stores, you can get a liter of O.J. for the price of a Coke or coffee. Look for *100% succo* or *senza zucchero* (without sugar) on the label—or be surprised by something diluted and sugary sweet.

Tè freddo (iced tea) is usually from a can—sweetened and flavored with lemon or peach. Lemonade is *limonata.*

If you want a hot drink other than coffee, *cioccolato* is hot chocolate, and *tè* is hot tea.

Coffee

The espresso-based style of coffee so popular in the US was born in Italy. If you ask for *"un caffè,"* you'll get a shot of espresso in a little cup. Most Italian coffee drinks begin with espresso, to which varying amounts of hot water and/or steamed or foamed milk are added. The closest thing to American-style drip coffee is a *caffè americano*—a shot of espresso diluted with hot water. Milky drinks, like cappuccino or *caffè latte,* are served to locals before noon and to tourists any time of day. To an Italian, cappuccino is a morning drink; they believe having milk after a big meal impairs digestion. If they add any milk after lunch, it's just a splash, in a *caffè macchiato.*

Italians like their coffee only warm—to get it very hot, request *"Molto caldo, per favore"* (MOHL-toh KAHL-doh pehr fah-VOH-ray). Any coffee drink is available decaffeinated—ask for it *decaffeinato* (deh-kah-feh-NAH-toh).

Cappuccino: Espresso with foamed milk on top (*cappuccino freddo* is an iced cappuccino)

Caffè latte: Espresso to which heated milk is added (ordering just a "latte" gets you only milk)

Caffè macchiato: Espresso "stained" with a splash of milk, in a small cup

Latte macchiato: Layers of hot milk and foam, "stained" with an espresso shot, in a tall glass. Note that if you order simply a *"macchiato,"* you'll probably get a *caffè macchiato* (see above).

Caffè corto/lungo: Concentrated espresso diluted with a tiny bit of hot water, in a small cup. Get a **caffè lungo** if you want more water added.

Caffè americano: Espresso diluted with even more hot water, in a larger cup

Caffè corretto: Espresso "corrected" with a shot of grappa or sambuca

Marocchino: "Moroccan" coffee with espresso, foamed milk, and cocoa powder; the similar *mocaccino* has chocolate instead of cocoa

Caffè freddo: Sweet and iced espresso

Caffè crema (or crema di caffè): Espresso whipped with cream, then frozen; like a shot of coffee ice cream
Caffè hag: Instant decaf

Alcoholic Beverages

Beer: While Italy is traditionally considered wine country, the production of craft beer *(birra artigianale)* has seen a recent and passionate growth. Even in small towns, you'll see microbreweries slinging their own brews. What's on tap is often inspired by the same trends you'll find stateside—IPAs, ambers, stouts, saisons, sours, seasonal beers, and so on. You'll also find local (Messina, Peroni, and Moretti), as well as imports such as Heineken. Italians drink mainly lager beers. Beer on tap is *alla spina*. Get it *piccola* (33 cl, 11 oz), *media* (50 cl, about a pint), or *grande* (a liter). A *lattina* (lah-TEE-nah) is a can and a *bottiglia* (boh-TEEL-yah) is a bottle.

Cocktails and Spirits: Italians appreciate both *aperitivi* (palate-stimulating cocktails) and *digestivi* (after-dinner drinks designed to aid digestion).

The classic ***aperitivo*** is the *spritz:* prosecco (or white wine) and soda livened up with either Campari (carmine red bitters with a secret blend of herbs and orange peel) or Aperol (sweeter, softer, bright orange bitters with herbal, citrusy undertones). Vermouths (both red and white) from Carpano, Cinzano, Martini, or Riccadonna can be served straight, on the rocks, with a splash of soda, or as part of drinks like Punt e Mes (sweet red vermouth and red wine). Other choices include Americano (vermouth with bitters, brandy, and lemon peel), Garibaldi (also known as Campari-Orange, a mixture of Campari and orange juice), and Cynar (bitters flavored with artichoke).

Digestivo choices fall into three categories. First is the bittersweet, syrupy herbal drink called *amaro* (many restaurants have their own brew; popular commercial brands are Fernet Branca and Montenegro). For something sweeter, try *limoncello* (lemon), *amaretto* (almond), Frangelico (hazelnut), *sambuca* (anise), or Marsala wine. Grappa is a brandy distilled from grape skins and stems; *stravecchio* is an aged, mellower variation. *Acquavite* ("water of life") is similar to grappa, but distilled from fruit such as apples, berries, or plums.

Wine: The ancient Greeks who colonized Italy more than 2,000 years ago called it Oenotria—land of the grape. Centuries later, Galileo wrote, "Wine is light held together by water." Wine *(vino)* is certainly a part of the Italian culinary trinity—

Ordering Wine

To order a glass of red or white wine, say, *"Un bicchiere di vino rosso/bianco."* House wine comes in a carafe; choose from a quarter-liter pitcher (8.5 oz, *un quarto*), half-liter pitcher (17 oz, *un mezzo*), or one-liter pitcher (34 oz, *un litro*). When ordering, have some fun, gesture like a local, and you'll have no problems speaking the language of the *enoteca*. *Salute!*

English	Italian
wine	*vino* (VEE-noh)
house wine	*vino della casa* (VEE-noh DEH-lah KAH-zah)
glass	*bicchiere/calice* (bee-kee-EH-ray/KAH-lee-chay)
bottle	*bottiglia* (boh-TEEL-yah)
carafe	*caraffa* (kah-RAH-fah)
red	*rosso* (ROH-soh)
white	*bianco* (bee-AHN-koh)
rosé	*rosato* (roh-ZAH-toh)
sparkling	*spumante/frizzante* (spoo-MAHN-tay/freed-ZAHN-tay)
dry	*secco* (SEH-koh)
fruity	*fruttato* (froo-TAH-toh)
full-bodied	*corposo/pieno* (kor-POH-zoh/pee-EH-noh)
sweet	*dolce* (DOHL-chay)

grape, olive, and wheat. (I'd add gelato.) Ideal conditions for grapes (warm climate, well-draining soil, and an abundance of hillsides) make the Italian peninsula a paradise for grape growers, winemakers, and wine drinkers.

In most years, Italian winemakers produce more wine than any other country—more than 4 million liters annually. Production is mainly red *(rosso)* and white *(bianco)* wines. Rosé *(rosato)* is less traditional—though as it's become trendy stateside and elsewhere, more Italian vintners are experimenting with it. A sparkling wine is *frizzante* or *spumante*; prosecco is a bubbly white wine from northeastern Italy.

Even if you're clueless about wine, the information on an Italian wine label can help you choose something decent. Terms you may see on the bottle include *classico* (from a defined, select area), *annata* (year of harvest), *vendemmia* (harvest), and *imbottigliato dal produttore all'origine* (bottled by producers).

In general, Italy designates its wines by one of four official categories:

Vino da Tavola (VDT) is table wine made from grapes grown anywhere in Italy. It's often inexpensive, but Italy's wines are so

> ## Sicilian Wines
>
> Wine has been produced on the shores of Sicily since the time of the Greeks. The island, with a variety of grape-growing areas with differing characteristics, is one of the biggest producers of wine in Italy. While once considered the land of cheap and cheery table wine, you'll now find upscale wineries ranging from big producers like Planeta to small family operations. Some of the grape varieties grown here are common on the mainland, but others, such as the red nerello grape, can be found only in Sicily.
>
>
>
> **Western Sicily:** More than half of the vineyards in Sicily are in the relatively small area around Trapani, on the west coast. These wines are inexpensive and generally good; you can buy a decent bottle at a wine shop for less than €10. The common white grape varieties are catarratto, grillo, grecanico, zibibbo, and inzolia. Among the red varieties is perricone.
>
> But western Sicily is best known for its Marsala wine, a fortified wine that earned the first DOC designation (indication of quality) in Italy. Marsala is made with four local grape varieties (grillo, inzolia, catarratto, and damaschino), and comes in sweet, dry, and semidry versions. Most local cooks keep a bottle of Marsala handy—this grade, called "fine," is only aged one year. The grades (and prices) go up depending on age, from 2 to 10 years or more. For more on Marsala wine, see page 172.
>
> **Eastern Sicily:** On this side, wines are grown from the south coast around Ragusa and Noto to the slopes of Mount Etna. Sicily's most famous and plentiful variety, Nero d'Avola, is grown all over the island but originates in the southeastern corner. In recent years, the rich volcanic soil and old vines of the Etna area have become a magnet for boutique producers. Wineries cluster around the north slope, like a Sicilian Napa Valley. Look for the native nerello and carricante varieties here. For more on Etna wines, see page 378.

good that, for many people, a basic *vino da tavola* is just fine with a meal. Many restaurants, even modest ones, take pride in their house wine *(vino della casa)*, bottling their own or working with wineries. These days a *vino da tavola* can also be a high-end niche wine—the price will tell you.

Denominazione di Origine Controllata (DOC) meets national standards for high-quality wine. Made from grapes in a defined area, these are usually quite affordable and good.

Denominazione di Origine Controllata e Guarantita (DOCG), the highest grade, meets national standards for the highest-quality wine (made with grapes from a defined area whose quality is "controlled and guaranteed"). These wines can be identified by the pink or green label on the neck...and the high price. (*Riserva* indicates a DOC or DOCG wine that's been aged for even longer than required.) Sicily has just one DOCG wine, but you'll find lots of budget-friendly, high-quality DOC options.

Indicazione Geografica Tipica (IGT) is a broad group of wines that don't meet the standard for DOC or DOCG status but have been designated as "typical" of a particular region.

If you're on a tight budget, try looking for a more affordable alternative. For example, in Tuscany, the world-famous Brunello di Montalcino (a DOCG) can break the bank, but Rosso di Montalcino (a DOC)—made in the same zone with similar grapes, in a similar way, but aged for a shorter period of time—costs half as much.

Transportation

Figuring out how to get around in Europe is one of your biggest decisions. **Cars** work well for two or more traveling together (especially families with small kids), those packing heavy, and those delving into the countryside. **Trains** and **buses** are best for solo travelers, blitz tourists, city-to-city travelers, and those who want to leave the driving to others. Short-hop **flights** within Europe can creatively connect the dots. Be aware of the potential downside of each option: A car is an expensive headache in any major city; with trains and buses, you're at the mercy of a timetable; flying entails a trek to and from a usually distant airport and leaves a larger carbon footprint.

If your itinerary mixes cities and countryside, my advice is to connect cities by train or bus and to explore rural areas by car. Arrange to pick up your car in the last big city you'll visit, then use it to lace together small towns and explore the countryside. For more detailed information on transportation throughout Europe, see ricksteves.com/transportation.

TRAINS

To travel by train affordably within Italy, you can simply buy tickets as you go. For travelers ready to lock in dates and times weeks or months in advance for longer trips, buying nonrefundable tickets online can cut costs in half. Note that the Italy rail pass is generally not a good value, but if your travel extends beyond Italy, then a Eurail Global Pass might be worth looking into. For advice on figuring out the smartest train-ticket or rail-pass options for your trip, visit the Trains & Rail Passes section of my website at ricksteves.com/rail.

Note that the train system in Sicily is not extensive and does not connect the entire island. The train line on the west coast, for example, does not connect to any other lines. Most trains are slow, and in some cases, the bus is a better option.

Types of Trains

Most trains in Sicily are operated by the state-run **Trenitalia** company (trenitalia.com, aka Ferrovie dello Stato Italiane, abbreviated FS). Ticket prices depend on the speed of the train, so it helps to know the different types of trains: pokey Regionale (R or REG), medium-speed Regionale Veloce (RV), and fast InterCity (IC). Note that high-speed Frecce and Italo trains don't run in Sicily.

Trenitalia's regional trains in Sicily have a set second-class ticket price for each route, no advance-purchase discount, open seating only, and often no first-class option. InterCity trains have assigned seats, which are built into your ticket for a specific date and time. Few trains in Sicily require seat reservations, which are important only on routes that connect the island to the mainland.

The **Circumetnea** railway provides service from Paternò to the west and north sides of Mount Etna (circumetnea.it; see page 375).

Schedules

Check schedules at trenitalia.it or use their app (for international trips, use bahn.com, Germany's excellent all-Europe schedule website). At the train station, the easiest way to check schedules is at a ticket machine. Enter the desired date, time, and destination to see all your options. Printed schedules are also posted at the station (yellow posters show departures—*partenze;* white posters show arrivals).

Buying Point-to-Point Tickets

You can buy tickets online, with an app, at train station ticket windows, from ticket machines, or at travel agencies. For long-haul runs or travel on a busy weekend or holiday, it can be cheaper to buy tickets in advance and lock in a seat assignment. But because most Italian trains run frequently and there's no deadline to buy

Connecting Sicily with Mainland Italy

If your trip to Sicily is part of a longer European trip, you may want to connect directly to mainland Italy. The easiest and fastest way is to fly to or from Palermo, Catania, or Trapani; flights can be inexpensive if booked in advance (especially for connections to Rome).

Budget travelers and those who enjoy the scenic route can consider linking by ferry, train, or bus. Long-distance buses (cheapest) and trains depart daily to most major cities on the mainland. Buses cross overnight via ferry at the Strait of Messina, at Sicily's northeast coast (for details, see saistrasporti.it or autoservizisalemi.it), while trains have special cars that are loaded onto a ferry and rejoin the tracks on the other side. If taking an overnight train, you can reserve a sleeping car in advance.

The quickest ferry trip is via the Strait of Messina to locations at the tip of Italy's boot. Ferries carrying both cars and walk-on passengers depart from Messina for Villa San Giovanni (30 minutes, carontetourist.it); a hydrofoil links Messina with Reggio di Calabria in 30 minutes (foot passengers only, libertylines.it). Long-haul ferries take 8-15 hours to connect Sicilian ports (including Palermo and Catania) with Naples, Civitavecchia (near Rome), or Livorno (near Florence).

---

tickets, for the most part I prefer to keep my travel plans flexible by purchasing tickets as I go.

It's easy to buy Trenitalia tickets **online.** At the website, choose English and be sure to read the pricing info, as many of the cheaper tickets are not refundable or changeable. You can keep the ticket on your mobile device (either as a PDF or with a QR code), or you can print it out. Or download the Trenitalia **app** to your phone—it has an English version that makes ticket-buying a breeze.

At the train station, avoid lines by using **ticket machines** for travel within Italy, seat reservations, and even booking a *cuccetta* (koo-CHEH-tah; overnight berth). If you do use the **ticket windows,** be sure you're in the correct line: *biglietti* (general tickets), *prenotazioni* (reservations), *nazionali* (domestic), and *internazionali*.

Trenitalia's ticket machines are user-friendly and found in all but the tiniest stations in Italy. You can pay with cash (change given when indicated) or by credit card (even for small amounts, but you may need to enter your PIN—even when using "tap-to-pay"). Select English, then your destination. If you don't immediately see the city you're traveling to, keep keying in the spelling until it's listed. You can choose from first- and second-class seats, request tickets for more than one traveler, and pick seats, when applicable. Don't select a discount rate without being sure that you meet the

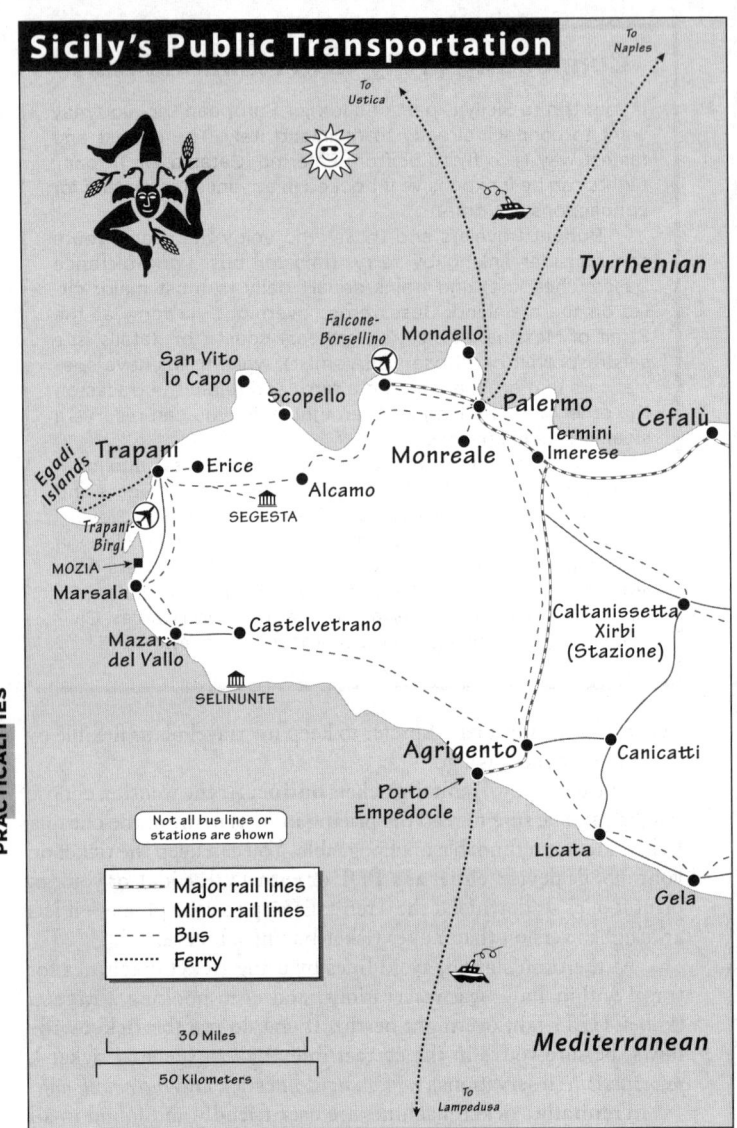

criteria (for example, Americans are not eligible for certain EU or resident discounts).

Some **international tickets** can't be bought online or from machines; for these tickets and anything else that requires a real person, you must go to a ticket window at the station. A good alternative, though, is to drop by a local travel agency. Agencies sell domestic and international tickets and make reservations. They

Transportation 485

charge a small fee, but the language barrier (and the lines) can be smaller than at the station's ticket windows.

Rail Passes

The single-country Eurail Italy Pass may save you money if you take several long train rides or prefer first-class travel, but for most people it's not a good value. In Sicily, no train trip within the island would warrant a rail pass, as it's cheaper to buy point-to-point tickets instead. Furthermore, a rail pass doesn't offer much hop-on convenience in Italy, since with a rail pass, seat reservations are required for InterCity, EuroCity, and Frecce trains.

Train Tips

Validating Tickets: An open ticket (generally for a *regionale* train) bought from a ticket desk or machine must be validated (date-stamped) before you board (the ticket may say *da convalidare* or *convalida*). To validate it, before getting on the train, stamp your ticket in the machine near the platform (usually marked *convalida biglietti* or *vidimazione*). Once you validate a ticket, you must complete your trip within the stamped timeframe (usually about four hours). If you forget to validate your ticket, go right away to the train conductor or you'll pay a fine. *Regionale* tickets purchased online are for specific trains, but the date and time can be changed up until 23:59 the day before your trip. On the day of travel, you can only change the time of your journey and only before the scheduled departure (at that point, the ticket is automatically validated).

In big-city stations, you may need to show your ticket to a staff member to access the tracks. Tickets for fast trains, which include a reserved seat *(biglietto con prenotazione),* don't need validation; you can just get on board.

Getting a Seat: If you're taking an unreserved *regionale* train that originates at your departure point (e.g., you're catching the Palermo-Agrigento train in Palermo), arriving at least 15 minutes before the departure time will help you snare a seat.

Baggage Storage: Many Italian stations have *deposito bagagli* where you can safely leave your bag for a standardized but steep price (double-check closing hours; they may ask to photocopy your passport). Due to security concerns, no Italian stations have lockers.

Theft: Italian trains are famous for their thieves. Never leave a bag unattended. Police do ride the trains, cutting down on theft.

Strikes: Strikes, which are common, generally last a day (often a Friday). Train employees will simply explain, *"Sciopero"* (SHOH-peh-roh, strike). But in actuality, a minimum amount of "essential" or "guaranteed" *(garantito)* main-line service is maintained (by law) during strikes. When a strike is pending, travel agencies, savvy hoteliers, and station personnel can check to see when the strike will go into effect and which trains will continue to run. Revised schedules may be posted online and in Italian at stations. Visit trenitalia.com, choose English, then "Information and Contacts" and "In Case of Strike" (but detailed info will be in Italian).

If your train is canceled, your reserved-seat ticket will likely be accepted on any similar train running that day (either earlier or later than the original departure time) but you won't have a seat assignment. Tickets for canceled trains should also be exchangeable without penalty ahead of the original departure time, or can be refunded (have an agent mark it "unused," and check refund deadlines). A rail pass works on any train still operating, but partially used rail passes can't be refunded—so make full use of any pass you have to continue your trip.

BUSES

You can usually get anywhere you want in Sicily by bus, as long as you're not in a hurry and you plan ahead (view bus schedules online or at local TIs or bus stations). For reaching small towns, buses are sometimes the only option if you don't have a car.

Long-distance buses in Sicily are a great alternative to the train. They are usually cheaper, more direct, more frequent, and occasionally (unlike trains) have free Wi-Fi.

Unfortunately, no single bus company handles every Sicilian route. Instead, multiple regional bus companies operate various routes around the island. These include Salemi (autoservizisalemi.it), SAIS Autolinee (saisautolinee.it), SAIS Trasporti (saistrasporti.it), AST (aziendasicilianatrasporti.it), and Interbus/Segesta/Etna Trasporti (interbus.it), to name a few. It's smart to confirm routes and times locally.

To save time, buy your ticket online or from a travel agency (usually for a small fee). Many bus companies use etickets (they'll scan your emailed QR code as you board).

Traveling by bus on Sundays and holidays can be problematic; even from large cities, schedules are sparse, departing buses are jam-packed, and ticket offices are often closed. Plan ahead and buy your ticket in advance.

Larger towns have a (usually chaotic) long-distance bus station *(stazione degli autobus* or *autostazione)*, with ticket windows and several stalls (usually labeled *corsia, stallo,* or *binario)*. Smaller towns—where buses are more useful—often have a central bus stop *(fermata)*, likely along the main road or on the main square, and maybe several more scattered around town. In small towns, buy bus tickets at newsstands or tobacco shops (with the big *T* signs). When buying your ticket, confirm the departure point *("Dov'è la fermata?")*.

Before boarding, confirm the destination with the driver. You are expected to stow big bags underneath the bus (if the compartment is closed, ask the driver for help; which compartment you use may depend on your destination).

TAXIS AND RIDE-BOOKING SERVICES

Most Italian taxis are reliable and cheap. Often, two people can travel short distances by cab for little more than the cost of bus or subway tickets. In Palermo and Catania, you can use an app called **Free Now** to hail a taxi. This can be a convenient alternative to calling a dispatcher or finding a taxi stand; prices are fixed up front, and you can pay with a credit card through the app. Note that **Uber** operates only in Palermo.

RENTING A CAR

It's cheaper to arrange most car rentals from the US, so research and compare rates before you go. Most of the major US rental agencies (including Avis, Budget, Enterprise, Hertz, and Thrifty) have offices throughout Europe. Also consider the two major Europe-based agencies, Europcar and Sixt. Consolidators such as Auto Europe (autoeurope.com—or the sometimes cheaper autoeurope.eu) compare rates at several companies to get you the best deal.

Wherever you book, always read the fine print. Check for add-on charges—such as one-way drop-off fees, airport surcharges, additional driver fees, or mandatory insurance policies—that aren't included in the quoted price.

Rental Costs and Considerations

If you book well in advance, expect to pay $350-500 for a one-week rental for a basic compact car. Allow extra for supplemental insurance, fuel, tolls, and parking. To save money on fuel, request a diesel car.

Manual vs. Automatic: Cars with manual transmission are more common in Europe and generally cheaper than automatic. If you need an automatic, it's wise to book well in advance. When selecting a car, don't go for a larger model, as it won't be as maneuverable on narrow, winding roads or when squeezing into tight parking lots.

Fuel vs. Electric: Electric cars are becoming more common in Europe and are generally cheaper to rent than fuel-engine cars (in some cities, they may even grant you access to limited traffic zones). Before you select an all-electric vehicle, think carefully about how much you plan to drive each day and where you can recharge.

Age Restrictions: Some rental companies impose minimum and maximum age limits—check the rental policies and rules section of car-rental websites.

Choosing Pickup/Drop-off Locations: Always check the hours of the location you choose: Many rental offices close from midday Saturday until Monday morning and, in smaller towns, at lunchtime. When selecting an office, confirm the location on a map. A downtown site might seem more convenient than the airport but could actually be in the suburbs or buried deep in big-city streets.

Pedestrianized and one-way streets can make navigation

tricky when returning a car at a big-city office or urban train station. For example, it's far easier to pick up and return a rental car to the Palermo or Catania airport. Both are just outside the city, easy to reach by bus or taxi from the center, and offer quick, easy access to the main highways.

Wherever you select, get precise details on the location and allow ample time to find it. And be aware that some Sicilian cities—including Palermo, Cefalù, and Siracusa—have a "ZTL" (limited traffic zone) that's carefully monitored by cameras. If your drop-off point is near this zone, get clear directions on how to get there to avoid getting a big fine.

Have the Right License: In addition to your driver's license, you're required to carry an International Driving Permit—an official translation of your license ($30, apply online at aaa.com/vacation/idpf.html). This is being enforced more strictly every year.

Picking Up Your Car: Before driving off, check the car thoroughly and make sure any dents or scratches are noted on your rental agreement (or take photos of any damage). Rental agencies in Europe tend to charge for even minor damage, so be sure to mark everything. Find out how your car's gearshift, lights, turn signals, wipers, dashboard display, and fuel cap function, and know what kind of fuel the car takes (diesel or unleaded). When you return the car, make sure the agent verifies its condition with you.

Car Insurance Options

When you rent a car in Europe, the price typically includes liability insurance, which covers harm to other cars or motorists—but not the rental car itself. To limit your financial risk in case of damage to the rental, choose one of these options: Buy a Collision Damage Waiver (CDW; also called "loss damage waiver" or LDW by some firms) with a low or zero deductible from the car-rental company (roughly 30-40 percent extra); get coverage through your credit card (essentially "free," but more complicated if you need to use it); or get collision insurance as part of a larger travel-insurance policy.

Basic **CDW** costs $15–30 a day and typically comes with a $1,000-2,000 deductible, reducing but not eliminating your financial responsibility. When you reserve or pick up the car, you'll be offered the chance to "buy down" the deductible to zero (for an additional $10–30/day; this is sometimes called "super CDW" or "zero-deductible coverage").

In Italy, most car-rental rates automatically include CDW coverage. Even if you try to decline CDW when you reserve your car, you may find when you show up at the counter that you must buy it after all (along with mandatory theft insurance, about $15–20 a day).

Getting a car with complete coverage will save you stress in Sicily. I pay for super CDW here, and drive care-free.

For more on car-rental insurance, see ricksteves.com/cdw.

Navigation

Using Your Phone: The mapping app on your phone works fine for navigating Europe's roads. Remember to bring your phone's car charger. In newer rental cars, you can plug your phone directly into a USB port (or connect with Bluetooth) and display GPS directions on the car's dashboard screen.

To save on data, most mapping apps allow you to download maps for offline use (do this before you need them, when you have a strong Wi-Fi signal). Some apps—including Google Maps—provide offline route directions, but you'll need to be online for current traffic.

Dashboard GPS: Some rental cars come with their own dashboard GPS system. Ask about enabling this in advance; it's sometimes an add-on cost (usually about $15-20/day).

Paper Maps and Atlases: Be wary of relying solely on GPS in Sicily, particularly on country roads. Aside from highways and state roads, routes that appear to be major on an online map can quickly turn into gravel donkey trails. If something doesn't look right, turn around and stop to ask a local. Before setting out, confirm the best route with your hotelier, particularly for farmhouse or countryside lodgings.

Even when navigating primarily with GPS, I always have a paper map, ideally a big, detailed regional road map. It's invaluable for getting the big picture, understanding alternate routes, and filling in if my phone's GPS stops working. It's smart to buy a good map before you go, or pick one up at a local TI, gas station, bookshop, newsstand, or tourist shop.

DRIVING

Driving in Sicily can be unnerving. Locals drive fast, tailgate, and honk frequently. They pass where Americans are taught not to—on blind corners and just before tunnels. Roads have narrow shoulders or none at all. Driving in the countryside is less stressful than driving through urban areas or on busy highways, but stay alert. On one-lane roads, larger vehicles have the right-of-way.

Road Rules: Stay out of restricted traffic zones or you'll risk huge fines. Car traffic is restricted in many city centers. Don't drive or park in any area that has a sign reading *Zona Traffico Limitato* (*ZTL*, often shown above a red circle—see image). If you do, your license plate will likely be photographed and a hefty (€80-plus) ticket mailed to your home without your ever having met a cop. Bumbling in and out of these zones can net you multiple fines. If your hotel is within a restricted area, ask your hotelier to direct you to parking outside the zone. (Although your hotelier can register your car as an authorized vehicle permitted to enter the zone, this usually isn't worth the hassle.) If you get a ticket, it could take months to show up (for more about traffic tickets in Italy, see bella-toscana.com/traffic_violations_italy.htm).

Be aware of typical European road rules; for example, many countries strictly enforce zero tolerance laws for driving under the influence of alcohol. Most require headlights at all times, and nearly all forbid handheld phone use. Seatbelts are mandatory, and children under age 12 must ride in child-safety or booster seats. In Europe, you're not allowed to turn right on a red light unless a sign or signal specifically authorizes it, and on expressways it's illegal to pass drivers on the right. Ask your car-rental company about these rules, or check the "International Travel" section at travel.state.gov (enter Italy in the "Learn About Your Destination" box, then click "Travel and Transportation").

Drive Defensively: Italians are aggressive drivers. Turn signals are optional. If a driver is tailgating you on the highway, pull to the side to let them pass, even if that means driving on the shoulder. If you're traveling in the right-hand lane on the highway, keep an eye out for slow-moving cars that appear out of nowhere. Also, if you brake quickly, it's customary to put on your hazard lights to warn the driver behind you. All this is normal for locals, who may colorfully gesture at you. Don't take it personally.

Sicilians don't follow expected right-of-way rules; observe and follow suit. For example, drivers making a left turn onto a busy street will slowly roll their car into oncoming traffic until everyone stops for them. It's best to stop when you see someone doing this. This makes roundabouts particularly challenging—simply forget everything you've learned about who has the right of way, and approach each roundabout as a unique experience. On country roads, you'll occasionally run into a "Sicilian traffic jam" (livestock blocking the road). There's nothing you can do but wait for the shepherd to move them along. Feel free to wave to make sure they see you waiting.

Motor scooters are very popular, and scooter drivers often see themselves as exempt from rules that apply to automobiles.

Tolls: You'll pay tolls for some stretches of freeway (autostrada; for costs, use the trip-planning tool at autostrade.it or search "European Tolls" on theaa.com). When approaching a tollbooth, skip lanes marked *Telepass;* for an attended booth, choose a lane

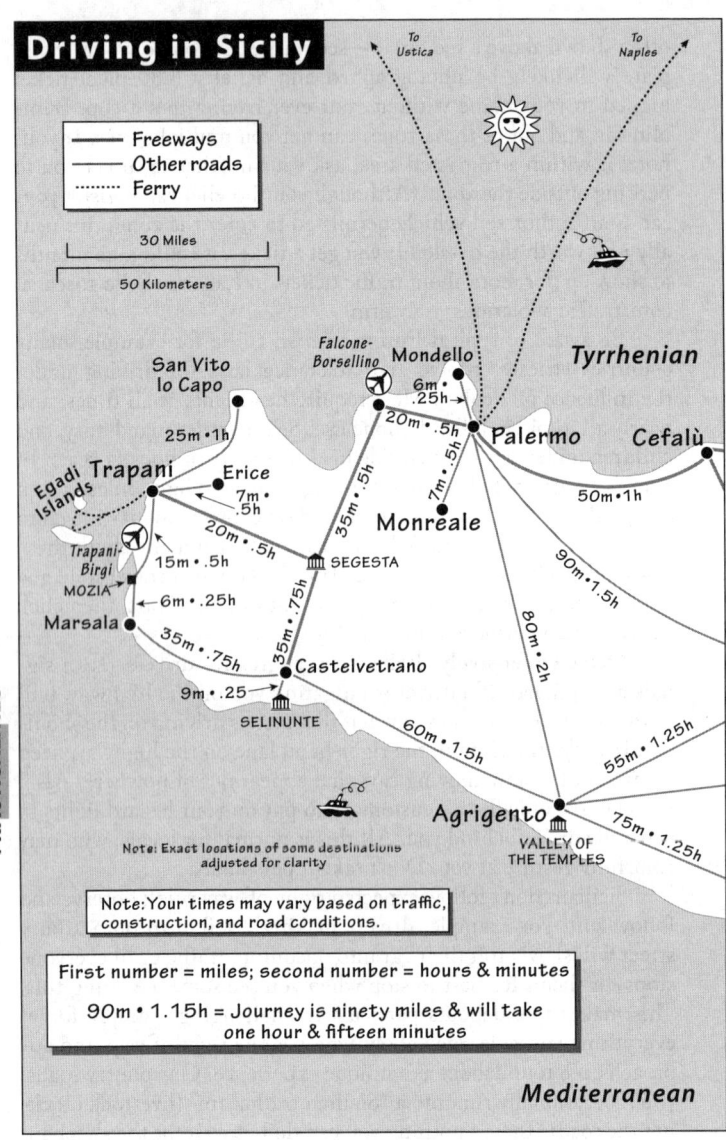

with a sign that shows a hand or coins or a credit card. If you don't have a tap-to-pay card, stick to the cash lane.

While I favor freeways because I feel they're safer and less nerve-racking than smaller roads, savvy local drivers know which toll-free *superstrade* are actually faster and more direct than the autostrada (e.g., Palermo to Cefalù). In some cases, if you have some time to spare, smaller roads can be worth the extra hassle.

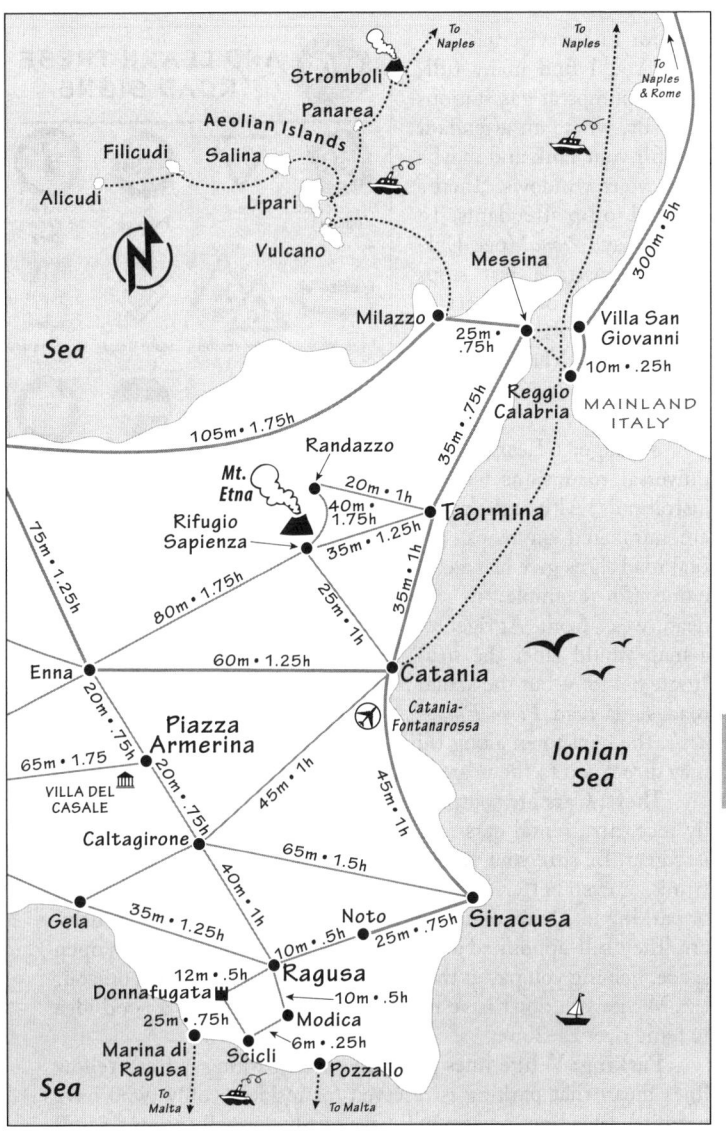

Fuel: Fuel is expensive—often about $6.50 per gallon. Diesel cars are more common in Europe than back home, so be sure you know what type of fuel your car takes before you fill up. Diesel costs less, about $6 per gallon. Some pumps are color-coded: Unleaded pumps *(senza piombo)* are green and labeled "E," while diesel pumps (*gasolio;* often yellow or black) are labeled "B." You'll also see the term *benzina*, which is standard fuel. If you are unsure or need help, stop for full-service gas *(servito)*. You'll find many full-service pumps at gas stations in Sicily, where an attendant will fill your tank and maybe wash your windows. There's no need to tip attendants. To fill up, say *"Pieno"* (pee-EH-noh). Autostrada rest stops can have full- or self-service stations (open daily without a siesta break). Many 24-hour stations are entirely automated.

Signage: Learn the universal road signs (see illustration). Although roads are numbered on maps, actual road signs give just a city name (for example, if you head west from Agrigento, a map would label the road "route S-115"—but the actual road signs read *Porto Empedocle,* the next town along this route). Signs are inconsistent: They may direct you to the nearest big city or simply the next town.

Theft: Cars are routinely vandalized and stolen. Thieves easily recognize rental cars and assume they are filled with a tourist's gear. Be sure your valuables are out of sight and locked in the trunk, or even better, with you or in your room. On any city street or parking lot, "attendants" may be hanging around to "help" drivers. Their self-appointed jobs may include directing you to an open space, helping you pay at the machine, and keeping an eye on your car. While you don't have to give them anything, it's a good idea to hand over €1-2.

Parking: White lines generally mean parking is free. Yellow lines mean that parking is reserved for residents only (who have permits). Blue lines mean you'll have to pay—usually around €1.50 per hour (use machine, leave time-stamped receipt on dashboard). Study the signs. Free zones often have a 30- or 60-minute time limit. Signs showing a street cleaner and a day of the week indicate which day the street is cleaned; there's a €100 tow fee—incentive to learn the days of the week in Italian.

Zona disco has nothing to do with dancing. Your rental car might come equipped with a time disc (a cardboard clock), which you can use in a *zona disco*—set the clock to your arrival time and leave it on the dashboard. (If your rental car doesn't come with a *disco,* pick one up at a tobacco shop or just write your arrival time on a piece of paper and place it on the dashboard.) These are generally used in areas where parking is free but has a time limit.

Garages are safe, save time, and help you avoid the stress of parking tickets. Take the parking voucher with you to pay the cashier before you leave.

Before your trip, consider downloading the **Easy Park** app—it simplifies pay parking, allowing you to extend your parking time and pay only for the time you use.

FLIGHTS

To compare flights to Europe, begin with a search engine such as Google Flights or Kayak, then book directly on your preferred airline's website. Skyscanner is the best search engine for inexpensive flights within Europe. Before you book, be sure to read the small print about change or cancellation policies, and the costs for "extras" such as reserving a seat, checking a bag, or printing a boarding pass.

Flights to Europe: Start looking for international flights about four to six months before your trip, especially for peak-season travel. Depending on your itinerary, it can be efficient and no more expensive to fly into one city and out of another.

Flights Within Europe: Flying between European cities can be surprisingly affordable, though it leaves a larger carbon footprint than a train or bus. Before buying a long-distance train or bus ticket, check the cost of a flight on one of Europe's airlines, whether a major carrier or a no-frills outfit like Easyjet or Ryanair. Be aware that flying with a discount airline can have drawbacks, such as minimal customer service, strict carry-on size or weight limits, hidden fees (read the fine print carefully), and time-consuming treks to secondary airports.

EU Air Passenger Rights: Tourists are covered by Europe's generous consumer protections for airline passengers. For flights departing from an EU airport (including Norway, Iceland, and Switzerland) or run by an EU airline, you're entitled to compensation for delays of three or more hours (or if your flight is canceled or rescheduled, or a connection is missed). The service flightright.com walks you through the steps to apply for compensation.

Conversions

NUMBERS AND STUMBLERS

- Europeans write a few of their numbers differently than we do. 1 =1, 4 =4, 7 =7.
- In Europe, dates appear as day/month, so Christmas is 25/12.
- Commas are decimal points and decimals are commas. A dollar and a half is 1,50, one thousand is 1.000, and there are 5.280 feet in a mile.
- When counting with fingers, start with your thumb. If you hold up your first finger to request one item, you'll probably get two.
- What Americans call the second floor of a building is the first floor in Europe.
- On escalators and moving sidewalks, Europeans keep the left "lane" open for passing. Keep to the right.

METRIC CONVERSIONS

A **kilogram** equals 1,000 grams (about 2.2 pounds). One hundred **grams** (a common unit at markets) is about a quarter-pound. One **liter** is about a quart, or almost four to a gallon.

A **kilometer** is six-tenths of a mile. To convert kilometers to miles, cut the kilometers in half and add back 10 percent of the original (120 km: 60 + 12 = 72 miles). One **meter** is 39 inches—just over a yard.

1 foot = 0.3 meter	1 square yard = 0.8 square meter
1 yard = 0.9 meter	1 square mile = 2.6 square kilometers
1 mile = 1.6 kilometers	1 ounce = 28 grams
1 centimeter = 0.4 inch	1 quart = 0.95 liter
1 meter = 39.4 inches	1 kilogram = 2.2 pounds
1 kilometer = 0.62 mile	32°F = 0°C

ROMAN NUMERALS

In the US, you'll see Roman numerals—which originated in ancient Rome—used for copyright dates, clocks, and the Super Bowl. In Italy, you're likely to observe these numbers chiseled on statues and buildings. If you want to do some numeric detective work, here's how: In Roman numerals, as in ours, the highest numbers (thousands, hundreds) come first, followed by smaller numbers. Many numbers are made by combining numerals into sets: V = 5, so VIII = 8 (5 plus 3). Roman numerals follow a subtraction principle for multiples of fours (4, 40, 400, etc.) and nines (9, 90, 900, etc.). The number four, for example, is written as IV (1 subtracted from 5), rather than IIII. The number nine is IX (1 subtracted from 10).

Big numbers such as dates can look daunting at first. The easiest way to handle them is to read the numbers in discrete chunks.

For example, Michelangelo was born in MCDLXXV: M (1,000) + CD (100 subtracted from 500, or 400) + LXX (50 + 10 + 10, or 70) + V (5) = 1475. It was a very good year.

M = 1000	XL = 40
CM = 900	X = 10
D = 500	IX = 9
CD = 400	V = 5
C = 100	IV = 4
XC = 90	I = duh
L = 50	

CLOTHING SIZES

When shopping for clothing, use these US-to-European comparisons as general guidelines (but note that no conversion is perfect).

Women: For pants and dresses, add 36 in Italy (US 10 = Italian 46). For blouses and sweaters, add 32 for most of Europe (US 8 = European 40). For shoes, add 30-31 (US 7 = European 37/38).

Men: For dress shirts, multiply by 2 and add about 8 (US 15 = European 38). For jackets and suits, add 10. For shoes, add 32-34.

Children: Clothing is sized by height—in centimeters (2.5 cm = 1 inch), so a US size 8 roughly equates to 132-140. For shoes up to size 13, add 16-18, and for sizes 1 and up, add 30-32.

Packing Checklist

Whether you're traveling for five days or five weeks, you won't need more than this. Pack light to enjoy the sweet freedom of true mobility.

Clothing

- ☐ 5 shirts: long- & short-sleeve
- ☐ 2 pairs pants (or skirts/capris)
- ☐ 1 pair shorts
- ☐ 5 pairs underwear & socks
- ☐ 1 pair walking shoes
- ☐ Sweater or warm layer
- ☐ Rainproof jacket with hood
- ☐ Tie, scarf, belt, and/or hat
- ☐ Swimsuit
- ☐ Sleepwear/loungewear

Toiletries

- ☐ Basics: soap, shampoo, toothbrush, toothpaste, floss, deodorant, sunscreen, brush/comb, etc.
- ☐ Medicines & vitamins
- ☐ First-aid kit
- ☐ Glasses/contacts/sunglasses
- ☐ Face masks & hand sanitizer
- ☐ Sewing kit
- ☐ Packet of tissues (for WC)
- ☐ Earplugs

Money

- ☐ Debit & credit cards
- ☐ Hard cash (US $100-200)
- ☐ Money belt

Electronics

- ☐ Mobile phone
- ☐ Camera & related gear
- ☐ Tablet/ebook reader/laptop
- ☐ Headphones/earbuds
- ☐ Chargers & batteries
- ☐ Plug adapters

Documents

- ☐ Passport (with ETIAS/ETA if required)
- ☐ Driver's license, International Driving Permit (if required), student ID, etc.
- ☐ Tickets & confirmations: flights, hotels, trains, rail pass, car rental, sight entries
- ☐ Copies of important documents
- ☐ Insurance details
- ☐ Guidebooks & maps

Miscellaneous

- ☐ Laundry supplies
- ☐ Small umbrella
- ☐ Travel alarm/watch
- ☐ Water bottle

Optional Extras

- ☐ Second pair of shoes
- ☐ Travel hairdryer
- ☐ Picnic supplies
- ☐ Disinfecting wipes
- ☐ Fold-up tote bag
- ☐ Small flashlight
- ☐ Small towel or washcloth
- ☐ Inflatable pillow/neck rest
- ☐ Tiny lock
- ☐ Extra passport photos

Italian Survival Phrases

Hello. (informal)	Ciao.	chow
Good day.	Buongiorno.	bwohn-**jor**-noh
Do you speak English?	Parla inglese?	**par**-lah een-**gleh**-zay
Yes. / No.	Si. / No.	see / noh
I (don't) understand.	(Non) capisco.	(nohn) kah-**pees**-koh
Please.	Per favore.	pehr fah-**voh**-ray
Thank you.	Grazie.	**graht**-see-ay
You're welcome.	Prego.	**preh**-go
I'm sorry.	Mi dispiace.	mee dee-spee-**ah**-chay
Excuse me.	Mi scusi.	mee **skoo**-zee
No problem.	Non c'è problema.	nohn cheh proh-**bleh**-mah
Goodbye.	Arrivederci.	ah-ree-veh-**dehr**-chee
one / two / three	uno / due / tre	**oo**-noh / **doo**-ay / tray
four / five / six	quattro / cinque / sei	**kwah**-troh / **cheeng**-kway / **seh**-ee
seven / eight	sette / otto	**seh**-tay / **oh**-toh
nine / ten	nove / dieci	**noh**-vay / dee-**ay**-chee
How much is it?	Quanto costa?	**kwahn**-toh **koh**-stah
Write it?	Me lo scrive?	may loh **skree**-vay
Is it free?	È gratis?	eh **grah**-tees
Is it included?	È incluso?	eh een-**kloo**-zoh
Where can I buy / find...?	Dove posso comprare / trovare...?	**doh**-vay **poh**-soh kohm-**prah**-ray / troh-**vah**-ray
I'd like / We'd like...	Vorrei / Vorremmo...	voh-**reh**-ee / voh-**reh**-moh
...a room.	...una camera.	**oo**-nah **kah**-meh-rah
...a ticket to ___.	...un biglietto per ___.	oon beel-**yeh**-toh pehr ___
Is it possible?	È possibile?	eh poh-**see**-bee-lay
Where is...?	Dov'è...?	doh-**veh**
...the train station	...la stazione	lah staht-see-**oh**-nay
...tourist information	...informazioni turisti	een-for-maht-see-**oh**-nee too-**ree**-stee
...the bathroom	...il bagno	eel **bahn**-yoh
men / women	uomini, signori / donne, signore	**woh**-mee-nee, seen-**yoh**-ree / **doh**-nay, seen-**yoh**-ray
left / right / straight	sinistra / destra / sempre dritto	see-**nee**-strah / **deh**-strah / **sehm**-pray **dree**-toh
What time does this open / close?	A che ora apre / chiude?	ah kay **oh**-rah **ah**-pray / kee-**oo**-day
At what time?	A che ora?	ah kay **oh**-rah
Just a moment.	Un momento.	oon moh-**mehn**-toh
now / soon / later	adesso / presto / tardi	ah-**deh**-soh / **preh**-stoh / **tar**-dee
today / tomorrow	oggi / domani	**oh**-jee / doh-**mah**-nee

In an Italian Restaurant

I'd like / We'd like...	Vorrei / Vorremmo...	voh-**reh**-ee / voh-**reh**-moh
...to reserve a table for one / two.	...prenotare un tavolo per uno / due. preh-noh-**tah**-ray oon **tah**-voh-loh pehr **oo**-noh / **doo**-ay	
...the menu (in English).	...il menù (in inglese). eel meh-**noo** (een een-**gleh**-zay)	
Is this seat free?	È libero questo posto? eh **lee**-beh-roh **kweh**-stoh **poh**-stoh	
service (not) included	servizio (non) compreso sehr-**veet**-see-oh (nohn) kohm-**pray**-zoh	
cover charge	(pane e) coperto	(**pah**-nay ay) koh-**pehr**-toh
to go	da portar via	dah **por**-tar **vee**-ah
with / without	con / senza	kohn / **sehnt**-sah
and / or	e / o	ay / oh
breakfast / lunch / dinner	(prima) colazione / pranzo / cena (**pree**-mah) koh-laht-zee-**oh**-nay / **prahn**-zoh / **chay**-nah	
fixed-price meal (of the day)	menù (del giorno)	meh-**noo** (dehl **jor**-noh)
specialty of the house	specialità della casa speh-chah-lee-**tah** deh-lah **kah**-zah	
appetizer	antipasto	ahn-tee-**pah**-stoh
first course	primo (piatto)	**pree**-moh (pee-**ah**-toh)
main course	secondo (piatto)	seh-**kohn**-doh (pee-**ah**-toh)
side dishes	contorni	kohn-**tor**-nee
cold cuts / bread / cheese	salumi / pane / formaggio sah-**loo**-mee / **pah**-nay / for-**mah**-joh	
sandwich	panino	pah-**nee**-noh
soup / salad	zuppa / insalata	**tsoo**-pah / een-sah-**lah**-tah
meat / chicken	carne / pollo	**kar**-nay / **poh**-loh
fish / seafood	pesce / frutti di mare **peh**-shay / **froo**-tee dee **mah**-ray	
fruit / vegetables	frutta / verdure	**froo**-tah / vehr-**doo**-ray
dessert	dolce	**dohl**-chay
tap water	acqua del rubinetto	**ah**-kwah dehl roo-bee-**neh**-toh
mineral water	acqua minerale	**ah**-kwah mee-neh-**rah**-lay
still / sparkling	naturale / frizzante	nah-too-**rah**-lay / freet-**zahn**-tay
(orange) juice	succo (d'arancia)	**soo**-koh (dah-**rahn**-chah)
coffee / tea / milk	caffè / tè / latte	kah-**feh** / teh / **lah**-tay
wine / beer	vino / birra	**vee**-noh / **bee**-rah
red / white	rosso / bianco	**roh**-soh / bee-**ahn**-koh
glass / bottle	bicchiere / bottiglia	bee-kee-**eh**-ray / boh-**teel**-yah
Cheers!	Salute! / Cin cin!	sah-**loo**-tay / cheen cheen
The bill, please.	Il conto, per favore.	eel **kohn**-toh pehr fah-**voh**-ray
Do you accept credit cards?	Accettate carte di credito? ah-cheh-**tah**-tay **kar**-tay dee **kreh**-dee-toh	
Delicious!	Delizioso!	day-leet-see-**oh**-zoh

For more user-friendly Italian phrases, check out *Rick Steves Italian Phrase Book* or *Rick Steves French, Italian, & German Phrase Book*.

INDEX

A

Abbazia Sant'Anastasia (Castelbuono): 148–149
Accommodations: *See* Sleeping; *and specific destinations*
Aci Castello: sleeping, 355–356
Aeolian Islands: 139, 413; tours, 139, 393
Africa, Museum of Italy in (Ragusa): 267
Agatha, Saint (Sant'Agata): 306, 338, 342, 343, 344
Agrigento: 15, 203–232; eating, 230–232; maps, 205, 224–225; planning tips, 204; sights, 206–223; sleeping, 228–230; tours, 206; transportation, 204–206, 223–225, 232; walking tour, 225–228
Agriturismi: 458–460; near Agrigento, 229–230; near Villa Romana del Casale, 249–250
Aidone: 247, 248–249
Aidone Archaeological Museum: 248–249
Airbnb: 89, 454, 457–458
Air-conditioning, in hotels: 455
Airfares (airlines): 21, 24, 495
Airports: Catania, 358, 390–391; Palermo, 103–104; Trapani, 173
Alcantara Gorge Botanical and Geological Park: 413; tours, 392–393
Alicudi: 139
Almanac: 424–425
Altar of Hieron II (Siracusa): 314
Amphitheaters (Catania), 347; (Siracusa), 316–317
Antica Focacceria San Francesco (Palermo): 49, 101
Antiques, shopping for, in Palermo: 85
Antiquity smuggling: 247
Apartment rentals: 89, 454, 457–458
Aperitivo: 32, 85, 147, 467
Apps: 25, 446; messaging, 446; navigation and maps, 448–449, 490; payment, 25, 441; sightseeing, 451; user reviews, 459

Aqueducts: 236–237, 315
Arab Sicily: 32, 53, 425, 427
Arancina: 98, 474
Archaeological museums: Aidone Archaeological Museum, 248–249; Paolo Orsi Archaeological Museum (Siracusa), 296, 319–323; Pietro Griffo Archaeological Museum (Agrigento), 216–223; Salinas Regional Archaeological Museum (Palermo), 39, 45, 60–64
Archaeological sites: near Aidone, 248–249; Neapolis Archaeological Park (Siracusa), 296, 313–317; Valley of the Temples Archaeological Park, 207–216; Villa Romana del Casale, 236–248. *See also* Greeks, ancient
Archimedes: 297, 299, 301, 422
Arethusa Fountain (Siracusa): 307
Arezzo Family Palazzi (Ragusa): 260
Art museums: Bellomo Palace Gallery (Siracusa), 310; Fondazione Mazzullo (Taormina), 397; Galleria d'Arte Moderna (Palermo), 52, 65; Mandralisca Museum (Cefalù), 143–144; Palazzo Butera (Palermo), 76–77; Palermo Regional Art Gallery, 39, 75–76; Pepoli Museum (Trapani), 166; Whitaker Museum (Mozia), 190–192
ATMs: 25, 440–443
Audio Europe, Rick Steves: 25, 436

B

Balio Towers (Erice): 179
Ballarò (Palermo): 33, 78; eating, 102; sights, 78; sleeping, 94
Ballarò Market (Palermo): 38, 56, 79, 83; eating, 95–97
Bars and cafés: overview, 465–466
Bastione di Capo Marchiafava (Cefalù): 140
Beaches: general tips, 147; Cefalù, 134, 136, 146; Donnalucata, 280; Favignana, 184; Giardini Naxos,

412; Letojanni, 412; Marina di Ragusa, 281; Mazzeo, 412; Mondello, 110; Punta Secca, 281; Selinunte, 198–199; Taormina, 390, 406–409, 412; Trapani, 157
Becket, Thomas: 119–120
Bed-and-breakfasts (B&Bs): overview, 456–457
Beer: overview, 478
Bellomo Palace Gallery (Siracusa): 310
Benanti Winery: 379
Benedictine Monastery and Church of San Nicolò (Catania): 350–351
Beverages: 476–481. *See also* Wine and vineyards
Biking (bike rentals): Favignana, 183–184; Palermo, 36, 40
Birgi Airport (Trapani): 173
Boat travel and cruises: Palermo, 105; Siracusa, 297; Taormina, 393, 408. *See also* Ferries
Breakfast: overview, 461–462
Brioche: 272, 418–419, 462
Bronte: 380, 386–387
Budgeting (budget tips): 21. *See also* Money-saving tips
Buses: 487; Agrigento, 205, 224, 232; best one-week trip, 19; Catania, 338–339, 358–359; map, 484–485; Monreale Cathedral, 112; Mount Etna Volcano, 366–367; Noto, 289; Palermo, 33, 36–40, 104–105; Ragusa, 253–254, 255, 272–273; Siracusa, 294, 295, 333; Taormina, 390, 391–392, 409, 419; Trapani, 155, 158, 173, 175; Valley of the Temples, 205, 207; Villa Romana del Casale, 235
Business hours: 439

C

Cable cars (gondolas): Erice, 174–175; Mount Etna Volcano, 373–374; Taormina, 407–408
Cabs: *See* Taxis
Café Concordia (Agrigento): 227, 231
Caffetteria Donnafugata (Ragusa): 260, 272
Caffé Wunderbar (Taormina): 401
Camilleri, Andrea: 206, 226, 227, 277
Cannoli: 8, 279–280
Capo Market (Palermo): 39, 79, 95–97, 99
Cappella Palatina (Palermo): 38, 69–72
Capuchin Crypt (Palermo): 38, 80–83; map, 81
Car and driver: Mount Etna Volcano, 367; Mozia Island, 188; Palermo, 40; Siracusa, 296–297; Trapani, 158; Villa Romana del Casale, 235
Caravaggio: 39, 51, 64–65, 324
Car insurance: 489–490
Car navigation: 490
Car rentals: 21, 488–489
Carthaginians: overview, 188–189, 420, 422
Car travel (driving): 490–495; Agrigento, 204–205, 224–225, 232; Catania, 338; Cefalù, 134, 151; distances and times, 492–493; Erice, 175; Monreale Cathedral, 112–113; Mount Etna Volcano, 365; Mount Etna Wine Country, 379–386; Palermo, 36, 106; Ragusa, 252, 253; road signs, 494; Segesta, 129; Selinunte, 197; Siracusa, 294, 333; Southeast Countryside, 273–283; Taormina, 390, 409–410, 419; Trapani, 155, 173, 175; Valley of the Temples, 204–205, 206–207; Villa Romana del Casale, 234–235; ZTL zones, 36, 45, 89, 106, 294, 490–491
Casa dei Mosaici (Mozia): 192
Cassata: 7–8, 475, 476
Castello di Donnafugata: 281–283
Castello di Venere (Erice): 180
Castello Maniace (Siracusa): 311–312
Castello Ursino (Catania): 351
Castelmola: 410–411; transportation, 409–410
Castelvetrano: 197–198
Castelvetrano olives: 470
Catacombe dei Cappuccini (Palermo): 38, 80–83; map, 81
Catacombs of San Filippo Apostolo (Siracusa): 296, 310–311
Catacombs of San Giovanni (Siracusa): 296, 323
Catania: 16, 334–359; eating, 356–

357; helpful hints, 338; maps, 336–337, 341, 354; orientation, 335; planning tips, 335; sights, 347–353; sleeping, 353–356; tourist information, 335; tours, 339; transportation, 335, 338–339, 358–359; walking tour, 340–347
Catania Cathedral: 340, 342–343
Catania City Walls: 340
Catania Civic Museum: 351
Catania Fish Market: 338, 340, 344–345, 347–349
Catania Town Hall: 344
Cattedrale Metropolitana della Santa Vergine Maria Assunta (Palermo): 39, 56, 66–69
Cefalino River: 137
Cefalù: 15, 133–151; eating, 149–151; map, 135; nightlife, 147; planning tips, 133; sights/activities, 141–147; sleeping, 147–149; tourist information, 134; transportation, 134, 151, 419; walking tour, 134–141
Cefalù Cathedral: 141–143
Cefalù Pier: 138
Cefalù Town Hall: 140
Ceramics and pottery, shopping for: 83, 84, 193, 325, 402
Cheese: 348–349, 470, 474–475
Chiesa del Collegio dei Gesuiti (Trapani): 162
Chiesa delle Anime Sante del Purgatorio (Ragusa): 263
Chiesa delle Anime Sante del Purgatorio (Trapani): 159–161
Chiesa Madre (Erice): 176–178
Chiesa Madre di San Ignazio de Loyola (Scicli): 278–279
Christ Pantocrator mosaics: 72, 119–120, 121, 142–143
Churches and cathedrals: architecture, 426; sightseeing tips, 451; Benedictine Monastery and Church (Catania), 350–351; Catania Cathedral, 340, 342–343; Cefalù Cathedral, 141–143; Chiesa del Collegio dei Gesuiti (Trapani), 162; Chiesa Madre (Erice), 176–178; Chiesa Madre di San Ignazio de Loyola (Scicli), 278–279; La Martorana Church (Palermo), 38, 52, 58–59; Madonna of Tears (Siracusa), 296, 318–319; Montevergini Church (Noto), 287; Palermo Cathedral, 39, 56, 66–69; Purgatorio Church (Ragusa), 263; Purgatorio Church (Trapani), 159–161; San Carlo (Noto), 287–288; San Cataldo (Palermo), 38, 52, 59; San Domenico (Noto), 288; San Domenico (Palermo), 46; San Filippo Apostolo (Siracusa), 310–311; San Francesco (Catania), 346; San Francesco d'Assisi (Palermo), 49; San Giorgio Cathedral (Ragusa), 261–262; San Giovanni Battista Cathedral (Ragusa), 268; San Lorenzo (Agrigento), 226; San Michele (Taormina), 398; San Nicolò (Siracusa), 317; San Nicolò Cathedral (Noto), 286; San Pietro Cathedral (Modica), 275; Santa Caterina (Palermo), 38, 52, 56–57; Santa Caterina of Alexandria (Taormina), 403; Sant'Agata alla Badia (Catania), 343–344; Santa Lucia alla Badia (Siracusa), 305, 307; Santa Lucia al Sepolcro Basilica (Siracusa), 296, 323–325; Santa Maria dei Greci (Agrigento), 228; Santa Maria delle Scale (Ragusa), 264–266; Santa Maria dell'Itria (Ragusa), 263; Santa Maria del Piliere (Taormina), 402–403; Sant'Anna (Palermo), 52; Santa Rosalia (Agrigento), 226; Siracusa Cathedral, 296, 304–305, 308–310; Taormina Cathedral, 398–399; Trapani Cathedral, 161–162. *See also* Monreale Cathedral
Cinabro Carrettieri (Ragusa): 259–260
Cinema Paradiso (movie): 138, 356
Cioccolato di Modica: 275
Circolo di Conversazione (Ragusa): 261
Circumetnea Railway: 375–376, 382–383, 482
Classroom Europe, Rick Steves: 25, 436
Climate: 17, 20, 30, 424
Clothing sizes: 497
Coffee: overview, 477–478
Comiso: 281
Consulates: 438–439

Cooking classes, in Palermo: 41, 93
Coral business, in Trapani: 164
Corso Giacomo Matteotti (Siracusa): 301–302
Corso Italia (Ragusa): 266
Corso Umberto (Taormina): 389
Corso Umberto I (Taormina): 399, 402–403
Corso Vittorio Emanuele (Noto): 285, 287
Corso Vittorio Emanuele (Trapani): 155, 161
Corso XXV Aprile (Ragusa): 257–258
Costs of trip: 21
Costume Museum (Donnafugata): 282
Credit cards: 440–443
Cuisine: 9, 468–476; courses, 463–464; pastries, 7–8; street food, 98, 471
Currency and exchange: 442
Customs regulations: 445

D

Debit cards: 440–443
Department store, in Palermo: 45, 84
Diocesan Museum (Catania): 340
Diocesan Museum (Monreale Cathedral): 114
Discounts: *See* Money-saving tips
Donnafugata Castle: 281–283
Donnalucata: 280–281
Drinking water: 294, 476
Drinks: 476–481. *See also* Wine and vineyards
Driving: *See* Car travel

E

Ear of Dionysius (Siracusa): 315–316
Eating: 460–476; atipping and cover, 444, 463; courses, 463–464; Italian phrases, 500; money-saving tips, 22, 465–468; ordering tips, 464–465; restaurant pricing and hours, 461; seasonal foods, 472. *See also specific destinations*
Economy: 425
Egadi Islands: 154, 182–186; ferries, 183; tours, 158
Eleanor of Aragon: 76
Electricity: 439
Elymians: 129, 174, 199, 420–421
Embassies: 438–439
Emergencies: 438
Emigration: 431
Emilio Sciacca Winery: 376–377
Environmental footprint (going green): 440
Erice: 154, 174–182; eating, 182; map, 176–177; shopping, 180–181; sleeping, 182; tourist information, 175; transportation, 174–175; walking tour, 175–181
Erice Town Hall: 181
ETIAS (European Travel Information and Authorization System): 24, 436–437
Etna: *See* Mount Etna
Etna Wine School: 376
Ettore and Infersa Salt Mill (Mozia): 196
Euro currency: 442

F

Falcone, Giovanni: 46, 51, 434
Falcone-Borsellino Airport (Palermo): 103–104
Favignana: 154, 182–186; eating, 185–186
Feast of Saint Pancrazio (Taormina): 391
Feast of San Giorgio (Ragusa): 254
Feast of Santa Lucia (Siracusa): 306
Feltrinelli (Palermo): 84
Fera 'o Luni (Catania): 338, 347
Ferragosto: 146, 147
Ferries: Egadi Islands, 183; Favignana, 183; Malta, 254–255; map, 484–485; Mozia Island, 187–188; Palermo, 105
Festa di Sant'Agata (Catania): 338, 343, 344
Festival of Saint Agatha (Catania): 338, 343, 344
Festivals: 438. *See also specific festivals*
Filicudi: 139
Filippo Grasso Winery: 377, 379, 383
Flag, Sicilian: 425
Fondazione Mazzullo (Taormina): 397
Fontana dell'Amenano (Catania): 344
Fontana Pretoria (Palermo): 52–54
Fontanarossa Airport (Catania): 358
Fonte Aretusa (Siracusa): 307

Food: shopping for, in Palermo, 83–84. *See also* Cuisine; Eating; Markets
Food tours: Catania, 339; Palermo, 41
Fornazzo: 382
Forza d'Agrò: 413
Fountain of Arethusa (Siracusa): 307
Fountain of Shame (Palermo): 52–54
Four Seasons San Domenico Palace (Taormina): 398

G

Galleria d'Arte Moderna (Palermo): 52, 65
Galleria Regionale di Palazzo Bellomo (Siracusa): 310
Garibaldi, Giuseppe: 159, 160, 166, 400–401, 431–432
Gelato (granita): 8, 475–476; Agrigento, 226, 231; Catania, 347, 357; Cefalù, 139–140; Noto, 287; Palermo, 100; Ragusa, 258, 260, 272; Siracusa, 302, 332; Taormina, 418–419; Trapani, 170
Genie of Palermo: 48
Geography: 424
George, Saint (San Giorgio): 254, 257, 261–262
Giardini della Villa Comunale (Taormina): 405–406
Giardini Naxos: 412
Giardino Ibleo (Ragusa): 257
Goddess of Morgantina: 247–249
Godfather, The (movies): 44, 50, 392–393, 413
Goethe, Johann Wolfgang: 107, 396, 397
Gondolas: *See* Cable cars
Government: 425
Grand Tour: about, 397
Granita: 8, 26–27, 462, 475. *See also* Gelato
Greek-Roman Theater (Taormina): 403, 404–405
Greeks, ancient (Greek sites): 9, 47, 60–61, 146, 164, 303, 421–423; Agrigento, 209–223, 228; best sights, 422–423; Catania, 334; Giardini Naxos, 412; map, 422; Mount Etna, 370; Segesta, 129–132; Selinunte, 197–202; Siracusa, 290, 300, 313–317, 321–322; Taormina, 393–394, 399, 404–405; Valley of the Temples, 207–216
Greek Theater (Siracusa): 315, 326, 328
Greek vs. Roman theaters: 406–407
Guidebooks: 459; Rick Steves, 437

H

Head of the Moor: 400
Hiking: Cefalù, 144–146; Mount Etna Volcano, 370–375; Ragusa, 262–268; Taormina, 409
History: 420–433
Holidays: 17, 20, 30, 438
Hostels: overview, 456–457, 460. *See also specific destinations*
Hotels: overview, 453–456; rates and deals, 452–453; reservations, 456–457. *See also specific destinations*
Hotel Excelsior Palace (Taormina): 395–396
House of the Mosaics (Mozia): 192

I

Infiorata di Noto: 287
Inquisition Cells at Palazzo Chiaramonte Steri (Palermo): 39, 74–75
Inspector Montalbano (TV series): 277, 279, 281
International Museum of Marionettes (Palermo): 77
Internet security: 446
Isola Bella (Taormina): 390, 406–408
Italian restaurant phrases: 500
Italian survival phrases: 499
Itineraries: Agrigento, 204; best one-week trip by bus and train, 19; best two-week trip by car, 18–19; Catania, 335; Cefalu, 133; designing your own, 17, 20, 23; Monreale Cathedral, 113–114; Mount Etna, 360–361, 364; Palermo, 30–32; Ragusa, 251–252; Siracusa, 291; Taormina, 388–389; Trapani, 152, 154; Valley of the Temples, 204; Villa Romana del Casale, 235

K

Kalsa (Palermo): *See* La Kalsa
Kasbah (Agrigento): 223, 227–228
King Roger II's Palace (Cefalù): 143
King Roger's Hall (Palermo): 73

Kolymbethra Gardens (Agrigento): 216
Kothon (Mozia): 193

L

La Kalsa (Palermo): 33, 49, 74–77; eating, 101–102; shopping, 83, 85; sights, 74–77; sleeping, 93
La Martorana Church (Palermo): 38, 52, 58–59
Language: 27–28, 424–425; online translation tips, 440; restaurant phrases, 500; survival phrases, 499; wine terms, 479
Language barrier: 448–449
Largo XXV Luglio (Siracusa): 301–302
La Rinascente (Palermo): 45, 84
La Rocca: 133, 138, 144–146
La Vucciria Market (Palermo): 47–48, 80; eating, 48, 99; nightlife, 88
Leopard, The (Lampedusa): 74, 93
Letojanni: 412
Levanzo: 163, 182
Ligny Tower (Trapani): 166–167
Linguaglossa: 383
Lipari: 139, 143–144
Lucy, Saint (Santa Lucia): 304, 306, 309
Lungomare Dante Alighieri (Trapani): 164–165

M

Madonna della Rocca: 411–412; tours, 392; transportation, 409–410
Madonna of Tears (Siracusa): 296, 318–319
Mafia: 29, 46, 64–65, 420, 432; about, 50–51
Mandralisca Museum (Cefalù): 143–144
Maniace Castle (Siracusa): 311–312
Marettimo: 182
Margaret of Navarre: 119–120, 125
Marina di Ragusa: 281
Marionettes: *See* Puppets
Markets: 9, 467–468; Catania, 338, 344–345, 347–349; Cefalù, 134; Palermo, 29, 36, 41, 78–80, 83–84, 85, 95–97, 99; Ragusa, 254; seasonal foods, 472; Siracusa, 295, 300, 332; Taormina, 391; Trapani, 156

Marsala wine: 172, 480
Massimo Theater (Palermo): 38, 42–44, 59–60, 85; eating near, 102
Mazzarò Beach (Taormina): 408–409
Mazzeo: 412
Medical help: 438
Messina, Antonello da: 76, 144, 145, 310, 425
Metric system: 496–497
Milo: 382
Minnuzze di Sant'Agata: 344
Mobile phones: 25, 445–448. *See also* Apps
Modica: 275–276
Monastero e Chiesa dei Benedettini di San Nicolò l'Arena (Catania): 350–351
Mondello: 110–111; tours, 40
Money: 440–445; average daily expenses, 21; budgeting, 21
Money belts: 36, 439, 443
Money-saving tips: 21; eating, 465–468; sights, 450; sleeping, 452–453
Monreale (town): 111–128; eating, 114; map, 113
Monreale Cathedral: 15, 111–128; maps, 118, 121; orientation, 114–115; planning tips, 113–114; self-guided tour, 115–128; transportation, 112–113
Monte Pellegrino: 68, 107–108
Monte San Giuliano: 165, 182
Montevergini Church (Noto): 287
"Moor head" planters: 400
Morgantina: 249
Mount Etna: 16, 360–387; maps, 362–363, 380–381; planning tips, 360–361, 364
Mount Etna Volcano: 361, 364–375; about, 368; activities, 370–375; helpful hints, 367, 369; lava rock, about, 372; in myth, 370; orientation, 365; tours, 369–370; transportation, 365–367
Mount Etna Wine Country: 375–387; map, 380–381; north slope driving tour, 379–386; overview of wines, 378; planning tips, 361; tours, 376; wineries, 376–379
Mount Santa Caterina: 183

Index

Mozia Island: 154, 186–194; map, 187; transportation, 187–188
Mozia Island Barracks: 192–193
Mulino delle Saline Ettore e Infersa (Mozia): 196
Museo Antonio Pasqualino (Palermo): 77
Museo Archeologico Regionale Antonino Salinas (Palermo): 39, 45, 60–64
Museo Archeologico Regionale Paolo Orsi (Siracusa): 296, 319–323; map, 320
Museo Archeologico Regionale Pietro Griffo (Agrigento): 216–223; map, 217; self-guided tour, 218–223
Museo Civico (Catania): 351
Museo Civico L'Italia in Africa (Ragusa): 267
Museo dei Pupi (Siracusa): 296, 312
Museo del Costume (Donnafugata): 282
Museo del Sale (Trapani): 196
Museo Mandralisca (Cefalù): 143–144
Museo Regionale Agostino Pepoli (Trapani): 166
Museo Storico dello Sbarco in Sicilia—1943 (Catania): 347, 352–353
Museum of Italy in Africa (Ragusa): 267
Museum of Salt (Trapani): 196
Museum of the Allied Landings in Sicily (Catania): 347, 352–353
Mussolini, Benito: 45, 50, 74, 192, 267, 301–302, 352, 432, 433

N

Naumachie (Taormina): 402
Neapolis Archaeological Park (Siracusa): 296, 313–317, 326; map, 313
Nelson, Horatio: 172, 386–387
Nietzsche, Friedrich: 396
Norman Palace (Palermo): 38, 69–73
Normans: overview, 47, 427
Noto: 283–289; eating, 288–289; map, 284; tourist information, 283; transportation, 283–284, 289; walking tour, 284–288
Noto City Hall: 286
Noto Flower Festival: 287

O

Olive oil: 84, 230, 256, 377
Opera: Catania, 351; Palermo, 38, 42–44, 59–60, 85
Operation Husky: 160, 352–353, 384, 433
Oratory of San Lorenzo (Palermo): 39, 50–51, 64–65
Ortigia (Siracusa): 291, 297–308; at a glance, 296; eating, 330–332; maps, 298, 329; market, 295, 300, 332; shopping, 325; sights, 308–312; sleeping, 328–330; walking tour, 297–308
Ortigia Street Market (Siracusa): 295, 300, 332
Orto Botanico (Palermo): 77
Ottobrata (Zafferana): 382

P

Packing tips and checklist: 25, 498; Mount Etna, 367, 369
Palatine Chapel (Palermo): 38, 69–72
Palazzo Abatellis (Palermo): 39, 75–76
Palazzo Alliata di Pietratagliata (Palermo): 46
Palazzo Arezzo di Donnafugata (Ragusa): 260
Palazzo Arezzo di Trifiletti (Ragusa): 260
Palazzo Bellomo (Siracusa): 310
Palazzo Beneventano (Siracusa): 305
Palazzo Bertini (Ragusa): 266–267
Palazzo Biscari (Catania): 350
Palazzo Burgio (Trapani): 163
Palazzo Butera (Palermo): 76–77
Palazzo Cavarretta (Trapani): 162
Palazzo Chiaramonte Steri (Palermo): 39, 74–75
Palazzo Conte Federico (Palermo): 39, 78
Palazzo Corvaja (Taormina): 403
Palazzo Cosentini (Ragusa): 263
Palazzo dei Chierici (Catania): 344
Palazzo della Cancelleria (Ragusa): 263
Palazzo Duchi di Santo Stefano (Taormina): 397
Palazzo Florio (Favignana): 184
Palazzo La Rocca (Ragusa): 262
Palazzo Nicolaci (Noto): 287

Palazzo Normanni (Palermo): 38, 69–73
Palazzo Pretorio (Palermo): 54
Palazzo Spadaro (Scicli): 279
Palermo: 12, 29–106; at a glance, 38–39; arrival in, 33, 36; best views, 37; day trips, 15, 107–132; eating, 95–103; helpful hints, 36–37; history of, 29 74, 47, 53; layout of, 32–33; maps, 30–31, 34–35, 42–43, 86–87, 90–91, 96–97, 108; nightlife, 85–89; orientation, 32–33; planning tips, 30–32; shopping, 83–85; sights, 56–83; sleeping, 89–95; tourist information, 33; tours, 40–41; transportation, 33, 36, 37–40, 103–106; walking tours, 41–56
Palermo Botanical Garden: 77
Palermo Cathedral: 39, 56, 66–69
Palermo City Hall: 54
Palermo Classica: 86
Palermo Regional Art Gallery: 39, 75–76
Panarea: 139
Paolo Orsi Archaeological Museum (Siracusa): 296, 319–323; map, 320
Parco Archeologico della Neapolis (Siracusa): 296, 313–317; map, 313
Passopisciaro: 383
Passports: 24, 436
Pasta: overview, 469, 472–473
Pasta di mandorla: 7, 84
Pasticceria Infurna (Agrigento): 226, 231
Pasticceria Maria Grammatico (Erice): 181
Pastries: overview, 7–8
Pepoli Museum (Trapani): 166
Phones: 445–448. *See also* Apps
Piazza Aragona (Palermo): 52, 83
Piazza Archimede (Siracusa): 302
Piazza Armerina: 248; map, 234; transportation, 233–235
Piazza Ballarò (Palermo): 79
Piazza Bellini (Palermo): 52; churches, 52, 56–59
Piazza Caracciolo (Palermo): 48, 80, 99
Piazza Carlo Alberto (Catania): 338
Piazza Chiesa Madre (Castelmona): 411

Piazza Cristoforo Colombo (Cefalù): 136
Piazza del Duomo (Catania): 340, 343–344
Piazza del Duomo (Cefalù): 140, 147, 150
Piazza della Loggia (Erice): 181
Piazza della Repubblica (Ragusa): 262, 263
Piazza Duomo (Siracusa): 302, 305, 307, 331–332
Piazza Duomo (Taormina): 398–399, 418
Piazza Europa (Favignana): 184–185
Piazza Garibaldi (Cefalù): 134
Piazza Garibaldi (Trapani): 159
Piazza Garraffello (Palermo): 48–49
Piazza Guglielmo II (Monreale): 115–116, 125, 128
Piazza Italia (Scicli): 277, 278
Piazza IX Aprile (Taormina): 400–402
Piazza Jolanda (Trapani): eating, 170–171
Piazza Madrice (Favignana): 184–185
Piazza Marina (Cefalù): 138–139
Piazza Marina (Palermo): 85
Piazza Mazzini (Catania): 345–346
Piazza Mercato del Pesce (Trapani): 165
Piazza Municipio (Noto): 286
Piazza Pancali (Siracusa): 299
Piazza Pardo (Catania): 348
Piazza Pirandello (Agrigento): 227, 231
Piazza Pola (Ragusa): 258
Piazza Pretoria (Palermo): 52–54
Piazza Rivoluzione (Palermo): 87–88
Piazza San Domenico (Palermo): 46
Piazza San Francesco (Catania): 346
Piazza San Francesco (Palermo): 49–50, 51
Piazza San Francesco all'Immacolata (Noto): 285
Piazza Sant'Antonio (Castelmona): 410, 411
Piazza Sant'Antonio Abate (Taormina): 393
Piazza Sinatra (Agrigento): 227
Piazza Stesicoro (Catania): 347
Piazza Verdi (Palermo): 43
Piazza Vittorio Veneto (Trapani): 163–164

Piazza XVI Maggio (Noto): 288
Piazzetta della Canna (Palermo): 88–89
Piazzetta San Domenico (Erice): 181
Pickpockets: 26, 438, 443
Pietro Griffo Archaeological Museum (Agrigento): 216–223; map, 217; self-guided tour, 218–223
Pirandello, Luigi: 227
Pistachios: 386–387, 470
Pizzerias (pizza): overview, 465, 468–469. *See also specific destinations*
Planeta Sciaranuova Winery: 377, 383
Police: 438
Ponte Santa Lucia (Siracusa): 291, 297
Ponte Umberto I (Siracusa): 291, 297, 299
Porta Carini (Palermo): 79
Porta Catania (Taormina): 389, 393–396
Porta di Mola (Castelmola): 410
Porta di Ponte Gate (Agrigento): 226
Portale San Giorgio (Ragusa): 257
Porta Messina (Taormina): 389, 403
Porta Pescara (Cefalù): 137–138
Porta Reale (Noto): 285
Porta Trapani (Erice): 175–176
Porta Uzeda (Catania): 340
Post offices: Ortigia, 299; Palermo, 45; Ragusa, 267; Trapani, 158, 164
Pottery, shopping for: *See* Ceramics and pottery, shopping for
Prestipino (Catania): 344, 349, 356
Puccio, Signore: 44
Puglisi, Giuseppe "Pino": 51, 69
Punta Secca: 281
Puppet Museum (Siracusa): 312
Puppets: 84; about, 327; International Museum of Marionettes (Palermo), 77; Puppet Museum (Siracusa), 312; Teatro dei Pupi (Palermo), 44–45
Puppet Theater (Palermo): 44–45
Puppet Theater (Siracusa): 296, 326
Purgatorio Church (Ragusa): 263
Purgatorio Church (Taormina): 401
Purgatorio Church (Trapani): 159–161

Q
Quarry of Paradise (Siracusa): 316
Quattro Canti (Palermo): 32–33, 54–56
Quota Mille: 384, 386

R
Ragusa: 16, 251–273; eating, 270–272; helpful hints, 254–255; maps, 254–255, 258–259, 264–265, 270–271; orientation, 253; planning tips, 251–252; sleeping, 268–270; tourist information, 253; tours, 256; transportation, 252–256, 272–273; walking tours, 256–268
Ragusa Ibla: 253, 256–262; eating, 270–272; maps, 258–259, 270–271; sleeping, 268–270
Ragusa Public Garden: 257
Ragusa Superiore: 253, 262–268; eating, 272; map, 264–265; sleeping, 270
Rail passes: 437, 485–486
Rail travel: *See* Train travel
Randazzo: 384–386; eating, 385
Regional Art Gallery at Palazzo Abatellis (Palermo): 39, 75–76
Rental properties: 89, 454, 457–458
Resources from Rick Steves: 436–437
Restaurants: *See* Eating; *and specific destinations*
Rifugio Sapienza: 365–375, 381; activities, 370–375; eating, 369; helpful hints, 367, 369; map, 366; orientation, 365; sleeping, 369; transportation, 365–367
Rinascente (Palermo): 45, 84
Risorgimento: overview, 431–432
Roman Amphitheaters (Catania), 347; (Siracusa), 316–317
Roman Catholicism: 10. *See also* Churches and cathedrals
Roman mosaics: about, 243
Roman numerals: 496–497
Roman Theater and Odeum (Catania): 349
Roman vs. Greek theaters: 406–407
Rosalia, Saint: *See* Santa Rosalia
Rossocorallo (Trapani): 164
Rosticcerie: overview, 466, 468
Royal Apartments (Palermo): 72
Royal Gardens (Palermo): 73

S

Safety: *See* Theft alerts
Salesiani Don Bosco (Taormina): 401
Salina: 139
Salinas Regional Archaeological Museum (Palermo): 39, 45, 60–64
Salita Commendatore (Ragusa): 263–264
Salt flats: 154, 163, 186, 194–196
Salt harvesting: 195, 196
Salt Museum (Trapani): 196
Salumi: 473–474
San Carlo Church (Noto): 287–288
San Cataldo Church (Palermo): 38, 52, 59
Sanctuary of Cappiddazzu (Mozia): 194
Sanctuary of Madonna della Rocca: 411–412; tours, 392; transportation, 409–410
Sanctuary of Santa Rosalia: 107–109
Sanctuary of the Madonna of Tears (Siracusa): 296, 318–319
San Domenico Church (Noto): 288
San Domenico Church (Palermo): 46
San Domenico Convent (Taormina): 398
San Filippo Apostolo Underground (Siracusa): 296, 310–311
San Francesco Church (Catania): 346
San Francesco d'Assisi Church (Palermo): 49
San Giorgio Cathedral (Modica): 276
San Giorgio Cathedral (Ragusa): 261–262
San Giorgio Church (Castelmola): 411
San Giovanni Battista Cathedral (Ragusa): 268
San Giovanni Catacombs (Siracusa): 296, 323
San Giovanni dei Cavalieri di Malta (Taormina): 399–400
San Giovanni Evangelista (Scicli): 279
San Giuseppe Church (Ragusa): 258
San Giuseppe Church (Taormina): 401
San Leone: eating, 231–232
San Lorenzo Church (Agrigento): 226
San Lorenzo Oratory (Palermo): 39, 50–51, 64–65
San Michele Church (Taormina): 398
San Nicolò Benedictine Monastery and Church (Catania): 350–351
San Nicolò Cathedral (Noto): 286
San Nicolò Church (Siracusa): 317
San Pietro Cathedral (Modica): 275
Santa Caterina Church (Palermo): 38, 52, 56–57
Santa Caterina da Siena (Donnalucata): 280
Santa Caterina of Alexandria Church (Taormina): 403
Santa Croce Camerina: 281
Sant'Agata alla Badia Church (Catania): 343–344
Santa Lucia alla Badia Church (Siracusa): 305, 307
Santa Lucia al Sepolcro Basilica (Siracusa): 296, 323–325
Santa Lucia Bridge (Siracusa): 297, 299
Santa Maria dei Greci Church (Agrigento): 228
Santa Maria dell'Ammiraglio (Palermo): 38, 52, 58–59
Santa Maria delle Scale Church (Ragusa): 264–266
Santa Maria dell'Itria Church (Ragusa): 263
Santa Maria del Piliere Church (Taormina): 402–403
Santa Maria Maddalena Church (Ragusa): 258
Sant'Anna Church (Palermo): 52
Sant'Antonio Abate (Taormina): 396
Santa Rosalia: 54, 68, 226; biographical sketch, 110; Sanctuary of Santa Rosalia, 107–109
Santa Rosalia Church (Agrigento): 226
Santa Vergine Maria Assunta (Palermo): 65–69, 66–69
Santuario della Madonna delle Lacrime (Siracusa): 296, 318–319
Saracen Castle: 412
Savoca: 413
Scams: 439
Sciascia, Leonard: 227
Scicli: 277–280

Index 511

Seasons: 17, 20, 30
Segesta: 15, 129–132; map, 130
Segesta Temple: 130–131
Segesta Theater: 131–132
Selinunte: 154, 197–202; map, 198
Shopping: clothing sizes, 497; hours, 439; VAT refunds, 444–445. *See also* Markets; *and specific destinations*
Sicilian puppets: *See* Puppets
Sicilian Regional Assembly (Palermo): 72
Sicilian street food: 98, 471
Sicilian Symphony Orchestra: 85
Sicily earthquake of 1693: 251, 252, 257, 265–266, 267, 273, 277, 278, 283, 290, 309, 316, 323, 340, 342, 345–346, 350, 351, 430
Sightseeing (sights): budget tips, 21; general tips, 450–451; maps and navigation tools, 448–449; must-see destinations, 12; planning tips, 449–450; top destinations, 11; worth-it destinations, 15–16. *See also* Itineraries; *and specific sights and destinations*
Silvestri Crater (Mount Etna): 370–373
SIM cards: 446–447
Siracusa: 12, 290–333; at a glance, 296; eating, 330–332; entertainment, 326, 328; helpful hints, 294–295; history of, 303, 306; maps, 292–293, 298, 329; orientation, 291; planning tips, 291; shopping, 302, 325; sights, 308–325; sleeping, 328–330; tourist information, 291, 294; tours, 295–297; transportation, 297–308; walking tour, 294, 295, 333
Siracusa Cathedral: 296, 304–305, 308–310
Siracusa City Hall: 305
Siracusa harbor: 299, 332
Sleep code: 452
Sleeping: 451–460; money-saving tips, 21, 452–453; reservations, 24, 456–457; types of accommodations, 453–460. *See also specific destinations*
Smartphones: 25, 445–448. *See also* Apps
Solicchiata: 383; eating, 384

Southeast Sicily: 16, 251–289; driving tour, 273–283; map, 274. *See also* Ragusa
Stabilimento Florio (Favignana): 185
Streaty Tours (Catania), 339; (Palermo), 41
Stromboli: 139

T

Taormina: 16, 388–419; day trips, 413; eating, 415–419; helpful hints, 391; maps, 389, 394–395, 416–417; orientation, 389–390; planning tips, 388–389; sights/activities, 404–412; sleeping, 414–415; tourist information, 390; tours, 392–393; transportation, 151, 380, 390–392, 419; walking tour, 393–403
Taormina Cathedral: 398–399
Taormina City Hall: 399
Taormina Public Gardens: 405–406
Tavola calda: overview, 466
Taxes: VAT refunds, 444–445
Taxis: 487–488; Catania, 335, 339; Cefalù, 134; Palermo, 39–40, 104; Ragusa, 255–256; Siracusa, 295; Taormina, 392, 409; tipping, 444; Valley of the Temples, 205; Villa Romana del Casale, 235
Teatro Antico (Taormina): 403, 404–405
Teatro dei Pupi (Palermo): 44–45
Teatro dei Pupi (Siracusa): 296, 326
Teatro Greco (Siracusa): 315, 328, 330
Teatro Massimo (Palermo): 38, 42–44, 59–60, 85; eating near, 102
Teatro Massimo Bellini (Catania): 351
Teatro Pirandello (Agrigento): 227
Teatro Politeama (Palermo): 85
Teatro Romano e Odeon (Catania): 349
Teatro Tina di Lorenzo (Noto): 288
Telephones: 445–448. *See also* Apps
Temple of Apollo (Siracusa): 300
Temple of Castor and Pollux (Agrigento): 215–216
Temple of Concordia (Agrigento): 212–213
Temple of Diana (Cefalù): 146
Temple of Hercules (Agrigento): 214

Temple of Juno (Agrigento): 210–211
Temple of Olympian Zeus (Agrigento): 214–215
Temple of the Sepulcher (Siracusa): 325
Tenuta di Fessina Winery: 377, 383
Theft alerts: 26, 438, 439, 443, 486, 494; Catania, 338; Palermo, 36
Time zones: 439
Tipping: 443–444
Tobacco shops *(tabacchi):* 439–440
Torre di Ligny (Trapani): 166–167
Torri del Balio (Erice): 179
Tour guides: tipping, 444. *See also specific destinations*
Tourist information: 437–438. *See also specific destinations*
Tours: Rick Steves, 437. *See also specific destinations*
Tower of the Winds (Palermo): 73
Train travel: 481–487; Agrigento, 223–224; best one-week trip, 19; Catania, 335, 358; Cefalù, 134, 151; Circumetnea Railway, 375–376, 382–383, 482; general tips, 486–487; map, 484–485; Noto, 289; Palermo, 33, 36, 105; Ragusa, 253–254; schedules, 482; Siracusa, 294, 333; Taormina, 390, 419; tickets, 482–485
Transportation: 481–495; budgeting, 21; map, 484–485; planning tips, 20, 23, 24. *See also* Buses; Car travel; Ferries; Train travel
Trapani: 15, 154–173; day trips, 174–202; eating, 168–171; helpful hints, 155–157; maps, 153, 156–157, 170–171; orientation, 155; planning tips, 152, 154; sights, 166–167; sleeping, 167–168; tourist information, 155; tours, 158; transportation, 155, 158, 173; walking tour, 158–166
Trapani Cathedral: 161–162
Trapani City Hall: 164
Travel advisories: 435–436
Travel documents: 24
Travel insurance: 25, 441
Travel smarts: 26–28
Travel tips: 435–440
Trinacria: 55, 56, 84, 425
Trip costs: 21
Tuna, canned: 84, 184, 185, 470
Tuna fishing: 165, 182, 184, 185

U
Umberto I Bridge (Siracusa): 291, 297, 299
University of Catania: 350
University of Palermo: 77

V
Valley of the Temples: 203, 206–216; eating, 231; map, 208–209; planning tips, 204; sights, 207–223; sleeping, 229; tours, 206; transportation, 204–207
Valley of the Temples Archaeological Park: 207–216; self-guided tour, 210–216
VAT refunds: 444–445
Vetrine e Balconi in Fiore (Taormina): 391
Via Alessandro Manzoni (Catania): 346
Via Alessandro Paternostro (Palermo): 49, 52, 83, 88
Via Alloro (Palermo): 83
Via Atenea (Agrigento): 223, 226, 227, 230
Via Auteri (Catania): 345
Via Bandiera (Palermo): 46
Via Bara all'Olivella (Palermo): 44–45
Via Capitano Bocchieri (Ragusa): 262
Via Carlo Ortolani di Bordonaro (Cefalù): 139–140, 147
Via Cavour (Siracusa): 302, 325, 331
Via Corrado Nicolaci (Noto): 287–288
Via Crociferi (Catania): 346
Via del Ghetto (Taormina): 396–397
Via della Libertà (Palermo): 85
Via Emanuele de Benedictis (Siracusa): 295, 300, 332
Via Etnea (Catania): 335, 344, 347
Via Francesco M. Penna (Scicli): 279
Via Garibaldi (Trapani): 155, 162–163
Via Giovanni Battista Fardella (Trapani): 163–164
Via Gisira (Catania): 345
Via Guarnotti (Erice): 181
Via Maqueda (Palermo): 33, 54, 56, 85; eating near, 102–103
Via Neve (Agrigento): 226–227
Via Orfanotrofio (Ragusa): 259
Via Pardo (Catania): 349

Index 513

Via Principe di Belmonte (Palermo): 89
Via Roma (Erice): 180–181
Via Roma (Palermo): 33, 45–46, 52; eating, 100–101
Via Roma (Siracusa): 325
Via Ruggiero Settimo (Palermo): 84
Via San Francesco (Erice): 178–179
Via Santa Filomena (Catania): 347, 357
Via Torrearsa (Trapani): 155
Via Vittorio Emanuele (Cefalù): 137
Via Vittorio Emanuele (Palermo): 33, 54, 56; eating, 99–100; nightlife, 85
Via Zappalà-Gemelli (Catania): 345
Vico de Spuches (Taormina): 396
Villa Bellini (Catania): 347, 357
Villa Comunale di Taormina: 405–406
Villa Romana del Casale: 15, 233–250; eating near, 250; maps, 234, 238–239; orientation, 236; planning tips, 235; self-guided tour, 236–248; sleeping near, 249–250; transportation, 233–235
Visitor information: 437–438. *See also specific destinations*
Vucciria Market (Palermo): 47–48, 80; eating, 48, 99; nightlife, 88
Vulcano: 139

W

Walking tours: Agrigento, 225–228; Catania, 340–347; Cefalù, 134–141; Erice, 175–181; Mozia Island, 190–194; Noto, 284–288; Palermo, 41–56; guided, 41; Ragusa, 256–268; guided, 256; Siracusa, 297–308; Taormina, 393–403; Trapani, 158–166
Weather: 26–27
Weeping Madonna of Siracusa: 296, 318–319
West Coast: 15, 152–202; at a glance, 154; map, 153. *See also* Trapani
Whitaker Museum (Mozia): 190–192
White Lotus, The (TV show): 388, 398
Wi-Fi: 25, 445–446, 456
William II: 68, 110, 112, 115–116, 117, 119–120, 124, 125, 128, 427
Wine and vineyards: 84, 478–481; glossary of terms, 479. *See also* Marsala wine; Mount Etna Wine Country
Wine bars *(enoteche):* overview, 466–467
World War II: 48–49, 160, 163, 305, 334, 384, 398, 402, 432, 433; Museum of the Allied Landings in Sicily (Catania), 347, 352–353

Z

Zafferana Etnea: 381–382

MAP INDEX

Color Maps: Front of Book
Sicily's Top Destinations: 11
Sicily by Car: 19

Color Maps: Back of Book
Sicily
Palermo
Etna Area

Palermo
Palermo Area: 30–31
Palermo: 34–35
Palermo City Walk: 42–43
Capuchin Crypt: 81
Palermo Shopping & Nightlife: 86–87
Palermo Hotels: 90–91
Palermo Restaurants: 96–97

Day Trips from Palermo
Near Palermo: 108
Monreale Town: 113
Monreale Cathedral: 118
Monreale Mosaics: 121
Segesta: 130

Cefalù
Cefalù: 135

Trapani & the West Coast
Trapani & the West Coast: 153
Trapani: 156–157
Trapani Hotels & Restaurants: 170–171
Erice: 176–177
Mozia: 187
Selinunte: 198

Agrigento & the Valley of the Temples
Agrigento Area: 205
Agrigento's Valley of the Temples: 208–209
Pietro Griffo Archaeological Museum: 217
Agrigento: 224–225

Villa Romana del Casale
Piazza Armerina Area: 234
Villa Romana del Casale: 238–239

Ragusa & the Southeast
Ragusa: 254–255
Ragusa Ibla: 258–259
Ragusa Superiore: 264–265
Ragusa Ibla Hotels & Restaurants: 270–271
Southeast Countryside Drive: 274
Noto: 284

Siracusa
Siracusa: 292–293
Ortigia Walk: 298
Neapolis Archaeological Park: 313
Paolo Orsi Archaeological Museum: 320
Ortigia Hotels & Restaurants: 329

Catania
Catania: 336–337
Catania City Walk: 341
Catania Center Hotels & Restaurants: 354

Mount Etna
Etna Area: 362–363
Rifugio Sapienza: 366
Mount Etna North Slope Wine Country: 380–381

Taormina
Greater Taormina: 389
Taormina: 394–395
Taormina Hotels & Restaurants: 416–417

Sicilian History
Sicily's Waves of Invasions: 421
Ancient Greek World: 422
Sicilian History & Art Timeline: 428–429

Practicalities
Sicily's Public Transportation: 484–485
Driving in Sicily: 492–493
Road Signs: 494

Start your trip at

Our website enhances this book and turns

Explore Europe

At ricksteves.com you can browse through thousands of articles, videos, photos and radio interviews, plus find a wealth of money-saving travel tips for planning your dream trip. And with our mobile-friendly website, you can easily access all this great travel information anywhere you go.

TV Shows

Preview the places you'll visit by watching entire half-hour episodes of *Rick Steves' Europe* (choose from all 100 shows) on-demand, for free.

ricksteves.com

your travel dreams into affordable reality

Radio Interviews

Enjoy ready access to Rick's vast library of radio interviews covering travel tips and cultural insights that relate specifically to your Europe travel plans.

Travel Forums

Learn, ask, share! Our online community of savvy travelers is a great resource for first-time travelers to Europe, as well as seasoned pros.

Travel News

Subscribe to our free Travel News e-newsletter, and get monthly updates from Rick on what's happening in Europe.

Classroom Europe®

Check out our free resource for educators with 500 short video clips from the *Rick Steves' Europe* TV show.

Audio Europe™

Rick's Free Travel App

Get your FREE **Rick Steves Audio Europe™** app to enjoy…

- Dozens of self-guided tours of Europe's top museums, sights and historic walks
- Hundreds of tracks filled with cultural insights and sightseeing tips from Rick's radio interviews
- All organized into handy geographic playlists
- For Apple and Android

With Rick whispering in your ear, Europe gets even better.

Find out more at ricksteves.com

Pack Light and Right

Gear up for your next adventure at ricksteves.com

Light Luggage
Pack light and right with Rick Steves' affordable, custom-designed rolling carry-on bags, backpacks, day packs and shoulder bags.

Accessories
From packing cubes to moneybelts and beyond, Rick has personally selected the travel goodies that will help your trip go smoother.

Shop at ricksteves.com

Rick Steves has

Experience maximum Europe

Save time and energy

This guidebook is your independent-travel toolkit. But for all it delivers, it's still up to you to devote the time and energy it takes to manage the preparation and logistics that are essential for a happy trip. If that's a hassle, there's a solution.

Rick Steves Tours

A Rick Steves tour takes you to Europe's most interesting places with great

great tours, too!

with minimum stress

guides and small groups. We follow Rick's favorite itineraries, ride in comfy buses, stay in family-run hotels, and bring you intimately close to the Europe you've traveled so far to see. Most importantly, we take away the logistical headaches so you can focus on the fun.

Join the fun

This year we'll take thousands of free-spirited travelers—nearly half of them repeat customers—along with us on 50 different itineraries, from Athens to Istanbul. Is a Rick Steves tour the right fit for your travel dreams?

Find out at ricksteves.com, where you can also check seat availability and sign up. Europe is best experienced with happy travel partners. We hope you can join us.

See our itineraries at ricksteves.com

A Guide for Every Trip

BEST OF GUIDES

Full-color guides in an easy-to-scan format. Focused on top sights and experiences in the most popular European destinations

Best of England
Best of Europe
Best of France
Best of Germany
Best of Ireland
Best of Italy
Best of Portugal (coming in 2026)
Best of Scotland
Best of Spain

COMPREHENSIVE GUIDES

City, country, and regional guides printed on Bible-thin paper. Packed with detailed coverage for exploring iconic sights and venturing off the beaten path

Amsterdam & the Netherlands
Barcelona
Belgium: Bruges, Brussels, Antwerp & Ghent
Berlin
Budapest
Central Europe
Croatia & Slovenia
England
Florence & Tuscany
France
Germany
Great Britain
Greece
Iceland
Ireland
Istanbul
Italy
London
Naples & the Amalfi Coast
Paris
Portugal
Prague & the Czech Republic
Provence & the French Riviera
Rome
Rome, Florence & Venice
Scandinavia
Scotland
Sicily
Spain
Switzerland
Venice
Vienna, Salzburg & Tirol

Rick Steves books are available from your favorite bookseller. Most guides are available as ebooks.

POCKET GUIDES
Compact color guides for shorter trips

Amsterdam
Athens
Barcelona
Florence
Italy's Cinque Terre
London
Munich & Salzburg
Paris
Prague
Rome
Venice
Vienna

SNAPSHOT GUIDES
Focused single-destination coverage

Basque Country: Spain & France
Copenhagen & the Best of Denmark
Dublin
Edinburgh
Krakow, Warsaw & Gdansk
Lisbon
Madrid & Toledo
Milan & the Italian Lakes District
Nice & the French Riviera
Normandy
Norway
Sevilla, Granada & Andalucía

TRAVEL SKILLS & SPECIALTY GUIDES
References for smart travel, eating well in Italy, and cruise ports of call

Europe Through the Back Door
Italy for Food Lovers
Mediterranean Cruise Ports

Complete your library with...

CULTURE & TRAVELOGUES
Gain insight on history and culture

Europe 101
Europe's Top 100 Masterpieces
European Christmas
European Easter
European Festivals
For the Love of Europe
On the Hippie Trail
Travel as a Political Act

PHRASE BOOKS & DICTIONARIES
Print alternative to online translators

French
French, Italian & German
German
Italian
Portuguese
Spanish

PLANNING MAPS
Uncluttered and round-trip tough

Britain & Ireland with London
Europe
France with Paris
Germany, Austria & Switzerland
Iceland
Ireland
Italy
Portugal
Scotland
Spain & Portugal

Credits

For help with this edition, Rick relied on...

RESEARCHERS
Virginia Agostinelli

Virginia was born and raised in Abruzzo, in central Italy. After graduation she moved to Seattle, where she taught Italian studies at the University of Washington while finishing her doctorate. Besides travel and teaching, Virginia has a passion for Italian cinema and detective fiction. When not leading a Rick Steves' Europe tour, she spends her time in the Pacific Northwest swimming, reading, and sipping a cappuccino at the nearest coffeehouse.

Alfio Di Mauro

After receiving his Ph.D., Alfio, a native of Sicily, began his career as a professor of organic chemistry with a specialty in Sicilian blood oranges and their uses. He took his expertise in food and wine on the road, becoming a tour guide for Rick Steves' Europe in 2005. His passions are history, photography, his two young sons, and sharing his homeland with visitors. He lives in Catania, on the slopes of Mount Etna.

Robyn Stencil

Robyn's adventurous spirit sprouted from childhood explorations of the Pacific Northwest and the competitive sports circuit. After studying in Rome, she joined Rick Steves' Europe, where she's become devoted to Europe's friendly locals, lived-in cities, and vibrant cultures. When she's not researching, climbing mountains, or running marathons, Robyn calls Everett, Washington, home and works as the program manager of tours at Rick Steves' Europe.

CONTRIBUTOR
Cameron Hewitt

Cameron Hewitt was born in Denver, grew up in Central Ohio, and moved to Seattle in 2000 to work for Rick Steves' Europe. Since then, he has spent about 100 days each year in Europe—researching and writing guidebooks, blogging, tour guiding, and making travel TV (described in his memoir, *The Temporary European*). Cameron married his high-school sweetheart, Shawna, and enjoys taking pictures, trying new restaurants, and planning his next trip.

ACKNOWLEDGMENTS

Grazie assai to Alfio Di Mauro and Sarah Murdoch for their contributions to the first edition of *Rick Steves Sicily*. We also wish to say *grazie* to the following people whose travel savvy and expertise helped shape this book: Michele Gallo, Jackie Alio, Elena Buscemi, Benjamin Spencer, Susan Lusty, and Boris Behncke. Thanks to Rainer Metzger for lending his critical eye and additional Sicily expertise. Finally, a sincere thank you to Risa Laib for her 25-plus years of dedication to the Rick Steves guidebook series.

PHOTO CREDITS

Front Cover: Piazza Bellini, Palermo © Alessandro Saffo, Sime, eStock Photo

Back Cover (Dreamstime.com, left to right): Quattro Canti, Palermo © Dudlajzov; granita © Vladimir Koshkin; mosaics, Villa Romana del Casale © Diego Barucco

Title Page: Ballarò Street Market, Palermo © Dominic Arizona Bonuccelli

Alamy: 62 REDA

Dreamstime.com: 7 (top) © Tanialerro; 7 (middle) © Mkos83; 73 (top and bottom) © Stefanovalerigm; 139 © Thecriss; 276 (top) © Marcobrivio6; 374 (bottom) © Giontzis; 385 (top) © Fotokon; 442 © Areg43

Additional Credits: 431 © 2015 Everett Collection, Shutterstock

Additional Photography: Dominic Arizona Bonuccelli, Mary Ann Cameron, Alfi Di Mauro, Orin Dubrow, Cameron Hewitt, Suzanne Kotz, Cathy Lu, Carrie Shepherd, Robyn Stencil, Rick Steves, Laura Van Deventer, Andrew Wakeling. Photos are used by permission and are the property of the original copyright owners.

Avalon Travel
Hachette Book Group
555 12th Street, Suite 1850
Oakland, CA 94607

Text © 2026 by Rick Steves' Europe, Inc. All rights reserved.
Maps © 2026 by Rick Steves' Europe, Inc. All rights reserved.

Printed in China by RR Donnelley
Third Edition. First printing April 2026.

ISBN 978-1-64171-685-7

For the latest on Rick's talks, guidebooks, tours, public television series, and public radio show, contact Rick Steves' Europe, 130 Fourth Avenue North, Edmonds, WA 98020, +1 425 771 8303, ricksteves.com, rick@ricksteves.com.

Hachette Book Group supports the right to free expression and the value of copyright. The purpose of copyright is to encourage writers and artists to produce the creative works that enrich our culture. The scanning, uploading, and distribution of this book without permission is a theft of the author's intellectual property. If you would like permission to use material from the book (other than for review purposes), please contact permissions@hbgusa.com. Thank you for your support of the author's rights.

The publisher is not responsible for websites (or their content) that are not owned by the publisher.

Rick Steves' Europe
Managing Editor: Jennifer Madison Davis
Editorial Group Manager: Cathy Lu
Editors: Jim Davis, Kim Eckart, Glenn Eriksen, Ellen Hurst, Suzanne Kotz, Rosie Leutzinger, Matthew Lombardi, Teresa Nemeth, Jessica Shaw, Carrie Shepherd, Chelsea Wing
Researchers: Virginia Agostinelli, Alfio Di Mauro, Robyn Stencil
Contributor: Cameron Hewitt
Creative Director: Sandra Hundacker
Maps & Graphics: Claire Conway, Orin Dubrow, David C. Hoerlein, Lauren Mills, Mary Rostad

Avalon Travel
Senior Managing Editor: Madhu Prasher
Managing Editors: Jamie Andrade Martinez, Sierra Machado
Copy Editor: Nikki Ioakimedes
Proofreader: Elizabeth Jang
Indexer: Stephen Callahan
Production & Typesetting: Lisi Baldwin, Jane Musser
Cover Design: Kimberly Glyder Design
Maps & Graphics: Kat Bennett

Although every effort was made to ensure that the information was correct at the time of going to press, the author and publisher do not assume and hereby disclaim any liability to any party for any loss or damage caused by errors, omissions, soggy cannoli, or any potential travel disruption due to labor or financial difficulty, whether such errors or omissions result from negligence, accident, or any other cause.

COLOR MAPS

Sicily • Palermo • Etna Area

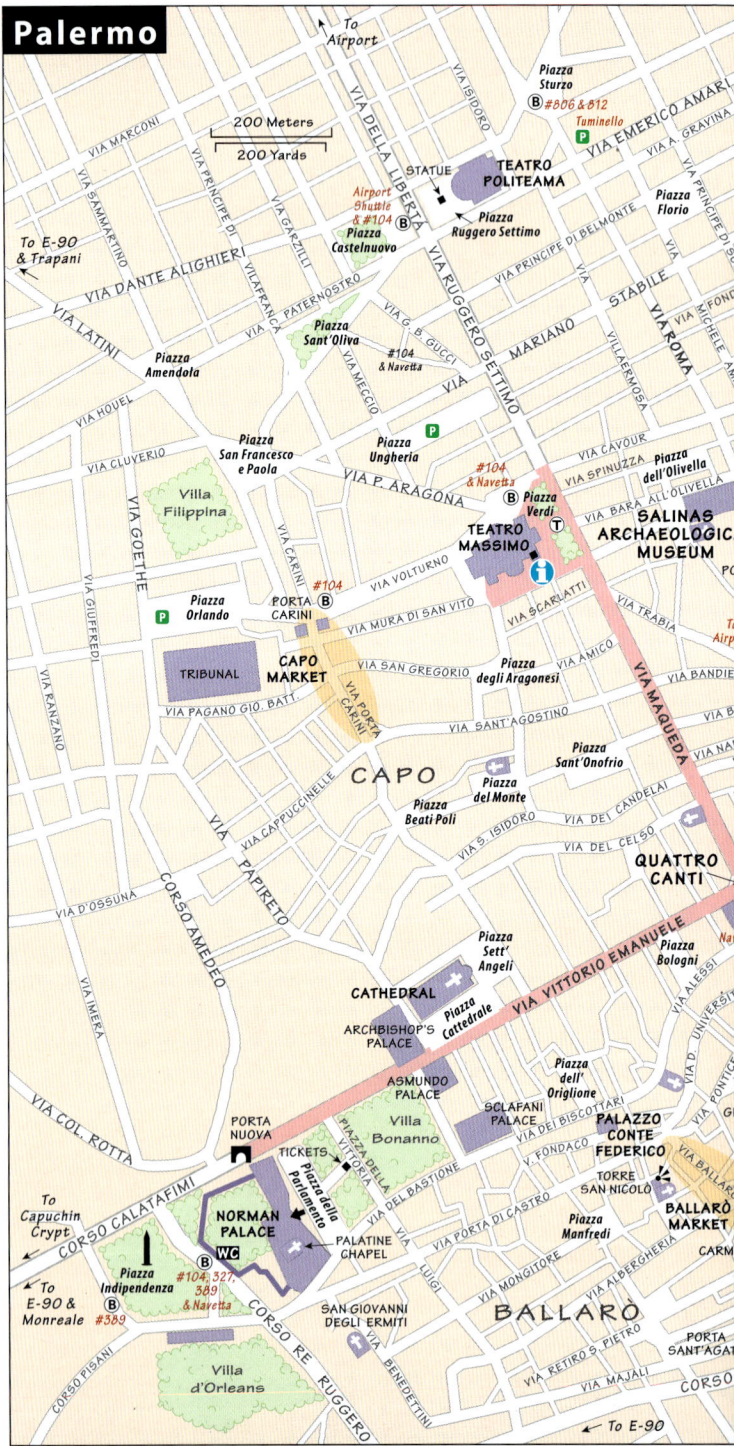

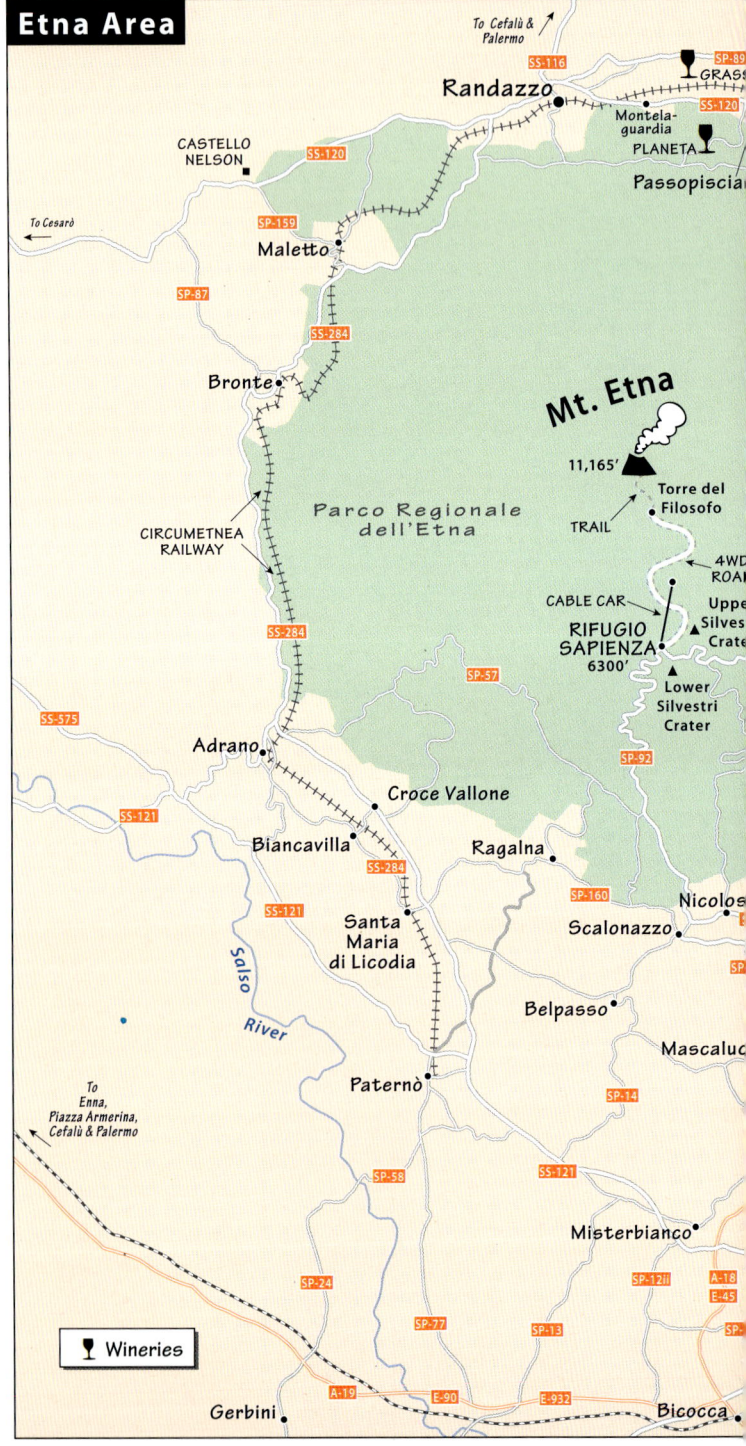

Let's Keep on Travelin'

Your trip doesn't need to end.

Follow Rick on social media!